World History

Journeys from Past to Present

D0708557

Candice Goucher
Linda Walton

Routledge
Taylor & Francis Group
NEW YORK AND LONDON

THE
PAUL HAMLYN
LIBRARY

WITHDRAWN

DONATED BY
THE PAUL HAMLYN

FOUNDATION

TO THE

BRITISH MUSEUM

opened December 2000

First published 2008 by Routledge
270 Madison Ave, New York, NY 10016

Simultaneously published in the UK
by Routledge
2 Park Square, Milton Park, Abingdon, Oxon OX14 4RN

*Routledge is an imprint of the Taylor & Francis Group, an informa
business*

© 2008 Candice Goucher and Linda Walton

Typeset in Adobe Garamond and Univers by
Keystroke, 28 High Street, Tettenhall, Wolverhampton
Printed and bound in the USA

All rights reserved. No part of this book may be reprinted or reproduced
or utilised in any form or by any electronic, mechanical, or other means,
now known or hereafter invented, including photocopying and
recording, or in any information storage or retrieval system, without
permission in writing from the publishers.

British Library Cataloguing in Publication Data
A catalogue record for this book is available from the British Library

Library of Congress Cataloging-in-Publication Data
Goucher, Candice Lee
    World history: journeys from past to present/Candice Goucher and
    Linda Walton.
        p. cm.
    1. World history.   I. Walton, Linda A.   II. Title.
    D20.G67 2007
    909–dc22   2007020802

ISBN 10: 0–415–77136–6 (hbk)
ISBN 10: 0–415–77137–4 (pbk)

ISBN13: 978–0–415–77136–8 (hbk)
ISBN13: 978–0–415–77137–5 (pbk)

THE
WITHDRAWN
THE PAUL HAMLYN LIBRARY

Contents

Illustrations and acknowledgments

FIGURES

MAPS

UNNUMBERED FIGURES

BOXES

Preface

This book's journey reflects the theme of collaboration. The original collaboration began nearly two decades ago and culminated in a two-volume work, *In the Balance: Themes in Global History* (Boston: McGraw-Hill, 1998), co-authored by Candice L. Goucher, Linda A. Walton, and Charles A. LeGuin. We are grateful to Charles for the many teaching and writing hours that he committed to the original project as we hammered out possible themes that seemed to interconnect our diverse areas of specialization in Africa and the Caribbean, East Asia, and Europe, respectively. Now out of print, *In the Balance* nonetheless inspired and helped to develop a thematic framework for the multimedia project *Bridging World History* (Annenberg/Corporation for Public Broadcasting [2004] can be accessed at <http://www.learner.org/resources/series197.html>), for which Goucher and Walton were lead scholars. And it has inspired the book you read today, a grandchild of the world history field, reflecting significant advances in the scholarship and teaching of world history in the intervening years since we began our collaboration. Each chapter-ending of the present book contains a link to the relevant section of the multimedia project. There is also a support website to *World History: Journeys from Past to Present* at <www.routledge.com/textbooks/9780415771375> that provides discussion questions for classroom use for each chapter, appropriate for use in college and AP high school world history survey courses as well as in upper division comparative world history and world civilizations courses.

Like all histories, this book is selective in tracing the journey of the human past from the earliest prehistory of human origins to the present age of globalization. World historians who favor "big history" incorporate the narratives of planetary and cosmic pasts within the scope of world history, and they use the longest possible timescale, billions of years long. They argue that choosing the distance from the beginning of time allows a different "mapping" or conceptualization of the shorter human past to occur. That different focus can bring new understanding to familiar topics. The approach we adopt here uses the narrower chronology of the past reflected in the fortunes of the human species alone. Our starting point for the human journey is the origin of the human species, and as we follow the many thematic pathways of that journey we rely on a variety of evidence and multidisciplinary interpretations. We make use of archaeology and allied sciences throughout the book, and include in each chapter primary sources and visual images that enrich the text content.

In this book we have challenged ourselves to be much braver in our thematic aspirations than before. From the humans who conquered the planet through a multitude of movements and moments that carry us to the present, the eleven chapters of this book portray through different thematic lenses both the diversity and the commonality of the human experience. Themes in human history provide a dynamic framework for the study of the vast reaches of our common past. Themes can also shape our understanding of differences that emerge from change over time and help us discover insights into what connects past and present. As we pursue our examination of peoples in the various places they inhabit, from their origins until today, we focus on a number of common themes: on the mobility and interrelationship of peoples; on their connections with the environment; on the patterns of dominance and submission embedded in the ways people organize themselves politically, economically, and socially; how people constructed and expressed cultures through ideas, religion, and art; and how technologies both shaped and reflected societies.

Thinking, teaching, and learning thematically offers particular advantages by presenting readers with the chance to bridge the familiar and new, the past and the present. Recursive elements reinforce learning, making it possible to build pathways of complex learning by returning to view the same event or ancient society through multiple thematic lenses. While the themes of world history are in some ways infinite, the themes of shared humanity and human purpose have guided our journey through world history just as surely as they did the journeys of our ancestors when they moved out from the prehistoric African forests and savannas to create new worlds.

CHAPTER 1

Human migration

World history in motion

The first Hadar field season in 1975 witnessed a line of National Science Foundation research tents camped in the center of the Afar desert overlooking the dry beds of the Awash River in Ethiopia. A young paleo-anthropologist, Donald Johanson, on his first exped-ition, was wondering what would happen if he failed to find the fossils he had written about in his grant application. Out surveying late one afternoon, Johanson describes kicking at what looked like a hippo rib sticking up out of the ground. On closer exam-ination it appeared to be the bone of a small primate. As he wrote down in his notebook the detailed location, he spotted two other pieces of bone nearby; the rest is history. These bones placed together by Johanson fitted at a surprising angle. They were the femur and tibia of an upright walker and part of an amazing early hominid skeleton, nearly 40 percent complete, that the archaeological team went on to locate. They had identified the remarkable remains of a single female individual of a new species, *Australopithecus afarensis*. The camp rocked with excitement as its members began to realize how significant the finds of an upright-walking 3-million-year-old female hominid were. As they celebrated, a Beatles tape played on a cassette recorder: "Lucy in the Sky with Diamonds." They affectionately called the fossil "Lucy."

Shortly after the Hadar discovery, the archaeologist Mary Leakey and her assistant found a remarkable pair of 3.6-million-year-old footprints in the volcanic tuffs at Laetoli, a prehistoric site in Tanzania. On a relatively flat surface, two early hominids had walked in the freshly littered shower of ash from a nearby volcano, leaving behind their footprints. The subsequent onset of the region's annual rainy season then created a cement of water and ash that preserved the footprints. The possible mother and child pair, whose footprints preserved a moment in prehistory, most likely were tree-dwelling creatures.

Most narratives of the human past examine change over time, rather than a single-moment event of the past as the Laetoli footprints represent. Viewing change over time requires world historians to distance themselves from the single moment and to view instead the broader patterns and processes that emerge. The processes that led to the point in time when modern human ancestors actually came down from the trees permanently triggered routine bipedalism. Walking upright on two feet is a strategy that allowed these human ancestors the distinct advantage of seeing over the tall grasses that replaced forests during an era of climatic change. This terrestrial locomotion occurred first in Africa, and it began the long march of human history.

Figure 1.1 Mary Leakey excavating. Between 1976 and 1981, British archaeologist Mary Leakey and her staff worked to uncover the Laetoli hominid footprint trail that was left in volcanic ashes more than 3.6 million years ago.

INTRODUCTION

Today we take the amazing mobility of humans for granted. With ever-increasing speed, humans travel from one side of the globe to the other. Since their origins, human migrations have had important consequences for the planet and all species. While historians rarely have the actual footprints left by humans on the move, they do rely on a staggering variety of historical and scientific evidence to trace the history of human migrations that begin long before the development of writing. For example, paleontology studies the history of life on earth based on fossil records and focuses only on selected chapters in our biological evolution, such as the major adaptation of bipedalism or changes in brain capacity. Other important chapters in prehistory, such as the development of omnivorous behavior (consuming both animals and plants) or the emergence of culture (distinct patterns or styles of behavior), are less well documented because such evidence is less tangible and permanent. The history of human migration points to the single place of origin and many destinations. Migration is also one of the main forces that have shaped the genetic and cultural diversity of human populations. How did early human migrations out of Africa people the planet? What are the varied sources for studying the patterns and impact of human migrations? How did later migrations shape the human experience? Finally, what are the causes and consequences of a world history continuously in motion?

EVOLUTIONARY FOOTPRINTS: HUMAN ORIGINS IN AFRICA

The discovery at Hadar suggested to archaeologists what may have been a new evolutionary branch of the human species family tree. This classification was used to develop a model for the appearance of the species *Homo* (humans or their ancestors). It pushed back hominid origins and human prehistory to 3.6 million years ago. Since Lucy, the fossils of many more hominid, or human, ancestors have been uncovered. The fossil evidence now suggests that at least twelve distinct species, including our own *Homo sapiens sapiens*, split from a common ancestor with the African ape and

walked on the earth over the course of the past 7 or 8 million years. Only our species, which evolved about 100,000 years ago, remains. These discoveries have caused world historians to reconsider what makes the human species unique. They have also reminded us how what we know about the past is dependent upon a range of supporting evidence, from oral traditions that describe ancient landscapes to the geology that documents changes over thousands of years.

Another major site of hominid research in East Africa has been the Great Rift Valley, including Olduvai Gorge in Tanzania, investigated over two generations by a family of scientists: Louis Leakey (1903–72), Mary Leakey (1913–96, his British wife), their son, Richard, and their daughter-in-law, Meave. In the sand, gravel, and other detrital material deposited by running water in the Olduvai Gorge, the Leakeys discovered stone tools and other evidence from about 2.5 million years ago. The stone tools excavated at Olduvai Gorge by the Leakeys and others provide part of the long chain of evidence of stone tool use that continued to several thousand years before the present. Early hominids have also been found recently in Chad in Central Africa, and they may have roamed across West Africa, too.

TRACING MIGRATION ROUTES

Eventually the movements of hominids connected continents as they traveled beyond Africa to Eurasia. The first intercontinental travel occurred nearly two million years ago (written as 2 MYR), when upright and bipedal hominids moved out of Africa. Bigger brains and long limbs, once thought to have spurred the exodus, were likely not needed for those early journeys. Walking upright on two legs freed the hands of these hominids and led to increasingly specialized tool use.

Sometime around two million years ago some of the early hominids may have taken up running, an activity that the genus *Homo* uniquely developed and is still developing. The endurance ability of hominids to run long distances not only helped early hunters and scavengers but also led to changes in the balancing mechanism of the inner ears, wide sturdy knee joints, and prominent buttocks. About this same time one or another species of hominid could be found across Afroeurasia. Eventually hominds spread to Southeast Asia and to China. Finally they reached southeastern Australia by about 50,000 to 46,000 years ago. Most of the continental area encompassing Africa, Europe, and Asia received migrants from East Africa by about 1.5 MYR. Hominids dated to about 1.8 MYR have been found in ex-Soviet Georgia, where they would have encountered cool seasonal grasslands. Two Eurasian sites associated with the species that spread out of Africa (usually identified as *Homo erectus*), one in Israel and one in the Caucasus Mountains of Central Asia, are dated to about 1.6 MYR. Elsewhere, on the Deccan Plateau of the Indian subcontinent, locally produced stone hand axes dating to about the same time have been found, while in Central Asia locally manufactured pebble tools attest to human occupation after 750,000 years ago. Although archaeological evidence of early human habitation in tropical parts of Asia has not been discovered, it is possible that hominids there would have used perishable material such as bamboo rather than stone for their tools, thus making it much more difficult for archaeologists to locate sites.

The most well-known hominid remains found in East Asia are those of the *Homo erectus* "Peking Man," first discovered in the cave complex at Zhoukoudian near Beijing in north China beginning in the 1920s. Dated to as early as half a million years ago, the earliest collection of fossils from this site disappeared in the turmoil of the Second World War and have never been recovered. Working from excellent casts of the fossils, and with additional remains recovered up through the 1960s, Chinese and international paleoanthropologists have continued to refine their understanding of the various layers of this site. Peking Man (and Woman) ate the meat of wild animals, whether as scavengers or hunters, and used stone tools. It was initially believed that they also knew how to use fire, but recent testing of the ash indicates that the fire may not have been made intentionally by humans. More recently discovered fossil fragments of *Homo erectus* from several other sites, spread geographically from far northeast to far southwest present-day China, have been dated to almost 2 million years ago. Recent revised dating of "Java Man" fossils in Southeast Asia indicates that these *Homo erectus* ancestors lived around the Solo River and at Sangiran on the island of Java in present-day Indonesia from 1.6–1.8 MYR. Pushing back the original dates of these remains by 800,000 years indicates that *Homo erectus* was in Southeast Asia, as well as East Asia, as early as in Africa, and that the move out of Africa may have begun about 2 million years ago, far earlier than originally believed.

Due to the slow retreat of the glaciers, the environment of Europe 2 million years ago was less inviting to the African migrants than that of Asia. As the glaciers retreated around 500,000 years ago, Europe became more attractive to hominids. As the climate improved, so did the food supplies: animal life underwent significant changes, and new species of deer, bovid, rhino, and horse appeared as more favorable foraging conditions emerged. The earliest, most widely distributed European hominid remains are not those of *Homo erectus* but those of the more recent Neanderthal, a name derived from discoveries made at a site in the Neanderthal Valley in modern Germany. Available evidence suggests that a second wave of migration out of Africa accounts for the appearance of anatomically modern humans elsewhere. Other Late Stone Age peoples, including the anatomically modern *Homo sapiens*, appear to have moved into Europe from West Asia during the earliest retreat of what is called the Würm glaciation, about 35,000 years ago. These migrants, called Cro-Magnon after a site in the Dordogne Valley in France, eventually displaced earlier ones. However, for more than 15,000 years after modern *Homo sapiens* appeared in Europe, the northern parts of the continent remained unoccupied because of its uncertain climate and unpredictable food resources.

The origins and spread of anatomically modern humans from Africa is supported by new evidence from paleoanthropology (the study of fossil human remains), recent dating techniques, computer simulations that model human differences, and genetic studies. One of the most significant scientific projects of the twenty-first century, the Human Genome Project (1990–2003), has demonstrated the similarity (down to 99.9 percent) of all genetic patterns across the human species. Genetic evidence from DNA analysis of blood samples from peoples around the world shows minute variations compared to other species. The genetic evidence from studying mitochondrial DNA (found in cells and inherited from the mother) also confirms the tracing of a single lineage back to the African homeland. The peoples within Africa show the greatest genetic variability compared to insignificant variation across the rest of the world's racial groupings, demonstrating that there is no genetic basis for classifying humans into racial types.

The migratory routes that interconnect the planet also have been scientifically tracked by studying the genetic similarities and differences among modern populations and tracing them back to a common ancestor in Africa. The genetic evidence confirms that the original out-of-Africa movement began as early as about 2 MYR. Sites with anatomically modern human remains are common in Africa during the Middle Stone Age (200,000–40,000 years ago), confirming the second migratory wave out of Africa perhaps around 100,000 years ago. Even if these human ancestors were anatomically modern, did they possess fully modern human characteristics such as culture? Did a genetic mutation or some other event trigger the changes that enabled the sudden appearance of the capability to produce tools and art?

COLONIZATION OF THE PLANET

The most significant migration event of world prehistory is the colonization of the planet: humans are the only animals to have achieved near-global distribution. Prehistorians had long considered that the movement of humans in prehistory reflects their purposefulness; but how did this sense of purpose arise? Understanding the process of global colonization raises the questions of how and where humans emerged as a species and how and why humans moved across the earth's landscapes to occupy all environments found on this planet. After leaving Africa, anatomically modern humans eventually spread by land and by sea to all the inhabitable parts of the planet. Why these earliest migrants left Africa to colonize the world is a complex, important question. The answer is likely to be found in a web of interrelated factors centered on human behavior, specifically behavior selected to reduce risk and increase individuals' fitness for survival. Calculated migration must have resulted from information sharing, alliance building, memory, and the ability to negotiate – all skills that

necessarily accompanied increasingly complex social and cultural groups. The increasing complexity of existence inevitably led hominids out of Africa, resulting in a global distribution of diverse human groups. Increasing population may have prodded the migration of some groups. Armed with the attributes of culture, the distinctive, complex patterns of behavior shared by human groups, humans eventually adapted to and conquered virtually all global environments.

Whatever the nature of human origins, whenever or wherever human societies and cultures first appeared, the peopling of our globe has been a product of migration from place to place. Given the small numbers of people and the vast distances they traversed, and considering their technologically limited modes of transportation, the movement of people around the globe seems miraculous. It was undertaken entirely by people who walked on foot and perhaps floated on rafts, who gathered and hunted food, and who thrived in diverse and difficult environments.

Most historians agree that symbolic cultural expression helps make the human species unique. Recent evidence of the symbols, including the red piece of iron incised with cross hatchings, has been found in southern Africa and dated to about 70,000 years ago. The evidence supports the theory that the second wave of African ancestors left the continent with the cultural advantages that would have furthered their migration. Some researchers believe that the key cultural roots included the development of widespread use of social networks, an important human marker. Successful adaptations enabled these populations to survive in different ecological zones and, competing with Neanderthal populations, eventually win out in Afroeurasia.

Many examples of global colonization depended on interactions between people and between people and their environments. Gradually, sometime during the Middle Stone Age (perhaps 100,000 to 200,000 years ago), distinct patterns of interaction emerged among humans and between them and the landscapes in which they lived. Because the distinctive physical and social environments to which humans adapted were themselves constantly changing, cultures too continually changed. That early humans acquired technological and social skills can be inferred from widespread evidence of their material culture – stone

Figure 1.2 Saharan rock art. Rock art reflects early human expression and can be used by historians to document change over time, such as population movements, environmental changes, and the otherwise impermanent or intangible past, from hairstyle to body art.

tools and utensils, carved figurines, rock and cave art, and the like, dating from about 40,000 years ago – that has been found in most parts of the globe.

LANGUAGE AND COMMUNICATION

Humans also developed language and language sharing, the highest level of communication skill and one still regarded as unique to humans. As they spread around the globe, our human ancestors developed efficient and various languages as the means of remembering and transmitting information within shared social contexts. Exactly how or when languages emerged remains obscure, but when they did language and the ability to reason abstractly separated humans from their hominid ancestors, and both reinforced the uniqueness of the species and confirmed its humanity.

Language would have been critical to communicating ideas, planning itineraries, and transmitting culture across the approximately 5,000 generations that separate us from our common human ancestor. The key physical adaptation, which may have occurred only about 200,000 years ago, was the lowering of the larynx in the human throat, enabling us to produce speech by modifying passing air. No other species is capable of modifying and reinventing its behavior through speech. Scientists also use the changes in language to trace the evolution of speech and the movements of speakers across the landscape.

All human languages are similar in being capable of expressing the needs, desires, and history of their speakers. Few would disagree that the ability to communicate verbally and symbolically is at the core of the behaviors and increasingly complex social structures of human beings. Communication has extended the impact of collective human learning across multiple generations. Humans are distinctive as a species because of their ability to inherit knowledge. The development of language unquestionably furthered the social and technological evolution of humans and facilitated systems of reciprocity and social exchange. For example, the division of labor in food production and the exchange and transportation of goods and products were greatly expedited by speech. Being able to assign different tasks to different individuals furthered cooperation and fueled the processes of social and cultural evolution. Sharing information greatly accelerated the adaptation and ultimate impact of the human species on the planet.

The evolution of increasing specialization in language and technology were parallel and likely interrelated developments. From the available evidence of stone technology worldwide about 500,000 years ago, tool types would have appeared very similar. By about 50,000 years ago, distinctive differences had appeared: regional specialization in toolmaking reflected cultural evolution and the occupation of different environments requiring different tools. On the basis of available evidence and its chronological pattern, the soundest judgment seems to be that continuous migration from the African continent peopled the adjacent landmass of West Asia and there created an ancient crossroads of cultural interaction. Scattered temporary settlements of Stone Age hominid culture appeared in West Asia as they did in most of the habitable world. Evidence of human societies in West Asia dating to about 35,000 BCE is well established. Since there is no evidence of a significant migration of new peoples into West Asia between 1.5 million years ago and 35,000 BCE, the people who settled there were probably descendants of the early migrants from Africa. After about 10,000 years ago, their descendants gathered and later planted wild grain, and they were soon building the first West Asian cities.

Long after the first global migration of hominids from Africa to Australia beginning about 50,000 years ago, the continuity of cultural style suggests the endurance of a population made up of only two or three language groups related to African languages. The development of West Asian culture and social structures was a product of slow change from within rather than an influx of new people coming from without. The early movement of people likely followed the fringe of the Indian Ocean into the tropical areas of the Pacific world. Movements into northern (and colder) lands occurred over time.

DEMOGRAPHY, ANIMALS, AND CLIMATE

As prehistoric cultures evolved, peoples moved into previously uninhabited areas. It is likely that human population increases were largely responsible for these migrations. The influence of demographic changes, increases or decreases in population size or characteristics, interacted with other aspects of ecology, including cultural and environmental changes, to encourage people to move. Population pressures on scarce or limited resources forced people into ever more restrictive environments that in turn required adaptive strategies. Deserts and arid lands could be colonized by early humans with effective tools, food storage, and social cooperation.

We have already seen that the earliest African migrations extended the achievements of human evolution to other parts of the globe. Since these migrations, more than a million years ago, no part of the globe has ever been truly isolated. Not all migration was permanent, and descendants of early migrants sometimes returned to Africa, resulting in an interchange of peoples, products, and ideas between Africa, West Asia, and the lands bordering the Mediterranean and the Red Sea. The Indian Ocean coast of East Africa and Eurasia was also an entry point for peoples and their cultures, creatures, and crops, such as bananas

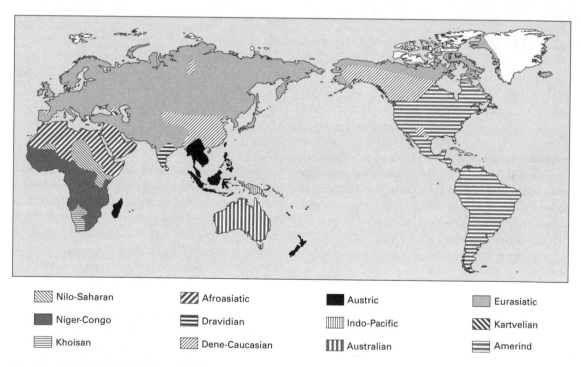

Nilo-Saharan	Afroasiatic	Austric	Eurasiatic
Niger-Congo	Dravidian	Indo-Pacific	Kartvelian
Khoisan	Dene-Caucasian	Australian	Amerind

Map 1.1 World language groups.

Source: Patrick Mannning, *Migration in World History* (London and New York: Routledge, 2005), figure 2.1, p. 29

(beginning sometime before about 6,000 years ago). Descendants of Africans themselves also ventured on voyages across the Indian Ocean to the Indian subcontinent and ultimately connected the story of human migration to China, Australia, and New Guinea. Humans were not the only populations to spread across the landscape. For example, the highly variable climate of the Sahara, the world's largest desert covering almost one-third of the African continent, has experienced severe drying conditions between roughly 8,000 and 7,000 years ago and again after about 5,000 years ago, leading to today's parched environment. The dramatic shift from lakes and humid climate to dry conditions led to the migration of animal species like the elephant, as well as to human migration. After the last dessication, humans adapted by developing irrigation and farming.

The domestication of animals further increased human mobility. On foot, mobility was estimated to be about 72 kilometers (45 miles) per century. Earlier animal migrations had spread the species most useful to human movements – the camelid (including camels, alpacas, and llamas) and the equid (including horse, ass, onager, and zebra) families from North America to Eurasia some 13 MYR. The harnessing of the Asian camel, the South American llama, and the Eurasian horse or donkey occurred much later (tamed in the wild by about 6000 BCE) when they expanded the migratory activity of early human groups just as humans were settling down. Their use was costly but speeded up journeys and made contacts between increasingly settled regions of the world more frequent. For more recent eras, world historians rely on evidence as diverse as language and archaeology to trace human movements. Social networks, defined by the communication between individuals and groups, probably shaped the earliest human migrations and have constituted the single most significant factor shaping all migration ever since.

LINGUISTIC EVIDENCE OF MIGRATION

The earliest beginnings of language makes humans distinct from other animals. The study of language can also offer important clues about the historic migration of peoples around the world. All human languages can be divided into approximately twelve classificatory groupings: Nilo-Saharan, Niger-Congo, Khoisan, Afroasiatic, Dravidian, Dene-Caucasian, Austric, Indo-Pacific, Australian, Eurasiatic, Kartvelian, and Amerind. There is disagreement over exactly when each of these groupings emerged. Most historians would place their emergence between about 10,000 and 20,000 years before the present, based on the current distribution of descendent speakers of related languages. The oldest and widest spread of language groups also suggests two key periods of migrations. The first was from Africa to the Pacific along waterborne routes and through tropical locales between 80,000 and 50,000 years ago. The subsequent human migration identifies dispersions through temperate zones between 40,000 and 30,000 years ago, reaching the more extreme environmental zones. This later distribution also suggests that human groups differentiated into subgroups more rapidly and even before the great Ice Age.

Distinctive linguistic features, such as click sounds, can reveal patterns of movement if they are found in geographically distant populations. Also, similar words in different languages can demonstrate common origins. Substantial movements from the savanna areas of eastern and southern Africa are reflected in the distribution and history of Khoisan languages sometime after 80,000 years ago. Speakers of Nilo-Saharan languages who moved eastwards into the Indian Ocean world may eventually account for the similarities between African, tropical Asian, and Oceanic language groups.

The Bantu migrations in Africa demonstrate ways the study of language can help scholars trace human movement in the distant past. Between 6,000 and 1,000 years ago, Bantu speakers from the Lake Chad region slowly spread across most of sub-Saharan Africa. By about 1000 BCE, the pace of their migrations quickened. They may have been aided in this process by their ability to make and use iron tools and weapons, which could have given them an advantage over other human communities. The incorporation of words from other language groups into Bantu languages, including words related to agriculture and herding, both provides evidence of other groups Bantu speakers encountered and indicates that they may have acquired knowledge of these processes from non-Bantu speakers.

The Bantu expansion involved speakers of related languages that now make up the populations of the southern half of the African continent. This largest and longest of recent African migrations also accounts for the shared cultural and political patterns that have helped to mitigate that continent's environmental and cultural diversity. The movement of Bantu speakers, like the spread of Asian peoples into the Pacific, may initially have been the result of dramatic climatic fluctuation. Both the Bantu and Asian migrations have been documented by archaeological and linguistic evidence, including the similar styles of and decoration on excavated pottery and the shared vocabulary of distant peoples.

One day it may be possible to trace in greater detail the pattern of all early human migrations using linguistic evidence. For the present time, historians have limited and fragmentary evidence of how (and when) the world's twelve or more language groups emerged and whether those groups are related ancestrally. For example, the speakers of early Indo-European languages appear to belong to one large super-family of languages (Eurasiatic) that emerged sometime after about 40,000 years ago. Historians do not agree on the exact location of their homeland. Later migrations can be traced between the areas occupied by the ancestors of Celtic groups and Central Asian peoples, and likely resulted in shared physical and cultural characteristics. For example, by about 4,000 years ago, a community in the Tarim Basin buried their dead in dry and sometimes salty soils, which preserved and mummified the bodies. Archaeologists have been able to detect distinctively Caucasian features, fair skin and light-colored hair from the remains of these Indo-European migrants, who once lived near the modern Chinese city of Urumchi.

Much later migrations can be studied by examining the similarities and differences in language groups. The Late Stone Age migration of the Celtic people who inhabited the trans-Alpine area north of the Mediterranean basin and west of the Urals was one of the most widespread movements of peoples in Europe. Better conditions and the lure of other cultures drew the Celts south to the Mediterranean and West Asia and west toward the Atlantic and the British Isles, where they settled during the first millennium BCE.

THE END OF THE ICE AGE

The recession of glaciation permitted migration and settlement from West Asia to Europe, and by the time the Ice Age ended (c. 10,000 BCE) distinctive societies and cultures had evolved there. The end of the Ice Age was of similar significance in East Asia, where it allowed early humans to develop a more complex array of subsistence strategies that included hunting, fishing, gathering, and the use of diversified and specialized tools. For these and other early migrations, historians have only the most general chronological outlines for thousands of people over generations.

What all migrations have in common is the evidence each provides for the extraordinary success story of early human populations. From East Africa to other continents, human populations steadily increased in number and human groups increased in size and complexity. Expanding populations sent new migrants into the next valley or across the sea to the next port, to occupy virtually every conceivable environmental niche on this planet. Population increase has been the single most critical factor shaping the human story.

The peopling of the landmasses we now call Africa and Eurasia was largely accomplished mostly on foot across land, over hundreds of centuries, and by hundreds of generations. Some migrations to other parts of Asia, the Pacific, and the Americas required long-distance travel across water, either by boats or across the temporary land bridges that appeared in various parts of the world during the glacial lowering of the world's sea levels, approximately 50,000 years ago. For some parts of the world – Australia and New Guinea, for example – both land bridges and rafts or boats would have been necessary for successful human migrations.

Reaching the Americas

It is generally recognized that the earliest inhabitants of the Americas were immigrants from Asia, though the picture of migration to the Americas is less clear than elsewhere. Biological evidence from blood types and dental patterns indicates that the nearest relatives of the earliest Americans are found in northeast Asia. Disagreement over dating has resulted in debate about who exactly the immigrants were and how and when they arrived. It has long been hypothesized that people came from Eurasia (Siberia) to the northernmost reaches of North America. Pebble tools discovered at a Siberian site only tentatively dated to between 1.5 and 2 million years ago suggest hominid inhabitants in Asia at that date, far earlier than the appearance of humans in Beringia, the area of the connecting bridge between Asia and North America. There is also a lack of evidence south of the ice sheet in the Americas. Consequently, informed opinion places migration from Eurasia across Beringia to the Americas during the period between 12,000 and 35,000 years ago.

The least controversial dates for the peopling of the Americas, 11,000 to 11,500 years ago, are based on evidence of human habitation far to the south of Beringia, at a Clovis, New Mexico, site. There are possibly earlier sites of human habitation that may date back as far as 19,000 years ago in North America and to 33,000 years ago in South America. This evidence includes sites that some historians speculate may have been reached by migrants across the North Atlantic from Europe west to the Americas Though all the dates are controversial, widely accepted evidence indicates that the Americas were most likely inhabited by humans around 12,000 years ago. This dating is supported by the widespread evidence in the eastern Arctic regions of Greenland, Canada, and northeast Asia. Colonization of the Arctic took place as ice sheets retreated at the end of what is known as the Wisconsin glaciation about 10,000 years ago.

The Beringian theory of the arrival of Eurasians in the Americas holds that at the time of the migration to the Americas, Siberia and central Alaska were connected by a land bridge across what is now the Bering Sea. Having crossed this bridge into the Americas, people found that there were two great fluctuating ice sheets, one covering the area around and south from Hudson Bay, another flowing down the Rockies. Between the two was an ice-free corridor, a route south roughly from the Yukon down through Montana, which humans and animals took as they occupied what had been a land without people.

Another theory of settlement of the Americas is that the Eurasian migrants might have sailed south along an ice-free Pacific coast. The close connection of the culture of Pacific coast peoples with marine resources might lend credence to the idea that migration to the Americas was by sea. Important adaptive strategies were developed by Pacific coast peoples to utilize marine resources: specialized harpoons have been discovered that, with seaworthy canoes, allowed Pacific coast peoples to kill sea mammals. Some historians have gone as far as suggesting that migration from Asia to the Americas was entirely by boat, across the Pacific Ocean. Similar theories of migration to the Americas across the Atlantic from Africa have also been proposed. None has found general acceptance.

Reaching the Pacific islands

Human settlement of the Pacific island world, Australia, and New Guinea may have begun as early as 50,000 years ago, although recently excavated Australian rock-shelter sites may testify to human presence there earlier than 60,000 years ago. This was a period of fluctuating glaciation when the sea level was temporarily low. Even so, as much as 50 kilometers (31 miles) of open sea would have had to be crossed to reach Australia, since at no time in the last 3 million years was there a complete land bridge between the Asian and Australian continents. Whether humans arrived as castaways, adrift on logs or other vegetation, or on boats or canoes deliberately constructed for intended voyages, they would have found themselves isolated once the glaciers retreated and the sea returned to its former levels. Along with the human inhabitants of Australia, the fauna and flora were also isolated, each to evolve in ways unique to its isolated environment: kangaroos, for example, are one product of the separation and isolated evolution of species. Recent dating of discoveries of rock engravings, red ochre, and stone artifacts at a site called Jinmium in northwestern Australia may push back the dates of the earliest migrations to between 75,000 and 116,000 years ago, suggesting to some researchers that the first artists were not modern humans at all but rather an earlier, archaic species of *Homo sapiens*. Perhaps art may not be a defining characteristic of human behavior.

Though scattered Early Stone Age sites have been found across much of Australia and New Guinea, full-scale and continuous occupation of these difficult environments began as a result of later migrations during the last glacial age, around 12,000 BCE, when Indonesia, Malaya, and Borneo were once again attached to one another and to the Asian mainland. Bands of gathering and hunting people moved steadily eastward and southward. From Indonesia, some crossed by canoe or raft to the continent of New Guinea–Australia–Tasmania. The presence of these new migrants can be documented by linguists, who have studied the distribution and relatedness of Australian Aboriginal languages. Both the expansion of land created by the lowering sea levels and the eventual restriction of lands as the sea rose again effected demographic changes and the movement of peoples.

A much more recent migration of people culturally related to the Southeast Asian mainland has been dated to 7,000 years ago. This Late Stone Age migration is divided into four distinct groups, and it is clear that people from both the islands and the mainland of Southeast Asia participated. Were they pushed south by the cold of the extended glaciers or by other northern peoples fleeing harsh environmental changes? Were they propelled by the pressures of expanding populations? The evidence is insufficient to provide an answer. As was the case for most coastal and island settlements, early sites dating to the period of actual migration have been destroyed by the changing sea level.

The rise and fall of global sea levels had a significant impact on the migrations into the Pacific and Americas. The earth's last dramatic climate change was a glacial retreat ending about 10,000 years ago and placing us in an interglacial period. The glaciers melted significantly and the oceans rose to the present level of shorelines (although global warming has subsequently produced continued glacial melting). The previous land bridges were submerged, and today's archipelagos and islands were created. Until recently it was thought that not long afterward another wave of migrants, mainland Malays, moved by canoe into Indonesia, the Philippines, Melanesia, and finally Micronesia. There only the easternmost Pacific island world of Polynesia remained unpeopled, to be settled between 1000 BCE and 1300 CE. These late dates have recently been questioned by archaeological finds dated to about 30,000 BCE in Melanesia, on the islands of New Britain and New Ireland, and in the East China Sea on Okinawa.

The crossing and settling of the Pacific were no more extraordinary than crossing the ice and drifting snow of Beringia to reach the Americas. Both movements are impressive evidence of the wide range of potential human response to environmental change. The final settlement of Polynesia testifies to this flexibility: Polynesians moved from an equatorial tropical zone that had no winter to the cool, seasonal world of New Zealand and eventually to the semi-tropics of the Hawaiian islands. Thousands of miles separated these colonies, and a thousand years or more separated their initial settlements. Each colony developed different material cultures in response to different environments. Yet today, as a result of continuous migration, all the Polynesian settlements share related languages and systems of belief.

CROSSING BOUNDARIES: LATER MIGRATIONS

The earliest human migrations that populated the planet involved travel across both land and sea, expanding the boundaries of human interaction and human settlement. The genetic, environmental, and linguistic evidence of these early migrations have helped identify patterns in both the large-scale and the brief movements of many individuals and groups. Historians often have been able to identify and document migration only once small-scale movements accumulated from a significant number of individuals and groups of migrants and were observed over long periods of time.

Once the planet was colonized and humans settled in one place, the human urge to migrate was undiminished. Migrations continued to create historical patterns that were complex and varied. What distinguishes later movements from the earliest colonization is that all of them can be characterized as crossing boundaries – boundaries that were geographic, environmental, linguistic, cultural, and political. From about 12,000 years ago, the earliest human settlements distinguished boundaries between the natural and human realms. After cities arose in all parts of the world, urban–rural boundaries were crossed by migrants attracted to cities for their amazing array of opportunities, where larger concentrations of populations could interact and exchange goods, genes, and ideas (see Chapter 3). The establishment of polities – like city-states and empires – depended upon the boundaries of trade and territory being protected from the threat of invasion, often by standing armies (see Chapters 7 and 10). Imperial expansion created new opportunities for migration, which increasingly meant leaving one's familiar birthplace and native language for a vastly different and possibly more complicated grouping of communities.

Technology also played a role in enabling migrations on both land and water (see Chapter 2). The available mode of transport and the reason for moving have changed ever more rapidly. The introduction of the camel to West Africa, the domestication or use of load-bearing animals like the horse, llama, donkey, and elephant, were critical changes in human–animal relations that regularized contacts between communities and created systematic networks that furthered migration to and between sites. Whereas the llama could easily climb the steps of fifteenth-century CE Incan roads, the Spanish horses (in 1532) could not. These technological adaptations were specific to the cultural and environmental contexts in which they occurred and they helped determine the direction and motivations of willing migrants. Intercontinental migrations relied on maritime and other technologies – including horses, guns, ships, and sails. The eventual harnessing of wind, steam, and other kinds of energy allowed sailing and steamships, airplanes, railroads, and automobiles to serve migratory interests of human populations with ever-increasing speed. Today, in the terminology of the "information superhighway," the worldwide web users conjure up a metaphor of migratory interconnectedness to describe the virtual communities of the digital age.

As connections by land and sea began to be constructed in all parts of the globe, they provided new limitations and opportunities for individuals and groups to participate in migration. Not all members of the human community participated equally. Women usually migrated shorter distances and men migrated longer distances. In some societies the access to distant destinations translated into access to power and wealth. Indeed, trade was one of the most powerful motivating forces in luring humans onto roads and waterways. The pull of trade, the push and pull of war, the expansion of polities, pandemic disease, and persistent exploration of new communities – all contributed to

the continuing role of migration in shaping human history.

CREATING DIASPORA

All migrations share a common feature of displacement. People leave their homeland community and travel to a new location some distance away. Most travelers – whether as settlers, conquerors, or refugees – were absorbed gradually by their new communities, changing one language and culture for another. A distinctive type of community formed when migrants came in sufficient numbers to enable them to retain their original culture and language. The term "diaspora" comes from the Greek word meaning "a sowing or scattering of seeds" and refers to a dispersal of people who survive as a community. The common features of a diaspora persisted whether the migrants were victims, laborers, traders, cultural travelers, or participants in empires. For example, the Jewish Diaspora was created by the successive movements of Jews out of Palestine, to Babylonia after the Assyrian invasion in 722 BCE, and eventually to the Iberian Peninsula after the defeat by the Romans in 70 CE. Jews, who were later expelled from Iberia (1492–7 CE), settled in Eastern Europe; finally the Nazi era (during the Second World War) led to subsequent migrations, extending their religious and cultural diaspora to the Americas and modern state of Israel. Sequences of migrations created a South Asian trading diaspora, as early as the second century CE, connecting the Indian Ocean maritime trade with the Southeast Asian network of ports. People known as "Roma" were laborers on the fringes of the caste system, sent as slaves to other parts of West Asia between the eighth and eleventh centuries CE and, after about 1300 CE, on to Europe, where Romani-speaking "gypsies," who, by keeping their distinctive language and culture intact, maintained a separate identity. Later migrations of South Asian and East Asian indentured and contract laborers after the fourteenth century CE created diaspora communities extending to Australia, Africa, Europe, and the Americas, especially in the Caribbean between about 1834 and 1924.

The opportunities provided by the expansion of trade, empire, and religion furthered the number of travelers and increased the likelihood of large-scale and permanent migration – relocating in the faraway trade ports. Trading diasporas accounted for the gradual dispersal of peoples, sometimes aided by the territorial extent of large empires like the Mongol or Mali (see Chapter 7). For example, Muslim merchants spread from Saudi Arabia to Egypt and across North Africa after the seventh century CE. As Islam penetrated the trans-Saharan trading networks in the thirteenth and fourteenth centuries, Muslim merchants created a trading diaspora through the cultural connections of the Mali empire. Merchant diasporas had their own life cycles, contracting and expanding as trade opportunities were won or lost. Other merchant diasporas eventually connected the traders of Yemen, the West African Hausa, South Asians, Chinese, and Lebanese Christians, among the many groups over the past 2,000 years whose trading activities led to migrations across land. Trade also accounted for the peregrination of many human groups, who lived along waterways, notably the Pacific Islanders and the Vikings, whose continuous migration eventually led to long-term changes in language and culture.

CROSSING THE SEAS: THE VIKINGS AND POLYNESIANS

Colonization usually replaced, absorbed or displaced earlier groups in their control of communities and only rarely established new communities. Viking migrations created diasporas or dispersals that reached from North Russia to Newfoundland and south to North Africa. According to written accounts and archaeology, their incursions were both peaceful and violent. During the ninth century CE, the harshness of the Scandinavian environment and the pressure of an increased population on lands of limited productivity, along with the lure of profit and adventure, stimulated ambitious Norse or Viking rulers to set their people into motion. As immigrants, conquerors, and traders, Vikings left their northern homelands in open boats of 21 to 24 meters (70 to 80 feet) in length. Long and narrow, elegant and efficient, these were primarily rowed ships with a supplementary square sail, with high sides but a shallow draft. They could carry as many as sixty or seventy people across the open sea as well as down the quieter waters of inland rivers.

They first appeared as plunderers and adventurers; they stayed as traders and mercenaries and encompassed many cultural groups, not just the Norse. In their remarkable boats they followed river routes further south to the Black Sea and imposed their control over the various disunited Slavic peoples among whom they appeared. By 850 CE they had gained control of Novgorod and soon thereafter Kiev.

Other Vikings, principally from Norway and Denmark, went west and south. Before the end of the eighth century, they were skirting and raiding Scotland and Ireland. By 830, they were establishing villages there and on the offshore islands; they used these small colonies as bases from which to raid and plunder the rich monastic establishments on the fringes of Christian Europe. From their stations in Ireland and the North Sea islands, the Vikings sailed westward across the open North Atlantic.

Shortly after the middle of the ninth century they reached Iceland and settled there permanently; from Iceland they were lured on to Greenland, where Erik the Red set up a colony in 981. From there, Erik's son, Thorvald Eriksson – who had been told about a place called "Vinland" (an Old Norse term for "grassland" or "pasture") by his brother Leif, who had reached this land (actually thought to be Nova Scotia) about the year 1000 – pushed westward to Labrador and southward to Newfoundland, on whose northernmost point, at L'Anse aux Meadows, the first known "European" colony in North America was established. Vikings may also have sailed further south to Massachusetts and Martha's Vineyard, but their colony at L'Anse aux Meadows lasted scarcely a year and their connection with the eastern shores of North America was not permanent.

On the opposite side of the Americas, both in contrast to the western expansion of the Vikings and much earlier, Polynesian migrations moved from west to east across the Pacific Ocean. Evidence from linguistics and archaeology suggests that the thousands of islands that lay scattered over the face of Pacific Oceania remained isolated from the connections that had been established between Africans, Asians, and Europeans before 1250 CE. Pacific Oceania is divided into Melanesia, Polynesia, and Micronesia. Later migrations colonized these distant habitats, creating new communities. The peoples who inhabited these islands established their own regional connections across the Pacific as early as the first and second millennia BCE, when maritime traders identified with the Lapita cultural tradition began to settle in Melanesia, the islands south of the equator from Papua New Guinea to the west to Fiji to the east.

The Lapita culture, named for an archaeological site in New Caledonia, was probably an extension of much earlier migrations to the Pacific islands from Southeast Asia. As sedentary agriculturalists, the Lapita brought with them domesticated plants and animals, along with a distinctive pottery style. They cultivated crops such as taro, yams, bananas, breadfruit, and coconuts, which were spread by occasional voyages among the islands. By 1300 BCE these people had reached the outer boundary of Fiji and soon after made their way to Polynesia by way of Tonga and Samoa. Regional exchange networks accounted for the spread of Lapita culture to Vanuatu, one of the major island groups in central Melanesia. Polynesia, bounded by Hawaii, New Zealand, and Easter Island, was subject to changes brought about by fluctuations in contact as well as by migration of peoples across extensive sea routes.

The Polynesians who settled in New Zealand, the Maori, provide a well-documented example of how Polynesians explored and settled the Pacific in decked vessels capable of carrying 100 to 200 persons, with water and stores sufficient for voyages of some weeks. They had knowledge of the stars and were able to determine favorable seasons for voyages. They were keen navigators, setting their courses from familiar landmarks and steering by the sun and stars and the direction of winds and waves.

Polynesian settlement of New Zealand presented an enormous ecological challenge, since most of the domesticated plants and animals from the Marquesas either failed to survive the long voyage or died out soon after in the different climate. Polynesian settlers adapted to the new environment by becoming hunter-farmers, which led to environmental changes and in turn to the necessity to adopt new strategies for survival that were no longer linked to their Marquesan origins. Exploits over such distances produced daring sailors

and skilled navigators. To maintain the connections among their islands, Micronesians mastered the intricacies of seasons, currents, and winds and even developed representational charts to guide them on their long voyages.

GLOBALIZATION: FORCED AND VOLUNTARY LABOR MIGRATIONS

The patterns of human migration eventually connected all the oceans of the globe. By about 1200 CE, most of the world's migrations were occurring on a small scale into lands already occupied by other communities. Not all migrations were matters of individual or group choice. Expanding empires between 1400 and 1600 helped to create migrations as Mongol, Ming, Ottoman, and Mughal administrators, merchants, and settlers followed in the wake of imperial soldiers. The forced expulsion of unwanted community members was one way in which a community protected its boundaries, maintained political control, and enforced cultural and social values. Through rituals, community action, economic disparity, judicial separation, or enslavement, individuals could be forcibly removed from their home community.

Forced migrations

A significant development in the history of migration was the globalization of coerced labor after 1500 CE. The trade in convicts and slaves followed most of the world's known long-distance routes throughout history, since most other commodities could be converted into the value of prisoners or slaves or their labor. Slaves had traveled the internal land and maritime trade routes in the Americas, Africa and Eurasia for more than a thousand years. In West Africa, trading caravans linked environments across the Sahara as early as the first centuries CE, through trade in slaves, salt, gold, and other goods. The rise of capitalism and imperial expansion spread plantations and encouraged a resurgence of slave trading and the reliance on slave labor (see Chapters 6 and 8). The Eurasian and the North and East African routes carrying slaves met in the Indian Ocean by about the thirteenth century, and crossed the Atlantic and Pacific Oceans in the fifteenth century, where plantations reflected opportunities for overseas economic growth and created an era of increasing exploitation by the eighteenth century.

Involuntary migration patterns were created when people were forced to move against their will. While slaves, convicts, and prisoners of war had always taken part in migrations, their numbers increased significantly with the globalization of trade. Under the impact of capitalism new systems of slavery created migrations of enslaved Africans, who were treated as commodities. Slavery grew in the Americas as the demand for labor in mines and on plantations grew, stimulating the demand for slaves in other parts of the world. After 1500, the introduction of new food crops to Asia led to huge population increases. One consequence was to make larger numbers of forced laborers available for maritime markets. The accelerated migration of East and South Asians after 1800 involved an estimated 80 million individuals, a number that dwarfs the better-studied African Atlantic slave trade.

In the Atlantic era, the West and Central African coasts also became magnets for urban migration after the fifteenth century, attracting trade and people to the opportunities of seaport towns, while redirecting interior trade routes in gold and slaves. Slaves, convicts, and indentured laborers supported new economic activities in new parts of the world, most notably the Americas, but also in Asia and the Pacific between about 1500 and 1800. For example, the colonization of Australia and parts of the Caribbean were largely undertaken through British importation of prisoners, with about 15,000 convicts crossing the Atlantic between 1760 and 1820. In contrast, more than 12 million Africans forcibly migrated to South and North America between 1500 and 1900.

Ecology of migration

The impact of modern migrations was more than economic. Both willing and unwilling migrants transformed the peoples and places of the Americas,

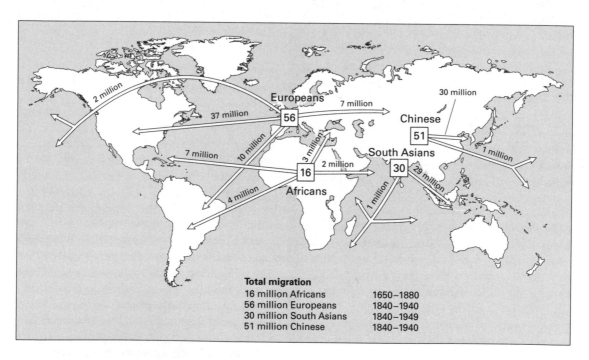

Map 1.2 Global patterns of migration, 1650–1940.

Source: Adapted from Patrick Manning, *Migration in World History* (London and New York: Routledge, 2005), figure 8.1, p. 146

Southeast Asia, and North Asia. Population decreases and available territory encouraged the initial strands of global migration. Undoubtedly, the most immediate and dramatic impact of post-Columbian migration on the transatlantic world was epidemiological. The effect of diseases brought by the earliest Europeans and Africans was both horrendous and prophetic. Disease resulted in the obliteration of whole indigenous peoples, from the Caribes of the Caribbean basin to the Beothuks of Newfoundland, and the general decimation of most populations was common. For example, the indigenous population of central Mexico in 1519 was estimated at 25 million; by 1580, after the Spanish conquest, it was less than 2 million. Within decades after contact with Europeans, an estimated 90 percent of indigenous American peoples had disappeared from some islands and regions. The Amerindian populations had no immunity to diseases common in Europe and Africa, such as swine flu and smallpox. Introduced by animal and human carriers, these virulent diseases brought from Europe and Africa killed most indigenous adults upon contact in the Americas, opening new areas for conquest and settlement.

Migrants moved with the ideas and familiar cultures of their homelands and they encountered new people, products, and ideas. The dominance of European migrants in the Americas was also expedited by a process described by historian Alfred Crosby and others as ecological imperialism, given the fact that the introduction of plants, animals, and diseases had an overwhelmingly dominant impact on the relationships between local communities and environments. The success of Europeans, backed by guns and governmental policies, gained control over both American continents and resulted in the disarray of indigenous populations and their cultures. The migrants established new communities and built new identities. Accelerated migration fostered the mixing of races and ethnic groups.

Willing migrants

As cities around the world increasingly became the destinations of willing migrants in the nineteenth century, their urban industrial and commercial activities created opportunities for small-scale migrations on land and trans-continental maritime migrations.

Imperialism furthered the movements of peoples both away from and to the lands of conquest in Africa, Asia, and the Americas. Migrants on land and across oceans responded to the expansion of boundaries and to the establishment of new settlements. The oceangoing steamships of the mid-nineteenth century helped shorten travel times and increased the overall number of journeys between the world's continents.

Voyages carried new migrants, returning sailors, and written correspondence between the new community and the old homeland. In 1854, the voyage of *L'Aquitaine*, the first ocean-going steamship between Bordeaux, France, and Saint-Louis, Senegal, created one of many oceanic paths of migration that would foster a series of intercontinental connections across generations. Migrant laborers in the Gambia were known as *navetane*, a word borrowed by the French colonizers from the Wolof language and used to describe seasonal laborers. During the colonial era many *navetane* were not only voluntary but came predominantly from wealthy and elite families, who sent family members away to France to reinforce their traditional positions. Some migrants became scholars or entrepreneurs, some never returned, some returned with wealth and prestige, and some were the sailors celebrated in local *navetane* songs:

> Mamadu the wealthy sailor has come back home
> Suuleyman the wealthy sailor has come back home
> Can the little birds serve as food to bats?
> Listen all
> And you the leaders of prayer
> Listen
> Our father Mamadu Konte, the chief of sailors has come back home and Jama Majigi who has come down from the ships to see again his mother Jele Alu and his aunt Awa Samba.
>
> (Manchuelle 1997: 198–9)

Continuous migration in the Senegal River Valley sought commercial opportunities before, during, and after the colonial era. By the 1950s and 1960s, the Soninke from this region made up the vast majority of Africans in France.

Between the 1840s and 1940s, there were multiple flows of migrants to world regions that together created the largest era of world migration in human history. These included three major waves of more than 30 million persons each. Fifty million migrants went from Europe to the Americas; another 30 million from South Asia, and 50 million from China went to Southeast Asia, the South Pacific, the Caribbean and Americas, and the Indian Ocean, and from northeastern Asia and Russia to Siberia, Manchuria, Central Asia, and Japan.

Global migrations caused significant shifts in world populations. The destination areas contained 10 percent of the world's population in the mid-nineteenth century and nearly 25 percent a century later. Migration to Southeast Asia and the Indian Ocean and South Pacific was undertaken by Asians, many of whom took part in one of a number of private and governmental labor recruitment schemes. The North Asian migrations were encouraged by government policies, the possibilities of homesteading, and labor opportunities. The rise of a global economy also provided the context for increased long-distance migration, largely in the hands of Europeans who controlled more than half the world's populations by the early twentieth century.

IMPERIALISM, INDUSTRIALIZATION, AND URBANIZATION

Industry, empire, and world wars combined to create the conditions for these massive modern migrations.

Figure 1.3 Chinese workers at a California gold mine. Chinese contract laborers worked in mines in Australia, South Africa, and the Americas in the nineteenth century.

The spread of industrial capitalism and the creation of empire required the movement of goods and peoples around the world. Innovations in transportation technology enabled increasingly rapid and relatively inexpensive transfers to occur. Adding to the global scale of movements in the last two centuries have been the linked processes of industrialization and urbanization (see also Chapters 2 and 3). From its beginnings, the Industrial Revolution was a global enterprise that relied heavily on the movement of raw materials and human labor. Willing migrants flocked to the cities created by new industry and to the industrialized enterprises devoted to mining and cash crops like palm oil or rubber. Global industrialization also relied on the movement of migrants into under-populated and vulnerable frontier areas in southern Africa, Australia, and New Zealand, where their presence furthered conquest. Indentured labor from South and East Asia built railroads, harvested sugar cane, and mined ores from South America to Australia, the American West to South Africa.

Capitalists sought labor, markets, and resources and transported all of them for the maximization of profit. Industrialization, wherever it occurred, furthered the migration of capital and *laborers*, while creating world markets. This was particularly true for industries like mining and manufacturing. The expansion of empires accelerated migration. The colonial enterprise relied on taxation and forced the colonized to seek wage labor opportunities.. Europeans and North Americans left their original homelands for the purpose of establishing colonial outposts. These migrations furthered the aims of empire, creating labor pools and consuming markets for manufactured goods. Post-colonial migrations have continuously pulled the populations of former colonies back to metropoles like Paris and London, where economic and educational advantages have been sought, but not always received, by the immigrants. Non-Europeans were key players in the expansion and integration of the global economy. In the world's largest cities, willing migrants swept streets and drove taxis. Their children forged new identities. The patterned movements of migrants intersected with the forces of nationalism. As nation-states expanded in the nineteenth century, their increasing recognition of territorial boundaries culminated in a world of passports, wars, and refugees.

DISLOCATIONS OF WAR

The dislocations of war have been a powerful determinant of human migration in the modern world. Prisoners of war have always been unwilling migrants. Fleeing from wars and oppression, migrants have found new opportunities in their ability to relocate halfway across the world. Economic and political refugees during and after the twentieth century's two world wars resulted in major dislocations of population and brought into being a legal international definition of refugee status. A refugee was someone displaced by economic or violent conditions, and who would seek asylum in response to war, famine, persecution or oppression. Moreover the growth of the nation-state during the nineteenth and twentieth centuries resulted in the imperial imperatives for new territory, resources, and labor and the increasing ability to control the crossing of national boundaries by establishing intervening obstacles to the sending and receiving of migrants. For example, League of Nations mandates opened Palestine to large-scale colonization by immigrants whose goal was to create a Jewish state in that territory. Benefiting from Western support and concern for the fate of the Jews following the Holocaust and a major influx of European refugees, especially women and children, Jewish settlers displaced long-time Palestinian residents. Arab opposition to the taking of lands that had been in families for many generations led to an attack on the new state of Israel and created many more refugees. Conflicts in Rwanda, Sudan, Kosovo, Iraq, Afghanistan, and Southeast Asia have similarly created significant refugee populations around the world in the late twentieth and early twenty-first centuries.

INEQUALITY AND ANTI-IMMIGRATION LEGISLATION

Not all factors in global politics have favored waves of migration. The American Chinese Exclusion Act of 1882 was an immigration policy based on racial fears and designed to restrict Chinese laborers from immigrating to the United States. During and after the world wars, the United States Congress limited immigration

BOX 1.1 RELOCATION GOODBYES, MANZANAR RELOCATION CENTER

War and discriminatory policy combined to create a relocation program targeting Japanese-American families and including more than 110,000 men, women and children, in the 1940s. Manzanar Relocation Camp in the California desert was one of ten military-style camps, situated in remote areas where Japanese American citizens and resident aliens were interned during the Second World War. This photograph captures a poignant image of one woman and raises questions about the broader context in which it was taken. Like any photograph, it is a primary document that conveys "first-hand" information about the place, people, and events from the time of the photograph.

The photographer Ansel Adams was invited to photograph Manzanar in Fall 1943 by Ralph Merritt (the camp director). The photographs he took did not include anything that might have made the camp look like a detention center. The historian might ask of this photograph, as of any historical document, questions about what is visible and what might be missing. Who is the intended audience and what was the artist's vision? The image does not include guards, barbed wire or guard towers. Other photographs by Adams document smiling families playing baseball. Yet we know from personal accounts that intense emotions and harsh conditions were the experience of detainees.

Neither does the photo express the circumstances that led to the relocation of so many people. Across the Pacific, the Japanese attack on Pearl Harbor (December 7, 1941) caused widespread public, media and government outcries, sanctioning fears and suspicion of people of Japanese descent. In 1942, President Franklin Roosevelt signed Executive Order 9606 that authorized the establishment of military areas to house those persons who were believed to pose a threat to the war efforts. According to one detainee, targeted families had about a week to dispose of everything they owned, except what they could carry with them on the bus. They did not know where they were going or how long they would be gone. Although Ansel's photograph does not appear to be posed, the woman's expression seems to reflect the uncertainty of the arrival or departure in which she was involved.

Photographs constitute a rich source of evidence for the world historian. Since photography's invention and widespread use after the 1840s, photographic images were thought to be "written with light." They have captured places and peoples from all parts of the globe with the immediacy and often intimate gaze of the camera. They also reflect the struggle of world historians to place such singular, local moments as this "relocation goodbye" in the context of larger patterns and global processes.

through subsequent laws. Throughout the nineteenth and twentieth centuries, US immigration policy was severely biased against nonwhites, except for purposes of importing male workers for hard labor. The policy was later imitated by Australia (1901) and Canada (1923), but eventually repealed. Today, many nation-states and multinational entities continue to struggle with the issues of international migration that test and compromise the national boundaries and transform identities (see Chapter 10). Victims of famines and repressive national regimes have also tried to take flight to safer havens; again, African and Asian refugees have been less successful in their attempts to migrate. Still, immigration to the United States has been exceptional in its size and in the diversity of the sending countries.

STUDYING MIGRATION

In the last two centuries, ever larger numbers of immigrants stimulated the scholarly study of migration. Many scholars have noted the uneven patterns of migration with regards to gender. E.G. Ravenstein's *Laws of Migration* was first published in 1885. Ravenstein had argued that despite the attention paid to long-distance (international) migration, most migration is local (rural to urban) and occurs in stages. This observation constituted the origins of network theory in the social sciences. Writing in a period that had just witnessed the onset of transoceanic travel by steamship, Ravenstein talked about patterns of migration like currents or cross-currents of population movement. He argued that women predominate in local migration and men in long-distance migration. Other typologies have distinguished among the types and motivations involved in migration, including migration as a response to an environmental shift, forced migration (the slave trade), coerced (indentured labor), free migration, and mass movements. His observations about disparity of opportunity hold partially true today. Significantly more men migrate longer distances and women enjoy far fewer opportunities for relocation. Yet many individual migrations have been instigated by women as wives and mothers. For example, the potato famine in Ireland encouraged nearly equal numbers of Irish male and female migrants, who sought relief from the harsh conditions and starvation their families faced.

CONCLUSIONS

Since the spread of *Homo sapiens*, human beings have also remained mobile creatures. The mobility of the earliest humans was one of their most astounding achievements, as they covered vast areas without benefit of horsepower or the wheel, much less the benefits of jet-propelled, air-conditioned comfort and speed. Throughout their history, people have continued to move about. Migration, variously occurring from no fixed locales, was the product of many things: the need for food and work; the need for protection; and because of population pressures, conflict with others, or the sense of adventure.

Migration was the result of and sometimes the catalyst for major shifts in population throughout world history. United Nations sources have estimated approximately 14–16 million refugees, 20–25 million displaced people, and 35 million "economic migrants" in the Northern Hemisphere at the beginning of the twenty-first century. Modern migration is not just fueled by war and conflict. It has been as frequently the consequence of desire, the quest for educational gain, poverty, hunger, terrorism, and environmental destruction. The modern condition of mobility reflects the most glaring and widening gaps between wealthy

Figure 1.4 Footprint from moon landing by astronaut Neil Armstrong. More than 3 million years after the hominid footprints preserved at Laetoli (see Figure 1.1) the human species took their first steps to colonize other parts of the solar system.

and impoverished groups. Most modern migration reflects the systematic ways that societies fail to meet basic human needs, even while it is perceived as providing opportunities for self-betterment. Most recently, international space programs have extended human migration into outer space, with the first landing on the moon in 1969 and the first permanent community on the International Space Station, a joint project of the United States, Russian Federation, Japan, Canada, and Europe, since 2000. How a world history in motion has balanced the dual needs for change and continuity underlies the most compelling themes connecting our global past, present, and future.

SELECTED REFERENCES

Chang, Kwang-chih (1986) *The Archaeology of Ancient China*, New Haven, Conn.: Yale University Press. Revised fourth edition of a classic work by a leading anthropologist-archaeologist. Detailed illustrations and account of human beginnings in China.

Christian, David (2003) *Maps of Time: An Introduction to Big History*, Berkeley: University of California Press. An integrative approach to world history framed by placing human history within the context of the history of life, the earth, and the universe.

Crosby, Alfred W. (2004) *Ecological Imperialism: The Biological Expansion of Europe, 900–1900*, Cambridge: Cambridge University Press. Investigates the roots of European domination in the transformation of ecological relationships.

Ehret, Christopher (2002) *The Civilizations of Africa: A History to 1800*, Charlottesville, Va.: University Press of Virginia. Emphasizes linguistic mapping of migrations.

Eltis, David, ed. (2002) *Coerced and Free Migration: Global Perspectives*, Palo Alto, Calif.: Stanford University Press. Examines the peoples, values, and cultures of post-1500 CE migrations, emphasizing similarities between free and coerced migration

Hoerder, Dick (2002) *Cultures in Contact: World Migrations in the Second Millennium*, Durham, N.C. and London: Duke University Press. Explores the roles of power and perspective in human migration, with emphasis on the last 500 years.

Jones, Steve, Robert Martin, and David Pilbeam, eds (1992) *The Cambridge Encyclopedia of Human Evolution*, Cambridge: Cambridge University Press. Presents the major issues in human evolution.

Manchuelle, François (1997) *Willing Migrants: Soninke Labor Diasporas, 1848–1960*, Athens, Ohio and London: Ohio University Press and James Currey Publishers. Uses the long lens of migration to understand the meaning of modern African choices.

Manning, Patrick (2005) *Migration in World History*, New York: Routledge. Uses human migration as a single thematic lens through which to view world history.

Olson, Steve (2003) *Mapping Human History: Genes, Race, and Our Common Origins*, Boston, Mass.: Houghton Mifflin. Synthesizes human origins and early migrations.

Stringer, Christopher and Robin McKie (1996) *African Exodus: The Origins of Modern Humanity*, New York: Henry Holt. Surveys the genetic and archaeological interpretation of human evolution and migration.

ONLINE RESOURCES

Annenberg/CPB Bridging World History (2004) <http://www.learner.org/channel/courses/world history/>. Multimedia project with interactive website and videos on demand; see especially Units 3 Human Migrations and 26 World History and Identity.

The National Geographic Society *The Genographic Project: Atlas of the Human Journey* (2006) <https://www3.nationalgeographic.com/genographic/index.html>. The site maps genetic markers and journey highlights of the migrations out of Africa and around the globe between about 200,000 BCE and 10,000 BCE.

Migration DRC (University of Sussex) *The World Migration Map* (Updated 2007) <http://www.migrationdrc.org/research/typesofmigration/global_migrant_origin_database.html>. Provides access to data from the Global Migrant Origin Database, developed by the University of Sussex's Development Research Centre on Migration, Globalisation and Poverty, allowing users to see the origins and destinations of migrants to and from nearly every country in the world.

CHAPTER 2

Technology, environment, and transformations in world history

The Roman writer Pliny the Younger described the eruption of Mount Vesuvius on the Italian peninsula on 24 August 79 CE, a natural event that destroyed and buried the towns of Pompeii and Herculaneum. After reporting his uncle's heroic efforts to rescue people with ships of the fleet he commanded off the coast, Pliny records his own escape:

> the flames remained some distance off; then darkness came on once more and ashes began to fall again, this time in heavy showers. We rose from time to time and shook them off, otherwise we should have been buried and crushed beneath their weight. I could boast that not a groan or cry of fear escaped me in these perils, but I admit that I derived some poor consolation in my mortal lot from the belief that the whole world was dying with me and I with it . . . At last the darkness thinned and dispersed like smoke or cloud; then there was genuine daylight, and the sun actually shone out, but yellowish as it is during an eclipse. We were terrified to see everything changed, buried deep in ashes like snowdrifts. We returned to Misenum where we attended to our physical needs as best we could and then spent an anxious night alternating between hope and fear. Fear predominated, for the earthquakes went on, and several hysterical individuals made their own and other people's calamities seem ludicrous in comparison with their frightful predictions.
>
> (Pliny the Younger, "The Eruption of Vesuvius, 24 August, AD 79," in John Carey, ed., *Eyewitness to History*, New York: Avon Books, 1987, pp. 19–20)

Not all interactions between humans and their landscapes were as terrifyingly dramatic as either the volcanic eruption of Mount Vesuvius described by Pliny the Younger or the recent tsunami that devastated the Indian Ocean region almost two thousand years later, but all such interactions were characteristic of one important theme in world history: the changing relationships between technology and environment and their interaction with human communities.

INTRODUCTION

Global migration and colonization of the planet by early humans presented a sequence of changing landscapes and eventually brought people into intimate contact with every natural environment the globe offers. The planet has undergone great geological, climatic, and environmental change in the past and continues to do so today. Relatively little of the past 4 billion years of environmental change was human-induced. Astronomical and geological events, such as the eruption of Mount Vesuvius, account for the most dramatic impact to date.

Humans also created technologies that wrought unprecedented processes of environmental change, unmatched by other species. The human story intensifies the scope and scale of its impact on ecological change in the last century. In this chapter, we examine the different ways in which humans have been part of ecosystems and the patterns by which environmental and human histories are intricately woven together. Key eras in human environmental history can be identified with significant changes in four areas of human life: food, metals, towns, and energy systems. We ask the interrelated questions of how environments have shaped world history and how humans have shaped the environment. What has been the impact of changing world environments on human societies? In

Figure 2.1 Eruption of Mount Fuji. The eruption of Mount Fuji on the island of Japan occurred in 1707, before the artist Katsushika Hokusai was born. The volcano's plume is depicted as a dragon, a symbol of supernatural powers and the mythical animal whose active energy "yang" was thought to reign over the universe. The Japanese borrowed the concept of yin and yang as balancing forces from China.

what ways has the course of technological change been shaped by environment? And how has technology also transformed the environment?

TECHNOLOGY DEFINES HUMAN CULTURE

Technology is a defining feature of the human cultural experience. Culture is the patterned behaviors which a social group develops to understand, use, and survive in their environment. Culture is shaped by human and natural forces; it encompasses both ideas and artifacts and includes such things as technology, language, beliefs, and values. Transmitted both consciously and unintentionally, culture perpetuates itself as learned behavior, molding the ways societies behave across generations. Though individuals make use of inherited cultural knowledge to guide their actions and interpret their experiences, cultures are not permanently fixed. They undergo change as members of a society learn new things and encounter and respond to new experiences, ideas, and peoples. In this way cultures reproduce themselves.

The earliest cultures have been identified by studying archaeological finds; patterned cultural variations called style can be observed in the evidence of material culture, such as 2-million-year-old stone tools or the rock art that began to appear about 40,000 years ago. Anthropologists believe that about 250,000 years ago, wild swings in global climate forced hominid species to adapt or become extinct. So human evolution – especially the evolution of brains and advanced human cognition – was itself an adaptation to a challenging environment. The use of cultural memory systems (see Chapter 9) helped these human ancestors adapt to change itself rather than to any specific environmental niche. Cultural variation or style helped ensure continuity of peoples and their groups, and it enabled groups to retain the memory of valuable information, such as the manufacturing process to create a hand ax, by transmitting it beyond a single lifetime. As groups spread out across the globe, this communication and its historical memory became critical to the community's survival.

No aspect of culture had a greater impact on human history than did technology, the totality of means used to create objects necessary for human survival and comfort. Even in the case of the earliest stone tools, it has been estimated that more than 100 separate, precise blows were needed to shape an individual stone into a useful tool, and thousands of intricate stitches created a single basket. Technology includes ideas as well as tools because it relies on human memory. The continuity of technological styles required the communication of complex processes from one generation to the next. Technological change became the cutting edge, so to speak, of human history, as tools replaced biological evolution as the main source of change. The transformation of the "big history" into human history may be measured by the names of periods assigned to the past. These eras are not defined by environmental or climatic changes, but rather by their technological characteristics. Beyond their cultural styles, technologies have contributed to defining the significant periods from the "Stone Age" to the "Nuclear Age."

Tools have always required the control of knowledge. By about 20,000 years ago, some of the earliest human artifacts appear to be associated with the control of specialized information. These magical objects of carved antler or bone are called batons by archaeologists, who interpret their use as devices for extending human memory. Engraved markings on many of these objects, like the paintings and engravings on cave and rock shelter walls, refer to observed patterns of nature, such as lunar phases or seasonal migrations of animals. Possession of batons would have enabled those skilled in their translation to predict changes in the landscape. Such tools also created and altered people's inner landscapes, how humans perceived the world around themselves. Symbols that could be used and reused to manipulate the world constituted a source of power. The power was accumulated by those specialists, who recognized the imagined possibilities of technology and who could express them successfully in the physical world, whether in the identification of seasons or the shaping of stone tools. No further biological adaptations were necessary for human expansion into new environments. Cultural innovations would be needed and their evolution enabled the successful human career. Using tools, human communities began to thrive in the new environments into which they expanded, and they altered the physical landscape as they conquered the globe.

ENVIRONMENT AND TECHNOLOGY

Important among the determinants of cultural variation, including technologies, are the environmental contexts or landscapes in which people lived. Throughout history, cultures have been influenced by the natural worlds in which they are rooted. Although humans moved from place to place – collectively, an average of about 200 miles per year in their earliest migrations – they also became attached to specific landscapes. Environment thus plays a major role in the construction of culture and in cultural variation. For example, Inuit technology and culture, shaped by its Arctic environment, allowed adaptation to the extremely cold temperatures of a world of ice and snow and provided specialized tools of bone and stone for fishing and hunting seals. The stable freshwater lakes of East Africa, on the other hand, provided vastly different conditions for establishing scavenging, hunting, and fishing technologies in its warm, prehistoric wooded savanna and grassland environment.

Just as contacts with other ethnic groups resulted in cultural readjustment and change (as, for instance, the recent Euro-American impact has destroyed the nomadic Inuit culture), so too did ancient environmental change contribute to cultural change. For example, Saharan desiccation occurred recently, only after about 15,000 years ago, drying up the region's great lakes and rivers and creating a vast desert in which hippopotamus and elephant could no longer survive. The dramatic environmental shift caused major changes in early African cultures and required equally dramatic shifts in lifestyles and technologies, even the forced migration of populations. Archaeologists have identified tool kits among the artifacts carried by the early emigrants in their global colonization, suggesting the importance of retaining technological information in times of changing environments.

EARLY HUMAN ECOLOGIES

Ecology is the relationship between organisms and their environments. The cultural relationship between humans and their environment varied according to people's perceptions of the landscape. In this way, technology and culture altered both the inner landscape of the individual and the physical landscape of the natural world. Though in the modern world, influenced by the powerful impact of industrialization, we tend to see nature as something to be dominated and controlled by human effort, early human cultures were shaped and informed by an awareness of the power of nature. Even in modern times, many peoples, such as the Fang in Central Africa, believe that humans must seek a balance between themselves and the natural world, not try to dominate or control it. The human-built order of the Fang village and its dependence on the surrounding Central African rain forest was a balancing act shaping the Fang culture. Modern ecology similarly derives its core notion of the essential relationship between human society and nature from this kind of thinking.

Although concern with the order of human society and the arts of human culture became predominant characteristics of Chinese thought, the school of thought in early China known as Daoism displayed a sharp sensitivity to the need for humans to live in harmony with nature, to acknowledge and appreciate the patterns of human birth, life, and death as part of the constant transformations of nature. Based on a belief in the oneness of all things – humans, stones, trees, water, animals – Native American cultures were shaped by the environments in which they took form. Native Americans of the Northwest Coast regulated their activities around the natural life patterns of the salmon; the pattern of Inuit life was determined by the seasons: caribou hunts and fishing in the summer, seal hunts and ice fishing in the winter. Even their homes were seasonally determined: tentlike structures in the summer, ice structures in the winter. Such societies minimized their demands on their ecosystems by moving their settlements in accordance with natural patterns. For these societies, cultural activity and the cycle of environmental change were interdependent.

What these differing views have in common is an acknowledgment that the relationship between human society and the environment, whatever it is, is fundamental to survival. The influence of nature on human societies and the ways different cultures have responded to their places in the natural world are crucial elements of historical understanding and basic to the ways in which cultures explain their pasts. Studying these relationships also increases our understanding of the past as process. Seeing human historical events in the context of long-term ecological or geological time produces a perspective on human history and a set of historical concerns very different from one based on single historical events or the accomplishments of individuals. Approaches to the human past that focus on the related history of the lands and oceans have had a profound influence on contemporary world historians, encouraging them to set the study of historical events into the context of slow geological time that unfolds across millennia and stressing the relationship between human history and the environment.

Awareness of the relationship between environment and historical cultures has also been heightened and intensified by current ecological concerns and the rise of systems science in the past century. How the Romans polluted their water sources, the extent to which West African iron smelters deforested their environment, the relationship between population and resources in Chinese history – these historical problems echo familiarly in recent times. The roles of environment and technology were intertwined and provided both limits and opportunities to the human experience.

SUBSISTENCE AND ENVIRONMENT

Technological changes related to food strategies were fundamental in forming relationships between humans and their environment. Until trade altered the equation, the food that early hunters and gatherers consumed was limited to what was available locally. For most of human history people lived in relatively small groups, gathering and hunting what they needed from their immediate environments. Success was ultimately measured by the group's survival. Sometimes effective subsistence strategies depended on people's seasonal movements, sometimes on their cooperation, and sometimes on the occasional sharing, storage, and exchange of foods. For tens of thousands of years and, in some parts of the world throughout the twentieth century, such subsistence patterns supported human populations. Gathering, hunting, and fishing were

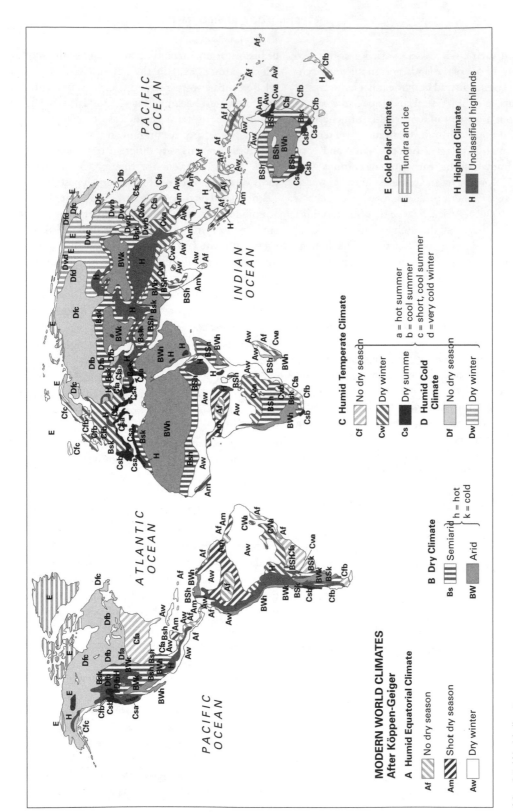

Map 2.1 World climates.

essential activities of the earliest world cultures as they provided the basic food supplies.

Dramatic climatic changes made adjustments in the relationship between humans and their environments necessary. The climatic changes were often slow, natural processes, as for example the gradual process through which the African Sahara became a vast, dry desert. Change may also have been the result of human intervention, sustained manipulation of the natural world, and overexploitation of natural resources; such environmental abuse is not confined to the present day. Extensive alteration of the environment, whether of natural or human origin, made it essential that humans change their subsistence patterns. For example, evidence indicates that prehistoric peoples in the Western Cape region of southern Africa exploited marine resources part of the year and then moved inland, where they followed territorial herds of small mammals and intensively collected plants and tubers in other seasons. Beginning 20,000 years ago, the culture of these peoples was based on a complex, interactive pattern of land use and technology adapted to their region.

Beyond the recurring seasonal cycles were larger global climate patterns. Daily and seasonal weather are the products of interlocking systems of cycles that are created by the earth's movement and the fact that the earth is globe-shaped. Because there is an inherent difference in the way the sun heats the closer middle (equator) and the more distant ends (poles) of the earth, the poles are colder than the tropics and an exchange of warming and cooling air sets off pathways of movement we call wind and weather. Scientists are beginning to identify cycles that track the movements linked to corresponding areas of warm water in the Pacific. The formation of each mass of warm water, or "El Niño," produces a countervailing pattern before reverting back. These shifts correspond to the most challenging environmental crises in world history and helped to integrate large parts of the planet even before they were connected by human interactions.

Hunting and gathering strategies were less vulnerable to climatic change than were systems of agriculture. The traditions of earlier gathering-hunting peoples were retained rather than abandoned by succeeding agriculturalists. The knowledge of flora and fauna that were not normally a part of later agricultural diets (such as edible insects, grubs, and wild plants) was used by farmers during famines and droughts. Although they can seem to be archaeologically "invisible" next to the splendor of later villages, towns, and monumental architecture, the gathering-hunting populations and their unique patterns of relationships between environment and society remained important to the herders, sedentary farmers, and townsfolk who succeeded them.

The earliest gathering-hunting societies had a profound effect on their environments. Even though early humans had no more than stone or bone tools at their disposal, they altered the environment more significantly than other species with which they shared the planet. Early gathering-hunting societies, which might be expected to have been less destructive of their environments than later agricultural and sedentary societies with their greater potential for ecological abuse, did not enjoy an unchanging relationship with nature.

Both the persistence of the nomadic lifestyle and the successful increase in societies in which hunters and gatherers settled more permanently in a favored locale were dependent on continuous cultural innovations. Technology was especially significant in negotiating the changing environmental conditions. The relationship between demographic change and technical innovation has led some scholars to suggest that constant population increase should be considered one defining characteristic of human achievement. While neither demography nor any other single factor can explain human history, the increasing size of human communities has challenged their members throughout world history by providing both an impetus for change and a reminder that humans live within the context and limits of a natural world.

FROM EARLY STONE TOOLS TO PYROTECHNOLOGY

Even the earliest human communities were dependent on tools that enabled them to sustain themselves by exploiting their environments more efficiently. Appropriate technology was basic to the ways humans organized themselves to utilize the natural resources available to them. Gathering-hunting communities relied on stone tools ranging from crude stone pounders for crushing grain, seed, and nuts to intricate, refined small stone instruments, or microliths, such as scrapers and knives, in addition to wooden digging sticks and implements fashioned from bone and other organic materials. The technology involved in tool production became increasingly proficient with experience and need. It is clear, for example, that a well-fashioned Late Stone Age tool involves greater technological expertise than a stone whose intrinsic size and shape enabled it to be used as a tool without much modification. Technology continually developed as it kept up with the changing environments and changing demands of various cultures around the world, and, as both accompaniment and cause, its impact reached revolutionary proportions during the global transitions from hunting-gathering to sedentary agrarian lifestyles.

The application of fire was one of the earliest tools that transformed the physical landscape. Fire produced dramatic changes in the lives of early humans. Its application to the sciences of cooking and fermentation altered mental landscapes, as the many examples of early alcoholic drinks attest. The modern scientific study of the dregs of ancient Egyptian beer has made it possible to identify the sophisticated technology of brewing used by the Egyptians. As the role of technology in transforming society continues to be studied and debated, there is little doubt that technology also helped fuel the lively social interactions of ancient peoples around the globe.

Fire allowed human groups to conquer new environments and probably encouraged the development of social networks and advances in communication

Figure 2.2 Egyptian tomb model of baking and brewing. In ancient Egypt domesticated barley and emmer were used for brewing a popular beverage drunk through tubes from ceramic cups. As early as 1400 BCE, pharaohs and workers consumed beer called "Joy Bringer" in taverns. Early rice beers in Asia, palm wines in West Africa, and the fermented juice of cactus in Mesoamerica intoxicated people throughout history.

through the sharing of food and shelter. The ability to cook foods expanded the diets and improved the health of early populations. Yet the simplest levels of technology were also capable of altering the environment and adversely affecting users' health. Smoke from fires in small, closed, poorly ventilated houses would have caused chronic pulmonary disease in Stone Age humans. Human-built fires, especially the burning of forests and fields, left a residue of pollutants that can be found in the past 100,000 years of polar ice strata. Pollutants such as lead aerosols, produced by ancient metallurgical technologies, have been detected in polar strata dating to periods as early as 800 BCE.

The botanical evidence available in lake-bottom sediments in Asia and East Africa suggests that significant modifications in plant and animal communities took place there as a result of prehistoric human activities such as the manufacture and use of substances that turned out to be poisonous to plants and fish. Intensive resource collecting, even ancient over-hunting and overgrazing, also created disequilibrium and change in early ecologies. For example, the hunting of the Australian marsupial lion to extinction or the overexploitation of marine mammals in the northern Pacific argue for significant human-induced changes. The loss of primary forest cover and destruction of the world's rain forests, currently a major global ecological concern, first began as a result of the systematic application of fire as an aid to hunting and food preparation with the spread of *Homo erectus* from around 500,000 years ago.

AGRICULTURAL BEGINNINGS

Today scholars and the public debate the wisdom of the genetic modification and manipulation of world flora and fauna. That process of modification began with the domestication of species and the rise of agriculture. Agricultural change is only one way in which increasingly populated societies adapted their cultural lifestyles to the changing landscape. Agriculture is the domestication of plants and animals to make them more productive. The development of agriculture began about 15,000 years ago, following the late stages of the last Ice Age. First identified from archaeological evidence in West Asia, agricultural

technology was an adaptation of forager-hunters some 4,000 years before who had begun first to harvest wild varieties of wheat and barley. Their descendants established semi-permanent villages. Striking out from their settlements, early food producers gathered useful grains like emmer, einkorn, barley and rye, leading to long-term genetic changes that made the plants dependent on human interference. The processes of deforestation accelerated with the introduction of agricultural practices and the intensified use and genetic manipulation of plants and animals to make them more productive. Other new technologies, such as pottery making and metallurgy, utilized fire and brought about even more changes in the landscape. Pollution and deforestation have been the seemingly inevitable artifacts of human technological history from ancient to contemporary times.

The movement from hunting and gathering to agriculture followed many different and seemingly independent paths around the world in response to a variety of specific environments. The movement to agricultural life was usually more difficult and labor intensive than hunting and gathering. Once established, however, agricultural societies could support larger and more complex societies than hunter-gatherer societies. As settled societies grew larger, they became stratified, revealing greater social inequality and a propensity to be more destructive of their environments.

The far-flung foraging and hunting peoples and their farming and herding descendants were impelled toward a new, intensive approach to food production. Wherever settled agricultural communities eventually appeared, so did population increases, environmental stresses, and technological innovations. While this change in the course of human history – sometimes referred to as the Neolithic Revolution – was indeed momentous, it was neither sudden nor straightforward. Rather, the "revolution" took place over thousands of years, occurred independently in different world regions, and relied heavily on the character of specific environments.

Efforts to pinpoint the earliest plant domesticates (agricultural crops) are complicated by the characteristics of the plants themselves. Cereal grains, with their hard-shelled seeds, were often burned (carbonized) during preparation and thereby preserved for archaeological discovery and analysis. In contrast, domesticated root crops lack hard, burnable parts and are otherwise difficult to distinguish from their wild ancestors. Consequently, such root crops as potatoes, yams, and manioc in the Americas, Africa, and Asia could have been domesticated even earlier than the cereals for which there is good evidence.

Sometime between 9000 and 6000 BCE, gathering and hunting peoples in West Asia gradually became both sedentary and reliant on domesticated plants and animals that they had previously collected wild. The emergence of agriculture in West Asia followed the creation of permanent settlements. The earliest such settlements found thus far are in Iran, Iraq, Syria, and Turkey, located in hill country between mountains and plains, near but not on rivers and streams. These are regions of complex ecology that offer a changing variety of wild food sources throughout the year.

Without exception, early agricultural societies became socially and materially complex communities. By at least the sixth millennium BCE, people who inhabited various regions of what we now know as China also practiced sedentary agriculture, ceramic technology, social stratification observable in burial forms, human and animal sacrifices, and systems of notation or proto-writing. The traditional Chinese view of the origins of agriculture attributed it to a sage-king called the "Heavenly Husbandman," who taught the people how to cultivate the land:

> In the time of the Heavenly Husbandman, millet fell as rain from the heavens. The Heavenly Husbandman then tilled the land and planted the millet . . . he fashioned plows and hoes with which he opened up the wasteland.
>
> (Francesca Bray, "Swords into Plowshares: A Study of Agricultural Technology and Society in Early China," *Technology and Culture*, 19 (1978): 3)

Domestication of grains and other plants depended on the use of the hoe and the digging stick, a tool also

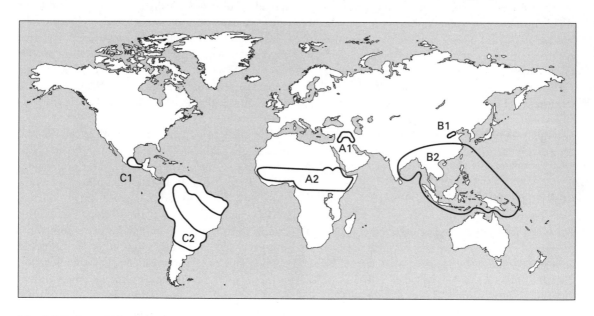

Map 2.2 Early world food crops.

Source: Cambridge Encyclopedia of Human Evolution, edited by Steve Jones, Robert Martin, and David Pilbeam (Cambridge: Cambridge University Press, 1992), p. 376.

Different regions of the world gave rise to the main food crops: A1, Near East (barley, wheat, peas, lentils and chickpeas); A2, Africa (millets, sorghum, groundnuts, yams, dates, coffee, and melons); B1, North China (millets and rice); B2, Southeast Asia (rice, bananas, sugar-cane, citrus fruits, coconuts, taro, and yams); C1, Mesoamerica (maize, squash, beans, and pumpkins); C2, South America (lima beans, potatoes, sweet potatoes, manioc, and peanuts).

used around the world by gatherers. In some areas, particularly the heavily wooded parts of northwestern Eurasia, it was necessary to use slash-and-burn techniques in order to make the transition to agriculture. Dense forests were cleared and burned, and the cleared area was cultivated until the soil was exhausted. Without properly spaced fallow periods or fertilizer, cultivation caused soil to lose its fertility rapidly. This resulted in frequent relocation, which meant, in essence, repeating the slash-and-burn techniques in a new area. Elsewhere, temporary settlements and horticulture, combined with gathering and hunting, continued for a millennium or so. The introduction of the plow was significant only in working certain soils. Technological changes in agriculture would benefit greatly from the application of oxen or horsepower to the plowing of fields, using iron plowshares around the third century BCE in China, and after about 800 CE in Europe, where the plow was combined with other innovations such as the introduction of the harness from the nomadic peoples of Asia, or the even earlier (c. 100 BCE) use of water and wind power for grinding grain that also had an impact on productivity .

WATER CONTROL AND THE ROLE OF ENVIRONMENT

What role did the environment play in the rise of agriculture? Clearly the environment provided an array of available plant and animal species for possible domestication. What factors led humans to select and invest intensively in specific species? Part of the answer rests in the attachment of human societies to the cultural memories associated with the landscapes of birth and death. Agriculture often required an investment in a single environment and sometimes in a single species. The intimate knowledge of a landscape was transmitted from one generation to the next generation, whose survival depended on it.

The success of early civilizations depended on the ability of societies to ensure their stability by adapting to changing environmental conditions and by controlling them when possible. As in Egypt and Mesopotamia, the control of water in early China was an important factor in increasing technological and political complexity. One theory has characterized such

communities as "hydraulic" societies, arguing that the demands of water control led to a concentration of power and authority. In China the need for dikes, built to prevent the Yellow River from flooding its banks and for irrigation to support wet rice agriculture, brought about the growth of a centralized bureaucratic state. While the concept of a hydraulic society may be overly deterministic, water control did play a role in dynastic changes by undermining political stability when dikes ruptured and floods destroyed homes and fields. China's two main waterways, the Yellow and Yangzi rivers, were connected by the Grand Canal, a product of human engineering in the sixth century CE that enabled grain, especially rice grown in the fertile Yangzi Delta area, to be transported to the capital area. Other smaller river systems and canals and waterways enabled the expansion of markets and a commercial economy from the eighth century onward.

The history of agriculture in the Americas suggests the importance of an ecological consideration for the list of possible explanations for the rise of farming. There is little doubt that reliance on a narrowed territory and familiar range of plants and animals made societies more susceptible to the vagaries of droughts and unpredictable weather than did the options offered by a wider range of foraging and hunting. A dramatic crisis, often referred to as the Long Drought, affected the region of the southwest of the present United States and northern Mexico; it began around 8000 BCE, reached a peak about 5500 BCE, and lasted until around 2000 BCE. The Long Drought, a period of desiccation or extended drought, was very likely the major impetus for the emergence of agriculture in North America and suggests that the transition to agriculture in parts of the Western Hemisphere is chronologically comparable to the development of agrarian practices in other parts of the world. Both the maize culture of Mesoamerica and the root culture of northwestern South America were well established by the mid-sixth millennium BCE. The emergence of "maize culture" as an alternative or supplement to poor gathering-hunting conditions was a corollary to drought. At the time of this transition to plant cultivation, animals were also being domesticated, but not for food; it appears that the essential American diet as agriculture emerged was largely vegetarian, supplemented by hunting and fishing.

FROM LOCAL TO GLOBAL FOOD SOURCES

Archaeological work in the highland Tehuacan Valley suggests that the intentional cultivation of maize first took place sometime after 6000 BCE, though the primitive maize of this early era was not yet a dietary staple. The earliest cultivators of maize were probably driven by extended droughts that had diminished the supply of wild foods across the highland region. Still, these people, living in small bands, remained primarily foragers and hunters, occupying various camps during their seasonal rounds in search of meat and other foods. Later excavation levels at Tehuacan begin to show a different picture. After 5000 BCE, a growing, somewhat less mobile Tehuacan population increased the proportion of both wild *and* domesticated plant foods in their diet while the proportion of meat decreased.

The Aztec called the domesticated plant *teocentli*, meaning "God's ear of corn." The potency of corn was believed by the early Mesomericans to be both spiritual and physical. According to Aztec beliefs, the first human couple cast kernels of maize to divine their future. With corn and other selected plants, the vision of that future would include the eventual creation of permanent, settled communities and large ceremonial complexes. Yet as the eventual staple of Mesoamerica and much of North and South America, corn initially did not necessarily have a great immediate impact wherever it appeared. Archaeologists have been able to measure the carbon atoms in human bone excavated from sites in the Americas in order to identify how much corn ancient people did eat, whether this corn was eaten in combination with other particular foods such as marine resources, and whether those populations were mobile, thus adding another scientific means of determining the dates, diffusion, and impact of the crop. The exchange of world foods after Columbus brought corn to other parts of the world, where the impact on population growth was significant.

Today the post-Columbian processes of globalization have brought people into contact with the foods of new continents. Plants like the chili pepper, native to the Americas, have conquered the cuisines of the planet. Peanuts, maize, soy, and improved strains of rice have supported dramatic population changes and altered the destinies of world societies. The eventual reliance of humans on global rather than local food has been debated since at least the time of the eighteenth-century French philosopher Rousseau, who expressed suspicion regarding foods that were imported from far-away lands. The transfer of foods from original habitats to new ones was accelerated by the processes some historians have identified as ecological imperialism, acknowledging the impact of the European-dominated transfer of plants, animals, and diseases.

VILLAGES, TOWNS, AND ENVIRONMENT

The entrenchment and spread of agricultural systems in the millennia between 12,000 and 2000 BCE set off explosions in both food production and population. Deliberate agriculture in most world regions fostered impressive increases in population, which in turn gave rise to the spread of early agricultural peoples to new areas of the globe. However, as agricultural peoples overtook foraging and hunting peoples, the relationship of humans to their environment began to change dramatically. Nonetheless, the transition to agriculture worldwide presents such a range of examples that no single explanatory model satisfies. The emergence of various agricultural systems and sedentary societies occurred quite independently at vastly different times and followed different scenarios in many different parts of the world, ranging from river valleys to dry, temperate upland areas.

Greater numbers of people living together in relatively stable communities, with domesticated animals also living close by, gave rise to infectious diseases and other illnesses that were easily spread by settled peoples and rare among the peripatetic forager-hunters. For example, because of its long urban tradition, China domesticated crowd diseases like measles and smallpox early on. Once animal husbandry was adopted, China, unlike the Americas, had experience with diseases shared with animals, such as influenza. The peoples of the Americas were devastated by their first contact with diseases carried by pigs introduced during the European conquest. The greater concentrations of sedentary human communities, geared to an *intensive* relationship with their environment rather than an *extensive* one, also resulted in frequent cases of environmental degradation: polluted wells, contaminated rivers and streams, and defoliated landscapes. So, while birth rates rose (in part because of changes in weaning, nursing, and birth spacing) among the settled agricultural populations, diets became narrower, labor became more routinized, and life expectancies fell.

THE AGE OF METALS

The second major area of human impact on the environment resulted from the use of metals, long indicative of technological "advances" synonymous with definitions of civilization. The impact of the increasingly complex material culture was visible even in the earliest communities: the cutting down of trees for firewood contributed to the early evidence of deforestation that has continued until today. Wood fueled the firing of pottery used to store food and the working of metals to be made into implements. About the time fired pottery generally came into use (c. 6000 BCE), technologies for working metal were developed. Metallurgical technologies were used to produce tools that had a great effect on agriculture – and commerce and war as well – at the time the transition to sedentary societies was occurring.

The "age of metals" varied from place to place and came earlier to some places than others. Not all societies developed technologies for the same metals. In West Asia, the Balkans, Spain, and the Aegean, for instance, copper metallurgy was the first to develop (between 6000 BCE and 2500 BCE). After iron metallurgy was developed (at least as early as c. 2500 BCE with the working of meteoritic iron and after about 1600 BCE by smelting iron ores), it began to supersede all others in areas where iron ore was available. Iron, being a harder, stronger metal able to retain sharp edges, could be used to create more durable and useful tools. As the demand for metal tools increased, the uneven distribution of ores around the globe endowed some societies with riches and others with the need to trade. Tin-bronzes, alloys or mixtures of copper and tin (or lead or antimony) are found at Velikent in Daghestan (in the Caucasus region) in the third millennium. By about 1500 BCE, the demand for superior bronze, metals harder than copper (though not as hard as iron), resulted in the importation of tin from as far away as Cornwall (in West England) or Central Asia to West and Southeast Asia for use in bronze metallurgy. Unlike the working of stone, a material that remained essentially unchanged except in shape, metalworking represented a fundamental

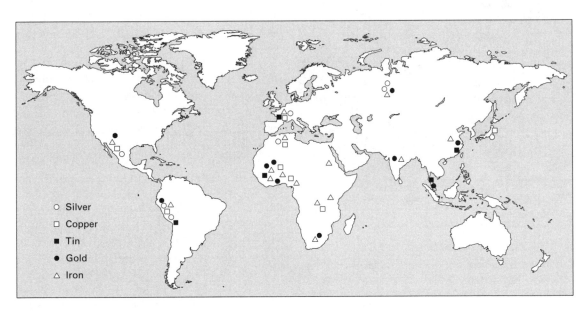

Map 2.3 Early metal sources before 1500 CE.

alchemy: the very nature of matter was changed by human skill and technology.

Metallurgy had a devastating impact on the environment everywhere it was employed. Mining activities themselves were destructive, as Neolithic miners of silex (chalk), flint, and obsidian demonstrated around the world. The first use of native copper required no underground extraction, but soon afterward the copper and tin of most ancient workings began to be found in veins or lodes in older, harder rock. Its extraction required the use of fire and specialized stone hammers, and ultimately the construction of shafts and support and drainage systems. Deforestation

and soil erosion were common consequences of mining and working of metals.

Metallurgy in Africa and the Americas

In West Africa, the production of iron and steel (probably after 2000 BCE) was perceived to harness both technical and spiritual forces. Adept in changing the very nature of matter, metallurgy specialists emerged as powerful members of the community. Their powers depended on the most powerful deities: those controlling the manufacture of iron tools and weapons. The site of Meroe (c. 400 BCE) in the middle Nile is an example of the intensive exploitation of pyrotechnological knowledge. Substantial quantities of slag, the waste product of iron smelting, together with surviving tools, including spears, tweezers, adzes, axes, hoe blades, and shears, suggest an impressive industry. The fuel consumption of major African metallurgical centers such as that at Meroe created serious problems of deforestation, and industries eventually declined as forests disappeared. The specialists – workers in iron, copper, gold, and glass – who altered the environment with such devastating impact were held in awe, both revered and feared. Control over technology, in Africa as elsewhere, served as a vehicle for the expression of social and political dominance and subordination. Metals acquired symbolic importance as expressions of power and social distinctions.

In the Andean zone of western South America (modern Peru, Bolivia, Ecuador, and Colombia), metals played only a minor role in warfare: there were no Andean bronze- or steel-tipped weapons, and cloth and worked fibers provided weaponry (slings for projectiles) and protective armor. Obsidian, a naturally formed volcanic glass, was highly prized and widely traded in its raw form, which was shaped into arrowheads and spear points. The role of metals was relegated to non-utilitarian realms. In the Andean region, copper, gold, and silver were used decoratively and artistically to convey both secular and religious status and power. The Andean craft worker was interested in a metal's color and appearance, not in its strength or durability. Sophisticated techniques of alloying, gilding, and silvering that used electrochemical methods of surface alteration dominated the

Figure 2.3 Iron smelting furnace, Bassari region, Togo, West Africa. The study of recent technological practices has aided the interpretation of archaeological remains of metalworking. Tall, natural-draft furnaces produced high-carbon iron and steel. Specialist knowledge required for their operation was restricted to the men in certain lineages.

repertoire of metalsmiths in Andean societies during the first millennium CE.

Complex copper metallurgies helped to shape South American societies. As early as 500 BCE, peoples on the northern Peruvian coast worked copper and gold. Later artisans also produced a copper–gold alloy well suited to sheet-metal working. At a reconstructed Peruvian site dating to between 900 and 1500 CE, archaeologists have excavated the earliest evidence in the world of intensive smelting of copper–arsenic alloys. The furnace openings revealed elaborate sacrificial offerings of llamas and food. Ceramic-tipped cane blowing tubes were used to raise the furnace temperatures, and additives were used to help remove impurities so that nearly pure copper could be produced. Each smelting would have produced only about 0.3 to 0.6 of a kilogram (0.66 to 1.32 pounds) of metallic copper, yet used enormous quantities of fuel. Accordingly, the burial of a leader with about 500 kilograms (1,100 pounds) of copper objects was an ostentatious statement of power and wealth.

Copper–silver and copper–gold alloys expressed significant cultural aspects of Andean value systems. For example, when copper encased or was alloyed with pure gold, the hidden or disguised gold was thought to represent the divine quality of a seemingly human ruler. In South America as elsewhere, technology reflected cultural preoccupations and provides critical evidence for understanding gender and status in early societies and cultures. Ironically, South American silver would play a major role in globalization and environmental loss after 1500 CE.

Metallurgy in Eurasia

This pattern of metallurgical development in Africa and the Americas stands in contrast to Eurasia, where the Copper Age was followed by the Bronze Age, and then by the Iron Age. The technology that dominated in each of these new eras was defined by the inevitable replacement of the older metal by the newer one. By the third millennium BCE, communities in China, the Indus Valley, and the western Mediterranean basin constituted examples of Bronze Age culture as a result of their significant advances in metallurgical expertise. Bronze (an alloy combining copper and tin) was an elaboration of the earliest copper metallurgy, which

had developed in areas adjacent to abundant ancient copper sources such as those near the Balkans, in the Sinai, and in East and Southeast Asia. In Thailand, where the earliest evidence of a tin and copper alloy was once thought to predate the third millennium, development of bronze is not thought to have begun before 2000 BCE. The Egyptians had previously added arsenic to copper (probably around 3000 BCE) to produce silvered bronze mirrors with reflective surfaces; they did not alloy copper with tin before about 2000 BCE. In China, bronze weapons were used by the founders of the first historic dynasty, the Shang (c. 1600–1045 BCE), which emerged on the north China plain in the early part of the second millennium BCE. In addition to weapons, bronze ritual vessels were cast for use in ceremonies sanctioning the political legitimacy of the Shang kings.

The transition from bronze to iron in the Mediterranean basin and Europe was late and sporadic. Bronze metallurgy there dates variously from the second millennium BCE; it was accompanied by the rise of increasingly hierarchical communities with growing populations. Eurasian metallurgy and deforestation in the early Bronze Age may contribute to quantifying and understanding human interactions with the climate system over time. Bronze fulfilled Europeans' needs for perhaps a thousand years before it was superseded by iron. From the sixth century BCE, Greek and Roman societies relied on iron for tools and weapons, but as early as the eighth century BCE the Greek poet Hesiod (fl. c. 776 BCE) had lamented the new Iron Age: "I wish that I were not any part of the fifth generation of men. . . . For here now is the age of iron." Hesiod's doubts about the effects of iron weapons on Greek culture were hardly an enthusiastic endorsement of inevitable or progressive change. Technological innovations have produced mixed responses throughout history.

One important factor in the adoption of iron for use in weapons was its relatively widespread availability. The environmental costs were high because of the dense woods required to produce consistently high temperatures inside the smelting furnaces. Though iron ore was difficult to extract and purify, once successful metallurgical techniques could produce useful amounts, iron superseded all previous metals for weapons and tools. It was the principal form of iron produced in Europe until the nineteenth century, when new techniques revolutionized iron metallurgy there.

In China, the preferred iron products were cast iron and steel, high-carbon alloys that were much harder. Chinese artisans were producing cast iron and steel by the fourth century BCE. Both were widely used in the era known as the Warring States (481–221 BCE). The introduction and widespread use of iron were related to the dramatic social and economic changes that resulted from conflict and frequent shifts of power during this period. Iron was used for weapons, and warfare created conditions in which those with access to iron technology were at an advantage. A third-century BCE text refers to "spearheads of steel . . . sharp as a bee's sting." Iron was also used by the time of the Warring States for the share, or blade, of the ox-drawn plow, probably based on wooden plows used by Chinese farmers in wet ricelands.

Despite the chaotic conditions in China resulting from war, or perhaps in part because of them, iron acquired great value – and even commercial exchange utilized iron currency. Merchants grew rich on its profits and agriculture prospered, aided by the use of iron tools. After the unification of the empire in the third century BCE, the government quickly grasped the importance of controlling iron production as a source of revenue. In the second century BCE, Emperor Wu of the Han dynasty (202 BCE–220 CE) created government monopolies of salt and iron. Criticisms by Confucian scholars such as those preserved in the *Debates on Salt and Iron* (81 BCE), did not succeed in ending the monopolies, and later dynasties continued to control the production and sale of salt and iron (along with other metals such as tin, copper, lead).

By the first millennium CE, cast-iron technology was commonly used to manufacture household items such as scissors and to build temples, pagodas, and bridges. But the environmental costs were great: before the end of the first millennium, north China was deforested. The expansion of iron production after this depended on the use of coal or coke. By the Song dynasty (960–1279) the technological and production levels of the iron industry in north China equaled that of the early stages of the Industrial Revolution in England over five hundred years later. Mining continued to be a lucrative and essential enterprise controlled by the state, which licensed the production of iron and other metals. An eighteenth-century poem reveals something of the conditions experienced by mine workers:

Lament for the Copper-bearing Hills
by Wang Taiyue

They gather, at dawn, by the mouth of the shaft,
Standing there naked, their garments stripped
    off,
Lamps strapped to their heads in carrying-
    baskets,
To probe in the darkness the fathomless bottom
    . . .

In the chill of the winter, their bodies will
    tremble,
Hands blistered with chillblains. Their feet will
    be chapped.
Down the mine, for this reason, they huddle
    together,
But hardly revive, life-force at a standstill . . .

The wood they must hunt is no longer available.
The woods are shaved bald, like a convict's
    head. Blighted,
Only now they regret – felling day after day
Has left them no way to provide for their
    firewood.
                    (Elvin and Liu Ts'ui-jung, 1998: 10–11)

Everywhere metallurgy was practiced, the impact on the environment was visible. Wang Taiyue's poem suggests the human and ecological dimensions of exploitation. Chinese miners' livelihoods grew increasingly difficult as the ore became scarce and the wood needed for smelting was used up.

TECHNOLOGY AND ENVIRONMENT: FUELING INDUSTRY

The demand for iron and steel accelerated in Europe after about 1000 CE because of an increased demand for weapons of war and conquest and a growing population's need of more implements for farm, house, and industry. As a result, the scarcity of wood for charcoal, an essential ingredient of the smelting process, soon jeopardized the English and other

European iron industries. One effect of the charcoal shortage was to shift the center of iron metallurgy from one country to another. Sweden, for example, which had plenty of trees as well as iron ore, became the leading European iron producer by the eighteenth century, replacing Germany and France. In countries such as Great Britain, the shortage of trees resulted in the replacement of charcoal with pit coal, which was abundant there.

The key to increasing the production of iron and steel, once the major processes were in place, was clearly fuel, but the use of coal presented complicated problems. At all stages of iron-making and steel-making, the use of coal impaired the quality of the product by introducing impurities. In 1614 a method was discovered for using coal in converting bar iron into a high-carbon product (steel), but for almost a hundred years no advance was made toward the use of coal in the all-important blast furnace in which iron could be smelted in huge and continuous quantities.

In the seventeenth century some brewers in Derbyshire, England, tried using coal to dry their malt. The presence of sulfur in coal ruined the taste of their beer, but when they refined the coal by heating it to produce coke, a new coal fuel, they got rid of the sulfur and brewed a famous beer. This industrial tale did not escape the notice of charcoal-short, thirsty iron makers. The first successful experiment in coke iron-making was conducted at Coalbrookdale, in Shropshire, England, in 1709 by Abraham Darby (1677–1721), who had served his apprenticeship in the malt mill of a brewery. Darby's use of coke in his blast furnace was not taken up quickly by others; because it remained an expensive process until the application of steam power, only six other coke furnaces were built in Great Britain in the next half century. Coke smelting gradually opened a new phase in iron technology and ranks with the steam engine as a major component in the European Industrial Revolution, which occurred between 1750 and 1850. What might have happened if West African iron industries could have exploited new sources of fuel as their forests dwindled? This was not an option since there were no suitable coal deposits available to be mined. In China, much earlier use of coal had shaped the cast-iron industry, but the technological development occurred in a vastly different economic and political context. In this way,

the Industrial Revolution favored the industries of some parts of the world over others.

SCIENCE, TECHNOLOGY, AND THE INDUSTRIAL REVOLUTION

Practical applications of most early European scientific knowledge were few and far between, but the scientific revolution of the sixteenth and seventeenth centuries led to a new habit of mind: a new way of analyzing particular problems to solve them. Technological innovations took place in spheres far removed from the rarefied and well-educated arenas of abstract scientific philosophy and theory, but they also relied on the research and reasoning skills of science. For example, potters and machinists were members of the British Royal Society and French Academy of Science (founded in 1660 and 1666 respectively), and they used experimentation and scientific reasoning to solve major technological problems related to commercial production and overseas commerce – from reproducing Chinese porcelain to constructing clocks and mechanical toys. Innovations that materially transformed Europe sometimes developed in the workshops of uneducated craftsmen. Such innovation was not based on abstractions or theory but from experience in working with the commoner elements of base metals and sooty fuel. Among important European technological changes that accompanied the development of theoretical science were those in metallurgy, especially the production of iron. Innovations in iron production supported the advances that made the European Industrial Revolution possible.

Beginning after about 1700, the onset of the Industrial Revolution brought about unprecedented levels of exploitation, measured by costs in human and natural resources. Many global changes in material culture can be linked to the rise of industrial capitalism worldwide. At the heart of these material transformations were profound changes in the ways people perceived themselves in relation to the natural world. Dramatic technological changes and equally dramatic economic transformations resulted in changes in the physical and social organization of life. While many of these changes occurred first in Europe, their impact was not limited to European territory. Around the globe the products and impact of industrialism altered everyday lives. The rapidity of change began to create a greater awareness of the age-old experience of globalization.

The acceleration of technology in the eighteenth century was termed an "industrial revolution," and like other clustered innovations in world history it provided new materials and means of production. The Industrial Revolution did not occur in isolation, but soon had a global scope. Eighteenth-century technological innovations coupled with expanding capitalism to revolutionize first European and American societies and their relationship with the non-European world. Other parts of the world soon followed. The Industrial Revolution also introduced new iron technology; indeed the parameters of the revolution may be set by the introduction of coke as a substitute for charcoal in the smelting process (eighteenth century) and eventually the perfection of a new and successful process for steel-making (nineteenth century). The French writer Emile Zola described the potentialities of the era in his novel *Germinal* (1885):

> Beneath the blazing of the sun, in that morning of new growth, the countryside rang with song, as its belly swelled with a black and avenging army of men, germinating slowly in its furrows, growing upwards in readiness for harvests to come, until one day soon their ripening would burst open the earth itself.

The scope of technological achievements that begin in the mid-eighteenth century, their relationship to global economic changes, and their broad impact perhaps justify the use of the term "global industrial revolution."

Steam power

Technological innovations in the eighteenth century took place principally in industries such as mining, metallurgy, and textiles. Most industrial innovations were produced by mechanics, craftsmen connected with the enterprises their innovations helped transform. Steam power was a dramatic leap from harnessing the power of water, horses, or heat; harnessing steam required a mechanical application. Since steam

Figure 2.4 Edgar Thomson's steel works. The artist Joseph Pennell (1857–1926) sketched the grittiness of the local steel industry, capturing its precarious approach of powerlines and transportation systems, as well as its visible impact on skyline and landscape.

power is so much associated with the eighteenth-century Industrial Revolution, the building of a steam engine in 1712 by Thomas Newcomen, a mechanic, may be taken as its inaugural event: all modern engines, either in factories or applied to locomotion, are descendants of Newcomen's engine. The earliest steam engines were solely pumping engines, restricted to coal mines; they were not very efficient and were expensive to operate. Eventually, however, their applications would create powerful tools for the expansion of Europe and the processes of urbanization and industrialization globally.

New machines created a textile revolution, but not until they were harnessed to the Watt engine. The new power-driven machinery, which was responsible for increased textile production, depended on the increased availability of metal, particularly iron. Thus the innovations in metallurgy were as important as the steam engine in generating the Industrial Revolution. But the problem of dwindling fuel supplies remained a chief obstacle to large-scale production. The substitution of coke for charcoal provided fuel for the full-scale application of steam to industry without which there might not have been an industrial revolution. Without the increased supplies of iron, Watt and Boulton could not have produced steam engines on a commercial scale, and without steam engines the European transformation from domestic industry to the factory system is difficult to imagine. Equally important were the sources of capital, labor, and raw materials, and the markets that consumed the increased production. Underpinning all these innovations was the Atlantic slave trade, which provided labor and markets and produced capital for investment in industry.

INDUSTRIAL CAPITALISM, TRANSPORTATION, AND PRODUCTION

The demands for increased production, and the rise of global markets, were at the heart of the new system of industrial capitalism (see Chapter 6). The ability to capitalize on the global market and to exploit global resources relied on new forms of transportation. Improvements in transportation affected industrial production of every type. Efficient and cheap movement of goods was instrumental in providing supplies necessary for the growth of production and satisfying the market demand necessary to sustain it. These technological changes took place in a global context. By 1829 a practical steam locomotive was developed by George Stephenson in England, and shortly thereafter railway construction proceeded rapidly. In England alone railway track grew from 49 miles in 1830 to 15,300 in 1870. By the end of the century, Europe was knit together by a network of rail lines, and by 1905 travelers could go from Paris to Moscow and on to Vladivostok on the Pacific via the lengthy (9,288 kilometres or 5,772 miles long) trans-Siberian railway. Imperialists in Africa dreamed of a Cape to Cairo version of the same.

Equally important to industrial growth in Europe was the development of practical ocean-going steam-ships, which made all parts of the world readily available as sources of raw materials and markets for finished products of European factories. As early as 1785, a steamboat had plied the Potomac River in the United States, but less than sixty years later regular trans-Atlantic passenger steamship lines were inaugurated – and mail and commercial applications soon followed. More than any other invention, the railroad came to symbolize the global reach of the Industrial Revolution. Railways spread across North America and Europe. The Trans-Continental Railroad in the United States was completed in 1869 when tracks connected Omaha and Sacramento (2,826 km or 1,756 miles) and the Orient Express originally (c. 1869) connected Paris and Istanbul (2,254 km or 1,400 miles). Railways also connected the interior reaches of African colonies to coastal ports and furthered the military control of imperial Asia. These innovations relied on iron and coal.

Demands for supplies and for finished goods doubled every few years with the expansion of global markets. For example, iron production, basic to the machine age, increased a hundredfold in the nineteenth century. Innovations in metallurgy, an important aspect of the eighteenth-century beginnings of capitalist industrialization, continued in the nineteenth century. An English engineer, Henry Bessemer (1813–83), patented a process for the efficient conversion of iron to hard steel in 1856, and about the same time William Siemens (1823–83), a German who had settled in England, perfected an alternative process. These innovations in turn relied on new sources of fuel. Many new industries appeared in the decades after 1850, and this tendency accelerated in the twentieth century.

GLOBAL TRANSFORMATIONS

Among the more important new industries appearing in the second half of the nineteenth century were those connected to new sources of power such as electricity. Dynamos (electrical generators capable of delivering power) and motors (converting electricity into a mechanical motion) were improved and multiplied, and new kinds of engines resulted in the development of industrial production unheard of during the initial eighteenth-century phase of the capitalist Industrial Revolution. This status was especially true of the internal combustion engine, which would result in the twentieth-century triumph of motorized vehicles and, among other things, cause the world production of petroleum to leap 1,000 percent in the first thirty years of the twentieth century.

At the same time a conspicuous growth of essential consumer industries occurred, producing aids to individual comfort that greatly improved both the style and standard of material life – first in much of the western world and ultimately around the globe. For example, in 1879 Thomas A. Edison (1847–1931) patented the greatest of his inventions, the incandescent lamp, which would rapidly become a necessary luxury. Artificial fabrics, such as rayon, patented by the French chemist Hilaire Chardonnet (1836–1924), and artificial dyes, made finery widely and cheaply available. None of these technological changes occurred without access to the full range of global products, especially tropical ones like palm oil and rubber. In this way, the Industrial Revolution was a global affair. But its impact was not felt equally by all nations. The exploitation of the new industrial cash crops replaced local agricultural production for subsistence in favor of manufacturing enterprises around the globe (especially in European colonies), with growing consequences for the dependency relationships and underdevelopment of much of the planet (see Chapter 8).

Refrigeration, first used on ships in 1877, added immeasurably to the availability and variety of foodstuffs. British Guyanese in South America could eat "ice apples," the fruit of North America carried on ice in steamer ships; while children in Detroit ate tropical oranges. The world became the garden for urban industrial workers who could not raise their own food in the rapidly expanding cities where they were confined. A member of the wealthy elite in any number of world cities might sit down to a meal gathered from five continents, and commoners who could afford to do so indulged in foods and supplies that even kings of an earlier age could not have imagined. Coal- and oil-burning furnaces kept people warm and comfortable, and trains, ships, trams, bicycles, and in time the automobile kept the population mobile. The impact of a number of technological innovations was to make the vagaries of environment uniformly hospitable for some, regardless of climate and season, day or night.

ELECTRIFYING CHANGE

Technology has shaped both urban and rural environments, and the daily lives of people who migrated to cities and those who remained in rural areas. Developments in technology altered the quality, conduct, and even length of daily life. Industrialization took place not only in factories, public transport systems or marketplaces but also in the home. Although Michael Faraday built the first electric motor in 1831, more than half a century passed before Nicola Tesla, working for the Westinghouse Company, successfully patented a small electric motor for use as an electric fan (1889). In the 1890s electric current was still a luxury discussed everywhere, but generally agreed upon as being too expensive for common use. Inventors like Tesla, on the other hand, predicted that electricity would soon be used as casually as water. The electrification of the home took place in industrialized parts of the world first: electric lights rapidly replaced gas lamps between 1918 and 1928, making the reliance on natural daylight obsolete for many.

Changes in the lighting of community streets and individual homes were not the most profound effects of electrification. The advent of electric lighting increased the length of the work day and altered material life. In the United States and other industrialized parts of the world in the 1920s, electric irons and electric washing machines became widespread symbols of the Industrial Revolution in the home. Yet these and other innovations and appliances did not reduce the amount of household labor performed by women; the number of tasks multiplied and increased awareness of such things as germs and hygiene required more frequent washing as new standards imposed additional tasks.

The increased consumption of material goods created by industrial technology in turn brought women to the forefront of a consuming public. A study in Oregon in 1928 revealed that farm wives (many without electricity) spent 61 hours a week on housework; "electrified" town wives spent 63.4 hours. Just after the Second World War, economists reported that farm wives spent 60.55 hours on housework each week,

Figure 2.5 Tokyo traffic, *c.* 1957. Traffic gridlocks in world cities began with congestion by horse-drawn omnibus traffic in the early nineteenth century and led to public transportation systems, including London's subway in 1863, Paris's in 1900, New York's in 1904, and Tokyo's in 1927. Even the automobile was once hailed as a transportation solution because it was quiet and less visibly polluting of streets.

women in small cities spent 78.35 hours, and women in large cities spent 80.57 hours – a trend that some historians have viewed as contributing to the call for a women's liberation movement of the late twentieth century. In turn, inventions that rely on electricity, such as the radio, television, and computer have changed the nature of family and household life. Whereas listening to the radio in the 1940s or watching television in the 1950s was often a family ritual that linked isolated households to the larger community, technological changes have made these innovations more widely available to individuals, with the result that their use is less social. Finally, the dependence on electricity has led to the need to harness the power of an ever-larger number of waterways, contributing to the growing imbalance between human societies and their relationships to the natural world.

THE LANDSCAPES OF IMPERIALISM

European Enlightenment attitudes toward nature as a force to be harnessed, controlled, and exploited by civilization intersected with the expansion of imperialism in the nineteenth century (see Chapter 7). This philosophical notion of conquering nature has increasingly become the model and pattern for non-Western societies, and its global acceptance has brought humanity to the threshold of ecological disaster at the end of the twentieth century. Ecological imperialism was intertwined with the political aims of colonial powers. For example, the British Raj exploited and destroyed the forests of the western Himalayas between 1815 and 1914 while building the most sophisticated forestry service in the colonial world. The colonization of nature was viewed as just as inevitable as the subjugation of peoples by colonial powers.

Europeans considered fenced and cultivated gardens as the most appealing and idyllic landscapes during the nineteenth century, a kind of colonization of nature. The landscape legacy of this colonization is found in the national parks of the world: from Kenya to Ghana to Yosemite, protected landscapes became necessary to preserve at least some semblance of the wilderness and its wildlife that was nearly lost to the nineteenth- and early twentieth-century rampages of imperialism. Colonial officers and other Europeans collected plants and animals from around the world to create botanical gardens and zoological parks, as well as mine them for valuable knowledge and marketable products. Through what some scholars have called "bioprospecting," the global encounters of colonizers with new environments threatened those without power. For example, both African slaves and Amerindians used abortifacients and other plants to control female fertility and resist oppression; but knowledge of those plants was never transferred to Europe, possibly the consequence of the male-dominated colonial enterprise. Today, multinational corporations vie for the "copyright" control over new species of highly productive plants.

From Thailand to the Amazon to equatorial Africa to the Pacific Northwest of the United States and Canada, the exploitation of forests changed global landscapes dramatically and impinged on centuries-long patterns of land and resource use. Scientific study aided the ability of societies to further comprehend and exploit the natural world. The global trend toward deforestation was not so much a response to the pressure of growing population as it was a consequence of world market forces, generated by global demands for commodities and raw materials. In particular, the markets of industrialized nations have demanded timber for construction, newsprint, and other paper products. A product of the collaboration between wealthy and less-developed nations, deforestation made many rural populations more dependent on international market needs and external control. The irony is that in many parts of the world, as scientific information about the forest systems was increasing, the forests themselves, increasingly exploited, disappeared. By the end of the twentieth century, an estimated 20.4 million hectares of tropical forest was being lost annually. Largely due to deforestation, approximately 1.4 percent of the world's environments now contain roughly half of the planet's biodiversity, making the future loss of forests even more critical.

WATER WARS

Deforestation is but one aspect of the global attack on environmental balance. Since the earliest "hydraulic civilizations," the control over water has symbolized and amassed political and economic power. Growing demands for electric power created by the needs of expanding technology and population have resulted in massive alterations in the landscape and the environment. Beginning in the 1920s dams in the Americas helped create agricultural stability at high environmental costs. The Alvaro Obregon Dam built in 1926 supplies the Yacqui Valley in Sonora, Mexico, with water for its wheat and sunflower fields. The Hoover Dam, completed in 1936, similarly waters the deserts of California, creating agricultural fields. The Aswan High Dam along the southern Nile was built in the 1960s at a cost of $1 billion to provide hydroelectric power. Supported in part by Soviet aid, the dam created a 300-mile-long lake, named Lake Nasser after Egypt's president, and inundated many villages along the Nile as well as some historical monuments. In the 1990s China began construction of the enormous Three Gorges Dam along the upper reaches of the Yangtze River at a projected cost of as much as $75 billion. When completed in 2009, this dam will constitute the world's largest hydroelectric plant. Its construction will inundate farmland and villages to create a 400-mile-long reservoir, forcing the evacuation of an estimated 1.5–2 million people from their homes. Criticism by environmental groups sensitive to its impact on landscape and people has delayed international financing for the project, which was to come largely from American, Canadian, and European banks. The trans-state and international trade of water and water rights, encouraged by greed and wasteful consumption, has increasingly threatened lives around the globe.

TECHNOLOGY AND WAR

Control over the environment has also been the direct consequence of technological advantages in warfare. Many of the earliest human tools were also weapons. The utilization of horse-mounted warriors, while limited to specific environmental conditions, similarly enabled some political entities to gain advantages through warfare. Some scholars have even argued that the earliest age of male warriors altered gender balances within societies and created worldwide systems of male domination.

Control over technology and territory went hand in hand. A Chinese invention, gunpowder, when combined with the production of iron, had dramatic consequences not only for the Chinese but also for the world. The first evidence of knowledge of gunpowder dates from the ninth century and was connected to Daoist alchemical experimentation, by which Daoists sought ways to transform one element into another. By the year 1000, the combination of charcoal, saltpeter (potassium nitrate), and sulfur that yields gunpowder was being used by the Chinese in small incendiary devices. Gradually more complex and sophisticated weapons were used in Song warfare against their northern nomadic neighbors, and both the discovery of gunpowder and the advanced state of

Figure 2.6 Seller of water bottles, Mexico City, *c.* 1910–15. Technology has redistributed scarce world resources, including water.

the iron industry in north China would seem to have made the Chinese formidable foes. But in the early twelfth century, north China was conquered by the Jurchen people from Manchuria whose horsemanship and military skill enabled them to defeat the Chinese. With the Jurchen conquest of north China, an early form of technology transfer took place that eventually put both iron and gunpowder (in the form of fire-lances and bombs, not yet guns) into the hands of the Mongols, who succeeded the Jurchen, and contributed significantly to the Mongol conquest of Eurasia in the thirteenth century (see Chapter 7).

Five centuries later the transfer of technology played a key role in expanding empires; it was not only transportation and communication innovations but weapons themselves that became tools of empire. The reliance on fossil fuels since the invention of the automobile in the late nineteenth century has resulted in the industrialized world's desire to control oilfields; this in turn has had environmental and human costs. In the Gulf War, the Kuwait desert and shoreline were subjected to oil spills, fires, and bombing. The earlier Vietnam War included levels of bombing that defoliated the tropical forest canopy, leaving behind craters and destroying much of the land's productivity. Toxic waste remains a threat from Cambodia to Europe.

Nuclear power also emerged in the context of the Second World War. The atomic bomb was the most controversial technology of the Second World War. Its use by the United States against Japan in August 1945 created the threat of global warfare and environmental destruction ever after. Satellite technology, first given an impetus from the use of captured German V-2 rockets to make measurements in the upper atmosphere, eventually allowed for long-term global observations of the land surface, biosphere, atmosphere, and oceans of the planet. Yet the view of the planet from space is an increasingly troubled one.

ECOLOGY, TECHNOLOGY, AND GLOBAL WARMING

The soaring forces of globalization continue to have a direct impact on the environment today. Two factors decide how much damage each person does to the environment: (1) consumption patterns, and (2) technological style (the kind of technology used and the waste and pollution it creates). While in industrialized countries, the "top billion" have lower birth rates, they are responsible for the largest share of resources used, waste created, damage to the ozone layer, acidification, and roughly two-thirds of global warming. The combination of poverty and population growth among the "bottom billion" is, of course, also damaging the environment through deforestation and land degradation. Most scientists agree that the resultant climate change called "global warming" is a major threat to human life. According to the 2007 report from the Intergovernmental Panel on Climate Change, the projected rise in temperature in the next half century is significant (perhaps as high as 2.8 degrees Celsius) and is creating a climate shift unmatched in human history. For centuries to come, continued warming would be expected to cause melting of the ice sheets and rises in sea levels with implications for increased hurricanes and cyclones, tropical diseases, droughts, and loss of habitats

Much of the responsibility for the world's ecological crisis lies in the kind of technology developed since the middle of the last century. Contemporary technology is potentially cleaner than the coal-produced iron technology of the eighteenth-century Industrial Revolution, but most technical developments in the last half century have been more harmful than earlier ones and they continue to burn fossil fuels and emit greenhouse gases at alarming rates. The main difference is the development of synthetic products to replace natural, organic ones. Compounding the technological and ecological changes is the expanding scale of human impact. In the 1970s industrial pollution became a serious national issue in Japan and revealed the most negative aspects of Japan's rapid economic growth over the last century. Mercury poisoning was suspected in the town of Minamata on the southernmost island of Kyûshû, but authorities refused to recognize the obvious source of pollution, a chemical company that was pouring wastes into the bay where most of the residents caught fish for food. Although the link between effluents discharged into Minamata Bay by the company and the cases of mercury poisoning began to be made as early as 1953, twenty years passed before formal legal action was taken and before any compensation was awarded to the more than 10,000 victims

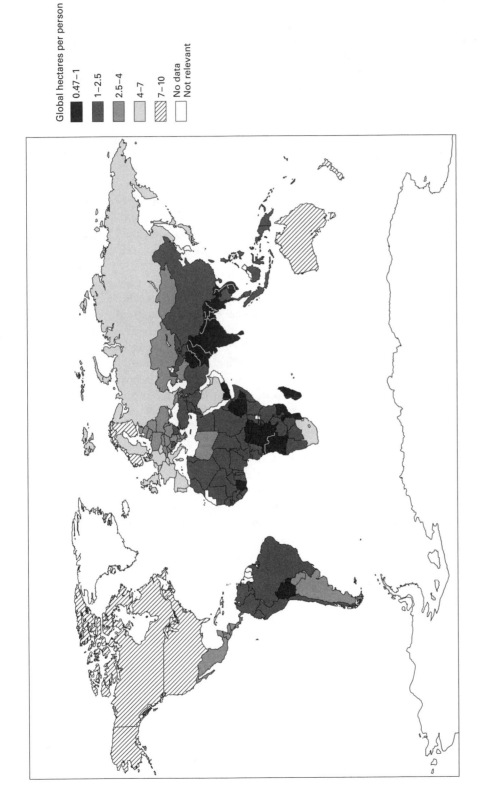

Global hectares per person

- ▉ 0.47–1
- ▉ 1–2.5
- ▉ 2.5–4
- ▢ 4–7
- ▨ 7–10
- ▨ No data
- ▢ Not relevant

Map 2.4 Ecological footprint.

Source: Adapted from <http://globalis.gvu.unu.edu/?840>. *Living Planet*, 2002 (WWF)

The Ecological footprint (EF) is a measure of the consumption of renewable natural resources by a human population. A country's EF is the total area of productive land or sea required to produce all the crops, meat, seafood, wood, and fiber it consumes to sustain its energy consumption and to give space for its infrastructure. The EF can be compared with the biologically productive capacity of the land and sea available to that country's population.

To calculate the number of hectares available per capita, one adds up the biologically productive land per capita worldwide of arable land, pasture, forest, built-up land, and sea space, excluding room for the 30 million fellow species with whom humanity shares this planet. At least 12 percent of the ecological capacity, representing 12 percent as the magic number for biodiversity protection. Accepting 12 percent as the magic number for biodiversity preservation, one can calculate that from the approximately 2 hectares per capita of biologically procuctive area that exists on our planet only 1.8 hectares per capita are available for human use.

of "Minamata disease," a severe neurological disorder caused by mercury poisoning. Reluctant to jeopardize its relations with business and to threaten productivity, the government hesitated to pursue the claims of victims until it could no longer ignore the evidence.

In the twentieth century, many multinational corporations found developing countries to be ripe for the largely unregulated location of dangerous industrial plants and dumping grounds for chemical and hazardous waste. When the pesticide plant in the city of Bophal, India, turned out to be an unprofitable venture for Union Carbide, the enterprise was partially abandoned. In 1984, a leaking toxic gas cloud killed more than 3,000 victims in a single night. As many as 15,000 subsequent deaths and the debilitating exposure to the occupants of a squatter community affected as many as 150,000 more victims, making this the single most deadly industrial disaster in world history.

The greatest source of urban pollution and consequential global warming has been the automobile's reliance on fossil fuels. The global dependence on fossil fuels has also created a structural divide between the energy consumption of the haves and the have-nots. For example, an individual in the United States consumes as much as a hundred times the amount of energy consumed by the average Bangladeshi, despite sharing the planet's future in common.

CONCLUSIONS

Since the beginning of human history technology and ideas have been intertwined in their impact on the landscape. Technological transformations have not produced an unquestioned rise in the quality of life. Technological innovations have had a profound impact on the consumption of resources, while transforming the physical landscape. Though humans have altered their landscapes since prehistoric times through the use of fire and other manipulations of the environment, the human impact on the landscape has intensified dramatically in the past two centuries. The two greatest environmental changes in last 3,000 years have been destruction of forests and reorganization of surface waters (irrigation, dams, etc.), both of which have been accelerated after the Industrial Revolution. The period between 1800 and 1914 witnessed an unprecedented expansion of agriculture and population growth throughout the world, both of which had devastating effects on world resources and the physical landscape. These forces can be held directly responsible for the increasing pressures of global deforestation beginning in the nineteenth century.

Since the Second World War, technology's ecological impact has reached crisis proportions. In the United States alone, pollution levels have risen between 200 and 2,000 percent since 1946. This situation is not the result of population growth or affluence alone, but to the unqualified uses of late-twentieth-century technology. New technologies – and the profits made from them – account for as much as 95 percent of the added environmental pollution of the last quarter century.

The twentieth-century technological explosion has helped create the first worldwide culture. It has resulted in fundamental environmental problems that, as the century drew to an end, were truly global concerns and the ultimate concerns of our time. Air pollution in China is experienced in the Pacific Northwest. In the twenty-first century, with its comfortable and rapid means of transportation, the movement of peoples (even in virtual space) continues unabated. New kinds of human interaction and movements are taking place in virtual space using digital technology. Forces propelling contemporary migrations are political (flight from war or oppression), economic, and environmental. At the same time, ecological destruction in the twenty-first century may make nomads of us all again, while reducing alternative possibilities of habitation and survival of the world's environmental diversity.

SELECTED REFERENCES

Crosby, Alfred (1986) *Ecological Imperialism: The Biological Expansion of Europe, 600–1900*, New York: Cambridge University Press. Examines the ecological implications of population movements and displacements, especially the European advantages in post-1500 expansion to the favorable agricultural lands in the Americas.

Diamond, Jared (1997) *Guns, Germs, and Steel: The Fates of Human Societies*, New York: W. W. Norton. Debates the roles of environment and culture in determining historical developments in different parts of the world since about 11,000 BCE.

Elvin, Mark (2004) *The Retreat of the Elephants: An Environmental History of China*, New Haven, Conn. and London: Yale University Press. Examines China's past and potential future impacts on the environment since the extinction of the elephant there over 4,000 years ago through the changing understanding of relationships between nature and culture.

Elvin, Mark and Liu Ts'ui-jung, eds (1998) *Sediments of Time: Environment and Society in Chinese History*, Cambridge: Cambridge University Press. Selected articles on the environmental history of China, including demography, climate, water and forest resources,

Fagan, Brian (1999) *Floods, Famines, and Emperors: El Niño and the Fate of Civilizations*, New York: Basic Books. Explores some of the unusual weather events and climatic shifts in human history and considers their causes and consequences.

Jones, Steve, Robert Martin, and David Pillbeam, eds (2000) *The Cambridge Encyclopedia of Human Evolution*, Cambridge: Cambridge University Press. Excellent world coverage of issues in primate (hominid and human) evolution; see useful tables and charts.

Keightley, David N., ed. (1983) *The Origins of Chinese Civilization*, Berkeley: University of California Press. Articles by specialists on such topics as environment and agriculture, Neolithic cultures and peoples, metallurgy, writing, and early political organization.

McNeill, J. R. (2000) *Something New Under the Sun: An Environmental History of the Twentieth-Century World*, New York: W.W. Norton & Company. An environmental history of the modern world emphasizing the impact of the industrialized world on deforestation and pollution.

McNeill, William H. (1977) *Plagues and People*, Garden City, N.Y.: Doubleday. A provocative study of the relationship of disease to demography and its effect on global history.

Schmidt, Peter R., ed. (1996) *The Culture and Technology of African Iron Production*, Gainesville, Fla.: University of Florida Press. Good introduction to current issues in African Iron Age studies.

Wertime, Theodore A. and James E. Muhly (1980) *The Coming of the Age of Iron*, New Haven, Conn.: Yale University Press. Although somewhat outdated, presents a comparative look at the age of iron in various cultural settings of world regions.

Williams, Michael (2003) *Deforesting the Earth: From Prehistory to Global Crisis*, Chicago: University of Chicago Press. Examines 10,000 years of human impact on the earth's forests.

Worster, Donald (1977) *Nature's Economy: A History of Ecological Ideas*, New York: Cambridge University Press. An essential history of human relationship with the natural world and how this has been expressed in human thought.

ONLINE RESOURCES

Annenberg/CPB Bridging World History (2004) <http://www.learner.org/channel/courses/world history/>. Multimedia project with interactive website and free, downloadable videos; see especially Unit 4 Agricultural and Urban Revolutions; Unit 19 Global Industrialization; and Unit 24 Globalization and Economics.

PBS Nova Program: Tracking El Niño (1998) <http://www.pbs.org/wgbh/nova/elnino/>. Examines the current and historical impact of meteorological events.

PBS Nova Program: Evolution (2001) <http://www.pbs.org/wgbh/evolution/index.html>. One episode and supporting site investigates human origins.

CHAPTER 3

Cities and city life in world history

The diversity and variety of life increased dramatically with the rise of urban centers. Ever since the earliest village, larger communities of people were themselves magnets of population growth and they drew the keen interest of travelers. In the third century CE, a southern Indian poet recounted his visit to the city of Madurai, vividly portraying the social, economic, and religious life of this city on the southern tip of the South Asian subcontinent:

> The poet enters the city by its great gate, the posts of which are carved with the images of the goddess Lakshmi. It is a festival day, and the city is gay with flags; some, presented by the king to commemorate brave deeds, fly over the houses of captains; others wave over the shops which sell toddy [a fermented drink made from blossoms of the palm tree]. The streets are broad rivers of people of every race, buying and selling in the market place or singing to the music of wandering minstrels.
>
> The drum beats and a royal procession passes down the street, with elephants leading and the sound of conches [shell trumpets] . . . Stall keepers ply their trade, selling sweet cakes, garlands of flowers, scented powder, and rolls of betel nut [to chew]. Old women go from house to house selling nosegays and trinkets. Noblemen drive through the streets in their chariots, their gold-sheathed swords flashing, wearing brightly dyed garments and wreaths of flowers. The jewels of the perfumed women watching from balconies and turrets flash in the sun . . . Craftsmen work in their shops, bangle-makers, goldsmiths, cloth weavers, coppersmiths, flower sellers, wood carvers, and painters. Food shops are busily selling mangoes, sugar candy, cooked rice, and chunks of cooked meat. In the evening, the city's prostitutes entertain their patrons with dancing and singing to the accompaniment of the lute. The streets are filled with music. Drunken villagers, in town for the festival, reel about in the streets. Respectable women visit the temples in the evening with their children and friends, carrying lighted lamps as offerings. They dance in the temple courts, which resound with their singing and chatter. At last the city sleeps . . . all but the ghosts and goblins who haunt the dark and the housebreakers, armed with rope ladders, swords, and chisels. But the watchmen are also vigilant, and the city passes the night in peace. Morning comes with the sounds of brahmins intoning their sacred verses. The wandering bands renew their singing, and the shopkeepers open their booths. The toddy-sellers ply their trade for thirsty early morning travelers. The drunkards stagger to their feet. All over the city the sound is heard of doors opening. Women sweep the faded flowers of the festival from their courtyards. The busy everyday life of the city is resumed.
>
> (A. L. Basham, *The Wonder That Was India*, New York: Grove Press, 1954, pp. 203–4)

In many ways this strikes us as being much like any modern city. Food and goods in dizzying amounts and varieties can be bought, day and night. Craftsmen, noblemen, prostitutes, shopkeepers, minstrels, captains, royalty – all are thrust together in the fabric of city life. At night, a different world emerges – that of "ghosts and goblins" but also of well-provisioned thieves and the watchmen who safeguard the city while it sleeps. Because it is a festival day, there is a vibrant religious atmosphere. But religion is also more deeply and permanently present, from the images of the goddess carved into the posts of the city gate to the temples that dot the urban landscape. What is striking, and characteristic even of some modern Indian cities, is the atmosphere of a festival day. We might say that the particular religious cast of these festivities is something culturally distinctive to Indian society, although not unique to urban sites. But what is common to the origins of cities throughout the world, and what is distinctive about cities as they evolve in different cultural settings and change over time? Why do people congregate in cities, and what benefits and drawbacks are there to urban life?

INTRODUCTION

Human population increase on a global scale has been a constant factor in changing community forms and evolving relationships between humans and their environments, despite dramatic, though usually short-term and regionally limited, decreases due to war or disease. The city is one particular form of human organization emerging where sedentary peoples were concentrated in densely populated, complex settlements. Complexity was both a necessary condition for and a consequence of large, growing communities.

Complexity appeared in the form of bureaucracies that registered populations, taxed them, and maintained order, as well as in the form of systems of trade, communication, and defense. No less important were rituals of public order, both religious and secular, and aspects of everyday life such as going to the market to buy food or taking part in an annual festival. In this chapter we explore a wide array of forces and circumstances that encouraged human settlement in early urban forms. What were the relationships between early urban communities and their environments? How were the changing structures of more recent urban communities shaped by the forces of global industrialization and colonialism? As we consider the creation of modern cities, we examine the human experience of post-industrial city life, its benefits and the global challenges created by dramatic demographic change.

WORLD DEMOGRAPHY: CROWDED DAILY LIVES

The creation of a sedentary community relied on groups of people who found a common purpose in staying in one place. Settling down may have eventually occurred around the world, but what were the dynamic forces

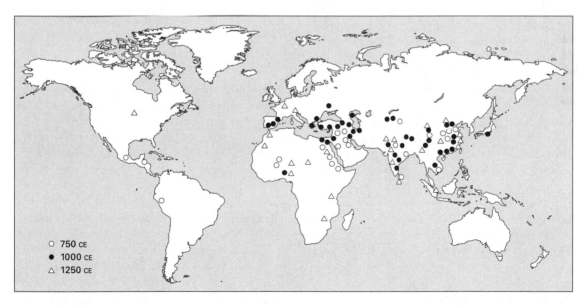

Map 3.1 Early centers of population, *c.* 750–1250 CE.

that set the process of urbanization in motion? The interplay of population increase and agricultural innovations reinforced continuity and created the conditions for a revolutionary change in the patterns of subsistence and in the shifting concentrations and locations of early communities. Above all, agriculture both created and sustained increasing populations around the world. Reliance on agriculture made necessary the commitment to staying in one place. Disease control became a new requirement of larger populations aggregated in permanent settlements, whose complexity included management of water resources, parasites, and infectious diseases previously unknown to more mobile populations. And wherever cities came into being they did not do so in isolation from rural hinterlands, which continued to feed the city folk.

The major feature of world populations through time has been their increasing numbers, in spite of disease, famine, and warfare. Historical demography is the study of changes in population throughout history. The natural biological increase of early human populations reflected the initial success of the species in adapting to a variety of changing environments. It is likely that many early human migrations resulted from the pressure of such demographic increases on limited food resources. Although the long-term, cumulative trend of human populations has been in the direction of a regular increase over time, increases were not always possible or desirable in the shorter-term historical experience of individual groups and societies. Disease, drought, famine, war, and natural disasters figure among the causes of temporary declines of populations in parts of the world, but they did not alter the basic overall trend of population increase.

From a global perspective, the biggest consequence of the establishment of sedentary farming communities (villages) between 4,000 and 12,000 years ago was the increased rate of population growth. Larger, denser village settlements were common to every continent. Agricultural peoples experienced more than the annoyances of crowded circumstances. Focused reliance on single agricultural crops resulted in resource consumption that was less diverse. Often this led to less well-balanced diets, tooth decay due to the increased consumption of processed foods, especially carbohydrates (such as grain porridges and breads), and

more susceptibility to contagious diseases, possibly as a result of their closer association with domesticated animals and animal viruses. Despite these downsides to crowded daily lives, the early inhabitants of villages, towns, and cities occasionally had longer life spans.

According to historical demographers, who study changes in population through history, most of the demographic increases common to prehistory also were not the result of migrations or shifts in mortality rates; rather they appear to have been associated with higher fertility rates. Why settled agriculturalists gave birth to more children is a matter of speculation. Demographic studies of contemporary gathering and hunting peoples provide a possible clue. Although many factors can affect the number of births to each female during her lifetime, birth spacing as a result of breast-feeding has been observed in many populations. Nursing a child stimulates hormones that suppress ovulation and menstruation (called lactational amenorrhea) with the consequence of producing a birth-spacing pattern that reduces fertility rates. Because infant formulas (high-carbohydrate, easy-to-digest cereals, and animal milk) were more readily available in the diets of agriculturalists than those of gatherers and hunters, infants were weaned off mother's milk at an earlier age, and the space between births became considerably shorter. The result was a trend in population growth that has characterized a more crowded human history ever since.

EMERGING COMPLEXITY

Increasing economic, social, and political complexity also accompanied the formation of cities. This complexity meant that many peoples, occupations, goods, and ideas came together into a single settlement that satisfied diverse needs. Though cities appear around the world, they were not a universal stage in the development of civilization, a term derived from the Latin word for "city," *civitas*, nor were they the logical and necessary culmination of earlier forms of community. While agriculture was common to many cities, it didn't automatically lead to urbanization. In some parts of the world (Mexico, Panama, and Ecuador, for example) plant domestication was around for almost 5,000 years before people began to settle in cities. The most common definitions of "civilization" include the presence of some or all of the traits commonly found in the large-scale, complex communities we call cities: monumental architecture, usually religious in nature; writing or other formal systems of record keeping and communication; trade, formal governmental structures, social stratification, and representational art. What forces brought these people together in large communities? What encouraged the particular form of complex social and economic organization characteristic of the city?

ANCIENT SETTLEMENTS BECOME CITIES

Urbanism was no accident. It was clearly a preferred form of human community as populations sought the variety, stimulus, and security of large settlements. Urbanism has been more extensively studied in West Asia than in almost any other part of the world. This is partly due to the abundant and well-preserved evidence, the product of dry conditions and less-acidic soils, and partly the result of scholarly interest in studying what were thought to have been the world's first cities. The earliest West Asian cities were based on gathering and hunting as well as on the cultivation of domesticated crops by sedentary farmers. Hunting and gathering continued to supply needs after groups became sedentary. By around 6500 BCE, West Asian settlements such as Jericho in Palestine were large enough to be considered small cities. They initially served their hinterlands, the surrounding rural areas, as exchange centers for goods and services, culture, and ideology. In turn, the strategic control of the hinterland's resources was necessary for urban survival, giving rise to standing armies.

Jericho was an older, year-round settlement, dating back to as early as 9000 BCE, when the site was established as a sanctuary beside a spring for hunter-gatherers. Over the next millennium, their descendants made the transition from a wandering to a settled existence. By the eighth millennium BCE, Jericho had an estimated population of about 2,000. The community was surrounded by defensive and protective walls to which were attached such monumental architectural features as a heavy stone tower. Jericho seems to have been only incidentally a farming community.

It perhaps drew its wealth from trade, the exchange of goods that traveled from the Red Sea to Anatolia. Around 7000 BCE, Jericho was abandoned and replaced by a more modest and straightforward farming community with houses and walls built of sun-dried mudbrick, a material widely used throughout West Asia at this time. The decline and replacement of Jericho seem indicative of a pattern in West Asia. Like Jericho, there were many other settlements that appeared and declined, expanded and contracted, as cities eventually became more closely connected with the agricultural development of their hinterlands.

AGRICULTURE AND THE DEVELOPMENT OF URBAN LIFE

The development of agriculture was important to the rise of most cities across the world, since agriculture supported the population growth that cities housed (see Chapter 2). Surplus food produced as a result of technological innovations in the intensive cultivation of plants or specialization in herding animals allowed people to settle in communities that grew in size and density and became cities. Reliable food supplies were essential to the emergence and survival of cities. The resources needed for expanding densely settled populations could be obtained by trade or by other means such as war, as well as by integrating agricultural hinterlands with the concentration of population in an urban center.

The size of later cities reflected, in most cases, the agricultural potential of the immediately surrounding region. One of these cities, Çatalhöyük in central Turkey, is an example of a complex urban society that developed without agriculture. By 5800 BCE, the city had a population of some 5,000 people settled in a thousand densely built houses surrounded by a well-watered plain. Yet people there exploited wild plants and animals. Unlike many early cities, the site of Çatalhöyük lacks any indication of a central authority or social stratification. There is evidence from elaborate murals, clay figurines, and burials that the people of this community had constructed a complex religious and social life.

The activities associated with religious specialists were commonly found in cities. Other specialists were

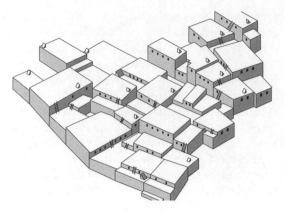

Figure 3.1 Reconstruction of a section of Çatalhöyük. Excavations at this site have changed historical views of urban origins.

skilled laborers or artisans, some of whom passed on the valuable secrets of their trade through family or household relationships. At Çatalhöyük, for example, there was a specialized labor force producing stone implements and excellent woolen textiles, metal goods, and pottery for the marketplace. Like other city dwellers, specialists were dependent on their rural counterparts, who remained full-time food producers, and it is likely that trade and exchange sustained the community over its thousand-year history.

Çatalhöyük's society and culture, taken together with that of the earlier and smaller Jericho, underlines the difficulty of making a unilinear connection between agriculture and the emergence of cities. The process of urbanization was a slow one of trial and error, complicated by environmental and other accidental factors. The interplay of environment, food supply, and the establishment of cities was a dynamic social process. No "first city" emerged in this or any part of the world during this earliest period, only many towns, each in its own way seeking to sustain a society that became more densely settled and complex. Some were successful and some were not; success, in some cases, meant building larger, ever more complex urban systems and political orders. Elsewhere, success meant survival of populations in smaller human communities and the disappearance of urban centers.

ENVIRONMENTAL FACTORS AND URBAN GROWTH

Environmental factors also offer clues to the process by which some people established cities. Situated in the shifting environmental context of southern Mesopotamia, Sumer was an attractive area for settlement in the late fourth millennium BCE. Although rainfall was limited, the region's lands were made fertile by silt deposited by the Tigris and Euphrates rivers. Established populations had cultivated the marshes for a thousand years and developed small town settlements scattered along the Persian/Arabian Gulf coast. Farming and irrigation techniques supported canals, dikes and reservoirs that greatly increased agricultural production, which in turn attracted more people and created denser settlements. Uruk was one of several cities that emerged in Sumer following the climatic changes that occurred with the end of the Holocene and the onset of a dry period after about 3500 BCE.

Ensuring a water supply became a major activity in Uruk. As the years of drying continued, major projects were undertaken to straighten and clean river courses and canals, which were cut away from the rivers to the fields in ever more complex patterns. Uruk provides an example of the complex relationships between environment and the emergence of cities. By 2800 BCE, the plains of Sumer were no longer profusely dotted with small settlements. Instead, there were lines of cities – Uruk, Lagash, Nippur, Kish – each with its hinterland of associated settlements that followed the lines of the rivers and main canals. They used complex irrigation methods to adapt to the increasingly dry conditions and scarcity of food. Full-time urban specialists like scribes, priests, and artisans were supported by rations of barley and other foods. The organization of these cities represented the communal strategies for coping with potential adversity.

Northeast Africa

Northeast Africa (Egypt) was settled rather slowly, probably at first by peoples who moved in from areas in east-central Africa, perhaps as early as 13,000 BCE. These peoples domesticated and raised barley and wheat in communities scattered along the Nile Valley. Arable land was found only along the narrow confines of the river banks. As in Sumer, with the climatic changes brought on by the end of the last glaciation, desiccation and changes in the Nile Delta intensified the land problem in the Nile Valley. As people were forced onto smaller pieces of irrigable land near water sources, they had to live in denser settlements, which survived only by intensively exploiting resources and controlling their distribution. By the end of the fourth millennium BCE, when cities developed, they were sustained by the relationships between those situated on the river and those in the hinterland of the earlier agricultural-herding communities.

The settlement of Thebes in Upper Egypt and Memphis in the Lower Egypt delta were the consequence of religious and political developments that centered around the remarkable environmental conditions of the Nile itself. By the end of the fourth millennium BCE, responses to environmental factors had helped shape a stable agricultural society in the Nile Valley, based on irrigated farming in the natural floodplains and delta of the Nile. Variation in regional rainfall and the short- and long-term trends of Nile flooding required systematic responses. Community efforts to control water required the organization of labor, responses that reflected the growing complexity of activity in Egyptian cities. Supported by their agricultural hinterlands to the south, cities became centers of both exchange and a distinctive culture.

Establishing successful agricultural systems and being able to predict Nile flooding became vital to effective religious and political leadership. One of the pharaoh's most important tasks was feeding the people. Famine and plenty were seen as indicative of a cosmic order, from the flooding of the Nile to the growth of vegetation and the increase of flocks. As settlements became more crowded, living space was expanded upward to city rooftops and sometimes to second stories. Traders traveled up and down the Nile carrying on their transactions from boats that defined cities as land-based as well as floating hubs of activity. Never far from the Nile waters, the ancient Egyptians lived as part of an elaborate system that linked the river, land, and labor to a world of belief.

South Asia

The earliest South Asian cities, like those of Sumer and the Nile, appeared in a river valley, the valley of the Indus, in the area that is now Pakistan. The Harappan culture of the Indus Valley flourished from *c.* 2300 to *c.* 1500 BCE. The Harappan culture emerged as a network of communities based on herding and the limited practice of grain cultivation, not unlike the Tigris–Euphrates region. Sites indicate numerous village communities of mudbrick scattered along the Indus and its tributaries and along the shores of the Arabian Sea. The eventual appearance of large cities, some of which housed populations estimated at more than 35,000, suggests that the sort of desiccation that contributed to urbanization in Sumer and Egypt may also have been a factor in the development of urban settlements in the Indus Valley.

Mohenjo-Daro, the best-documented site, was located midway along the Indus River, and Harappa lay about 6,500 kilometers (4,000 miles) to the northeast on a tributary of the Indus. The annual inundation of the Indus Valley, along with simple irrigation techniques, made possible the settling of relatively large communities in the region by the third millennium BCE. Harappan cities were part of systems of local trade and economy linking rural producers to urban centers of occupational specialists. They also became centers of long-distance trade, establishing contacts with the Persian Gulf and Mesopotamia, Persia, Afghanistan, and areas to the south of the Indus River on the Indian subcontinent.

Shortly after 1750 BCE the character of this civilization was disrupted by a series of floods and the changing course of the river, which contributed to the depletion of resources. When the Indus River changed its course, the patterning of irrigation strategies was altered, destroying the food surplus and commercial activity. Successive waves of migrations may have included squatters from neighboring villages, nomadic communities replacing the urban population, and crumbling walls replacing the glorious citadels. Other chariot-riding peoples laid claim to the remains of Harappan culture, bringing their semi-nomadic way of life, new languages, and vastly different ideas about food, social organization, and religion. These new-comers gradually settled the region in much smaller communities, including some which surrounded the other great river system of northern India, the Ganges. By the sixth century BCE, the Ganges Valley was the primary center of population, productivity, cities, and commerce in South Asia.

CITIES AS CEREMONIAL AND COMMERCIAL CENTERS

Many early cities were ceremonial or religious centers, as remarkable for their monumental structures as for the technology of city planning employed by the people who built them (see Chapter 4). Trade could be both a catalyst for urbanization and also its consequence. As regional systems of trade and exchange developed, they included larger concentrations of activity and settlement. Centers that were ceremonial might also lead to the growth of commercial activity serving large populations. In general, once material needs of large populations were being satisfied, one characteristic urban form that emerged was the ceremonial complex.

Indus Valley

Indus cities were among those early centers boasting monumental architecture. Temple sites are found in each urban center, where worshipers gathered to conduct rituals. Water purification rites, still found in modern Indian culture, were an important part of ancient rituals, and evidence of public baths has been excavated. The urban societies of the Indus were literate. Their script, dated to about 2500 BCE, is unlike any early West Asian script and remains mostly undeci-phered. As symbols of cosmic, social, and moral order, public ceremonial structures such as pyramids, mounds, and temples were centers of political, social, and sacred space. Staffed by priests in service to rulers, these monu-ments suggest the essential redistribution of resources embedded therein. Sustaining the economic relation-ships that supported elites relied on protecting the connections between an urban center and its agri-cultural hinterland. Religious practices often served as a symbolic means of redistributing resources, providing strategic access without resorting to the use of armies.

The Americas

Urban processes could be triggered by the attraction of large populations to sacred sites. One of the earliest cities in South America was Chavin de Huantar, located in the northern highlands of modern Peru from about 1000 to 100 BCE. Substantial stone buildings, probably used for ceremonial or religious purposes, were erected on temple platforms. Outside the city center and surrounding its religious core were the inhabited dwellings, which were made of perishable materials. Here is where people traded and practiced their crafts. The specialists of Chavin produced a distinctive pottery: "Chavin" has become the name attached to culture associated with a style of pottery that portrayed snarling jaguars and birds of prey. Evidence indicates that there were contacts and trade between the people of Chavin and other pilgrimage sites, which included the Mochica, Nazca, and Chimu coastal kingdoms and the highland empires of Tiahuanaco and Huari.

Along the coasts of and inland from the Gulf of Mexico are the important archaeological remains – monumental stone architecture and sculpture – from the urban society of the Olmec people, who flourished between 1200 and 900 BCE As elsewhere in the Americas, buildings were primarily ceremonial in nature – temple-crowned pyramids facing vast plazas – and they were generally set outside the city sites. Evidence of irrigation systems that suggest reliance on an agricultural hinterland has been found, and both artifacts and the widespread influence of Olmec artistic style and motifs suggest that the Olmecs engaged in long-distance trade in raw materials such as shells, stone and obsidian.

In the Valley of Mexico, Teotihuacán was a sacred ceremonial center founded about 100 BCE and lasted until about 750 CE, when the city was burned to the ground. Approximately 2600 buildings have been excavated at its site not far from present-day Mexico City. Its earliest phases may be associated with a sacred cave shrine, which attracted a coalescence of small hamlets into a larger sacred center. The palaces, temples, apartment compounds, ceremonial plazas, and markets of Teotihuacán at its height were laid out in an orderly grid pattern, which was occupied by at least 100,000 city dwellers. The uniform large apartment compounds

Figure 3.2 Teotihuacán mural. Murals such as this were painted on thinly plastered walls of apartment compounds throughout the city of Teotihuacán. Their flat, linear style and primary colors depict images associated with male and female deities.

organized around patios, each with its own drainage system, may have been inhabited by clans or guilds. Quarters for priests and storehouses flank the Pyramid of the Sun.

Life in the city of Teotihuacán was crowded and animated by the constant arrival of daily visitors. Brightly colored parrot and quetzal feathers, foods from rural fields, prisoners of war to be sacrificed in the urban capital – all manner of ordinary and exotic goods and peoples entered the city. The inner city's residents were mainly the wealthy elite and their servants who lived in luxurious dwellings that consisted of rooms around a common courtyard. Laborers and specialists lived on the outskirts of the city, but daily markets must have brought many of them to the city center for trade and exchange. Life inside the city probably also included many masked performers in splendid costumes. The mural art of these and other activities shows a rich vocabulary of images, masked figures, and deities. The laws of the city were embodiments of the natural order of the universe, as harsh and demanding as it was a lush and bountiful paradise. Supporting a population of more than 100,000 meant that overcrowding, problems of sanitation, and poverty were ever present.

Other Classic Mayan (250–900 CE) cities include the southern sites of Tikal, Palenque, Copán and Clakmul, in addition to a network of cities in the northern lowlands. Some sites are marked by pyramids or palaces, evidence of religious and ceremonial importance. Other sites used natural features (like caves or hills) to command a presence. Carved stone slabs called stelae depict rulers and describe the accomplishments of war and trade. In the lowlands of the Yucatán peninsula, where the Maya (Classic Maya fl. *c.* 250–900 CE) were concentrated, there were around fifty cities, ceremonial centers for the practice of religious ritual on graduated-platform mounds. Tikal, one of the main Mayan cities, boasted a population of nearly 50,000. Mayan cities controlled outlying territories and extracted the resources of these areas to support the rich material life of the urban centers. Mayan cities vied for religious prestige as well as resources. The economy of the Maya was based on the cultivation of maize, and most of the urban population was supported by the labor of farmers. Other resources were gathered through coercion, and warfare conducted by shaman-kings had a distinctive ritual basis.

China

The earliest cities in East Asia were also ceremonial centers. The rise of urbanism in China was directly related to the formation of early political orders, in particular the first dynastic state, the Shang (*c.* 1600–1027 BCE). Shang kings based their political authority on their claim of descent from ancestors who were able to intercede with the central deity of Shang religion. Because political authority was legitimized by religion, the royal capital where the ruler lived was a sacred ceremonial center that embodied the close relationship between kingship and urbanism in early China. Shang rulers moved their capitals several times during the course of the dynasty, possibly in response to shifting defense needs or access to resources.

Like earlier Shang capitals, Anyang was a ceremonial center, including royal tombs containing evidence of human sacrifices as well as a rich material culture such as bronze vessels, chariots, and jade. Near the modern city of Anyang on the north China plain lie the ruins of the late Shang capital, which was excavated in the early twentieth century. The "palace" itself, like other buildings at the Anyang complex, was made of wattle-and-daub construction (interlaced rods of wood plastered with mud) on a pounded-earth foundation, creating a dirt floor that over time would become polished by use. Storage pits and drainage ditches fulfilled the practical needs of the concentrated population, many of whom lived in subterranean "pit" dwellings built into the ground. Social stratification was evident in the distinction between the nobility's ground-level dwellings with their pounded-earth floors and the 4-meter-deep (13-foot-deep) pit dwellings of urban commoners, which resembled those of their social status who lived in the countryside.

The ability of a relative few – the Shang king and nobility – to claim the right to the fruits of labor of the many – farmers and producers – made possible the settlement of urban sites by allowing ruling elites to be fed and supported by the labor of those subject to their political control. Not only the evidence of rich material culture displayed in tomb artifacts, but also articles and foodstuffs that supported daily life, were produced by artisans and farmers whose labor was controlled by a small elite.

After the unification of the empire in the third century BCE, the Chinese capital cities retained their earlier ceremonial functions. Imperial capitals and other urban sites were administrative and political centers rather than primarily centers of settlement, production, and trade. Sites were chosen using principles of geomancy; that is, landscapes were selected with topographical properties believed to confer benefits on the residents of the city. In the imperial capital, the ruler's palace and other important buildings were built in a south-facing direction to take advantage of the benevolent southern winds. Chang'an, the imperial capital during the Han (206 BCE–220 CE) and Tang (618–907 CE) dynasties, located in northwest China, was also the eastern terminus of the Silk Road. The city itself was laid out in a regular square, with thoroughfares running north–south and east–west, embodying symmetry and order as the imperial capital manifested the patterned order of the empire.

URBANIZATION, CONQUEST, AND COMMERCIAL GROWTH

In the mid-eighth century CE, Chang'an was probably the largest city in the world, with a population of over a million enclosed within the city walls and immediate suburban surroundings. As the terminus of the Silk Road, the city received goods from the great caravan route across Central Asia, which also carried Chinese silks and spices to other parts of the Eurasian continent. Thus Chang'an was both an imperial capital – a ceremonial political center – and a center of international trade. Beginning in the late Tang, towns and cities increasingly grew up as centers of commerce, but these commercial cities existed side by side with administrative towns that were walled enclaves of political authority.

West Africa

While cities sometimes emerged as commercial centers in response to the stimulus of external trade, the origins of other cities are found in local urban systems that slowly expanded over time. Slower evolutionary development of urban systems integrated a hierarchy of interlinked sites. Evidence from the archaeological excavations of Jenne-Jeno, in modern-day Mali confirmed an indigenous growth of urbanism in the western Sudan. Radiocarbon dates document the continuous settlement of Jenne-Jeno from before 250 BCE. In the early phases of the site, its inhabitants fished, hunted, used pottery, and had domesticated the cow. By the first century CE, they were cultivating African rice. About the same time, people began to build more permanent mud structures and the size of the settlement increased to an area of more than 10 hectares (approximately 25 acres); at the height of the settlement (400–900 CE), Jenne-Jeno had spread to more than three times that size. Its population reached between 7,000 and 10,000 inhabitants. Finds of pottery and terracotta sculpture, copper, iron slag, and gold indicate a rich material culture, craft specialization, and the involvement of the city in long-distance trade.

The early Jenne-Jeno was a commercial city without monumental architecture. A large wall, however, that measured about 3 meters (10 feet) across was built around the city. As was characteristic of West African urban wall-building traditions, the Jenne-Jeno wall was probably not built for defensive purposes. Jenne's walls served to define the settlement's identity and allow the city's elite to protect and tax the flow of goods, caravans, and people, thus sharing in common with other early cities the distinction between town and countryside. Sometime before the twelfth century, Islamic merchant clerics joined the trading caravans plying the Saharan trade. In Islamic West Africa, the need for protection of the long-distance trade routes connecting cities also led to the creation of military states, which grew powerful through their strategic access to resources. Eventually West African Islamic cities like Jenne acquired the defining urban feature – the mosque.

Like a number of other West African urban centers, Jenne-Jeno was located at the intersection of major trade routes. The city was an important collecting point for gold and other goods and was critical to the development of West African commercial relations. Like other centers of social, economic, and political complexity, Jenne-Jeno enjoyed a stable agricultural base. Farmers on the rich floodplains of the inland Niger Delta produced a considerable surplus in rice, sorghum, and millet and produced these and other foodstuffs, such as smoked and dried fish, for trade. Well placed on the axis between the savanna and the region of the edge of the desert called the Sahel, and situated at the highest point for reliable transport by canoe along the Niger River, Jenne played an important role in regional trade networks. This in turn made possible the rapid expansion of trade with Arabs in later centuries.

The example of Jenne-Jeno suggests that a city should be thought of together with its countryside. Indigenous trade and independent urban development effectively related to the city's relationship with its own hinterland in an integrated regional system. Archaeologists have surveyed about a 1,100 square-kilometer (425-square-mile) area of Jenne-Jeno's rural hinterland and sampled some forty-two contemporary sites. On the basis of their size and diversity, it is clear that these sites functioned in a hierarchical relationship to Jenne-Jeno with Jenne-Jeno as their center and increasingly smaller settlements spaced at further distances as though along spokes on a wheel. Their patterning further supports the presence of a high degree of urbanism and an intra-regional economy with Jenne-Jeno as its center point. Jenne-Jeno flourished not in isolation but within a rich and ancient urban system.

North America

Complex agricultural systems and urban centers of trade comparable to those that developed in other world regions also appeared in North America in an area that is now the southeastern United States, between the Atlantic and the Great Plains, the Mississippi and Ohio valleys, and the Gulf of Mexico. This is the area of the Mississippian culture, in which the largest cities emerged as attempts to integrate the region's economy.

Mississippian culture began developing before 700 CE and spanned the next 700 years. A pattern of cultivation of beans, corn, and squash similar to that of Mesoamerica made it possible for full-time agriculture to sustain an increasing population. The Mississippians – a general name for many different peoples and cultures scattered over thousands of square miles – lived on farms and in villages, towns, and cities. None can compare, however, with Cahokia, clearly the principal center of Mississippian culture, which was located in present-day southern Illinois just across the river from the modern city of Saint Louis, Missouri. About 25,000 people lived in Cahokia at its peak around 1100 CE, and it was the focus of a much larger group of people who lived in the hamlets and villages that constituted its hinterland. With the increasing complexity of the urban center at Cahokia, these smaller hinterland settlements adapted to meet the demands of increasingly structured obligations and opportunities by altering their production of goods, provision of services, and participation in ceremonies that linked them ritually to the urban center. Urban development thus affected not only the people living in cities but also people outside the cities.

Cahokia, like other Mississippian towns, was part of a trading network that stretched from Hudson Bay to the Gulf of Mexico and probably on into Mesoamerica, and from the Atlantic to the Rocky Mountains (see Chapter 6). Graves at Cahokia reveal the extent of the trade that was centered there. In them, copper from Lake Superior, flints from the areas of Oklahoma and North Carolina, and many art objects from afar have been found. Cahokia covered almost 16 square kilometers (6 square miles) and was protected by a series of stockades and bastions. It contained more than a hundred human-made earthen mounds, dominated by the largest earthen mound in North America, Monk's Mound, the base of which covers 37 hectares (about 91 acres). Standing a hundred feet high, Monk's Mound was one of the largest human-made structures in the Americas before the European conquest. Mounds, which were common to Mississippian towns, account for the description of the Mississippians as "Mound Builders." As in Mesoamerica and South America, the mounds were used for ritual and ceremonial purposes, as temple or burial mounds, but they also served a key economic role by visibly integrating the countryside. They were built with great effort of the most readily available local material: dirt, every grain of which was carried and put into place by humans. The Mississippian culture reached its peak sometime between 1200 and 1300 CE, after which its *populations began to decline* and cities were abandoned. The cause of Cahokia's demise is not fully understood, but regional competition for economic and political power led to the development of other centers.

Mediterranean cities

Cities in the Mediterranean region also reflected the rise of complex political orders that integrated the commercial wealth of urban centers. Early urban development in the Mediterranean can be seen in Athens, where the remains of walls, early fortifications, pieces of a tower, and tomb, suggest a settlement as early as 1500 BCE. These remains indicate a small place of minor significance, a settlement primarily of local importance. The Greek poet Homer (*c.* 800 BCE) made scant mention of Attica or the abrupt hill – the Acropolis – on which Athenians erected their earliest settlement. Eventually it was the city's role as the reserved precinct of the goddesses and gods of Attica that distinguished Athens as the urban center for the farmland and villages that made up its hinterland.

The most important festival in ancient Athens was the Panathenaia, the annual state festival honoring the city's patron deity, the goddess Athena Polias ("of the city") (see Chapter 4). Every four years the festival was celebrated on a grand scale, including musical competitions, recitations of Homer's epic poetry, gymnastic and equestrian contests, and a long, colorful procession through the city to the goddess Athena's shrine on the Acropolis. The culmination of this spectacle was the presentation of a *peplos*, a richly woven robe, to the cult statue of Athena. Spinning and weaving occupied most of women's time, even that of elite Athenian women.

The agora, or market, where everyone had a right to trade agricultural surplus or manufactured articles, was the focus of commercial life. No elites controlled the access to or distribution of valuable goods. The agora was a civic forum too, where, after worship and marketing, property owners might discuss common community issues – such as customs duties or the issues of government or war – in a sort of open-air town council. It was accepted in Athens that decisions made in common were preferable to any made by a single person.

Small farmers were always of decisive importance to Athens, as they provided the connection between independent agrarian village life and urban society. As infantrymen they protected the city. Farmers went to the urban center on market days, for religious occasions, or to attend the town council. The first Athenians to abandon this pattern and become permanent residents in the city were artisans and craftspeople, blacksmiths, potters, weavers, and tanners. These skilled workers held both rural laborers and the urban poor in contempt. Between 750 and 550 BCE the number of city dwellers swelled as the result of a population explosion, which lessened the already sparse amount of arable land in Attica. Increasing urbanization led to expanding trade beyond the city as well as increasing complexity within it.

Athenians looked to the sea. Trade and entrepreneurship resulted in overseas connections and expansion. Commerce and values associated with commerce became triumphant. Great fortunes were made by merchants who traded across the Mediterranean, and by the fifth century BCE numerous commercial middlemen had begun to share in the profits of that trade. Athens began to develop specialties and, as it did so, to import much of its raw materials and food: two-thirds of the grain consumed by Athenians was imported from beyond the city's borders. Early city planners recognized that the success of the complex public and political functions of Athens, a city-state with its distinctive participatory government, relied on limiting the population growth or expanding beyond its borders.

South Asia

Athenians may have been aware of flourishing cities as far away as the South Asian subcontinent. In 331 BCE, Alexander the Great defeated the Persian army of Darius at Gaugamela and then turned his attention to the Indian subcontinent. A fourth-century BCE account by the Greek Megasthenes (c. 350–290 BCE) describes the city of Pataliputra, a political and economic center strategically located along the Ganges River trade route. Pataliputra was the capital of the Mauryan empire founded by Chandragupta Maurya in 322 BCE. At the time Megasthenes' account was written, and for perhaps two centuries afterward, Pataliputra was probably the largest, most sophisticated city in the world. Surrounded by large wooden walls with 570 towers and 64 gates, Pataliputra was the center of a wealthy, highly organized economic system that included farms, granaries, textile industries, and shipyards that built ships for seaborne trade. Pataliputra was also the seat of a famous university and library, along with palaces, temples, gardens, and parks.

Several centuries later, in the third century CE, the city of Madurai, capital of a southern Indian state, flourished as a cultural, economic, religious, and political center. Like other south Indian cities of the time, Madurai was enriched by maritime trade, largely with Southeast Asia, and dominated by a temple complex. As described in the introduction to this chapter, Madurai displayed the social, economic, and cultural complexity characteristic of other cities found throughout the world in the first centuries CE.

Urban culture on the Indian subcontinent was greatly affected by repeated conquests. Traditional Indian cities of all sizes had two focuses: the palace and the temple. The homes of the urban poor were humble huts of wood, reed, and mudbrick, thatched with straw. Many urban poor had no shelter and slept openly wherever they could in the city. Both temples and palaces were often surrounded by open areas that featured trees and expanses of water – lakes, pools, and basins. Fortified cities were encircled by moats, some of which contained earthworks covered with spiny shrubs, and by high walls with numerous towers and balconies for defending troops.

The Islamic world

The vast interactive sphere of the Islamic world depended on the existence of large cities, which served as centers for faith and commercial activity. In turn, the flourishing trade often relied on conquest for its expansion. The ancient Hindu city of Delhi was the site of Muslim invasions between 1000 and 1200 CE and became a capital during the Muslim sultanate (1206–1526). One of the most noticeable alterations of the city was the destruction of Hindu temples, the materials of which were used to build the mosque and the citadel. Buddhist monasteries and nunneries in the northwest frontier of India also became the target of the sultans' incursions between the thirteenth and sixteenth centuries.

Not only on the South Asian subcontinent, but elsewhere in Eurasia and Africa, the creation of Muslim empires led to the growth of large cities. The complexities and demands of urban life gave direction and impetus to long-distance trade that served the populations of Islamic cities. The great Islamic cities such as Baghdad or Constantinople were centers of trade and manufacturing. Surrounding the stable urban population of merchants, shopkeepers, and craftsmen was a larger population of unskilled workers, peddlers, street cleaners, and the semi-employed, a stratum that included a large proportion of rural immigrants. Market gardens were situated on the outskirts of the city and attracted a fluctuating labor force from the countryside.

The structure of Islamic cities reflected economic and other roles: trade and manufacturing, religion and scholarship, government and justice. Two or more complexes of major buildings were part of every Islamic city. One complex was the main mosque, surrounded by the chief courts, schools of higher learning, shops that sold objects of piety, and possibly the shrine of a saint identified with the life of the city. Another complex included the central marketplace (the main point of exchange), offices of money-changers, store-houses, and shops that sold locally made or imported goods. A third complex might be government offices. The power of government was present in everyday urban life (as watchmen, market supervisors, and police), but it was expressed as well in large and sometimes ostentatious public buildings.

Wealthy traders, merchants, and craftsmen resided near their buildings, and scholars and religious leaders near theirs, but most of the urban population lived outside the center in quarters that were a tangle of small streets and cul-de-sacs. Each quarter had its mosque (or shrine or church or synagogue), local market, and public bath. The tendency was for each quarter to house specific religious or ethnic groups. Farthest from the center, near or beyond the walls of the city, were the poorer quarters of rural immigrants and the workshops of noisy or malodorous crafts (such as tanning or butchering). Also outside the city walls were cemeteries.

Non-Muslims in Islamic cities were set apart from the families of believers. They paid a special tax (*jizya*), and Islamic law required that they show signs of their difference by dressing in special ways and avoiding colors (especially green) associated with Islam. They were prohibited from carrying weapons or riding horses (much as native populations in Spanish America were) and could not build new places of worship or repair pre-Islamic ones without permission. Laws about marriage were strictly enforced: non-Muslims could not marry or inherit from Muslims. And though Christians or Jews might occupy positions of importance in certain economic activities such as the arts, they were virtually excluded from others such as food preparation.

While all Islamic cities shared a commercial role, some originated as imperial administrative centers. Baghdad was founded from about 750 CE as the capital of the Islamic Abbasid empire and the home of the caliph (regent of the Prophet on earth). For more than five centuries, the city was a world center of education and culture. Under Abbasid rule, Baghdad became a city of museums, hospitals, libraries, mosques, and baths:

> The baths in the city cannot be counted, but one of the town's sheikhs told us that, in the eastern and western parts together, there are about two thousand. Most of them are faced with bitumen, so that the beholder might conceive them to be of black, polished marble; and almost all the baths of these parts are of this type because of the large amount of bitumen they have . . . The ordinary mosques in both the eastern and the western parts

cannot be estimated, much less counted. The colleges are about thirty, and all in the eastern part; and there is not one of them that does not outdo the finest palace. The greatest and most famous of them is the Nizamiya, which was built by Nizam Al-Mulk and restored in 504 AH. These colleges have large endowments and tied properties that give sustenance to the faqihs who teach in them, and are dispensed on the scholars.

> (R. J. C. Broadhurst, *The Travels of Ibn Jubayr*, London: Jonathan Cape, 1952)

The rise and decline of empires had an impact on the fortunes of cities. Constantinople was the capital city of the Byzantine empire after the fall of the Roman empire. It was also the western terminus of the Silk Road, and in 1432 it became the capital of the Ottoman empire. Baghdad was conquered and destroyed by the Mongols in 1258. The new rulers established the Il-Khan empire in Persia and Iraq with its new capital at Tabriz in northern Persia. Baghdad was reduced to a secondary city in the new Mongol empire and its role as the leading city of the Muslim world was overtaken by Cairo, where the caliphate was restored and through which most trade then passed from the Mediterranean to the Indian Ocean.

As noted by Ibn Battuta in the fourteenth century, Cairo was a lively, prosperous city. Called by some the "mother [city] of the world," Cairo flourished in the thirteenth, fourteenth, and even early fifteenth centuries, though its population peaked at a half million in the first half of the fourteenth century. Well before Cairo's elevation to its key role in east–west trade during the thirteenth century, prosperous merchants were part of a vital commercial life in the city (see Chapter 6). Like Constantinople or Istanbul, the capital of the Ottoman empire and a city as large as any in Europe, Cairo's importance increased as a result of Muslim conquest. By the fourteenth century, when the Ottomans gained control of Egypt, Cairo had become a major world city with 250,000 inhabitants. Its population would climb to an estimated 300,000 by the end of the seventeenth century, when it continued to be a major center of trade and cultural exchange among Africa, West Asia, and Europe.

THE EXPANSION OF COMMERCIAL CITIES

In 1000 CE, Europe's population was approximately the same as it had been during the heyday of imperial Rome a millennium earlier – approximately 36 million. During the twelfth and thirteenth centuries it rose rapidly as a result of expanded cultivation of marginal lands and technological innovation, reaching about 80 million. But the demographic climb in most cities was also punctuated by periods of disease and decline. The Black Death, as it came to be known, devastatingly reduced populations across Eurasia as it spread more rapidly through large cities. The disease probably erupted from the Yunnan region of southwestern China and was spread first through the military incursions of the Mongols and later through Afro-Eurasian trade routes. In the Hebei Province (near the modern city of Beijing) about 90 percent of the population died. In many parts of Europe, where the plague continued, populations declined to an estimated 19 million in 1400.

Not only disease but hunger plagued the poor in cities (see Chapter 8). Early Paris had suffered the growing pains of many expanding population centers. Sometime before the fourth century BCE, the settlement of Paris was established on an island in the Seine much smaller than the present Île de la Cité, both a central and a defensible location. From this location its people navigated the lower course of the Seine and perhaps reached the coast of Britain. As Paris expanded its river commerce and grew in wealth, it also became a religious center. Romans built a temple to Jupiter there, and subsequently Christians located one of their earliest north European bishops there, probably in the third century CE. By becoming the seat of a bishop, Paris, as Christians reckoned it, became a city. It took another thousand years for it to become a major urban center – of secular government, commerce, industry, and culture.

The divisions between countryside and urban life were often blurred. Streets were muddy pastureland where sheep and pigs grazed on grass and garbage. A twelfth-century CE Parisian "traffic jam" caused a pig to run between the legs of a horse, upsetting his rider, the heir to the royal throne. Individual households sometimes had gardens and vineyards (on the other side of town walls) to supplement the availability and offset the high cost of foods. Still, there were many poor and many hungry. Even the wealthy Parisian could not escape the unpleasantness and pollution that was the consequence of an increasing urban population.

The concentration of specialists such as leatherworkers, metalworkers, weavers, and other craftsmen, who flocked to cities to produce and sell their wares in the great city markets contributed to a significant decline in the quality of water and hygiene, even as it helped develop the city's trade and economy. The city government in Paris faced enormous problems and complaints about activities it tried to regulate and control. Blood and carcasses from slaughterhouses and the urine, alkalines, and salts used in tanneries, waste products from smelting, choking smoke from the burning of coal and other fuels, noisy industrial activities – all created undesirable living conditions for city residents. Disease and vermin, such as rats, were rampant. Filth was everywhere a condition of urban existence. Public baths – in contrast to Baghdad, there were only thirty-two in all of Paris in 1268 CE – were eventually banned by the Church because of their noted contribution to rampant promiscuity. By the time of the plague, the urban concentration in Paris was especially vulnerable to the spread of disease, which likely killed about one-third of the inhabitants in a single year. Ties between cities and their surrounding countryside remained close, especially where, as in Italy and the Netherlands, cities were numerous, and the balance of power and dominance slowly shifted from the countryside to the city, from the land to the markets increasingly linked to maritime worlds.

Despite major setbacks like plagues, epidemics, and famines, by 1500 CE world population reached roughly 450 million. These levels would double in the following three hundred years – meaning that the planet would be home to about 900 million humans in 1800 CE. Between 1500 and 1800, unprecedented shifts in population also occurred around the globe. Shifting demographic centers brought new cities into being, rebuilt and enlarged others, and left obsolete locales abandoned on the margins of the new maritime power.

The globalization of trade from about 1500 CE wrought commercial and technological changes that had their most powerful impact in cities. As centers of population, production, and consumption of material goods, cities were sites of transformation. They acted as magnets, drawing population from the countryside and mixing people of diverse classes, regional backgrounds, and cultures. Cities were technological and artistic centers where material goods were produced in profusion. At the same time cities were centers of consumption that provided huge markets for consumer goods produced with increasing efficiency by regional specialization and transported with relative speed along well-maintained highway networks. Cities were also cultural centers that provided entertainment and cultural activities for residents and visitors, and thus significant sites of transformation.

EARLY MODERN URBAN CULTURES IN EAST ASIA

In seventeenth-century Japan, as much as the government of the Tokugawa shoguns (military dictators) sought to ignore commerce and promote a rigid social and economic order based on agriculture, commerce flourished, merchants prospered, and expanding urban areas became the centers of a lively popular culture. Concentrated in the cities of Osaka, Kyoto, and the capital of Edo, this new urban culture was a product of merchant patronage. With a population of more than half a million, Edo was the world's largest city by the end of the seventeenth century, while the populations of Osaka and Kyoto approached those of sixteenth-century London and Paris, the two largest cities in contemporary Europe.

Merchants who patronized the arts in urban Japan under the Tokugawa did so as members of a lowly social class that lacked political power. The children of merchants, for example, were forbidden to marry children of samurai. Merchant wealth was not translatable into either political power or higher social status, but it could be used to patronize artists whose work portrayed the lives and world of the urban townspeople. The new urban culture of Tokugawa Japan patronized by merchants included the colorful *kabuki* theater, the sophisticated and elaborate puppet

theater (*bunraku*), woodblock prints of the *ukiyo* – the "floating world" of the urban pleasure quarters – and popular fiction.

Despite the rapid growth of urbanization in China in the fifteenth and sixteenth centuries, before the nineteenth century most Chinese lived in rural areas and engaged primarily in agriculture. However, the rapid rate of increase in urban populations in the early modern era (1500–1800) is significant in China and elsewhere. The fact that the lives of even rural villagers were increasingly tied to the commercial economy and

Figure 3.3 A Mirror of Actors' Likenesses from *An Album of Toyokuni Actor Portraits*. Portrait series of thirty-three Edo *kabuki* actors, illustrated by Utagawa Toyokuni I (1769–1825). *Kabuki* was a colorful and vibrant form of theater that flourished in Tokugawa Japan (1600–1867), attracting large audiences of merchants and other residents of cities such as Edo and Osaka. Shown here is Bandô Yasosuke I (1759–1814), a *kabuki* actor. The portraits of famous *kabuki* actors were popular souvenirs sold as single-sheet prints.

cultural life of cities is even more important. Hierarchies of sites were created, linking smaller villages, larger towns, and big cities into urbanized regional systems. By late imperial times in China, people in the countryside everywhere were influenced by what went on in the cities. Though there was no increase in the general rate of urbanization in the eighteenth century, a hierarchy of central places became more widely developed and refined throughout every region of the Manchu empire (see Chapter 10). Marketing networks and regional merchant associations tied rural markets to the cities.

By the seventeenth century the city of Nanjing, an imperial cultural center, had been eclipsed by the areas of Yangzhou, Suzhou, and Beijing. Like Nanjing, Yangzhou and Suzhou were cities of the Yangzi delta, whereas Beijing, like Edo in Japan, was the capital and thus distinct from other urban centers. Suzhou, somewhat like Venice, was known for its canals; its population growth resulted from conditions of economic prosperity, not because of the administrative needs of the government. Urban centers such as Suzhou, Hangzhou, and Nanjing were also sites of urban riots and disturbances in the late imperial period (Ming [1368–1644] and Qing [1644–1911]). Wealthy scholars and merchants lived lives of conspicuous consumption, collecting art and books and building elegant gardens. Urban workers (in the textile industry in Suzhou, for example) barely eked out a living and were also forced to fulfill service levies by performing municipal duties maintaining order, hygiene, and other tasks necessary to urban life.

CITIES AS SITES OF GLOBAL COMMERCIAL INTERACTION

Urban centers became zones of global commercial and cultural interaction. The mobility of labor between continents was one consequence of maritime trade after 1500, bringing new cultures into contact. The expansion of European maritime trade sent traders from the cities of one continent to the cities of other continents. These were cities of "strangers," as the English writer Thomas Mun (1571–1641) described them. The urban anonymity of the era's economics was based on selling more to strangers than would be consumed in

return by one's own society. Mun did not have in mind the tremendous growth of cities beyond Europe when he was writing his economic treatise *A Discourse of Trade from England unto the East Indies* (1621).

Cities like Malacca emerged as strategic entrepôts for European commercial empires. Long a Southeast Asian river port town, Malacca was situated on the southwestern coast of the Malay peninsula. Its maritime expansion in the fifteenth century was as an Islamic city-state, whose large fleet policed the length of the strait against Thai armies. Indian, Arab, Persian, Chinese, and later European traders set up headquarters there. After conquest by the Portuguese in 1511, Malacca was guarded by 200 soldiers and 300 mercenaries, a recognition of the commercial wealth found along maritime routes in the Indian Ocean.

In most of Africa, Europeans built trading communities, but, with only a few exceptions, they did not colonize parts of the continent until they had gained technological advantages in the late nineteenth century. During the first three centuries of African–European interaction, between 1450 and 1750, intensification of commercial activity and the consequent impact of European culture were felt in new coastal cities such as Lagos or Luanda, where Africans acted as agents of existing African states and corporations. Their adoption of European languages and dress became signs of the new merchant culture and status symbols. Manchester cottons and Chinese silks could be found in almost every village, just as Moroccan leather and West African gold regularly made their way to the markets and fairs of Normandy and Britain. As coastal markets and their communities grew in size and complexity, the urban centers became sites of cultural and social transformations and magnets for migration.

A few ancient African cities such as Ife and Benin remained sites of contested economic and political autonomy where the African rulers struggled with Portuguese, Dutch and English traders to maintain control over the production of exports and the price and demand for imports:

> [In the West African city of Benin] the king's court is square, and is certainly as large as the town of Haarlem [in the Netherlands], and entirely surrounded by a special wall, like that which

encircles the town. It is divided into many magnificent palaces, houses, and apartments of the courtiers, and comprises beautiful and long square galleries, about as large as the Exchange at Amsterdam, but one larger than another, resting on wooden pillars, from top to bottom covered with cast copper, on which are engraved the pictures of their war exploits and battles, and are kept very clean.

(H. Ling Roth, *Great Benin: Its Customs, Art, and Horrors*, London: Routledge, 1968, p. 160)

In contrast, European travelers described the Portuguese-built Central African city of Luanda as small and squalid. The marginal placement of European traders in separate quarters for visitors was a widespread and traditional strategy for organizing the inhabitants of settlements.

From Luanda to Nagasaki, European traders often were separated from independent and local urban processes. Between 1609 and 1641, the Dutch maintained a trading post at Hirado, an island off the coast of Kyushu. Then the Japanese granted the Dutch trading rights and placed them together with Chinese traders on a man-made island in Nagasaki Bay, where they remained until the "opening" of Japan in 1853.

From the seventeenth century onward, European influences were most marked in certain Indian urban centers, especially Bombay, Madras, and Calcutta. These cities became administrative centers, creating an urban tripod on which the British East India Company based its monopoly of power. At each center the company erected a fort around which an urban complex expanded, attracting Indians as agents or servants of company officials. Each British settler community consisted of only a few hundred men, merchants, administrators, and troops, at least until the end of the eighteenth century. At first the British residents clung to European culture and isolated themselves, closing the great gate at night. Eventually, cultural interaction won out, and many European merchants lived with Indian women, wore Indian-style clothing, and ate Indian foods. A further cultural layer was added in the case of Madras and Calcutta, where members of the Hindu mercantile elite provided the continuity with the pre-colonial city structure and preserved ritual resources until the nineteenth century.

CITIES OF CONQUEST AND COLONIZATION

Other cities were defined by European conquest and domination. European views of the landscape of North America, particularly what would be known as New England, illustrate both a lack of ecological understanding and a desire to create commodities from the presumed abundance resources attracting European settlement. While Native Americans were greatly reduced in numbers by genocide and disease during the Columbian contact and exchange, European populationss increased in size. The indigenous peoples were forced onto less desirable agricultural lands, while the Europeans who supplanted them wrought great changes to the landscape. Lands became bounded by

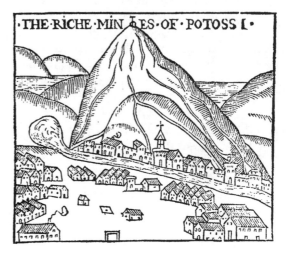

THE
DISCOVERIE AND CONQVEST
of the Prouinces of *PERV*, and the *Nauigation in the South* Sea, along that Coaſt. And alſo of the ritche *Mines* of *POTOSI*.

Figure 3.4 Anonymous, illustration of town of Potosi in mountains (1581). The site of *cerro rico* ("rich mountain"), the colonial town, is portrayed in this drawing, including the prominent church, some patrician houses, and the *barrios mitayos*, the areas where the workers lived.

concepts of property rights in the forms of fences and maps; forests were cleared to plant crops and to permit the Europeans' domesticated cattle and sheep to graze. The abundant animal wildlife rapidly disappeared. Dandelions and rats from Europe and Asia were introduced to the North American continent, and they and other pests and crop diseases spread in the cleared areas of European settlement.

The most profound transformations of native cultures in the Americas took place in the crucibles of urban life. Spanish conquest resulted in the imposition of European urban patterns that transformed the lives of the indigenous peoples of Central and South America and in the Caribbean. From the time of their arrival, the Spanish replaced pre-Columbian towns and cities with new ones organized and functioning on the Spanish model. For example, Cuzco, capital of the Incan empire, gave way to the Spanish imperial city of Lima, which was built over the ancient Inca city walls. Central to these new Spanish urban centers were European economic and cultural systems, values, and moral judgments regarding just about everything from dress to marriage, which were forced upon the conquered peoples. Elsewhere, a combination of conquest and disease provided inroads for settlement and city building by English, Dutch, and French colonists.

Cities were the most conspicuous feature of colonial America. Even mining towns like Potosi (the largest city in the Western Hemisphere in 1600, with an estimated population of 150,000), where indigenous laborers dominated the population, took on a distinctly European style. Its coat of arms read:

> I am rich Potosi,
> Treasure of the world.
> The king of all mountains,
> And the envy of all kings.
> (Quoted by John Demos, "The High Place: Potosi," *Common-Place* (Special Issue on Early Cities of the Americas), vol. 3, no. 4 (2003), n.p.)

During the sixteenth century about 200 colonial towns in Spanish America appeared; by 1600 there were 250; by the mid-seventeenth century aristocratic and luxurious Lima, with a population of 170,000, had become the largest city in Spanish America. When the Spanish conquest was completed by about 1700, an urban-dominated imperial system was in place.

Spanish colonial cities were distinguished by grants of land (4 square leagues or 18,000 acres) and by groups of ten to a hundred Spanish heads of families who settled on the grants. As cities grew, they became centers of European culture. Like towns in Spain, each had its own plaza, parks, imposing churches and monasteries, schools, and substantial government buildings. Within a decade of its founding, San Domingo had become a thoroughly Iberian city with convents, schools, and a bishop. Similarly, the French established Quebec in 1608 as the only walled city in North America. When it became the center of the diocese of New France, it accordingly became a city by European definitions.

Urban attitudes were a part of the cultural baggage of many seventeenth- and eighteenth-century migrants. Even early village settlements performed urban functions, including the exchange of goods, services, and ideas drawn from the global economy through their contact with larger urban centers. In the seventeenth century, colonists established small urban centers extending the length of the Atlantic coastline and into the Saint Lawrence Valley. Some colonial cities grew out of the fortified outposts that protected inhabitants from indigenous peoples or competing European powers. Other towns were established with the support of governments or joint-stock companies to increase profits by more efficiently exploiting hinterland resources. Still other cities were created from the push westward into new territories claimed by imperial expansion.

Colonial cities were frequently coastal settlements, small by contemporary standards. Boston, the largest seventeenth-century town in British North America, hardly surpassed a population of 7,000. Contemporary Philadelphia and New York scarcely reached 4,000, though in the next century they surged ahead. Toward the end of the eighteenth century, Philadelphia had 40,000 inhabitants, making it one of the four largest cities in the British empire. Yet the coastal position of the new North American towns enabled them to participate in global trade routes, to which they supplied fish, furs, wheat, rice, tobacco, indigo, and lumber. Shipbuilding expanded to support the urban mercantile base. By 1720 Boston boasted fourteen

BOX 3.1 EIGHTEENTH-CENTURY VIEW OF THE OLD SQUARE, THE PRINCIPAL MARKETPLACE OF HAVANA

The Caribbean city of Havana on the island of Cuba was an early crucible for globalization. Seen in this view of the old square, the city is portrayed as a site that blended transplanted European architecture (modified for a tropical climate) and a most diverse group of peoples who met and interacted in a marketplace typical of Africa. At the beginning of the eighteenth century, the population of Havana was over 27,000, more than half the population of the entire island of Cuba. Probably one-third of this population was of African descent. The illustration of the marketplace accurately reflected this racial diversity in the foreground scenes of interaction. Caribbean markets relied heavily on the bargaining skills of specialist traders – often enslaved African women traders called "higglers." Higglers were known to spread information from one plantation to another through their trading networks – often fueling rebellions and resistance.

The market square was teeming with life and human drama – domesticated pigs, chickens, sheep, caged birds, and human cargoes. Like other Caribbean cities, the port of Havana attracted pirates, thieves, tourists, sailors, and merchants. Hundreds of travelers sought American souvenirs and were not disappointed in the trinkets and goods they could purchase. Freight arrived almost every day from Asia, other parts of the Americas, Africa, and Europe, and market goods included

everything from locally grown fruits and vegetables to imported basic staples like wheat and wine. The market square was the site of more than trade. Wealthy residents would have watched executions, religious processions, bullfights, and fiestas from their upstairs balconies overlooking the square. This was a marketplace of ideas as well as goods. Political debates and social observations connected the citizens of the city.

Illustrated travel accounts became increasingly popular leisure reading in the eighteenth and nineteenth centuries. Many early European engravings of faraway cities were composed at least partially of scenes concocted by artists who had never visited them and who emphasized the romantic and exotic locales by sometimes inserting stereotypical images like oriental domes and fancifully imagined dress. Travel accounts and their illustrations thus reveal as much about the author's and artist's preconceived notions about a place as they provide actual historically accurate details about local life. Yet in this instance some of the buildings in the illustration can be matched to existing structures in Havana today, suggesting that the artist was more than an armchair traveler.

shipyards and produced more than two hundred ships annually.

The global position of the colonies in relation to the Atlantic economy also influenced the development of colonial urbanism. Though the Puritan colony at Boston began as a reformist religious community that was not dissimilar to Calvin's Geneva, the expansion of trade after 1650 weakened Boston's social homogeneity and ultimately undermined the power of the Puritan community's leaders. The growth of maritime commerce affected all elements of the city. Though as late as the last quarter of the seventeenth century small farmers still cultivated much of the peninsula on which the city was situated, new immigrants from Africa and Europe crowded together along the waterfront.

The site of Montreal was originally the Indian village of Hochelaga, reached by the French explorer Jacques Cartier in 1535. As the seventeenth-century French came to dominate the settlement, it became a key trading port for the continental interior. Both internal and international commerce were responsible for Montreal's growth. Like other far northern cities, it was a grim place with houses and public buildings made of cold grey stone. Montreal did not get drinking water from public aqueducts until 1801. The city's narrow streets were dimly lit with oil lamps, and policing consisted of a few constables and a night watch. Though enormous profits were made from the fur trade, most of the wealth was funneled through Montreal back to Europe.

Mexico City was built on and from the ruins of the Aztec city Tenochtitlán, conquered by Cortes in 1521 and rebuilt as the viceroyalty of New Spain. For indigenous peoples life in the colonial cities was only marginally better than rural life. City life certainly offered them greater freedom and mobility than the life people in the rural land and labor system known as *encomienda* enjoyed (see also Chapter 6). It did not mean less labor. In the craft workshops of the towns, people were transformed from tillers of the soil to wage earners and were potentially liberated from the servile status to which conquest and the new economy had assigned them; city workers earned higher cash wages than rural manual workers, but they also had higher living expenses. Women worked outside the home in both rural and urban Spanish America. Some skilled textile manufacturing was completely in their hands, and in Mexico City, as early as the sixteenth century, there were associated female guilds and guild officers. Much of the art and architecture in Spanish America was ecclesiastical, and people were trained to quarry stone for churches, monasteries, and schools and to become the masons who erected them. They were trained as carpenters and cabinetmakers, sculptors and painters, musical instrument makers and performers, all in the service of religion.

Figure 3.5 Dakar, Senegal, West Africa. Dakar's wide city boulevards were an imported design of colonial planners. Industrial development did not occur until after independence.

The colonial era brought enormous changes to world cities, creating new magnets for growth and emphasizing an urban–rural divide. By the twentieth century, economic and political forces – especially in the interwar years (1920s and 1930s) – brought Africans and Asians to towns where the woefully inadequate social provisions of colonial administrations were fueling economic grievances. Urban centers attracted migrant (male) labor as workers sought cash to pay taxes and buy imported goods. From Nairobi to Calcutta, cities became crucibles for social and political change. By the 1940s an era of rapidly growing wage-labor and labor unrest in the cities was underway, joining an equally threatening period of rural discontent. Only the coalition of these forces – urban intelligentsia, organized urban laborers, and rural mass protest – could create successful nationalist movements in postwar Africa and Asia. They did so in the form of dockworker and railway strikes in Dakar (from 1922 to the 1940s), or the cocoa boycotts and protests in Ghana (1930 and 1938), or the salt and textile protests in South Asian cities (1930–42). Resistance before this time rarely had anything to do with sovereignty or racial identity; rather it resulted from widespread crises in the material world and was related more closely to class conflicts.

URBAN CULTURAL LANDSCAPES AND GLOBAL INDUSTRIALIZATION

Increasingly the growth of many modern cities would be directly linked to the spread of global industry and the markets that industry created. Because the modern urban cultures that emerged in various parts of the world sometimes grew on the sites of earlier cities, they were not necessarily new phenomena, but their influence was growing as the processes of global industrialization shaped lives worldwide. The impact of commerce, industrialization, and urbanization was uneven. Around the globe cities became sites for industrialization and the collection of goods and reflected the global processes involved in the movement of labor, resources, and capital.

Cities around the world received an impetus to growth from the expansion of global industrialization. The commercial and information networks that connected resources, manufacturing processes, and markets created interlinked forces of urbanization, especially in seaport cities. The technological innovations after about 1850, like steamships, electricity, telegraph, telephone, and other inventions relied on the organization of capital and labor into ever-larger available pools. Credit systems were city-based. Industries were built near ports that delivered natural resources and labor from around the globe. Seemingly overnight, in the following century, nations of rural populations became urban. Russia was typical in the extent of dramatic urbanization in the twentieth century, as the nation of peasants before 1900 CE became roughly 50 percent urban-dwelling by 1970.

Elsewhere, railroads and other technologies constructed the new paths of urban cultural growth. Industrialization and rail transport in the 1840s began to create magnets for migration to cities. The demographic shifts of the nineteenth and twentieth centuries were partly accomplished by the pull of mass migration to urban areas as people sought employment and other opportunities. For example, cities dotted the trans-American rail system and carried African Americans from the agricultural south to northern industrial cities. Other cities like Paris never lost their density of settlement, which in times of epidemics could be deadly. The cholera epidemics of 1832 and 1849 claimed tens of thousands of Parisian lives. The city's wide avenues were created as a pinnacle of engineering achievements during the 1889 exposition, and architectural monuments like the Eiffel Tower (the world's tallest building until 1930) were erected later in the century. In turn, rapid urbanization brought problems of sanitation, health care, crime, and unemployment, exacerbating the environmental and economic disparities of the modern world. Indeed, no city of the

modern era has avoided the experience of wealthy urbanites rubbing shoulders with the poor and penniless.

Once the age of steam-generated industries in iron and steel was underway, cityscapes around the globe were increasingly defined by their tall buildings and their smokestacks. During the Meiji Restoration, the industrialization of the Japanese economy was intensely promoted by the government. Edo was renamed Tokyo and along with Osaka became a commercial and industrial as well as a political center. Western influences pervaded city life as the Japanese economy emulated Western industrial capitalism. A late-nineteenth-century anthem of the Japanese city of Yawata extolled the "billows of smoke filling the sky, our steel plant, grandeur unmatched."

When the Communists took over China in 1949 they saw cities as centers of Western imperialism as well as of the Nationalists and Japanese they had fought. Peasants were the heroes of the revolution, not urban capitalists and merchants. Cities were suspect, but over time they became the most desirable places to live for everyone because of access to education, health care, and goods that were not available in the countryside. The People's Republic of China (PRC) government issued ration cards for essentials such as cooking oil and soap, and these could only be redeemed in the places where people were officially assigned and registered. Nonetheless, as China's economy has grown and cities have become even wealthier, large numbers of the "floating population" migrate into the cities and work as peddlers or day laborers or otherwise try to get by.

Shanghai began as a fishing village that became a market town in the eleventh century and subsequently flourished as a commercial center well before it became a treaty port city as a result of the Opium War (1839–41). As a treaty port, Shanghai was divided into the Chinese city, the International Settlement, and the French Concession, mirroring the penetration of China by foreign powers, who controlled their parts of the city and kept Chinese out. Shanghai was also a center of industry as well as commerce, and the workers of Shanghai played a key role in the organized labor movement in the early twentieth century. It was also the site of large-scale organized crime, prostitution, and international drug and spy rings. At the beginning of the twenty-first century, Shanghai was once again an international city, a center of banking, finance, and trade, with a modernist landscape of new buildings that jut up against the famous Bund, the European-style buildings that line the banks of the Huangpu River and once housed the banks and consular offices of foreign imperial powers.

Hong Kong was nothing more than a rocky promontory distant from centers of culture and power when it was ceded to the British as a result of the Treaty of Nanjing (1842) that ended the Opium War. By the time it reverted to Chinese control in 1997, Hong Kong was a center of international finance and commerce populated by Chinese who were British citizens, spoke English as well as Cantonese, and did not easily fit into the political or economic structure of the PRC.

Across the Pacific, in North America, the poet Carl Sandburg had once portrayed Chicago (1916) as the "stormy, husky, brawling, City of the Big Shoulders," even while alluding to the grim violence, hardships, and prostitution. Urban centers clearly meant more than dirt and grime and industrial pollution. The cities of the modern world became synonymous with the cultural pleasures of an earlier era's palaces and castles. Cities inspired cultural production and they housed art museums and universities, newspapers and publishing houses, jazz bands, symphonies and ballet companies. Part of the modern urban appeal has been the concentration of cultural resources on tap for city-dweller consumption. At the Chicago World's Fair (Columbian Exposition) held in 1893, artists and architects collaborated to create the "White City," an ideal model city. To keep the exhibit white, the planners had to institute a ban on the use of coal during the Fair. Using the classical Roman style, they awkwardly constructed a perfectly ordered city to house elephants, gondolas, Greek statues, the "Ottoman's Arab Wild East Show," and Japanese woodblock prints, among other diverse world cultural artifacts.

Not only diversity but anonymity has been a feature of urban cultural life. By the twenty-first century the cities of "strangers" described by Thomas Mun had materialized in cultures on every continent. On the crowded streets of Senegal's capital, Dakar, the image of Sheikh Amadou Bamba (1853–1927) can be found almost everywhere, from the brightly painted buses, to the walls of the city's buildings. Bamba, a poet and Sufi saint, is the spiritual leader of 4 million Muslims in Senegal and thousands who follow his teachings around the world. His image derives from a single photograph in which his features are hidden under a shroud of cloth and shadow. Today anonymous urban art is probably best exemplified by the work of graffiti artists on subway cars and sidewalk "galleries." Together with hip-hop culture, graffiti reflects the extent that modern urban streets have generated crime and culture with equal ferocity.

CITIES AND POPULATION GROWTH

Both the size and scale of cities have changed dramatically over time. As urbanization led to significantly larger concentrations of population and a proliferation of human achievements, cities became the focus for questioning the global impact of population growth. After all, cities have absorbed two-thirds of the world's population growth since the mid-twentieth century. The increased rates of population growth themselves have long drawn public scrutiny. The effect of human population growth has been debated at least since the eighteenth century. Thomas Malthus, in his influential *Essay on Population* (1798), expressed the belief that population grew at a rate exceeding that of resources; this theory led many to conclude that surplus population means too many people and not enough resources. Others attributed the perception of overpopulation to the inequitable division of resources in society. Nineteenth-century capitalists, in contrast, welcomed increased numbers of laborers and consumers who created the expanded markets necessary for capitalist industrial growth.

Population growth was even encouraged by some political leaders in the twentieth century, such as Stalin in the Soviet Union and Mussolini in Italy, both of whom gave awards for motherhood. During the 1950s Mao Zedong urged his people to expand their already huge population, arguing that the country could make up in people what it lacked in industry and other resources. But this policy was dramatically reversed with the introduction of the "one child" policy in the 1960s, in which only one child was allowed per family, a strategy intended to slow China's birth rate and population growth.

Tremendous postwar population increases were noted with alarm by many in the twentieth century, including the biologist Paul Ehrlich who described the "problem" of growth in his book *The Population Bomb* (1968) at a time when there were 3.5 billion human beings, five times the population of Malthus's world.

More than 90 percent of the current population growth occurs in the poorest countries of the world, and a billion of the current 6.6 billion inhabitants of the world, the "bottom billion," live in poverty, a fact that suggests that a large part of the crisis at the crossroads is political and economic. This global crisis

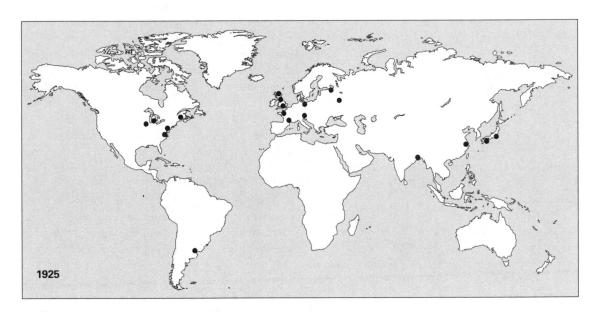

1925

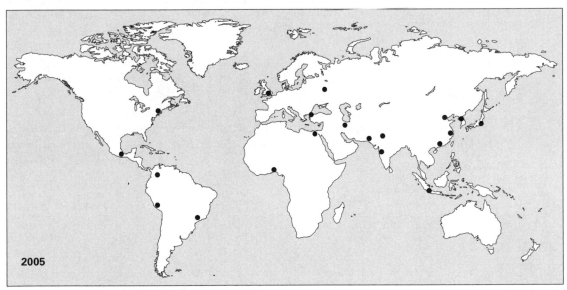

2005

Map 3.2 Changing distribution of the world's largest cities.

has altered the character of world cities, which now house about half the world's population in urban slums. What it means to be a world city today (controlling capital and information flows) may not hold true in the next generation.

CONCLUSIONS

This chapter has provided examples of the transition from early settled communities to urban centers beginning as early as the sixth millennium BCE. Some, like Memphis, which became Cairo, have survived the millennia, while others have declined and disappeared. The early cities were concentrations of increasingly diverse and highly stratified populations. Many originated as, or became, ceremonial centers, drawing large numbers of people to participate in rituals that were believed to propitiate deities, to encourage good agricultural harvests, or to request the support of the gods in war against their enemies.

Cities, since their origin, existed on a continuum of urban–rural relationships. Gradually they transcended their original primary functions. They were the centers from which ideology, institutions, material goods, and other urban "products" were transmitted to their hinterlands, on which they in turn depended. Such systems were also recipients of goods, peoples, and ideas from areas beyond their radii. The degree of urbanism in any part of the world was dependent on the ability of each large community to maintain an integrative system between itself and its hinterland. Though cities flourished around the world, most people still did not live in cities before the nineteenth century; most did, however, live in intricate relationship with them, visiting them, trading with them, and supporting them with food and other necessary and valued goods and services. The commercial revolution and global industrialization resulted in the further pull of populations towards urban centers in the past few centuries.

Wherever urban systems appeared, they had common characteristics. Urban society became more complex. It involved larger numbers of people and greater management and control of resources and environments, resulting in a wider variety of economic activity and a more rigid structuring and organization

of the city's inhabitants. In addition to more opportunities and the availability of more goods and services, urban life often meant the intensification of inequality and rigid divisions along lines of class, status, and gender. The systems of authority and relationships of inequality found in urban settings grew out of earlier patterns of larger social groupings and evolved to suit the conditions of urban life: complex and large communities of varied, interdependent parts required the mechanisms of control and centralized decision-making to negotiate these differences. For example, gender differences and relations became more clearly defined. Even in early agricultural communities, male dominance was more accentuated than it had been in gathering-hunting societies, an accentuation that was powerfully confirmed and perpetuated in urban societies. Sometimes male gods were credited with the growth of cities, and male warriors and rulers protected the trade routes that connected cities with their supporting hinterlands.

As later cities became centers for capital accumulation, they also wielded political power and furthered divisions based on gender and class. Overcrowded and polluted cities, especially in less-developed regions of the world, have become sites of instability and tremendous social and economic change. Between 1950 and 1990 there was a fivefold increase in the number of urban residents in less-developed countries, a far more rapid increase than for the world as a whole. Prior to the twenty-first century, the vast majority of the world's peoples lived on farms in rural settings, and their lifestyles, while culturally distinct, shared certain technological similarities. The gaps between highly industrialized and "developing" societies began to emerge during the colonial era, as capitalist industrialism spread and encouraged the growth of urban centers. Yet today our "planet of slums" now boasts many cities with sprawling poverty and no modern industry. Today more people live in cities than in rural areas for the first time in human history.

It is impossible to understand the historical rise of urbanism without taking into account the functional relationship between the urban center and its surrounding area. The process of successful integration of city and countryside, of constructing a larger political or community identity from increasingly diverse and divergent parts, is common to all the urban societies described in this chapter. Cities remain a constant throughout history after their appearance in the sixth millennium BCE, and both cultural and historical circumstances determine the changing nature of cities and their variety. In the twenty-first century the process of urbanization is escalating, with the sharpest growth in cities in less-developed parts of the world. In 1950, fewer than 30 percent of the world's people lived in cities; now at the beginning of the twenty-first century more than half do – and the number is steadily increasing. Tokyo is currently the only world city with a population of more than 20 million, but it likely will be joined by Bombay, Lagos, Shanghai, Jakarta, São Paulo, and Karachi, with Beijing, Dhaka, and Mexico City close behind. By the year 2025 it is estimated that more than two-thirds of the world's population will be city dwellers, making the urban experience one of the few truly common denominators among humankind.

SELECTED REFERENCES

Allchin, F. R. (1995) *The Archaeology of Early South Asia: The Emergence of Cities and States*, Cambridge: Cambridge University Press. Useful source on south Asian urbanism.

Balter, Michael (2006) *The Goddess and the Bull, Çatalhöyük: An Archaeological Journey to the Dawn of Civilization*, Walnut Creek, Calif.: Left Coast Press. Highly readable case study of how archaeologists study how and why people settled down in the first cities.

Cipolla, Carlo M. (1967) *The Economic History of World Population*, Harmondsworth: Penguin. Brief, stimulating view of demographic and economic development tracing the history of the great trends in population and wealth that have affected global societies as a whole.

Esherick, Joseph W. (2000) *Remaking the Chinese City: Modernity and National Identity, 1900–1950*, Honolulu: University of Hawai'i Press. A collection of articles on urban transformations in relation to modernity and national identity during the first half of the twentieth century, drawing comparisons with similar developments outside of China.

Heng, Chye Kiang (1999) *Cities of Aristocrats and Bureaucrats: The Development of Medieval Chinese Cityscapes*, Honolulu: University of Hawai'i Press. A study contrasting the regular grid pattern cityscape of the Tang (618–907) capital, Chang'an, with that of the irregular design of Song (96–1279) cities, using the northern capital, Kaifeng, as the principal example.

Johnson, Linda Cooke, ed. (1993) *Cities of Jiangnan in Late Imperial China*, Albany, N.Y.: State University of New York Press. A collection of articles on urban economic, social, cultural, and political life in the Yangzi delta cities of Suzhou, Hangzhou, Yangzhou, and Shanghai.

McEvedy, Colin and Richard Jones (1978) *Atlas of World Population*, London: Allan Lane/Penguin. Fully illustrated (with graphs, maps, and diagrams) history of world demography.

McIntosh, Roderick J. (2005) *Ancient Middle Niger: Urbanism and the Self-organizing Landscape*, Cambridge: Cambridge University Press. Summarizes key research on early West African urbanism at one site, exploring concepts of settlement hierarchy in a global context.

Morris, A. E. J. (1994) *History of Urban Form: Before the Industrial Revolution*, New York: Longman Scientific and Technical. Third edition of the classic introduction to the historical evolution of cities.

Roberts, Allen F. *et al.* (2003) *A Saint in the City: Sufi Arts of Urban Senegal*, Los Angeles: University of California, Fowler Museum. Places the visual culture of urban Senegal in the longer history of Islamic arts in Africa

UN-Habitat (2003) *The Challenge of the Slums: Global Report on Human Settlements (2003)*, London: United Nations. United Nations study on twenty-first century trends in urban poverty.

Whitfield, Peter (2005) *Cities of the World: A History in Maps*, Berkeley: University of California Press. An illustrated overview of more than sixty world cities.

ONLINE RESOURCES

Annenberg/CPB Bridging World History (2004) <http://www.learner.org/channel/courses/world history/> Multimedia project with interactive website and videos on demand; see especially Units

4 Agricultural and Urban Origins, 9 Connections Across Land, 10 Connections Across Water, 19 Global Industrialization, 24 Globalization and Economics, and 25 Global Popular Culture.

Hodder, Ian *Çatalhöyük Research Project* (2007) <http://www.catalhoyuk.com/>. The official site of the ongoing excavations of the Neolithic village in Anatolia.

UNESCO World Heritage Site (2007) <http://whc.unesco.org/en/list/>. Documents the most valuable of known sites, including the remains of most early cities and their monuments.

Waugh, Daniel Silk Road Seattle Project (Simpson Center for the Humanities, University of Washington) (2007) <http://depts.washington.edu/silkroad/cities/cities.html>. Cities along the Silk Road.

CHAPTER 4

Cosmos, community, and conflict

Religion in world history

On New Year's Day, 1946, Emperor Hirohito complied with orders from Allied occupation forces and made a radio broadcast to the Japanese people denying his divinity as a descendant of the Shinto gods. According to Shinto tradition, Hirohito and his imperial ancestors were descended from Amaterasu Ōmikami, the Sun Goddess. The Sun line, as the imperial family was known, represented an unbroken link to the founding of Japan and the very creation of the world. Yet that tradition – identifying the Japanese nation with the Shinto religion – was in fact quite recent, a product of the Meiji Restoration in the mid-nineteenth century that "restored" imperial rule and legitimized the emperor as a descendant of the gods. In the twentieth century, Shinto was officially adopted as the state religion by the wartime government, intensifying the identification of the Japanese nation with Shinto. Despite the fact that relatively few Japanese still believed in the divine descent of the emperor, the symbolic power of this idea as a cornerstone of state Shinto was sufficient to convince occupation authorities after the Second World War to demand a public renunciation by Emperor Hirohito. From the perspective of the Allied occupation, the union of state and religion in wartime Japan had contributed to militarism and fascism and therefore had to be dissolved.

Beyond its association with the imperial family and identification with the state, what is the meaning of Shinto as a religion? The name literally means "Way of the Gods," and was adopted only after the introduction of Buddhism to Japan created a need to distinguish native customs by which people protected their communities, ensured safe childbirth and sufficient food sources, and sought solace in the face of death. Unlike Buddhism and many other religions in world history, Shinto has no founder, no core sacred texts, and no moral or ethical code, yet it is still regarded as a religion. How can understanding Shinto help us to unravel the densely woven and thickly textured fabric of religion in world history?

INTRODUCTION

Evidence of what we now call Shinto practices among early human inhabitants of the Japanese archipelago can be traced through archaeology. Clay figurines known as *haniwa* that mark the borders of tombs, for example, include male and female dancers whose roles are suggested from later textual sources that describe ritual performances. A third-century Chinese chronicle provides some of the earliest textual records of Shinto mourning ritual:

> When death occurs, the family observes mourning for more than ten days, during which period no meat is eaten. The head mourner wails and cries, while others sing, dance and drink liquor. When the funeral is over, the entire family goes into the water to cleanse themselves in a manner similar to the Chinese in their rites of purification.
>
> (*Wei zhi* [History of Wei], cited in David J. Lu, ed., *Sources of Japanese History*, Vol. 1 (1974), p. 9)

Traces of such purification rites remain in the stone basins of water for ritual cleansing found at the entrances to Shinto shrines in modern Japan. Visitors to these shrines today perform the symbolic act of pouring water out of a bamboo ladle over their hands, but the origin of this purification ritual may have been protection of the community from the possible spread of disease associated with the dead.

As rituals designed to sustain and protect the community, Shinto provided the basis for a common identity among peoples who inhabited the Japanese archipelago. The transformation of unnamed community-based practices to a named religion after the advent of Buddhism, and then to a modern state religion that supported the rule of the Sun line, illustrates key aspects of the theme developed in this chapter: How did people around the globe understand and interpret their place in the cosmos? How did religion help to construct and to make sense of the social and political worlds people inhabited?

Religion is one of the most powerful and important ways people have responded to the need to understand themselves and the world around them. Religion is also one of the most difficult topics to address in world history. The study of religion in world history asks us to investigate the notoriously elusive realm of belief as well as historically visible traditions and practices. The expression of belief can take many forms – oral, written, artistic, performed – and these are the only sources the historian has to describe belief. We can't know precisely what people believed at any time in the past or present – even if we know exactly what they said about what they believed – but we *can* trace the evidence of belief through its expression in oral traditions, texts, artifacts, and performance as these changed over time. Nevertheless, we must acknowledge the particular difficulty and complexity of accessing belief in the past. As we necessarily use terms such as Shinto or Buddhism to label religious beliefs and practices, we risk reducing the lived experience of people in the past to fixed characteristics defined by these labels.

Religion can express personal longings or social meanings, negotiating the place of individuals or communities in relation to the natural or spiritual worlds, as in early Shinto. Religion can be shaped by, or become intertwined with, politics, reinforcing power relations by lending legitimacy to social hierarchies or political orders, exemplified in the use of Shinto to sanction imperial rule in Japan. Religion has the capacity to integrate communities and nurture a common identity, as Shinto did in early Japan; but it can also easily become either a divisive force that rends the social fabric or a source of resistance to institutionalized forms of authority and structures of power.

The introduction of Buddhism to Japan both stimulated the naming of native beliefs and practices as Shinto and confronted people with an entirely new conception of religion. Unlike Shinto, which was directly tied to the origins and identity of the Japanese people, Buddhism brought a message of universal appeal that transcended ethnic identities, cultural origins, and geographic space. However, when Buddhism encountered native beliefs and practices in Japan, as elsewhere, it was influenced by local traditions as much as it reshaped religious life there. We might say that Shinto was local and Buddhism global, but there was a dynamic relationship between them that serves as a guide for the content of this chapter: How did local, community-based religions interact with institutionalized, "portable," or so-called "world" religions?

This chapter will also address the question of local and global from the perspective of both "world" religions spread by adherents and community-based religions that moved with the migration of peoples (see Chapter 1). Unlike "world" religions transmitted by missionaries, merchants, and even soldiers, other religions – such as Judaism or African religions in the Americas – moved across the globe through the diaspora of peoples, who carried their religion with them as they were pushed and pulled to establish communities in new places. How did the forces of globalization reshape the contexts for religion, challenging adherents to seek new ways of accessing spiritual power and expressing their faith?

READING THE ARCHAEOLOGICAL RECORD

Evidence of prehistoric practices that may reflect belief in unseen forces with power over life and death dates from as early as 600,000 years ago, when archaic *Homo sapiens* used hematite in Neanderthal burials to decorate the bodies of the dead. The ritual use of hematite, an iron ore used to create red ochre pigments, suggests a link with the color of blood or life force. Subsequent evidence of red pigments used in burials and rock art is spread around the world from Europe to southern Africa, to Indonesia, Australia, and the Americas. Evidence of the actual mining of hematite dates from the Middle Stone Age, about 28,000 years ago in southern Africa.

The discovery of Chauvet cave in the French Pyrenees in 1994 thrilled archaeologists with its stunning wall paintings depicting red and black rhinos, bears, lions, horses, and even human hand prints, created more than 30,000 years ago. Like much later cave art from Lascaux in southern France, Altamira in northern Spain (20,000–15,000 BP), or still later petroglyphs from southern Africa, Australia, or western North America, these images provide tantalizing evidence of our early ancestors' attempts to convey their experiences of the world they inhabited and perhaps to communicate with an unseen world. Were they pictorial representations of sympathetic magic, drawn for ritual gatherings of increasing human populations in the areas surrounding the caves, designed to ensure plentiful game or to propitiate the spirits of animals killed for food and clothing? Or were they simply records of human activities and animal populations used to teach the young, transmitting vital information to succeeding generations?

Although animal and human statuettes of equal antiquity to the earliest cave paintings have been found in southern Germany and France, beginning around 25,000 years ago there was a marked increase in the production of female figurines across a broad swath of Eurasia, from western Europe to Siberia. Fashioned of stone, ivory, or clay, many of these figures portray well-developed, or even obese, females with heavily accentuated sexual features. It seems plausible to associate these "Venus" figures with the idea of fertility, and to speculate that the exaggerated breasts, abdomens, vulvae, and buttocks were designed to evoke human reproduction. Since at most half of the images found to date are female – most are simply anthropomorphic, neither clearly female nor clearly male – and there are images of animals as well, we cannot say more than that female reproduction was (obviously) valued and that the representation of the female form with signs of pregnancy may have been an effort to encourage reproduction.

A large number of female figurines have been found in Neolithic (c. 7000–3500 BCE) sites in the circum-Mediterranean area and southeastern Europe, leading to speculation that these represent the continuation of a much earlier fertility cult. But the striking diversity of figurines produced over many thousands of years suggests that this is too simplistic an interpretation: lumping them all together as "fertility images" may distort the historical understanding of the variety of female roles in societies ranging from nomadic hunter-gatherers to sedentary farmers. Whether female, male, or animal, we do not really know how these images were used – in religious rituals, as toys, to teach (childbirth, for example) – so we cannot necessarily assume their role in a fertility cult as such, although we can associate images of obviously fecund women with concerns for the reproduction of labor needed for grain farming in Neolithic times. Small clay figurines from the Mesoamerican site of Chalcatzingo in southern Mexico from the mid-first millennium BCE, for example, depict women in various life-cycle stages: puberty, pregnancy, and child-rearing – and they are thought to have been used in female-focused life-crisis ceremonies, rather than as objects of worship in religious rituals. The increasing production of anthropomorphic images, whether female or male, does seem to contrast with the depiction of animals on cave paintings and the dominance of animal imagery in late Paleolithic times, which may reflect primary concern with the human relationship to the animal world.

As representations of humans increased, considerable evidence attests to the continuing importance of animals in the religious life of Neolithic peoples around the world. Clay and stone seals dating to as early as 3200 BCE from Mehrgarh in present-day Pakistan and other Harappan sites in the Indus River Valley depict animals, along with human figures in yogic postures, horned deities, and trees. One particularly complex seal shows a horned deity standing between two branches of a tree, and a kneeling figure with folded hands, behind which is a sacrificial goat. At the bottom of the seal are seven figures with distinctive headwear and hairstyle, priests perhaps. Animals were used as sacrificial offerings because they were valuable, and their representation on artifacts testifies to their importance. Unicorns and bulls are frequently depicted, sometimes together with incense burners, indicating ritual activity.

Symbols inscribed on the seals have not been fully deciphered, but we can speculate that, although the seals may have been used for practical functions such as authenticating goods in commercial transactions, as well as for amulets, the artisans who produced them took the opportunity to portray important aspects of religious and ritual life in Harappan society that were characteristic of later beliefs and practices. The zebu (*Bos indicus*) found on Harappan seals, for example, became the bovine animal sacred in later Hindu ("of the Indus") tradition, although the transformation of this creature into the "sacred cow" of modern India was a long and complex process. The apotheosis of the zebu was related both to its ecological value as a resource and to its metaphorical use as a representation of cosmic unity. Similar importance as a religious icon was attached to the cow elsewhere too, likely because of its value as a food resource. The Egyptian goddess Hathor, for example, was represented as a cow or a cow-headed deity nourishing the living with her milk. Hathor was sometimes depicted as nursing the pharaoh, thus sustaining human society.

Ecological differences determined the role of specific animals in human cultures and religious life around the world. Early Chinese (*c.* 1500 BCE) bronze ritual vessels were sometimes cast in the shape of elephants or rhinoceroses, animals that roamed the plains of north China in those early times, or decorated with the "monster mask" design, representing a flattened symmetrical animal face. Jaguar imagery abounds in Mesoamerica from the early Olmecs (*c.* 1250–400 BCE) to the Aztecs (*c.* 1350–1521 CE). There was both a physical and a symbolic association between large predatory cats, warfare, and high social status. Images of felines, feline-like creatures, and warriors with feline attributes or apparel are found in an assortment of chronologically and spatially separated cultures. Mayan (*c.* 200 BCE–900 CE) rulers are sometimes depicted wearing jaguar pelts, or elaborate headdresses shaped like jaguar heads. The physical association with the jaguar in his apparel symbolized the ruler's strength and power.

Among the Olmecs and some later Mesoamerican peoples, caimans (Central and South American crocodiles) also had religious significance. A major food source, caimans (like jaguars) were predators of humans, and their representation thus projected power. Caiman imagery was used to portray both political and religious authority. A ruler, for example, might be depicted wearing a caiman pelt. Caimans

were also associated with fertility because of their ability to reproduce even in circumstances of limited food supply.

THE WORLD OF SPIRITS: ANIMISM AND SHAMANISM

Recognizing natural forces and their ability to affect human lives, many early human communities developed belief systems based on the idea that the natural and animal worlds are endowed with spiritual power (animism). In Shinto these forces are called *kami* and may include everything from waterfalls and mountains to deities with human characteristics like the Sun Goddess. Among many Mesoamerican peoples, including the Zapotec (*c.* 500 BCE–500 CE) and Maya, the notion of animistic breath, wind or spirit embodied in natural forces and the natural world was fundamental to their cosmologies: everything that moved should be respected as the reflection of a single, incorporeal creator. These forces were then personified as gods or goddesses.

Early human communities also practiced shamanism, beliefs and practices focused on individuals with special abilities that enable them to communicate with spirits. Shamanism persists in the contemporary world, in places ranging from Korea to North America and Africa. Shamans, who can be either female or male, are thought to communicate with anthropomorphic or other spiritual beings on behalf of the community through ceremonial trances. In modern Korean society, reflecting practices that can be traced to the earliest inhabitants of the Korean peninsula, female shamans perform ceremonies to assist their clients in seeking help with a current misfortune or ensuring a future benefit.

Some rock art has been interpreted as representing shamanistic experiences, notably examples in southern Africa, western North America, and Australia. Among the San people of southern Africa, shamans were believed to influence the herds of eland, a kind of antelope they hunted. Recent and ancient rock art imagery of anthropomorphic (part human-part eland) figures may refer to their trance experiences, in which shamans became eland. Similarly, utilizing both ethnographic and archaeological evidence, modern scholars have interpreted 4,000-year-old rock art in the lower Pecos River region of southwest Texas and northern Mexico that depicts anthropomorphic figures passing through an opening in a serpentine arch as a pictographic representation of a shamanic journey into the spirit world.

Along with rock art, the earliest artifacts that give us a hint about religious ideas and practices in North America are smoking pipes with carved human figures on the bowl who appear to be in trance. Such pipes, dating to as early as 3,000 years ago, were likely used in shamanic ceremonies in which smoking a substance produced a trance-like state that enabled the shaman to communicate with the spirit world. The pipes appear when North American Moundbuilders were beginning to erect platforms where ceremonies – which presumably might use such pipes – could be held on the summits of huge earthen mounds.

MOUNDS, MEGALITHS, AND MORTUARY MONUMENTS

The alteration of the landscape by the Moundbuilders in North America was dramatic, seen today still in the bird-shaped mound at Poverty Point (c. 1000 BCE) in Louisiana and later effigy mounds such as the Great Serpent Mound (c. 500–1000 CE) in southern Ohio. These mounds were architectural monuments that often played a role in religious life through ceremonial platforms built on the top.

Although the materials and the design differed considerably, the ziggurat at the Mesopotamian city of Ur, built around 2000 BCE, was a stepped pyramid representing a mountain on which the city god's temple was built. Similarly, like other Mesoamerican pyramids, the Pyramid of the Sun in Teotihuacán, a large urban site in the Valley of Mexico that flourished between about 100 BCE and 600 CE, served as the base for a temple on top. The Pyramid of the Sun represented a sacred mountain, as the city itself – later called "the Place of the Gods" by the Aztecs – was a sacred realm.

Elsewhere in the world, people built elaborate tombs to house the dead. Egyptian pyramids may be among the most impressive – the largest, at Giza, was built around 2500 BCE – but Bronze Age (2000–1300 BCE) *kurgans* in southeastern Europe, barrow mounds in the British Isles, and later (c. 300–500 CE) keyhole-shaped

tumuli in Japan all testify to the labor and resources that were lavished on erecting these monuments to the dead. Along with the erection of huge stones (megaliths) to mark the sites of graves or for other ritual activities, such as those at Stonehenge in England (c. 2400 BCE), tomb structures are also evidence of increasingly sharp stratification in society, in which the elite dead were entombed with elaborate rituals and conspicuous wealth. Bronze Age royal tombs in China, such as those at Anyang (c. 1400 BCE), provide vivid examples of this. Buried with large, highly decorated bronze ritual vessels and the remains of servants, slaves, and animals executed to accompany and serve the deceased in the afterlife, Shang kings displayed in death their power and status as ancestral divinities who could communicate with the supreme god of the Shang people.

INTERPRETING MYTHOLOGICAL TRADITIONS

Around the world, as people sought to locate themselves in time and space, they developed explanations of how the world began – creation myths – and stories about how human beings became a part of the world – origin myths. The Judeo-Christian biblical account of creation is contained in the Book of Genesis: "And God created the heavens and the earth." The Mayan *Popol Vuh*, orally transmitted until the sixteenth century, describes the origins of the K'iche' Maya people within the story of creation:

> the fourfold siding, fourfold cornering, measuring, fourfold staking, halving the cord, stretching the cord in the sky, on the earth, the four sides, the four corners . . . by the Maker, Modeler, mother-father of life, of humankind, giver of breath, giver of heart, bearer, upbringer in the light that lasts of those born in the light, begotten in the light; worrier, knower of everything, whatever there is: sky-earth, lake-sea.
>
> (From *Popul Vuh*, trans. Dennis Tedlock, New York: Simon & Schuster, 1985, pp. 71–2; quoted in Thomas Sanders et al., *Encounters in World History*, Vol. I, Boston: McGraw-Hill, 2006, p. 53)

Versions of their origins unique to Australian Aboriginals reflect archaeologically proven migrations that took place perhaps 50,000 years ago. The legends refer to the era of creation as the "Dreamtime," and they explain the migration of their ancestors to Australia in terms of beliefs about superhuman spirit ancestors who lived during the Dreamtime. The Kakadu people of Australia believe that the arrival of Imberombera, the Great Earth Mother ancestress, was by canoe, a mythical version of an event that archaeologists and prehistorians accept, even though no canoes – since they are perishable artifacts – have survived. Kakadu legend further explains the populating of Australia by the fact that when Imberombera came to Australia she was pregnant, her womb filled with children. Once on the continent, she created the natural landscape – hills, creeks, plants, and animals – and peopled it with her children.

Like Imberombera, the actors in the dramas of creation are often anthropomorphic deities – gods and goddesses – who create the earth, generate the cosmos, and even give birth to human rulers. According to Japanese mythology, a pair of gods, Izanami and Izanagi, gave birth to the Japanese islands and a host of deities:

> When the primeval matter had congealed but breath and form had not yet appeared, there were no names and no action. Who can know its form? However, when heaven and earth were first divided, the three deities became the first of all creation. The Male and Female here began, and the two spirits (Izanagi and Izanami) were the ancestors of all creation.
>
> (Donald L. Philippi, trans., *Kojiki*, Tokyo: Tokyo University Press, 1983, p. 37)

The progeny of these two gods included Amaterasu, the Sun Goddess, who became the central Shinto deity, ancestor of the imperial family, and one of many solar deities, male or female, found worldwide. When the Sun Goddess's brother annoyed her, she retreated into a cave and drew a stone across the entrance, bringing darkness to the world until she was drawn out again by the dances and laughter of other deities. This was an early Japanese explanation for a solar eclipse, and portrays the role of Shinto dances and ritual performance in propitiating the Sun Goddess to ensure the light and warmth of the sun needed for plentiful harvests.

THE DIVERSITY OF DIVINITY: GODDESSES, GODS, AND GOD-KINGS

According to Japanese mythology, Amaterasu sent her grandson down from her heavenly abode to establish the rule of the Sun line, thus creating the link between the Sun Goddess and the lineage of the imperial family. The relationship between gods and humans was central to the development of religion throughout the world.

The goddess Inanna first appears in the late fourth millennium BCE as the tutelary deity of Uruk, an urban center in the region of Sumer in southern Mesopotamia. She was the deity of the city's central storehouse, suggesting the connection between the rise of urban life dependent on the storage of food and the protection of those resources (see Chapter 3). Like other deities in the region, she had a human consort, a priest-king who ruled through the favor of the goddess. Mistress of life and death, Inanna was both compassionate and fierce – protector, temptress, demon, and lover. By the mid-second millennium BCE, Inanna had merged with her northern Mesopotamian counterpart, Ishtar, the tutelary deity of the city-state of Akkad, and exhibited a multifaceted, androgynous character.

In the third millennium BCE, the Sumerian city of Nippur seems to have acquired a uniquely sacred status, thus elevating its city deity, the warrior god Enlil, to a position of dominance over other gods. Later conquerors, including the Akkadian ruler Sargon I (*c.* 2300 BCE), legitimized their rule with the sanction of Enlil: religious inscriptions from the time promote the idea that Sargon I had been appointed to rule by Enlil.

Gods such as Enlil could sanction the rule of men, but some rulers were believed to be god-kings. By the third millennium BCE there was a pantheon of Egyptian gods and goddesses who supported the rule of god-kings. The Egyptian ruler, pharaoh, was worshiped as a living god who was the point of contact between the human and divine realms. It was the pharaoh's responsibility to preserve and maintain *ma'at*, the order of the universe and the harmony of human society. Pharaohs claimed to be descended from Amun-Ra, the sun god. Immediately below Amun-Ra were three principal deities who reflected the ecological conditions of the Nile Valley essential to the survival of humans in that region: Osiris represented the fertilizing power of the annual Nile floods; his wife Isis, the fertility of the earth; and their son Horus, the vital force of vegetation resulting from the union of Isis and Osiris. Pharaoh was believed to be the embodiment of Horus.

A written script known as hieroglyphics ("sacred carvings") was used for inscriptions on stone as well as for writing on papyrus. Both murals on tomb chambers in the pyramids and accompanying hieroglyphic inscriptions portray an array of deities and describe the afterlife in the underworld, which was presided over by Osiris. Egyptian funerary beliefs were collected in the Book of the Dead, dating to the era of the New Kingdom (c. 1530–1070 BCE) and containing an illustrated set of hymns, prayers, and magic formulas to guide and protect the soul in its journey.

By the time of the New Kingdom in Egypt, the introduction of bronze technology had led to the rise of the Shang state (c. 1700–1045 BCE) in the Yellow River Valley from Neolithic centers on the north China plain. The rule of chariot-riding Shang kings was validated through a religious cult that linked their political authority to the ability of royal ancestors to intercede with a supreme deity, Di. Skillful artisans crafted elaborate bronze vessels that were used to present offerings of food and wine to the ancestors of the Shang kings. Divination practices also sanctioned the rule of Shang kings. Oracle bones, the shoulder blades of oxen or sheep or turtle plastrons (the flat underside of turtle shells), were inscribed with questions such as "Will there be a good harvest?" or "Will we [the Shang] be successful in battle against our enemies?" Written in archaic Chinese script, the questions were addressed to Di, and the answers were read by interpreting cracks made in the bones when heated over a fire. These divination practices were carried out by shaman scribes, who served Shang rulers as a kind of priesthood in control of the technology of writing and thus communication with ancestral spirits.

Beginning around 1500 BCE, nomadic cattle herders and warriors from Southwest Asia moved into the realm of the Indus Valley civilization. Technologically well equipped with horse-drawn chariots and inspired by their warrior god, Indra, they conquered the remnants of the Indus Valley civilization and settled there. These invaders assimilated indigenous ideas and gradually integrated the early Indus Valley beliefs with their own. The new social and political order was sanctioned by a pantheon of deities, who were manifestations of cosmic forces, and by texts, the Vedas ("knowledge"), a collection of orally transmitted ritual hymns that were compiled as written texts between around 1200 and 600 BCE. Culminating over centuries in the rich Hindu pantheon of gods and goddesses, the original triumvirate of central deities included Brahma, the creator, Shiva the destroyer, and Vishnu the preserver. Goddesses figure in the Vedic pantheon only in relatively minor ways until much later (c. 400–800 CE), when female divine power (shakti) was recognized and the image of the mother goddess as a supreme being became an important part of Hindu tradition. The consorts of Shiva and Vishnu, for example, are incarnations of Devi, the great goddess. Durga is the warrior form of Shiva's consort, and Kali is the demonic version, a grim goddess associated with death and destruction.

Contemporary with invasions of the Indus Valley civilization in South Asia, various Indo-European peoples invaded the Aegean basin, where they conquered and absorbed centers of earlier (third to first millennium BCE) Mediterranean culture such as the Minoan palace at Knossos on the island of Crete and the citadel of Mycenae on the Greek mainland. Figurines from the palace at Knossos wearing dresses that expose and emphasize the breasts represent priestesses of Minoan religion, or perhaps images of a goddess with power over nature shown in her grasp of writhing snakes in both hands. Shrines on Crete dated to 1400 BCE contain terracotta goddess statues, and by the second millennium BCE the Myceneans had an elaborate pantheon of gods and goddesses. This pantheon included the later Greek gods Zeus, Poseidon, and Dionysus, all of whom dwelt on sacred Mount Olympus.

The Greek poets Homer and Hesiod (c. eighth century BCE) described the gods and goddesses of the Olympic pantheon as anthropomorphic figures who both controlled the forces of nature and interacted with human beings. By the sixth century BCE, the polis (city-state) of Athens could boast of a full-fledged civic religion, centered around the Olympian goddess Athena Polias, the patron deity of Athens, at her temple on the Acropolis (see Chapter 3). The Pananthenaia festival celebrated the goddess with a public procession, sacrifices, hymns, and dances.

In contrast to practice of this civic religion, the fifth century BCE Greek philosopher Plato undertook to create a system of thought that united the natural and the theoretical and to provide a world-view that was both ordered and beautiful. In his *Timaeus*, Plato returned to the traditions of ancient Greek beliefs and postulated a creator god who designs an orderly world that is maintained by the actions of gods. The duty of humans is to carry on with the gods' efforts through the performance of religious sacrifices, which ensures harmony and order.

Contemporary with the practice of civic religion that was communal and public, mystery religions that prized secret knowledge known only to initiates also flourished. Mystery religions promised rebirth or regeneration, demanding secrecy of their initiates in exchange for benefits in life or after death. The shrine to the Olympian goddess of crops and fertile earth, Demeter, at Eleusis near Athens, became the center of the Eleusinian mysteries, which focused on life, death, and the sprouting of the new crop. Like Demeter, the Egyptian goddess Isis was also associated with the renewal of life. Although Isis was known to the Greeks as early as the fifth century BCE, a mystery religion dedicated to her appeared only in the last two centuries BCE when it spread throughout the eastern end of the Mediterranean.

Even more popular than the cult to Isis, worship of the great mother goddess Cybele originated during the early first millennium BCE in Anatolia (modern Turkey) and spread throughout the Greco-Roman world. Known as Meter (mother) in Greece, Cybele was officially venerated in Rome by the end of the third century BCE as *Magna Mater*, Latin for "Great Mother." Her worshipers participated in ecstatic dancing, and bull slaughtering was part of a ritual performance that produced blood with which initiates were sprinkled. Followers of both Cybele and Isis were found all over the Greco-Roman world, and the two goddesses were often conflated. In a work of the second century CE, Isis announces herself by describing the

various names by which she is known throughout the Mediterranean world, beginning with the Phrygian (Anatolian) Mother of the Gods, the antecedent of Cybele:

> The Phrygians, earliest of humans, call me the . . . Mother of the Gods; . . . to the Eleusinians I am the ancient goddess Ceres [Demeter], to others Juno . . . and the Ethiopians who are illuminated by the first rays of the sun, the Africans, and the Egyptians full of ancient lore and wisdom honor me with the true rites and call me with the true name: Isis.
>
> (Apuleius, *The Golden Ass*, quoted in Fritz Graf, "What is Ancient Mediterranean Religion?," in Sarah Iles Johnston, ed., *Religions of the Ancient World*, Cambridge, Mass.: Belknap Press of Harvard University Press, 2004, p. 3)

Alongside the worship of Cybele, belief in Mithras, based on an old Indo-Iranian sun god, flourished among soldiers of the Roman empire by the first century CE. Bull slaughter was also central to the Mithraic religion, which appealed to soldiers by emphasizing bonds of brotherhood cemented through initiation ceremonies, including a shared meal. Followers of Mithras could be found throughout the Roman empire, as far afield as Britain.

Despite recognition of Magna Mater and the popularity of the Mithras cult, the Roman government was suspicious of popular cults that appealed to citizens and non-citizens alike. Although a temple to Isis and her husband, Sarapis (the Greco-Roman version of Osiris), was built in Rome in 43 BCE, persecutions of the Isis cult were ongoing at the same time that the Roman state began to promote veneration of the emperors as deities. In a reversal of the spread of the goddess Cybele from Anatolia much earlier, Emperor Augustus was deified after his death and worshiped in Anatolia and other parts of the Roman empire.

The initial acceptance of diverse deities from Egypt and Anatolia in the Greek city-states and later in Rome may have been a response to ethnic diversity and social disparities based on gender and class: popular mystery religions provided an outlet for both men and women otherwise disenfranchised. But such groups could also become a threat to the power of the state, an example of the way in which religion can express divisions in society and pose a challenge to the social and political order. By deifying emperors, or by identifying Roman gods with local ones (Minerva, for example, was identified with the Celtic god Sulis in Roman Bath), the Roman state sought to regain control by asserting its authority through religion.

While belief in Isis and Cybele spread throughout the Mediterranean and the Roman empire promoted worship of deified emperors, on the opposite side of the globe the rulers of contemporary Teotihuacán associated their rule with the Feathered Serpent, Quetzalcoatl, whose temple lay near one end of the ceremonial plaza at the center of the city, and also with the primal deity, Tlaloc, whose shrine was the Pyramid of the Sun. Extant images of a powerful goddess (see Figure 3.2), perhaps associated with the Pyramid of the Moon at the other end of the ceremonial plaza, convey aspects of war and fertility, both central to Teotihuacán's identity as a dominant power in the region until the sixth century CE.

Rulers of Mayan kingdoms that coexisted with Teotihuacán in the Mesoamerican lowland rain forests of the tropical Yucatán Peninsula warred over control of territory but shared each other's gods. The Mayan pantheon included numerous deities, manifestations of the cosmic breath that animated the natural and human worlds. The names of Mayan gods and goddesses, as well as events aligned with the complex Mayan calendrical system, were recorded in a hieroglyphic script inscribed on the walls of temples and monuments. Blood sacrifice was believed to be required to nourish the gods, either through self-inflicted blood-letting (earlobes and tongues) or the sacrifice of prisoners of war.

Unlike god-kings such as the Egyptian pharaohs, Mesoamerican rulers, including the Maya, were believed to rule for the gods but were not themselves gods. Deceased royal ancestors could, however, share the realm of the gods. Mayan gods and ancestors of Mayan kings often are portrayed as hovering in the same realm, and at times share common attributes. A major deity associated with Mayan rulers is the Maize God, who cyclically dies and is reborn as corn is harvested and planted. A vessel from the Mayan city-state of Tikal dated to c. 250–600 CE depicting King "Great Jaguar Paw" as the Maize God is inscribed with titles that link the ruler to the god as his protector deity.

In Eurasia and North Africa as early as the third millennium BCE, similar belief systems developed that were focused on gods who sanctioned the power of kings to rule. In Egypt, the pharaohs were considered to be "living gods," while elsewhere kings ruled with the divine sanction of gods, as in Sumer, where goddesses or gods were consorts of rulers, or in Shang China, where royal ancestors interceded with a supreme deity. Drawing on earlier animistic and shamanistic beliefs, as in Mayan Mesoamerica, priests and scribes played important roles in confirming the authority of rulers by claiming to communicate with gods and ensuring the legitimacy of rulers. Sacred scripts aided rulers in preserving the records of their relationships with deities and thus sanctioning their rule.

In sub-Saharan Africa, beliefs about divine kings and other ancestors were common features of community life. In the sacred city of Ife in the first millennium CE (and in the successor kingdom of Benin), life portrait masks and commemorative heads were cast in copper alloys and placed on altars. The ruler (oba) was portrayed as having mudfish legs, a trait thought to enable the oba to travel across the watery reaches of the spirit world. From West to Central Africa, iron objects were symbols of the power of transformation thought to be required of divine kingship at least from about 800 CE. Concurrent with religious ideas that supported and validated political power were beliefs in spirits and ancestors, who were reborn as children. Both ancestral and other spirits were believed to interact with the living through dreams, divination, and ritual, thus reproducing the world's seen and unseen realms.

By the end of the first millennium BCE, smaller, diverse religions distinct from civic or state religions appealed to people at all levels of society and flourished throughout the world. Religions dedicated to the goddesses Isis and Cybele, at times appropriated by rulers and at times subversive of the state, spread throughout the Mediterranean world from Spain to Anatolia (modern Turkey) and from North Africa to Europe (as far as modern Germany). Around the world, from Mesoamerica to the Mediterranean, visions of the afterlife provided solace in the face of the universal experience of death and vividly portrayed

Figure 4.1 Stone bust of the Maize God, Mayan, Late Classic period (CE 600–800), from Copán, Honduras. The Maize God is represented here as a handsome youth, with corn silk hair and a corn cob protruding as his headdress. As related in the *Popol Vuh*, the Ki'che' Maya people were created from corn, so this deity and the motif of corn are prominent features of religious art.

realms of the dead, often furnished with material goods offered up by the living. In the proliferation of local traditions, peoples everywhere sought to gain security in the face of change.

PRIESTS, PREACHERS, AND PROPHETS

As early as the second millennium BCE, religious ideas that did not focus on goddesses, gods, or god-kings began to take shape in Eurasia. New belief systems challenged the power of shamans, priests, and god-kings and focused instead on ethical questions of right and wrong, explanations of good and evil, and on the meaning of human existence and suffering.

Judaism

The roots of Judaism can be traced among the semipastoral peoples of Iraq in the second millennium BCE, and the early history of the religion is intimately tied to the historical experience of one group, the Hebrews. They moved westward early in the second millennium under the leadership of the patriarch Abraham. According to the Bible, Abraham abhorred the idol worship found in his birthplace, Ur, in Mesopotamia, and moved his family and herds through the Syrian desert to a new home in Palestine at the eastern end of the Mediterranean, where they continued to worship their ancestral clan divinity.

Around the middle of the second millennium BCE, the Hebrews moved to Egypt, where eventually they were enslaved. About 1250 BCE, following a leader named Moses, the Hebrews fled Egypt and resettled in Palestine. Under the guidance of Moses, Yahweh, originally the most powerful of numerous gods, emerged as the favored god of the Hebrew tribes. Moses claimed that God (Yahweh) had transmitted to him the sacred laws by which the community should live. These were the Ten Commandments, and they were sealed up in a box called the "Ark of the Covenant," reflecting the covenant, or pact, with God made by the Hebrew people.

Under Moses' successor, Joshua, the twelve Hebrew tribes that traced their descent from Abraham and his sons staked out territory in Palestine, and in the

eleventh century BCE Saul became the first king of Israel. Under the rule of his son David (r. c. 1000–960 BCE) the transition from a tribal confederacy to a unified monarchy was completed. The Ark of the Covenant was brought to David's new capital of Jerusalem, which became the political and religious center of the kingdom of Israel. The First Temple was built by David's son and successor, Solomon (r. c. 960–920 BCE), after which the kingdom split into two, divided between Israel in the north and Judah in the south.

The Assyrians destroyed Israel in 721 BCE and deported many Israelites to the east. It was during this time of tribulation that the teachings of a series of great social and moral critics and reformers – the prophets Ezekiel, Amos, and Isaiah, among others – confirmed Abraham's tribal god, Yahweh, as not just the most powerful god but the only god. In 587 BCE, the Babylonians captured Jerusalem, destroyed the Temple, and deported many leading Jewish families to Babylon, along with skilled workers such as blacksmiths and scribes. This was the origin of the diaspora (Greek for "scattering" or "dispersal") in which Jews were forcibly deported or fled their homelands to settle elsewhere.

In addition to religious ritual focused on the Temple in Jerusalem or on a synagogue elsewhere, a central issue of Hebrew belief became just and moral behavior among human beings. Such behavior was the result of obeying Yahweh's laws, while transgression of his laws led to punishment. In the fifth century BCE, the Temple was rebuilt and a code of laws was introduced to guide the Hebrew people so that they would not err again. By this time, Judaism was a cosmology based on one god, who was the creator and lawgiver, and on humans, who ideally ruled the earth justly, guided by God's laws.

Zoroastrianism

At the time when the Hebrews were creating a religious community based on belief in one god and their shared historical experience, the Medes and Persians, who ruled Iran in the seventh century BCE, were part of an Indo-Iranian cultural and religious world: they spoke an Indo-European language, used Sanskrit texts, and believed in a pantheon of Hindu gods and goddesses. They saw existence, the world, and themselves as moving through eternal cycles on the Hindu "Wheel of Life." Their place on that wheel was defined by birth into a rigid caste system.

This was the context in which an Indo-Iranian priest, known to us by his Greek name of Zoroaster, began preaching to farmers and semi-sedentary herders who lived south of the Aral Sea in eastern Iran. This traditional borderland between settled Iran and the wide-ranging nomads of the Central Asian steppe was subject to frequent border raids and wars. The sixth century BCE was no exception to this perennial instability, and Zoroaster's ideas gained a receptive audience because they spoke to the difficulties experienced by people in this region and called for change.

In place of the numerous Indo-Iranian gods and goddesses, Zoroaster proposed a dualistic pairing of gods: Ahura Mazda, the "Wise Lord," who represented the ethical good, and Ahriman, the embodiment of darkness and falsehood. Life was a constant moral war between two forces, and human beings had to choose between lies and truth, darkness and light. The teachings and principles of Zoroaster are found in the Avesta, a collection of hymns and sayings made sometime after his death. Zoroaster's ideas attracted the support of the Persian empire's ruling aristocracy, and for the next 1,200 years some variation of Zoroastrianism continued to find followers in Persia and the territories it controlled. Zoroastrian ideas were also influential in shaping later Judaism, particularly the dualism of God and Satan and of Heaven and Hell.

Hinduism

While Zoroaster responded to turmoil in the borderlands of the Persian empire, commercial expansion, social conflict, and new religious ideas transformed the rich Ganges River plain of northern India, dotted with more than a dozen kingdoms. In this setting challenges emerged from within the Vedic tradition that opposed the domination of Brahman priests and reinterpreted the meaning of Vedic ritual. Unlike the Brahmanas ("sacred utterances"), Vedic texts that emphasize ritual as a means to regulate the social order according to caste divisions, the later Upanishads ("sessions," referring to esoteric knowledge gained from sitting at the feet of a master) represent a speculative tradition that seeks to explain the meaning of human existence.

According to the Upanishads, the goal of human existence should be to escape the endless cause–effect sequence of the continuous cycles of existence and achieve individual identification with a unified cosmic essence. Because of their focus on metaphysical or abstract questions concerning human existence rather than rigid adherence to ritual, the tradition of the Upanishads greatly reduced the role of priests and the importance of ritual and set the stage for the emergence of Jainism and Buddhism. Both religions were rooted in a "wandering ascetic" movement that opposed the power of Vedic priests; both also rejected caste ideology and the sacrificial rituals of the Vedic religion, drawing on the critical intellectual tradition associated with the Upanishads.

Jainism

Mahavira (c. 540–468 BCE), whose name means "Great Conqueror," was the founder of Jainism (for Jina, "Victor"). He abandoned his comfortable life as the son of a tribal chief to become a wandering ascetic at about the age of thirty. He reacted to priestly ritualism by promoting ascetic practices for his followers. Jains believe that everything in nature is alive and endowed with a form of spiritual essence; they also believe in the doctrine of nonviolence, which has had a profound influence on Indian culture and society into modern times. Jainism, however, never gained a wide following, either in India or elsewhere.

Buddhism

The teachings of the man later known as Buddha were profoundly shaped by concepts developed in the Upanishads, such as *samsara*, the cycle and bondage of rebirth, and *karma*, the cumulative causality of actions that propels humans through life after life. Born during the sixth century BCE to the ruler of a kingdom in the Himalayan foothills, young Prince Siddhartha grew up amid the luxurious surroundings of palace life. As he matured, he began to recognize the existence of suffering, sickness, and death. He sought an understanding of the causes of human suffering by following the teachings of various ascetics and holy men. Dissatisfied with their teachings, Buddha eventually achieved *nirvana* (the extinction of forces that cause rebirth), "enlightenment," or the realization of the true nature of existence through a combination of meditation and ascetic practices. The Buddha, his life and teachings that comprise the fundamental law (*dharma*), and the *sangha* (community of monks) became known as the "Three Treasures," the core of Buddhist doctrine.

The Four Noble Truths, taught by Buddha in a famous sermon at the Deer Park in Sarnath, contain the basic precepts of Buddhist belief: that life is suffering; that the cause of suffering is desire; that in order to stop suffering, one must stop desire; and that the way to accomplish this is through the Eightfold Path, which includes ascetic practices and mental disciplines followed by monks, holy men who live apart from society and have committed their lives to religious practice. After Buddha's death, disciples continued to spread his doctrines. Gradually, the orally transmitted teachings were written down as scripture (*sutra*) and collected into the Buddhist canon. Divisions arose about interpretations of the Buddha's teachings, and councils were held to resolve and clarify doctrinal disputes.

One of these councils was called by Ashoka (*c.* 272–232 BCE), ruler of the Mauryan empire that stretched across northern India from the Indus Valley to the Ganges. Ashoka adopted and patronized Buddhism, erecting inscribed pillars and *stupas* marking sacred sites connected with the Buddha throughout his empire. In these inscriptions, Ashoka is called "Beloved of the Gods"; he is described as regretting the death and destruction that accompanied his conquests and looking on to the next life rather than taking pleasure in the power and luxury of his role as king. The adoption of Buddhism by Ashoka helped to establish legitimacy for his rule over many different ethnic groups by claiming to be the first true *chakravartin* ("he for whom the Wheel of the Law turns"), or universal monarch.

During the first two centuries CE, Buddhist believers divided into Mahayana ("Greater Vehicle") and Theravada ("Doctrine of the Elders") traditions. Mahayana Buddhists emphasized universal salvation through devotional practices accessible to lay believers. This contrasted with the Theravada (also known pejoratively as Hinayana, or "Lesser Vehicle") concentration on the discipline of renunciation, spiritual self-cultivation, and meditation characteristic of monastic life, and the belief that only those who devoted their lives to Buddhist practice could attain enlightenment. As the goal shifted from enlightenment, at the heart of early Buddhism, to salvation in Mahayana Buddhism, there was a profound change in the fundamental orientation of Buddhist believers.

The central religious goal of Mahayana belief was that of the *bodhisattva*, one who seeks enlightenment for the purpose of aiding other beings in the pursuit of awakening, in contrast to the Theravada *arhat*, who was concerned only with individual spiritual liberation. The *bodhisattva* ideal was rooted in the altruism of Buddha in his former lives, when he sought to help other living beings, and it was represented in Mahayana Buddhism by the Buddhas and *bodhisattvas* who became the focus of worship by Mahayana believers, such as the *bodhisattva* Avalokiteshvara or the Buddha Amitabha, both of whom became the center of sectarian Buddhist beliefs and practice in Central and East Asia. As Buddhism was transmitted from India across Asia, the Mahayana tradition came to dominate Central and East Asia, while Theravada became dominant in Southeast Asia, and these differences continue to the present day.

CHRISTIANITY, MANICHAEISM, AND ISLAM

Christianity, Manichaeism, and Islam originated in the same geographical and cultural setting and drew from the ancient traditions of that region, particularly that of the Jewish people and Judaism, as well as Zoroastrianism. Like Abraham, Moses, and Zoroaster, the founders of Christianity, Manichaeism, and Islam were preachers and prophets whose charismatic leadership and teachings attracted devoted disciples and eventually generated movements that spread far beyond their places of origin.

Christianity and Manichaeism

At the beginning of the first millennium CE in Palestine, then a province of the Roman empire, a Jew named Jesus was born in the town of Bethlehem. Palestine had come under Roman control about 65 BCE, but some Jewish groups continued to resist the

Figure 4.2 Buddha preaching, Sarnath, fifth century CE. Sarnath, near the modern city of Varanasi, was the place where Buddha gave his first sermon to five disciples and formed the *sangha*, the community of monks.

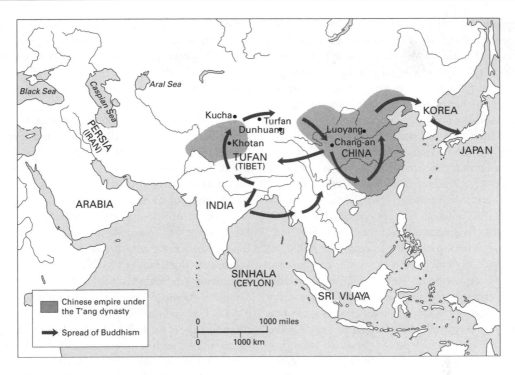

Map 4.1 Spread of Buddhism from South to East Asia.

Roman occupation. Jewish political activists called "Zealots," a small minority of the Jewish population, carried out guerrilla attacks against the Roman government. Another group of Jews, the Essenes, chose to withdraw from the tensions of everyday life under Roman occupation and settle in communities to await the imminent end of the world that would usher in a new age. When he was about thirty years old, Jesus set out to preach reform in this Palestinian milieu of many religious beliefs and practices. He spoke against narrow reliance on ritual, attacked the legalistic and too-worldly character of community religious leaders, and again and again warned of the imminent end of the world, the resurrection of the dead, judgment, and the establishment of the Kingdom of God. After three years of preaching to increasingly receptive audiences, the Romans tried Jesus on two counts: for blasphemy and for claims of being "king of the Jews." He was convicted of the charges and executed by crucifixion around 35 CE.

In the decades following Jesus's crucifixion, aided by the zealous missionary activities of Saul of Tarsus, an Anatolian Jew later known as Paul, Christian communities grew throughout the eastern end of the Mediterranean. By about 100 CE, the sacred texts of Christianity had been established. There were four Gospels, or "Good Stories," written in Greek by four of Jesus's apostles. These described the sayings and deeds of Jesus and spelt out collectively how these sayings and deeds were to be understood. To these Gospels were added the Epistles of Paul, couched in the form of advisory letters and sermons written by him to early Christian communities in need of advice. These texts (the "New Testament") were attached to the Judaic sacred scriptures (the "Old Testament").

Within a century after the death of Jesus, there were small communities of Christians scattered around the eastern end of the Mediterranean. The number of Christians expanded through the second and third centuries. In the early fourth century CE, the Christian movement was given enormous encouragement by the ruler of the eastern half of the Roman empire. In 312, on the eve of a major battle, the Emperor Constantine (r. 306–37) promised to declare for the Christian god in the event he won. The victorious Constantine was true to his pledge, sanctioning Christianity by giving it legal status and favoring Christians the rest of his life. In 380 Christianity became the imperial state religion, a recognition granted it by Emperor Theodosius. After 380, emperors at the capital of the eastern half of the Roman empire, Byzantium (renamed Constantinople) reigned over the Byzantine empire and ruled as "vicars of God" with religious authority equal to that of the Apostles. Following the fall of the Roman empire in the west, the bishop of Rome (*il papa*, "the father" or pope) gradually emerged as the leader of Christian communities in western Europe. The pope became head of the Church of Rome, and the Byzantine emperor head of the Church in the east, thus dividing Christianity between Roman Catholicism and Eastern Orthodoxy. In the fourth century, however, before this division, Christianity rivaled both Persian Zoroastrianism and its later manifestation, Manichaeism, in influence in West Asia.

The familiar Zoroastrian concept of an ongoing war between Good and Evil, Light and Dark, provided crucial background for the development of Manichaeism, named after its founder Mani (*c.* 216–77 CE), an itinerant preacher and physician from southern Iraq. According to Mani, humanity was created to be soldiers on the side of Light but through defeats and setbacks had become hopelessly entangled in the material Dark world. A series of messengers and prophets had been sent down to earth to offer salvation from the swamp of evil darkness that is earth; Buddha had been one of them, Zoroaster another, and Jesus had been one of the greatest of them. Following him, Mani came as the "seal of the prophet," the "apostle of Jesus Christ," to enlighten humanity on how to identify and venerate its spark of Light. Manichaeism offered, through its learned priesthood, a path to salvation from the troubles of the world.

Although Mani was executed as a heretic at the Persian court, during the late third and fourth centuries, Manichaeism gained many adherents in West and Central Asia, North Africa, and Europe, eventually spreading as far as China. Some Manichaean ideas influenced the early Christian Church. The North African Augustine (354–430 CE), one of the great Christian thinkers and a "Church father," professed Manichaean beliefs before he converted to Christianity.

Augustine's conversion took place in Italy, but Christianity was already flourishing on the African continent when he returned to North Africa. Well before Augustine's birth and close to the time that Constantine adopted Christianity, King Ezana, the ruler of the state of Axum in the Ethiopian highlands of northeast Africa, also converted to the new faith. Christianity had reached the Nile Valley during Roman times, eventually spreading into Nubia and the Ethiopian highlands. The official introduction of Christianity has been attributed to the first consecrated bishop of Axum, Frumentius of Constantinople, in 315 CE. One of the primary motivations for the fourth-century conversion to Christianity by King Ezana of Axum was the trading advantage offered to Axum as a result of religious connections with the Byzantine world; status as a Christian polity conferred certain guarantees of prices and trading partners. Pre-Axumite and early Axumite religions included the moon god, of south Arabian origin, and Mahrem, a god of war. Their associated symbols, the crescent moon and disc, eventually gave way to the cross, which appeared exclusively on stone stelae and coins minted from the time of King Ezana.

Christian missionaries also carried their faith north and west to Gaul, Spain, and the British Isles, where Christianity merged with native traditions, such as Celtic beliefs and practices in Ireland. By the second half of the first millennium CE, Christian communities were to be found throughout the Mediterranean basin and the Nile Valley, north and west to Britain and the Iberian peninsula, and eastward to the fringes of Asia and beyond. Nestorian Christianity, emphasizing the human rather than the divine nature of Jesus, was deemed a heresy by Christian Church authorities in the fifth century. Nestorians subsequently made their way to Central Asia, India, and as far east as China, where communities of believers remained active for several centuries.

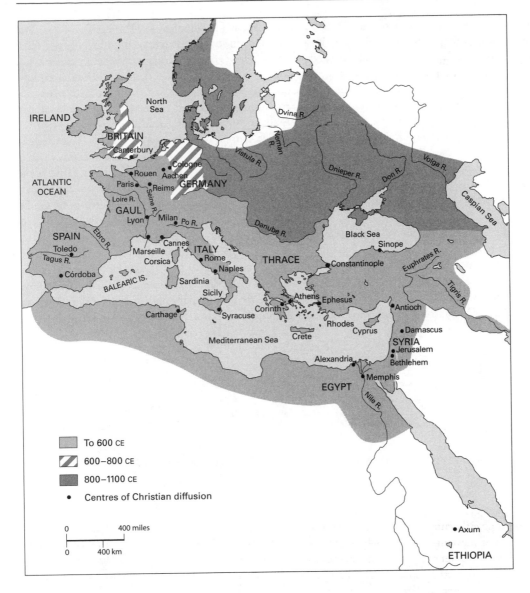

Map 4.2 Spread of Christianity in the Mediterranean, Europe, and North Africa before 1100 CE.

Islam

Christianity was already a well-established religion by the time Islam appeared in the seventh century CE in Mecca, a flourishing trade city located halfway up the Red Sea coast between Egypt and the Indian Ocean. The people of Mecca knew Zoroastrianism through trading contacts in Iraq and the Persian Gulf, and Christianity through trading trips north to Syria and Egypt or across to Christian Ethiopia. They knew something of Judaism, not only because of business but also because large numbers of Jews lived in Yemen and even closer in the agricultural town that would later be known as Medina.

In the year 610, one of the businessmen of Mecca, Muhammad, experienced a vision in which he was enjoined by the angel Gabriel to speak God's word, to warn humanity of the imminent coming of the day of judgment and the need to correct greedy and immoral ways. Persuaded that he had been chosen to be a messenger of God, he dedicated the rest of his life to exhortation and action: exhortation to lead a just and moral life, and action to establish a godly community in which all members accepted, or submitted to, God's plan and laws. Islam is the Arabic word for "acceptance" or "submission," and a Muslim is one who follows Islam.

Muhammad's attacks on the morals of the wealthy and powerful and on the false gods of Mecca led to his persecution. In 622, persecution led to the migration (*hejira*) of Muhammad and his now fairly sizable group of followers to the town of Medina, 300 miles north of Mecca. There the first Muslim community was formally established. To commemorate this event, the Muslim calendar, one calculated in lunar months, begins in 622. After a few years of struggle, Muhammad and his supporters returned to Mecca in 630. The city rapidly became Muslim, and over the next two years the community expanded to include the whole of the Arabian peninsula and part of southern Syria as well.

The Qur'an is the Muslims' sacred book. A collection made in 651 of Muhammad's revelations written down by followers as he uttered them, this book contains all the principles and precepts necessary to live life according to God's plan. Considered to be God's word and eternal, the Qur'an was revealed and copied down in Arabic. In addition to the Qur'an and its language, Islamic law and daily ritual held the Islamic community together in faith as it rapidly expanded to include many diverse cultures. *Shari'a*, or Islamic law, took its final shape in the ninth century. Like the Jewish Talmud, it is comprehensive, dealing with dietary laws

Figure 4.3 Verse from the Qur'an written in *kufic* script, an angular form named for the city of Kufa in southern Iraq. This verse is from *sura* (chapter) 38, verses 87–8, and says: "This is a message to the world. And you will certainly know the truth"; and *sura* 39, verse 1: This is a revelation of the scripture, from God, the Almighty, the wise."

and prayer ritual as well as with building codes and punishment for murder. The *shari'a* is based on the Qur'an, which functions in effect as the constitution of God. For cases not clearly addressed by the Qur'an, local customs, *hadith* (stories about the sayings and actions of Muhammad), general consensus, and analogy were used to modify and extend the *shari'a*,

which became the law of the land wherever Muslim governments held sway.

While the *shari'a* defined legal relations in the Islamic world, the "Five Pillars of Islam" guided everyday individual practice of Islam. To be a Muslim, one must follow the five primary rules spelled out in the Qur'an. The first is that Muslims must bear witness or

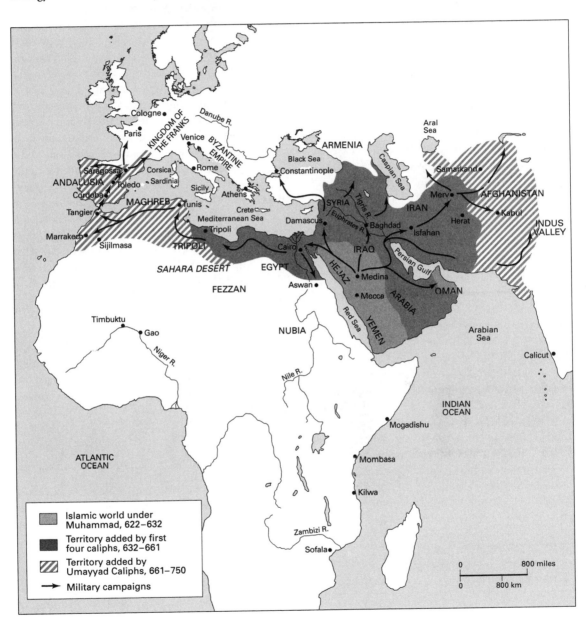

Map 4.3 Spread of Islam and early Islamic empires.

testify that they believe in the one and only God and that Muhammad was his last prophet. The second is that they must pray daily. Five times per day is specified in the Qur'an, and they must pray especially on Friday, when the whole community gathers to hear a sermon. Third, Muslims must voluntarily give a tenth of their annual income to provide for the poor of the community. Fourth, during one month of the year, Ramadan, all Muslims must fast during daylight hours. Finally, at least once in their lives, they should go to Mecca on pilgrimage.

After Muhammad's death in 632, the expansion of Islam continued. The Islamic state expanded out of Arabia in the mid-seventh century. Rapidly seizing Palestine, Syria, and Iraq by 640, the armies moved steadily west through Egypt and across north Africa into Spain, east through Iran, and south into India. Even as Arab armies made huge territorial gains across Eurasia and Africa, a doctrinal split ruptured the Muslim community. This originated as a political dispute over government succession following the death of Muhammad. Some felt that a member of his family should succeed him, while others thought it should be someone elected by and from the general council of community leaders. The latter was the Sunni, or "traditional" way, and it won out. The other was the way of the Shi'i, or "partisans" of the Prophet's family and their descendants. Over the centuries, the orthodox Sunnis faced not only the political and religious challenge of Shi'ism but also the task of coming to terms with popular mysticism, or Sufism. Sufism coexisted uneasily with Sunni orthodoxy for several centuries after the rise of Islam. It developed out of an ascetic movement that appeared in the first Muslim century in reaction to the great material wealth generated by the Arab conquests. Sufi mysticism emphasized a special spiritual love of God and, above all, provided the means for direct personal religious experience of the divine, which held great appeal for the common believer.

THE SPREAD OF "WORLD RELIGIONS": BUDDHISMS, CHRISTIANITIES, AND ISLAMS

Often referred to as "world" religions, Buddhism, Christianity, and Islam were rooted in ethical and religious traditions where they began in South and West Asia, but eventually transcended their local places of origin to expand and spread across every region of the globe. Like Christianity and Islam, Buddhism was a proselytizing religion: Buddhists, Christians, and Muslims all tried to convert others to their beliefs. Also like Christianity and Islam, Buddhism was at times patronized by rulers and became entangled in the politics of states in South, East, and Southeast Asia. But Buddhism did not become the kind of political force that both Christianity and Islam did, inspiring conquest and empire.

As they spread through Africa and Eurasia, Christianity and Islam encountered other belief systems and cultures, which were variously absorbed and adapted by Christian and Islamic rulers. Buddhism similarly engaged the religious beliefs and cultural ideals of the societies its missionaries penetrated. In contrast to the monotheistic background of Christianity and Islam, Buddhism grew in a cultural and philosophical environment that recognized the coexistence of many deities, even many different pantheons. As it spread from India to China, Korea, Japan, and Southeast Asia, it encountered and adapted to many different cultures, changing them as Buddhism itself was transformed by exposure to these cultures. Because of the diversity of beliefs and practices reflected in evolving forms of Buddhism, Christianity, and Islam as they spread across continents and cultures, referring to them in the plural – Buddhisms, Christianities, Islams – captures the multiplicity engendered by such encounters and reduces the tendency to see these "world religions" as monolithic.

BUDDHISMS IN ASIA

By the beginning of the first century CE, Buddhist missionaries were carrying their beliefs and practices beyond India to Central, East and Southeast Asia along the Silk Roads and over maritime routes. Buddhist missionaries in China were challenged to teach this new religion in the context of indigenous beliefs and practices, especially those ideas commonly referred to as Confucianism and Daoism. The teachings of Confucius (551–479 BCE), recorded by his disciples in the *Analects*, exhorted people to follow the models of the sage kings of antiquity and to bring order to both family and society through the practice of ritual. Confucius paid little attention to the spiritual realm because he preferred to deal with what he could know through experience of human society. In contrast to the Confucian focus on ritual order in family and society, knowing how to correlate one's life with *qi*, the "vital breath" of the cosmos that animates nature, humans, and gods, is the aim of teachings and practices loosely termed Daoism. The early Daoist texts, *Daodejing* and *Zhuangzi*, were composed not long after the Confucian *Analects* and articulate in part a philosophy of mysticism as the Dao, the "way" or "path."

At the time Buddhism was introduced into China, many people followed Daoist paths to seek immortality through life-prolonging elixirs and other physical means, and a rich assortment of deities were worshiped. One of the most important deities was the Queen Mother of the West, who empowered believers to achieve spiritual transcendence. People believed in the ability of spirits to intervene in human life and the need to propitiate these spirits. Both malevolent and benevolent spirits filled the cosmos, and among them were the ghosts of departed ancestors who required ritual veneration.

Central Asian monks played a key role in the transmission of Buddhism to China. Fluent in Sanskrit and Pali, the languages of the Buddhist *sutras*, these monks translated Buddhist sacred texts into Chinese, often under the patronage of rulers of north China. Transferring Buddhist ideas across the vast cultural frontier between India and China required translators to search for native vocabulary that could at least vaguely suggest the concepts they were trying to convey. But ultimately they were restricted to terminology that might be quite distant in meaning from what they began with. The translation of texts, however skillful, meant the transformation of ideas. For example, the concept of *nirvana* was rendered by the Daoist term, *wuwei* (literally "non-action"). Eventually new sectarian divisions of Buddhism developed in the Chinese environment, including Chan, which drew on indigenous Chinese ideas associated with Daoism.

Given the linguistic and cultural barriers Buddhist missionaries faced in proselytizing their faith, the patronage of the state was vital to the flourishing of Buddhism in China. Non-Chinese rulers of northern states adopted Buddhism to help unify the non-Chinese and Chinese populations under their rule, since Buddhism provided a universal message that transcended both local beliefs of the Chinese and those of their rulers. Like the Indian ruler Ashoka, Chinese rulers of the Sui (589–617) and Tang (618–907) dynasties patronized Buddhism, supplying funds to carve giant cave temples, erect magnificent temples, and support huge monasteries even while they ruled as Confucian monarchs carrying out the Mandate of Heaven.

Though all *sutras* were supposed to be the teachings of Buddha, in fact they were highly inconsistent in the doctrines they taught, and this gave rise to differing sectarian traditions within Chinese Buddhism. One of the most important sectarian developments was the Pure Land school, said to have originated with a devotional cult to the Buddha Amitabha established by the learned cleric Huiyuan in the fourth century CE. Although the name of the Pure Land school is drawn from a sutra of the same name, the sutra that became the principal doctrinal source for Pure Land believers was the Lotus Sutra. The Pure Land school preaches the efficacy of complete faith in the precepts of Buddhism to attain salvation and practices worship of the Buddha Amitabha and the *bodhisattva* Avalokiteshvara, or Guanyin in Chinese. These two deities preside over the Western Paradise, the "Pure Land," where believers seek to go to attain enlightenment with the aid of Amitabha and Avalokiteshvara. The Pure Land school reached a far wider audience than did more text-based, scholastic doctrines.

Even as the Chinese state contributed to the wealth and power of institutionalized Buddhism, divergent religious beliefs and practices drew on Buddhist, Daoist, and other sources and created new images of faith and devotion that expressed resistance to the Confucian order of society as well as to the Buddhist and Daoist establishment. The White Lotus movement, founded by a Buddhist monk in the twelfth century, became the center of a folk Buddhist religion that emphasized congregational worship and the fellowship of believers in the saving grace of the compassionate Buddha, Amitabha, the "Lord of the Western Paradise."

Buddhist missionaries had carried the teachings to Korea during the fourth century, whence they were transmitted to Japan two centuries later. After a period of exposure to these new ideas and accommodation between native beliefs and the new religion, Buddhism gained a firm foothold in Japan with the patronage of the state. By the mid-eighth century, Japan was the new outpost of East Asian Buddhism, with the erection of the Great Buddha at the imperial capital of Nara in 752. Initially the audience for Buddhism in Japan was aristocratic, but over time, as in China and elsewhere, zealous priests devised methods of reaching a wider population.

Popular Buddhism in Japan, which developed in the late Heian period (794–1185) and flourished in the Kamakura period (1185–1333), brought an awakening of faith to the broad masses of the people. The Pure Land sect, focused on belief in salvation through faith in the compassion of Amitabha Buddha and his female attendant, the *bodhisattva* Avalokiteshvara, took root in eleventh-century Japan. In contrast to the ideals of enlightenment that animated more orthodox Buddhist sects, Pure Land followers believed that the saving grace of Amida (Japanese for Amitabha) would bring them to the Western Paradise, the "Pure Land." Like its counterpart and predecessor in China, Amidism in Japan reached out to a mass audience that was excluded from the complex and often esoteric doctrinal teachings of established orthodox scholastic sects such as the Heavenly Platform (in China, Tiantai; in Japan, Tendai).

Both Hinduism and Buddhism were transmitted to Southeast Asia as early as the first and second centuries CE. Buddhism grew rapidly in the Southeast Asian archipelago during the seventh century. Early stone inscriptions at Palembang, the capital of the Srivijayan empire (c. 683–1085) on the Malay peninsula and the island of Sumatra reveal a ruler there blending the local imagery of the sacred mountain and sea with the traditional veneration of ancestors into Buddhist symbols and ethics. Buddhist themes imposed upon indigenous traditions provided a common set of ideas that transcended local communities. To build regional prestige, Srivijayan rulers became major builders of Buddhist temples and patrons of Buddhist scholarship in their territories. In the late eighth century, rulers of Java constructed Borobudur, the largest Buddhist monument ever built.

Shortly thereafter, on the mainland of Southeast Asia, the Khmer state gained control over the Mekong River Valley and delta. Ruling for more than 600 years (802–1432), at its height in the twelfth century the Khmer empire controlled probably a million people in the area of modern Cambodia, Laos, Thailand, and parts of Burma, Vietnam, and the Malay peninsula. Both Hinduism and Buddhism provided sanction for the authority of rulers and built common cultural and religious bonds among the Khmer people.

Rulers initially blended Hinduism with indigenous beliefs to consolidate their power over their expanding territory, and the Sanskrit language was adopted by the Khmer court. Worship of the Hindu god Shiva, who was identified as the "Lord of the Mountain," was connected with indigenous beliefs in the sanctity of mountains, the home of ancestral spirits. Shiva was also associated with fertility, and similarly worship of Shiva was merged with local fertility beliefs in Shiva's representation by the stone or metal "phallus," the *lingam*, inserted upright into the circular "vulva," or *yoni*, at shrines dedicated to him in the Khmer state. The twelfth-century Hindu temple complex, Angkor Wat, eventually incorporated Buddhist images as rulers aligned themselves with Hindu, and later Buddhist, deities. On the walls of the Khmer capital Angkor Thom, also built in the twelfth century, are huge Buddhist images of whom the Khmer ruler was said to be a manifestation.

CRUSADES, CONFLICT, AND CHANGE: THE EXPANSION OF CHRISTIANITIES

Christianity and Islam were spread largely by the work of missionaries and traders, but both religions also spread as the consequence of conflict. Christianity collided with an expanding Islam and Islamic empires in the "Holy Land" of Palestine at the eastern end of the Mediterranean. In 1095, Pope Urban II urged Christian knights to take up arms to regain control of the Holy Land. Supported by European Christian monarchs, eight crusades were carried out over the next two centuries to restore Palestine to Christian control. They were initially successful and established Christian kingdoms in Palestine, but by the end of the thirteenth century their kingdoms had been lost to the Muslims.

Despite the losses of the Crusades, the Church continued to dominate European politics and society, as well as spiritual life. But the Church's domination of religious life in Europe also encountered resistance, some of which it suppressed and some of which it managed to incorporate, as it had done with pre-Christian beliefs and practices. Popular religious festivals frequently had pagan origins, which were masked behind Christian meanings. Aspects of popular belief in pre-Christian magic were transformed by the Church into belief in Christian miracles, and the veneration of pre-Christian deities was incorporated into the cults of saints. During the twelfth century, while scholastics were debating the boundaries of faith and reason, the miracles central to Christianity, including the birth of Jesus of Nazareth to a chaste mother, Mary, also were scrutinized. The veneration of the Virgin Mary became such a popular movement that it had to be incorporated into traditional ritual and practice.

The magical aspects of religious ritual and practice, such as transubstantiation (transformation of bread and wine into the body and blood of Christ) became a part of Christian dogma. Such "good" magic was orthodox, but there was other "black magic," such as sorcery, which the Church condemned and rejected as belonging to the realm of the Devil. The Church viewed witchcraft as a danger to orthodox standards and doctrines and considered those guilty of practicing heresy to be punishable. In times of social or economic crisis, the perception and perhaps the reality of unorthodox practices such as witchcraft increased. Heretical religious sects were also accused of satanic practices and suffered the same condemnation and persecution as individuals accused of sorcery.

Dramatic reform of the Church, however, came from within its own ranks. In the sixteenth century Martin Luther, a theologian and teacher at the University of Wittenberg, challenged the position of the Church by arguing that the individual did not need the intervention of the clergy or the Church to reach God. He claimed that salvation was instead a matter of individual faith. Luther's ideas had great appeal in sixteenth-century Germany, where rulers were struggling to assert their independence from the pope and where peasants were rebelling against their masters. The English king severed bonds with the Church in Rome and asserted his own authority over the Church in England (the Anglican Church).

The Protestant Reformation decisively split the Christian Church from the sixteenth century on, and its impact eventually spread well beyond Europe. John Calvin, a sixteenth-century Frenchman who underwent a sudden religious conversion, promoted the idea that God alone decides who shall be elected for salvation, and who shall be damned because of Adam's original sin. Lutheranism was essentially confined to Germany (and later Scandinavia), and other Protestant movements were equally localized. But Calvinism spread widely through France, the Rhine Valley, the Netherlands, Scotland, and parts of Central Europe. Calvinistic views of the world quickly stretched from North America, especially New England, to southern Africa.

Faced with the Lutheran and other Protestant revolts, the Catholic Church responded with its own movement, known as the Counter-Reformation. In addition to censoring books and persecuting heretics, in 1534 the Church chartered the Society of Jesus, a Catholic religious order whose members (Jesuits) helped to check the spread of Protestantism by preaching and teaching. Expanding beyond Europe, Jesuit missionaries brought Christianity to regions of Africa, the Americas, and Asia in tandem with the emerging global reach of European states. In the sixteenth century, Christianity, commerce, and colonization combined to spread Christianity across the globe. By the nineteenth century, an even more zealous brand of Protestant Christian missionary movement linked its fortunes to the new imperialism as colonization intensified in parts of Africa and Asia.

THE SPREAD OF ISLAMS: CONQUEST, COMMERCE, AND CONVERSION

Following the expansion of Islam through the creation of Islamic empires that stretched from the Iberian peninsula to northern India, Arab traders carried the faith across the Indian Ocean to southern coasts of India, the east coast of Africa, and Southeast Asia. Caravans along the Gold Roads of Africa and the Silk Roads of Eurasia transported Islam, along with gold, silk, and other commodities. By unifying a vast swath of Eurasia in the thirteenth century, the Mongols helped to spread Islam through Central and into East

Asia. Like the spread of Christianity beyond Europe, a combination of conquest, commerce, and conversion brought Islam to the farthest reaches of Africa and Asia.

Beginning in the eighth century, Muslim invaders encountered both Hinduism and Buddhism among the populations they conquered in north India, as well as the strict social hierarchy shaped by the caste system. Previous invaders had been absorbed by the ancient civilization of the subcontinent, but the Muslims were bearers of a proselytizing religious faith with a powerful social and political ideology that sharply challenged the cultural and social, as well as political, orders of India. After the Muslim invasions that began in the eighth century, India became a land where Muslim mosques and Hindu temples stood side by side.

By the twelfth century, several Sufi orders had migrated from West Asia into the Indian subcontinent. Sufism found many parallels in Hindu *bhakti*, which was focused on devotion to a personal god, through common language, imagery, and motifs. Sufism in India provided a means of establishing contact between Muslims and Hindus, was responsible for many conversions to Islam, and contributed to Hindu-Islam syncretic movements. In Hindu *bhakti*, God was seen as having three forms: Vishnu (generally in the incarnation of either Rama or Krishna), Shiva, and *shakti* (the female form). No caste or social distinctions were made among people in *bhakti*, although the movement was typically led by brahmans. *Bhakti* can be seen as a reaction against the highly ritualized, exclusive Brahmanism of the period.

Medieval *bhakti* figures influenced the development of the Sikh (Sanskrit for "disciple") religion, which was founded by the guru (master or teacher) Nanak (1469–1533). Nanak had a revelation that God was a unitary spiritual force shared by all religions and that social, ethnic, gender, caste, and other divisions were illusory. Together with a Muslim musician, Nanak wandered all over India and Islamic lands, composing and performing devotional songs, which were later recorded in the Sikh scripture, Adi Granth. This new community of faith flourished in the Punjab, drawing recruits from both Hindus and Muslims among the peasantry.

After the invasions of Egypt and North Africa beginning in the seventh century, Islam gradually began to penetrate further into the African continent through the influence of traders and clerics. On the East African coast, Islam arrived as early as the eighth century, coinciding with the increasing urbanization of the coast connected to Indian Ocean trade. Syncretism characterized the early spread of Islam in both East and West Africa. Trade with Arab merchants who traveled the caravan routes across the Sahara appealed to rulers of states in West Africa, who converted to Islam while retaining local religious beliefs and practices. By the twelfth century, the influence of Sunni and Sufi traditions had overtaken that of earlier Shi'ite converts. Sunni orthodoxy was largely dominant in towns where centers of Islamic learning, *madrasas*, were built. The more mystical Sufi tradition dominated in rural areas, spread largely through long-distance trade and by independent Sufi scholars.

Originating as an oasis market town for trans-Saharan trade before the twelfth century, from the fourteenth through eighteenth centuries Timbuktu was a center for the transmission of Islam in West Africa and had its own *madrasa*. Islam flourished in West Africa, though indigenous religious beliefs continued to dominate the lives of people outside the scholarly and commercial elites of urban centers such as Timbuktu. The influence of Islam was manifested in the flamboyant pilgrimage of the Mali ruler Mansa Musa to Mecca in 1324–5.

Islam in Africa also sparked movements for social and political change. Beginning in the sixteenth century, a wave of *jihads* (holy wars) swept over parts of West and West-Central Africa. Africans who studied in Mecca and Medina during their *hajj* (pilgrimage) absorbed ideas about *jihad* and conversion to Islam. When they returned to Africa, they took these ideas with them and helped to transform local political and social protests into Islamic reform movements. The *jihad* in the Senegambian region that established the Muslim-dominated state of Bundu in the 1690s is one example. Agricultural reforms accompanied the replacement of traditional elite by Muslim rulers. In contrast, the eighteenth-century victories at Fuuta Jaalo, south of the Gambia, installed Muslim rulers but did little more than convert their slaves to Islam.

The slow diffusion of Islam across the Sahara through commerce and the cultural influence of Muslim clerics compares well to the expansion of Islam across the Indian Ocean and into Indonesia. Arab and

Indian Muslim traders were active in Southeast Asian waters as early as the eighth century. During the late thirteenth century, Marco Polo visited Sumatra and noted that many residents of towns and cities had converted to Islam, while those living in the countryside and the hills continued to follow earlier traditions – likely a combination of native, Hindu, and Buddhist practices. By the time Marco Polo made his observation, Sufi saints were traveling the same roads and in the same ships as Muslim merchants, prepared to seek followers of their own version of Islam in the region.

Evidence of the conversion of local rulers to Islam begins in the later thirteenth century with the ruler of Samudra-Pasai. The first state in the region to convert officially to Islam, by the fourteenth century it was a center of Islamic studies. By the end of the fifteenth century, Islam was to be found throughout maritime Southeast Asia, though not on the Southeast Asian mainland where Buddhism and Hinduism continued as the dominant cultural and religious influences along with indigenous beliefs.

Between 1500 and 1800, beginning from coastal fringes on the Malay peninsula and around the island of Sumatra, Islam made substantial inroads into Southeast Asia, acquiring a political role as well as a religious one. Islam interacted with indigenous beliefs, as well as with Hinduism and Buddhism, in reshaping Southeast Asian societies during the period of European expansion into this area of the world. European influences formed yet another stratum in the complex, multilayered societies of Southeast Asia. Unlike the earlier expansion of Islam through military conquest, in Southeast Asia Islam was carried by Arab and other Muslim merchants who plied the waters surrounding the Malay peninsula and the Indonesian archipelago. Its gradual and relatively peaceful spread was much like the course of Islam in West and East Africa.

In the sixteenth century, increasing numbers of merchants from the southern part of the Arabian peninsula followed Indian Ocean trade routes and settled in port cities from East Africa to Southeast Asia. Many of these merchants held a special religious position in their homeland through the claim of descent from a descendant of Ali who had emigrated to the southern Arabian peninsula, and in the Indian Ocean ports where they settled they were often given special standing as religious authorities, which in turn conferred economic and political opportunities. Rulers of states that rose and fell in the region often made use of Islam to sanction their rule, as their predecessors had relied on Buddhism, Hinduism, and indigenous beliefs in earlier times. For example, Islam was adopted in the central Javanese state of Mataram, whose ruler, Agung (1613–45), assumed the title of sultan and established the Islamic calendrical system in Java.

RENEWAL AND REFORM IN THE ISLAMIC WORLD

Like the Protestant reformations of the sixteenth century in European Christianity, the eighteenth century was a time of intense renewal and reform in the world of Islam. As in European Christianity, the idea of change was not new, but both the degree of intensity and the impact of reform were unprecedented.

Probably the most influential reformer was Muhammad Ibn Abd al-Wahhab (1703–92), who moved scholarly debate to the field of action. Abd al-Wahhab received an orthodox Islamic education from his father, combining the holy scripture of the Qur'an, the *hadith* (traditions of the Prophet), and works of jurisprudence that comprised the *shar'ia* (Islamic law). He was also exposed to Sufi mysticism, which emphasized the search for a direct experience of God and the power of saints as channels for God's action in the world, personified in scholar-mystics, ecstatic preachers, and miracle-working holy men.

After his formal education at home in the Najd region of the Arabian peninsula, Abd al-Wahhab traveled widely for two decades – to Mecca, Baghdad, Damascus, Isfahan and beyond. After his return home, he began to preach Orthodox teachings and anti-Sufism as a result of the corruption and laxity in religious practice he observed during his travels. Abd al-Wahhab's puritanism suggested the overthrow of the medieval superstructure of Islam and a return to the "pure" authority of the Qur'an and *hadith*. In 1744 he managed to convert Ibn Sa'ud and other members of his family, and the two men swore an oath to make God's word prevail in Arabia and neighboring lands. The tribal leader and the religious reformer pooled their interests and talents, and by the beginning of the nineteenth century they had firmly established the Saudi state on the Arabian peninsula.

Other reform movements also appeared elsewhere in the Islamic world. One of the most powerful Islamic reform movements flourished among the Fulani people in what is today northern Nigeria. Led by a Fulani Muslim cleric, Usman dan Fodio (1754–1817), this Islamic revitalization movement attached the loose religious practices of the old Hausa rulers of this region and eventually created a large Islamic empire in this part of West Africa. Dan Fodio belonged to a Sufi brotherhood, one of many Sufi orders that had helped spread Islam into West Africa beginning in the sixteenth century. The revolt Dan Fodio led in 1804 toppled the Hausa rulers and created a confederation of Islamic emirates under the control of the Fulani. Together with his brother and son, Dan Fodio established the Sokoto caliphate (Islamic government) in 1809 and spread Islam throughout the region.

The obligation of the *hajj*, the obligatory pilgrimage to Mecca, meant that many Muslims would spend time in this holy city, converging with pilgrims from all over the Islamic world. It was a perfect opportunity for the exchange of ideas and the inspiration for renewal and reform. Throughout the nineteenth century, there were pilgrims who returned from Mecca and tried to revitalize Islam in their homelands, from Africa to India to Southeast Asia.

GLOBALIZATION AND RELIGIOUS CHANGE

In the nineteenth century dar al-Islam, the "world of Islam," stretched from West Africa to Southeast Asia. While reformers energized the faithful and revitalized the religion, political leaders adopted Islam and promoted it through the building of mosques, the support of clerics, and the application of *shar'ia*. Christianity likewise secured a global reach by the nineteenth century. Though Catholic missionaries – Jesuits, Dominicans, and Franciscans – accompanied the sixteenth-century expansion of Europe and had a lasting influence in Asia and Africa, they were most successful in the Americas (see Chapter 10). In the nineteenth century, however, the Protestant missionary

movement provided ideological support for the new imperialism, especially in Asia and Africa. The biblical command "Go ye into all the world, and preach the gospel to every creature" was literally taken up by Protestant men and women as they moved out from their homes, cultures, and societies to make their own particular contributions to the new imperialism through evangelization, converting other peoples to Christianity. Although movements for religious revitalization as a form of resistance to the grip of empire were not new – Druid resistance to Roman rule of Gaul and Britain is one example – the global reach of the entwined forces of Christianity and colonialism set the stage for many and varied responses shaped by diverse cultural and historical experiences.

The impact of proselytization could be wildly unpredictable, as in the Taiping Rebellion in nineteenth-century China. Protestant missionaries preaching the gospel in the southern Chinese port of Canton engaged the imagination of a young man named Hong Xiuquan from the Hakka minority who was disappointed in his attempts to pass the imperial Chinese civil service examinations and thus denied access to the world of the scholarly elite. The Old Testament message of a Baptist missionary pamphlet inspired Hong's vision that he was the younger brother of Jesus Christ, sent by God the father to save people in China and return them to the way of their Heavenly Father. There was a fit between the idea of outcaste, oppressed people – the Hebrew (read Hakka) people – and the economic and social distress of people at the lower rungs of the social order in southern China. These were the people most affected by the impact of the Opium Wars when British gunboats forcibly opened China, perpetuating the lucrative drug trade for British entrepreneurs. Kindled by Hong's own frustration and visionary charisma, Christianity was a spark that ignited a massive rebellion, causing the deaths of as many as 20 million people before it was over. The Boxer movement in the late 1890s, in contrast, used traditional religious beliefs and practices to resist the foreign presence in China, most visible to rural, disaffected, and uneducated Chinese in the form of Christian missionaries.

In New Zealand, one Maori response to conflicts with Europeans and the oppression of the colonial government took the form of a religious movement known as the Pai Marire ("The Good and the Peaceful"), also called Hauhauism after its founder Te Ua Haumene. Te Ua had been baptized by a Christian missionary and had also been a follower of the Maori King movement that opposed land sales to Europeans. In 1862 Te Ua claimed to have had a vision of the angel Gabriel who told him to reject war. Te Ua preached a blend of New Testament Christianity and traditional Maori beliefs, including "peaceful arts" such as song, dance, and tattooing, that culminated in a millenarian prophecy of a new world free from pain, suffering, and oppression. When it peaked in the mid-1860s, approximately one-fifth of the Maori population were followers of the Pai Marire movement. Though its leader preached peace and virtuous behavior, more radical elements of the Pai Marire engaged in violence against Europeans, leading to divisions within Maori society between those who resisted European encoachment and those who cooperated with the Europeans and gained some benefits as a result.

A series of catastrophes in the eastern Cape province of South Africa left the Xhosa, whose ancestral lands had been annexed to the British empire in 1847, landless migrant laborers. An epidemic of disease destroyed nearly 100,000 head of cattle, the mainstay of Xhosa livelihood and traditional culture. One response to these desperate circumstances came in the form of a cattle-killing prophecy revealed in a vision experienced by a 15-year-old Xhosa girl named Nongquwase, who claimed that "the whole nation will rise from the dead if all the living cattle are slaughtered because these have been reared with defiled hands, since there are people who have been practicing witchcraft" (J. B. Pieres, "The Central Beliefs of the Xhosa Cattle-Killing," *Journal of African History*, 27 (1987): 43). Also embedded in the visions of the young girl were notions of hastening change through sacrifice.

Since the London Missionary Society established its first station in Xhosaland in 1817, Christian ideas had penetrated Xhosa beliefs. Nongquwase's prophecy represented an amalgam of traditional Xhosa beliefs in the omnipresence of the spirits of dead kinsmen and Christian and African ideas of sacrifice to achieve a desired end (resurrection in Christian terms, but political change in Xhosa tradition). Most Xhosa

followed Nongquwase's instructions, and by the end of 1857 more than 400,000 head of cattle had been destroyed with the result that more than 40,000 Xhosa died of starvation. In the aftermath of this tragedy, the Xhosa were divided into those who believed in following traditional ways, despite the devastation caused by the cattle killing, and those who were now without any recourse and ready to seek opportunities from the colonial presence and opposed the cattle killing as senseless.

Although prophetic movements were not new among native American peoples, one of the most dramatic examples took place in the late nineteenth century in response to decades of deprivation and loss among the Sioux. Desperate economic conditions on the Great Sioux reservation in the winter of 1889 led the Sioux to turn to the Ghost Dance religion, based on the teachings of Wovoka, a Paiute shaman from western Nevada. In the 1880s, under the influence of Protestant evangelists, Wovoka had seen a vision of the reunion of the living and dead. Wovoka commanded his followers to perform the round (or ghost) dance in which men and women joined in a circle with fingers interlocked as the key to the regeneration of the world. Wovoka's vision and the Ghost Dance spread to the Arapaho and Shoshoni in Wyoming, the Cheyenne in Oklahoma, as well as the Sioux in the Dakotas. United States government agents saw the Ghost Dance movement as threatening and moved to suppress it among the Sioux, with the result that some Ghost Dancers became militant. Conflict erupted between the federal government and the Lakota Sioux, climaxing in the massacre at Wounded Knee in the winter of 1890.

Despite the deadly outcome, Wovoka's prophetic movement, as others before it, drew on native traditions (the Sun Dance) as well as new Christian ideas in an effort to cope with a new world. Millenarian visions of utopian worlds (see Chapter 11) that integrated Christianity and local religion – like that of the Sioux, Taiping, Xhosa, or Pai Marire – were empowering responses to the dystopian realities confronted by peoples living with the consequences of colonialism and Christian conversion.

SLAVERY, SYNCRETISM, AND SPIRITUALITY

The creation of the African diaspora, while originating from slavery and conditions of extreme oppression, nonetheless is also synonymous with the creation of vibrant, syncretic belief systems among people of African descent in the Atlantic world. Slaves carried their beliefs from the West and Central African regions of the Guinea Coast, the Slave Coast, the Bight of Benin, Kongo, Angola, and everywhere in between to the Americas, where they were used to alter and even subvert the condition of enslavement. The African Atlantic world was a spiritually empowered and interactive universe of living persons, spirits, and ancestors who functioned as critical links to the past; that is, to human memory of the past.

African-derived religions survived from the wide variety of beliefs practiced in communities of enslaved Africans, who were Muslims, Christians, and practitioners of indigenous African belief systems. New syncretic religions blended the disparate Kongolese, Yoruba, Catholic, Masonic, and other beliefs into coherent forms of spirituality, which promoted resistance by preserving historical memory in the form of *candomblé*, Santeria, Vodun, and other religions. Today the living legacy of these beliefs can even be seen in their application to modern technology. For example, Ogun (the Yoruba god of iron) is the protector of taxis and airplanes; his imagery appears across the

Figure 4.4 Followers of African-Brazilian religious sects in Rio de Janeiro, Brazil, dance and pray next to offerings to Yemanja, an African water goddess. The offerings will then be taken in procession to a beach. On Yemanja's day, which corresponds with the Catholic feast of Our Lady of Navigators, thousands of followers go to the beach with offerings of flowers, perfume, and jewels.

Atlantic world and even in extensions of Yoruba religion as far from West Africa and the Caribbean as London, Toronto, Brooklyn and Los Angeles.

RELIGION AND REVOLUTIONARY CHANGE

Religion can inspire social and political change as well as support the forces of institutionalized oppression. Since the introduction of Catholicism during the European conquest in the sixteenth century, the Roman Catholic Church has played a sometimes contradictory role in historical change in Latin America. Beginning in the nineteenth century, Protestant missionaries made inroads, especially with the poor, though the Catholic Church continued to dominate Latin America. The victory of the Cuban revolution in 1959 brought home to the Church in Latin America (and its foreign supporters) the realities of the political and economic crises of the region. Gradually during the 1960s and 1970s, the role of the Church as defender of the state and the landed aristocracies began to be transformed. Pope Paul VI issued several papal encyclicals in the 1960s that condemned capitalism, and put forward a policy of supporting economic and social development as part of the Church's mission to abolish injustice. The historic Medellin Conference of Latin American bishops in 1968 went even further to declare that what was holding back development was oppression; liberation required political action and the establishment of socialism. Parallel developments occurred within the Protestant clerical community.

Christian involvement in revolutionary movements in Nicaragua, El Salvador, and Guatemala came to be described as following a "liberation theology," a Christian ideology that emphasizes the revolutionary and subversive power of the Gospel as historic testimony to the possibility of radical social and political change. Liberation theology inspired both social and political activism, including support for guerrilla warfare. As a consequence, many churches became enemies of autocratic states; church leaders, including archbishops, were martyred.

In response to attacks on Christian communities, a resurgence of traditional Mayan religious ideas in Guatemala replaced liberation theology, focusing instead on indigenous beliefs in justice, struggle, and the protection of the earth. This is a local response, but it is framed in a setting of global awareness – of indigenous peoples' movements and environmental consciousness. Contemporary concerns about the disappearance of the rain forest and other transformations of nature caused by humans encourage reconnection with earlier religious traditions that focused on veneration of nature.

Buddhism also has provided support for peaceful political change in the modern world. The Dhammayietra is an annual peace walk in Cambodia that originated with the repatriation of refugees from Thai border camps in the transition to democracy in 1992. Though grounded in traditional Khmer Buddhism, the walk represents the connection to global Buddhism beyond the local space of the Cambodian nation. One of the most powerful spiritual figures in the world is the leader of the Tibetan exile community, the Dalai Lama, whose voice has been a constant reminder of nonviolence, even in the face of the threatened destruction of Tibetan culture by the policies of the Chinese government.

In the last quarter of the twentieth century, Islam became a powerful political force, unseating the Shah of Iran in the 1979 Iranian Revolution and replacing his Westernized rule with that of Ayatollah Ruhollah Khomeini, a Shi'ite cleric. Many Muslims rejected the Western notion of the social contract as the basis for the state in favor of the Islamic idea of the "community of true believers." By the end of the century, the goals of Islamic revolutionary change, shaped by the revival of eighteenth-century Wahhabism, were distorted by the strategic means of terrorism aimed at undermining or destroying Jewish and Christian states, institutions, and communities. Echoes of the twelfth-century Crusades were heard in the calls for *jihad* against non-Muslims and in the twenty-first century conflict between Islam and the West.

CONCLUSIONS

One of the most revolutionary aspects of religion in the modern world is the transformation of world religions as they have been transported all over the globe. The very meaning of "world religion" has changed, since Judaism, Hinduism, Yoruba, and other religions identified with particular cultures or communities have also spread throughout many places in the world with the movements of peoples. Diasporas of Jews, Chinese, Indians, and Africans have established new communities in places far distant from their homelands whether voluntarily or not (see Chapter 1). Growing Muslim populations in Europe and North America are changing the religious landscape of these centers of Christianity.

Christianity itself is undergoing dramatic change as Pentecostal Christianity draws ever greater numbers of believers, especially in Africa and Latin America. Spreading from its base in a run-down section of Los Angeles in 1906, Pentecostalism has grown to be an international movement within Protestant Christianity, claiming more than 500 million followers worldwide on its hundredth anniversary in 2006. Pentecostals believe in the individual experience of the Holy Spirit and in the power of faith for both physical and spiritual healing. Emphasis on experience over doctrine enables believers to adapt a wide variety of practices from other religions, including everything from spirit possession and ancestor worship to faith healing and shamanism. This ability to absorb and adapt, along with the missionary zeal to evangelize, helps to account for rapid growth in places such as Kenya and Brazil, where Pentecostals now account for half the population. Like radical Islam, which has deep roots in economic deprivation and political struggles in the modern world, Pentecostalism began among poor and oppressed people, who found solace, hope, and agency through their individual ability to experience grace and connect to the divine.

Christianity is by far the world's largest faith, with over 2 billion believers, and expected to grow to over 2.6 billion by 2025, when 50 percent of the world's Christians will be in Africa and Latin America. Reflecting the legacy of Jesuit success in the sixteenth century and after, by 2025 nearly three-quarters of the world's Catholics will be found in Africa, Asia, and Latin America, dramatically altering the face of Catholicism. The largest Jesuit order is now in India. Muslims are slightly more than half the numbers of Christians, but they are spread equally far and wide, from Asia to the Americas. Buddhism is found not only in its historic birthplace of Asia but also in parts of the world where other religions have been dominant, such as North America – where nearly a million people claim to be converts to some form of Buddhism – and Europe.

As global as the movements of Buddhisms, Christianities, and Islams are, in each place these world religions take on new and different characteristics that enable them to survive and flourish in local settings. As suggested in the Introducton, it is in the interaction between "world religions" – whether carried by missionaries, pilgrims, and converts or by diasporic communities – and local beliefs that the key to understanding religion in world history lies. A compelling example of this can be found in a scene that took place in 2006 in the world's most populous Muslim nation, Indonesia. A Muslim cleric officiated at an annual ceremony presenting offerings to the goddess of the sea. The cleric blessed the offerings – silk, curry, bananas, hair and toenail clippings – before they were carried in a procession to the sea and thrown in. This ritual is deeply embedded in both Hindu and indigenous beliefs and practices, and for the participants in the ceremony, from the Muslim cleric to the public audience, the convergence of these diverse traditions was unexceptional.

From the earliest evidences of human consciousness of and communication with spiritual forces, people have sought to locate themselves as both individuals and communities in the cosmos. Religions have been constructed from manifold ways of accessing divine power in order to seek benefits for the living and comfort for the dead. Charismatic preachers and prophets have drawn followers to their ideas and institutions have developed to promote new faiths. Even for religious movements in the contemporary world that focus on individual experience, such as Pentecostalism, the ability to reach large audiences in far-flung places through electronic communication has dramatically expanded communities of believers and shaped collective identities across global cultural and national frontiers (see Chapters 7 and 10). Religions inspire conflict and support oppression, but they also provide powerful and compelling visions of human possibility. Although modernity was associated in the twentieth century with secularization and the assumed demise of religion, by the twenty-first century it was clear that religion was as potent a political, social, and cultural force as it ever had been in world history.

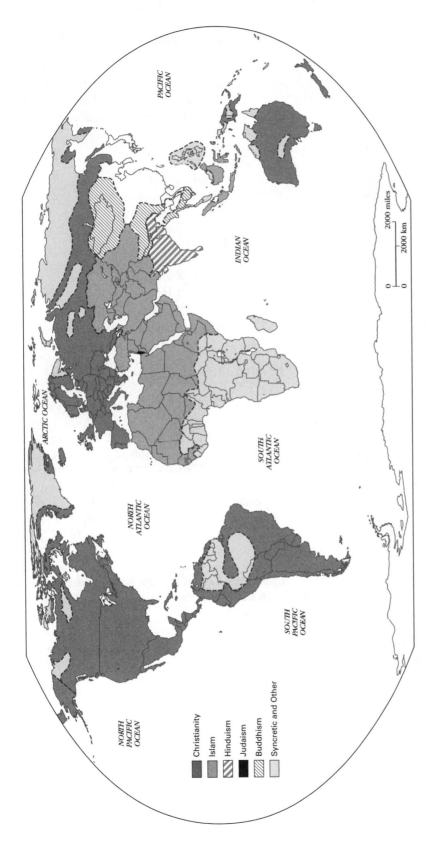

Map 4.4 Contemporary global religions.

SELECTED REFERENCES

Berkey, Jonathan P. (2003 (reprint 2005)) *The Formation of Islam: Religion and Society in the Near East, 600–1800*, New York: Cambridge University Press. A recent survey of the development of Islam in historical context.

Gill, Sam (1987) *Native American Religious Action: A Performance Approach to Religion*, Columbia: University of South Carolina Press. A collection of essays by an expert in Native American religion that confront the challenges of understanding the religious experiences of oral peoples through the medium of academic discourse.

Grube, Nikolai, ed. (2000) *Maya: Divine Kings of the Rainforest*, Cologne: Könemann. A richly illustrated overview of recent research on the Maya, including religion, with contributions from many different scholars.

Hayden, Brian (2003) *Shamans, Sorcerers, and Saints: A Prehistory of Religion*, Washington, DC: Smithsonian Books. An archaeological and historical survey of early religion from a cultural materialist perspective.

Herman, A. L. (1991) *A Brief Introduction to Hinduism: Religion, Philosophy, and Ways of Liberation*, Boulder, Colo.: Westview Press. Historical foundations and key texts of Hinduism related to modern religious leaders and movements.

Jenkins, Philip (2002) *The Next Christendom: The Coming of Global Christianity*, New York: Oxford University Press. A compelling presentation of the dramatic transformations taking place through the growth of Christianity in Africa, Asia, and Latin America.

Johnston, Sarah Iles, ed. (2004) *Religions of the Ancient World: A Guide*, Cambridge, Mass.: The Belknap Press of Harvard University Press. Topical and historical guide to religions in the ancient Mediterranean world.

Jolly, Karen Louise (1997) *Tradition and Diversity: Christianity in a World Context to 1500*, Armonk, N.Y.: M.E. Sharpe. A collection of primary sources chosen to illustrate the historical development of Christianity both in its traditional European context and from the perspective of other voices outside that tradition.

Kitagawa, Joseph, ed. (1987 (reprint 1989)) *The Religious Traditions of Asia*, New York: Macmillan. A collection of articles from *The Encyclopedia of Religion* on Hinduism, Buddhism, Islam and other religious traditions of Central, East, South, and Southeast Asia.

Stark, Rodney (2001) *One True God: Historical Consequences of Monotheism*, Princeton, N.J.: Princeton University Press. A provocative analysis of the role of monotheism in world history.

ONLINE RESOURCES

Annenberg/CPB Bridging World History (2004) <http://www.learner.org/channel/courses/world history/>. Multimedia project with interactive website and videos on demand; see especially Units 5 Early Belief Systems, 7 The Spread of Religions.

Buddhism in China <http://depts.washington.edu/chinaciv/bud/5budhism.htm>. Part of "A Visual Sourcebook of Chinese Civilization," this website portrays the impact of Buddhism on Chinese society and the Chinese transformation of Buddhist belief and practice.

Islam: Empire of Faith <http://www.pbs.org/empires/islam/>. Companion website to this PBS film on Islam.

Pew Forum on Religion and Public Life <http://pewforum.org/>. Information on a wide range of issues related to intersection of religion and politics in the contemporary world.

CHAPTER 5

Finding family in world history

In late twelfth-century China, the author of a guide for family life named Yuan Cai matter-of-factly explained the origins of the bond between parents and children:

> Babies are closely attached to their parents, and parents are extremely generous with their love for their babies, doing everything possible to care for them. The reason would seem to be that not long has passed since they were one flesh and blood, and besides, a baby's sounds, smiles, and gestures are such that they bring out the love in people. Furthermore, the Creator has made such attachment a principle of nature, to ensure that the succession of births will continue uninterrupted. Even the most insignificant insect, bird, or animal behaves in this way. When the young first emerges from the womb or shell, these creatures suckle it or feed it pre-chewed food, going to all lengths to care for it. If something threatens their young, they protect it, heedless of their own safety.
>
> When human beings are full grown, distinctions in status become stricter and distance becomes established: parents then are expected to express fully their kindness and children their filial duty. By contrast, when insects, birds, and animals mature a little, they no longer recognize their mothers nor their mothers them. This difference separates human beings from other creatures.
>
> (Patricia Buckley Ebrey, trans., *Family and Property in Sung China: Yüan Ts'ai's Precepts for Social Life*, Princeton, N.J.: Princeton University Press, 1984, pp. 188–9)

Yuan believed that family ties began with the dependence of a child on its parent during infancy, when feeding and protection were essential for survival. The bond established between parent and child through that experience, he argued, is a principle of nature and can be seen in all living creatures. According to Yuan, what distinguishes human from animal life is the evolution of this bond when children reach adulthood. In the human world, parents care for their children when they are young; after they are grown, children treat their parents with gratitude, love, and obedience. Yuan Cai's audience would have been familiar with this concept, rendered into English as "filial piety". The sense of duty and moral obligation that children owe parents for their lives, filial piety was a value Yuan believed everyone in his society shared, or should share.

We may agree with Yuan Cai on the common biological basis for family life rooted in the reproduction and survival of the human species, but question his reasoning that the sentiment of filial piety flows naturally from this biological process. From the perspective of world history, filial piety is not a universal feature of all human families but a distinctively Chinese family value. World history reveals as many variations in family values as in the organization of family life, and in the very meaning of family. How has "family" been defined differently across cultures and over time, and what can this tell us about patterns and processes in world history?

INTRODUCTION

Seeking the earliest evidence of family life, we might begin with a collection of hominid fossils that have been dubbed "The First Family." The fossils came from at least thirteen individuals who likely died together some 3.2 million years ago under unknown circumstances (perhaps a flood?). This is the first evidence of hominids living together in groups, but we do not know whether the individuals were related in such a way that we could call them a family. Other sites with evidence of tool use or butchering also provide possible glimpses into early human cooperation and sharing. When does this behavior approach anything like what we may call "family life"? At the site of Shanidar Cave in Iraq (dated to between 70,000 and 40,000 years ago), the burial of an older person who was partially blind, one-armed, with impaired mobility, suggested to archaeologists that there was some care of the elderly, perhaps as members of multi-generational families.

As remote and tentative as this evidence is, even in later historical times, it has often been difficult to piece together the history of families and family life from recalcitrant textual sources. Even when sources do exist, they are frequently ones that treat the family as an object of state control for taxation purposes or as the target of moral rulings from religious authorities. However, historians can also look to a multitude of sources beyond standard historical documents that illuminate the intimate realms of family and household in world history: oral testimony, mythology, genealogies, life histories, legal codes, archaeological finds, language, and literature.

Agents of economic production as well as biological reproduction, families and households were shaped by social, cultural, political, economic, and ideological forces. Every aspect of family and household – from the most intimate and personal to the most public and formal – intersects with and reflects larger patterns of historical change: migration, urbanization, the rise and fall of states and empires, the spread of religions, industrialization, and political revolutions. Understanding continuities as well as changes in family and household over time and across cultures illuminates the dynamic relationship between broader processes of historical change and the most intimate realms of human interaction.

FAMILY AND HOUSEHOLD IN ROMAN LAW AND SOCIETY

Throughout the vast Roman empire, stretching at its height from North Africa to the British Isles and from the Black Sea to the Iberian peninsula, there was enormous variety in the structures of family and household. Viewed even from the limited perspective of the urban center, Rome, however, we can identify aspects of family institutions that continued to influence Mediterranean and later European societies long after the fall of the Roman empire.

The English word "family" comes directly from the Latin word *familia*, but the meanings of the two words are almost completely different. In its broadest usage, *familia* referred to all persons and property under the control (*patria potestas*) of the head of the family (*paterfamilias*), including servants and slaves as well as kin. Although Romans had no term for the conjugal unit of father–mother–children, this triad was central to Roman family life, even in situations of extended and multigenerational families. The key relationships were those of husband and wife and parents and children, even though elite households also included numerous servants and slaves who attended the master and mistress, cared for their children as wet-nurses, nannies, and foster mothers, and managed the estates and businesses belonging to the *paterfamilias*. Although slaves were not legally free to marry, they often did form unions within the *familia*; freed slaves also tended to marry within the *familia* and took the family name (*nomen*) of their former owners. The *domus*, the Roman house and household, was for elite Romans a public space as well as a domain of family intimacy and privacy. The atrium, the main public area of the house, was the place where rites of passage were marked and celebrated, and births and deaths were announced to the outside world by decorations on the threshold. Both the location of the house and the house itself were the physical expression of a family's place in society.

The Roman government implemented policies to encourage childbearing and to discourage celibacy or childless marriages among the elite. Julius Caesar's law of 59 BCE, for example, made land available to fathers of three or more children. In 18 BCE and again in 9 CE, Emperor Augustus issued legislation to promote childbearing. Political preference was given to fathers of three or more children, and women who had borne three children were exempted from the need for a male guardian. The encouragement of childbearing emphasized in legislation under Augustus continued throughout the later Roman empire. Roman coinage of the second century CE, for example, was used to advertise ideals of Roman motherhood, often in association with women of the imperial family.

Roman women enjoyed a relatively high degree of independence in marriage. Upon marriage, a woman transferred from her father's authority to that of her husband, and her dowry went along with her to become part of her husband's property. But on the death of her husband, the wife was entitled to an equal share of her husband's property along with her children. A wife could also divorce her husband and take much of her dowry with her, giving a wealthy wife a good deal of independence.

Apart from legal prescriptions over divorce and property rights, however, there is plentiful evidence of companionate marriages in which husbands and wives shared mutual respect and affection for each other and for their children. The valediction of a letter written from exile in 58–57 BCE by the Roman orator Cicero to his wife, Terentia, expresses the emotional attachment he felt for her and their children: "My dear Terentia, most faithful and best of wives, and my darling little daughter, and that last hope of my race, Cicero, goodbye!" (Cicero, *Letters*, Harvard Classics, 1909, p. 14).

However, Cicero's devotion to Terentia did not prevent him from divorcing her about ten years after he wrote this letter. Cicero was not a wealthy man, and he had great difficulty in repaying Terentia's dowry, as he was required to do upon divorce. Both Cicero and Terentia remarried, also a common occurrence among the Roman elite due both to mortality and to divorce, leading to the proliferation of complicated households of step-parents, siblings, and other relatives.

Roman leaders and authors often promoted an idealized view of the Roman family under the firm authority of the *paterfamilias* in which wives were faithful, children obedient, and slaves submissive. The satirist Juvenal (60?–140?), for example, described

Figure 5.1 A Roman Couple. Painted by the Flemish artist Peter Paul Rubens in the early seventeenth century, this portrait was based on the classical Roman sculpture Rubens had seen in Italy. It reflects the idealized Roman marriage, and may be a representation of Germanicus Caesar, an accomplished military leader and his wife Agrippina, known for her marital devotion.

exemplary virtuous women of archaic Rome in contrast to the decadent, adulterous women of his own day. Youth, too, were seen as disrespectful and disobedient, unlike those of earlier times under the domination of patriarchs who could determine life or death. The disruption of patriarchal order in the family and the violation of family bonds was linked by many commentators to social breakdown. Laments of moral decay within the family echoed throughout the later Roman empire, to be exploited by early Christian communities who criticized the decadence of Roman life.

CHRISTIANITY, FAMILY, AND HOUSEHOLD IN MEDIEVAL AND EARLY MODERN EUROPE

With the conversion of the Roman emperor Constantine (306–37) to Christianity, this new religion gained the support of the state. Spreading throughout the realms of the Roman and Byzantine empires, Christianity gradually transformed society, including ideas about family and household. Although another well-known convert to Christianity, the North African Augustine (354–430), wrote extensively in his *Confessions* and in *The City of God* about the family as a unit of society based on the conjugal union of husband and wife, in other ways Christianity challenged the model of the conjugal family by offering alternatives to marriage and procreation for both men and women. By the time of Augustine, monasticism provided opportunities to live outside the structures of family and household within a religious community. The early Christian community thus created bonds of fellowship that transcended and replaced family bonds. But Christians also drew on the social symbolism of kinship relations and family life in creating their new religious communities. Beginning with the concept of Jesus as the "son of God" and the idea of "God the father," the symbolism of the family was a powerful model in Christian ideology.

In the centuries between the fall of the Roman empire and the crowning of Charlemagne as Holy Roman emperor by the pope in 800, Christianity penetrated beyond urban centers such as Rome and Constantinople to the countryside. Along with Christianity, economic changes began to transform rural society. The peasant household replaced Roman slave-based agriculture as the means of economic production. The head of the household, much like the Roman *paterfamilias*, exercised control over the household members and was the link between the household and the world beyond the house and fields. The dwellings and diet of the rural poor were spare and simple, a mud and thatch hut shared with animals, built around an open fire for heat, with turnips, beer, bread, and perhaps some cheese to eat. The bed was the most important item of furniture, and even the poorest peasant household had at least a mattress, if not a bedstead, which would often be shared by both adults and children.

By the ninth century, the establishment of Christian parishes throughout the European countryside transformed the daily lives of peasants who labored on the manors and estates of landlords and attended local parish churches regularly. Although marriage did not officially become a sacrament of the Church until the twelfth century, eventually parish registers recorded the births, deaths, and marriages of both the aristocracy and the peasantry. According to the Church, marriage was a matter of consent affirmed through the exchange of vows between bride and groom; once a conjugal union was formed it was regarded as indissoluble. The Church's intrusion into family life went beyond its control of the marriage sacrament. The practice of regular confession to a priest who prescribed penance meant that the Church through its clergy exercised control over family behavior. In addition to mandating celibacy for the priesthood and idealizing the religious life of chastity, poverty, and obedience, the Church excluded women from the priesthood.

With the gradual disappearance of serfdom in the eleventh and twelfth centuries, towns and cities increased in size and number. Between 1300 and 1800, the number of towns with populations of more than 10,000 nearly doubled, from 5.6 to 10 percent. Migration from rural areas accounts for most of this growth as rural laborers sought work in urban businesses and industries. Families and households adapted to new opportunities for work offered in urban settings, sending their sons and daughters to work as domestic servants or as apprentices. In fourteenth- and fifteenth-century Toulouse in southern France, for example,

Figure 5.2 Medieval woodcut showing birth of a child. Medieval childbirth was difficult and dangerous, and required the help of a community of women beyond the immediate household to care for the mother and the child.

over half of the apprentices and young male servants came from outside the city, including many as young as eight to twelve years old. Sending children to work in the cities was an economic strategy adopted by many rural families that enabled them to survive the uncertainties of dependence on agriculture. But urban life also took its toll, since mortality rates were high. Dense populations and poor sanitation created conditions for disease that were absent in rural villages. Whether as long-term urban residents or newly arrived immigrants, urban women worked in large numbers at a variety of occupations – from weaving wool to hawking food – that provided important sources of income for themselves and their families.

Individuals who migrated to cities left behind whatever network of family support they had. Some of these migrants remained single, and some married and established their own households. But many were left on their own to seek help in times of crisis. Children were the most vulnerable, both infants and orphans. The earliest foundling hospitals for abandoned infants were established in Italy during the thirteenth century, and the institution spread over the next two centuries through Spain, Portugal, and France. Other charitable institutions developed as well to provide food, clothing, and health care. Many of these institutions were the product of religious charity and donations made to churches, monasteries, and convents.

Like the influence of the Church on medieval European family life, the Protestant Reformation had a profound impact on family life in sixteenth-century Europe. Martin Luther and other leaders of the Reformation promoted the idea of the home as the cradle of citizenship, extending its values and example into the world around it. Marriage was described as a shared responsibility between husband and wife, with clearly defined roles and expectations. A wife was the "mother of the house," a position of authority and respect, but clearly subordinate to the husband and father. An evangelical treatise of 1524 stated:

> For it is written, the head of the wife is the husband, the head of the husband is Christ, and the head of Christ is God . . . there is no nobler, greater authority on earth than that of parents over children, since they have both spiritual and worldly authority over them.
>
> (Quoted in Kertzer and Barbagli 2001: xxv–xxvi)

DEMOGRAPHIC CHANGE, FAMILY, AND HOUSEHOLD IN EARLY MODERN EUROPE

Along with the impact of the Reformation, European families in the sixteenth and seventeenth centuries were subjected to a variety of economic and social pressures, as well as the effects of religious wars and political change. Over the three centuries from about 1500 to 1800, however, European population more than doubled, from 81 to 180 million, although some of this growth was cyclical in nature and it was uneven regionally. Historians have made use of population records and other kinds of sources to examine the demography of family and household in this era. Demographer John Hajnal in 1965 first charted the remarkable phenomenon of late marriage age in early modern Europe, a discovery with profound implications for understanding the relationship between family and household and larger processes of historical change. Although the Church sanctioned marriage for men at age 14 and for women at age 12, from 1500 to 1800 men were more likely to be in their mid- to late twenties and women in their early to mid-twenties when they married. During the medieval period, even though marriage was a holy sacrament, the private exchange of vows officiated by a father, for example, had been recognized by the Church. After the Reformation, public vows in church were increasingly required before a marriage was regarded as valid, and so marriages tended to take place at later ages.

Late marriage can also be explained in part by demography: population growth in the late fifteenth and sixteenth centuries, spurred by recovery after the ravages of the Black Death, meant there were more children to share inheritances, and it was thus more difficult for young men and women to establish independent households because they lacked the economic resources to live apart from their parents. What many young people did do in order to set aside resources to establish their own households was to work outside their parental homes as servants or agricultural laborers. These circumstances provided a good deal of flexibility to agricultural families as their need for labor fluctuated with the seasons, and young workers from outside the family may also have supported cottage industries in the early stages of the Industrial Revolution. While it is not yet clear to what extent or in what precise ways the phenomenon of late marriage age – along with a high rate of celibacy or non-marriage, as much as 10 percent – may have contributed to the expansion of the European economy in the eighteenth century, it is possible to recognize the benefits of years of women's labor within the household or outside it before marriage and childbearing began in the mid-twenties. Individual and collective family decisions about work and wedding may well have played a significant role in underpinning the European Industrial Revolution, turning on its head the assumption that all families can do is to respond to changes imposed by external forces – political, social, and economic.

By the eighteenth century, there appears to have been a rise in illegitimate births, a consequence of disruptions in social life caused by the beginnings of industrialization and urbanization. The appearance of institutions to care for abandoned children, such as the Paris Foundling Hospital (1670) and the London Foundling Hospital (1739), testifies both to the increase in illegitimate births and to the growing concern for the welfare of illegitimate children, espoused by both religious and political authorities. One possible means to provide for these children – adoption – had virtually disappeared in Europe under the influence of the Christian Church, which banned it. Fostering – sending children to work or to be cared for in another household – remained a common practice, as did wet-nursing, even though the Church took a dim view of the former and tried unsuccessfully to ban the latter.

The French philosopher Jean-Jacques Rousseau (1712–78) famously campaigned against wet-nursing, urging aristocratic women to nurse their own children as part of the model family that would sustain the new form of state based on the social contract (see Chapter 7). Yet in an egregious demonstration of the gulf between thought and action, Rousseau himself abandoned his own children by his mistress to the Paris Foundling Hospital. There are two points we might note from this: the existence of community institutions – particularly in urban settings such as Paris – that provided a safety net of sorts for children who ended up without the support of kin, and the contrast between ideal and reality in the history of family and household.

THE IMPACT OF ISLAM ON FAMILY AND HOUSEHOLD

Like Christianity's influence on family and household in European society, Islam brought important changes to family and household where it began on the Arabian peninsula and eventually to other parts of the world where the faith spread (see Chapter 4). The critical change that accompanied the introduction of Islam to the Arabian peninsula lay in the imposition of a written religious text, the Qur'an, as a guide to social and political order and the interpretation of this text into a code of law, or *shari'a*. The foundations of *shari'a* were the unambiguous commands and prohibitions found in the Qur'an, systematically ordered into codes of behavior beginning in the eighth and ninth centuries with the work of several schools of legal scholars. The legal code regulated individual and family life within the community, which was defined as consisting of those who were "true believers" in Islam.

Written codes, by their very nature, changed social customs because they removed practices common to members of a society from their everyday context and transformed them into general principles to be applied across the Islamic world without regard to context. In addition to the Qur'an and the *shari'a*, there was another source of wisdom known as *hadith*, or oral sayings. The intersection of these two authorities, written and fixed, oral and fluid, provided the guidelines for relations between men and women and between parents and children, the managing of families and households, and the division and inheritance of property.

The family was portrayed in the Qur'an and in the *shari'a* as the primary social, economic, and political unit of the community. Both Muhammad's revelations and the legal code they inspired emerged from a society based on strong kinship bonds and lineage solidarity. Although blood ties were key to social organization in sedentary communities on the Arabian peninsula, they were perhaps most deeply felt among the tribal clans of nomadic pastoralists. Writing centuries after the establishment of Islam, the North African historian Ibn Khaldun (1332–1406) described the concept of "group feeling" (*'asabiyya*) that he observed among the Bedouins of his homeland:

> Respect for blood ties is something natural among men, with the rarest exceptions. It leads to affection for one's relations and blood relatives, (the feeling that) no harm ought to befall them nor any destruction come upon them. One feels shame when one's relatives are treated unjustly or attacked, and one wishes to intervene between them and whatever peril or destruction threatens them. This is a natural urge in man, for as long as there have been human beings.
>
> (Ibn Khaldun, *Muqaddimah*, trans. Franz Rosenthal, Princeton, N.J.: Princeton University Press/Bollingen Foundation, 1969 reprint, p. 98)

The "group feeling" characteristic of Bedouin society as Ibn Khaldun portrayed it provided core social values that were transposed to the urban, commercial world of Mecca by Muhammad, a merchant in this caravan trading center on the Arabian peninsula. At the heart of Islam's teachings relating to family and household is the desire to ensure that the bonds of patrilineal kinship are protected, the patriarchal order is upheld, and that family property is fairly divided and transmitted. As elsewhere, however, the authority of written codes of behavior to regulate family and household was subject to enormous variation. In the case of Islam in particular, as it spread through vastly different cultures and geographical regions, Islamic law adapted to local custom and tradition and in turn these were influenced by Islamic law.

Housing varied throughout the Islamic world, depending on the pre-Islamic culture, climate, available building materials, and geography. However, two household concerns were widely shared: the right of the family to keep its affairs private and the impact of Islamic law and religious practice on women. Wealth, social interactions, and the intimate areas of family life remained hidden inside the household. Nothing of a house's façade revealed the inner workings or material comfort of the group. The family lived around a courtyard often ornamented with trees and fountains. According to the Qur'an, believers should "not enter the dwellings of other men until [they] have asked their owners' permission and wished them peace." If visitors were entertained, they were admitted only as far as a men's reception area. Women remained secluded in their own separate area (harem) with apartments.

In his *Book on the Etiquette of Marriage*, the eleventh-century Muslim religious scholar al-Ghazālī wrote that there were five advantages to marriage: procreation, satisfying sexual desire, ordering the household, providing companionship, and disciplining the self (Madelain Farah, *Marriage and Sexuality in Islam: A Translation of Al-Ghazālī's Book on the Etiquette of Marriage from the Ihyā'*, Salt Lake City: University of Utah Press, 1984, p. 53). Marriage in Islam was based on mutual consent and was therefore a contractual relationship that involved both economic and social obligations. The legal contract of marriage, whether written or not, linked the resources of two families and was the single most important event in an individual's

life. It required at least two witnesses, and if a court lay within a reasonable distance, it was recorded there. The contract might specify gifts of land or other family property to the woman or her family. Muslim women could marry only Muslim men, a restriction that prevented the flow of property and population from the Muslim community to other groups. Depending on what the contract stipulated, a woman might retain control of her dowry. A man was required to provide maintenance for his wife, and he could have more than one wife – up to four – as long as he treated them all equally as the Qur'an dictated. Early West Asian society also included significant numbers of slaves, who were largely integrated into free Muslim family units. Many female slaves became concubines, and their children were accorded the same rights as children born to married partners.

Unlike Christianity, which regarded marriage as a sacrament and thus indissoluble, the contractual basis of Islamic marriage meant that if the obligations were not met the marriage could be dissolved. Divorce was relatively easy for men: they had only to repudiate their wives three times in order to divorce them. It was more difficult and complicated for women, who could only initiate divorce by appeal to a court judge and only for specific reasons. Both divorce and remarriage were common throughout the Islamic world, among both elite and commoners.

The relative ease of divorce and remarriage, even for those at the bottom rungs of the social ladder, can be glimpsed in three consecutive marriage contracts preserved in a court archive for a freed slave-girl named Zumurrud, a resident of Jerusalem in the late fourteenth century. In early 1389 she married a milkman who was obliged by the terms of the contract to provide a marriage gift to her of three gold coins, payable in installments. He divorced Zumurrud a little over a year later, and she forfeited the remainder of her marriage gift. She soon wed another freed slave, Sabīh, though without waiting for three months as divorced women were required to do before remarrying. In addition to a modest monetary marriage gift, he pledged to support Zumurrud's son by her previous husband, who had legal custodial rights he apparently chose not to exercise. Six months later, Sabīh divorced Zumurrud, and shortly thereafter she was once again remarried, this time to a weaver who also pledged a marriage gift

Figure 5.3 Divorcing husband and wife accuse each other before a judge (*qadi*). Here a scribe listens and records the complaints. Most divorces took place without the intervention of a judge.

to be paid in installments (Rapoport 2005: 64–8). Evident from the tale of Zumurrud's marriages is not only the ease with which the marriage contracts were made and revoked but also the complicated financial negotiations that underpinned the contracts.

For centuries, from the lively urban center of Cairo to al-Andalus on the Iberian peninsula, Islamic law provided a degree of coherence in regulating family and household practices across culturally diverse societies that rimmed the Mediterranean. This continued with the expansion of the Ottoman empire in the fifteenth and sixteenth centuries throughout much of West Asia, eastern Europe, and the eastern end of the Mediterranean. Records from Ottoman Bulgaria illustrate the role of Islamic courts in marriages, divorces, and other family issues such as inheritance within a society

composed largely of Orthodox Christians, including Bulgarians, Greeks, and Wallachians, along with Armenians and Muslims. One marriage contract, dated 1715, was written in Arabic and read: "In the name of Allah and in compliance with the *shari'a*, the Rousse town judge Abdullah, son of Alhaj Ibrahim, performed a marriage between Abdalhata and Hava, at a bride-price of 100,000 *akçes*, in the presence of two witnesses" (Svetlana Ivanova, "The Divorce Between Zubaida Hatun and Esseid Osman Ağa: Women in the Eighteenth-Century *Shari'a* Court of Rumelia," in *Women, the Family, and Divorce Laws in Islamic History*, edited by Amira El Azhary Sonbol, Syracuse, N.Y.: Syracuse University Press, 1996, p. 115). In the same region, Osman Ağa and his wife Zubaida Hatun were divorced by decision of the local court (Ivanova, pp. 112–13). As earlier and elsewhere in the Islamic world, marriage was a contractual relationship registered in courts and often dissolved through divorce proceedings adjudicated by Islamic judges.

AFRICAN FAMILIES AND HOUSEHOLDS: MATRILINEALITY AND MOTHERHOOD

The degree to which Islamic ideas about family and household varied according to local custom and tradition can be seen in the Muslim traveler Ibn Battuta's observations of matriliny in fourteenth-century Mali:

> Their women are of surpassing beauty, and are shown more respect than the men. The state of affairs amongst these people is indeed extra-ordinary. Their men show no signs of jealousy whatever; no one claims descent from his father, but on the contrary from his mother's brother. A person's heirs are his sister's sons, not his own sons. This is a thing which I have seen nowhere in the world except among the Indians of Malabar. But those are heathens; these people are Muslims, punctilious in observing the hours of prayer, studying books of law, and memorizing the Qur'an. Yet their women show no bashfulness before men and do not veil themselves, though they are assiduous in attending the prayers.
>
> (Quoted in Erik Gilbert and Jonathan R. Reynolds, *Africa in World History: From Prehistory to the Present*, Upper Saddle River, N.J.: Pearson Prentice-Hall, 2004, p. 93)

Ibn Battuta was startled by these matrilineal customs, which were typical of many African societies, even those which had converted to Islam. Both matriliny and the prominent role of women in society surprised this Islamic traveler because such customs turned upside down the Islamic patrilineal and patriarchal order with which Ibn Battuta was most familiar.

As elsewhere across the globe, a pervasive concern of African societies throughout history was continuity, the ability of the family and group to reproduce itself. An adult's sense of social completeness was dependent on his or her ability to sire or bear children. Motherhood was an essential aspect of female identity in most societies. Children guaranteed the well-being of an individual in old age and ensured the transition of the parent's spirit to the community of the ancestors, who would be honored by their descendants. The prevalent belief in reincarnation of ancestors as newborn members of the lineage meant that children were highly valued as visible symbols of the continuity of life. The pragmatic concern of many African women and men over fertility ensured a large and productive household labor force.

Among the Batammaliba of northern Togo and Benin, who lived in dispersed, stateless settlements in the fifteenth century, the same word designated both the extended family and the house in which its members lived. The meaning of household (those sharing physical space) and family (those sharing social space) was a conceptual continuity. Lacking a household, an individual would be without social and spiritual support. The house was dressed in human clothes, and its parts were identified with parts of the human body as well as with specific human ancestors in its lineage.

The Batammaliba house also reflected the importance of historical ancestors in the identity of the family's compound. Every house served to symbolize a tomb; without the death of an elder there was believed to be no new life. The arrangement of a settlement's cemetery was identical to the placement of family houses within the village, reinforcing the complementarity of house and tomb, present and past. In the house, family history was evoked and manipulated through daily contact between living family members and their ancestors.

The Akan people of Ghana created some of West Africa's most powerful forest states and empires, beginning around the fourteenth century and culminating in the Asante empire in the late seventeenth century. Central to Akan identity was the matrilineal structure of society centered on the *abusua* (which referred to family or matrilineage, as well as clan). Matrilineal descent in Akan society refers to the pattern by which Akan men and women marked their place in the continuum of ancestors, by reference to the female side of the family. It had no special connotations for the distribution of political power, which as elsewhere in large-scale states worked in favor of men.

The Akan concern with fertility and bearing children was a recognition of the importance of the *abusua* in acquiring individual and community identity. Individuals had recognized rights only through their positions within an *abusua*. Without the protection afforded to members they were considered without ancestors and without sexual identity. The uncertainty and ambiguity inherent in the lack of ancestry and status are best exemplified by the fact that enemies captured by the expanding Akan state became permanent slaves unless they were integrated into an *abusua* through adoption or marriage. During the expansion of the Akan state during and after the fourteenth and fifteenth centuries, neither women nor children gained position or power. The emphasis on warfare resulted in men gaining status, and the increased numbers of slaves available to perform household tasks generally devalued women's labor and diminished their influence even further.

One of the best-known sculptural traditions from the Akan region is the small, abstracted carving of a human figure known as *akuaba*, literally "Akua's child." Oral traditions claim that a woman named Akua, desperate to produce children, once approached a local priest. He consulted the spirit world and then instructed Akua to commission the carving of a small wooden child. She was told to carry the child on her back, feed it, and care for it as if it were real. The whole village laughed at her until she succeeded in her quest to become pregnant and gave birth to a beautiful daughter. The tradition illustrates the high status and importance associated with motherhood in matrilineal societies, even ones in which women are politically subordinated. Children had relatively few rights, since knowledge and power, considered to be the basis of rights, were thought to accumulate with age. Still, children were accorded respect because they were believed to be the reincarnation of ancestors. The *akuaba* fertility figures suggest the important role of children in reflecting spiritual harmony, ideals of individual beauty, and the well-being of the family order.

The extent to which such a unit as the household-family was mediated by the Akan state or local political authority varied according to the status of its members.

Typically, interference in the creation of marriage alliances allowed a patriarchy to control the labor of women and their children and thus the accumulation of any household surplus. Even when wealth was inherited through the female line, most women were excluded from most political offices. Exceptions were made for elite Akan women who were beyond their childbearing years. The female office of queen mother

Figure 5.4 Akuaba fertility figure. The idealized image reflects the desirability of children believed to be the reincarnation of ancestors.

was secondary to that of the king, but she was omni-present and consulted in the ascension of the head of state. Women acted as priestesses and even diplomats who could find themselves making significant contributions to statecraft and foreign policy.

CASTE, FAMILY, AND HOUSEHOLD IN SOUTH ASIA

In his disapproving description of matrilineal society in fourteenth-century Mali, the Muslim traveler Ibn Battuta mentioned that he knew of only one other similar instance and that was "among the Indians of Malabar." Ibn Battuta was referring to a system of marriage practiced along the Malabar coast of India in which *sudra* (the lowest caste) women of one ethnic group who lived in matrilineal and matrilocal joint families married with *brahman* (the highest caste) men who lived in patrilineal and patrilocal joint families. This custom entails a complicated series of arrangements that ultimately result in the joint family being formed around the mother and her children under the authority of the eldest male member of the matri-lineage. But this regional tradition is also clearly an exception to the patterns of patriarchy, patriliny, and caste boundaries that predominated throughout most of the South Asian subcontinent.

Inherited divisions of society based on corporate membership, common descent, and endogamy, determined what people should do with their lives, whom they should marry, with whom they should eat and work, and where they should live (see Chapter 8). Caste helped to shape families since it determined the boundaries of group membership and placed restrictions on marriage, though families were shaped by other factors as well. The patriarchal and patrilineal extended joint family – sons or brothers, their wives and children, grandsons, and their wives and children – was the basic structure of family life. The family was bound together by rites of ancestral commemoration, in which three generations of descendants of the deceased participated. This group formed the core of the joint family, and the head of the family managed its property on behalf of all.

Marriages were arranged by families, and sons brought their wives into the parental home and reared their children there. Women were usually married at a very early age – before puberty – in theory to protect them from engaging in sexual activity before marriage and humiliating both themselves and their families. Polygamy (having multiple spouses, especially wives) was customary, although there were many variations, even polyandry (having multiple husbands). Widows were expected to follow a harsh regimen of daily life to honor their dead husbands, and in some upper classes widows even threw themselves onto their husbands' funeral pyres to demonstrate their fidelity.

The three purposes of marriage were religious (the performance of ancestral rites), continuation of the family line, and sexual pleasure. Marriage practices varied greatly according to region as well as caste. For example, in south India cross-cousin marriage (marriage of a son to his father's brother's daughter) was not only permitted but encouraged. For Hindus in north India such marriages were generally prohibited, while Muslims in the north often chose spouses from within the patrilineal clan or lineage and thus married a cross-cousin.

As in many other societies, marriage was often a means of establishing alliances between families and of balancing economic against political or social status; for example, a wealthy family might form an alliance with a politically powerful family by contracting a marriage for their daughter with a son of that family. These goals in marrying, however, were always tempered in the case of India by the caste system. In most castes, inheritance was through the male line, but in some castes family property was inherited through the female line. In both north and south India, however, and for Muslims as well as Hindus, marriage as economic exchange involved both bride-price and dowry. The custom of purdah (an Urdu word) – the rigorous seclusion of women and the requirement that they cover their faces in all company except that of the immediate family – came to India following the Muslim invasions beginning in the eighth century and appears to have spread over northern India during the fifteenth and sixteenth centuries. Although this practice may have primarily affected elite women and lower-class women may have never observed complete purdah, women did tend to keep out of sight when men were present.

SOUTHEAST ASIAN FAMILY AND HOUSEHOLD: INDIGENOUS TRADITIONS AND ISLAMIC INFLUENCE

Between 1500 and 1800, beginning from coastal fringes on the Malay peninsula and around the island of Sumatra, Islam made substantial inroads into Southeast Asia, where it interacted with indigenous beliefs, as well as with Hinduism and Buddhism (see Chapters 4 and 6). In matters of personal law, such as marriage and divorce, traditional local ideas and practices tended to shape the application of Islamic law and to moderate its harsher aspects. By traditional custom monogamy prevailed, in part because divorce was easily obtained by either partner and divorce was frequent. Both property and children were divided on a more or less equal basis. Daughters were highly valued, and, through marriage, wealth passed from the male to the female side in the form of bridewealth. In contrast to dowry, which follows a daughter into her marriage, bridewealth shows the high value placed on women.

The court diary of the seventeenth-century state of Makassar details an elite woman's marital history that helps to illustrate the pattern of relatively easy divorce rooted in local custom in contrast to Islamic law, which typically would not allow such freedom for a woman to divorce as she does. Karaeng Balla-Jawaya (b. 1634), daughter of one of the highest Makassar lineages, was married at the age of thirteen to Karaeng Bonto-marannu, who eventually became one of the greatest Makassar warriors. At twenty-five, she separated from him and soon married his rival, Karaeng Karunrung, the prime minister. In 1666, at the age of thirty-one, she separated from him, and she later married Arung Palakka, who was in the process of conquering her country with the aid of the Dutch. At thirty-six she separated from him, and she lived another fifty years (Anthony Reid, *Southeast Asia in the Age of Commerce, 1450–1680*, Vol. I: *The Lands Below the Winds*, New Haven, Conn. and London: Yale University Press, 1988, pp. 152–3).

The relative freedom of sexual relations and marital practices in Southeast Asia conflicted sharply with both Islamic and Christian beliefs, which were increasingly influential after the fifteenth century. Both Islam and Christianity forbade premarital sexual relations, and Islam in particular imposed harsh punishments for transgressions. Islamic beliefs gradually imposed restraints on indigenous ways of life and influenced Southeast Asian societies on the Malay peninsula and throughout the Indonesian archipelago. This is particularly clear with regard to the position of Southeast Asian women, who had been independent and active participants in commerce and public social life and equal partners with men in matters of love and domestic life before the imposition of Islam.

CONFUCIANISM AND THE CHINESE FAMILY

Like Christianity in Europe and Islam in West Asia, Confucianism profoundly shaped family life in China and throughout East Asia. Born into an age of political and social disorder in the sixth century BCE, the thinker known in the West as Confucius considered the family to be the foundation of society. He encouraged families to venerate their ancestors, so the performance of ancestral rites became an important activity of the Confucian family. Each generation was obliged to produce male heirs so that succeeding generations could continue to honor their ancestors.

State and society were modeled on the family. The ruler was to treat his subjects as a father treats his sons, and vice versa. The virtue of filial piety ideally characterized this relationship: the father had absolute authority within the family and absolute obedience was required from the son. In addition to the relationship between ruler and subject, the father–son relationship, along with that between elder brother and younger brother and between husband and wife, was among the five fundamental human relationships (the fifth was between friends). Certain aspects of these relationships as prescribed by Confucius are apparent: the dominance of age over youth, and male over female. Age and gender determined hierarchy within the family. Women, no matter how old they became, could not escape the authority of men. As daughters, they were dependants and subordinates of their fathers; as wives, of their husbands; and as widows, of their sons.

One of the most influential interpreters of Confucian ideals with regard to the roles of women in the family was Ban Zhao (*c.* 45–115 CE), the daughter of a famous scholarly family of the time and a noted scholar in her own right. She compiled the *Admonitions for Women*, a treatise concerning the moral and ethical principles by which women should order their lives. This work also provided guidance for the practical concerns of everyday life for daughters, wives, and mothers. Some of the chapter titles of this work suggest Ban Zhao's themes: humility, respect and caution, devotion, obedience, harmony. She urged women to yield to others, respect others, and to put others first. Among other things, she addressed the role of women and men within the family: "If a wife does not serve her husband, then the proper relationship between men and women and the natural order of things are neglected and destroyed" (Alfred J. Andrea and James H. Overfield, eds, *The Human Record: Sources of Global History*, Vol. I: *To 1700*, 2nd edn, Boston, Mass.: Houghton Mifflin, 1994, p. 454)

Apart from prescribed behavior written about in classical texts, we know relatively little from standard sources about the intimate details of family life or about the practical operation of households in early imperial China of roughly the first millennium CE. But in part due to the remarkable finds made in the early twentieth century at Dunhuang in the arid northwest of China, we have some household registration records compiled by government officials around 750 for the purpose of taxation. These records tell us something of family members, their ages, and the generations that comprise a household. One household includes the head, whose age is given as 56; a widowed stepmother, 60; wife, 58; two younger brothers (of the household head), 28, 42; son, 18; one younger brother's wife, 25; five daughters, ranging in age from 13 to 31; two sons of a deceased elder brother, 23 and 17; and a younger sister (of the household head), 43. (Patricia B. Ebrey, *Chinese Civilization: A Sourcebook*, New York: Free Press, 1993, pp. 125–6).

By around 1000 CE we begin to have much more documentation available to reconstruct the Chinese family and household, and literary sources, especially poetry, provide personal and private perspectives that greatly enhance what we can learn from official records. Literary sources can open a different kind of window on family life in the past, documenting emotional and psychological dimensions of family relationships and

suggesting how stated ideals were lived in practice. Despite the apparently rigid demarcation of gender roles in marriage suggested in Ban Zhao's *Admonitions for Women*, emotional ties between husband and wife could often be deep.

A profound emotional and intellectual tie existed between a woman poet named Li Qingzhao (1084?–*c.* 1151) and her husband. Like other women of her time, she married at a young age, 16 or 17. After her husband's death she wrote a moving recollection of their marriage as an intimate scholarly partnership. Li Qingzhao and her husband lived in an era when marriage ties were often used as a strategy to enhance a family's political, social, or economic status. Wealth was an important factor, but even more important was the status achieved by those who passed the imperial civil service examinations. For example, a wealthy family with no sons might marry their daughter to the son of a relatively poor family who had passed the examinations and thus had prospects of both wealth and power. Adoption could also be used as a means to gain a son with potential to achieve status through the examinations, particularly if a family had no male offspring. By the thirteenth century, the economic exchange involved in marriage shifted from bride-price (the transfer of wealth and property from the groom's family to the bride's) to dowry (wealth and property brought by the bride to the marriage), suggesting a relatively equal balance in terms of the exchange of property between the families of the bride and groom.

Marriage was more than simply a means to enhanced social or economic status, and families were more than units for the production of examination candidates or marriageable daughters. Marriage and family life reflected a complex of notions about the role and position of women and their relationships with men, and created complicated emotional ties that were often denied or thwarted by social custom and practice. Yuan Cai's guide for family life written in the twelfth century gave practical advice on how to deal with problems that affected family harmony, such as the treatment of women (as wives, concubines, servants, unmarried relatives, or widows) and how to maintain status. Rather than being the idealization of family life portrayed in Confucian texts, this guidebook was written from the perspective of the day-to-day concerns of family life and often showed a more flexible and tolerant attitude toward women and a more realistic view of human behavior from the perspective of daily life. Family genealogies in later imperial China (1300–1800) sometimes included instructions to family members on how to conduct themselves, what to wear, what to eat, what occupations were acceptable, and admonished descendants to honor their ancestors with the proper rites and not to spend their inheritance. In this way, the memories of family life served as imprints for future generations to decipher and order their own worlds.

FAMILY AND HOUSEHOLD IN THE AMERICAS

The kinds of historical evidence we have to describe family and household vary as widely as do the concepts themselves: English parish registers recording births, marriages, deaths; Islamic court records documenting marriages and divorces; Confucian family genealogies and guidebooks. In the absence of such records, the recovery of family history in the pre-Columbian Americas depends on a combination of written, archaeological, and orally transmitted sources.

The North American continent was home to a bewildering array of small-scale societies based on communities organized by lineage (see also Chapter 7). Multifamily dwellings, or longhouses, were common to communities in the Pacific Northwest Coast region, the Great Plains, and among the Eastern Woodland Iroquois. At the beginning of the sixteenth century, one of the earliest European observers of native peoples in the Americas, Amerigo Vespucci, wrote of hundreds of persons sleeping in shared households. In some cases, multifamily dwellings were associated with the development of agriculture, since joint residency encouraged the cooperative labor required by intensive food production, though they were also characteristic of the nonagricultural Pacific Northwest. More commonly, shared kinship was the basis for establishing multifamily dwellings, with membership in a lineage determining joint residence. Matrilineal and patrilineal descent were recognized in different societies, and in some cases, as in some Northwest Coast groups, bilateral descent (acknowledgment of both sides of one's ancestry) was recognized.

Matriliny, in which both descent and property were transmitted through females, was characteristic of the Iroquois of the Eastern Woodlands. The Iroquois lived by a combination of hunting, gathering, fishing, and subsistence agriculture in semi-permanent settlements dating from about 500. By 1000, the Iroquois had adopted improved hardy strains of the "three sisters" crops – beans, maize, and squash – which enabled them to shift toward a greater dependence on agriculture. This resulted in important changes in the organization of their society. The increased food supply made rapid population growth possible, and this meant that individual households began joining together and living in multifamily dwellings. Archaeological evidence suggests that each multifamily house in a village came to hold a lineage or a segment of one and bore an animal name, such as Bear, Turtle, and so on. Kinship relations were used to facilitate cooperative efforts (such as land clearing) and to maintain order in a society of increasing size and complexity. Multifamily longhouses were probably occupied by matrilineal families, connected by kinship through women who traced their descent from a common ancestress. The new importance of agriculture reinforced the importance of women in subsistence and domestic affairs, and males had no authority in the household. The longhouse was dominated by a matron assisted by a council of women.

On the opposite side of the North American continent, inhabitants of the Northwest Coast, such as the Tlingit, Haida, and Kwakiutl, prospered on the natural bounty produced by the temperate rainforest climate. Ocean currents and relatively warm air masses encourage natural food production, and rivers that descend from the mountains are filled with migratory fish during spring and summer. This environmentally rich area was home to dense populations settled in scattered sites. By about 1000, large, permanent settlements of several hundred people appeared, despite the absence of agriculture. Typically, Northwest Coast lineage or extended family groups lived in separate households, about thirty or so people living in a longhouse made of cedar logs or planks. Longhouses were headed by a chief – any man who owned a house was a chief – and each had its totem, such as a bear, a whale, or a raven, often decorating a totem pole located at the residence. The basic social unit among

Northwest Coast peoples was similar: politically autonomous groups of relatives, their spouses and children, aligned according to one of three methods. Some of them were based on matrilineal descent, wherein membership and inheritance came from the mother and her side of the family; others were patrilineal (wherein kinship, membership, and inheritance were through the father); still others followed a bilateral (determined through both the mother's and the father's line) reckoning of descent and membership.

The center of the North American continent was dominated by temperate grasslands, home to a number of grazing and burrowing animal species that provided bounty for hunting peoples. The earliest (before 900) Plains peoples banded together in their joint search for sustenance, based primarily on hunting bison. Membership in the group was determined by residence. Later, by the Plains Village horticultural period, membership in the community was fixed by heredity, which was achieved by consistently ignoring one side of the family and stressing the other. All persons of either sex descended from the male ancestor, through the male line only, formed a patrilineage community, or clan; all those descended from a female ancestor, through the female line only, formed a matrilineage community, or clan. Whereas the family unit recognized both parents, clans ignored one parent in favor of the other in determining membership. This sort of organization meant that one-half of one's ancestors, either maternal or paternal, counted for certain purposes (admission to a ceremony or feast or the sharing of an inheritance), while for other matters the other half might be equally important. Clans bore names, usually of animal origin, such as Wolf, Eagle, Elk, and Beaver, and some of them had distinctive ceremonial and political functions.

By around 1000, the Pueblo peoples of the arid American Southwest practiced intensive irrigated agriculture and lived in communal dwellings that consisted of contiguous flat-roofed stone or adobe houses, sometimes several stories high. Between about 1250 and 1500, archaeological evidence shows that Pueblo peoples moved often and in large numbers, likely due to changes in the ecological niches they inhabited. Rooms were built, occupied, abandoned, and later reoccupied. By the sixteenth century, the Pueblo Indians were a total population of less than 250,000 horticulturalists who resided in modest-sized towns and villages scattered throughout New Mexico and Arizona. Pueblo society was both matrilineal and matrilocal: when a woman married, her husband left his mother's house and came to live in her house, where he remained forever an outsider. The house and its possessions, the sacred objects and wealth, principally in the form of stored corn and access to the fields, belonged to the women who lived there. The typical household unit consisted of a grandmother and her husband, her sisters and their husbands, her daughters and their husbands, children, and perhaps an orphan or slave. While women remained attached to their natal homes throughout their lives, men moved according to their stage of life: in childhood a male lived with his mother; as a youth he moved to a kiva (male lodge and ritual chamber) to learn male ritual traditions; and then he took up residence in the home of his wife.

Written sources that reveal the nature of family and household in both Mexica-Aztec society in the Valley of Mexico and Incan society in the Andean highlands of South America are restricted for the most part to accounts recorded by Spanish scribes after the conquest. Integrating territory and peoples across a vast terrain, the Incas established their empire in the Andes in the early fifteenth century. Changes in gender roles, family and household accompanied territorial expansion. Men came to symbolize the conqueror, and women the conquered. As a result of the pervasive warfare, in which female enemies were incorporated into households as slaves and wives and male enemies were killed, the status of Incan women was devalued and the power they had once held because of their economic and reproductive roles was diminished. Warfare became as important as childbirth in increasing populations.

The family or *ayllu* provided the basis of Inca social organization, and was regarded by the Incan state as a unit of economic production (see Chapter 6). Families were provided with land by the state, which claimed everything produced and had the power to move family members and households to wherever their labor was needed. Men paid their tribute to the state through laboring on public works or in agriculture, or through military service; women spent much of their time weaving. Woven cloths had extraordinary ritual and

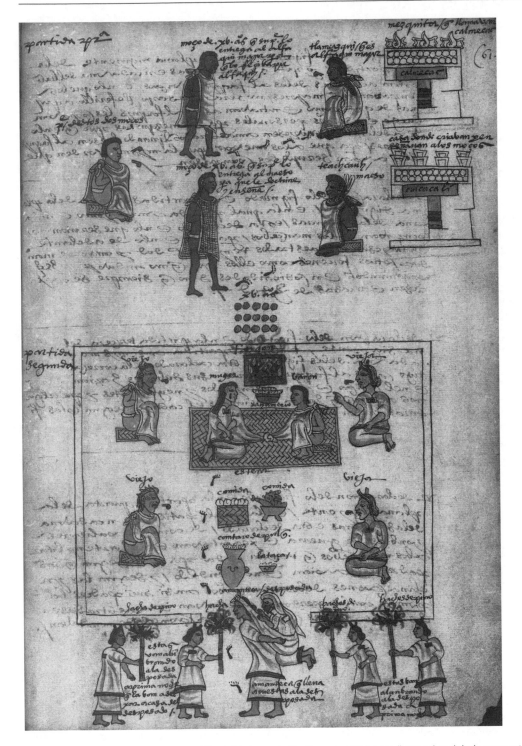

Figure 5.5 Aztec marriage ceremony. The bride is carried to the groom's house (bottom) and their garments are ritually knotted (above) to signify the union.

ceremonial value. A special public building served as a convent for Chosen Women, brought to the Incan capital to weave cloth and participate in rituals. Male dominance was maintained in the patriarchal Incan society by treating women as property. Adultery was considered theft of the female involved, and the male was punished for having committed a crime against property. Boys and girls were educated in separate schools.

Less is known of family and household in Aztec society, centered in the Valley of Mexico and reaching its peak in the fifteenth century, just before the European conquest. The complex tribute society of the Aztecs centered around the city of Tenochtitlán, founded in 1325. From this center, the Mexica-Aztecs ruled through seven *calpulli*, or tribal-kinship units. The cult of the warrior that dominated Aztec culture and society was reflected in the beliefs and practices associated with childbirth and child rearing. The metaphor of battle was used for childbirth, and the infant was described as a "captive," won in battle. Women giving birth were possessed by the spirit of the Earth Mother. If a woman died in childbirth, the Earth Mother would have to be appeased. From birth, female infants were carefully distinguished from their male counterparts by differences in care and feeding, according to the roles that each would fulfill in society. The social duty of the male was to be a warrior; that of the female was to be a wife. Marriage was a secular rite that symbolized the transfer of a young male from the care of his mother to that of his bride.

GLOBALIZATION AND CHANGING FAMILIES AND HOUSEHOLDS

Across the globe families and households were shaped by varying cultural traditions, religious institutions, economic and ecological conditions, and political structures. Even within broad geographical regions – Europe, the Americas, Africa, Asia – there was great variation in marriage systems, gender roles, and values concerning the relationship between men and women and between parents and children. Marriage itself was largely an economic or political transaction, marking the transfer of wealth and creating alliances between families. Religion, ranging from family veneration of

ancestors to institutions such as the Christian Church, had a powerful impact on families everywhere, sanctioning marriage, reinforcing patriarchy, and determining inheritance practices for the transmission of property. Families were equally shaped by economic considerations. Shifting patterns of economic activity and changing modes of production had profound effects on family and household.

After about 1500, the processes of globalization began to influence family and household everywhere by connecting regions, peoples, and cultures in new ways. The impact of Europe's expansion around the globe was felt in the intimate realms of family life as well as in the large-scale economic, social, and political worlds. Patterns of migration carried European patriarchal notions to encounter widely differing systems of family and household. Yet European women in frontier areas often had important economic roles and greater independence than before, and gradually challenges to patriarchy emerged among settler societies. By the latter half of the nineteenth century, women were gaining ground in education and in political life. For example, in 1893 women in New Zealand made up half of all university students and also gained the right to vote.

COLONIALISM AND FAMILY IN THE AMERICAS, ASIA, AND AFRICA

In areas of the "New World" where slavery provided essential labor on plantations and in mining, hybrid family systems developed out of the forced encounter of indigenous traditions with European patriarchal structures. In the Andean region of South America a hybrid or Creole system aligned with native Indian forms of marriage that could be traced back to Inca times. "Trial marriage," known in Quechua as *watanaki* or *servinakuy* (betrothal involving cohabiting), was widely practiced and fit well with the looser family structures of Creole society that allowed sexual experimentation, and relatively easy dissolution. A dual-family system gradually emerged in Latin America and in the Caribbean, in which an Iberian variant of the Western European marriage system – patriarchal, racially pure, strong marriage – contrasted with the ethnically mixed, informal, matrifocal native family.

In the mid-nineteenth century in the Brazilian state of Bahía, the family based on the marriage of a man and woman was the exception not the rule: one-third to one-half of the population of Salvador never married. Colonialism and plantation slavery accounted in part for this: there were serious impediments to interracial marriage, and huge economic and social differences meant that marriages could not be contracted between poor Indians and white colonists, although this didn't mean that sexual relations weren't possible. In 1900 the Andean Caribbean region had the most complex and multifaceted marriage and family systems of anywhere in the world due to the conjuncture of colonialism with indigenous cultures.

In the Caribbean, the situation of South Asians who came to work as indentured laborers contrasted with that of African slaves whose forced labor provided the basis of the plantation economy. In both cases, through either voluntary or forced migration, families were uprooted and, in the case of African slaves, destroyed. Enslaved men and women were not permitted to marry, but to breed and produce children as commodities to maintain the system of slavery. Slave women who bore children by their white masters often lost them to the master's family. Colonialism produced a sharp distinction between the protected, isolated white women and black, Indian, and mulatto women to whom white men had sexual access. The patriarchal, patrilineal white family contrasted with the matrilineal, matriarchal Afro-Creole family, whose male father and husband were emasculated by the brutal conditions of slavery and servitude. In the twentieth century, the Caribbean doctor and writer, Frantz Fanon, saw patriarchy and colonialism as related through the common idea of sexual domination.

The impact of colonialism on the family and household in regions of Eurasia where plantation slavery was not the dominant economic system differed. Marriage was viewed in Hindu society as a sacramental act, indissoluble and unrepeatable by a woman. When the sister-in-law of the Bengali Brahmin, Rammohan Roy, was forcibly burnt on his brother's funeral pyre in 1811, Roy became an ardent opponent of the custom of *sati* (widow immolation) and worked to eradicate it. In 1829 the British governor of Bengal issued legislation prohibiting the practice, and the instances of *sati* did decrease. The colonial government also issued legisla-

tion to prohibit infanticide and to permit the remarriage of widows and inter-caste marriage. In attempting to reform traditional family practices, the British government presented its policies as part of its "civilizing mission," and was joined by Indians like Roy who saw these changes as part of a necessary transformation of Indian society to become part of the modern world. But many Indian nationalists rejected some of these changes, including increasing the age of consent and permitting remarriage, because they saw them as leading to the Westernization of Indian women. Still, relatively little changed as the government reforms only penetrated at best the Anglicized middle and upper classes on the urban elite fringes of Indian society. In much of rural India, among the illiterate and away from direct contact with foreign influences, traditional practices held sway throughout the twentieth century. Marriage, for example, remained the primary goal for women: in 1901, 96 percent of women in India aged 20 to 24 were married.

As difficult as it is to generalize across the Islamic world or throughout South Asia because of religious, caste, and regional linguistic and cultural differences, it is even more difficult to make general statements about African family and household. Vast ethnic and regional differences characterize the African continent, and even within sub-Saharan Africa there are fundamental distinctions in marriage practices among peoples in West, East, and southern Africa. It may be more useful to recognize a range of difference, from coastal areas of West Africa – where the patrilineal Yoruba and Ibo dominated and where there was female autonomy under male sovereignty, particularly in trade and economic activities – to East and southern Africa where tight male control was exercised among the Ndebele in Zimbabwe, the Zulu in southern Africa, and the Luo in Kenya. Yet among the Akan in Ghana, matrilineality created conditions that allowed important roles to women, including having female co-chiefs.

The transport of 3 million slaves across the Atlantic in the nineteenth century, along with the imposition of colonial rule throughout much of the African continent, brought sweeping changes to African families and households, whatever the differences among them. One colonial legacy was uneven economic development dictated by European desires to extract the wealth of the continent through enterprises such as mining and cash crops. Demands for labor to operate mines and farms led eventually to a pattern of long-distance, long-term African male labor migration, leaving behind wives and families in an increasingly impoverished hinterland of subsistence agriculture. Urbanization accompanied colonialism, although again there were regional differences in the impact of colonial urbanization (see Chapter 3). Although cities such as Lagos and Abidjan were colonial creations, they built on pre-colonial traditions of urban trading centers that provided the basis for a relatively balanced population of men and women, and in which women had legitimate economic autonomy. But in East, southern, and Central Africa such traditions were largely absent, and so the urban population was predominantly male, with few female activities apart from prostitution and beer-brewing or bar-keeping. The destabilization of the African family through the colonial legacy of uneven economic development and urbanization was compounded by the contradictions of colonial family legislation that was rooted in European national traditions and Christianity but also recognized African customs. These conditions often led to dual legal systems with very different views of what constituted a legal marriage, grounds for divorce, or inheritance rights.

The disruption of the African family as a result of European contact and urban industrial development brought about perhaps the most drastic change in traditional family structures in the twentieth century. Family and kinship systems, which provided the essential structure of individual and social relationships, have been radically undermined where European influences have been strongest. Traditional family structures varied with different ethnic groups, but each form was strongly sanctioned by custom. In most communities the family or kinship group was a self-contained economic unit in which all shared for purposes of production and consumption. It was also a unit for childrearing. The authority of elders extended to all, so that immediate parents did not have full or unsupported responsibility for the young.

In the course of the twentieth century, family structures in many parts of Africa have been altered and reduced as a source of identity in cities and weakened in many parts of the countryside. Rural areas have been especially affected by Christian missionary teaching

and activity that, for example, attacked such practices as polygamy. Muslim influence has been less disruptive in that sense, since the Qur'an permits polygamy and religious leaders have not sought to stop it. Colonial administrators generally left customary family institutions intact unless they affected measures designed to deal with commerce and administration. Such measures sometimes contributed to undermining the family forms that held communities together. Yet, at times, the changes wrought by colonial rule were negotiated inside family and household institutions, as colonial courts recognized indigenous patterns of legal rights and inheritance.

The principal disruption of African family structures came from industrialization and urbanization promoted through European influence. In the early twentieth century, men who went away to work left the family group impaired and increased women's labor demands. A major breakdown occurred when women eventually accompanied men to urban areas and established urban family units in African cities such as Johannesburg, Nairobi, Dakar, Lagos, Accra, Mombasa, and Kinshasa. From one end of Africa to the other, the ever-growing number of urban African families represents a break with virtually every element of traditional African family structure, even though close ties are maintained with rural relatives.

Traditional familial economic self-sufficiency based on the contribution and shared consumption by all has virtually disappeared. The structure of authority has been undermined: elders no longer are able to reinforce parental authority over children, having been undermined by the forces of the state and Western education, yet parents are often inexperienced in carrying out their responsibilities alone. Urban African families have been forced to reconstruct themselves almost from the ground up; and coming from a society in which family structures ensured that no one should experience uncertainty as to who they are or what was expected of them, many twentieth-century urban Africans found themselves in a society in which these certainties have been swept away. Yet today many exiled Africans resident in the diaspora remain connected to and support rural family members in the continent's villages through cash remittances.

REFORM AND REVOLUTION: WOMEN AND FAMILY IN THE ISLAMIC WORLD AND CHINA

Reformist Islamic scholars as early as the turn of the twentieth century began to debate the issues of women and family in the modern urban world. The Indian Muslim scholar Mawlana Ashraf Ali Thanawi (1864–1943) argued that women should be expected to have all the Islamic knowledge that would enable them to establish Islamic rule inside their households. The struggle between secular state power and religious authority has made Muslim women's destinies the object of conflict. Although seen by some as the symbol of oppression, the veil also has become for other women the symbol of cultural authenticity that has permitted a new generation's movement into the changing public space of modernity – institutions of higher education, for example.

In Islamic countries the Muslim family became a focal point of conflict relating to social reform, especially in the second half of the twentieth century. Except in the most conservative Islamic countries, those known as Islamic republics, there has been some effort to establish monogamy, to liberate the women – one-tenth of the world's population – from restrictive practices of dress and custom, such as whether they should go covered or uncovered by veils, and to allow children increasing independence. This transformation of tradition is especially true in urban areas of countries such as Egypt or Turkey in which there has been the greatest interaction with the West. But even more conservative countries, such as Saudi Arabia or Afghanistan, have experienced some weakening of the traditional family system, at least in cities and before the rise of Islamic fundamentalist movements.

In China the traditional family and its institutions came under attack in the early part of the twentieth century during the May 4th Movement (1919) and became a major target following the establishment of a Communist regime in 1949 (see Chapter 7). Chinese women, Mao had written in 1927, were dominated by four thick ropes: those of political, clan, religious, and male domination. In the People's Republic of China, customary family practices such as arranged marriages, concubinage, and the selling of daughters have been replaced by emphasis on marriage as a matter of personal choice and responsibility and by government efforts to regulate and control family size. Confucian emphasis on respect for elders and family as the foundation of society were initially rejected by the regime as obstacles to Communist ideals of an egalitarian society, and collective ownership of land and enterprises replaced family ownership. Mao had accurately recognized that women's participation in labor would be a devastating blow to the feudal-patriarchal ideology.

The radical collectivization of the mid-1950s emphasized suprafamily units, such as the work team, production brigade, or large-scale agricultural collectives known as communes. More recently, especially in urban areas, the policy of limiting couples to having one child has produced a new phenomenon: the "little emperor" or "little empress," a term coined to describe an only child whose parents spare no cost to feed, dress, and educate their precious single offspring. In China, as in many other Asian societies, male children are preferred and fetal scanning, abortion, and female infanticide are practices that provide testimony to the persistence of sex-based discrimination despite major social and economic gains made by women.

FERTILITY AND FAMILY: THE DEMOGRAPHIC TRANSITION, 1750–2000

Beginning in the mid-eighteenth century, a worldwide demographic transition began to take place, a shift from conditions of slow growth through high fertility and high mortality to slow growth through low fertility and low mortality. It was not a smooth transition, but rather a long-term product of cyclical swings and regional variation. As advances in medical technology improved life expectancy for much of the world's population and therefore contributed to population expansion, other innovations made it possible to control the birth rate, both altering family size and changing the status of women by providing artificial means to plan births. Following the development of special material heating techniques (1839), a flexible rubber was commonly used for contraceptive devices such as the condom. The first major wave of fertility decline took place between the late nineteenth and early twentieth centuries, roughly from the 1880s to the 1930s. Precisely why this took place is not well understood. The availability of improved birth control devices may have provided the means, but understanding why large numbers of couples decided to limit the number of children they had needs to consider the historical conditions of industrialization and urbanization. Under twentieth-century urban conditions, children became economic liabilities rather than assets, because child labor laws and compulsory education postponed their economic contribution and lengthened their period of dependency.

The idea that the size of the family could be a matter of conscious planning and control emerged during the last quarter of the nineteenth century and spread rapidly in the twentieth. The work of nineteenth-century pioneers in family planning and birth control, such as the Dutch physician, Dr Aletta Jacobs, or Mrs Annie Besant in England, was developed in the twentieth century by the efforts of Dr Marie Stopes in Britain and Margaret Sanger (1883–1966), a public health nurse who was imprisoned during her fight for birth control, in the United States. The general downward spiral of the birth rate during the early twentieth century was attributed to the legalization of contraception and its widespread acceptance by the female population. According to Sanger:

> Today, however, woman is rising in fundamental revolt . . . Millions of women are asserting their right to voluntary motherhood. They are determined to decide for themselves whether they shall become mothers, under what conditions and when. This is the fundamental revolt referred to. It is for woman the key to the temple of liberty.
> (Margaret Sanger, *Woman and the New Race*, New York: Brentano's, 1920, p. 5; quoted in Helga Harrison, *Women in the Western Heritage*, Guilford, Conn.: Dushkin, 1995, p. 51)

Family reformers wanted to limit the family to the number of children it was able to support. Some were motivated by the belief that women should have reproductive choice and should not be subject to continuous or undesired childbearing. But states often resisted fertility decline by promoting childbearing as a national, patriotic duty (see Chapter 7). In both Nazi Germany and Stalinist Russia, for example, mothers were celebrated and rewarded for producing young citizens.

As the twentieth century progressed, emphasis shifted from the prevention of unwanted pregnancies to comprehensive family planning. The Birth Control League (founded in 1914) was replaced by Planned Parenthood, whose objective went beyond birth control to helping families have the number of healthy children they felt they could take care of. Clinics offered help in overcoming sterility as well as in using effective means of contraception. Oral contraceptives were introduced in 1954, followed 25 years later by the development of a method in which a set of small tubes implanted under a woman's skin was designed to release a hormone that prevented contraception for a period of five years. A second wave of fertility decline occurred in the last quarter of the twentieth century, from about 1975 to 2000. This wave was often pushed by states, which encouraged or even mandated population control. The best-known example of this is the notoriously draconian "one-child" policy carried out in China beginning in the 1970s, which was successful in halting China's population growth but also led to a skewed gender ratio because of the continued desirability of sons. Cultural traditions die hard, and the age-old preference for male heirs meant that many people did everything possible to ensure that the one child they could have was a male, including female infanticide and late-term abortion of female fetuses. By the end of the twentieth century, abandoned female infants in China had become transnational children through adoption to childless couples in the United States and elsewhere.

CONCLUSIONS

In many ways as industrialization and urbanization have spread throughout the world, families everywhere have been subjected to similar influences and processes of change. One important sign of this is the 40 percent decline in the fertility rate in the less-developed world by the last quarter of the twentieth century, contributing to the dip in worldwide human fertility from 4.9 to 2.7. Yet great diversity remains among families

Figure 5.6 Contemporary Chinese family. The one-child policy was only one influence on smaller family size. As more people lived in crowded urban settings, away from extended family networks of support, and as more women worked outside the home, couples tended to have fewer children.

and households across the globe, testifying to the resilience of cultural traditions in the face of economic, social, and political transformations associated with globalization. The assumption that, under the impact of industrialization and urbanization, families every-where would eventually become exactly alike is no longer tenable.

World historians, like all historians, look for change over time and often lose sight of continuities. Studies of family and household once supported a view of extended, multigenerational families as characteristic of preindustrial societies, gradually shifting to the nuclear or conjugal family unit as industrial workplaces and urban homes replaced farms and rural villages. It is now widely recognized that the conjugal unit can be found as a core constituent in many widely differing historical

and cultural settings. Similarly, childhood was once believed to be a modern development, a product of changing conditions that made children more valuable. High fertility and high mortality rates, it was argued, made the viability of infants fragile, and so parents did not invest very much emotionally or otherwise in young children. Once again, this notion has been undermined by much evidence that parents through-out history have mourned the deaths of their children, and that there was not a profound transformation in parent–child relations at a certain point in time. In short, the family may be a realm that displays relatively significant continuities over time and even across cultures, far more resistant to pressures from outside than we have tended to think.

From the efforts to promote childbearing by the Roman emperor Augustus to the Chinese govern-ment's "one-child" policy, states have sought to control the intimate domain of sexuality and reproduction at the core of family life. Both political and religious authorities such as the medieval Christian Church or the Islamic *shari'a* have defined and regulated the institution of marriage, viewing it as the bond between man and woman that provides the basis for family, the essential unit of social reproduction and economic production. Marriage remains in the contemporary world a realm of contention, as different models of marriage reflect changing views of sexuality and reproduction. Technology has made it possible not only to limit conception but also to expand it to couples who desire children but cannot conceive them. What remains a constant is the vital role of human agency in determining family and household. Individual decisions – whether, when, and how to marry, whether to have children or not and how many – made in the intimacy of private life, combined with changing historical conditions, have contributed to dramatic transformations in world history.

SELECTED REFERENCES

Burguière, André, Christiane Klapisch-Zuber, Martine Segalen, and Françoise Zonabend, eds (1996 (original French edition 1986)) *A History of the Family*, Vols. 1 and 2, Cambridge, Mass.: The Belknap Press of Harvard University Press. A collection of international scholarship on the family across the globe, with limited treatment of non-European societies.

Goitein, S. D. (1978) *A Mediterranean Society: The Jewish Communities of the Arab World as Portrayed in the Documents of the Cairo Geniza*, Vol. III: *The Family*, Berkeley, Los Angeles, London: University of California Press. A portrait of marriage and family life among Jewish, Christian, and Muslim families in medieval Cairo based on letters and other documents recovered from the Cairo *geniza*, a repository of discarded pages of writing.

Gutiérrez, Ramón A. (1991) *When Jesus Came, the Corn Mothers Went Away: Marriage, Sexuality, and Power in New Mexico, 1500–1846*, Stanford, Calif.: Stanford University Press. A path-breaking study of the Spanish colonial American empire and the Pueblo Indians as a dialogue between two cultures through the lens of marriage and sexuality practices.

Hartman, Mary S. (2004) *The Household and the Making of History: A Subversive View of the Western Past*, Cambridge: Cambridge University Press. The author argues that a unique late-marriage pattern identifiable in European society from as early as the Middle Ages lies at the root of changes that usher in the modern world after about 1500.

Kertzer, David I. and Marzio Barbagli, eds (2001) *Family Life in Early Modern Times, 1500–1789*, Vol. I: *The History of the European Family*, New Haven, Conn. and London: Yale University Press. A collection and synthesis of recent scholarship on the European family, including studies of demography, religion, material life, marriage, and childhood.

Lynch, Katherine A. (2003) *Individuals, Families, and Communities in Europe, 1200–1500: The Urban Foundations of Western Society*, Cambridge Studies in Population, Economy, and Society in Past Time 37, Cambridge: Cambridge University Press. Integration of the history of the family with the history of public life, seeing the family at the center of "civil society," and emphasizing the relationship between kinship and larger voluntary, collective organizations in European urban society.

Meriwether, Margaret L. (1999) *The Kin Who Count: Family and Society in Ottoman Aleppo, 1770–1840*, Austin: University of Texas. A study of one part of the later Ottoman empire, focusing on three aspects of family life: household, marriage, and inheritance.

Rapoport, Yossef (2005) *Marriage, Money, and Divorce in Medieval Islamic Society*, Cambridge: Cambridge University Press. A richly detailed and documented study of the economic, legal, and social causes of Muslim divorce in Cairo, Damascus, and Jerusalem in the Mamluk period (1250–1517).

Sonbol, Amira El Azhary, ed. (1998) *Women, the Family, and Divorce Laws in Islamic History*, Syracuse, N.Y.: Syracuse University Press. A collection of recent scholarship on marriage, divorce and family in Islamic societies.

Therborn, Göran (2004) *Between Sex and Power: Family in the Modern World, 1900–2000*, London and New York: Routledge. A sociologist's attempt to explain global transformations of the family in the modern world through interlocking historical shifts in patriarchy, marriage, and fertility.

Thornton, Arland (2005) *Reading History Sideways: The Fallacy and Enduring Impact of the Developmental Paradigm on Family Life*, Chicago, Ill. and London: University of Chicago Press. A provocative argument critiquing what the author calls the "developmental paradigm": seeing the institution of the family in Europe progressing from a traditional to a modern form through a linear series of stages.

ONLINE RESOURCES

Annenberg/CPB Bridging World History (2004) <http://www.learner.org/channel/courses/world history/>. Multimedia project with interactive website and videos on demand; see especially Unit 13 Family and Household.

Women in World History <http://chnm.gmu.edu/wwh/>. A project of the Center for History and New Media at George Mason University, this website provides a wide range of resources on women in world history.

CHAPTER 6

Making a living

World economies, past and present

Maps of Africa before 1500 invariably included an image of the king of Mali seated on his throne, holding a gold nugget nearly the size of his head. It was the fourteenth-century Malian ruler and his entourage, who had given away so much gold while on *hajj* (pilgrimage) to Mecca that the price of gold on the Cairo market had collapsed shortly thereafter. Egyptian chroniclers wrote about the event in the next century, and the traveler Ibn Battuta described the West African ruler around 1350: "[The sultan] has a lofty pavilion, of which the door is inside his house, where he sits for most of the time." His image of the gold-turbaned sultan under a silken dome stands in stark contrast to the vivid description of the desert caravans that actually carried goods such as highly prized salt and copper in exchange for gold. Ibn Battuta writes of the merchants of Sijilmasa that "they load their camels at late dawn, and march until the sun has risen, its light has become bright in the air, and the heat on the ground has become severe. . . . When the sun begins to decline and sink in the west, they set off [again]." Twenty-five days later, the caravans would reach Taghaza, a major salt-mining area. Describing the enormous amounts of gold traded in the grim and perilous mining town, Ibn Battuta says, "This is a village with nothing good about it. It is the most fly-ridden of places" (Ross E. Dunn, *The Adventures of Ibn Battuta: A Muslim Traveler of the 14th Century*, Los Angeles: University of California Press, 1989, pp. 302, 296–7).

Although they relied on what was produced and traded in their realms and beyond, gold-bedecked rulers like the king of Mali had little concern for – and probably little direct knowledge of – those who slaved in mines, labored in fields, or traveled near and far, providing goods to support their lavish way of life. But whether king or farmer, merchant or miner, each held a place in the economic order of their societies and each

was dependent on the smooth functioning of that economic order to secure food, shelter, and clothing. In this chapter we focus on the basic and universal question of how people made a living in the past. How did they gain access to what they needed to survive, and even prosper? How did societies create systems of exchange based on differing concepts of value? What was considered valuable: land, labor, commodities (gold, salt)? And finally, how did economic systems interact through trade, and how were economies knit together into regional and eventually global economic systems?

INTRODUCTION

After the spread of agriculture throughout much of the world, many people settled in villages and became farmers. The concentration of population in larger settlements led to the development of cities, which became dependent on food supplied by farmers in rural areas surrounding urban sites (see Chapter 3). Others, however, did not adopt a sedentary way of life in either cities or their hinterlands and continued to live as nomads, following animal herds as they moved across steppes, grasslands, and tundra. Pastoral peoples also often fished and hunted, and frequently combined horticulture – and even agriculture – with herding. Both pastoralism and agriculture were practiced in common and diverse ways shaped by the environments people inhabited and by the technologies they employed.

By the early first millennium CE, a regular pattern of relationships developed in many parts of the world between nomadic pastoral economies and sedentary agrarian ones. Across the frontiers that divided these two different ways of life, trading relationships and warfare were both common. Dwelling in the steppes of Mongolia during the early second millennium CE, the Mongols had a pastoral economy based on sheep, goats, and yaks for sustenance (food, clothing, and shelter), camels for trade-related transportation, and horses for hunting, herding, communication, and warfare. Because their economy was subject to the vagaries of drought and cold, as well as other potentially devastating problems such as animal diseases, the Mongols were dependent on trade in grain, textiles, tea, and other goods with their sedentary agricultural neighbors, particularly the Chinese. The Chinese likewise had need of goods from their nomadic neighbors, especially horses. The trade relations between the neighboring states periodically disintegrated into warfare, with Chinese raids on Mongol camps or Mongol raids on Chinese communities.

The success of the Mongols in their expansion across Eurasia in the thirteenth century relied heavily on the adaptation of the traditional technology of horse-breeding to the environment. Mongol horsebreeders had preserved an early form of domesticated horse, with a stocky body and thick, coarse mane that helped it to survive in the extremely cold and dry temperatures of Mongolia. When the Mongols created their empire, they became nomadic rulers of largely agrarian peoples, and exacted tribute from or taxed the population of conquered states (see Chapter 7). By unifying Eurasia, the Mongol conquest also facilitated trade along the Silk Road and connected caravan routes. As Janet Abu-Lughod has argued, Mongol domination of Eurasia helped to bring about a "thirteenth-century world system," a network of trading ties that extended across the Eurasian continent and linked the economic, political, social, and cultural lives of peoples in places as distant from each other as Hangzhou and Venice or Cairo and Palembang.

The Mongol empire illustrates key aspects of economic life considered in this chapter: the role of environment and technology in shaping economic systems (agriculture, pastoralism); the control and distribution of material resources by rulers and states through tribute and taxation systems; the role of trade in connecting different economies, as well as in exchanging goods within economies. Although beyond the realm of the Mongol empire, other parts of Asia, Africa, and the Americas experienced their own

varieties of agriculture, pastoralism, and trade, and the rise and decline of regional economies. Vast and powerful as the Mongol empire was, it extended across Eurasia, not the globe. It was Europeans who took the lead in this enterprise, linking together economies of Africa, the Americas, and Asia and ushering in a new age of globalization.

Competition among emerging European nation-states in the late fifteenth and early sixteenth centuries inspired the voyages of exploration that led to the shift of world trade and wealth, eventually to the Atlantic Ocean. Advances in maritime and commercial technology in Europe were essential to the development of capitalism and the expansion of Europe. By 1500, Europe was poised to reap, accumulate, and invest the profits of the developing capitalist economy of the new Atlantic frontier as the vital periphery to the expansion of the European core economy.

Between about 1500 and 1800, following Columbus's voyages, the economic relationships and societies of the Americas, Europe, parts of Africa, Asia, and the Pacific were transformed through the creation of an Atlantic world economy that provided the means for subsequent European expansion into Asia and the Pacific. Establishment of Atlantic connections had a profound impact on the lives and cultures of African peoples, particularly those of West and Central Africa, as well as those of the Americas. The new global connections upset the balance of the long-established relations among Asia, Africa, and Europe, replacing and redirecting their world systems of land-based and maritime, inter- and intra-regional commerce.

By 1800 capitalism and industrialism profoundly altered the economic lives of people in Europe and the Americas by transforming the ways they earned their livelihoods and the communities in which they lived. Changes in the mode of production from rural agriculture and handicraft industries, embedded in community life and shaped by personal relationships, to the Industrial Revolution's relatively impersonal and urbanized factory system had a dramatic effect on individual and family life. Through imperialism these transformations were extended across the globe, creating dramatic imbalances between European economies and the colonial economies controlled by Europeans. By the twentieth and twenty-first centuries, these imbalances had shifted, though they did not disappear, and a new era of globalization brought its own uneven development.

COWRIES, COINS, AND COMMERCE

Although globalization is a relatively recent phenomenon, the development of exchange networks is as old as human behavior itself. We know that between 1.9 and 1.6 million years ago hominids carried prized stones from their quarry sites to distant places, where they were shaped into useful tools. Evidence of trade in stone tools and specialized trade in amber and obsidian hint at the extent of early commercial interactions between cultures and regions. Prehistoric exchange networks in ores were among the first long distance trade routes. Tin was valued from the Mediterranean to Southeast Asia, and it has been speculated that the tin originated in Central Asian mines, suggesting an extensive exchange network.

Trade in precious metals and stones indicates extensive commercial contacts dealing in highly valued commodities. Although most early trade was carried out through the bartering of one good for another, there is evidence for the use of money, the earliest forms of which were materials that were rare, portable, and nearly impossible to counterfeit. Cowry shells fit this description. Cowry shells were a common form of currency in the Afro-Eurasian world from very early times until as late as 1800 CE. Cowry shells, actually several species including the *Cypraea moneta*, mined from the sea near the Maldives, and with a limited distribution, were used in China for commercial purposes as early as the seventh century BCE and even earlier as a sign of wealth. The tomb of one of the consorts of a king who lived around 1200 BCE contains over 7,000 cowries. Even after the development of metal currencies, cowries continued to be used in some places. As late as the eighth-century CE, Arab gold traders in the western Sudan and ancient Ghana found that African merchants demanded cowries in payment. A cowry-based system of exchange prevailed in southwestern China's Yunnan region from the ninth through the seventeenth centuries.

Other kinds of shell currencies were also used elsewhere, even into more recent times, such as the *quiripa* (string of shells) used in the Orinoco basin of South America as late as the eighteenth century. In North America, *wampum* (derived from an Algonquian word *wampumpeag*, meaning "white strings [of beads]") was used to refer to many pre-Columbian currency systems. In Papua New Guinea snail shells were collected and strung in specific lengths that corresponded to monetary values, and the *kina* (as the shell currency was known) is still used to refer to paper bank notes.

The first known coins were minted in the Anatolian kingdom of Lydia in the mid-seventh century BCE. Not long after that, rulers of kingdoms in China cast their own bronze coinage in the shapes of shovels, knives, and shells. Both the metal itself and the symbolic objects into which it was cast contributed to the coinage's economic value, since iron tools were important in agriculture and shells had been in use as a form of currency. Like iron, other metals in relatively scarce supply, such as lead, tin, copper, or bronze (an alloy of tin, copper, and lead), were made into coins, along with the even rarer gold and silver. Copper currency was used in sub-Saharan Africa, where it was traded for gold at least as early as 950 CE. But for Africa, copper was the "red gold," a scarce metal that was highly prized locally. To those outside the continent, West Africa was known by the Arabic name *bilad al-tibr* ("land of gold"), and its gold provided the main source for the Mediterranean world during medieval times.

By assuming monopolies over both the mining and the production of valuable metals and by establishing the weight, degree of adulteration, and value of metal coins, large and small states throughout the world began to mint and control currency. Some state currencies quickly became accepted as units of exchange thousands of miles distant from their origins. From the sixth through the twelfth centuries, the Byzantine gold coin, the *bezant*, was widely used throughout the Mediterranean as a medium of exchange. Following the Arab conquests of the seventh and eighth centuries that gave them access to rich sources of gold in Africa, the Arabic *dinar* was used in international trade throughout Afro-Eurasia. Eventually, however, both the *bezant* and the *dinar* declined in purity and weight and were replaced by gold coins of the Italian merchant city-states of Florence (the *florin* in 1252) and Venice (the *ducat* in 1284). It was the *ducat* that became the first true

BOX 6.1 TANG COIN

Round metal coins with a square hole in the center were minted by the earliest Chinese imperial government, the Qin (221 BCE–210 BCE), and this practice continued under subsequent dynasties. Coins were strung together through the square holes to make a unit of currency called a "string of cash" ("cash" is the translation of the generic term for money). This coin, like others of its kind, is made of bronze (an alloy of copper, tin, and lead) and stamped with a reign period that falls within the Tang dynasty (618–907), when China's power in East Asia was at its height.

Coins from many places and times are the bearers of rich historical information, so much so that a whole sub-field, numismatics, is devoted to the study of coins. Coins stamped with images of rulers, phrases, or designs reveal many different things to historians, and the metals from which the coins were made can also tell us about trade in metals by tracing the location of sources and connecting them with the sites of foundries that cast coins. The distribution of coins themselves can also yield information about cross-regional trading patterns. Tang coins, for example, have been found in sites from the Arabian coast to Southeast Asia and Japan, indicating the extent of commercial exchanges.

Like all governments, the Chinese imperial government had difficulty regulating the currency, because the value of the coins minted was relative to the metals used. During the Tang period, especially after the mid-eighth century when a devastating rebellion led to the closing of many copper mines, the number of coins minted fell precipitously. At the same time, the high percentage of copper (83 percent) in the coins meant that the value of the metal in the coin was greater than the value of the coin itself, and so people began to melt the coins to use the copper for other purposes, such as making tools and even Buddhist statues. The following dynasty, the Song (960–1279) tried to establish a standard currency from the varied kinds of coinage (including

copper, iron, and lead coins) in use throughout the empire. The unit of currency was the string, 1,000 coins per string, but in practice a string might contain only 700 or 800 coins. The Song government minted many times more coins than its predecessor, but it remained plagued by inability to control and regulate the currency. Even though the Song government drastically reduced the amount of copper in its coinage (to 46 percent), people still melted down coins for their copper value. To make matters worse, it was profitable to export copper, especially to Japan, which further reduced availability of this metal and increased its value domestically.

In time, these difficulties led to the creation of the world's first paper money. Some of the first paper money was known as "flying cash," elegantly describing the virtue of this currency as a speedy and light means for merchants to do business. The fullest development of paper currency took place in the Mongol Yuan (1279–1368) dynasty. The paper money was backed by silver and gold deposits as well as silk. Weights of silver, known as "ingots," were used as a standard of value in China for many centuries in addition to coins and paper money. When global connections made it possible in the sixteenth century, Ming China (1368–1644) became what some economic historians have called the world's "silver sink," drawing in huge amounts of silver mined in the Americas and transported across the Pacific in Manila galleons.

international coinage, maintaining its purity and thus its dominance for over 500 years.

OVER LAND AND SEA: SHIPS OF THE DESERT AND OCEAN

The desire for exchange drove the development of currencies, but exchange over long distances was made possible by merchants willing to take risks and by efficient transportation technologies. From very early times, by both land and sea, merchants moved luxury goods and bulk commodities between towns, regions, and continents, delaying or changing their shipments according to shifting markets, wars, rumors, and weather. Driven by hopes of profit, they sought out trade items that might increase their wealth. Luxury goods such as silk and everyday commodities such as salt, were commonly traded in both regional and international commerce by interlocking overland and maritime routes. Merchants who took risks on trade and grew wealthy or became impoverished were not alone in their commercial ventures. Rulers also tied their fortunes to trade. They increased their power and expanded their states by knitting together agricultural hinterlands with strategically located commercial centers and maritime ports, and by taking advantage of shifting international trade routes.

From the first century CE, people, goods, and ideas moved over several well-known and long-established routes: the Indian Ocean route by sea and the Central Asian Silk Road by land, as well as the two established African connections, the trans-Saharan roads and the East African coastal system. Africa, at the far western end of the Silk Road and Indian Ocean routes, in addition to participating in the east–west exchange, provided a south–north connection that added another dimension to established global commercial and cultural interaction. Across the huge continent, main highways were developed to link the inter-African markets and to connect them with Asia and Europe.

There were two major historical frontiers of global interconnection in Africa: the Red Sea and Indian Ocean frontier of East Africa, and West Africa's Sahara frontier. Although the commerce of the Red Sea–Indian Ocean frontier was maritime and that of the Sahara frontier was land-based, both seemed to border on oceans: the Sahara, a formidable desert some 3 million square miles in area, may be considered an ocean of sand. The Arabic word *sahel* translates as "coastline," and in the Sahel region that borders the desert's southern edge were situated many "ports" of entry. Like the oceans of the East African frontier, the desert sands were not a barrier but rather a space to be regularly traversed, which Africans did along well-established trade routes beginning at least as early as the second century.

Between 100 and 500 CE, the camel, the "ship of the desert," was introduced to the Sahara from West Asia via Egypt. The use of the camel was an innovation in African overland trade equivalent to improvements in maritime technology elsewhere. The camel led to faster, more frequent, and more regular commerce. Bred in different sizes and shapes for different terrains, the standard one-hump camel could carry loads of up to 250 kilograms (550 pounds) while traveling more than a week without water. The camel was used in overland caravans in both Africa and Asia.

SILK ROADS AND CENTRAL ASIAN CARAVAN ROUTES

For a thousand years before the Mongol conquest of Eurasia in the early thirteenth century (see Chapter 7), one of the most important east–west interconnections was the Silk Road across Central Asia, created between the second century BCE and the second century CE. By the first century CE, large and wealthy market zones lay at the eastern and western ends of Asia: Han China to the east and, to the west, the Parthian empire in Persia with its connections to the Roman empire in Europe. Routes through Central Asia linked trade between these markets, but there was little guaranteed security to reassure cautious merchants.

Before the Silk Road, goods moved sporadically and in small quantities. For 1500 years following its establishment, the Silk Road provided the main land connection over which people, technology, trade, and ideas moved between East and West Asia, Europe, and North Africa. As West Asian merchants and Roman soldiers reached eastward and Chinese merchants and Han armies stretched westward, Central Asian oasis states thrived along this caravan route. Gold was one of the most important items of trade, but spices, silks, and other luxury items were also traded.

Situated at the crossroads between an east–west lateral route and a north–south highway between India and Russia, Samarkand was one of the most ancient cities of Central Asia and played a major role in the caravan trade that traversed this region for more than a thousand years. Samarkand was ruled successively by Turks, Arabs, and Persians and was conquered again by the Mongols in 1220. An account of Samarkand written shortly after this portrays a garden-filled city surrounded by three concentric walls: an outer wall with twelve wooden gates, enclosing a second wall around the city itself, and an inner walled area that enclosed the main mosque and the walled citadel containing the ruler's palace. Samarkand and other oasis cities, such as Bukhara, Tabriz, or Turfan to the northwest of China, were essential to the caravan trade across Central Asia that connected China to West Asia and Europe. They provided necessary stopping places for water and provisions for the great caravans that traversed the deserts and steppes of Central Asia.

TRANS-SAHARAN CARAVANS AND COMMERCE

The trans-Saharan gold trade predated the North African expansion of Islam in the seventh century CE. More than seven centuries later, gold was still being loaded and carried on the backs of camels along the centuries-old routes that crossed the great desert. Once the camel and wheeled vehicles were adopted along the trans-Saharan caravan routes in Roman times, the patterns of commercial growth remained technologically stable until the introduction of firearms and horseback cavalries in the sixteenth century. The desert routes rarely changed course since they relied on the navigational abilities of African merchant families familiar with the location of oases. The incorporation of early trade routes into the larger Islamic world commercial network occurred gradually and mostly peacefully as Muslim merchant-clerics traveled afar engaged in trade and pilgrimage. There is no doubt that the increasing Islamization of West African societies furthered their participation in the land-based commercial world that stretched from the Atlantic to the Indian Ocean and beyond.

As essential as the trans-Saharan caravans were in the trading system of North and West Africa, caravans organized for the profit of North African merchants were only temporary associations of firms that happened to be bringing goods across the desert at the same time. Individual firms, not the caravans themselves, were the organizational core of the trans-Saharan caravan trade and these firms were joined together in the caravan enterprise by both formal and informal bonds. Islamic law provided the basis for drawing up written agreements of partnership in trading ventures or credit advances between independent merchants.

The trading city of Begho on the edge of the West African forest was strategically situated as an entrepôt for the Akan goldfields, shipping gold north to the Mande world and beyond through the trans-Saharan caravan routes interconnecting the Mediterranean and Islamic worlds. At its height (thirteenth–sixteenth centuries), Begho probably included some 15,000 people, including merchants from a vast number of cultural regions. Different language groups resided in distinct quarters of the town. Artisans lived and worked in a separate quarter, where they cast brass and bronze in crucibles, worked iron, steel, and ivory, and wove and dyed cotton cloth prized as far away as the Atlantic coast.

At Begho and other gold-trading cities, clay and brass weights in varying shapes and sizes were used by merchants to weigh gold, these being placed on counterbalance scales to weigh gold dust and nuggets. These weights conformed to an Islamic ounce system used in North Africa and across the western Sudan as early as the ninth century. The heaviest of the Islamic standards, the ounce of 31.5 grams, became known as the troy ounce in Europe. Gold traders traveled under the charge of a chief trader, and often in large groups as a protection against thieves.

Journeys across the Sahara were filled with danger, as the bones and debris of lost caravans show; they could last for months, and oases could be as far as ten days apart. Even once tolls and duties were paid to local authorities to ensure safe passage, caravans were under constant danger of attack by thieves and bandits. Shifting dunes and blowing sands could confound even experienced guides. The hazards were great, but so were the potential fortunes to be made. Reliable estimates of Akan gold production, a major source of Saharan trade, suggest that during the 1400s, 5,000 to 22,000 ounces of gold were produced each year. This enormous wealth was supplemented by fortunes to be made in the trading of brass vessels, kola nuts (chewed as a

stimulant), and salt mined in the Sahara. In addition, the Saharan commercial network served as a conduit for the transfer of technology and ideas. The great Saharan ports of Sijilmasa, Timbuktu, Gao, and others were the entry points for a lively exchange of peoples and cultures. Through these ports passed traders and travelers from Genoa, Venice, Ghana, Cairo, Morocco, and beyond.

In the centuries before 1500, trans-Saharan trade with Europe is documented by the regular appearance in European markets of such items as "Moroccan" leather, a product actually manufactured in the Sudanic region of present-day Nigeria. For centuries, no African goods captured the attention of world trade so much as West African gold. Like Siberian gold, that of Africa supported many contemporary European currencies. It was the rumor of gold, as well as other wealth on the African continent, that inspired the Portuguese and later European sea voyages that were to change the established global connections and significantly affect the global balance.

THE INDIAN OCEAN

The maritime routes of the Indian Ocean were established even earlier than the overland Eurasian Silk Roads and the trans-Saharan caravan routes in Africa, and were the primary competitor of these overland networks in east–west world trade. Sea routes were less subject to breakdowns of security and political disruptions than the overland routes were and consistently carried larger quantities of goods and people. Long-distance maritime trade in the western Indian Ocean existed from the third millennium BCE, and by the first century CE the number of ports had significantly expanded.

Shipping linked East Africa and Southwest Asia with India, Southeast Asia, and China. The earliest connections were made by ships that moved slowly, hugging the great northern loop of coastline between East and West. Early in the first century CE, at both the eastern and western ends of this long, complex route, market conditions and political circumstances forced a change in the pattern of coastal trade: the Indian Ocean route became a maritime highway spanning the ocean between eastern and western ports. Southeast

Asian ports served as a conduit for Chinese trade with Arab and African traders who sailed the Indian Ocean. Arabian frankincense, one of the main ingredients in incense used in religious ceremonies and also in many medicines, and African ivory, along with Southeast Asian spices, were among the staples of Indian Ocean trade destined for Chinese markets that passed through the ports of Southeast Asia. Chinese products in demand by its trading partners included silk, tea, and manufactured goods such as ceramics.

There were three interlocking circuits of trade in the Indian Ocean: the Arabian Sea, the Indian Ocean, and the South China Sea. The first was dominated by Muslims, the second included Muslim merchants from East Africa and Hindus from South and Southeast Asia, and the third was dominated by Chinese. No single state, culture, or ethnic group dominated Indian Ocean trade as a whole; rather, it was a multiethnic world where Arab merchants resided in Chinese ports, East African merchants in Indian ports, and Indian merchants in East African and Chinese ports. Goods and ideas were both exchanged in these encounters among merchants, and the monsoon winds determined when trade took place and how it was configured.

"LANDS BELOW THE WINDS": SOUTHEAST ASIA

The region we now know as Southeast Asia was shaped by the burgeoning east–west long-distance maritime trade through the Indian Ocean and beyond. Watered by the monsoons, heavy rains brought by winds that also moved sailing ships over the seas with great seasonal regularity, Southeast Asia was known to its inhabitants – and to outsiders who plied the waters of the Indian Ocean for trade – as the "Lands below the Winds." Both mainland and island Southeast Asia were dependent on the oceanborne trade carried by the monsoon winds, and certain port cities, such as Malacca on the tip of the Malaysian peninsula, existed solely as a result of maritime commerce in the Indian Ocean.

By the end of the first century CE, the area of present-day Vietnam, Cambodia, Thailand, and Burma, the great river plains of mainland Southeast Asia, was divided among a number of regional polities. Made fertile by the silts of regular and relatively gentle monsoon flooding, these plains were very productive for rain-fed and increasingly irrigated rice farming. They were, moreover, quite large and capable of supporting sizable and concentrated populations. The plains were also easy to dominate politically, in contrast to mountainous regions, where communication and transportation were more difficult. Sometime around 50 CE, what later Chinese sources would describe as the "Kingdom of Funan" emerged on the lower Mekong delta and along the coastline of Thailand to the west.

Early Funan was composed of a number of communities, each with its own ruler, linked loosely together by a common culture and by a shared economic pattern of rice farming supplemented with participation in the regional coastal trade. Funan's population was made up primarily of farming people in the hinterland and maritime traders in the coastal towns, who were economically interdependent. Surplus rice production found a ready market at the ports, where ships passing along the coast supplied themselves. Ship traders in turn had no difficulty paying for the rice and other agricultural products with goods brought from foreign ports. This nicely balanced exchange system, which may have been in place a hundred years or more previously, underwent a significant change between about 50 and 150. The change was brought about by external factors and reinforced internally by ambitious rulers, who transformed Funan into an empire. The catalyst for this transformation was a boom in the India–China maritime trade, which intensified the importance of exchange.

Funan, which began as a group of autonomous agricultural communities on the lower Mekong and Tonle Sap rivers, found that the growth of maritime shipping passing through the region brought enough profit through trade to support a larger population base. With an increased population, the leaders of Funan expanded their land's agricultural productivity by investing in more intensive irrigation, and they began to conquer neighboring communities. They also sought to monopolize the region's maritime trade by conquering rival coastal emporiums, or trading centers.

While Funan's origins lay in agriculture-based communities transformed into an empire by wealth and power that came from control of the international coastal trading networks, Srivijaya emerged from river-

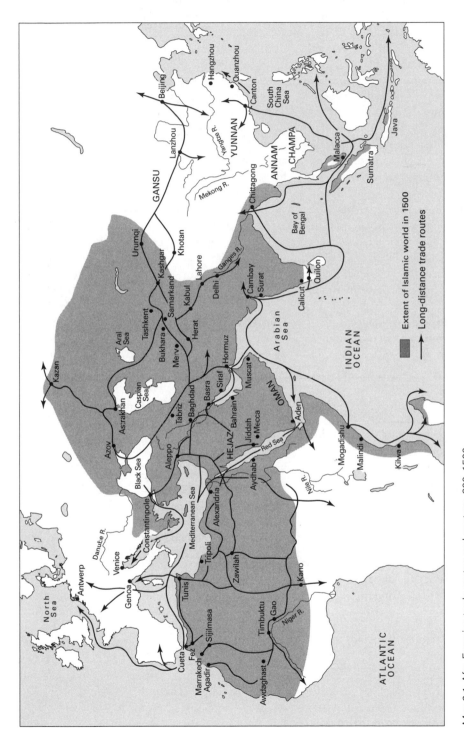

Map 6.1 Afro-Eurasian trade routes and centers, 600–1500.

Source: Francis Robinson, *Cambridge Illustrated History of the Islamic World* (Cambridge: Cambridge University Press, 1996), p. 126

based coastal trading communities that were joined together to form a maritime empire (see Chapter 7). By developing good relations with the agricultural hinterland in order to gain a dependable supply of commodities for trade, the founders of Srivijaya were able to support a larger maritime trade zone and thus to establish an empire that dominated the region from about 670 to 1025. Srivijaya's capital, Palembang, on the island of Sumatra in modern-day Indonesia, was strategically situated near the southern entrance of the Strait of Malacca. With its fleets and armies, it gradually established dominance of the coastlines and built a major coastal emporium on the southeast coast of Sumatra.

In Java during the declining years of Srivijaya, the east coast maritime trading region became unified under the government of Majapahit, a dynastic city-state and trading confederation. By the end of the thirteenth century, Majapahit had developed its own extensive and tightly controlled trade network with the Malay peninsula and islands to the north, including Sumatra, Borneo, Sulawesi, and the Moluccas.

From the thirteenth century on, Islamic influence grew steadily in the island world of Southeast Asia. The Muslim city-state of Malacca was founded in 1401. Malacca developed during the fifteenth century into a wealthy entrepôt (point of exchange or distribution), with a rapidly expanding volume of trade flowing through its strategically located port from north to south and south to north, through the narrow Strait of Malacca. Indian, Arab, and Persian traders set up their trading headquarters at Malacca, and the Malay language became the principal language of trade throughout Southeast Asia. Indian cotton was one of the main goods that passed through the port of Malacca, where it was traded for East Indian spices destined for the European market. By 1500, Malacca was the largest and most populous commercial emporium in the international trade world of Southeast Asia.

PORT CITIES, MERCHANTS, AND MARITIME TRADE

Across the Indian Ocean, East African city-states also grew as centers for the administration of maritime trade. Situated on islands off present-day Kenya and Tanzania on the East African coast, complex urban societies such as Kilwa, Pemba, Lamu, and Pate emerged (after the second century CE) from the background of early civilization on the African mainland. These coastal urban centers were the crucibles in which the Swahili language (based on a local Bantu linguistic core with Arab elements added) and culture emerged by around 1100 CE. The wealth and political importance of the Swahili were based on their control of the extensive Indian Ocean trading networks. Trading gold, ivory, slaves, iron, rare woods, and other goods obtained from the African hinterland for Chinese porcelains, Islamic glazed wares, glass vessels, and beads, wealthy sultans built luxurious entrepôts, commercial centers for importing and exporting, with collection and distribution functions.

Three key areas on the subcontinent engaged in Indian Ocean trade: the Gujarat peninsula, the Malabar coast on the west, and the Coromandel coast on the east. Ibn Battuta praised the beautiful architecture of the city of Cambay, the major port of Gujarat, constructed by foreign merchants, who made up the majority of its inhabitants. Gujarati merchants played an important role in international shipping and commerce and were prominent in East African port cities as well. Far south of Cambay, along the Malabar coast, the city of Calicut was a commercial complex where Gujarati and Jewish merchants engaged in trade. Calicut rose in the mid-thirteenth century, when Baghdad fell to the Mongols and the Persian Gulf was eclipsed in importance as a trade route when the Karimi of Cairo took over the spice trade from the Indian Ocean.

Karim (meaning "great") was an Arabic term used to distinguish large-scale wholesale merchants from petty entrepreneurs. Karimi merchants rose to prominence in Cairo during the late thirteenth and early fourteenth centuries, just as Cairo came into its prime in international trade. Although spices were the primary commodities traded by Karimi merchants, cloth, porcelain, precious stones, silk, and slaves (non-Muslims) were among other goods traded. Some Karimi merchants were bankers or shipowners. Like their counterparts in Italian city-states such as Venice and Genoa, Karimi merchants formed partnerships for one overseas venture at a time in which one partner put up two-thirds of the capital and the other contributed the remaining one-third, plus the labor to accompany the goods abroad. Profits were equally shared, once the transport and other costs of the venture were subtracted. This kind of partnership was known in Venice and Genoa as a *commenda* and was widely used by merchants there.

At the end of the eleventh century, the First Crusade had inaugurated a process of trade revival that reconnected European economies to those of Asia and Africa, with the result that Italian cities became commercial centers of long-distance trade. The effort to recapture the Holy Land proved a boon to trade, and Italian merchants reaped vast profits. Venice came into its own during the first four Crusades, vanquishing its rivals, such as Genoa, dominating the eastern Mediterranean, and reaping the riches of the trade routes between Constantinople and western Europe.

Situated at the head of the Adriatic Sea, Venice grew up on mudflat islands located in brackish lagoons between the mainland and the banks formed by the debris of a number of rivers, notably the Po, that emptied into the sea there. Though Venetians had to collect rain for drinking water, the sea served them in almost every other way. The sea was the major source of food, since land on the islets was scarce and most of it was unsuitable for agriculture. From early trade with the mainland in fish and salt to the virtual monopoly of east–west trade that Venice achieved by the thirteenth century, maritime commerce enriched Venetians and made Venice an important European power. As Venice was becoming wealthy and powerful on the bounty of Mediterranean trade and profits connected with the Crusades, how did people outside the setting of port cities dependent on trade make their livings?

MAKING A LIVING ON THE MANOR IN MEDIEVAL ENGLAND

Before about 1200, in both agricultural and pastoral economies across the globe, kinship relations defined the basic unit of production and consumption. In many parts of the world, households made up largely (though not exclusively) of individuals related by blood were organized into larger-scale units, as in the manorial economy of medieval England.

England in the late eleventh century was an agrarian society in which over 90 percent of the population made their living from the land. On Christmas Day, 1085, William the Conqueror, king of England, deliberated with his advisors about the people and the land of the kingdom he ruled. A contemporary chronicler recounts the outcome of these discussions:

> Then he sent his men over all England into every shire and had them find out how many hundred hides there were in the shire, or what land and cattle the king himself had in the country, or what dues he ought to have in twelve months from the shire. Also he had a record made of how much land his archbishops had, and his bishops and his abbots and his earls . . . what or how much everyone had who was occupying land in England, in land or cattle, and how much money it was worth.
>
> (Quoted in David Roffe, *Domesday: The Inquest and the Book*, Oxford: Oxford University Press, 2000, p. 1)

This survey was recorded in what later became known as the "Domesday Book," named for the Day of Judgment because of its unparalleled importance in the eyes of the inhabitants of England at the time. A precise and detailed account of wealth and property held by the king, his lords, the Church, and everyone else, the Domesday Book provides a snapshot of the distribution of wealth in England at one point in time. A rich portrait of economic life in late eleventh-century England can be drawn from the data recorded in its pages.

Fewer than 200 laymen and roughly a hundred major churches (including bishoprics, abbeys, and priories) together possessed about 75 percent of the assessed value of the entire country. Powerful lords rented out parcels of their estates to tenants who were often described as knights and thus belonged to the same social circles as the lord. Somewhere between a half and three-quarters of the estate was kept "in demesne" to provision the lord directly with the needs of his personal household with food and income. Most demesnes were leased for money rent, and the lessees constituted a landowning middle class, a gentry. But by far the largest number of people were either villeins, who held or rented some amount of land, or serfs, who were bound to the soil and labored at the behest of the landlord.

Fields under cultivation were divided into long, narrow strips, which were divided among the various claimants to land rights: the landlord, knight tenants, villeins, and serfs. To maintain tenure of even the modest strips assigned to them, serfs owed more than labor service to the landlord. Along with customary dues and rents, they were obliged to give a percentage of all they harvested to the lord, a tithe to the manor or village priest, and perhaps a share to the steward who oversaw and managed the lands of the estate. There were also extra obligations, such as gifts made to the landlord on certain holidays and other special occasions, and there was additional labor owed, called *boonwork*, such as collecting the lord's firewood or doing other errands for him and maintaining roads and bridges on the manor.

The landlord also had control of certain products of the manor known as *banalities*. These included products of the manorial winepress, gristmill, and oven, which belonged to the lord and which the residents of the manor had no choice but to use. Common land was held collectively by the village community, whereas forests, meadows, and waterways were controlled by the lords. Lords held hunting privileges, which were denied the peasants, and hunting rights included riding roughshod through fields in pursuit of prey.

Beginning in the eleventh century, there was an increase in agricultural productivity, boosted by further technological improvements such as the horseshoe and horse collar, which made it easier to harness horses to plow the fields. Combined with the proliferation of watermills to provide power for grinding grains and the clearing of additional lands for cultivation, technological innovations helped to speed demographic growth, which in turn led to a pronounced increase in towns and cities. Urban centers offered opportunities to peasants from the countryside to engage in trade, handicrafts, and other jobs as the development of a commercial economy surged. But the manor persisted as the primary basis of agriculture, even though some lords began to shift their crops to production for the market.

Over the next two centuries, there was overall growth in the population and some expansion of the economy through increased volume of trade in such goods as wool, cloth, and timber, but no agricultural or commercial revolution. Nor were there significant advances in industrial technology, and major industries remained essentially the same: mining, salt production, shipbuilding, sea fishing. England's foreign trade in the thirteenth century was controlled by Italian merchants operating out of the ports of Venice and Genoa. The Crusades of the eleventh to thirteenth centuries had reconnected northwestern Europe to the trading networks of the eastern Mediterranean and Afro-Eurasian land routes, but England remained on the periphery. Demands for English wool, however, did help to preserve the balance of trade and ensure that bullion flowed into England to maintain the coinage – the silver penny – at a consistent standard. And population growth between the late eleventh and thirteenth centuries meant the expansion at least of settlement and cultivation and the growth of towns. Between 1100 and 1300 approximately 140 new towns can be documented.

But the expansion of cultivation to marginal lands did not necessarily provide the productivity needed. In the thirteenth century attempts to farm arable land more intensively led to the widespread adoption of the three-field system in place of the two-field one. A pattern of cultivation that promoted "sustainable agriculture" by rotating crops among either two or three fields and leaving one field idle or fallow, both systems were designed to replenish the soil and maintain productivity. To preserve soil quality under more intensive cultivation – the effect of the shift from a two-field to a three-field system – necessitated more use of fertilizer, which in turn was dependent on livestock. And livestock pasturage was reduced as pastures and woodlands were both brought under cultivation.

There is some evidence that economic conditions were tightening up for the English peasant by the end of the thirteenth century, as population growth outpaced agricultural productivity. Estate records of the time indicate that at least the average size of tenant holdings was shrinking. And, although slavery had all but disappeared, perhaps as many as half the population were serfs subject to the demands of the lords on whose estates they labored. In the twelfth century the labor services owed by many serfs were converted to the payment of money rents. Around 1200 – and certainly with the impact of the Magna Carta (1215) in promoting the rule of law – the king's judges began to decide who had the right as a "free man" to be heard in court and who did not. The effect of this was to establish a two-tiered classification of society: half enserfed as unfree and half regarded as free. Whereas in the past lords were able freely to manipulate customary services owed by tenants, as a legalistic way of addressing disputes gained ground the arbitrary exactions of lords became more difficult to enforce. The bottom line, however, remained that people with or without land, free or unfree, often barely survived. Living on the margins of existence meant that even a relatively minor drop in harvest might have a major impact on mortality, either through starvation or diseases that were rooted in malnutrition.

Growth in population meant an increasing demand for food, an often devastating consequence for the poor but a rewarding development for the rich when prices rose, as they did around 1200 and again in the late thirteenth century. A related result of the population increase was the plentiful labor supply, which meant that money wages did not grow in tandem with the rise in prices. Wealthy landowners made large profits by selling their excess produce at markets, which were proliferating throughout the countryside. The increasing importance of production for the market led many landlords to take over management of their estates directly rather than leasing lands to tenants. For example, around 1200 Abbot Samson of Bury St. Edmunds took his estates into his own hands and appointed managers to run them in order to produce a surplus for sale on the open market. This managerial revolution and accompanying interest in agricultural technology benefited only some of England's inhabitants at the time. By the end of the thirteenth century population pressures were straining the traditional agricultural economy and heightening divisions between rich and poor.

By 1300 English peasants were living in a world where land was scarce, alternatives to farming were few (wages were low even if jobs could be found), and prices were high. England's population boom had reached its peak by 1300, and, by the mid-fourteenth century, lowered living standards for much of society

Figure 6.1 Peasants reaping the harvest under the supervision of the lord's official (*c.* 1300–25). The labor of peasants tilling the fields and harvesting the crops belonged in part to the lord, whose officials were responsible for ensuring that the land produced as rich a harvest as possible.

– produced by too many people trying to eke out a living on too little land – resulted in high mortality rates that brought a stop to demographic growth. A series of poor harvests due to bad weather and natural disasters in the first half of the fourteenth century showed the fragility and vulnerability of the economy and people's livelihoods and produced a temporary dip in the population. But it was the epidemic known as the Black Death that had the greatest impact on the population and on all levels of English society in the mid-fourteenth century.

Beginning in 1348, the plague spread throughout England and into Scotland, swiftly reducing population by about a third. The catastrophic decline in population did improve conditions for labor by raising demand and therefore wages, but the human physical and psychological cost was enormous. In the face of labor shortages, English landowners attempted to exert control over the peasantry, and the Crown likewise supported their efforts by rulings that tried to stabilize wages and return them to pre-plague levels. Peasant frustrations accumulated and erupted finally in the Peasants' Revolt in 1381, precipitated by yet another increase in the poll tax, a threefold increase in as many years. Opposition to this brought together a wide range of English society, from agricultural workers to townsmen, who finally converged on London to demand that King Richard II essentially dismantle serfdom. But the spontaneity that spawned the insurrection was unable to sustain its hold and the rebels quickly dispersed to their homes in town and countryside. Ultimately, the growth of commerce and urbanization would have the effect of breaking down the old manorial system and, to some extent at least, freeing the peasant.

MARKETS AND MONEY IN CHINA: THE COMMERICAL REVOLUTION

By the time that commercial changes were beginning to undermine the manorial system in England, Chinese peasants had already experienced a commercial revolution. The commercial revolution in China, however, was slowed and eventually halted by the invasions of nomadic peoples on their borders that culminated in the Mongol conquest in the late thirteenth century.

Although debates continue to swirl around the precise nature of landholding in China during the Song (960–1279), the era of the "commercial revolution," two things are certain: there was great regional variation in modes of landholding, and there was no widespread "manorial" system that generally bound peasants to the land. With a population of about 100 million in the year 1000, China began to experience a series of changes that catapulted its economy into rapid growth and the commercial revolution was well underway.

By the beginning of the eleventh century, the introduction of new strains of early-ripening and drought-resistant rice from Southeast Asia began to increase the supply of food. These imported strains of rice either allowed planting and harvesting more than one crop a year, because the rice plants matured quickly, or enabled farmers to plant rice in places that were not well irrigated and where it had not been possible to plant before. At the same time, improvements in dam technology allowed the reclamation of lowland swampy areas to open up new land for farming. The resulting increases in food production contributed to population expansion. Population growth, in turn, contributed to the expansion of markets for products. An expanded marketplace, coupled with efficient transportation networks facilitated by stable political conditions in the eleventh century, encouraged regional specialization of production for the market. Regions began to specialize in the production of textiles, such as silk – which required the cultivation of mulberry bushes and the feeding of silkworms as well as the skill of weavers – or in agricultural products, such as oranges or tea. Tea, for example, was produced in the southeastern coastal province of Fujian, but was marketed to regions all over China.

Trade with nomadic neighbors provided Chinese with markets for their own products and access to commodities they needed. They imported silver, hemp cloth, sheep, horses, and slaves from the north, and eventually exported tea, rice, porcelain, sugar, silk, and other goods in exchange for medicines, horses, and other items. Maritime trade had begun to prosper under the earlier Tang dynasty, when Indian and Arab merchants traveling Indian Ocean maritime routes established permanent communities at the southern port of Canton. With the commercial revolution of the

Song, maritime trade was recognized as a vital part of the economy and received official patronage and supervision. By the mid-twelfth century, profits from maritime commerce were about one-fifth of the state's total cash revenues.

In the eleventh century, state revenues from commercial taxes and state monopolies (principally iron and salt) equaled the yield from agrarian taxes; by the twelfth century, commercial revenues far exceeded the income from agrarian taxes. The increasing use of both metal and paper currency and the development of institutions of banking and credit that took place in the Song were both key aspects of the commercial revolution of the period. Between the eighth and eleventh centuries, for example, the output of currency quadrupled, while the population grew much more slowly.

The shift from localized economies based on barter or exchange of goods to an increasingly monetized economy of scale that integrated regional economies was aided by the use of paper currency and credit. The round bronze coin with a square hole, called "cash," which was strung in units of 1,000, was the basic unit of currency minted by the Song state, but it was heavy and cumbersome to use and transport in any great quantity. Innovations such as the use of certificates of credit or bills of exchange – documents showing that money deposited in one place could be exchanged for a receipt that could be used to pay for goods in another – made it possible for merchants to carry on trade across regions with ease. Paper had been invented in China by the beginning of the first millennium, and the use of paper currency also began in China among regional entrepreneurs in the tenth century. By the eleventh century, the Song government was printing official paper currency.

The development of printing technology – both movable type printing and woodblock printing – and a commercial printing industry facilitated the spread of other technologies by making available cheap books, for example, that instructed farmers in new agricultural methods. Advances in the textile industry improved production, the scale of which is suggested by an early fourteenth-century account of a mechanical spinning wheel that could spin 130 pounds of thread in 24 hours. Along with cotton and silk textiles, the pro-

duction of ceramics expanded, with both imperial and private commercial kilns scattered throughout the empire. The technique of making porcelain was perfected in the twelfth century, and a variety of ceramic art was produced.

For many centuries Chinese craftsmen had produced cast iron, and they also made steel, utilizing smelting techniques well in advance of Europe. By the early twelfth century, the production of crude iron concentrated in north China ranged between 35,000 and 125,000 tons, a level comparing favorably with that of England several centuries later on the eve of the Industrial Revolution. Since the north China plain was already deforested by the Tang, and therefore access to charcoal was limited, growth in the production of iron during the eleventh century was dependent on the use of coal, an innovation that Europe did not employ until the eighteenth century.

Cities grew and prospered as both marketplaces and centers of population (see Chapter 3). An account of the southern capital, Hangzhou, written in 1235, describes the vibrant commercial atmosphere of the urban markets there:

> During the morning hours, markets extend from Tranquility Gate of the palace all the way to the north and south sides of the New Boulevard. Here we find pearl, jade, talismans, exotic plants and fruits, seasonal catches from the sea, wild game – all the rarities of the world seem to be gathered here. The food and commodity markets . . . are all crowded and full of traffic.
>
> (Patricia B. Ebrey, ed., *Chinese Civilization: A Sourcebook*, New York: Free Press, 1993, p. 178)

Cities like Hangzhou became destinations for people from the countryside because the restaurants, shops, and entertainment houses offered jobs that seemed attractive in comparison with rural life. The populations of Hangzhou and other cities grew and the social life in urban areas created new cultural opportunities and brought about changes in gender roles and social status. Even though China's population was still overwhelmingly rural, by 1200, when the manorial system in England was at its peak, the commercial

Figure 6.2 Qiu Ying, *Spring Festival Up the River* (detail of a bridge), *c.* 1500. Attributed to a Ming dynasty (1368–1644) artist, this rendering of a famous scroll from the twelfth century depicting the lively commerce and other urban activities of that era may in fact be an even later copy. The original scroll was believed to portray the Northern Song (960–1126) capital city of Kaifeng, although it is now regarded as representing an idealized generic city.

revolution of the eleventh century had substantially altered the Chinese landscape – physically, socially, and, above all, economically.

TRADE AND TRIBUTE IN THE INCAN EMPIRE

As ecologically diverse as the varied landscapes of Eurasia were, enormous environmental differences were concentrated in a much smaller area in the Andean region of South America where the Inca empire rose early in the fifteenth century. Verticality was the defining characteristic of the environmental constraints on making a living here. Only 2 percent of the land is arable, compared with about 25 percent of the mountainous volcanic archipelago of Japan. The topography rises and falls thousands of feet in short distances, creating many microclimates and ecological niches that produce different products and are home to various animals on which the human inhabitants depend. Andean tubers – more than 470 different varieties of these "potatoes" have been identified today – and camelids such as the llama and alpaca are found on the *altiplano* (high plateau) 14,000 feet up. Maize and peppers are grown in the high valleys, 6,000 to 10,000 feet above sea level; coca, in the "eyebrow of the jungle" valleys 3,000 feet up. Honey, nuts, and birds are found in the Amazon rain forest, and salt and fish are traded along the dry Pacific coast. Access to a full range of these ecological niches is necessary to consume a complete basket of goods.

Gaining control of the varied regional economies of the numerous ecozones found along the Andean coast of South America, the Incas built on the experiences and institutions of their predecessors to craft an empire that ruled over 10 million people by commandeering both labor and material resources of communities scattered throughout the region. In order to do this, the Incas had to construct an economic system that integrated and utilized the wealth and productive capacities of ecologically and ethnically distinct communities that stretched for nearly 3,000 miles along the western coast of South America. The ability to transport goods from one part of the empire to another was vital. The 40,000 km Incan highway system was a vast network of roads that constituted both an essential achievement of the Inca rulers and a remarkable engineering feat. A Spanish observer commented:

> In human memory, I believe that there is no account of a road as great as this, running through deep valleys, high mountains, banks of snow, torrents of water, living rock, and wild rivers. . . . In all places it was clean and swept free of refuse, with lodgings, storehouses, Sun temples, and posts along the route.
>
> (Terence N. D'Altroy, *The Inkas*, Oxford: Blackwell, [2002] 2003, p. 3 [quoting Pedro Cieza de Leon])

The storehouses mentioned here played a similarly crucial role in the ability of the Inca state to extract wealth from the peoples it conquered and redistribute it. Storage is essential to maintain a stable supply of food through the uneven cycles of planting and harvest in agricultural subsistence economies. Storage facilities are equally important in political economies like that of the Inca empire. The Inca rulers commandeered resources through an elaborate system of reciprocity, in which provincial leaders (*kuraka*) supplied labor and goods in return for their local authority being recognized by the Incan state. Although labor services were regarded as the basic obligation in this reciprocal relationship and the main source of wealth for the Inca state, commodities such as coca were also supplied by local communities and stored for redistribution in the large storehouses that dotted the Incan landscape.

When the Incas conquered a region, they claimed all resources and allocated them among the state, the state religion, and the subject communities. By then reapportioning farming and grazing land back to the community, the Incan state demanded labor service (*mit'a*) in return. In Peru's Huanaco region, for example, people were assigned as many as thirty-one different duties for the state: farming, herding, masonry, military service or guard duty, mining, portage, and artisanry. At the level of the local community, the key unit was the *ayllu*, a corporate kin group that organized households and was the basis for the distribution of access to farmlands, pastures, and other resources. Elite members of the *ayllu* had rights to farm and pastoral labor, personal services, and some craft products, in return for their ceremonial, political, and military leadership, and for sponsoring festive events. They established their authority in part by distributing material goods and food to their people, including cloth, maize beer, and coca. This relationship – economic, political, and social – was mirrored in that between the provincial elites (especially their leaders, the *kuraka*) and the Incan state. As the diverse ecozones mandated, the regional economies varied greatly and so did the products they supplied, ranging from marine or farm products, to textiles, ceramics, and sandals.

Recognizing the great diversity of the peoples and economies controlled by the Incas, how might one region have functioned within the structure of the Inca state economy? The Wanka people of the Upper Mantaro Valley of the Peruvian central highlands were conquered by the Incas around 1460. The main Inca highway from the imperial capital Cuzco to Quito in the north ran through this valley. The total Wanka population was probably close to 200,000, and after the Inca conquest Wanka communities moved down from hilltop locations to reside in a more dispersed settlement pattern along the valley margins. As elsewhere, Wanka elites were drawn into the state administration as local representatives of the Inca rulers, and labor taxes were assessed on the local population. Wanka informants to the Spanish later revealed that they had, in effect, been required to produce staples for the state:

> they [the Wankas] were sent to tend fields of food and [to make] clothing and maids were named for

their wives; and native clothing and all [things] that they could produce were ordered put into storehouses, from which gifts were made to soldiers and to the lords and to the valiant Indians and to whomever appeared; and similarly, it was ordered that those who worked in their fields and houses receive something from the storehouses.

(Terence D'Altroy and Timothy K. Earle, "Staple Finance, Wealth Finance, and Storage in the Inka Political Economy," *Current Anthropology*, 26, 2 (April 1985), p. 193)

In addition to the staples supplied by conquered peoples like the Wanka, the Incan state continued earlier practices of the circulation of prestige goods such as gold and silver, shells, feathers, and semi-precious stones. The Incan state demanded "gifts" from local elites, which could include shell beads and gold, silver, or copper objects. Alternatively, staples collected from communities as tribute could be converted into the support of artisans at the capital who produced prestige goods. One of the most important of these goods was the fine cloth used for giving as bridewealth, buried in mummy bundles, sacrificed in rituals, and used as a status marker. Cloth was produced for state use either by craft specialists through their labor service, using wool provided by the state, or by displaced colonists and female weavers employed on a full-time basis by the Incan state. Colonies of craft producers included weavers, such as the inhabitants of a town near Cuzco, where a Wanka master weaver reported later to a Spanish chronicler that his father had held the position of head of 500 households there. Fine cloth, in effect, functioned as a unit of value that could be exchanged for other goods and services.

As the Incan state expanded, resources were brought under the control of royal and aristocratic kin groups at the center. Some of these resources were lands that were converted into private estates for living and dead kings, their descendant kin groups, and other aristocratic lineages. The most imposing of these royal estates lay in what was called the Sacred Valley of the Incas, between Pisac (near Cuzco) and Macchu Picchu. Inca rulers and elite carved out estates from virgin territory, commandeered lands that had already been developed, or increased their holdings by accepting "gifts" from

subjects (voluntary or otherwise). Royal estates were spread across the landscape to provide access to a wide range of resources. For example, the estate of one ruler contained croplands, pastures, settlements, forests, parks, a pond and a marsh, a hunting range, and salt fields. The workers who maintained this estate numbered 2,400 men and their families. Because of the ecological heterogeneity of the Andes, estates were spread across different zones and therefore are difficult to measure in size, but some imperial holdings probably covered thousands of hectares. As expansive and impressive as these royal estates may have been, and as diverse as their holdings were, they were concentrated at the heart of the empire. Throughout the farthest reaches of the Incan empire, however, it was the combined productive forces – both labor and goods – exploited by the Inca rulers that fueled the engine of the Incan state and characterized the distinctive Incan political economy.

MANORS, MARKETS, AND MONEY: SOME CONCLUSIONS AND COMPARISONS

Peasants working in the fields on manors in England, Chinese merchants using paper money to carry out transactions, and Wanka weavers producing fine cloth for their Inca rulers were all engaged in making a living. They shared the common goal of laboring to produce goods or services that would enable them to feed and shelter themselves and their families. But the ability to obtain these basic human needs was determined literally by where these individuals stood in the food chain – by their place in a complex web of economic relationships shaped by distinct political systems. In all three cases – manors in England, the commercial revolution in China, and the political economy of the Incan empire – ways of making a living were circumscribed by both economic and political structures that limited the ability of individuals to benefit from their own labor. But in the first two cases, England and China, it is clear that the development of markets and a money economy by the fourteenth century had begun to break down barriers between urban and rural and between lord and peasant. In contrast, the Incan empire functioned as a distinctly non-market economy, tightly controlled by the center.

It is impossible to know what might have evolved had the Spanish not appeared and imposed their own imperial order on the Incas, exploiting for their own economic benefit the system used so successfully by the Incas to commandeer the vast resources of their Andean empire (see Chapter 7). By the sixteenth century, peoples of the Incan empire were connected to their counterparts in England, Japan, and China by global forces of economic change that fundamentally transformed their ways of making a living.

TRADING NETWORKS IN THE AMERICAS

Long before the rise of the Incan empire, like the Eurasian Silk Roads and trans-Saharan caravan routes, trading networks in the Americas linked peoples, cultures, and regional economies to each other, and longer-distance routes even connected the two continents of North and South America. Unlike the extensive criss-crossing web of Indian Ocean highways, in the Americas maritime coastal and riverine routes transported goods by water using smaller and lighter vessels. Ecuadoran voyagers along the coast of South America, for example, used large, balsa-wood sailing rafts with movable centerboards and rigged sails for their Pacific travels.

In Mesoamerica, jade deposits in territory controlled by the Olmecs (fl. *c.* 1000 BCE) contributed to far-flung trade, from modern Costa Rica and Guatemala in the south to the Mexico Valley in the north. Teotihuacán (*c.* 100 BCE–650 CE) was involved in a wide trading network that probably linked all major contemporary Mesoamerican cultures. Teotihuacán obsidian, one of the most common materials used for weapons, has been found in widely distributed sites across the region.

Evidence suggests that the cultural brilliance of Teotihuacán was known to the early Maya (*c.* 300–900 CE) as a result of trade conducted between these two cultures. Mayan regional trade in salt, hard stone, and pottery brought together outlying districts and may have been a major basis for the integration of Mayan society. As early as Teotihuacán, there were also northern routes that extended westward into Arizona and New Mexico to the Anasazi of the Colorado plateau, where Mesoamerican feathers, gold, and cacao beans (then the major medium of monetary exchange) were traded for turquoise.

Between about 900 and 1200 the use of turquoise became widespread throughout Mesoamerica. Since the source mines containing this blue gem lie in North America, from California to Colorado, and turquoise objects have been found in many Mesoamerican sites, it is clear that turquoise was traded over long distances. Like gold in Africa and silk in Asia, turquoise was valued for its aesthetic appeal and rarity, but for Mesoamericans, it also had religious meaning. After it was mined and traded, it was worked into ceremonial objects and often placed in burial sites.

Mesoamericans also had intercontinental connections with South America. The appearance of maize in agriculture along the Peruvian coast about 1500 BCE suggests early connections with Mesoamerica, where maize was first domesticated. Regional connections in South America existed early, flourished, and were continuous. As early as the time of Chavin de Huantar (*c.* 1000–200 BCE), when the llama and alpaca were domesticated for transportation as well as wool, exchange routes were established along the west coast of South America. These were expanded by other cultures, such as the Chimu (*c.* 800–1400), and were ultimately brought under the sway of the Incas (1438–1536).

Mississippian regional connections in North America are better known. They focused on the great center at Cahokia (fl. *c.* 900–1300), a city built by native North Americans (see Chapter 3). Through extensive trading connections, Cahokia was in constant contact with other communities scattered across nearly a third of the North American continent. The ruling elite at Cahokia controlled trade in raw materials, such as seashells, coppers, flint, and mica, which were drawn from a wide radius extending from north of Lake Superior to the Gulf Coast shoals of Florida and from the Appalachians as far west as the plains of North and South Dakota and Nebraska. In addition, the Cahokians manufactured a variety of goods for export: salt, tools, jewelry, and ceremonial goods.

The exports and imports – it took a steady flow of some 25,000 to 30,000 pounds of food a day to feed the people of Cahokia – traveled mainly by water, since domesticated draft animals (other than dogs) were not in use. Much of the produce was transported on streams and lakes, perhaps linked by canals; the city may have been so interlaced with waterways that it would have resembled European Venice. Tons of goods carried in canoes up to 15 meters (50 feet) in length moved along water routes to satellite centers and outposts.

Similar in kind to those of Asia, Africa, and Europe, connections in the Americas bound two continents together and served as avenues for trade and cultural interchange. Extending over distances comparable to the east–west and north–south connections between Eurasia and Africa, they had unique features: for example, the lack of horses, donkeys and camels as draft animals on overland routes and the differences in ships used for maritime and riverine routes. They served the needs of peoples in the Americas before the European conquest and were reorganized and integrated into the shifting pattern of connections that underlay the establishment of European global dominance following 1500.

MERCANTILISM AND THE ATLANTIC WORLD, c. 1500–1750

The European economy began to be transformed when the self-sufficient feudal-manorial system of services and duties gave way to an urban economy based on money and trade and controlled by merchant-manufacturers. Because these merchant-manufacturers became very wealthy, rulers of city-states and monarchies – and even the pope – would turn to them and to their financiers for the cash wealth they needed to maintain and extend their power. In proportion to the princes' reliance on the wealthy merchant class, the political influence of this urban elite began to replace that of landholding feudal vassals. As their influence grew, the urban wealthy increasingly influenced state politics. What merchant-manufacturers needed and wanted most was freedom from the restrictions of a static medieval economy that was communal and largely self-sufficient, and in which production and trade for profit were constrained or limited by such regulations and restraints as tariffs, road duties, and the concepts of a just price and the prohibition of interest (usury). The demands of merchant-manufacturers and bankers to expand their enterprises and increase profits

brought them into conflict with the norms of medieval agrarian society. In order to tap the growing wealth of the commercial elite, ambitious rulers increasingly supported their demands for changes in the economy. Use of political power to promote and protect trade was necessary to increase commercial wealth, which would benefit both prince and merchant alike.

The partnership that evolved between rulers and merchant-manufacturers enhanced the wealth and power of both. It also produced a set of doctrines and practices known as mercantilism, which aimed to enhance state power by increasing wealth. Mercantilism was based on the use of government intervention to promote the accumulation of profits, which, it was believed, would secure the prosperity and self-sufficiency of the state while benefiting those who contributed most to it – the urban commercial elite.

The voyages of Christopher Columbus illustrate the role of the prince in mercantilism and the mutual benefits to be derived by both prince and merchant. Although Columbus was a native of Genoa, he sought financial backing for his voyages first from the king of Portugal and then from Isabella of Castile and Ferdinand of Aragon in Spain. The Spanish monarchs retained Columbus in their service, but it took about five years to convince them to provide the 2,500 ducats for the voyage. The person who finally persuaded Ferdinand and Isabella of the financial potential of the venture was a banker and papal tax gatherer from Valencia, who had successfully raised a number of loans for them and who had himself amassed a fortune as a shrewd businessman. Merchants, whose power rested on their wealth, were as necessary to mercantilist enterprises as kings, and they derived great advantage from them, at least until the mid-eighteenth century, when merchants began to assert their independence from government support and protection.

One of the components of the theory and practice of European mercantilism was bullionism. For ambitious rulers, bullionism, the acquisition of surplus bullion (precious metals, specifically gold and silver ingots) meant that more ships could be built, larger fleets and armies equipped, and territorial expansion financed. One strong reason for the decision to back Columbus's voyage was the Spanish monarchy's acute lack of currency (especially gold); the possibility of enormous profits from an entirely new set of trading networks loomed large enough to overshadow the risks of Columbus's venture. Another component of mercantilism was the fervent hope that European voyages of exploration would lead to the establishment of colonies, the extension of European activities overseas. The Portuguese took the lead in accomplishing this.

INTERLOPERS IN INTERNATIONAL TRADE: THE PORTUGUESE EMPIRE

From the time of the Crusades, the Italian city of Venice had dominated trade in the Mediterranean. Excluded from this trade, the small Atlantic-facing kingdom of Portugal on the Iberian peninsula was forced to seek its commercial fortunes elsewhere and so inaugurated the European voyages of exploration. The maritime voyages began as a latter-day "crusade." The Portuguese, together with the Spanish, had for centuries engaged in wars to expel Muslims and Jews from the Iberian peninsula and to reduce the power and influence of both groups in surrounding areas. In 1415, the Portuguese extended the Iberian "crusade" to North Africa with an attack on the city of Ceuta, a Muslim strategic and commercial center. The acquisition of Ceuta gave the Portuguese access to African trade and became a base for further Portuguese expeditions southward, down the western coast of Africa to the area of the Kongo, a major Central African kingdom, and on to the Cape of Good Hope, the southernmost point on the African continent, reached by the Portuguese in 1488.

From the cape, subsequent expeditions moved northward, attempting to replace centuries-old African and Arab merchant enterprises in port cities along the eastern coast of Africa. From East Africa, the Portuguese sailed across the Indian Ocean, reaching India in 1498. In their attempt to control the movement of goods, Portugal then built large fleets, which were used to conquer Aden, Hormuz, Diu, and Malacca, key strategic ports on the established east–west Indian Ocean trade route. Here, as elsewhere, they were successful interlopers in vast and ancient international commercial networks.

In this way, Portugal built a sixteenth-century commercial empire on the seas that, although it fell far short of global monopoly, was enormously profitable. By proving that Mediterranean trade was not the only way to commercial success, the Portuguese experience stimulated the eventual shift of European trade and wealth northward and westward to the Atlantic. The Portuguese success showed how profitable a seaborne empire could be, and later fifteenth- and sixteenth-century European explorations sought alternative routes to Asia.

THE CREATION OF AN ATLANTIC ECONOMY: SUGAR AND SLAVES

The European entry into the world of the Americas had catastrophic effects on the indigenous peoples, who succumbed to diseases and violence that accompanied the European conquest; and in the wake of Amerindian population decreases, other forms of coercive labor, including slavery, were exploited in the construction of the "New World" (see Chapter 8). Central to the growth of Atlantic commerce were two commodities: sugar and slaves. The history of Atlantic commerce is inseparable from the history of slavery, and the transfer of both labor and capital across the Atlantic is closely connected with the production of sugar. Technology and culture were intertwined in the development of the sugar industry, one of the mainstays of the new Atlantic economy.

Before the sixteenth century, northern Europe's only local source of sugar was bees. By the fourteenth century, the growing demand for sugar led first to cane sugar plantations on the Mediterranean coast and the islands of Cyprus and Sicily and then, by the fifteenth century, to Spanish and Portuguese plantations on Atlantic islands such as the Madeiras and São Tomé and Principe off the west-central African coast, where African slave labor was exploited, and finally in the Americas. Sugar sold for high prices as a rare spice or medicine. Its production and trade soon became enormously profitable.

With the increase in prices, expansion of sugar cultivation dominated the list of profitable Portuguese investments in Brazil and the Caribbean. The demand for sugar grew, and, as supplies also expanded, new uses for sugar were found. French and Dutch merchants vied for power. Europeans came to crave the taste of

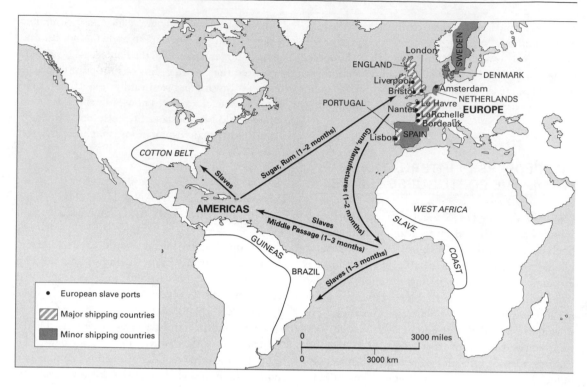

Map 6.2 Atlantic trade triangle, sixteenth to nineteenth centuries.

Source: Peter Ashdown, *Caribbean History in Maps* (Trinidad and Jamaica: Longman Caribbean, 1979), p. 16, top.

sugar, especially as a sweetener for two other products from the Afro-Asian world: coffee and tea. These became popular additions to the European diet, especially valued as stimulants and comforts by workers in European factories, the products of which in turn fed the markets of the Atlantic world with cheaply manufactured goods, such as hoes and cast-iron pots.

The Dutch were pioneers in the technology and trade of the Atlantic. The Dutch West India Company seized and controlled the richest sugar-producing area in Brazil (around Recife) from 1630 to 1654. Dutch sugar enterprises in Brazil served as models for other large-scale Caribbean ventures. Dutch merchants controlled the copper trade that supplied plantation boiling houses with pots. These entrepreneurs relied on the systems of credit, insurance, and finance that Dutch trading companies experimented with and that were necessary to risky overseas enterprise. Corporate

financing and state support jointly promoted the development of sugar plantations and, along with them, slavery. Creditors in Amsterdam, London, and other cities, who accumulated capital both from the sale of goods and people, financed shipping concerns involved in the transfer of these goods and people and invested their profits in manufacturing.

The system of plantation slavery that developed across the Caribbean was unprecedented as an economic, political, and social institution. The sugar plantation was a landed estate that specialized in export production. It combined large-scale tropical agriculture, African labor, European and African technology, European animal husbandry, Asian and American plants, and the climate and soils of the Americas. The typical sugar plantation was a big-business establishment, both farm and factory. Sugar-cane was grown, raw sugar manufactured, and molasses distilled into rum.

Figure 6.3 Sugar mill at work, West Indies (1849). This engraving published in the *Illustrated London News* portrays an idealized sugar mill in the Caribbean. The European overseer leans against a wall, observing the African laborers. The processing of cane was highly mechanized by the nineteenth century.

Plantation owners were often absentee proprietors, who used attorneys or other Europeans as overseers. Managers, bookkeepers, carpenters, blacksmiths, masons, coopers, and doctors provided essential services. Because the food supplies provided by the plantations were insufficient to maintain the slave population, slaves grew their own provisions to supplement their diets. In about 1740, Charles Leslie described how the slaves of Jamaica did this:

> Their owners set aside for each a small Parcel of Ground, and allow them the Sundays to manure it: In it they generally plant Maiz, Guiney Corn, Plantanes, Yams, Cocoes, Potatoes, &c. This is the Food which supports them, unless some of them who are more industrious than others, happen to raise a Stock of Fowls, which they carry to Markets on the Sundays (which is the only Market-day in Jamaica) and sell for a little Money, with which they purchase Salt-Beef or Pork to make their Oglios or Pepper-Pot.
>
> (Roger D. Abrahams and John F. Szwed, eds, *After Africa*, New Haven, Conn.: Yale University Press, 1983, p. 329)

The slaves developed an informal economy, based on West and Central African practices of bargaining and exchange, that often relied on specialized women traders called higglers. Higglers became critical agents of interplantation communication and slave resistance.

The effects of the slave trade on Europe are perhaps not quite so obvious but they are nevertheless profound. Europeans benefited not only from the profitable use of cheap labor in the Caribbean but also from their control of the Atlantic trade that connected Europe to Africa, Africa to the Americas and the Caribbean, and the Caribbean and the Americas to Europe. European merchants and business interests were involved as suppliers of goods traded for slaves, as shippers of those goods and of slaves, and as dealers of goods produced by slave labor. The organizational experience and demands of the Atlantic system produced unrivaled entrepreneurial expertise and capital. Europe's control of the Atlantic world provided the means for its later world dominance.

THE PACIFIC WORLD

The first documented link between the Americas and the islands of the Pacific was established by a Spanish expedition led by the Portuguese adventurer Ferdinand Magellan. Magellan's fleet sailed from Spain in the fall of 1519, wintered at Patagonia at the southern tip of South America, and then crossed into the Pacific through what is now known as the Strait of Magellan. After a hundred days at sea, Magellan's fleet reached a group of islands that they claimed under the terms of the 1494 Treaty of Tordesillas that divided the world between Spain and Portugal. The Spanish finally secured their claim to the islands in 1542, renaming them "Islas Filipinas" (the Philippines). Spanish occupation of the Philippines was confirmed in 1571, when a third expedition took control of Manila, an important trading center that became the principal Spanish entrepôt in Asia.

By the second half of the sixteenth century, following the Spanish conquest of the Philippines, complicated patterns of both legitimate and contraband trade grew up around routes connecting the Spanish settlement of Acapulco in Mexico with Manila, from whence it reached China, principally through the Portuguese entrepôt of Macao. By the 1560s, Spanish "pieces of eight" had become the currency of expanding world trade, and Spanish galleons bearing goods, including silver bullion, became the object of piracy, either private or sponsored by Spain's European rivals and enemies. In 1573, the first galleon sailing eastward from Manila across the Pacific to Spanish America carried Chinese silks, satins, porcelains, and spices to Acapulco, from whence it returned to Manila with silver from Spanish-American mines. Potosi, more than 15,000 feet high in the Andes, two and one-half months' journey from Lima, was the site of the richest silver mine in the history of the world (see Chapter 3). Found in 1545, Potosi's mountain of silver funded the Spanish empire until about the middle of the seventeenth century.

By the end of the sixteenth century, the amount of bullion flowing from Acapulco to Manila surpassed the sum that was involved in transatlantic shipments. Between 1570 and 1780, an estimated 4,000–5,000 tons of silver flowed to East Asia along the Acapulco–Manila route. As Spanish-American bullion flowed westward as well as eastward, both Asians and Europeans were enriched. This trade lasted until the first half of the nineteenth century, when Spanish rule in the Americas came to an end.

By the late sixteenth century, the Dutch had acquired the knowledge of navigation necessary to enter into world trade competition. Their initial target was the Portuguese-dominated spice trade in Southeast Asia. In 1602, the Dutch East India Company, a unified trading monopoly formed under state charter, began the administration of the Indonesian archipelago economy under Dutch control. By the 1640s, they had displaced the Portuguese and had consolidated their holdings across a vast sweep of islands from Ceylon in the west, through Malacca and Java (where they had an important administrative center at Batavia), to the Moluccas in the east. The Dutch had superior ships, arms, and organization, as well as more skilled merchants. They mixed piracy and missionary activities with trade.

Because of Dutch strength in Southeast Asia, British trade interests were diverted to South Asia, which became the base from which the British East India Company (1600) made inroads into Southeast and East Asia during the eighteenth century. In contrast to Spain, which reaped its wealth from the Americas, and Holland, which exploited the Indonesian archipelago, Britain concentrated, through its East India Company, on India and China, the heartlands of the two major Asian civilizations; the British government did not establish its ascendancy there until the nineteenth century, however. What all the seaborne European empires in Asia had in common by the eighteenth century was their starting point on the shores of the Atlantic.

Like the growing taste for sugar in Europe that fueled the plantation system of the Caribbean and contributed to the growth of the Atlantic economy, the introduction of products from Asia created new tastes among Europeans that drove trade in the Pacific and had global impact. Chinese tea was in great demand in European markets, to which it was introduced by Dutch merchants; by 1664 tea reached England and quickly became the national beverage. Tea importing became a major enterprise under the monopoly of the British East India Company and an important source of government tax revenue. China demanded payment in silver for its tea, and most of the silver flowing to China from European trade originated in the Americas.

CHINA AND THE WORLD ECONOMY, 1500–1800

As Europeans sailed into East Asian waters in the sixteenth century they encountered a world dominated by China, a civilization more ancient and sophisticated than any in Europe. European expansion in East Asia was limited during the sixteenth century to peripheral missionary and mercantile contacts; not until the nineteenth century would European power erode the dominance of China and shatter the stability of the East Asian world order. Nonetheless, the expansion of Europe and the creation of a global economy through the opening of the Atlantic frontier had an impact on China, the core economy of the East Asian world.

With the growth of the Chinese economy following the end of Mongol rule and the restoration of a native Chinese dynasty, the Ming (1368–1644), merchants became prosperous, and even powerful, members of society. The growth of domestic commerce, however, was not matched by that of foreign trade. Ming rulers generally followed policies designed to control foreign trade and bring it into the framework of the tributary system. Though the tributary system was conceived as a means of conducting diplomatic relations, trade was an important aspect of tribute relations. Tribute was paid in the form of gifts to the Chinese emperor from rulers of states surrounding China to express their homage to the Son of Heaven, the ruler of the center of the world. Return gifts from the Chinese court made tribute relations a kind of commodity exchange. Tribute missions in China from foreign countries were allowed to engage in trade as well. Merchants traveling with the tribute missions also conducted their own private trade. Despite the hostility of the Ming government to foreign trade, a substantial amount of such trade took place within the framework of the tributary system.

Ming prosperity was fueled by an agricultural revolution beginning around 1500 that saw the introduction of new crops from the Americas – corn, peanuts, and sweet potatoes – indirectly transmitted

to Asia by Europeans through their voyages of exploration (see Chapter 10). These crops contributed significantly to an increase in the food supply since they could be cultivated in marginal soils unsuitable for other crops and provided substantial nutrition. Partly as a result of increased food supply, population swelled from between 60 and 80 million (to which it had dropped as a result of the Mongol conquest) to at least 150 million by 1600.

The importation of new food crops was only one dimension of China's growing participation in a world economic system that would eventually be dominated by Europe. Though by the mid-fifteenth century, in contrast to European states' mercantilist policies, the Ming government had withdrawn its support from voyages of exploration, China could no longer remain entirely isolated from the world system being constructed through the expansion of Europe. By 1500, China was becoming part of a global monetary system through indirect links established by its Asian trading partners. East Asia in the age of European exploration and empire formed its own sector of the world economy, with silver flowing into Chinese coffers from Japan, Europe, and the Americas, often through intermediaries who used silver to pay for Chinese products, such as silks, spices, and porcelains, that were extremely profitable on the world market. The monetization of the Chinese economy that accompanied commercial growth during the Ming period made China susceptible to shifts in the global economy and made even the poorest peasants in the most remote villages victims of inflation that pushed prices of goods beyond their reach, costing them more bronze cash in taxes to make up the equivalent value of silver, which had appreciated on the international market.

Between about 1500 and 1800, following Columbus's voyages, the economic relationships and societies of the Americas, Europe, parts of Africa, Asia, and the Pacific were transformed through the creation of an Atlantic world economy that provided the means for subsequent European expansion into Asia and the Pacific. Establishment of Atlantic connections had a profound impact on the lives and cultures of African peoples, particularly those of West and Central Africa. The new global connections upset the balance of the long-established relations among Asia, Africa, and Europe, replacing and redirecting their world systems of land-based and maritime, inter- and intra-regional commerce.

Triangular connections among societies in Africa, Europe, and the Americas revolved primarily around an expanding Atlantic trade, with its foundations mired in slavery and merchant capitalism. Soon after its forging, the interconnected world of Atlantic commercial development was no longer a set of balanced relationships. European expansion into the Pacific added new global connections and constituted a westward shift of power away from earlier Afro-Eurasian centers such as the Indian Ocean trading world and the East Asian core economy of China. In the eighteenth century, new developments in Europe would provide the means to intensify European domination of the global economy.

THE INDUSTRIAL REVOLUTION

The acceleration of European technology in the eighteenth century was such that it became known as an "industrial revolution" (see Chapter 2). Under the impact of technological changes and expanding capitalism, first European economies and then economies around the globe were transformed. Technological innovations in eighteenth-century Europe took place principally in industries such as mining, metallurgy, and textiles. Before the textile revolution, cloth was produced by workers at home, using raw materials provided by merchants, who then gathered the completed cloth. Women spun thread and men generally did the weaving. The location, organization, and output of the industry changed dramatically during the Industrial Revolution. The introduction of new spinning and weaving equipment in Europe early in the eighteenth century began the process of moving textile production from the home to factories. In the case of textile production, the new machinery not only took work out of the home and agricultural villages but also (sometimes) reversed traditional gender-based tasks: in the industrialized factory, spinning became men's work rather than women's work because it took place outside the household. The factory replaced the home as the workplace, requiring large numbers of workers to travel daily to the city or move there.

The distinctive institution of the capitalist Industrial Revolution was the factory system of production, whereby workers were herded together in buildings for fixed hours of labor at power-driven machines. Factories were, however, slow to replace domestic industry, where workers spun and wove in their own homes, using their own spinning wheels and looms. Except in cotton spinning and weaving, as late as the 1830s many employers continued to find domestic industry more profitable and to prefer small shop production to large factory enterprise.

As factories multiplied, younger trainees, many of them women, who had no commitment to older modes of production, replaced traditional artisans and older workers. Factory work meant a loss of the artisan's independence and often a readjustment of family relationships, since production moved outside the home and altered the roles of individual workers. In 1831 a government committee in England investigating child labor in the textile industry uncovered the grim circumstances of daily life for many young children condemned to work in the mills to supplement family income.

Many people compared the factory to the workhouse, where the poor or ill were sent to work. Many factory owners, who believed themselves morally as well as physically justified in controlling and disciplining their workers, introduced strict work codes that regulated every aspect of the factory day as well as after-hours activities. Despite the reluctance of some entrepreneurs and the resistance of some workers, by the middle of the nineteenth century the factory system had become the common mode of production, and capitalist industrialists who owned the factories organized and controlled the economic, cultural, and even religious life of factory communities.

By the nineteenth century, the impact of the Industrial Revolution was seen across the globe. In Brazil, textile manufacture competed with that of the metropolitan capital of Lisbon. In Japan, rapid industrialization was encouraged after 1868 by the Meiji government policies. Silk production traditionally had been the work of Japanese women. When factories were built, they attracted large numbers of very young women, who worked long hours in dismal conditions. Women were given the most monotonous and lowest

Figure 6.4 Ichiyosai Kuniteru, *Interior of a Japanese Silk Factory* (1870). Kuniteru was a woodblock print artist in the tradition of Hiroshige, Hokusai, and others who portrayed both urban life and rural landscapes of traditional Japan in the eighteenth and nineteenth centuries. In contrast, Kuniteru was known for his depictions of industrial life and Western influences in late nineteenth-century Japan.

paying jobs, while men held specialized positions. The unequal division of labor continued well into the twentieth century. In Japan and around the globe, the factory replaced the home as the workplace, requiring large numbers of workers to travel daily to the city or move there. The migration of labor and capital led to the forces we recognize as globalization, interconnecting people, technology, and ideas. Innovations brought possibilities that extended the reach of global capital. Industrialization required resources from afar: cotton from Egypt and India fed the mills of England; rubber and oil from the tropics supplied the machines of America and Japan. The large-scale demand for goods quickened the tempo of change in systems of transportation and communication.

CAPITALISM

The Industrial Revolution was closely tied to the economic system of capitalism, the use or investment of money to make profits. The earliest form of capitalism was agricultural, where wealth was both made from the land and invested in its improvement and expansion. Localized, self-sufficient agriculture was only gradually replaced with market-oriented agriculture, which required capital investment. Commercial capitalism developed with the late-medieval revival of cities and trade and flourished as a result of global exploration, trade, and colonization beginning in the sixteenth century. Before the sixteenth century, the power of monarchs depended on their relationship with an agrarian–military aristocracy; with the development of commercial capitalism, monarchs were supported by their merchant partners in mercantilism.

Industrial capitalism took shape in the late eighteenth and early nineteenth centuries along the Atlantic frontier of western Europe and, perhaps earliest and most successfully, in England. Industrial capitalism was the result of many factors, including government-encouraged economic growth, new large-scale marketing, the availability of surplus capital, and technological innovations that had cumulatively developed since the sixteenth century. It developed earliest in industries such as machine tools, which are basic to all forms of industrial production, and textiles, which supply vast market demands. Enterprises such as

mining and metallurgy that were ancillary to machine-tool or textile production were also critical to early industrial capitalist development.

By the late eighteenth century, the investment of capital in industry, much of it derived from commerce and agriculture, began the vast expansion that would make industrial capitalism the dominant form of capitalism by the end of the nineteenth century in Europe. Older forms of capitalism were gradually subsumed in finance capitalism, in which bankers and financiers invested in industry, commerce, and even agriculture. Finance capitalists combined huge corporations and immense concentrations of money in economic activities that were increasingly global and intertwined with the expansion of European nation-states in the Americas, Asia, and Africa.

IMPERIALISM AND COLONIALISM AS ECONOMIC SYSTEMS

As the growth limits of industrial capitalism began to be reached in European economies during the second half of the nineteenth century, alternative markets and resources had to be found overseas. While there were still a few possibilities for more intensive utilization of European resources, increasingly Europeans turned to the exploitation of other parts of the world. Late nineteenth-century European imperialism completed the process of European domination of the world that began with the opening of the Atlantic frontier in the sixteenth century. Propelled by industrial capitalism and the nation-state, the new imperialism spread both industrialism and nationalism around the world. Europeans little realized, and less expected, that both might be used eventually by non-Europeans to challenge and readjust Europe's position in the world.

The trans-Atlantic slave trade had been central to commercial capitalist development and growth in West and Central Africa. Even after the abolition of slavery by European powers beginning about 1807, African societies' dependence on slave labor did not disappear. The slave trade era was followed by the era of "legitimate commerce," a period between about 1800 and 1870 during which African-European economic enterprises were forced to find other products to replace illegal human cargoes. In almost all instances the products sold to international markets were agricultural or forest products grown or collected for export to Europe. They included timber, rubber, palm oil, minerals, and ivory. Even when slaves were no longer exported, slavery and other forms of coerced labor remained essential to the production and transport of commodities. The era has also been termed a period of informal empire, suggesting that the economic relations characteristic of the subsequent formal empires of the colonial era were well underway by the end of the nineteenth century.

In some important ways the era of colonial rule was fundamentally different from what had preceded it. Before colonial rule Africans were independent, if not always equal, trading partners. After the establishment of colonial rule, the African economy became a European-dominated economy. Under post-Berlin Conference (after 1885) colonial rule, African political economies controlled by colonial powers – such as Great Britain, France, or Germany – were rapidly establishing Western-based capitalism that would inevitably reduce the power and economic opportunity of the African participants. While production remained largely in African hands, Europeans controlled credit and tariffs. Few Africans prospered during this era; colonial controls hampered the development of free enterprise, and European governments offset the high costs of extracting raw materials and transporting them to European-based manufacturing centers by providing price supports.

European economic and political hegemony depended on the development of the colonial system. African colonies supported many European industries that otherwise could not have been profitable. For example, the textile industry of France depended on the cheap cotton supplied by French West African colonies to remain competitive with technologically more advanced manufacturing in Great Britain and the United States. The other side of the colonial relationship was of course the development of markets in Africa. African markets continued to support the patterns of Western industrial growth as Africans became dependent consumers of European textiles, iron pots, agricultural implements, soap, and even foodstuffs.

The Opium War (1839–42) between Britain and China can serve as an example of the impact of European power in Asia (see Chapter 7). The insatiable appetite of British merchants for Chinese tea and other goods had been satisfied as long as there were plentiful supplies of silver to pay for them. After the American Revolution cut off British access to silver sources in the Americas, merchants were hard-pressed to purchase the commodities they desired. Britain's control of Bengal in India provided the answer: opium. Illegally imported into China by British merchants, and distributed through networks of Chinese agents, opium had a devastating impact on Chinese society. When the Chinese government tried to ban imports of the drug, the British retaliated with gunboats. China's humiliating defeat by Britain resulted in the forcible opening of treaty ports along the coast, entry points for foreign merchants into the commerce of the enormous Chinese empire. Although China was never directly colonized by any European power, it was carved up into "spheres of influence" that granted commercial and other rights to foreigners.

China's neighbor, Japan, was also visited and theatened by an American ship with an envoy from the US president in 1853, an event that swiftly sparked political change in the country. The Meiji Restoration in 1868 brought to power a group of leaders whose primary goals were to industrialize and militarize, using Western models but without colonial control by Western powers. The success of both economic and military modernization in Japan would have dramatic consequences for the global economy and global war.

Unlike its East Asian neighbors, India was colonized in the nineteenth century and the Indian economy was held hostage to British interests. The textile industry, beginning in the English Industrial Revolution, was typically one of the first industries to develop as an economy industrialized. Indian cotton had been known for centuries, but the production of Indian cotton was compromised in order to provide markets for British goods. When Mahatma Gandhi wore the traditional Indian dress, the *dhoti*, made of Indian cotton, he was opposing British colonial control of the Indian economy and people's livelihoods through a boycott of British goods (see Chapter 7). Gandhi had also experienced imperialism on another continent, in South Africa, and across every continent in the world examples of the economic grip of imperialism could be felt.

industrialized the Soviet Union on the backs of peasants, squeezing the necessary capital to fund heavy industry from agriculture and peasant labor. After the Second World War, Mao Zedong and the leaders of the new People's Republic of China, following their Soviet mentors, undertook a Five-Year Plan to industrialize the Chinese economy. Mao eventually resisted the Soviet model and challenged prevailing ideas about how to industrialize rapidly by extracting resources from the peasantry. He believed that the social (and political) costs were too high, and turned instead to reliance on agriculture in tandem with smaller-scale industrialization. This program ultimately was a drastic failure, creating conditions that led to mass starvation and millions of deaths.

National policies elsewhere in the postwar world attempted to provide for people through state-mandated and supported welfare programs, most notably in Scandinavia but also elsewhere in Europe and in the United States. The state became a kind of insurer of the infirm, elderly, and poor, as earlier the Church through charity and the family had been.

INTERNATIONAL ECONOMIC ORGANIZATIONS AND AGREEMENTS

Emerging from the latter days of the Second World War, a series of international agreements on financial operations was crafted by the victors. The World Bank and the International Monetary Fund were created in 1944, initially to prepare for the restoration of order in Europe after the war's end but later adapted in the postwar world to economic development in the "Third World." The notion of the Third World was applied to former – and continuing – colonies in Africa, Asia, and Latin America. Both organizations were controlled by the "First World," the most developed capitalist economies, including those that had profited most by imperialism. In 1971 the United States severed the dollar from the gold standard, effectively dismantling the 1944 Bretton Woods agreement that tied the value of international currencies to gold. This paved the way for other international currencies to break loose from their tie to the US dollar and created a more volatile and fluid international financial climate. This was a crucial point in the development of a new system of informal management across borders that replaced the more formal, institutionalized management of the World Bank and IMF. Commodities such as salt, gold, silk, and spices that were once traded along the networks of caravan routes and monsoon maritime routes have been replaced by oil, rubber, textiles, and narcotics.

GLOBALIZATION AND ITS DISCONTENTS

In 1995 the World Trade Organization (WTO) replaced the postwar (1947) General Agreement on Tariffs and Trade (GATT), designed to provide guidelines for and regulate world trade. The WTO provoked sharp opposition among many who saw it as a perpetuation of control by dominant economic and political powers over the world's poorest people who had no voice in its deliberations and decisions. China and Vietnam, once ardent communist economies transformed into market economies, became members of the WTO, a reflection of the increasingly important role that Asian economies have played in the postwar world and the power of the capitalist model, beginning with Japan. Regional trading blocs also emerged in the late twentieth century, the most notable of which is the European Union, promoting a unified currency and a common bank for member nations.

In the same year (1995) that the WTO was founded, a young software engineer, Pierre Omidyar, developed the code that would enable people to buy and sell items on the Internet through what became known as "eBay." A new kind of Silk Road, the Internet provided a cyber-route for commerce that was individualized, a direct contrast to the giant multinational corporations that dominated the global economy by the late twentieth century.

Hugely successful, the billionaire entrepreneur who began eBay turned his attention to the problem of how to solve global poverty. Following the lead of Muhammad Yunus, who won the Nobel Peace Prize in 2006, Omidyar and other wealthy philanthropists, such as the Microsoft magnate, Bill Gates, have invested in different ways in the process of microfinance or microcredit: awarding small loans to poor women (and sometimes men) to start their own businesses and gain a degree of economic independence. But whatever financial gains they make, their efforts are embedded in a local setting that is ultimately tied to global market forces and a capitalist world economy. Without large-scale structural change in the global economy – the control of capital, the banking system – it is difficult to see how global poverty can be eliminated, or even substantially reduced, through such incremental means.

CONCLUSIONS

The transnational economies of the early twenty-first century contrast sharply with the mercantilist economies of the sixteenth and seventeenth centuries. In the transnational economic world, merchant princes do team up with governments to promote common economic and political interests, but multinational corporations often transcend in power and influence the national economies from which they sprang. The heads of multinational corporations often command as much – or more – attention than the heads of states.

In early history, environmental conditions determined what kinds of economies developed, even as technology enabled people to alter their environments – by irrigation, by terracing hillsides, and so on (see Chapter 2). The technological changes introduced with the Industrial Revolution began a process that drastically altered the environment, from coal mining to chemical pollution. In some ways technology freed human beings from dependence on the environment, along with providing vastly enhanced material conditions for many. But the combination of increasing consumption of goods and the waste produced by excessive consumption has ravaged the global environment in ways that challenge people to confront how they live and what that means for how other people across the globe live and will live in the future.

SELECTED REFERENCES

Abu-Lughod, Janet L. (1989) *Before European Hegemony: The World System, A.D. 1250–1350*, New York and Oxford: Oxford University Press. A richly documented argument for the existence of an Afro-Eurasian world system before the sixteenth-century expansion of Europe and the creation of the world system defined by Immanuel Wallerstein.

Chaudhuri, K. N. (1990) *Asia Before Europe: Economy and Civilisation of the Indian Ocean from the Rise of Islam to 1750*, Cambridge: Cambridge University Press. A study of the dynamic interaction between economic life, society, and civilization around the Indian Ocean over a period of nearly a thousand years, modeled in part on Fernand Braudel's classic work on the Mediterranean.

Dyer, Christopher (2002) *Making a Living in the Middle Ages: The People of Britain, 850–1520*, New Haven, Conn.: Yale University Press. A thorough study of the ways in which people at all levels of society in medieval Britain provided for themselves and their families amidst changing economic circumstances.

Frank, Andre Gunder (1998) *ReOrient: Global Economy in the Asian Age*, Berkeley, Los Angeles, and London: University of California Press. A provocative study of the "rise of the West" as a temporary shift away from what had been an Asia-centered world economy and will be again.

Pomeranz, Kenneth (2000) *The Great Divergence: China, Europe, and the Making of the Modern World Economy*, Princeton, N.J. and Oxford: Princeton University Press. A comparative study of Chinese and European economic development in the nineteenth century, arguing that Europe's success was dependent on convenient access to coal and on trade with the Americas.

Pomeranz, Kenneth and Steven Topik (1999) *The World That Trade Created: Society, Culture, and the World Economy, 1400 to the Present*, Armonk, N.Y. and London: M.E. Sharpe. A highly readable work that traces the movements of goods through the actions of people across the globe and the often unpredictable outcomes of their interactions.

Reid, Anthony (1988) *Southeast Asia in the Age of Commerce, 1450–1680*, Vol. One: *The Lands Below the Winds*, New Haven, Conn. and London: Yale University Press. A comprehensive survey of daily life in Southeast Asia on the eve of European hegemony, including material culture, family, customs, religion, commerce, and law.

Shiba, Yoshinobu (trans. Mark Elvin) (1992 (1970, first translation; 1968, original Japanese publication)), *Commerce and Society in Sung China*, Ann Arbor: University of Michigan Center for Chinese Studies. A study of transportation, agricultural and handicraft products, markets, cities, and the organization of commerce in China between the tenth and thirteenth centuries.

Tracy, James D. (1991) *The Political Economy of Merchant Empires: State Power and World Trade, 1350–1750*, Cambridge: Cambridge University Press. A collection of articles relating to various aspects of world trade between the fourteenth and eighteenth centuries.

Wright, Donald (2004 (2nd edn)) *The World and a Very Small Place in Africa: A History of Globalization in Niumi, The Gambia*, Armonk, N.Y. and London: M.E. Sharpe. How global events and world systems affected the live of people over the past eight centuries in a small area in West Africa.

ONLINE RESOURCES

Annenberg/CPB Bridging World History (2004) <http://www.learner.org/channel/courses/world history/>. Multimedia project with interactive website and videos on demand; see especially Units 8 Early Economies, 9 Connections Across Land, 10 Connections Across Sea, 14 Land and Labor Relationships, 15 Early Global Commodities, 16 Food, Demographics, and Culture, 19 Global Industrialization, 24 Globalization and Economics

Asia for Educators: The Song Dynasty in China (960–1279) <http://afe.easia.columbia.edu/song/>. This interactive website makes use of the famous twelfth-century scroll, "Spring Festival on the River," to portray aspects of urban life and the economy in Song China.

CHAPTER 7

Creating order and disorder

States and empires, old and new

At the end of the Second World War, the Vietnamese nationalist leader Ho Chi Minh (1890–1969) wrote in the introduction to the Vietnamese Declaration of Independence:

> All men are created equal; they are endowed by their Creator with certain unalienable rights; among these are Life, Liberty, and the pursuit of Happiness.
>
> This immortal statement was made in the Declaration of Independence of the United States of America in 1776. In a broader sense, this means: All the peoples on the earth are equal from birth, all the peoples have a right to live, to be happy and free.
>
> The Declaration of the French Revolution made in 1791 on the Rights of Man and the Citizen also states: "All men are born free and with equal rights, and must always remain free and have equal rights."
>
> Those are undeniable truths.
>
> (Quoted in William D. Bowman, Frank M. Chiteji, and J. Megan Greene, *Imperialism in the Modern World: Sources and Interpretations*, Upper Saddle River, N.J.: Pearson Prentice-Hall, 2007, p. 248)

In quoting these two famous documents long after they were crafted in the American and French revolutions, Ho sets up the inspiring values they declare as an ironic prelude to his account of French (and Japanese) colonial oppression in his native land. Freed of French colonial control only by the Japanese occupation during the Second World War, once Allied victory was declared France reasserted its claims to "French Indochina." When the French were finally defeated, the United States attempted to control Vietnam in a long and bitter war directed against communism in Asia, and in turn was itself ultimately defeated by nationalist resistance and the heirs of Ho Chi Minh.

The experience of being controlled by a foreign power was not new to the people of Vietnam even in the nineteenth century when France first colonized their land. For over a thousand years (111 BCE–939 CE), much of what is now modern Vietnam was under the domination of the Chinese. Only in the tenth century did the Vietnamese establish their independence from China, and they still remained in the cultural shadow of China, drawing upon the Chinese imperial government model for their own. The modern name for Vietnam, in fact, derives from the Chinese name, "Yue nan," south of Yue, the southernmost region in China at the time Vietnam was brought under Chinese control. This geographical term described a region that was peopled by different ethnic groups who spoke distinct (though related) languages, and adapted their ways of living to varied landscapes, from mountains and hills to river deltas and coastlines.

In the twentieth-century postwar world, Vietnam's Declaration of Independence was a statement confirming its status as a modern, independent nation-state, created from the shared experience of recent colonialism, a common written and spoken language, and historical identity. Modern Vietnamese – Ho Chi Minh among them – could look to the heroic Trung sisters, who led resistance against the Chinese in the first century CE, as models of nationalist pride. They could also seek models of the modern nation-state in the principles articulated in the American and French revolutionary declarations.

Vietnam's historical experience provides a rich field for introducing the theme of this chapter. What is a state and why do people create states? When and how did the modern nation-state come into being in Europe and across the globe? What forces led to the creation of early empires (before 1500), and how are modern

Figure 7.1 Ho Chi Minh (1967). Born in Vietnam, Ho Chi Minh was brought up in a Confucian household and educated in a French secondary school. Later he lived and worked in the United States, England, and France, where he embraced communism. He spent time in China and the Soviet Union before returning to Vietnam in 1941 to lead the Viet Minh, the Vietnamese nationalist movement.

empires different? In the case of Vietnam, a common historical identity as a state and a people was forged in resistance to the Chinese empire's expansion, and modern nationalist identity was a product of resistance to French, Japanese, and ultimately American imperialism in the nineteenth and twentieth centuries. This chapter explores transformations in collective identities embodied in changing political formations, from the earliest states and empires to modern ones.

INTRODUCTION

As peoples around the world began to practice agriculture and move into cities, growing populations living together expanded the scale of human activities and led to increasing social complexity (see Chapter 3). The unequal distribution of resources – and thereby power – intensified as agricultural villages became cities, city-states, kingdoms, and even empires. Accompanying the concentration of population and resources was the growth of military forces to protect food stores, to defend territory, and eventually to expand control both of people (their labor) and land. Religious ideas and practices that had inspired and guided community life in earlier times were adapted to provide sanction for new rulers and forms of political organization, new social hierarchies, and new economic relationships. Inanna, the tutelary deity of the Sumerian city of Uruk, for example, protected the city's storehouse and had a human consort, a priest-king who ruled through her favor (see Chapter 4).

City-states were independent urban centers that controlled an agricultural hinterland, relied on trade, or both. They are one of the earliest political forms, evident as early as the fourth millennium BCE, but they are found throughout world history and into the present. Greek city-states in the fifth-century BCE Aegean region are examples, as are port cities that rimmed the Indian Ocean in the sixteenth and seventeenth centuries CE, and the modern city-state of Singapore. Kingdoms were larger in scale than city-states and directly controlled a territory that included more than one urban center. Examples of kingdoms can also be found throughout world history and across the globe, everywhere from the twelfth-century kingdom of Sicily in the Mediterranean to the nineteenth-century Zulu kingdom in southern Africa.

Empires were the largest-scale polities and resulted from the expansion of one polity, such as a kingdom or city-state, at the expense of others. Empires have been defined in many different ways, and the processes that led to the formation of empires are equally varied. What all empires appear to have in common are control of a large multiethnic polity by a strong center, and the successful promotion of an ideology that sanctions the exercise of imperial power. The Roman empire is a classic example: at its peak in the first century CE, the urban center of Rome lay claim to a vast area surrounding the Mediterranean, extending west and north to the Iberian peninsula and the isles of Britain and east to the edges of Central Asia. Roman legions policed this territory, and the Roman government exacted tribute from all over the empire to support its elite rulers, army, and administration. Roman emperors were eventually deified, deriving sanction to rule from association with Roman gods.

Differences of scale ranging from agricultural villages to empires imply differences in the nature of collective identities. Blood ties constitute the most basic, or primordial, source of identity beyond the individual, so kinship based on blood ties is one of the building blocks of collective identity. Although societies organize kinship relations in very different ways, kinship ties everywhere can be considered a primordial source of identity. Kinship as a constituent of collective identity is followed by larger-scale communities, states, and finally empires. Transformations in collective identities produced by cross-regional and cross-cultural interactions – including those linked to empire-building – dramatically intensified with the processes of globalization that began in the sixteenth century and continue unabated in the twenty-first.

In this chapter we will first consider the relationship between kinship ties and political orders, questioning the notion of a necessary progression from decentralized communities to centralized states and the assumption that kinship alliances necessarily wither in the face of the bureaucratization of power in large-scale states and empires. We will then compare "old" empires in different parts of the world before 1500, followed by early modern empires on land and sea, the rise of the modern nation-state, and, finally, new empires. We will address the questions of what constitutes an empire, how and why empires differ (both old and new), and trace the historical processes of nationalism, imperialism, and revolution. Across this broad canvas of historical change, the basic concern remains the shifting formulations of collective identity woven throughout transformations of states and empires, old and new.

A "STATELESS SOCIETY": ARCHAEOLOGY AND IGBO-UKWU

States, whatever the scale (city-state, kingdom, empire) are produced by the centralization of power, and enabled by control of technology and the forces of violence. State formation is a complex process, encompassing not only diverse paths but also different outcomes. There is no universal model with local variations, rather a multitude of different ways people assign power to individuals and groups according to hierarchical notions of status and authority. So-called "stateless" societies offer alternative visions of the distribution of power, as do societies that retain a looser organization of political power and authority, often rooted in kinship ties.

As societies grew in size and complexity, the web of social relations holding individuals in place and determining their positions became increasingly important. One form this web frequently took was the lineage, or descent group. The lineage was the perceived community of persons related by blood ties, by their belonging to a traced line of common descent from a real or fictive (imagined) ancestor. Providing a primary source of identity, lineage has endured as a vital building block of human communities and has had the power to shape large-scale political structures as well as individual destinies.

The archaeological complex called Igbo-Ukwu (c. 900), situated in a forested region of roughly 10,000 square kilometers (3,860 square miles), east of the Niger River in present-day southeastern Nigeria, provides evidence of an early decentralized polity in West Africa that was organized around lineages. Despite the region's high population density, neither large cities nor centralized states or empires are known to have existed there. Evidence of the lineage-based society here is primarily archaeological. Excavations of three sites have produced an extraordinary array of technically complex bronze sculptures and objects, imported glass beads and textiles, and human remains. Among the objects excavated is a horseman's hilt, perhaps once attached to a staff of office and depicting a seated male astride a horse. The seated figure bears signs of deliberate facial scarring identical to face designs found among Ibo-speaking peoples in the same area in modern times. Ibo oral traditions similarly attest to a millennium of ethnic continuity in the region.

In more recent times, the Ibo have been studied by anthropologists as an example of a "stateless" political system based on highly democratic, lineage-based connections. Unlike the hierarchical structure of highly centralized societies, the lineage-based society emphasized the common goals and achievements of the group. Membership in lineages was useful for settling disputes (since a member could be assured of the support and protection of other members) and redistributing wealth across generations. Belonging to the same lineage also meant that members shared a common spiritual heritage, central to which was the belief that ancestors were reborn within the same lineage. The Ibo religion included a creator deity, as well as a component that provided each reincarnated person with a personal chi, or deity guide, from the spirit world. Political power was thus a worldly reflection of individual spiritual achievement.

The rule by a council of titled elders at Igbo-Ukwu provided members with opportunities to develop to their highest abilities and increasingly accumulate wealth and wield influence over others. Through their control over social relationships, council members made group decisions and received support in return. Their power and influence were developed gradually and relied on group consensus and the fruits of patronage. Both spiritual and political power were recognized in the award of titles and ranks. The excavator of Igbo-Ukwu has interpreted one of the sites as a possible burial of a priest-king figure, the highest-ranking person within Ibo titled society. Evidence from the site of Igbo-Ukwu also confirms the existence of long-distance trade in which horses, metals, and other goods were imported across the Sahara in pre-Islamic times (before the tenth century). Involvement in such trade networks did not invariably lead to the establishment of a centralized authority. The society's organizational complexity should not be confused with its physical size. Many decentralized societies were large, involving hundreds or thousands of people in voluntary, cooperative endeavors.

LINEAGE SOCIETIES AND EMPIRE

The social, economic, and ideological systems of centralized empires and decentralized lineage polities were profoundly different. The ideology of lineage politics required the sharing out of resources, rather than their centralization (see Chapter 8). The web of reciprocity and patronage demanded constant negotiation and consensus, which was impractical at the level of political strategy and control in a polity the size of an empire.

The dynamic relationship between successive Islamic empires and lineage societies of the Arabian peninsula was characteristic of the relations between empires elsewhere and the lineage societies that bordered and interacted with them. The Muslim historian Ibn Khaldun (1332–1406) even theorized that the rise and fall of states were dependent as much on the interplay of lineage and other internal social factors as on military prowess, great leaders, or the power of gods. The histories of both the Chinese and the Roman empires were marked by shifting relations between an imperial center and lineage societies on their fringes: the Franks, Celts, and Picts for the Romans, and the Xiongnu and other northern nomads for the Chinese.

Nomadic peoples who confronted the Chinese empire across the Great Wall, traded with the Chinese, warred with them, and at times adopted Chinese political institutions came from societies organized by lineages into clans that extended into tribes. The Chinese historian Sima Qian (c. 145–90 BCE) recorded his observations of the social and political organization of nomadic life among the Xiongnu, Turkic, and Mongolic peoples who formed a large confederation in the second century BCE that periodically threatened the Chinese empire:

> They move about in search of water and grass [for their herds], having no cities, permanent dwellings, or agriculture. . . . Their leaders have under them a few thousand to ten thousand horsemen. There are twenty-four chiefs altogether, each titled a "ten-thousand horsemen." All of the major offices are hereditary. The three clans of the Huyan, Lan, and later the Xubu are the nobility.
>
> (Quoted in Patricia B. Ebrey, ed., *Chinese Civilization: A Sourcebook*, New York: Free Press, 1993, p. 55)

In later centuries other lineage-based societies also interacted with and at times threatened or even conquered the Chinese. Although these societies' nomadic or seminomadic way of life and their basic tribal and clan organization worked against the concentration of power characteristic of centralized states, the rise of a charismatic leader whose base of support through ties of personal allegiance was strong enough, could unite tribal leaders into a large confederation. Adopting some aspects of administration from the model of the Chinese state, which loomed large as an influence throughout the region, this confederation could be transformed into a powerful organization for rule of an extended territory as well as a highly skilled and mobile fighting force. The thirteenth-century unification of the Mongol tribes by Chinggis Khan is the best-known example of this process. Tension between the forces of centralization that led to the growth of large-scale polities such as empires, and the decentralized patterns of political life characteristic of societies ordered by lineage, both fueled historical change and highlighted the powerful continuities of kinship through lineage and clan ties.

The transformation of lineage societies into centralized, if temporary, confederations (and even empires) was not a universal pattern. Among Northwest Coast peoples of pre-conquest North America the basic social unit was similar to that of lineages and clans in Eurasia: politically autonomous groups of relatives, their spouses and children, aligned according to systems that reckoned descent or rank based on group affiliations. Social status was determined by both heredity and wealth.

Typically, Northwest Coast lineage or extended family groups lived in separate households, about thirty or so people living in a longhouse made of cedar logs. Longhouses were headed by a chief – any man who owned a house was a chief – and each had its totem, such as a bear, a whale, or a raven, often decorating a totem pole located at the residence. Chieftaincy was inherited both matrilineally and patrilineally, but chiefs were also dependent on the wealth and prestige of his (or her) lineage. The greater the collection of gifts accrued, the greater the potlatch (the manifestation of wealth) that could be created and the more important the chief and his clan. Alliances were sometimes made with similar social groupings for purposes of common defense or for ceremonial ends, but groups never surrendered to one another certain highly individual and important rights, such as totems, crests, and dances.

FEUDALISM: BETWEEN KINSHIP AND STATE

In Europe, a more formally structured style of decentralized political system developed that historians have called "feudalism." Although the term is problematic because it has sometimes been used in such a way as to blur important distinctions, it can still be fruitfully applied to compare patterns of power relationships. Feudalism in this sense can be considered an alternative to societies based primarily on either the personal ties of kinship or the impersonal bureaucratic structures of centralized polities. Broadly defined, feudalism describes a hierarchy of power in which land (from the Latin *feudum* or fief) constitutes the principal form of wealth and provides the basis for political and social orders as well as economic structures. The institutions and practices of European feudalism developed after the power of a strong centralized state (the Roman empire) had shifted onto local political units. Feudalism in its various forms was prevalent in western Europe from the ninth to thirteenth centuries; in parts of eastern Europe, feudalism developed later and lasted longer.

Central to feudalism was the personal, specifically military, relationship between lord (patron) and vassal (client). The basis of all feudal relationships was the contract, a powerful legal and cultural force for cohesion in a world that was effectively localized and decentralized. A contract took the form of an oath of fealty (loyalty), by which homage was sworn by the vassal to the overlord for the grant of a fief.

The term "feudalism" has also been used to describe Japanese political and social institutions from the twelfth to nineteenth centuries. Whether or not the term is precisely appropriate in the case of Japan, there are similarities in the evolution of Japanese society during this period that make comparison meaningful. Both European and Japanese feudal institutions emerged from the crumbling of a centralized imperial government and its legal-administrative apparatus: the weakening of the Roman empire and Roman law in the case of Europe and that of the Japanese state of the Nara and Heian periods (eighth to twelfth centuries), modeled on the imperial government of Tang China (618–907). The development of contractual relationships between patrons and clients in both cases rested on prior legal and administrative foundations.

Japanese feudalism evolved from the reassertion during the Heian (794–1185) period of a lineage-based aristocratic social tradition in which patron–client relations were the basis of political organization and the means of governing the state, exemplified by the rule of the Fujiwara family during the ninth to eleventh centuries. The Heian nobility lived a life of great luxury and refinement, supported by the income from landed estates that lay outside the capital, often in provinces far distant from the center of cultural and political life at the Heian court. They were absentee landholders, dependent on estate managers to supervise their landholdings and secure their income. Control of the manors gradually slipped out of the hands of the court aristocrats and into those of the local managers and military men, who in the absence of imperial authority protected the manors from assault.

As with European feudalism, Japanese feudalism was based on two institutions: the manor (*shoen*), to which was connected the idea of rights to the land, and the military power of a warrior elite. With the decline of Fujiwara power in the late twelfth century and the subsequent weakening of central authority, a new warrior elite, known as *bushi* or samurai, developed outside the capital. Samurai replaced the court aristocracy as a social and political elite whose power was consolidated through personal ties of loyalty and military service.

MARITIME AND MAINLAND EMPIRES IN SOUTHEAST ASIA: SRIVIJAYA AND KHMER

The importance of personal alliances – whether based on kinship ties or contractual relationships as in feudalism – can be seen in the form even empires took in some parts of the world. Southeast Asian states may be thought of as complex systems of personal loyalties that formed the basis for power relations, rather than as territories with defined boundaries administered by representatives of one or another ruler. The precise boundaries of the territory controlled by a ruler were not of primary concern; what mattered was the network of loyalties on which that ruler could depend. Both maritime and mainland empires in Southeast Asia are examples of this.

The large Srivijayan island empire (*c.* 670–1025) was built on the wealth produced by maritime trade (see Chapter 6), along with a combination of military force and the political acumen of the *datus* (chiefs or rulers) of the capital, Palembang, on the island of Sumatra. Given the fluctuations in international trade and variations in human abilities, military power and political skill alone were insufficient to ensure the survival of Srivijaya. The rulers also needed a belief system that could unite conquered regions with differing religious and ethnic groups under a common loyalty to Palembang. Srivijaya's rulers found such a unifying ideology in the universal religion of Buddhism.

Buddhism grew rapidly in the Southeast Asian archipelago during the seventh century (see Chapter 4). Early stone inscriptions at Palembang reveal a ruler there blending the local imagery of the sacred mountain and sea with the traditional veneration of ancestors into Buddhist symbols and ethics. Buddhist themes imposed upon indigenous traditions provided a common set of ideas that transcended local communities. To reinforce this ideology and build regional prestige upon it, the Srivijayan rulers used some of the profits of their empire to become patrons of Buddhist scholarship in their territories and major builders of Buddhist temples, such as the great eighth-century Buddhist monument Borobudur on the island of Java. By the tenth and eleventh centuries, the empire was dedicating temples as far away as Bengal and the southeast coast of India.

On the Southeast Asian mainland, the Khmer empire (802–1432), at its height in the twelfth century, controlled probably a million people in the area of modern Cambodia, Laos, Thailand, and parts of Burma, Vietnam, and the Malay peninsula. A network of canals used for both transportation and irrigation linked the Khmer state physically, and reservoirs helped control the uneven rainfall of a monsoon climate by storing monsoon rainwater for later use.

Both Hinduism and Buddhism provided sanction for the authority of rulers and the common cultural and religious bonds among the Khmer people (see Chapter 4). Their rulers initially blended Hinduism with indigenous beliefs to consolidate their power over their expanding territory, and the Sanskrit language was adopted by the Khmer court. Worship of the Hindu god Shiva, who was identified as the "Lord of the Mountain," was connected with indigenous beliefs in the sanctity of mountains, the home of ancestral spirits. Shiva worship was formalized in the *devaraja* (god-king) cult of the ruler Jayavarman II (770–834),

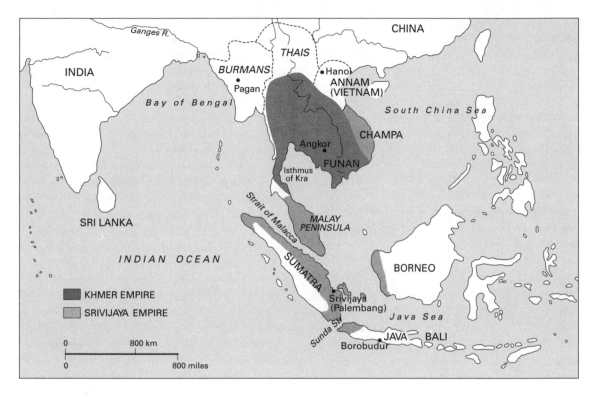

Map 7.1 Srivijayan and Khmer empires.

Source: Anonymous, "Early South East Asia" (Boston, Mass.: Houghton Mifflin, 2001)

who built the Khmer state through a combination of conquest and the formation of a network of personal alliances. Following Jayavarman, statues of gods were fused with the person of the ruler, symbolized by the merging of the monarch's personal title with the name of a god. After the twelfth century, at the capital city of Angkor Thom, Buddhist dominance was reflected in the Bayon temple complex façade, which portrayed the Buddhist deity Lokeshvara. This Buddhist deity was identified with the builder of Angkor Thom, Jayavarman VII (r. 1181–1218?), whose authority was reinforced through the new Buddharaja (Buddha-king) cult.

Massive public works projects carried out by the Khmer monarchy, such as the Hindu temple complex of Angkor Wat (*wat* means "temple") built in the twelfth century, are testimony to the ability of the Khmer state to collect and redistribute economic resources on a huge scale. This was accomplished through a network of temples, which served as centers of redistribution from villages to local temples and on up through a hierarchy to the central temple in the king's capital. In this way both material wealth and symbolic capital, the cultural and religious symbols used to integrate Khmer society, were distributed through a complex temple network spread throughout the realm.

Although the Khmer did not control sea trade that would have allowed them to connect the agricultural hinterland with maritime commerce, as did Srivijaya, both empires controlled massive resources, incorporated different peoples and cultures within their realms, and created ideological foundations using both Hinduism and Buddhism that unified the region under their control. In both the Srivijayan and Khmer empires, new collective identities were constructed through religion and supported by economic wealth produced by the labor of people who engaged in agriculture or both riverine and maritime trade. Temples and other religious monuments were vital expressions of collective identity as they manifested the material wealth commanded by rulers and sanctioned by religion. Personal alliances lay at the core of both empires, and no doubt at the local level where they were part of everyday life that remained unrecorded. People continued to identify closely with kin and village, even as they dwelt in the shadow of mighty empires.

TRADE, TECHNOLOGY, ECOLOGY, AND CULTURE: THE MALI EMPIRE IN WEST AFRICA

Mali was not the first empire to occupy the large grasslands region of West Africa that straddled the Sahara, the semiarid edge of the desert known as the "Sahel" (literally the "shore" of the great ocean of sand, in Arabic) and the inland delta of the Niger River. The Mali empire (c. thirteenth to sixteenth centuries) developed from the conquest and union of several smaller states. At its height, Mali covered much of West Africa and incorporated into one polity hunters, herders, nomads, merchants and farmers from many different language groups. Oral traditions credit a single legendary and heroic figure with the final act of unification: Sundiata, the most powerful of the Mali rulers, finally subjected the Soso people to the authority of Mande languages and culture, with the ascendancy of the Keita clan. The praises of Sundiata today are sung by every *griot*, or Mande oral historian, on behalf of the royal clan. In this way, history was – and still is – used to legitimize the Mali empire and its heirs.

The epic of Sundiata devotes a major portion of its tale to sorcery and its relationship to political power. All great exploits, including the founding of empires, require control of the supernatural, or *nyama*, which the Mande view as both natural and mystical energy. Access to sorcery is a component of political leadership and as such is needed to wage successful military campaigns, to subdue enemies, and even to protect one's personal fortune. Like many African divine rulers, Sundiata overcame obstacles, exile, and a physical handicap (the inability to walk from birth) in order to demonstrate his power (*nyama*). The *griots*

generally attribute most of the empire's administrative structures and innovations to the reign of Sundiata, who was probably responsible for the division of the empire into two military regions and for the codification of hereditary craft clans. During and after his reign, blacksmithing, leatherworking, and other specialist activities became associated with statecraft. The products of such activities supported the expansion of trade and empire.

Management of the trans-Saharan trade was a central feature of the Mali empire, as well as of its predecessor (Ghana) and successor (Songhai). Mali was situated on an ecotone, an area that straddled the borders of desert, Sahel, and savanna. The exchange between these regions, which supplied quite different products, also created a lucrative source of income. Internal trade and occasional tributary relations, with outlying regions being tapped for support, proved necessary to the functioning of the empire. Centers of trade such as Jenne, Gao, and Timbuktu were similarly situated on ecotones. However, exchange among zones was not the only way in which ecology played a role in the fortunes of the Mali empire: much of the expansion of the empire was made possible by Mande military use of the horse, which made them dependent on certain ecological conditions for its breeding and survival, and these conditions existed in the savanna grasslands of Mali.

Ecological factors played a paramount role in defining and limiting the extent of the spread of Mande culture and society. In tropical Africa, the humidity and presence of the tsetse fly limited the use of the horse. The tsetse fly thrived in damp and swampy conditions and spread diseases that were deadly to horses. Thus, the occurrence of a dry climatic period in West Africa between 1100 and 1500 was particularly significant. Horse breeders, warriors, and traders alike derived great advantage from that progressive desiccation, which inhibited the spread of the tsetse fly. With the onset of a drier climate, expansion on horseback was favored over a much wider area. Sundiata's military success over his rival was closely associated with cavalry warfare. Also, the regions occupied by Sahelian and savanna vegetation pushed southward at the expense of the southern forests, increasing the territory in which horses could survive. The elliptical lines of Mande expansion with the aid of

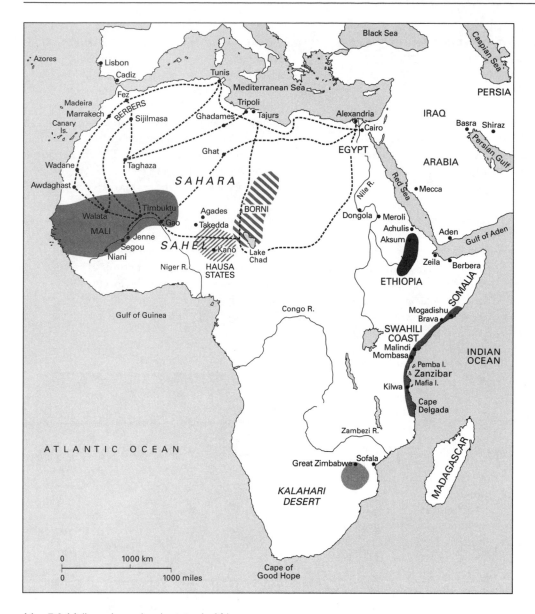

Map 7.2 Mali empire and early states in Africa.

Source: Anonymous, "Africa, 1200–1500" (Boston, Mass.: Houghton Mifflin, 2001)

their cavalry could then extend east and west. Only the rainforest zone, where other ethnic groups lived, remained inhospitable to the empire's warriors and their horses. Conversely, changing ecological conditions during the wet period between about 1500 and 1630 also influenced the fortunes of the empire, which

had begun to collapse toward the end of the fifteenth century. Wetter conditions limited the use of cavalry and put the Mali military at a disadvantage.

The Mali empire's fortuitous combination of technological skills, cultural control, and ecological circumstances came to an end in the late fifteenth

BOX 7.1 EQUESTRIAN FIGURE, INLAND NIGER DELTA STYLE, INLAND NIGER DELTA REGION, MALI (THIRTEENTH TO FIFTEENTH CENTURY)

The terracotta horse and its larger-than-life rider depicted here may suggest the rising prestige associated with cavalries, either Mali's own warrior culture or those of smaller states and towns, resisting state expansion. Although horses were not native to the West African Sahel and forest regions, the horse and rider image constitutes a common symbol of power and prestige. It is likely that only the very wealthy could have afforded the purchase and upkeep of horses. Although probably introduced to West Africa in the early first millennium BCE, horses became essential in warfare around the thirteenth century CE, corresponding to the rise of many small states and notable large ones like Mali. It is said that the ruler Mansa Musa's cavalry was 100,000 strong, a remarkable show of wealth and military strength that would have required considerable resources to acquire and maintain animals, fodder, harnesses, weapons, equipment, and warriors.

Archaeological research has uncovered the ancient artistic heritage of modern-day Mali. Terracotta or fired clay sculptures depict urban life in the region, with idealized human figures exuding calm and assuredness. This sculpture is in the style of art from Jenne-Jeno and the inland Niger Delta region, where art was used in rituals to extend control over the environment. Like other equestrian figures made in clay, bronze, and iron, this particular sculpture exaggerates the size of the rider relative to the horse. In doing so it makes a definitive statement about the role of the horse in elevating one's status and authority. Likely a warrior, the rider sits upright and is dressed in military gear, including knives and quiver, the leather case to hold the bow and arrows of the court archer. His arms hold the horse's bridle and his legs join to those of the animal's, creating a powerful unity of form and function in anthropomorphic profile. The horse is also decorated, perhaps with bells that could summon spirits or deities for speed and strength. Both heads look upward in a ritual pose.

The inland delta region is an area in which flooding occurs annually and the lack or overabundance of water is a constant historical theme. One Dogon myth features the tale of the heavenly ark, containing all of life. The ark falls to earth and is then pulled to water by a horse. No doubt the association of the horse with ecological well-being derives from how precarious existence could be. States could rise and fall, depending on the vagaries of climate, resources, and ancestral sanction. Created by craftsmen working leather, clay and iron, some of the most powerful of ritual art objects reflect the belief in the inevitability of the spiritually endowed to control the outcome of all activities – from war to agriculture.

century, but the legacy of the Mali empire would be felt far and wide for centuries. There remained as well the voices of the *griots*, whose ancestors had created the heroes of the Mande world and who continued to sing the praises of Sundiata, recalling the events of past centuries. In so doing, they both expressed and cemented the collective identity of peoples encompassed by the Mali empire, and breathed life into its history long after the walls of its palaces had crumbled.

NOMADS AND EMPIRE IN EURASIA: THE MONGOL EMPIRE

In the early thirteenth century the foundations were laid for what has been called the largest contiguous land-based empire in human history. The Mongol empire endured for only a century, but it had a profound impact on world history. Sometime around the close of the eleventh century and the beginning of the twelfth, Mongol clans began to organize into tribal collectives under the leadership of chieftains whose power was based on personal loyalty. By 1200, the Mongol tribes had joined together in a large confederation. Under the leadership of Chinggis (*c.* 1162–1227), who was elected khan (chief) in 1206 by an assembly of tribal chieftains, they began to bring other tribes, such as the Turkic Uighurs, under their control. With this step, the Mongol conquest of Asia began. Chinggis was a charismatic political leader who organized the Mongol tribes, and a brilliant military strategist who led the Mongol armies to victory. Along with the military strength that made conquest possible, the Mongols were driven to conquest by the uncertain nature of their economic base, which depended in part on the fluctuating fortunes of trade and was made more precarious by a climatic change that produced colder weather and consequently poorer pasturage for their animals.

Religious sanction for the authority of Chinggis Khan and the conquest of the world came from the sky god, the principal deity of the steppe. Under Chinggis's leadership a written script, adapted from Uighur Turkic, was created for the Mongol language, and a law code was issued to provide guidance first for the administration of the Mongol tribes and later, as it was

modified, for the governing of conquered lands and peoples. Succession to the position of khan, however, was not institutionalized, and at Chinggis's death, despite his stated will that he be succeeded by his third son, Ögödei (1186–1241), there was no clear successor. In 1229, two years after Chinggis's death, the territories under Mongol control were divided among Chinggis's grandson Batu (d. 1255), who became the khan of the Golden Horde (the western lands, eventually including Russia); Chinggis's son Chaghadai (*c.* 1185–1242), who assumed control of Central Asia; and another son, who was assigned responsibility for the Mongolian homeland and north China. In a gesture of compliance with Chinggis's will, Ögödei became the khaghan, or khan of khans, ruler over all Mongol domains.

During the next generation, the Mongol empire expanded into China, Russia, and Islamic lands in West Asia, confronting vastly different political, religious, and social conditions in each region. Despite continuing conflicts among themselves over leadership, Mongol rulers in each khanate (territory ruled by a khan) of the empire were able to implement an efficient administrative system that integrated Chinese, Muslim, Turkic, and native elements.

Chinggis and his successors in the thirteenth and early fourteenth centuries had succeeded in creating a huge empire by their military prowess, discipline, and strength, and by their strategic and logistical skill at maneuvering large numbers of troops over long distances. Their military abilities were grounded in their superior horsemanship, honed in the course of Mongol life as nomadic herders and hunters. Their efficient communication network in the form of a courier system operated by riders on horseback was an essential part of their military operations. But their expansion and conquest of the Eurasian world would have stopped short of creating an empire had they not been able to successfully make use of the human and material resources of the lands they conquered to fuel the machinery of expansion and to provide the tools of empire.

Mongol armies linked vast areas of the Eurasian continent, bringing about an era known as the *pax Mongolica*, the "Mongolian peace." What is remarkable about the Mongol empire is not that it was relatively short-lived but that an empire of such scale

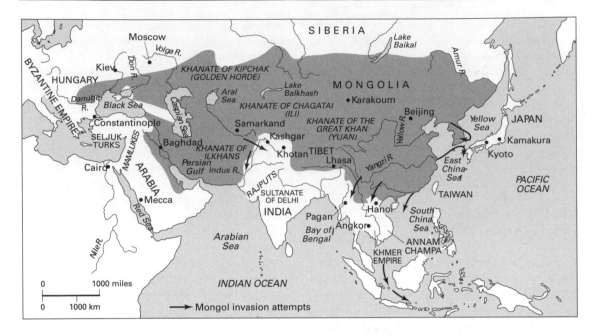

Map 7.3 The Mongol empire.

and complexity existed at all at a time when communication and transportation were largely dependent on the horse, donkey, and camel. The Mongol courier system was known for its speed and efficiency, and the effectiveness of this communication network, along with military skill and administrative ability, accounts in large part for the rise of the Mongols from a lineage-based society, to a tribal confederation, to one of the most powerful empires in world history. Its very size, however, also contributed to its fragility and brevity, since the Mongol empire incorporated so many different peoples, cultures, and ecologies that it was impossible to create a unitary collective identity with the technological limitations in communication and transportation of the time.

MARITIME AND LAND-BASED EMPIRES, *c.* 1500–1800

In contrast to the land-based Mongol empire, the empires of expanding European states in the sixteenth and seventeenth centuries – Portuguese, Spanish, Dutch, and English – were seaborne. Each of these maritime empires moved along ancient routes, especially in the Indian Ocean, and opened up new routes, across the Atlantic and the Pacific. The Portuguese established outposts that rimmed the coastlines of Africa, India, and Southeast Asia, from Ceuta (1415) on the northwest coast of Africa to Goa (1510) on the Malabar coast of India, the Southeast Asian port of Malacca (1511), and Macao (1517) on the southern coast of China. After the pope divided the world between the Portuguese and Spanish in 1494 with the Treaty of Tordesillas, these two European states shared the oceans. In the Indian Ocean and in Southeast Asian waters, Portuguese traders competed with Muslim merchants for control of the seas, while the Spanish encountered Chinese merchants in the Asian Pacific. By the late sixteenth and early seventeenth centuries, the Dutch and English had begun to encroach on Portuguese and Spanish claims in Asia. On land, expanding European empires confronted land-based empires across Africa, the Americas, and Eurasia. In Eurasia, the Ottoman, Safavid, and Mughal, Russian and Chinese empires dominated a region from the Mediterranean to the edges of the Pacific during the sixteenth to the eighteenth centuries. In the Americas, the Aztec and Incan empires reached their peaks in the sixteenth century, when they faced destruction and conquest by the Spanish.

During the sixteenth century, well before the English, French, and Dutch colonized North America, Spanish and Portuguese *conquistadors* established themselves in a wide geographic range, from the southern parts of North America to the tip of South America. Following the conquests of Mexico and Peru, a well-organized colonial administration, which was controlled from Spain by the Council of the Indies, supported the mercantilist goals of the kingdom, selling goods in America and shipping to Spain as much precious metal as possible. By the eighteenth century, the Spanish monarchy had established "viceroyalities," administrative units presided over by the king's representative (the viceroy), in New Spain (Mexico); New Granada (Colombia, Ecuador, and Venezuela), from which one for Peru was separated; and finally Argentina (1776). Viceroys, responsible to the Council of the Indies and the European king, headed the well-defined hierarchical system with an easily recognizable chain of command. The viceregal and mercantilist system by which Spain and Portugal controlled their American colonies created a European elite in Latin America, consisting of *peninsulares* (those who had come to America from the Iberian peninsula) and *creoles* (Iberians who were born in America) who controlled wealth and exercised power, neither of which they willingly shared with *mestizos* (a "new race" resulting from European and Native American unions). Both the European monopoly on wealth and power and the complicated relations between the native populations of South America and the Europeans became important components in the nationalist struggles in Latin America during the nineteenth and twentieth centuries.

The expansion of Europeans across the globe during the early modern era (*c.* 1500–1800) was stimulated by the mercantilist impulse (see Chapter 6), and in the meantime the European states that promoted and supported maritime empires through the establishment of trading companies such as the British East India Company (founded 1600) were experiencing changes that would have profound implications for subsequent global ventures and for transformations in collective identities around the world.

THE NATION-STATE AND REVOLUTIONS IN THE ATLANTIC WORLD

Sixteenth-century Europe was a conglomeration of more than 500 different polities, ranging from city-states such as Venice to the Holy Roman (German) empire. The transformation of this dizzying array of polities into nation-states took place in a variety of ways and at different paces. Beginning with the transformation of the English monarchy in the seventeenth century and the American and French revolutions in the eighteenth, the personal ties that bound the privileged aristocracy to their rulers in dynastic states were replaced in nation-states by the abstract ideal of a constitutional contract regulating the relationship between ruler and ruled. The contractual nature of society was acknowledged by political guarantees of legal equality and personal freedom, though gender and social class often determined the extent to which these principles were enacted. States based on the social contract can be distinguished as nation-states – those in which the state is the property of all the people who make up the nation, not of the ruler alone. The nation-state is thus based on the construction of a common historic and cultural identity of ruler and ruled, and nationalism – evinced in language, culture, history – provides the ideological sanction for the nation-state.

English monarchy and revolution

The transformation of the English monarchy from absolutism to constitutional monarchy, in which the king shared power with a representative body called parliament, was a long-term process that encompassed evolutionary change, civil war, and revolution. The Magna Carta, granted by King John in 1215, declared that the king was subject to the same laws as those he ruled and could not arbitrarily impose his will. In 1295 Edward I summoned the first or "model parliament," an assembly of rural nobles and representatives from the cities, to lend support for war with France. Over the centuries the summoning of parliaments became regularized, though they remained elite bodies whose role in governing was controlled by strong kings.

In the seventeenth century, a series of conflicts culminating in what became known as the "Glorious

Revolution" decisively defined the relationship between king and parliament: the king was henceforth expected to act in and through parliament and only with parliamentary approval and support. The "Glorious Revolution" inspired the English philosopher John Locke (1632–1704) to suggest that anyone in authority who exceeds the power given to him by the law or who encroaches on the rights of individuals forfeits the right to rule. Having done so, he may be opposed and resisted just as "any other man who by force invades the right of another." John Locke's justification of revolution not only inspired the American revolutionaries who sought independence from England and its king but also foreshadowed the upheavals of the French Revolution at the end of the eighteenth century.

The American Revolution

The American Revolution (1776–83) occurred soon after the apex of British imperial power in the Americas was reached in the mid-eighteenth century when the British gained control of most of the North American continent by their victory over the French (1763). Thus the American Revolution was a response to British imperialism, even though the colonists themselves for the most part were originally British. Discontent with British colonial policy mounted as innumerable specific incidents further exacerbated relations between the seaboard colonies and the imperial government. Discontent fueled resistance, and resistance became rebellion. Colonists became more radical as they convinced themselves that the liberties they believed belonged to them as British subjects were endangered. They embraced the concepts of the social contract proposed by Locke and were influenced by French Enlightenment thinkers, as well as by Benjamin Franklin, one of their own. Resistance to the British imperial government's restraints on expansion, control of the economy and, above all, "taxation without representation," flared into armed conflict in the last quarter of the eighteenth century. Supported by European governments (France, Spain, the Netherlands), who had their own anti-British national motivations, the colonists finally defeated the British and declared their independence.

The Declaration of Independence distilled eighteenth-century ideals of rights common and equal to all and the concept of the social contract: "all men

are created equal . . . [and] endowed with certain inalienable Rights, that among these are Life, Liberty and the pursuit of Happiness . . . Governments derive their just powers from the consent of the governed." The Declaration explicitly justified the American rebellion: "To secure these rights, Governments are instituted among Men . . . whenever any Form of Government becomes destructive of these ends, it is the Right of the People to alter or abolish it, and to institute new Government." It took nearly a decade to translate these ideals into the principles and structures of government and embody them in a contract, the Constitution of 1789. Like the Declaration of Independence, the Constitution reflects eighteenth-century ideas and ideals such as the separation of Church and state.

The French Revolution

Unlike their English counterparts, on the European continent absolute monarchs of the seventeenth and eighteenth centuries, such as Louis XIV of France (r. 1642–1715), thought of themselves as the embodiment of the state, as he famously declared: "L'état c'est moi" (I am the state). Though the first French parliament, known as the "Estates-General" and representing the three "estates" of clergy, nobility, and commoners, was summoned at about the same time as the English model parliament, the French parliament never evolved into a body that actively participated in governing. When it questioned royal policy, it was simply dismissed. Tensions between the monarch and aristocracy continued during the seventeenth and eighteenth centuries until a severe fiscal crisis was reached in 1789 that forced the king, Louis XVI, to summon the Estates-General for the first time in 175 years.

The most powerful ideas inspiring the actions of the representatives of the Third Estate (commoners) came from the writings of Enlightenment thinkers, especially Jean-Jacques Rousseau (1712–78), whose *Social Contract* became the guiding principle of the Third Estate. Rousseau argued that the social contract between rulers and ruled required rulers to obey the "general will" of the people. If they failed to do so, then the people had the right to overthrow them. These ideas were embodied in the Declaration of the Rights of Man and the Citizen, adopted in 1789. This "solemn declaration of the natural, inalienable, and sacred rights of man" declared that sovereignty is located in the people who constitute the nation, and that "no body, no individual can exercise authority" unless it is granted by the people.

Though women were denied civic rights and equality with men, they took active roles in the popular revolutionary *journées*, which were often inspired by hunger and began as bread riots led by women. For example, the October 1789 women's march on Versailles brought the royal family – popularly referred to as "the baker, the baker's wife, and the baker's son" – back to Paris. Participation in *journées* provided women with political opportunities and experience. Militant women responded to being shut out of the political process by organizing political clubs and exerting pressure by speaking out at rallies and during riots. One militant woman revolutionary, Olympe de Gouges (1748–93), responded to the Declaration of the Rights of Man by publishing a Declaration of the Rights of Women (1791), which proclaimed that "woman is born free and lives equal to man in her rights."

The initial Constitution of 1791 was invalidated because of tensions between the king and the Estates-General and opposition on the part of still disenfranchised members of the population including all women. The Constitution of 1793 much more closely reflected Rousseau's vision of a social contract based on the general will. It provided universal male suffrage, freed slaves in France and its territories, and gave citizens the right to work and the right to revolt. Internal struggles and the dangers posed by external enemies – revolutionary France was at war with the rest of Europe – offered a young Corsican artillery officer, Napoleon Bonaparte (1769–1821), his opportunity to seize power. Napoleon's command of the army enabled him to control the state and even to convert it from a republic to an empire, but he accepted the revolutionary ideal that "sovereignty is located in essence in the nation" and that "law is the expression of the general will."

The Haitian Revolution

Eighteenth-century European ideals, such as "men are born free and equal in rights" and "liberty, equality, and fraternity," also spread to Caribbean shores, where they were translated into the issues of property, labor,

and race. Soon after the outbreak of the French Revolution (1789), white planters in St Domingue (the western third of the island of Hispaniola, today's Haiti) were given control of colonial assemblies and a large measure of autonomy. Then in 1791 the National Assembly in Paris, responding to pressures from a European abolitionist society, Les Amis des Noirs ("The Friends of Blacks"), further extended rights to all free persons, including mulattoes (those of mixed race), decreeing that "persons of color, born of free parents" should have voting rights in the colonial assemblies. White planters demanded the law be repealed and threatened to join the British empire if it was not. Both whites and mulattoes began to arm themselves, and the conflict that broke out between them offered slaves their opportunity to revolt.

The potential threat of slave revolt on St Domingue was great. Most of the slaves, unlike those in the US, were African born, and they formed the majority population, outnumbering other ethnic groups by a ratio of thirteen to one. Since the colony's mountainous interior afforded ample inaccessible hiding places, there were numerous maroon (freedom-fighter) communities. Common beliefs, such as the African-derived religion of Vodun (Voodoo), and shared myths and heroes, united diverse slave populations (see Chapter 4). In 1791 slaves in northern St Domingue demanded their own liberty and rebelled; during much of the period from 1791 to 1792, slave strikes and revolts spread across the island. Reluctantly, France sent troops in. Attempts at negotiation to restore colonial order failed to gain the support of slaves. In 1793 the French National Assembly granted emancipation to the slaves, an act further angering the planters and the free coloreds, who accepted aid from the British (who were alarmed at the possibility that the slave rebellion might spread to their colonies) against the rebellious slaves.

More than 100,000 slaves participated in the rebellion under the leadership of Toussaint L'Ouverture (*c.* 1746–1803), the educated son of African slave parents. In his efforts to liberate his fellow black slaves, Toussaint fought for a decade against intervention and blockades by slave-owning nations (France, Britain, Spain, and the United States), and even against mulatto opposition. By 1801 he and his supporters controlled the entire island of Hispaniola, but many more battles were fought before a final victory established the independent nation-state of Haiti.

Once Napoleon was firmly in control in France, he dispatched a huge army to invade St Domingue. L'Ouverture was induced to meet with the French, treacherously seized, carried to Europe, and imprisoned, where he died in 1803. Jean-Jacques Dessalines and Henri Christophe continued the struggle in Haiti, and black strength and yellow fever defeated the massive French effort to regain control of St Domingue. On January 1, 1804, the independence of the western half of Hispaniola was proclaimed, and the new nation was given the name Haiti. But independence came at a high price, leaving the country poor and plagued by political strife for the next 200 years.

NEW NATIONS FROM AN OLD EMPIRE: HISPANIC AMERICA

Like the colonists in North America who rebelled against the British imperial government in the late eighteenth century, descendants of Spanish colonists and Native Americans rebelled against Spain in the early nineteenth century. The turmoil of the French Revolution and Napoleonic decades led to the collapse of the Spanish empire in the Americas. By the beginning of the nineteenth century Spain was severely weakened in Europe as well as in its colonial possessions in the Americas. In 1807 Napoleon invaded the Iberian peninsula, causing the Portuguese king to seek refuge in his Brazilian colony, and replaced the Spanish king with Joseph Bonaparte. Spain's sea power had been destroyed, a development fatal to an overseas empire.

The disarray of the Spanish monarchy enabled peoples of South America to liberate themselves from Spanish control. Many leading *creoles* whose loyalties to the lands of their birth were greater than to Spain and who saw independence as a chance to replace *peninsulares* in power, took leading roles in the uprisings that became wars of independence. The Spanish government was unable to win over the rebels by either compromise or force, and a number of South American revolutions essentially ended Spanish imperial control in the Americas.

Simon Bolivar (1783–1830), educated in Caracas, Venezuela, and in Spain, was one of the heroes of the struggle for South American independence from Spain. Like so many of his contemporaries in North America and Europe, Bolivar was influenced by Enlightenment ideas such as the social contract of Rousseau; these ideas inspired his efforts to achieve independence for his homeland. In his fight against Spain in Venezuela, Bolivar was defeated many times before independence was finally achieved in 1817. During the struggle against Spain, he visited Haiti seeking support, and while living in temporary exile in Jamaica in 1815, Bolivar composed a letter to the island's British governor in which he eloquently stated his views on independence:

> Americans either defend their rights or suffer repression at the hands of Spain, which, although once the world's greatest empire, is now too weak, with what little is left her, to rule the new hemisphere or even to maintain herself in the old. And shall Europe, the civilized, the merchant, the lover of liberty allow an aged serpent, bent only on satisfying its venomous rage, devour the fairest part of our globe? . . .

> [I]f she [Spain] will fix herself on her own precincts she can build her prosperity and power upon more solid foundations than doubtful conquests, precarious commerce, and forceful exactions from remote and powerful peoples.
> (Quoted in Alfred J. Andrea and James H. Overfield, eds, *The Human Record: Sources of Global History*, Boston, Mass.: Houghton Mifflin, 1994, p. 187)

Two years later Bolivar led his army across the Andes to liberate Colombia, which was then united with Venezuela. In 1822 Ecuador was liberated, followed by Peru, the southern part of which was named Bolivia.

Bolivar was aided in the liberation of Latin America by others, such as José de San Martín (1778–1850), an Argentine who led an army of liberation across the Andes in 1817, and, with the Chilean leader Bernardo O'Higgins (1778–1842), freed Chile in 1818, invaded Peru, and captured Lima in 1821. Bolivar had a vision of a united Latin America and tried to achieve political unity among the territories he liberated from the Spanish. His dream was destroyed by political factionalism and rivalry among liberation leaders and by tension and suspicion among *creoles, peninsulares,* and *mestizos* inherited from the colonial era.

Portuguese Brazil, unlike its South American neighbors, did not break away from its imperial master as a result of a nationalist revolution. When the French invaded the Iberian peninsula in 1807, the Portuguese government simply moved to Brazil, and Rio de Janeiro, instead of Lisbon, became the seat of Portuguese government. In 1815 King Joao declared that the viceroyalty was a kingdom and decided to remain in Brazil even though the French occupation of

Map 7.4 New nations in Latin America.

Portugal had ended. In 1820 leaders of a revolution in Portugal demanded that the government return to Lisbon and that Brazil be reduced to colonial status. When Joao returned to Lisbon, he left his son, Pedro, to continue Portuguese control; but in 1822 when independence was declared, Pedro became emperor of Brazil, which kept the monarchical government until 1889.

In nineteenth-century Brazil political conflicts between the old and new orders highlighted characteristics of the age of global imperialism. The ties between this former Portuguese colony and the Atlantic economy were perhaps the most entrenched of the region. Slavery lasted longer and the ties to West and Central Africa were more numerous and enduring (see Chapter 8). Between 1850 and 1874 the number of slaves had been cut by more than half, but still remained about a million. When slavery was finally abolished in 1888, planters felt betrayed by the Brazilian monarchy; this opposition fueled the impetus for a military coup and the creation of a new republic. Its motto was "Order and Progress," and both were sought with often contradictory results in the following generations.

SETTLER SOCIETIES AND NEW NATIONS: CANADA, AUSTRALIA, NEW ZEALAND, SOUTH AFRICA

Settler colonies had come into existence during the early maritime expansion of Britain and other European nations, and immigrant ambitions had particularly significant consequences on vast land masses in North America and the Pacific. Such communities not only extended European hegemony through conquest and colonization but also provided examples of the rise of new nationalist identities in conflict and competition with the old. In Canada, Australia, and New Zealand expansion came at the expense of the subjugation of indigenous peoples. Immigrant communities also struggled with conflicts between their new colonial identities and ties to their homelands.

Canada

Canada, like so much of the globe, became an arena for competing European imperial ambitions following the sixteenth- and seventeenth-century voyages of exploration and subsequent colonization. Because parts of this vast northern half of the North American continent were claimed, explored, and settled by both France and Great Britain, it became an extension of their competition for dominance in Europe. In 1763, at the Treaty of Paris, the issue was resolved: Canada, including those parts claimed and settled by the French for 200 years, became wholly a part of the British empire. Canadians eventually became restive with their status as colonial subjects. The desire to control their own destinies independent of London became a motivating force in their politics and led to independence in the twentieth century.

The American Civil War (1861–5) was crucial to the Canadian nationalist desire for confederation. It once again aroused Canadian concern with the threat from the south, and it reaffirmed the Canadian sense of dependence on England. Although the threat of American invasion subsided when the war was over, the danger of American competition and ambition continued. Three and a half million Canadians could hardly ignore 35 million Americans whose national energies and ambitions, finally freed from their internal conflict, turned toward western expansion. Canadian nationalism grew too as Canadians recognized that British government interest in and commitment to North America was waning. As a result, negotiations between Canadians and the British Colonial Office led to the creation of the Canadian confederation through the British North America Act of 1867, which officially declared the Dominion of Canada.

The development of Canadian nationalism also took place against the background of expansionist claims against indigenous peoples, those known in modern Canada as the "First Nations." Some native peoples resisted being moved to "reserves." At least one important Plains chief, Big Bear (c. 1825–88), joined Métis (mixed) discontents in a rebellion (1885) against the encroachment of government policy and immigrants into the western Great Plains. The Big Bear–Métis rebellion was suppressed, and Indian policy remained directed by the interests of settlers. After 1885 First Nations were pushed out of sight of settlement and "pacified" on reserves from the Atlantic to the Pacific.

Australia

Australia's history bore some similarities to that of Canada, but also differed in ways that shaped its own distinctive experience of British imperialism and the growth of nationalism. Although the Dutch were the first Europeans to reach Australia, the first British settlements there during the late eighteenth century and the early nineteenth were penal colonies for felons transported from Britain. The spread of European settlers into the interior of the continent destroyed the fragile ecology of the Australian Aborigines, the indigenous people who were forced into the deep interior and whose way of life was virtually destroyed by the incursions of European settlement.

The growth of a world market in wool and technological advances in shipping and refrigeration contributed to a developing commercial economy. The largely British and European population remained predominantly in the major cities, especially Melbourne and Sydney, despite important mineral discoveries that led to gold rushes in the 1850s and again in the 1890s. The individual colonies of Tasmania, Western Australia, South Australia, Victoria, and Queensland were united into a federation as the Commonwealth of Australia in 1901, part of the British empire.

New Zealand

Like Australia, the settlement of New Zealand dates from the late eighteenth century in the wake of the voyages of Captain Cook; and, like both Australia and Canada, New Zealand became a self-governing dominion within the British empire in the early twentieth century (1907). As with other dominions in the British empire, the settlement of New Zealand by Europeans came at the expense of native peoples. Britain claimed sovereignty over New Zealand and its native inhabitants, the Maori people, in the 1840 Treaty of Waitangi, though the terms of this treaty as understood by Maoris and British differed.

Granted a constitution in 1852, New Zealand was governed according to a British provincial system. In the 1850s an influx of European settlers into the colony led to disputes over land between the "Pakehas," as the Europeans were known, and the Maoris. In response to European demand for land, Maoris formed a pan-tribal anti-land sales league known as the "Maori King movement." Land wars beginning in 1860 led finally to the confiscation of much Maori land, and in 1864 the Maoris were confined to reservations.

The Natives Land Act in 1865, and the Native Schools Act and the Native Representation Act in 1867, promoted the assimilation of the Maoris by education, some representation, and a Native Land Court. The individualization of land tenure was the outcome of the Natives Land Act, and the Native Land Court proved a difficult place for Maoris to confirm their claims to land through legal means. Many Maoris actually were forced to sell their lands to pay the legal fees necessary to prove their claims to the land. By the 1890s the bulk of New Zealand had been shifted to Pakeha ownership, and many Maoris were left in poverty.

South Africa

In South Africa, as in Canada, Australia, and New Zealand, European settlers claimed African territories that they eventually considered as their own homelands. Isolated from their European roots and marginalized by shifting global relations, these "white" settlers – the Afrikaners – found themselves competing with Africans and European empires for control over territory and resources. They were descendants of early Dutch settlers who began arriving only in the seventeenth century; by the nineteenth century they displayed a language and culture born of two centuries of interaction with African populations and began to develop a cultural nationalism that would eventually turn political.

For the Afrikaner the history of South Africa began in 1652, the year of the first permanent settlement in the Cape. From that century onwards their history took on mythic proportions. With motives they considered of divine origin and therefore pure (the claiming of lands by God's chosen people), and with their God's protection, the descendants of these early European settlers found themselves pitted against two traditional sets of enemies: the British, who acquired control over Cape Colony in 1815, and the Africans. In the Afrikaner view of history, the central saga is the so-called "Great Trek" of 1838, the era of the Afrikaner migration northward out of the Cape when both sets of enemies opposed the expansion of the Afrikaner state.

For the Zulu, Madlathule was a famine that devastated southern Africa from the 1790s until about 1810, setting the stage for the rise of the great Zulu kingdom. During the famine, larger villages were needed to defend grain storage from the attacks of marauders. The control of cattle over a larger area was also necessary to compensate for the decrease in palatable grasses. One powerful and charismatic leader known as Shaka (r. 1818–28) exploited the crisis. He utilized revolutionary military tactics (the use of a new weapon, the short stabbing spear; a new formation known as the "cow-horn" formation), and he converted the traditional age-grade system into a military organization. The system was an association of similar-aged males, who from boyhood to manhood created regiments in a unified army.

Through his control over marriage (and thus population and production), Shaka was able to revolutionize Zulu social relations. Marriage practices had potentially important economic and political consequences. As social and political transactions, marriages transferred wealth and created strategic alliances between families. Shaka, by delaying the marriage of his young soldiers, was able to control the movement of a significant proportion of the kingdom's power and production. With marriages delayed and warfare increased, Shaka was able to resolve the population pressures that the Madlathule had induced.

The era after the famine came to be called the Mfecane, the "time of the crushing." The forces and peoples of the Mfecane transformed the region, and societies that could not resist Shaka's armies became starving, landless refugees. Survivors were highly militarized. Small political units were no longer viable; populations were dramatically redistributed across southern Africa. The Great Trek era (1836–54) of Afrikaner history was the collision of Boer expansion with these forces.

The mid-nineteenth century presents a momentary balance of power: the independent states of the Zulu and other Africans, independent Boer "republics" (not much more than lumps of settlements), and British control over two southern African colonies, Cape and Natal. The Mfecane had left large unpopulated areas vulnerable to European imperialists. This was the eve

of the country's mineral revolution: the European discovery of diamonds and gold in 1868 and 1886 dramatically altered the role of land and capital. Mineral exploitation spurred British expansion into the interior of South Africa, where it met with the resistance of Africans and Boers, the descendant "white" farmers from Dutch and racially mixed frontier mercantile and farming societies at the Cape.

Conflicts over land and ideology erupted between farmers and capitalist interests. Known as the Anglo-Boer War (1899–1902), this period of conflict witnessed the birth of Afrikaner nationalism, which was based on a sense of shared religion and historical experience of the Boers. The Anglo-Boer War was basically about who should dominate South Africa: the British, who controlled mining, or the Boers, who controlled politics.

This conflict set the stage for the social, political, and economic reconstruction after British victory in

Figure 7.2 Restoration and defense of British liberty in South Africa (*c.* 1900). Soldiers posed with their rifles in front of a woman and flag to create a souvenir image of masculinity protecting the innocence of British values during the Boer War. This brutal conflict witnessed the first use of the English term "concentration camp" to describe the British internment of women, children, and enemy soldiers.

1902 and for unitary white rule under the British crown in 1910. British and other foreign investment in agricultural production further removed Africans from their landholdings in an era of expanding foreign capital. Against this background customary policies of segregation and discrimination became entrenched in laws between 1905 and 1945. Black Africans continued to be denied participation in the machinery of government; they could neither vote nor hold office until the end of apartheid in the 1990s.

EUROPEAN NATION-STATES, NATIONALISM, AND THE "NEW" IMPERIALISM

While new nations and national identities were being forged in the crucibles of empire in the Americas, Africa, and Australia, the map of Europe was being redrawn in the wake of the French Revolution and the Napoleonic wars. European monarchies that had resisted both revolution and Napoleon – Great Britain, Russia, Prussia, Austria – tried to stem the tide of revolutionary nationalism, but they were only temporarily successful. For most of the nineteenth century attempts to create nation-states based on contractual constitutions were made all over Europe, from the Baltic eastward to the Black Sea and south to the Mediterranean. In 1835 the Italian nationalist and patriot Giuseppe Mazzini (1805–72), who mobilized Italian national aspirations, expressed his understanding of nation:

> A nation is an association of those who are brought together by language, by given geographical conditions or by the role assigned them by history, who acknowledge the same principles and who march together to the conquest of a single definite goal under the rule of a uniform body of law.
>
> (Herbert H. Rowen, ed., *Absolutism to Revolution, 1648–1848* (2nd edn), Englewood Cliffs, N.J.: Prentice Hall, 1969, p. 277)

In 1848 revolutions demanding constitutions, parliaments, and political independence based on ethnic identities swept Europe. Although the revolu-

tions of 1848 were suppressed, their legacy was apparent in the unification of Italian territories into the kingdom of Italy in 1861 and the creation of the Second (the first existed in medieval times) German Reich (empire) in 1871.

The notion of a shared past played a vital role in shaping national identities, so views of history – what it meant, how it was practiced, and how it was used – were critical in the formation and maintenance of nationalism. The writing of history became a professional discipline in nineteenth-century Europe, and its development was closely connected with the emergence of the European nation-state and nationalist ideology. Leopold von Ranke (1795–1886), a German historian, played a defining role in the creation of history as a modern academic discipline. According to Ranke, the task of the historian is to reconstruct the past as objectively and comprehensively as possible, to present the past "wie es eigentlich gewesen" (as it actually was). The historian performs this task through the critical use of evidence contained in written texts collected in national archives, or other official repositories of documents. Historians were key participants in the construction of new collective identities in

Figure 7.3 The French Revolution: Burning the Royal Carriages at the Chateau d'Eu (1848). Published by the famous American printmakers Currier and Ives, who produced over a million prints for the mass market between 1835 and 1907, this lively lithograph portrays an attack at the royal residence of the French king, Louis-Philippe, during the revolutionary upheavals of 1848. It was titled *The French Revolution*, both describing the events of the time, when French citizens rebelled against the restoration of the French monarchy, and recalling the violence of the original French Revolution of 1789.

European nation-states during the nineteenth century. But Rankean objectivity was not always the best way to promote nationalism. A century before Benedict Anderson coined the term "imagined community" to evoke the constructed nature of nationalism, Ranke's contemporary, Ernst Renan, observed that "Forgetting, I would even go so far as to say historical error, is a crucial factor in the creation of a nation" (Eley and Suny 1996: 45). Renan's point was that the manipulation of the past to enhance national consciousness was as important as the archival work of historians.

Competition among new nationalisms in Europe began a process that spread the idea of the nation across the globe through the new imperialism. As the growth limits of industrial capitalism (see Chapter 6) began to be felt in European economies during the second half of the nineteenth century, alternative markets and resources had to be found overseas. While there were still a few possibilities for more intensive utilization of European resources, increasingly Europeans turned to the exploitation of other parts of the world. Late nineteenth-century European imperialism completed the process of European domination of the world that began with the opening of the Atlantic frontier in the sixteenth century. Engendered by capitalist industrialism and the nation-state, the new imperialism spread both industrialism and nationalism around the world. Nothing stimulated imperialism more than national rivalry, as new nation-states competed for power and territory. The new economic forces unleashed by capitalist industrialism stretched the tentacles of empire around the globe and heightened this rivalry.

The principle of balance of power among European nation-states – that is, no single state should be allowed to dominate territory or economic control – guided the diplomatic and political decisions underlying global expansion through imperialism. As European nation-states created empires and colonies, the balance of power came to be applied on a global scale. As a

Map 7.5 Nineteenth-century European nation-states bordered by the Ottoman and Russian empires.

global balance among European nations was sought, however, the imbalance between European powers and those they colonized was heightened. Between 1800 and 1914 the dissolution of old empires and states produced new nationalisms in Europe and around the world that would eventually alter the global balance of power in the twentieth century (see Chapter 11).

THE NEW IMPERIALISM, COLONIALISM, AND RESISTANCE IN AFRICA

Africa, which Europeans called the "dark continent" because its interior was still virtually unknown to them, was colonized by conquest from one end of the continent to the other. At the Berlin Conference (1884–5), European powers and the United States met to protect their "spheres of influence" (areas of special economic and political interests) and to establish mechanisms for making new territorial claims (see Chapter 10). The scramble for African territory was underway. Political independence was lost as one territory after another was conquered. Although post-Berlin Conference colonial rule followed decades and even centuries of involvement, its imposition was swift. The use of military force was necessary everywhere to establish and maintain European control of African territories.

The European "tools of empire," from quinine (to treat malaria) to the steamboat, railway, and machine gun, all enabled the penetration and conquest to be complete. In some places, such as the Benin kingdom of Nigeria in 1897, Europeans forcibly removed the local rulers (the oba and his chiefs) from power and sent them into exile. Cultural treasures that expressed power and recorded the Benin kingship's historically sanctioned legitimization were stolen and taken to Europe, where they were auctioned to offset the costs of the expedition. Accordingly, the Benin bronzes and ivories are found today in world museums, from Berlin to London and New York.

Conquest and exploitation through the use of force brought about immediate resistance in all parts of the colonized continent. In 1890 in southern Tanganyika, the main opponents were the German commander Hermann von Wissman and Macemba, ruling chief of the Yao people. When Wissman demanded subordination by Macemba, the African ruler replied by way of a letter written in Kiswahili:

> I have listened to your words but can find no reason why I should obey you – I would rather die first . . . I look for some reason why I should obey you and find not the smallest. If it should be friendship that you desire, then I am ready for it, today and always; but not to be your subject, that I cannot be. If it should be war you desire, then I am ready, but never to be your subject. I do not fall at your feet, for you are God's creature just as I am. I am sultan here in my land. You are sultan there in yours. Yet listen, I do not say to you that you should obey me; for I know that you are a free man. As for me, I will not come to you, and if you are strong enough, then come and fetch me.
>
> (Quoted in Basil Davidson, *African Civilization Revisited from Antiquity to Modern Times*, Trenton, N.J.: Africa World Press, 1991, pp. 417–18)

Macemba's reply was characteristic of a great many African responses. With no technological match for advanced European weaponry, the failure of African resistance was endemic until well into the twentieth century, when the educated elite and masses eventually found common political, and sometimes even nationalist, grounds.

At times even traditional strategies of resistance could be employed to oppose colonial rule. The Ibo Women's War of 1929 was a protest against one of the basic mechanisms of colonial rule: taxation. Led by approximately 10,000 women of southeast Nigeria, the war was actually a traditional response to injustice experienced by Ibo women, a response known as "sitting on a man." When an individual woman could not resolve a conflict with a man, she utilized marketing and kinship-based organizations to spread the word about the grievance and produce the participation of other women in solidarity with her.

The specific grievance in 1929 was begun by an African assistant to the local colonial officer, who had been sent to count a certain woman's goats. Fearing that this inventorying of her property would mean eventual taxation, the woman refused to cooperate and was eventually struck by the colonial employee. Shortly after the incident, thousands of nude women carrying men's weapons (sticks and spears) surrounded the houses of the accused parties and sang ridiculing songs in the ritual of "sitting on a man." This protest traditionally would have effectively isolated the accused until he provided reparations. However, the British response to the peaceful assembly of women was swift and violent, and about fifty women were killed or injured. Eventually the tax was imposed.

The British won the war, and their language prevailed in the way in which the event was known. In colonial documents, the "war" was termed "Aba Riots" by the British, even though the event was neither chaotic nor was it confined to the single village of Aba. The African women were "invisible" in the British terminology. One of the consequences of colonial rule was that the colonizers controlled the language and content of history. However, traditional forms of resistance such as sitting on a man survived in the inspirational oral history of Ibo women. Their strategy of resistance also survived into the 1990s, when it was witnessed by corrupt government officials in post-independence Nigeria. The widespread resistance to the violent imposition of colonial rule was not successful but had a lasting legacy.

FROM EMPIRE TO NATION: THE OTTOMAN EMPIRE AND TURKEY

The process that led to the weakening and disintegration of the Ottoman empire pitted the rising forces of European nationalism against the once powerful Ottomans. By the eighteenth century the Ottomans were no longer the formidable enemy that had threatened Europe for centuries; rather, it was Europe that threatened the Ottomans.

During the eighteenth century, the enormous confidence that had characterized the seemingly invincible and expanding Ottoman empire gradually eroded in the face of expanding and powerful European nation-states. Many Muslims in the Ottoman empire viewed their reversal of fortune as punishment from God and called for a return to "true" Islam. Others, especially those in the government, took a more pragmatic approach. They were convinced that

the empire could return to its former power and influence only if systematic reforms were introduced to eliminate corruption and modernize the government and the armed forces. By the early nineteenth century, a series of reforms were carried out to Westernize and modernize Ottoman rule. The most intensely Western of these reform eras was called "Tanzimat" (reorganization).

Most European states, including Britain, actually supported the reforms as a means of strengthening the Ottoman empire and guaranteeing special rights for Christian minorities. Europeans tended to encourage the national aspirations of these minorities, and this stance caused resentment among Muslims, thus adding to the forces opposing the state. The Tanzimat continued for the remainder of the nineteenth century. Europeans were invited to help streamline the government, teach in technical schools, train the army and navy, and improve the state's infrastructure. Unfortunately, all of this activity cost money, which had to be borrowed heavily from Europe. When the empire went bankrupt, it was forced to surrender its finances to European governments and bankers.

At the beginning of the twentieth century, a group of young "Westernized" Turks formed a clandestine organization, the Young Turk Party, which spread among the intelligentsia and the army. In 1908 the party engineered a *coup d'état* and forced the sultan to restore the constitution. This event opened a brief period of political freedom in which the roles of Turkism, Arabism, Islam, and Westernization were intensively discussed. During this period the Young Turks began to equate "Ottoman" with "Turkish." When the Young Turks seized power for themselves in another coup in 1913, the new government leaned toward Germany, which appeared to be a model of modernization and seemed to have no designs on the Ottoman empire.

Germany's defeat in the First World War meant that the Allies treated the Ottoman empire as a defeated power, aiming to dissolve it (see Chapter 11). Organized Turkish resistance soon found a leader in the person of Mustafa Kemal (1881–1938), a general in the Ottoman army who had earlier been associated with the reformist Young Turk movement against the autocratic rule of the Ottomans. Kemal drove out the occupiers of Anatolia one by one, and in 1923 he was elected the first president of the Turkish Republic. Subsequently, he led the adoption of an ambitious series of measures aimed at changing Turkey into a modern Western country. Kemal, who acquired the honorific title "Ataturk" (Father Turk), and the Turkish nationalists believed that modernization (which they understood as Westernization) was essential for their country's survival and prosperity. They demanded that Turkey be coequal with the leading European states in almost every respect.

The new government took many actions concerning religion: it abolished the caliphate (the religious leadership of the Muslim world that had generally been appropriated by later Ottoman sultans); replaced religious courts with civil courts and civil law based on European models; disbanded the religious brotherhoods; abolished the fez (male headgear) and veil for women, which were symbols of religious conservatism; replaced the Muslim calendar with the European calendar; and officially disestablished Islam as the state religion. Turkey became the first secular Muslim state. Other measures were equally far-reaching. The Latin alphabet replaced the Arabic alphabet. Polygamy was abolished, and women were given the right to vote and hold all public offices and professions in the country. A system of public schools and universities was established.

From 1923 until his death in 1938, Ataturk ruled Turkey as a kind of benevolent dictator through a one-party government. In addition to Western models of political authority, the construction of the modern Turkish nation-state entailed the forced inclusion of ethnic groups that were unwilling to be Turks, such as the Kurds, who live within the political boundaries of more than one modern nation-state (Iraq as well as Turkey), along with the eradication of others (Armenians) who were seen to be hostile to modern Turkish national identity.

FROM EMPIRE TO NATION: THE BRITISH RAJ AND INDIA

Like other parts of the globe, the Indian subcontinent became a pawn of European politics and ultimately of the conflicting designs of imperialists. By the seventeenth century, the Mughal empire, which once controlled large parts of the subcontinent, had weakened so that it became easier for Europeans to make their presence felt. By this time the major European powers there were France and Britain, and the French lost their position (excepting a few coastal trading stations) and influence to the British at the Peace of Paris in 1763 following defeat in the Seven Years War.

Initially, British interests were represented by the British East India Company, but over time British control was increasingly formalized through mechanisms that linked policies on the subcontinent to oversight in London. In 1857 the so-called Sepoy Mutiny of Indian soldiers provided the pretext on which the British acted to bring the subcontinent under direct control as a formal colony. The 1858 Government of India Act and subsequent laws made India part of the British empire. The East India Company disappeared from the scene, and the governor-general became a viceroy representing Queen Victoria, who was proclaimed empress of India in 1876 and to whose imperial crown was thus added the "jewel" of India.

The agency of Indian nationalism was an organization called the Indian National Congress, which was formed in 1885 by members of the largely English-educated urban elite. But resistance to the Raj was widespread across regions and social classes, and so Indian nationalist thought was not limited to its expression through the Indian National Congress. The convergence of the demand for independence from British rule among urban intellectuals with popular resistance movements such as the *ulgulan* (great tumult) of 1899–1900 carried out by the Munda tribe on the Bengal–Bihar border was critical to the ultimate success of the Indian National Congress.

At first the demands of the Indian National Congress were moderate, reformist rather than revolutionary, aiming to give Indians a voice in running their own country. Congress's practical suggestion for achieving this goal included reorganizing the Indian Civil Service to give Indians more opportunity to participate in the British-controlled government known as the "Raj." The progress of the Indian nationalist movement was slow and fraught with regional and religious differences, of which the divisions between Hindu and Muslim were the most difficult.

The young Indian lawyer Mohandas K. Gandhi (1869–1948) went to South Africa in 1893, where he developed his philosophy of nonviolence and many of his techniques of civil disobedience. In South Africa Gandhi experienced discrimination, including beatings by white South Africans, and was even thrown off a first-class passenger train because of his skin color. When he returned from South Africa in 1906 to attend the Indian National Congress, he incorporated his South African experiences into a deeper understanding of resistance to injustice. Gandhi began to wear the Indian *dhoti* (dress), rather than an English-tailored suit, and adopted the diet of a poor Indian peasant. He used techniques such as boycotts, defiance, strikes, and marches to protest British rule. When the Indian National Congress met in 1906 it adopted the goal of self-government, *swaraj*; as Gandhi used the term, it meant political independence, economic independence, and personal psychological self-control.

One particularly effective boycott that Gandhi supported through his symbolic wearing of the *dhoti* was the *swadeshi* ("of our own country") movement, which originated in 1905 in Bengal in opposition to the British partition of Bengal into Hindu and Muslim majority areas. This boycott of British goods was intended to support the indigenous textile industry as well as to protest the partition of Bengal. Beginning with petitions and pleas, the *swadeshi* boycott turned into a widespread nationalist movement, with bonfires burning British-made saris (Indian women's dress). By 1908 the boycott was so successful that textile imports were down by 25 percent.

When the Raj adopted a new policy in 1919 aimed at controlling political activities, a demonstration against this new policy at Amritsar, a center of Indian resistance to British rule as well as the holy city of the Sikhs, brought about a confrontation between unarmed Indian demonstrators and British troops. When the troops fired on the crowd, 400 demonstrators were killed. The Amritsar Massacre intensified Indian resistance to British rule and pressure for independence; it also galvanized support throughout the country for Gandhi's movement.

One of Gandhi's most famous protests came in 1930, in a peaceful march against British taxation, especially the salt tax, which he had encouraged his followers to refuse to pay. On the anniversary of the Amritsar Massacre Gandhi and hundreds of his followers marched over 200 miles to the sea. When they reached the sea, Gandhi waded into the surf and picked up a lump of natural salt. By this act, Gandhi and his followers openly defied the British salt monopoly, which forbade the independent manufacture or sale of salt, an essential commodity. The British responded to this challenge to its authority with violence, arresting and imprisoning tens of thousands of nationalist leaders and followers, including Gandhi himself. The Indian Independence League proclaimed their conviction that the only resolution to the situation of intensified conflict and violence lay in prompt and complete independence from British rule.

With the outbreak of the Second World War, England was unable to count on wholesale Indian support and loyalty. The Indian National Army was formed to support the Japanese effort to overrun British Asian possessions and it assisted in the Japanese occupation of British Burma. Many Indians apparently believed that if they must be subjects of foreign imperial rule, Asian rule was preferable to European. The destructive effects of the Second World War on Great Britain enabled Indian nationalists to realize their dreams at last. An Indian Independence Act was finally adopted by the British government in 1947.

Independence, however, did not bring peace, but violence and partition. The subcontinent was partitioned between India, a Hindu state, and Pakistan, which was Muslim, a compromise carved from the religious and ethnic divisions that had plagued Indian nationalism from its beginnings. The new nations provided frameworks for the construction of modern national identities from the complex ethnic and religious mix of their populations. The two countries chose to become members of the loose economic and cultural organization known as the British Commonwealth of Nations. British authority in India formally ended on August 15, 1947 when the Union Jack was hauled down and replaced with flags of the two new states. Gandhi himself barely had time to witness the fulfillment of Indian independence. He was assassinated in 1948 by a Hindu extremist who opposed Gandhi's inclusion of Muslims.

IMPERIALISM, MARXISM, AND REVOLUTION

As much as violence peppered the transformation of the British Raj into India and Pakistan, change was still relatively slow and evolutionary. Models for revolutionary change in the twentieth century begin with the American Revolutionary struggle for independence from Britain; the eighteenth-century popular uprisings of the French Revolution; and the cultural, ethnic, and political complexities of the Haitian Revolution. The revolutions of 1848 in Europe inspired Karl Marx's ruminations on the relationship between capitalist industrialism and the nation-state and led to the formulation of the Marxist model of revolutionary historical change (see also Chapter 11). According to this model, modes of production or economic systems and the class relationships they generate provide the dynamic forces that propel and direct historical change. The first major impact of Marxist political ideology came with the Russian Revolution of 1917. When Marx created his model of historical change based on observation of mid-nineteenth century European capitalist industrial society, he was dismissive of the non-European world and even of Russia, which was "backward" in comparison with western Europe at the time. He saw in parts of the non-European world such as India and China examples of what he called the "Asiatic mode of production," which was based on feudal landlord–tenant relations.

Marx assigned no revolutionary role to peasant cultivators in any society, including that of Europe, arguing that because farmers were by the nature of their livelihood isolated, individualistic, and self-interested – concerned only with what they could produce on their own plots of land – they lacked consciousness of their condition of oppression as a class and would remain a conservative force in society. In contrast, the urban proletariat, the industrial working class, by the nature of their labor in factories, subject to the oppressive management of capitalist entrepreneurs who exacted surplus value from their labor, would develop the class consciousness necessary for revolutionary change.

Marx knew little about the non-European world, and he could not foresee the impact of imperialism and colonialism on the capitalist industrialism he was familiar with in Europe. In the generation after Marx, in the backwater of the European industrial revolution that was Russia at the turn of the century, V. I. Lenin (1870–1924) saw beyond Marx's vision to the realities of his own time. While the First World War was in progress, Lenin wrote *Imperialism, the Highest Stage of Capitalism* (1916–17), arguing that imperialism had extended the life of capitalism by improving conditions for the proletariat in the advanced industrialized nations and therefore enabling capitalist societies to avoid revolution.

According to Lenin, Marx's prediction that the worsening condition of the working classes in advanced industrial societies would lead to revolution had not come true because imperialism had allowed the expansion of capitalist economies. Even though harsh economic inequities persisted, overall growth meant that conditions for the working classes had not worsened and may even have improved. Lenin concluded that Marx was not wrong about the process, only the timetable, since the unforeseen effects of imperialism had provided the means to extend the life of capitalism. However, in Lenin's view, imperialism carried within it the seeds of its own destruction. He believed he was witnessing this destruction in the First World War, the result of the clash of imperialist rivalries that led to militarism, war, and widespread popular discontent. Lenin appeared to be right about Russia at least. The First World War contributed significantly to the breakdown of the Russian monarchy and the opportunity for Lenin's party, the Bolsheviks, to seize power, as they did in 1917.

The success of the Bolshevik Revolution impressed many intellectuals from the colonial world and attracted them to the study of Marxism. The model of the Russian Revolution was exported to China in the early 1920s, when Russian and other agents of the Communist International (Comintern) helped to organize the fledgling Communist Party. Because of its ideological focus on the urban proletariat and the necessity of an industrial base, the Russian Revolution had limited applicability to Asia and Africa, which were overwhelmingly agricultural. In contrast, the Mexican Revolution (1910–13) yielded a very different model of revolutionary change: agrarian reform, the redistribution of land as the basis of wealth. This model of revolutionary change, flawed though the outcome was in Mexico, provided an example for ongoing revolutions in much of the colonized and semicolonized world in the twentieth century, where land reform was still the key issue for most of the disenfranchised population.

The key transformation in Marxist ideology that made Marxism into a model of revolutionary change for agrarian societies took place in China where the urbanized, industrialized sector of society was far smaller even than that of Russia and where the peasantry was the vast majority of the population. Though early Chinese Marxist revolutionaries were inspired by the Russian Revolution, guided by Russian mentors, and looked to an urban proletariat for support, the young Mao Zedong (1893–1976) challenged the Marxist view of the revolutionary consciousness of urban industrial workers with his own vision of the peasantry as the key to revolutionary change:

> A revolution is an uprising, an act of violence whereby one class overthrows another. A rural revolution is a revolution by which the peasantry overthrows the authority of the feudal landlord class.... If the peasants do not use the maximum of their strength, they can never overthrow the authority of the landlords which has been deeply rooted for thousands of years.... In a very short time ... several hundred million peasants will rise like a tornado or tempest, a force so extraordinarily swift and violent that no power however great will be able to suppress it.
>
> (Quoted in James P. Harrison, *The Long March to Power: A History of the Chinese Communist Party, 1921–1972*, New York: Praeger, 1974, p. 84)

Written in 1927, Mao's words echo the revolutionary violence of the French Revolution, distant in time, context, and outcome though it was. Like his French revolutionary forebears influenced by Rousseau's idea of the social contract, Mao was a student of the new ideas of his time: Marxism. He participated in the heady intellectual world of the "Chinese Enlightenment" in Beijing around 1920, on the eve of the founding of the Chinese Communist Party.

Less than a decade after Mao wrote these words, he took control of the young Chinese Communist Party and eventually led this group, supported by the Red Army, to mobilize peasant support and organize guerrilla warfare against the Japanese in northwest China during the Second World War. Ultimately, collective action resulted in victory over the Nationalists in civil war after the end of the Second World War. A century of imperialist aggression beginning with the Opium Wars of the mid-nineteenth century and the "spheres of influence" of Western powers in China culminated in the establishment of the modern nation-state embodied in the People's Republic of China in 1949. To what extent the Chinese revolution was an agrarian revolution of peasants overthrowing centuries of oppression, both internal and more recently external, is debated by historians. As the history of the People's Republic unfolded in the last half of the twentieth century, the dilemmas of revolutionaries in power became more and more apparent. The revolutionary state had become a powerful oppressor in its own right, as the events of 1989 in Tiananmen Square revealed.

Everywhere that European imperialism had penetrated, whether through colonization or in less structured ways such as the "spheres of influence" in China, revolutionary change took the form of nationalism. Whether it originated in response to imperialism alone or in tandem with resistance to the traditional state, nationalism could become either a revolutionary force that overturned the traditional social order or it could overthrow the old state structure but not those in power. Revolutions tended to recreate hierarchies of power within the revolutionary state, which in turn generated resistance to the revolutionary leadership.

REFORM, REVOLUTION, AND ISLAMIC NATIONALISM

Two responses to nineteenth-century Western domination in the Islamic world had been reform and revolution. By the early twentieth century, world power had passed into European hands, and the last of the great Muslim empires, the Ottoman, was no more. The shrinking of territory and influence ushered in a period of readjustment and reconciliation between

Western science and technology, European imperialism, and Islamic cultural identity. The impact of modernist reform was experienced from North Africa to Central and Southeast Asia.

The Ikhwan al Muslimin (Muslim Brotherhood) was the leading Islamist force in West Asia and North Africa. Sometimes referred to as "fundamentalist," the movement was founded in Egypt in 1928 by Hasan al-Banna (1906–49). It disagreed with traditional orthodoxy about modernization and called for a revivalist Islam as a means of resisting the economic and political injustices of secular states. Between 1948 and 1981 the Brotherhood was banned and suppressed by the successive colonial and post-independence governments of Egypt. Syria, the Sudan, and Pakistan also struggled with Islamic forces. Sayyid Qutb (1906–66) was an Egyptian Muslim who became one of the most important intellectual figures in the Muslim Brotherhood. Author of a 30-volume commentary on the Qur'an, Qutb promoted a fundamentalist vision of Islam that demanded the highest standards of Muslim belief and practice from its followers. His execution by the Egyptian government made him a martyr to many members of the Muslim Brotherhood. His writings remain widely influential. By the late 1970s all Muslim societies came to contain at least an Islamist wing that resisted the contamination of their communities by Westernization.

Western influence had grown in Iran during the interwar years, beginning with the expansion of German political and economic interests after the First World War (see Chapter 11). The ruler of the Pahlavi dynasty, Reza Shah, like the Young Turks in Turkey, saw Germany as an important power that had no imperial designs. In 1941, after the Second World War (see Chapter 11) had begun, Britain and the Soviet Union demanded the expulsion of all Germans from Iran. They were concerned about the flow of oil and the ability of the Allies to provide war material to the Soviet Union, then under attack by Germany. Reza Shah refused and British and Soviet forces invaded Iran. The shah abdicated and was succeeded by his son, Muhammad Reza, who ruled Iran until 1979 when he was overthrown in a popular Islamic revolution under the leadership of Ayatollah Ruhollah Khomeini, a Shi'ite cleric who had been in exile in France since 1963. Both rejection of modernization based on

Western models and resistance to the continuation of monarchical rule lay at the heart of the Islamic fundamentalist movement that unseated the shah, a Westernized monarch whose policies favored a secular state rather than the Islamic ideal of the "community of true believers."

A broad spectrum of resistance movements and their interaction with new states formed by the overthrow of traditional monarchies characterized postwar developments in West Asia and North Africa. Islamic fundamentalism provided a key ideological source of resistance to Westernized authoritarian or one-party states, as Muslims rejected the Western notion of the social contract in favor of the Islamic belief in the "community of true believers" as the model for the nation-state. But there was no unitary Muslim ideal of the nation-state. For some, religion and state were to be a unified whole, and religious law was joined to state law in an Islamic state. For others, as in Turkey, the state was secular, and Islam was one component of a common national identity.

DECOLONIZATION, NATIONALISM, AND REVOLUTION IN ASIA AND AFRICA

In colonized regions of Asia and Africa, the postwar processes of decolonization were shaped by legacies of anticolonial resistance and by the nature and degree of colonial control. The declaration of Indian independence in 1947, for example, was the product of many years of organized nationalist resistance personified by Gandhi, but it was also influenced by the British-educated Indian elite (including Gandhi, who studied law in England) who took the reins of power.

Clashes between nationalist insurgents and colonial government forces took place in the aftermath of the Second World War in almost every state in Southeast Asia (see Chapter 11). Burma and Ceylon were freed from British control. In those parts of Southeast Asia that had been colonized by the French, nationalist leaders challenged French colonial authority and worked to overthrow traditional political and social orders. In Vietnam, a French colony since the 1860s, a nationalist movement began in the early twentieth century. Ho Chi Minh, who was introduced to

Marxism as a young man in Paris, played the leading role in the founding of the Communist-led national independence movement, the Viet Minh, which fought the Japanese occupation in the Second World War and was determined to resist the restoration of French colonialism after the war's end. After the defeat of the French in 1954, Americans eventually took over the role of colonial power, and by the 1960s were entangled in the Vietnam War. The Vietnamese communists declared victory in 1975 with the fall of the southern capital, Saigon, renamed Ho Chi Minh City after the nationalist leader.

Elsewhere in Southeast Asia, such as in Indonesia and the Philippines, the combination of colonial legacies with complex ethnic and religious compositions shaped new political and social orders. A movement for Indonesian independence from Dutch rule began in 1927 with the establishment of the Indonesian National Party, headed by a young engineer named Sukarno (1901–70). Dutch repression of Indonesian nationalism reached a peak in 1940 when Dutch colonial authorities prohibited the use of the name Indonesia. During the Second World War when Indonesia was occupied by the Japanese, the extent of opposition to the Dutch surfaced in the relatively passive acceptance of Japanese rule, which was regarded as no worse, and perhaps better, than Dutch rule. Though Indonesian independence was declared by a client government of the Japanese in 1943, and again at war's end in 1945 by Sukarno, Dutch recognition of Indonesian independence came only in 1949.

The complex colonial legacy of the Philippines includes Spanish domination beginning in the sixteenth century, followed by American hegemony after the Spanish–American War in 1898, and finally Japanese conquest during the Second World War. Strong resistance to American control surfaced under the leadership of Emilio Aguinaldo (1869–1964) between 1899 and 1902 and subsequently. The reconquest of the Philippines from the Japanese in the Second World War took place with the help of guerrilla groups such as the Communist Hukbalahap (from words in the Tagalog language meaning "People's Army against the Japanese") movement. The Huks, as they were known, represented an important rural resistance movement, like the Viet Minh, that challenged traditional social and economic hierarchies in the countryside and championed the interests of poor tenant farmers.

Africans were not unaware that the Second World War had swept away European colonialism in Asia. A key symbol of European hegemony in Africa was Algeria, a French colony since the mid-nineteenth century. Nationalist struggles there led to nearly a decade of civil war. Algerian independence in 1962 represented the culmination of mass political party activities of the Front National de la Libération (FLN) beginning in the period 1937 to 1946. Algerian women, socially and politically marginalized by traditional society, played critical roles in the revolution. They were spies, smugglers, and even took on combat roles. The escalation of the struggle in Algeria, where as many as 2 million French settlers resided, forced the French government to negotiate independence there and in other territories.

The emergence of independence movements brought an end to most of the traditional, aristocratic leadership that had predated the colonial era. Already undermined by the merchant middle class and the missionary- and colonial-educated elites, few traditional African leaders remained. The survivors became symbolic targets for mass political action, such as in the example of the armed Mau Mau revolt in Kenya between the 1940s and 1955, which began with the assassination of the senior chief, Waruhiu, and the onset of an intense period of grassroots guerrilla warfare. During the Mau Mau struggle, violent rural action terrorized British settlers, who had been given lands taken away from African farmers. Although the Mau Mau were defeated, the struggle convinced the British to accept the principle of African majority rule over the protests of white settlers. Kenya finally achieved independence in 1963.

In South Africa, a major turning point was the national election of 1948 through which the Nationalist Party came into power and implemented a national policy of segregation and oppression, known as "apartheid." Apartheid policies enforced a color code that favored whites over all others and dictated where the majority African populations could live, travel, and work. Blacks were systematically excluded from holding political office and from voting, yet their labor was essential to the processes of industrialization. Black Africans were required to carry identity passes that

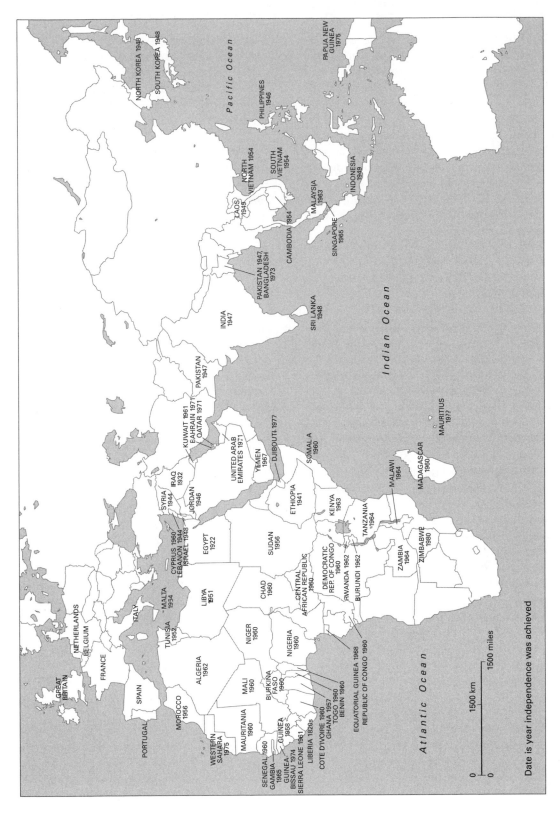

Map 7.6 Anonymous, "Decolonization, 1947–1990": new nations in Africa and Asia (Boston, Mass.: Houghton Mifflin, 2002).

revealed their racial classification. The white minority enacted "pass laws" to restrict African movements and particularly to control the influx of workers from rural to urban areas. Internal security acts legalized the violent repression of resistance to gross human rights violations. The African National Congress, founded in 1912, initially worked through nonviolent techniques of mass resistance to apartheid and eventually adopted a program of terrorism directed against the repressive South African state. Led by Nelson Mandela (b. 1918) and others, the ANC eventually succeeded, and in 1994 Mandela became the first African elected president of South Africa.

NEW STATES, NEW COLONIALISM, AND NEW EMPIRE

The twentieth century witnessed not only the dismantling of European new imperialism in the conflagrations of two world wars (see Chapter 11), but also the rise of a new kind of state. The totalitarian state (where total power resides in the state) took shape in diverse political settings, and expressed vastly different aspirations for the people it claimed to represent. In Soviet Russia, the totalitarian state emerged from anti-Tsarist and anti-imperialist Marxist revolution. German leaders promoted the idea that the Nazi state was heir to the pure tradition of a historic German *Volk* (people). Both claimed to embody the aspirations of people included in the definition of the nation, and both excluded those who did not belong to the same group: Jews, for example, in both Nazi Germany and Stalinist Russia were persecuted or murdered in an effort to "purify" the nation. Totalitarian states were possible in part because of technologies that made mass communication possible. Collective identities shaped by popular media and mass spectacles like the Hitler Youth rallies represented a new kind of nation-state far removed from the ideal of the social contract that inspired eighteenth-century revolutions in the Atlantic world.

The collapse of European empires and the independence of former colonies in the aftermath of the Second World War did not necessarily mean the end of dependence or the end of empire. To many, these events simply ushered in a new era of colonialism.

As Kwame Nkrumah (1909–72), the first post-independence president of Ghana, observed:

> Neo-Colonialism is . . . the worst form of imperialism. For those who practise it, it means power without responsibility and for those who suffer from it, it means exploitation without redress. In the days of old-fashioned colonialism, the imperial power had at least to explain and justify at home the actions it was taking abroad. In the colony those who served the ruling imperial power could at least look to its protection against any violent move by their opponents. With neo-colonialism neither is the case.
>
> (Kwame Nkrumah, *Neo-Colonialism: The Last Stage of Imperialism*, London: Thomas Nelson & Sons, 1965, p. xi)

Echoing Lenin's *Imperialism, the Highest Stage of Capitalism*, Nkrumah attempted to explain the ties of dependence that persisted after African states gained formal independence from colonial powers, as Ghana did in 1957. Nkrumah saw hope in pan-Africanism, uniting the continent to achieve economic, social, and true political independence. It proved a hope that could not be realized within his lifetime or even in the future, although Nkrumah's economic plan for African unity later became a blueprint for the European Economic Union.

As Nkrumah accurately perceived, in the postwar bipolar world that pitted the United States against the Soviet Union, former colonies in Asia and Africa that gained their formal political independence were often still under the domination of one of the two superpowers through economic aid and diplomatic pressure. Efforts to organize against this polarization, such as the Bandung (Indonesia) Conference of Non-Aligned Nations in 1955, were symbolically important but relatively ineffective.

One of the key participants in the Bandung Conference was the People's Republic of China. After another generation of political, social and economic upheaval, China finally emerged as a global power by the end of the twentieth century, again shifting attention to Asia following the postwar economic rise of Japan. Heir to the 2,000-year-old Chinese empire, the modern Chinese nation-state was a product of revolutionary nationalism in response to imperialism, even though China was never a direct colony of any European power. Modern Chinese identities are tied both to the sense of their ancient cultural legacy and to the painful memory of humiliation by Western powers and the century of war and revolution that followed.

CONCLUSIONS

Along with the rise of China, by the end of the twentieth century both the collapse of the Soviet Union in 1991 and the creation of the European Union also signalled shifts in global power. The European Union, inspired by the desire to build economic community, has moved in the opposite direction from that of the dissolution of the Soviet Union to create an umbrella organization that transcends, but does not eradicate or reduce, national identities.

Even more significant a development than the breakup of the Soviet Union, the rise of China, or the evolution of the European Union is the rapidly proliferating technological connection of peoples all over the world beyond the borders of states and empires. Transnational linkages – through family, work, language, and culture – drive individuals to identify with communities that are not defined by the territorial boundaries of the nation-state. As powerful as nationalism remains, it is a newer nationalism shaped by ethnic loyalties and shared histories rather than the geographic boundaries of nineteenth- and twentieth-century states (see Chapter 10). Religious-inspired nationalism, most prominently associated with Islam, offers a new model of collective identity to replace the notion of civil society based on a social contract independent of religious, cultural, ethnic, linguistic, or kinship ties (see Chapter 4). As much as the idea of modernity is identified with the rejection of religion in favor of secular rationality – the notion of the state as the personal property of the ruler replaced by the impersonal bureaucratic rationality of the modern state – religion as a source of political authority and collective identity has not disappeared. This is currently most visible in the Islamic world, but is certainly not exclusive to it.

Both gender and ethnicity shape modern nationalisms, as they were powerful elements in the collective identities of political formations beginning with the earliest states and empires. Terms such as "motherland" or "fatherland" are commonly used to refer to the nation, and motherhood has been promoted as a tool of the nation in urging women to give birth to citizens and soldiers, and rewarding them for reproducing the nation (see Chapter 5). In the French Revolution, which denied equal rights to women, a female image was used to symbolize the Revolution. The word "nation" is derived from the Latin *natio*, which means "birth," and thus underscores the idea of the place of one's birth determining citizenship in the modern world of nation-states that patrol their borders and require passports to document official citizenship. The ideal of the nineteenth-century nation in Europe was rooted in shared culture, history, language, and territory, and this notion was exported with the forces of European imperialism to the Americas, Africa, and Asia, where it interacted with other forms of collective identity based on ethnicity, culture, and religion.

Leaders of nation-states as they evolved in the nineteenth century had to develop new symbols, unconnected with the person or family of the ruler, that became the means by which citizens identified with them. Popular manifestations of nationalism, such as flags and the veneration and glorification of national heroes such as Simon Bolivar, Napoleon, Marcus Garvey, or George Washington, all contributed to the shaping and expression of national identities, as did theater, festivals, and mass celebrations.

Flags, like all symbols of the nation, are representations of collective identities that can be manipulated to accomplish goals of inclusion and exclusion and to favor certain definitions of the nation over others. In European dynastic states, the crest of the ruling family was the primary emblem on the flag. The crest of the Bourbon family in France exemplifies this, and the replacement of this with the French revolutionary tricolored flag was a powerful symbol of the revolutionaries' goals. The flag raised in 1947 to declare Indian independence from Britain used an ancient symbol, the *chakra*, the "Wheel of the Law," at its center to link modern India to the period of the ruler Ashoka (third century BCE), who claimed to rule as the Buddhist-inspired *chakravartin* ("he for whom the Wheel of the Law turns") king (see Chapter 4), but was also known for having expanded his empire across the north of the Indian subcontinent and beyond. Championed by India's first prime minister, Jawaharlal Nehru (1884–1969), this flag promoted an ancient historic identity for the Indian nation that differed significantly from an earlier version proposed by Gandhi that placed the spinning wheel – a symbol associated with the boycott of textiles produced in Britain and his campaigns for economic independence – at the center. As forces of globalization continue to reshape identities in the twenty-first century, ancient sources of identity rooted in language, culture, religion, and history have not been erased and continue to evoke powerful responses.

Like other sources of identity, nationalism, whether based on geographic boundaries, common language and culture or shared histories, is a construction that creates a sense of community (or collective identity) and survives as long as it empowers rather than weakens that community. That nationalism remains a potent force can be seen in the strong desire of Palestinians to

Figure 7.4 Indian national flag. Nehru's *chakra* symbol replaced the more limited vision of twentieth-century struggle embodied in Gandhi's spinning wheel to suggest continuity with a remote, but expansive and powerful past.

establish a state, as the state of Israel was created in the aftermath of the Second World War as a homeland for Jews. A sense of Palestinian national identity exists but the issue of boundaries for a Palestine nation-state remains unsettled.

Just as nationalism has not disappeared in the face of new global identities, neither have empires disappeared. Some see the United States in the twenty-first century as a new empire, arguing that the invasion of Iraq in 2003 was only one manifestation of its imperial role as the superpower in a unipolar world. Comparisons to the Roman and British empires fall short, however, because the contemporary world order is a very different one in which the actions of any individual state are circumscribed to some degree by global economic interdependence and international law. Newer forms of "empire" are instead built on global technological and economic links, and their power is exercised with far greater subtlety than in the past through international organizations, agencies, and aid. Some have even argued that globalization itself constitutes a new kind of empire, displacing the obsolete nation-state in its regulation of human activities. Others insist that the nation-state retains substantial control over people's economic and social, as well as political, lives, and that the power of nationalism has even increased in response to anxieties produced by international terrorism and global economic interdependence. Issues of global military, environmental, and economic security demand collective action across wide religious, national, and cultural gulfs to build a sense of collective identity – global citizenship – for all whose fortunes are at stake in the fate of the planet and the human species.

SELECTED REFERENCES

Anderson, Benedict ([1983] 2000) *Imagined Communities: Reflections on the Origins and Spread of Nationalism*, London: Verso. Path-breaking study of the relationship between the origins of print-capitalism and the birth of national consciousness in Europe and its global repercussions.

Burton, Antoinette, ed. (2003) *After the Imperial Turn: Thinking With and Through the Nation*, Durham, N.C.: Duke University Press. Collected essays on the nation-state as an analytic category in the study of history and culture and on related concepts such as imperialism.

Eley, Geoff and Ronald Grigor Suny, eds (1996) *Becoming National: A Reader*, New York and Oxford: Oxford University Press. Selections from a wide range of readings on nationalism and related issues such as colonialism.

Esherick, Joseph W., Hasan Kayah, and Erik Van Young, eds (2006) *Empire to Nation: Historical Perspectives on the Making of the Modern World*, Lanham, Md.: Rowman & Littlefield. A collection of conference articles questioning the historical narrative of empire to nation-state, focusing on the Spanish, Ottoman, Chinese, and Russian empires and their heirs.

Geary, Patrick (2002) *The Myth of Nations: The Medieval Origins of Europe*, Princeton, N.J. and Oxford: Princeton University Press. A historian of medieval Europe shows how modern European nationalisms are a product of mythic origins in the medieval period.

Hardt, Michael and Antonio Negri (2000) *Empire*, Cambridge, Mass. and London: Harvard University Press. A provocative and controversial argument that globalization constitutes a new form of empire distinct from the empires and imperialism of previous eras.

Levine, Philippa, ed. (2004) *Gender and Empire*, New York and Oxford: Oxford University Press. Collected essays focusing on the British empire seen through the lens of gender.

McIntosh, Susan Keech, ed. (1999) *Beyond Chiefdoms: Pathways to Complexity in Africa*, Cambridge: Cambridge University Press. An interdisciplinary collection of essays by archaeologists, anthropologists, and historians on how African cases challenge traditional models of chiefdoms and states.

Meeker, Michael E. (2002) *A Nation of Empire: The Ottoman Legacy of Turkish Modernity*, Berkeley: University of California Press. A study of the Black Sea district of Of and its relations with the Ottoman government in Istanbul and later with the Turkish government in Ankara.

Pagden, Anthony (1995) *Lords of All the World: Ideologies of Empire in Spain, Britain and France, c.*

1500–c. 1800, New Haven, Conn.: Yale University Press. A comparison of ideologies of empire in Spain, Britain, and France in relation to New World conquest and settlement.

Scott, James C. (1998) *Seeing Like a State: How Certain Schemes to Improve the Human Condition Have Failed*, New Haven, Conn. and London: Yale University Press. A comparative study of large-scale social engineering projects carried out by twentieth-century states that failed to produce the desired results and ended in increasing human misery.

Suny, Ronald Grigor (1994) *The Revenge of the Past: Nationalism, Revolution and the Collapse of the Soviet Union*, Stanford, Calif.: Stanford University Press, 1994. An analysis of class and nationality in the formation and disintegration of the Soviet Union.

Tilly, Charles (1990) *Coercion, Capital, and European States, A.D. 990–1990*, Oxford: Basil Blackwell. A provocative argument by a historical sociologist that the financial demands of making war were crucial in the formation of European national states.

ONLINE RESOURCES

Annenberg/CPB Bridging World History (2004) <http://www.learner.org/channel/courses/world history/>. Multimedia project with interactive website and videos on demand; see especially Units 6 Order and Early Societies, 11 Early Empires, 20 Imperial Designs, 21 Colonial Identities, 26 World History and Identity.

The Mongols in World History <http://afe.easia. columbia.edu/mongols/>. Part of the Asia for Educators website at Columbia University, this section provides useful background on various aspects of the Mongol empire.

CHAPTER 8

Experiencing inequalities

Dominance and resistance in world history

When reggae music legend Bob Marley (1945–81) sang "Get Up, Stand Up," it was a call to arms. Reggae had become the anthem of resistance in Jamaica, a former British colony where color, class, and capitalism churned in an urban crucible of poverty and under-development. The song's lyrics rang true for many people far from the Caribbean:

> Get up, stand up,
> Stand up for your rights,
> Get up, stand up,
> Don't give up the fight.

In its Jamaican homeland, reggae was linked to the Rastafarian religion, an African-derived philosophy that combined Christian biblical teachings with beliefs rooted in the historical crowning of the last Ethiopian emperor Haile Selassie I (r. 1930–74) as the living god of black people. Freedom songs were "songs of redemption." Emerging from Jamaican folk traditions and embracing multiple musical styles from local and imported sources, reggae music was also rooted in historical consciousness. Marley's song "War" was taken almost entirely from a speech by Haile Selassie. Other music sang of histories silenced by those in power; through the lyrics in "Buffalo Soldier," about the forgotten African-American soldiers who were freedom-fighters in the United States, Marley reminded his listeners that "If you'd know your history, then you would know where you're coming from."

Marley's artistry attracted the attention of Jamaica's political establishment, who were forced to take seriously the poor, mostly black underclass on the island. But reggae's message transcended political and religious boundaries. Bob Marley sang to the hopes and aspirations of the downtrodden and a new generation of young people and revolutionaries searching for alternative philosophies to challenge the status quo. He called for personal freedom through revolution. His songs hit the music charts in every part of the world and came to be associated with the struggles for black political independence. In 1980 Bob Marley was invited to Zimbabwe to perform at the African nation's independence ceremony. Although Marley died the next year, the political authenticity of reggae music provided a model for revolution and resistance beyond Jamaica in the years that followed. Moreover, it provided an anthem for the recognition of difference and the role it could play in both solidarity and change.

As suggested by the enduring music of Bob Marley, the ideas and circumstances that inspired revolutionary change in the twentieth century were found both in the experiences of oppressed peoples around the globe and in the historical examples of other resistance movements. History told from the viewpoint of those in power could be a tool for silencing other pasts; but historical memory could also be a means of empowerment for those who sought social and political changes.

INTRODUCTION

Although we tend to think that inequalities have begun to disappear in the modern world, they have surprisingly sharpened. They continue to reinforce and sometimes intensify the enduring social and economic disparities that can be traced to even the earliest settled societies. Inequality may be created by social or political forces and it can be measured by economic disparities, reflecting markedly different access to resources acquired by individuals or groups. The agents of inequality are varied – from gender, age, caste, or class to racial and other identities. Among the most important of world historical questions is the consideration of how and why humans persist in the hierarchical and gendered relationships that have placed some in dominant and others in subordinate positions. Expressions of inequality and difference have ranged from inherited or ascribed, to perceived categories. Inequalities have been expressed both through ideas and in material conditions. Differences give rise to positions of privilege that enable individuals and groups to achieve concentrations of power and exercise strategies for accumulating disproportionate wealth, power, and opportunity. While inequality has been institutionalized through a variety of means, among the most important occurred through unequal access to land, division of labor, and the creation of accompanying social, economic, and political hierarchies.

In the modern Jamaica of which Marley sang, the legacy of slavery and colonialism created lingering systems of exploitation based on race, gender, and class differences. Understanding inequality provides opportunities for exploring the counterbalancing efforts of those individuals and groups who have resisted systems of inequality and sought greater social justice throughout world history.

What are the origins of inequality? How is inequality institutionalized? The French philosopher Jean-Jacques Rousseau wrote a discourse on the subject in 1754, attempting to answer the question of whether or not inequality is sanctioned by natural laws. He asks, "For how shall we know the source of inequality between men, if we do not begin by knowing mankind?" Aside from the glaring exclusion of women in his question, for Rousseau and others, the story of world history provides us the opportunity to try to answer the question of inequality's origins. Rousseau believed that the answer resided in the material world; but there may be other factors at play. As the German philosopher Karl Marx (1818–83) later suggested, class divisions arise from differences within an economic system. Marx predicted that these conflicts would result in conditions favorable to labor, whether they were conflicts between slaves and masters as in ancient times or between modern industrial laborers and the owners of capital under modern imperialism.

This chapter examines the origins and experience of inequalities and how they change over time, including the history of inequalities based on the construction of gender, social and economic positions, and ethnic or racial identities. Can we identify any common or enduring agents of inequality from earliest societies to modern times? In what manner does the modern age of globalization stand apart from earlier eras? Although we may consider major periods significant to the history of inequality in complex societies, the sequence and timing are not uniform across the globe. Before about 500 BCE, most world regions witnessed the emergence of societies ordered by wealth and resource accumulation. These complex societies provided elites with new possibilities for the strategic control over land and labor, with technologies of warfare and resource control enabling the expansion of complexity and the flourishing of social, political, and economic divisions. Between about 500 BCE and 1800 CE, expanding systems of exploitation were built around unequal access to land and labor, although these were valued differently across societies. The globalization of both inequalities and resistance intensified with the worldwide movement of forms of coerced labor, giving birth to a global capitalist system of inequality. Modern imperialism in the nineteenth century reflects the worsening of patterns of inequality as institutionalized disparities have been compounded. Today the world has been described as a "planet of slums," suggesting the pervasiveness of globalizing forms of inequality. What insights might these periods offer us as we try to comprehend the causes and meaning of the significant divisions that characterize the modern world?

EMERGENCE OF GENDER INEQUALITIES AND SOCIAL HIERARCHIES

The most basic differences embedded in the human condition are the ones felt most personally – gender and age. What it means to be a child or an elder and how male and female identities are experienced vary dramatically across cultures and from one period in human history to another. Distinct from biological sex, gender can be used to describe the socially constructed roles and identities implicated in being male or female in a particular society. These roles and identities do not stand alone; rather they intersect with other realities. Their divisions express not only a differentiation of roles, but the attributes associated with socially constructed notions of power in society. When gender differentiation was employed oppressively to dominate and subordinate women, biological explanations were frequently adopted as the underlying ideology. For example, the justification of a gendered division of labor might be based on differences in male and female biology, construing menstruation or lactation as undesirable pollution or weakness. The meaning of those biological differences is ideologically constructed, not biologically determined.

Ideas about gender are neither stable across time and space nor are they universally fixed in the context of an individual's lifetime – rather they are transformed by their intersections with age, class, and other categories of understanding the world.

The earliest hunting and gathering societies are assumed to be more egalitarian and possibly even to have lacked hierarchy altogether. However, testing the evidence for gendered labor roles is problematic. Women as gatherers and men as hunters were common, but not universal divisions of roles. Some rock art depicts prehistoric women as hunters and some engravings reveal separate groupings of all-male and all-female composition. The stereotyped image of female gatherers and male hunters has been further exploded by the realization that gathered foods formed the substantial basis of the prehistoric diet. Yet in most known hunting and gathering contexts, although meat was hardly central to the diet, it was highly prized as prestige food. Greater interchangeability of roles would have been an advantage in small-scale, highly mobile hunting-and-gathering societies.

Anthropologists have traced male attempts to gain control of women's reproductive capacities. Gender inequality is linked to the increasing social complexity common in larger, settled societies. Control over biological and social reproduction appears to have gone hand in hand with the rise of patriarchy, a form of social organization in which the male is designated the head of the family or social unit. No matter the consequences – whether control over labor or wealth as measured by access to material things – the control over female reproductive capacity had important implications for the control over wealth since labor was as important as other resources that might be accumulated. Such control could be and was translated by male elites and specialists into creative and instrumental power.

The first widespread evidence of differentiation of status accompanies the first permanent human settlements, even if some aspects of patriarchy may pre-date settling down into communities (see Chapter 3). As societies became settled, the reliance on organized human labor became critical to the survival and thriving of communities. Living in one place for a long time encouraged elaboration of culture expression and the possession of items of material culture, which marked identity and status. As the possibilities for material accumulation expanded, so did the potential for wealth to be displayed and manipulated. The unequal distribution of resources and their strategic control intensified as societies became more complex. Although not all societies followed the same path of increasing hierarchy and centralization of power, these were common patterns that emerged and were expressed in a variety of forms across the globe from the fourth millennium BCE to the mid-first millennium BCE (see Chapter 7).

But why did the need for order generate increasingly centralized and hierarchical societies? Why did people appear to give up living in egalitarian societies in exchange for life in state-ordered stratified societies? The obvious, though not necessarily complete, answer is the desirability of community life, which includes the social complexity arising from the introduction of agriculture and the consequential specialization and trade characteristic of settled societies. Yet much of what historians know about urban societies comes from the prescriptive writings of the literate elite and it is unknown whether and to what extent non-literate peoples followed the same norms of inequality they described. Since, until recently, most people did not live in urban settings, how the vast majority of people used these models of inequality to order their own worlds may be difficult to answer.

In trying to understand the development of social complexity, social scientists have often assigned evolutionary stages – band, tribe, chiefdom, state – and have also assumed that inequality was an inevitable product of increasing complexity. But was this always the case, and therefore inevitable, or are there contrasting examples of societies that did not follow this evolutionary model and instead exhibited alternative ways of ordering the world? Historians now view the relationship between increasing social complexity and inequality as a complicated one. Age and sex are the primary differences between people in small-scale hunting and gathering societies. Gender roles differentiated between the activities engaged in by men and women; in most settled societies, men eventually became associated with hunting and women with domestic work. Elders gained more power than did the younger siblings in kinship groups; older males frequently subordinated young men and women. Older women beyond their childbearing years frequently gained status. Historians still struggle with the question of whether the construction of hierarchies based on age and gender was the inevitable outcome of increasing social complexity.

KINSHIP, LINEAGE, FAMILY, AND GENDER HIERARCHIES

Kinship provides a cultural framework for the construction of identity throughout world history, for a sense of belonging to and exclusion from groups. While the meanings ascribed to age and gender differences are constructed in a social context, these differences also interact with other social categories such as ethnicity, class, or social status. Other agents of inequality arise from the ordering of social groups. Powerful ideologies emerged from the most basic arrangements of persons related by blood and often living in a shared household. These ideas – of family and belonging as members or strangers to a social fabric – sometimes were influenced or sanctioned by larger political and social structures. Sometimes concepts of kinship helped define or legitimize power. Kinship relations could be shaped by genealogical claims, descent patterns, age and gender. An individual's standing within a family (for example, as a senior or junior member) or a family group's claims to land or rituals, rights and access to resources could all give rise to inequalities in rank and status. The attainment of status as an elder conferred respect in many societies and, over time, could be translated into inherited status available to descendants across generations.

Hierarchies of status existed among early lineage-based societies around the world. On the Arabian Peninsula, pre-Islamic nomadic camel-herding lineages carried the highest status even though they were the poorest in natural resources and wealth and probably represented no more than 25 percent of the population. Their status owed much to their military abilities and their mobility in the arid environment, an asset that allowed them greater independence. Raiding one another for animals was an ongoing part of the lives of these nomadic peoples, since ownership of animals meant life to those who subsisted in the parched environment. Beneath the camel herders were the nomadic and semi-nomadic sheep and goat herders, and lower still in the status line were the sedentary farmers and townspeople.

Even within each economic group, some lineages were thought to have more honor than others, honor being measured in terms of regional power, reputation for hospitality, and the security provided by members of the lineage. Within a lineage, certain families also had high status, and they usually provided perennial leadership to the lineage as a whole. Families who held leverage in lineage politics sometimes parlayed this into leadership. After the rise and spread of Islam, claiming lineage connections gave distinct advantages to Muslims whether they resided in East Africa or East Asia. For example, coastal Swahili in post-800 CE East Africa could gain prestige as traders by emphasizing their relation to royal sultanate families abroad, just as Arab traders became Swahilized in East Africa as it served their purposes.

Political and social orders based on genealogical ties can be found in most regions of the world, including Africa, the Americas, Asia, and Europe. For example, the Akan people of Ghana created some of West Africa's most powerful forest states and empires, beginning around the fourteenth century and culminating in the Asante empire in the late seventeenth century. Central to Akan identity was the matrilineal structure of society centered on the *abusua* (a term referring to the family grouping or matrilineage, as well as clan). Matrilineal descent in Akan society refers to the pattern by which Akan men and women marked their place in the continuum of ancestors, by reference to the female side of the family. It had no special connotations for the distribution of political power, which as elsewhere in large-scale states worked in favor of men.

The Akan concern with fertility and bearing children recognized the importance of the *abusua* in acquiring individual and community identity.

Individuals had recognized rights only through their positions within an *abusua*. Without the protection afforded to members, they were considered without ancestors and without sexual identity.

Not surprisingly, women had not played a prominent role in the pre-imperial male-dominated elite authority of West African society either. Women are rarely mentioned in the oral historical record, which was frequently controlled by male traditionalists (*griots*) and their male descendants until recently. In the fourteenth century Malian epic of Sundiata, women do appear as potential power sources – mothers, sisters, and sorceresses – despite their unequal access to instrumental political power. The manipulation of kinship for the purposes of domination was a common characteristic of increasingly hierarchical expressions of power and authority.

Around the world the family reflected and provided a model for the inequalities found in political orders. The code of the Mesopotamian king Hammurabi (*c.* 1792–1750 BCE) is one of the earliest written documents that provide explicit regulations concerning the family. This collection of case law reveals ideas about female chastity, contractual obligations, and the property dimensions of family, servants, and slaves. Among other things, the Code of Hammurabi viewed the family as an economic unit and made definite gender relationships and parental authority, as shown in the following example:

> If a man has taken a wife, and she has borne him children and that woman has gone to her fate, and he has taken a second wife, and she also has borne children; after the father has gone to his fate, the sons shall not share according to mothers, but each family shall take the marriage-portion of its mother, and all shall share the goods of their father's estate equally.
>
> (Mark Anthony Meyer, *Landmarks of Western Civilization*, Guilford, Conn.: Dushkin Publishing Group, 1994, p. 28, citing C. H. W. Johns, ed., *Babylonian and Assyrian Laws, Contracts, and Letters*, Library of Ancient Inscriptions, New York: Charles Scribner's Sons, 1904)

The ability of women to share equally in control over resources seems to have also depended on their role in reproducing society. Productivity could be increased by providing children for labor, establishing genealogical claims derived from giving birth to children, or by adding lands and labor through territorial expansion.

GENDER AND WARFARE

Some historians have argued that gendered inequalities have their origin with the technologies of human warfare and violence. Accompanying the concentration of population and resources was the growth of military forces: to protect food stores, to defend territory, and eventually to expand control of both people and land. The transformation of societies into warrior cultures promoted patriarchal domination through the control over such items as weapons, horses, and the wealth that conquest and raiding might produce. The gendered ordering followed the pattern of female association with childbirth and home and male association with warfare. In ancient Sumer there is some evidence of the gradual erosion of women's rights when women lost inheritance rights on behalf of families. This may have occurred as a result of chronic warfare (possibly reflecting scarcity of resources and an ecological crisis due to climate change that caused desiccation) and the growth of private property. Where kin-based control over resources existed, this control was centered in the household and dominated by women. The control over property by individuals rather than families tended to shift emphasis to the activities performed by men outside the household; this may have given way to male control and female dependence.

In most agricultural and warrior societies the division of labor could and did lead to the subordination of women. For example, ancient Egyptian society was patriarchal: men and their male heirs controlled the majority of relationships. In the realm of the household, elite Egyptian women controlled property, business, ritual, and family matters. This is not always obvious from the surviving records, which are frequently biased and, in the case of documents composed by the all-male scribes, directed toward an all-male audience of readers.

Egyptian women were accorded theoretical equality under most laws relating to property and inheritance. However, the absence of women from government posts and the realities of patriarchy (including differences in the ability of women to inherit and own property) prevented equal access to influential positions and limited the independent accumulation of wealth. Subordination was linked to the concept of fertility, which ascribed to a woman the responsibility and duty of reproduction as service to her husband. This is revealed by Old Kingdom (third millennium) authors, who advised men, "When you prosper, found your household. Take a hearty wife, a son will be born unto you" and "Gladden her [the wife's] heart as long as you live; she is a fertile field for her lord."

It is not surprising to recognize labor as a metaphor for the oppression of women. Not only gender but also distinctions in status and social divisions appeared in ancient agricultural societies. The artwork of tombs describes visual hieroglyphic (sacred picture writing) tales about the divided daily lives of rural and urban Egyptians, from the royal family to their slaves. Land and labor would remain arenas for both the expression of and resistance to growing inequalities, as they became more systematically enforced around the world.

Elsewhere there is evidence that contests the assumed correlation between male gender and warfare. In the vast and open landscape of the Ural steppes of southern Russia, at a place called Pokrovka, archaeologists have found the final resting place of the bones of a 13- or 14-year-old girl. She lived more than 2,500 years ago in a nomadic society of people who grazed their sheep and horses across the steppes, moving seasonally from pasture to pasture. The Greeks called such people "Sauromatians"; their contemporaries were best known from the description by the Greek historian Herodotus of the female warriors he called "Amazons" (those who are not breastfed). These daughters of nomads rode horses, used bows and arrows, and were required to have killed an enemy before they married.

From the bowed leg bones of the young girl's skeleton excavated at Pokrovka, it can be determined that she had spent her brief lifetime on horseback. Buried with her was an array of weapons, including a dagger and dozens of arrowheads in a wood and leather container. Around her neck she wore a bronze arrowhead amulet in a leather pouch. A great boar's tusk once probably suspended from her belt now lay at her feet. It is likely that the amulet and tusk had been worn to enhance her warrior abilities and ensure success.

Other excavations in the Russian steppes have shown that some Early Iron Age women held a unique position in society. They controlled wealth, performed family rituals, rode horseback, hunted, and fought. Such Amazons have been identified in other parts of the world, from West Africa to the Americas and Australia. These and other data from early societies suggest that women were not inherently more peaceful than men. However, there is also evidence that, in general, the militarism that accompanied the formation of complex societies also contributed to the subordination of women, who increasingly were excluded from warrior training and the high status it conferred.

If the impact of warfare on gendered inequalities was not universal, the interpretation of available evidence is critical. We know little of women in early periods of history in China, but evidence from a royal tomb suggests that women could hold military power virtually on a par with men. The tomb of Fu Hao, consort of a king who ruled about 1400 BCE, has yielded evidence that she controlled a large army in her own right. Apart from this, the limits of current knowledge make it difficult to say much about the position of women in Shang (c. 1750–1050 BCE) society and attitudes toward women. Though female fertility figures, which may represent a goddess, have been found in Neolithic sites in China, these do not appear in Shang and later sites when a patriarchal order was in place.

CASTE, CLIENTAGE, AND INEQUALITY

Not only family groups, but hereditary ties that transcended family were used to distinguish categories of unequal status. There are various theories about the historical origin of the South Asian system of castes, the division of society into rigid hierarchical ranks assigned by birth. Caste was a distinctive alternative to lineage and clientage as approaches to social organization and relations of power. The caste system may have been produced by the imposition of rule by Indo-European invaders over the indigenous population of the Indian subcontinent during the mid-second millennium BCE. Distinctions among castes were perhaps initially drawn according to skin color, since the Sanskrit term *varna* ("color") is the term first used to classify social groups. By about 1000 BCE, the population of the Indus River Valley and the Ganges plain had been divided into four groups: religious (priests), warriors, merchants or farmers, and finally servants or slaves. This division of society was justified and explained in the Vedic scriptures (the earliest surviving written literature of the region) as the result of the dismemberment of a cosmic being into four pieces. The system of castes, which became one of the key features of South Asian life, evolved from the complex division of society according to occupational and social differences.

The use of caste distinctions as a means of establishing social organization was neither rigid nor unchanging. Over time, caste divisions were further subdivided into increasingly complex occupational and ethnic groups, each with its own distinct rules of behavior. The hereditary system of social stratification is known as *jati*, literally meaning "births," a reference to the belief that one's station in life is ascribed at birth. The *jati* system was associated mostly with specific occupations and other distinctions based on geography. Inter-*jati* marriages, while defying the caste system, also constantly redefined it. The categories were intimately linked in complex webs of inter-dependency, including exchange of services, goods, and land rights.

The concept and practice of caste involved corporate membership, common descent, and endogamy: members of castes shared a common identity because they belonged to the same cultural and social group; they were descended from common ancestors; and their relatedness continued across generations through marriage practices restricting liaisons to others within the group. Three of the four initial groups were defined by occupation, although the fourth appears to have been an ethnic category.

Caste became a hereditary distinction that was demonstrated by rules forbidding marriage to outsiders, requiring that members eat together, and restricting other kinds of activities between members of different sub-castes. Members belonging to one caste were believed to be ritually impure by members of other castes; contact between different castes resulted in contamination. Notions such as ritual purity and pollution limited the contact between different caste groups and provided an ideological justification for caste, just as such ideas frequently were applied to gender categories. It is also likely that these practices resulted from the early social distinctions, rather than having generated them, and so helped maintain members and nonmembers in an orderly social and political structure. The use of caste distinctions as a means of establishing social organization was neither rigid nor unchanging. Over time, caste divisions were further subdivided into increasingly complex occupational and ethnic groups, each with its own distinct rules of behavior. Breaking these rules would lead to social ostracism, while following them rigidly might allow one to be reborn into a higher caste.

Caste has been debated as a concept applicable to other parts of the world beyond South Asia. Often described as a caste system, the social order of Tokugawa Japan (1600–1850) was rigidly structured around the ideal of a four-tier class system, imported from China and modified to fit Japanese society in the seventeenth century. Warriors (samurai) were placed at the top, farmers came second, artisans were third, and at the bottom were merchants. The Tokugawa government attempted to keep these groups strictly separate, and in theory the daughter of a merchant could not marry the son of a samurai. Such social prohibitions created tensions, richly illuminated in the popular theater of the time. Despite their low position in the social order, economic growth in the Tokugawa enriched merchants and made some of them among the wealthiest people in Japan. At the very bottom of the social order, beyond the four classes, were the *eta*, the "untouchables," who were given the polluting tasks of burying the dead, tanning hides, and other unsavory occupations. This group was not unlike the untouchables of the Indian caste system, and discrimination against them persists in contemporary Japan.

In some African societies, reliance on clientage, a relationship of dependence not necessarily based on kinship, was the essential cement for centralized political systems. It was commonly said in the oral traditions of West and Central Africa that a king was his people. For example, in pre-colonial Dahomey, the metaphor of a perforated pot was used to describe the state: the king was like the pot's water, which everyone had to help keep inside. In other words, authority figures were necessary and existed to serve the essential needs of members of the social group, including protection and the extraction of labor for large social enterprises. Membership in such societies was based not on blood ties or genealogy but on service to the king, a dependency relationship in which the king was the patron and the people his clients.

The presence of clientage relationships in African societies reveals the social and political inequalities that brought them into being. Whereas in some parts of the world clientage involved landowners providing land to the landless, these relationships in Africa rarely involved land. They did sometimes involve the transfer of other forms of property, such as human beings and the value of their labor. For example, around 1000 CE the king at Ife (Yoruba, Nigeria) did not own the land surrounding the city, but he controlled the available labor and assigned persons to work the land surrounding the royal city. His counterpart to the north of Nigeria, the ruler of Kanem in the eleventh century, was celebrated in a song that commemorates his ability to capture and control labor:

> The best you took (and sent home) as the first fruits of battle,
> The children crying on their mothers you snatched away from their mothers,
> You took the slave wife from a slave, and set them in lands far removed from one another.

In sub-Saharan Africa, where the population density remained low and land was valued less than people, authority was frequently expressed in personal rather than territorial terms. This was especially true in herding societies. In Rwanda, clientage was initiated by a cattle transaction between the owner of the cattle and the client herder: "Give milk, make me rich, be my father." In the Sena society of Mozambique, a pre-European system of clientage was the result of economic motives often arising during times of drought and famine, when a desperate lineage group could temporarily pawn a member's labor to a larger, wealthier household. It also frequently indicated the need for protection and was initiated by the ritual act of "breaking the mitate," literally walking into the potential patron's household and smashing a clay pot,

an act that created obligations and resulted in a period of servitude by the "offender." The various means of establishing reciprocal relationships resulted in the accumulation of human resources by the larger and wealthier groups, which in turn derived greater political importance. The political and social order of the nearby fifteenth-century Mwenemutapa empire in southern Africa was built on relationships of personal dependency that successfully expanded over a large territory. Individuals owed allegiance, service, and agricultural labor to the ruler, who in turn provided protection and other benefits.

The presence of clientage resulted in ties of obedience on the part of the client and obligation on the part of the patron. Reliance on clientage relations appears to occur when states are emerging or disappearing. The clientage system could be part of either the devolution of power (as in the breakup of polities) or of the emerging evolution of highly centralized states (such as empires). The African examples indicate a variety of flexible polities in which inequalities based on inherited positions with differing access to wealth and influence were integrated in such a way as to enable all parties – both the more powerful and the less powerful – to sustain their common social fabric in the face of external threats. These various systems were temporary and indigenous solutions to the central problem of holding hierarchical power relations together amid great social inequality. The defining features of social forms not only were reconstructed in response to changing political contours, such as the emergence of an empire or state, but were purposefully altered to serve the political interests of those in power.

ECONOMIC INEQUALITIES: FEUDALISM AND SERFDOM

The term "feudalism" has been used to describe a political system (see Chapter 7) that developed in some parts of Europe, when central government broke down and public functions, obligations, and privileges were taken over by individuals operating under a variety of private hierarchical arrangements created by personal obligation. In theory, all land was owned by the sovereign, and granted to his lords in the form of manors. Lords concentrated on making their manors self-sufficient, with free labor in the form of peasants. Free peasants continued to live in villages where much of the land was subject to family or community reallocation as necessity dictated. They owed labor (corvée) to the local lord who in turn protected them. Due to debt and the collapse of urban-based economies as viable employment options, some free peasants gave up their mobility (of labor) in order to have economic and military security for themselves and their families. Thus serfs became the unfree labor force of medieval Europe.

Europe

The economies of many early societies were based on self-sufficient agricultural estates. In feudal Europe between the eleventh and fourteenth centuries, roughly 90 percent of the population made their living from agricultural production. The principal social and economic unit organizing this production was the manor, an estate owned by a wealthy landowner and farmed by tenants who were either free peasants or serfs (people who owed obligations of produce or labor to the landowner).

Feudalism involved the relationship between land-owners, in which the most powerful landowners provided aid and protection to less powerful landowners who had enough wealth to own horses and arms. The less powerful landowners, in turn, owed allegiance and military service to the most powerful. The vassal (or client) gradually became identified as a knight, a warrior around whom evolved a highly elaborate culture and lifestyle. The knight's prestige depended upon fighting, and knights justified their existence by waging wars. Many knights were descended from elites through the male line, and they maintained their power through kinship networks and alliances with other powerful lords.

Japan

In Japan during roughly the same period, society was also largely based on agricultural estates known as *shoen*. Like manors, the *shoen* were owned by wealthy landowners and farmed mostly by peasants who rented the land. Unlike the manor system, however, Japanese landowners typically did not live on the *shoen*,

differentiating the practice from the institution of serfdom, based on hereditary rights to work the land, since everyone on the *shoen* held some legally recognized rights to the land. Inequalities in Japanese society evolved from the lineage-based aristocratic social tradition in which patron–client relations were the basis of political organization and the means of governing the state. This process was exemplified by the rule of the Fujiwara family during the ninth to eleventh centuries, the early part of the Heian period (794–1185), named for its capital city (modern Kyoto). The Heian nobility lived in luxury supported by the labor of peasants on landed estates that were distant from Heian court life. Eventually the control over manors was lost to local estate managers and military men, who were expected to protect the manors from assault.

Russia

In Russia, as in other parts of the world where obligation ordered the social systems and land was readily available, power and wealth were based on control of labor. There were no religious or ethnic differences between masters and serfs, nor was conquest involved. Serfdom evolved as forced agricultural labor in Russia, when the imperial governments expanded eastward under the post-Mongol Muscovy tsars and following the Ottoman capture of Constantinople in 1453. The expansion of the Muscovite state created a revolution in the system of landholding. The tsar was master and under him were elite servants, who called themselves "slaves." They were under the direct protection of the tsar. Thus, the Muscovite notion of subservience bound both master and servant to a set of reciprocal relationships and obligations. Outside the orbit of the tsar's protection were the "orphans" or "pilgrims" – powerless participants in a model of bondage as a blessed condition (just as they might achieve servitude to God). Only members of the ruling Kalita clan could inherit land – all others were granted the use of land across a vast and poor agricultural region, known for its harsh climate and poor communication. As the tsars rewarded military officers and nobles with enormous estates in the hinterlands, there was a correspondingly enormous labor shortage of peasants to work the estates. The solution was to limit the mobility of the peasants to the point where, by 1649, they were forbidden to leave their place of employment and the status was hereditary. By the 1660s, owners were buying and selling serfs without land, and by the eighteenth century the practice had become commonplace.

Narratives of serfs are rare, but like those of slaves elsewhere suggest the longings for passage from their state of bondage. The writings of Nikolai Shipov, who eventually escaped serfdom, suggest that a longing for his native land compounded the violence and loss of rights attached to his status as a serf. He wrote:

> They put me in a dungeon, take away my money, separate me from my wife and son and daughter, rule inside my home and give orders as they please; they send me away from my dear native place, and forbid me from shedding tears on the dust of my parents.
>
> (John MacKay, "'And Hold the Bondsman Still': Biogeography and Utopia in Slave and Serf Narratives," *Biogeography*, 25, 1 (2002): 110–29, at p.129)

Serfdom gradually evolved into chattel slavery by the end of Peter I's reign (1725). The combination of a revolution in landowning and an increasingly powerful state that could regulate and enforce laws about immobility of labor helped to cement the existence of an indigenous unfree labor force that survived until 1861.

SLAVERY AND OTHER SYSTEMS OF INEQUALITY

Among the most extreme forms of social inequality in history were systems of human bondage and enslavement. From Eurasia to the Americas and Africa, forms of coerced labor created a spectrum of intricate relationships of dependency and obligation. Social inequality as reflected in family, lineage, and clientage relationships constitutes one expression of the exploitation of difference common in smaller-scale societies. Beginning between about the middle of the first millennium BCE, systems of exploitation had also

begun to be built around the unequal access to land and labor in larger states. Slaves were found in almost all parts of the ancient world. Systems of slavery were situated at the extreme end of this continuum of inequality and exploitation. They appear in large-scale polities around the world. Historians do not always agree on when to apply the term "slavery" to the variety of cultural systems of inequality. Sometimes labor systems were imposed on conquered populations, resulting in loss of rights and labor obligations.

Greek and Roman slavery

Although enslavement originated through vastly different social, economic, and political processes, all slave systems were characterized by the threat or actual use of violence to coerce labor for the benefit of others. Enslavement resulted in the total loss of personal rights. Enslavement might be the consequence of capture in warfare or the internal processes of judicial judgment, punishment, or economic indebtedness. In Roman society most slaves originated as war captives, whose lives were spared. They were legally defined as people who were owned by someone else. High-ranking slaves might self-select the status in order to be attached to the wealthy households of others. In ancient Greece, slaves attached themselves to larger households or to shrines in times of famine or debt through a ritual process. In some societies, domestic slavery might be temporary or could gain permanency through marriage into an adopted household. For example, Roman slaves in urban households were adopted as domestic servants. Slaves in many cultures provided labor in mining, domestic households, and in highly specialized crafts and trades.

Slave trading was a principle activity of states which relied on military expansion. The cycle of imperial expansion resulted in war captives and was matched by increases in the slave population. Large-scale slave systems throughout world history supported the power and authority of rulers and enabled their extended access to labor. There was also an intimate link between land and the labor of the enslaved. As territorial conquests extended the control over land, conquered peoples were viewed as essential sources of labor or tribute.

Figure 8.1 A scene of a triumphal procession on this terracotta *"campana"* plaque shows chained captives in an open cart being taken through the streets of Rome. Early second century CE.

Hierarchies in the Inca tribute system

While economic motives may have underpinned the existence and spread of slavery, those systems could also be supported by complex beliefs and rituals. Like the Egyptian pharaohs who were living gods, the Sapa Inca, or "Sole Ruler," was believed to be a descendant of the sun god and his representative on earth. Incorporating the Andean traditions of ancestor worship, the mummified bodies of dead kings became the tangible link between the Incan people and their pantheon. To preserve this link and to ensure the continuity of their own political order, the Incas had to maintain the royal dead in fitting splendor for perpetuity; thus a constant income was necessary, and this could be supplied only by continual conquests. Upon every conquest, the Incas made a thorough inventory of the people, land, and resources they had conquered, all of which accrued to the Sapa Inca: all land, all gold and silver, all labor (a form of tax as well as a duty), all people. As in many other societies, women were considered a form of property. Adultery, therefore, was punished as a crime against property. Subjects of the Sapa Inca were all provided with land, although they might be moved from place to place

according to bureaucratic inventories of people and resources, as a guarantee against sedition and rebellion.

The Sapa Inca's authority was maintained by an elaborate hierarchical administrative system, by blood lineage ties, and by his religious function. All his subjects were divided into groups, arranged in an orderly fashion of responsibility; for example, fathers were responsible for their children's actions. Another organizational pattern had to do with labor: all subjects had assigned tasks. When the state expanded its control over territory it also included people's labor, sometimes termed corvée labor (meaning a labor obligation). The major labor obligation was cultivation of the land, which was divided into three types: what was necessary for the state, what was necessary for the cult of the sun, what was necessary for the people. Other general labor duties included keeping weaving; tending llama flocks, which were state-owned; and keeping up roads, bridges, and public monumental buildings.

West African states

The intersection of gender and other inequalities was dependent on complex cultural and social constructions that could and often did change over time. During the expansion of the Akan state (in West Africa) during and after the fourteenth and fifteenth centuries CE, neither women nor children gained position or power. The emphasis on warfare resulted in men gaining status, and the increased numbers of slaves available to perform household tasks generally devalued women's labor and diminished their influence even further. As Akan society became a slave society, dependent on slave labor, social classes became more entrenched and inequalities proliferated. The uncertainty and ambiguity inherent in the lack of ancestry and status are best exemplified by the fact that enemies captured by the expanding Akan state became permanent slaves unless they were integrated into an *abusua* through adoption or marriage.

A general feature of empires was the increased and more systematic exploitation of social inequality. An empire's territorial expansion ultimately relied on its increasing the supplies of food for its armies and other sources of wealth for trade. In addition to their reproductive role, women produced goods. Another important feature of imperial systems was the expansion of territorial control over land. The fourteenth-century Arab traveler Ibn Battuta described the extent of social inequality in Mali. One of the consequences of the expansion of empire through trade and military means was the capture of prisoners of war, who then became sources of male soldiers and female slaves. The Sahelian and Saharan towns of the Mali empire were organized as both staging posts in the long-distance caravan trade and trading centers for the various West African products. At Taghaza, for example, salt was exchanged; at Takedda, copper. Ibn Battuta observed the employment of slave labor in both towns. During most of his journey, Ibn Battuta traveled with a retinue that included slaves, most of whom carried goods for trade but would also be traded as slaves. On the return from Takedda to Morocco, his caravan transported 600 female slaves, suggesting that slavery was a substantial part of the commercial activity of the empire's fringes.

Imperial growth everywhere depended in part on women, the appropriation of female labor as well as the mechanisms for the exclusion of women from the sources of political and economic power. There were many more female slaves than male slaves traded in the empire, a fact that points out the inequality that existed between the genders. The variation in women's social positions increased with the growth of the empire's towns. Women, usually slaves, were valued porters in the trans-Saharan caravan trade. They sometimes served as concubines. Additionally, female labor produced salt, cloth for export, and most of the local foodstuffs essential to the provisions required by urban centers. Men were hunters, farmers, merchants, and specialists, in addition to frequently being conscripted as soldiers.

Whether or not a society's hierarchical structure monopolized labor, controlled access to strategic food or positions through farms, palaces, temples, or cities, power organized the relationships in society. The division of labor, ecological variability, and accumulation of material wealth resulted in the propensity for hierarchies to proliferate. The ability to appropriate labor and gain preferential access to strategic resources in turn created greater disparities. Enslavement was the most extreme form of social disempowerment and could result from the subjugation of labor, the transfer of rights over persons, or through sanctions that made an individual not only "unfree" but also kinless. Being made kinless was tantamount to denying an individual the right to belong to community.

Islam, imperial expansion, and slavery

Belonging to community was especially important in the world of Islam, By the fifteenth century CE, dar al-Islam stretched from the Arabian peninsula to the Iberian peninsula and North Africa, into sub-Saharan Africa, and then east to the three great Islamic empires of the Ottoman Turks, the Safavid Persians, Mughal India, and much of Southeast Asia. While the diverse peoples of dar al-Islam were spreading across three continents, land was not scarce. Dar al-Islam was a civilization of cities, where wealth and power were based on money and trade across vast reaches of land and sea. It was equally a system of interknit small communities in the hinterlands of those cities – hinterlands that provided townsfolk with essential food and the trade goods that sustained their commercial enterprises. Particularly in the more urban areas of Southwest Asia the common use for slave labor was in domestic situations and in the military. Islamic laws forbid the enslavement of fellow Muslims. To be Muslim was to be free. Therefore slaves could only be non-Muslims, and preferably not even "people of the book" (Christians and Jews). According to Ahmad Baba of Timbuktu (1556–1627):

> The reason for slavery is non-belief, and the Sudanese non-believers are like other *kafir* [non-believers] whether they are Christians, Jews, Persians, Berbers, or any others who stick to non-belief and do not embrace Islam . . . This means that there is no difference between all the *kafir* in this respect. Whoever is captured in a condition of non-belief, it is legal to own him, whosoever he may be, but not he who was converted to Islam voluntarily, from the start, to any nation he belongs, whether it is Bornu, Kano, Songhai, Katsina, Gobir, Mali, and some of Zakzak [Zazzau]. These are free Muslims, whose enslavement is not allowed in any way.
>
> (Quoted in Paul E. Lovejoy, *Transformations in Slavery: A History of Slavery in Africa*, Cambridge: Cambridge University Press, 1983, p. 30)

Debt slavery and loss of status in Southeast Asia

An alternative means of understanding enslavement occurred in societies in which slaves originated as persons disgraced or degraded in status. In Southeast Asia and some parts of Africa, slaves could be indigenous rather than perceived of as "others" (outside the social and kinship networks of familiar terrain). These societies were held together by vertical bonds of obligations between the elite and less powerful, and slavery was merely one of many options on a spectrum of obligation. Land was assumed to be abundant, and not therefore an index of power. Wealth and power lay in the manpower (and womanpower) one could gather. For the poor and weak, on the other hand, security and opportunity depended upon being bonded to somebody strong enough to look after them. Fundamental to success and wealth was the ability to succeed in gaining control over people not land.

The most common origin for this system of bondage was debt, although there were also war captives. When overwhelmed with debts (due to dowry payments, perhaps, or expensive rituals like slaughtering a buffalo upon the death of a family member), a man could sell himself and/or his wife and children to the creditor. Most often, he became a domestic slave, much like a junior member of the household, doing all its most menial jobs, yet closely bound in intimacy to it and sharing its triumphs as well as its disasters. The slave owner was likewise expected to provide for his slave, even procuring a wife. The debt-bondsman's labor had a definite value, however, and he could be sold , traded, and exchanged. Most importantly, the slave owner and ruler were tied directly or indirectly to the human drama of enslavement through various alliances and loyalties.

Although agriculture was by far the dominant activity in Southeast Asia, a slave mode of production did not seem to exist there: farm laborers owed a portion of their produce to their lord, but were not owned personally by the lord – even if they owed some form of tribute. The most characteristic roles for slaves were as domestics, entertainers, and as spinners and weavers of textiles. They also functioned as significant status symbols, and symbols of power. Kings and powerful nobles constantly struggled for control of men: the kings seeking to maximize the number of people obligated to him through corvée (unpaid state labor) and the nobles to withdraw men from the corvée for their own private uses. In the flourishing centers of Angkor, Ayudhuya, Malacca, Banten, Aceh, and Makassar, populations numbered up to one hundred thousand people each, and slaves were the single most important item of property. They symbolically conveyed status: it was important that the elite do no manual labor, and be seen always attended by a retinue of slaves. Likewise, foreign merchants could not function effectively unless they had men bonded to them. In these societies, the existence of slaves served to define the status of individuals and the bounds of community.

GLOBALIZING INEQUALITY

Between about 1500 and 1850, the globalization of slavery, indentured labor, and the slave trade defined the parameters for the rise of capitalism and the era of exploitation and conquest that followed. Long-distance trade in slaves linked regions of the world from Eurasia and Africa to the Americas. The Indian Ocean slave trade provided a nexus point for slaves from Europe, North Africa, East Africa, and Asia. The globalization of trade in humans as commodities would integrate these vastly different regions into a single, integrated system of exploitation and profit, thereby globalizing inequality.

Trading labor

The extensive world trade that followed the circumnavigation of the globe and European maritime expansion extended the markets and opportunities for the movement of enslaved populations. Slaves were carried across the Atlantic and Pacific oceans, but the land routes also continued. During the period between 1500 and 1800, slaves were traded across the Sahara and the Red Sea from Africa to the Muslim Mediterranean, in continuation of a trade that reached back to medieval times. North and east of the Mediterranean, a trade in Slavic-speaking and Caucasian peoples sent captives to the Ottoman empire. Captives from East Africa and Madagascar went to Asia, to

Indian Ocean islands, and eventually to Africa and the Americas. The slave trade of the Indian subcontinent and Southeast Asia went to places near and far in the web of the Indian Ocean network. The slave was always valuable property and a symbol of status and power for his or her owner. As merchant capital began to drive the global economy, the slave was bought and sold as a commodity. Through the process of sale, hundreds of thousands of Asians and Africans were transported to all points of the globe. The new slave trade changed the identities of millions more.

Early modern societies bore the legacies of many different ways of valuing land and labor. Some societies valued individual landholding, others royal land-holding, while still others stressed the significance of communal property, and others held no beliefs that land could be owned at all. In organizing their human communities, some societies stressed reciprocal social obligations to knit people together, while others stressed unbending hierarchical obedience from the bottom up. When Europeans came in contact with, and then conquered most of the Americas, they viewed their experiences within an understanding of the profound differences among the patterns of peoples and lands.

Slavery in the Americas

The first truly global industry – mining – relied heavily on slave labor. While the exploitation of silver in the Americas formed the basis for the rise of global trade with Asia, the creation of an Atlantic economy was based on two other commodities: sugar and slaves. The European entry into the world of the Americas had catastrophic effects on the indigenous peoples, who succumbed to the diseases and genocidal policies of Europeans; and in the wake of Amerindian population decreases, other forms of coercive labor, including slavery, were exploited in the construction of the "new world." Recently conquered non-Christian popula-tions were entrusted to the Spanish, who would assure their physical and spiritual well-being, in return for which they would labor and give a share of their produce. In actuality a slave system was created, although subsequently dismantled by the Crown. By then, the Crown had established its own draft labor, reviving the Inca *mit'a*. When the silver deposits at Potosí, in Peru, were identified, the Spanish con-

quistadors looked to local labor systems of the Inca, which had resettled millions of subjects. The corvée labor obligation system known as *mit'a* served to tax the labor of the population for the benefit of the ruler. In Spanish hands, it was brutal and coercive enslavement. The Spanish divided up populations and used them to mine, grow crops, or as servants. Entire indigenous communities fled to territories beyond the reach of the conquerors, some becoming serfs on *encomiendas* or Spanish estates, trading their labor for protection.

The history of Atlantic commerce is inseparable from the history of slavery, and the transfer of both labor and capital across the Atlantic is closely connected with the production of sugar. Technology and culture were intertwined in the development of the sugar industry. Very few Iberians of the sixteenth and seventeenth centuries objected to the use of African slaves, but enslavement of indigenous Americans was hotly contested in Spain. The labor required by plantations in the Americas was satisfied through conscription and coercion, establishing the relation-ships of inequity that have continued to plague the social structures of much of the Americas.

Inequality in the Caribbean

In the Americas it was not only silver mining but also sugar cultivation and ranching that required both large investments of capital and a steady supply of labor, and investors were needed who could guarantee both. In order for sugar production to return a profit, expensive plantations, large-scale plots of land at least 80 to 100 hectares (198 to 247 acres) in size, were essential. Many of the largest plantations were run as businesses by absentee landlords across the ocean. Their successful operation required both skilled and unskilled labor, as well as a supply of industrial equipment to support the processing of crops and products for export.

Providing labor for Caribbean plantations was a constant problem. Many indigenous peoples resisted and were killed, and others fled into the most inaccessible regions of the interior of large islands and the mainland. Those who were not as fortunate succumbed to European diseases. In Mesoamerica, the population declined from 25.2 million in 1519 to 16.8 million in 1532 and 0.75 million in 1622. As entire villages of Amerindians disappeared, Europeans turned to other available sources of labor, including European bond servants, people who were offered meager land grants (that often did not materialize) in return for providing labor on plantations, and European convicts and prisoners of war also were shipped by the hundreds and even thousands. In this way Scots and Irish prisoners, for example, were also brought to Jamaica. Later in the nineteenth century, South Asians were transported as indentured labor.

Neither the indigenous peoples nor Europeans adequately answered the labor needs of the plantations of the Americas. African slaves were brought across the Atlantic within a decade of Columbus's voyages. First in small numbers and later in astounding ones, regular supplies of slaves were provided by traders who had bought them in Africa, where most originated as war captives from conflicts between Africans. Even under appalling conditions, though, African slaves fared better than Amerindian slaves had. The African slave populations had come from often tropical environments, similar in many ways to the Caribbean; they were accustomed to heat and humidity. If they survived infancy and childhood, they already had, unlike adult Amerindians, developed resistance to the most deadly Old World (Afro-European) epidemics, including smallpox, and many tropical diseases.

Enslaved Africans

In the end, costs favored the use of slaves. The lower death rate of the enslaved Africans and their agricultural and technological skills, weighed against the hostility of European free and indentured laborers who knew the master's language, culture, and weaknesses, made African labor preferable. The reliance on slavery was so complete that by the eighteenth century Africans significantly outnumbered those of European descent in the circum-Caribbean region (by ratios typically as high as eleven or thirteen to one). Their darker skin colors also made them more easily identifiable as slaves, not free men; as "black" came to be synonymous with "slave," racism was born. Out of the European justification of the enslavement and trade of Africans emerged an ideology of superiority based on skin color. This ideology came to assert the superiority of white Europeans and their cultural values over the rest of the world's peoples.

Both private companies and companies enjoying government monopolies set up operations in African coastal towns, where they built forts and castles on land rented from African communities. Tropical diseases against which European adults had no immunity and a climate and environment considered harsh and difficult by Europeans prevented them from moving inland from the coast much before the nineteenth century. Moreover, their coastal trading stations satisfied the purposes for which they had come to Africa: they became the entrepôts for amassing wealth and promoting inequality.

Captains of slaving ships acquired their cargoes either by sailing along the West or Central African coast and purchasing slaves from several independent African dealers or by buying slaves directly from a European agent, called a factor, at one of the large coastal trading stations, called factories. These slaves were provided to the dealers mostly by African states. Slaves usually originated as war captives; they were victims of a period of numerous wars and a general atmosphere of political instability and personal insecurity that was common to many inland regions of the African continent during the era of the Atlantic slave trade. African hostilities, fueled by the possession of firearms acquired from European traders, became increasingly violent.

Originating as war prisoners, African slaves were sold to European traders in exchange for guns and other manufactured goods, such as cloth and metal, which were prestige goods used by African elites to enhance status. Slaves sold to European traders were most often males, whereas captured females were retained by African elites because they contributed to productivity. African slavery, conceived in social and political terms, eventually gave way to economic slavery, with states relying on a slave mode of production in which the production of wealth was dependent on slave labor. The Atlantic era resulted in the transformation of many Africans into dependent consumers of cheap European products living in increasingly violent slave societies. The historian Walter Rodney called this process "how Europe underdeveloped Africa." The interrelated tentacles of social, economic, and political inequality would characterize the colonial era, backed by the engines of capitalist industrialism.

Ideological and social changes resulted from the complex cultural and economic negotiation with European traders. Elite classes of merchants were created in some places – the *compradores* or merchant princes of West Africa, for example – and culturally and materially impoverished groups were the results elsewhere, such as the South African Hottentots, a derogatory term given by the Dutch to Khoisan servants, who adopted Dutch language and dress in a desperate attempt to buy back their land and cattle and who eventually were decimated or absorbed by their contact with Europeans. Especially in coastal regions, the impact of merchant capitalism was deepened by the transformations of slavery and the accompanying political and social violence. The acceptance of human labor as a commodity after the sixteenth century was reflected in the increased reliance of states on slavery and labor coercion, and in the rise of prostitution in urban areas. Alongside cheap European wares, women's bodies and the titled ranks of gentlemen could be purchased without reference to traditional, ritually sanctioned, and inherited cultural categories of identity and access to power. These and other contradictions would be recalled to form the basis of resistance to European colonialism in later centuries.

African and Asian diasporas

Slaves and indentured laborers supplied by the Indian Ocean and Atlantic systems of forced labor represented the largest known transfer of people prior to the nineteenth century (see Chapter 1). Between about 1518 and 1860 an estimated 12 to 20 million Africans were transported to the Americas. As many as 30 million South Asians formed part of the mass exodus of indentured labor in the nineteenth century, with perhaps as many as 6 million laborers settling into a diaspora community. The impact of the Atlantic slave trade on the circum-Caribbean region is most obvious in the patterns of plantation production and profits, the legacy of Caribbean economic dependency on Europe, and the region's ethnic diversity.

The creation of the African and South Asian diasporas (literally, "dispersals") across the Atlantic world relied on the survival of individuals and their ability to build a life in the Caribbean or Americas or Indian Ocean that owed much to their original African

and Asian heritage (see Chapter 1). There were obstacles to creating cultural continuity. For example, slave masters outlawed African drumming and separated persons speaking the same language in order to discourage communication and solidarity among slaves. Such conditions made African family life difficult and sometimes impossible. Yet the vitality of the hundreds of distinct African languages and cultures, together with the courage and resistance of African peoples in the Americas, ensured their continuity in the face of slavery and oppression even as they negotiated a new identity. Some slaves ran away; others sabotaged the operations of the system. Yet others participated in acts of armed rebellion. The South Asian diaspora was similarly diverse in language and religion.

During the second half of the nineteenth century, 2 million southern Chinese migrated to a wide variety of destinations, including Siberia, Manchuria, the Malay peninsula, Indonesia, the Philippines, Australia, Hawaii, Mexico, Peru, Cuba, and the United States. Many Chinese went as indentured workers to build railroads, mine, and farm. Some went abroad as merchants. People left nineteenth-century China because of adverse conditions resulting from conditions of famine, overpopulation, foreign invasion, and civil wars. Both social and geographical location were significant factors in determining migration patterns.

Inequality and identity

Facing discrimination in their new homelands, immigrants created identities over time that transcended national boundaries. At the same time as their global movements reinforced and defined the contours of modern global capitalism, resistance to the conditions brought about by capitalism was immediate and continuous. The success of resistance helped keep alive African or Asian cultures, while providing an ongoing source of African and Asian identity that promoted survival against great odds. Resistance was most violent in slave societies. Both within the communities of escaped freedom fighters and those of the plantations from which they came, cultural continuities in dance, language, food, informal economic systems, technology, music, dress, pottery, family organization, religion, and other areas are well documented in Caribbean and American life. They attest to the processes of transformation, in which both continuities and discontinuities create the patterns of historical change and determine its direction and scope.

The legacy of slavery and the forced migration of millions is a feature of the contemporary world. The expanding trade provided the basis for the growth of the new global economy. Comparative studies about attitudes toward coerced labor and slavery are essential to an understanding of societies' intellectual and economic transitions. Some historians have argued that the industrialization that gave rise to the modern global economic systems grew from the exploitation of slaves and others who were locked, to varying degrees, into coerced labor systems. Understanding today's world requires an understanding of the circumstances of the laborers who built the infrastructure.

GLOBAL INDUSTRIALIZATION AND INEQUALITY

The early patterns that emerged in the global exploitation of land and labor also characterized later processes of global industrialization (see Chapters 2 and 6). And both industrialization and urbanization were agents in the spread of inequalities. The distinctive institution of the capitalist Industrial Revolution was the factory system of production, whereby workers were assembled and sometimes locked in buildings for fixed hours of labor at power-driven machines. Factories were, however, slow to replace domestic industry, where workers spun and wove in their own homes, using their own spinning wheels and looms. Except in cotton spinning and weaving, as late as the 1830s many employers continued to find domestic industry more profitable and to prefer small shop production to large factory enterprise. Traditional workers also tended to resist the reorganization of the workplace. Workplaces remained segregated on the basis of gender and race.

The use of power-driven machinery under factory conditions, a feature that characterizes the Industrial Revolution, was made possible by venture capitalists who were willing and able to invest substantial sums in innovations and take risks in the quest for profits. Not all capitalists, however, were willing to take risks involved in developing new modes of production. As long as the traditional, labor-intensive methods of production were profitable, most capitalists continued to invest in them, rather than in machine-operated factory production. Labor-intensive industry remained a major mode of production well past 1800, even as machine production increased.

As factories multiplied, younger trainees, many of them women, who had no commitment to older modes of production, replaced traditional artisans and older workers. Factory work meant a loss of the artisan's independence and often a readjustment of family relationships, since production moved outside the home and altered the roles of individual workers. In 1831 a government committee in England investigating child labor in the textile industry uncovered the grim circumstances of daily life for many young children condemned to work in the mills to supplement family income. Elizabeth Bentley, a 23-year-old, described her work in a textile mill at the age of 6, laboring from 5 a.m. in the morning to 9 p.m., with meager portions of poor-quality food to sustain her. Bentley was interviewed by the social reformer Michael Sadler (1780–1835) who worried that the suffering of the poor would not be addressed by the government:

> [In a] society in which persons enjoyed unequal measures of economic freedom, it was not true that the individual pursuit of self-interest would necessarily lead to collective well-being.

Neither did Sadler blame the parents, without pointing to the structural causes of injustice:

> The parents rouse them in the morning and receive them tired and exhausted after the day has closed; they see them droop and sicken, and, in many cases, become cripples and die, before they reach their prime; and they do all this, because they must otherwise starve. It is a mockery to contend that these parents have a choice. They choose the lesser evil, and reluctantly resign their offspring to the captivity and pollution of the mill.
> (Michael Sadler, Speech in the House of Commons, March 16, 1832)

Many people compared the factory to the workhouse, where the poor or ill were sent to work. Many factory owners, who believed themselves morally as well as physically justified in controlling and disciplining their workers, introduced strict work codes that regulated every aspect of the factory day as well as after-hours activities. Despite the reluctance of some entrepreneurs and the resistance of some workers, by the middle of the nineteenth century the factory system had become the common mode of production, and capitalist industrialists who owned the factories organized and controlled the economic, cultural, and even religious life of factory communities.

This pattern of technological change and exploitation was echoed in the experiences of workers around the globe. In Japan, the industrialization of the silk industry after the Meiji Restoration (1868) resulted in social upheaval and change. Meiji policies encouraged rapid industrialization, and as a result many factories were built in the silk-producing regions of Japan. These factories attracted large numbers of very young women, who were required to work long hours in dismal conditions, and to live in unsanitary dormitories. Moreover, women were allocated the most menial, monotonous jobs in the factories, while the more specialized jobs were reserved for men. This unequal division of labor was reflected in unequal pay – so even though women came to dominate the workforce of the

Figure 8.2 *Slums* (Gustave Doré, *c.* 1880). This engraving depicts the grim and crowded daily lives of urban poor in the slums of London, celebrated by many as "the world's greatest city" at the end of the nineteenth century.

Japanese silk industry by the end of the nineteenth century, their wages remained much lower than men's wages well into the twentieth century.

In the wake of industrial capitalism, the growth of cities was neither quick nor regular. It was a slow, varied, and disjointed process by which prior social dynamics were merged into developing urban systems; but once underway, the process of accumulating levels of complexity and diversity continued without cessation or reversal. The new forms of technology and production relied on larger and more highly organized forms of labor. Factories provided employment for large numbers of otherwise homeless or poor, including women and children. The evolution of the welfare system in Britain began with the utilization of factory space as temporary poorhouses. A new market agriculture was required by the expanding urban centers. The profitability of industrialization increased the accumulation of capital in the centers of production and attracted even larger numbers of people to these frontiers of opportunity. Urban middle-class culture included well-built town palaces, in which tablecloths, napkins, fine china, and crystal could be found. Imported foods and wines were served to the middle class by household servants. With success, rich burghers took to wearing silks and velvets as aristocrats did. Yet their values were fundamentally different: they emphasized the "spirit of capitalism," the capacity to work hard, save, and invest. They became a true "middle class" between workers and aristocracy with its own culture.

While the lure of industrial urban life offered the possibility of material benefits, cultural variety, and excitement, as well as economic gain, for many people European cities were synonymous with poverty and homelessness. Traditionally, the Church had taken a primary role in providing relief to vagabonds and homeless persons, but gradually this role was taken over by the state. "Poor laws" passed in sixteenth-century England required local government officials to register the poor of each parish and forbade unlicensed beggars. This legislation also empowered local governments to levy taxes called "poor rates," which were intended for the support of the community's poor. In England a 1601 law created overseers of the poor and established poorhouses – as relief for the able-bodied. By the time the Industrial Revolution was in full swing, the poorhouse was institutionalized and served as a supplier of child and female labor for the new factories. Immortalized by Charles Dickens in his novel *David Copperfield* (1850), the horrors of Warren's boot-blacking factory, where the author was sent at age 12, are described against a grim backdrop of the debt imprisonment that befell Dickens's father. Even social reformers like Michael Sadler could not succeed in eliminating the underlying causes of social and economic inequalities. As the global Industrial Revolution spread the forces of urbanization around the globe, control over capital, land, and labor became increasingly linked to whether individuals and polities were victims or victors in capitalism's net.

IMPERIALISM, INEQUALITY, AND THE RISE OF GLOBAL RACISM

The globalization of slavery and other forms of coerced labor had an impact on perpetuating inequalities and the ideologies that supported those inequalities. The pseudoscientific foundations of racism in the nineteenth century were linked to the primacy of scientific method and to the notion that the world could be understood with certainty through the rational application of scientific principles.

Pseudoscience of race

Since the 1850s, race has been a powerful historical construct built on erroneous claims about human identity and difference. Humans were classified into distinct categories based on skin color, to which were attached stereotypes about ability and intelligence. For example, in his *An Essay on the Inequality of the Human Races* (1853), Joseph Arthur Comte de Gobineau divides races based on geography, arguing that ethnicity is the most important question in history and that inequality can be used to explain how the destinies of peoples are intertwined.

Scientific research eventually demonstrated that biologically distinct "races" do not exist. The human species is singular and no significant features, physical typologies (head size or skin color), or biological difference (such as blood type) can be demonstrated as being linked with identifying human groups as racial groups. Simply speaking, there is no such thing as biological race. Nonetheless, the erroneous concept has been used and is still widely used in the construction of identity. Emerging first in European society, the concept of race developed in the context of the historic persecution of or oppression of ethnic groups, including Jews and Africans. Racial discrimination became a global phenomenon associated with imperialism, and its use has been both overt (as in the physical separation of races in apartheid South Africa) and covert (as in the racial profiling of African-Americans). The consciousness of difference can be a powerful ingredient in individual and group identity whether or not it rests on supportable scientific facts. In the words of the African-American scholar Cornel West, "race matters."

Ideology and structures of inequalities

Not only ideology, but also political structures contributed to exacerbating inequalities in the modern world. Imperialism was more than the extension of territorial control. Since the 1880s, imperial forms of power and authority created new patterns of wealth that disproportionately increased the wealth of some nations at the expense of others. For example, in India, where the Mughal and British empires had privileged landlord property owners, investment in agriculture, health, and education stagnated, creating conditions of extreme inequality, poverty, and famine.

Most of the world's population experienced imperialism and colonialism – whether as colonizers or colonized – in the nineteenth and twentieth centuries. This common experience, although locally varied, helped integrate peoples of the world through trade, language, sports, food, music, and material culture. Colonialism also resulted in the formation of unequal relationships based on class, race, gender, and ethnicity. Understanding the experience of living under a colonial system is as essential to understanding the history of imperialism as economics or politics. Imperialism's leading ideology was based on the premise of the superiority and right of some nationals to rule over others. The colonial experience was not simply determined by the imposition of colonial rule by a foreign power. Rather, that experience was always negotiated and modified by the responses and reactions of colonized peoples. The colonial experience shaped the identities of both colonized and colonizing people.

In the American colonies, the abolition of slavery (1863) and the Fourteenth Amendment to the Constitution of the United States confirmed the constitutional rights of African-Americans at the end of the Civil War. Knowing that these were the stakes, many blacks enlisted as soldiers for the Northern cause, while Southern slaves were forced to assist their Confederate masters. The eighteenth-century ideals of equality, popular sovereignty, and the social contract, which were the bases for the American Revolution and the nation-state that resulted from it, were in theory legally recognized for all Americans. In practice, it took more than a century for African-Americans to begin to realize the rights recognized in the Fourteenth Amendment.

Intersecting inequalities

The nineteenth-century American historian Lydia Maria Child had argued against slaveholding in *The Duty of Disobedience to the Fugitive Slave Act* (1850), an anti-slavery tract. But in order to do so as a woman she was forced to defend her own right to speak to the legislature.

> I feel there is no need of apologizing to the Legislature of Massachusetts because a woman addresses them. Sir Walter Scott says: "The truth of Heaven was never committed to a tongue, however feeble, but it gave a right to that tongue to announce mercy, while it declared judgment." And in view of all that women have done, and are doing, intellectually and morally, for the advancement of the world, I presume no enlightened legislator will be disposed to deny that the "truth of Heaven" is often committed to them, and that they sometimes utter it with a degree of power that greatly influences the age in which they live. I therefore offer no excuses on that score. But I do feel as if it required some apology to attempt to convince men of ordinary humanity and common sense that the Fugitive Slave Bill is utterly wicked, and consequently ought never to be obeyed.
>
> (Lydia Maria Child, *The Duty of Disobedience to the Fugitive Slave Act*, Boston, Mass.: American Anti-Slavery Society, 1860)

The passage suggests not only that Child's lifetime was plagued by inequality but also that people sometimes struggled against the injustices they experienced, building coalitions across similar, but not identical experiences of oppression.

Imperialism helped to spread racial and economic inequalities, as well as revolution. Revolutionary voices in the following century included intellectuals and activists like Frantz Fanon (1925–61), born in Martinique but seeking justice and change in Africa. While in France, Fanon wrote his first book, *Black Skin, White Masks* (1952), an analysis of the effect of colonial subjugation and racism on the human psyche. His final work was *The Wretched of the Earth* (1961), which examines the role of class, race, national culture and violence in the struggle for national liberation. In it, Fanon describes the divisions created by colonialism:

> The colonial world is a world cut in two . . . The cause is the consequence; you are rich because you are white, you are white because you are rich . . . The violence that has ruled over the ordering of the colonial world . . . will be claimed and taken over by the native at the moment when, deciding to embody history in his own person, he surges into the forbidden quarters.
>
> (Frantz Fanon, *The Wretched of the Earth*, Paris, 1963, pp. 38–40)

Fanon's involvement in the Algerian liberation movement led to his recognition of the role of violence both as a cause and consequence of structural inequalities. It would take some nations on the African continent (South Africa, for example) until the end of the twentieth century to rid themselves of the shackles of systematic, structural racism. In the end, the intersection of inequalities became a powerful antidote to assuming world history to be an unending story of human progress.

Modern wars have also been used to sanction the enslavement of groups. Throughout the nineteenth and twentieth centuries, US immigration policy was severely biased against nonwhites, except for purposes of importing workers for hard labor. After the Japanese bombing of Pearl Harbor, the government initiated the summary incarceration of more than 110,000 persons of Japanese birth or ancestry on the Pacific coast. The general population was placed in relocation camps and suspected Japanese loyalists or troublemakers were resettled in internment camps between March and mid-August 1942, demonstrating the stark difference in the ways that European and non-European immigrants were viewed.

A US Supreme Court decision in 1943 (*Hirabayashi* v. *US*) upheld the right of the military to treat Japanese Americans as enemy aliens, despite protestations of loyalty and actions that confirmed loyalty. One example of this was the all-Japanese American US Army Unit 442, which fought effectively on Second World War battlefields and became the most highly decorated unit in the army's history. Japanese Americans also served the United States during the war as translators. The 150,000 Japanese living in Hawaii were not sent to internment camps because their labor was needed in agriculture and to rebuild the shipyards, unlike the West Coast Japanese whose confiscated agricultural lands and small businesses were desirable assets coveted by others.

Racial consciousness and racism have been key determinants in an individual's sense of belonging to a group and in a person's and group's exclusion from social and economic opportunities. Yet when peoples compete as individuals, racial boundaries sometimes dissolve. This was apparent in the history of South Africa, perhaps the most blatant example of a racially divided nation-state of the twentieth century. After the initial discovery of diamonds and gold (1867–84), individual whites found themselves ill-equipped to compete with Africans in a rapidly industrialized economy. Racial boundaries between groups were intentionally constructed to protect whites from competition from black South African workers. The racialized society intensified after the apartheid election of 1948. Yet by the 1980s the economic success of some of the African majority was beginning to blur, if not dissolve, the distinctiveness of the artificially constructed racial boundaries. The 1994 South African constitution was drafted to guarantee the rights of all – including the white minority oppressors – in a multiracial society. Historical forces propelling the mixing of peoples since the twentieth century are likely to continue to undermine the notion of race as a source of identity.

RESISTANCE AND ORGANIZED LABOR

As imperialism generated resistance movements throughout the colonized world, the impact of the Industrial Revolution on the conditions of people's lives also produced resistance through the organization of labor movements in industrialized nations. The factory system method of production in the Industrial Revolution, one of the key markers of the modern world, stimulated consciousness of common interests among industrial workers and led to the organization of labor. In the nineteenth century active resistance to the subordinate status of women gave birth to women's rights movements, which were complicated by divisions of race and class. By the twentieth century, international resistance movements on the fronts of labor and gender intersected with political revolutions that took place across both cultural and political boundaries.

In the early stages of the Industrial Revolution, governments prohibited workers from organizing to seek higher wages and better working conditions; with the expansion of male suffrage in the second half of the nineteenth century, European male workers were able to use their votes to reduce restraints on the organization of labor. Official recognition of labor unions came in England in 1871 and in France and Germany in the 1880s. The first nationwide American labor organization, the National Labor Union, was founded just after the Civil War (1866).

As membership in labor unions grew – 2 million in England and 850,000 in Germany by 1900 – their political influence increased. In the United States, 7.5 percent of workers belonged to unions in 1900 (about 2.2 million members). By voting as a bloc, labor was often able to support candidates that represented the interests of working people. In 1906 the British Labour Party had twenty-nine members elected to Parliament; after the First World War, the Labour Party became the second major party in Great Britain. By the outbreak of the First World War, German and French socialist parties supported by workers played major roles in parliamentary government.

When political representation of workers was inadequate and governments did not respond to the demands of labor unions, workers turned to the strike as a method to achieve their goals. However, the effects of economic depression – job loss and decreasing wages – precipitated more strikes than did the inaction or ineffectiveness of government. For example, depression in the United States in the mid-1870s produced the greatest American labor confrontation of the century, the railroad strike of 1877; during the serious depression in England at the end of the nineteenth century, a London dock strike (1889) closed the port of London for the first time since the French Revolution.

One of organized labor's most powerful tools of resistance is the general strike in which all workers abandon their jobs and bring society to a standstill. In 1886 union leaders in the United States called for a general strike in support of the eight-hour day. The specter of a nationwide strike frightened the public, though the strike, which began on International Labor Day, May 1, proved to be a fiasco. About 190,000 workers laid down their tools, but they were mostly in large cities such as New York and Chicago. In Chicago the situation was complicated by a separate strike against the McCormick Harvester Company during which strikers clashed with police and one man was killed. A protest meeting was called in the city's Haymarket Square; when police appeared, someone tossed a bomb, killing one policeman and injuring others. The police charged into the crowd with guns firing. Eight "anarchists" were convicted, four were hanged, and a backlash against labor was the result of what became known as the "Haymarket riot."

On a November night in 1909, thousands of shirtwaist makers gathered at New York's Cooper Union to protest working conditions and low wages in the city's garment industry. Mostly women and many of them immigrant women, the workers earned as little as $3.50 a week; some were forced to buy their own needles and thread and to pay for their own electricity. The meeting, called by the International Ladies Garment Workers Union (ILGWU), was orderly until interrupted by a young Russian woman who stood to announce that she too had "worked and suffered" but that she was tired of talking and moved that they go on general strike. By the next night more than 20,000 garment workers had walked off their jobs. Their plight received widespread sympathy. In rare cross-class solidarity, wealthy women's clubs, college students, and suffragists united with the garment workers. For the first time, women were at the forefront of a successful labor struggle in the United States.

INTERNATIONAL LABOR AND POLITICAL EMANCIPATION

The international migration of labor and industries helped spread the impact of labor organizations around the world in the twentieth century. Labor and trade unions also became increasingly political. In European colonies the struggle of labor (the workers) against capital (the government and its industries) fueled anticolonial and anti-imperialist sentiments. In the British Caribbean colony of Barbados, Grantley Adams, the leader of the Barbados Labour Party and Workers Union, expressed the connection between labor and universal suffrage in a Labor Day speech in 1946:

> Today I want to make a special appeal to you. The day is long past when the working man – the Broad Street clerk or the water-front worker – can afford to stand by himself and hope to win the fight with capital . . . I want every one of you to look upon this day as a milestone on the road to democracy in industry . . . The people of this country make the wealth of the country, and it is for the organized might of this country to say how that wealth is to be distributed. For centuries it has been the practice of the capitalist class to amass wealth out of the toil and sweat of the labourers. If it has been the unfortunate lot of the labourers not to have a vote in this government, it is our duty to change that . . . If we stand solidly together, we can, and should, be masters of this country.
>
> (Shirley C. Gordon, *Caribbean Generations*, New York: Longman Caribbean, 1983, pp. 239–40)

Barbados was not an isolated example of the link between economic and political empowerment. From Latin America to Africa and Asia workers were essential in the struggle for political and social justice.

The goals of organized labor were often as much political as economic, particularly in authoritarian political systems of either the left or right in which there was no effective institutionalized way to challenge state power. The student demonstrations that sparked the May 4th Movement in China in 1919 were supported by labor strikes and merchant boycotts in Beijing, Shanghai, and Canton, the major industrial and commercial centers. The organization of Chinese labor began with the May 4th Movement and intensified with the activities of anarcho-syndicalists, those who rejected working within the political system (anarchists) in favor of direct organization of workers to take over government (syndicalists).

In the early 1920s the principal focus of Chinese Communist Party activities was the organization of labor. They were greatly influenced by the ideas of trade unionists, especially the anarcho-syndicalists, who believed that the wage system and private ownership had created class divisions. The success of these efforts was evident in the Hong Kong Merchant Seamen's strike in early 1922 when 40,000 sailors, supported by sympathy strikes throughout south China, won wage increases. In Japan, during the same year, a strike of dockworkers at the port of Kobe demonstrated the potential of Japanese organized labor.

But in both China and Japan, early successes were compromised by failures that sharply revealed the weakness of organized labor coping with militaristic (warlord-controlled China) or unstable parliamentary (Japan) governments. A strike of 50,000 coal miners in north China in 1922 ended in failure, as did a strike in the silk spinning mills on the outskirts of Shanghai in the same year, though the latter was the first large strike by women in the history of China. Though it did not signal the beginning of a large-scale labor movement, a much earlier example of labor organization in the textile industry – key to the Industrial Revolution in England and elsewhere – was the strike of 100 women workers in the Amamiya silk mill in northern Japan in 1886. When the owners of seventy-three silk mills in the area formed an organization to tighten control over some 4,500 female workers they employed, 100 women refused to work; the employers granted some concessions and the dispute ended.

One of the most tragic failures in Chinese labor history was the 1923 strike of the United Syndicate of Railway Workers of the Beijing-Hankou System, a line that served the territory of a warlord whose soldiers attacked the striking railway workers and killed sixty-five. Anti-union activity escalated in China during the next two years, but in 1925, when English police in the International Settlement in Shanghai fired on a group of demonstrators and killed ten, a general strike was organized in response to this brutality. The strike involved 150,000 workers, merchants, and students and lasted for three months, though sympathizers throughout China contributed money, boycotted foreign goods, and staged strikes for more than a year. This event became known as the May 30th Movement and was the peak of organized labor's success during this early period.

The potential of organized labor to bring about political change, however, was demonstrated in Communist Poland during the 1980s, when scattered strikes ballooned into a working-class revolt. A variety of unions united under the name "Solidarity," a national movement that used its focus on the economic ills of the country to rally support for the transformation of Poland from a state run by the Communist Party to one governed by the elected representatives of the people. By the summer of 1989, members of the Solidarity movement had been elected to parliament (previously controlled entirely by the Polish Communist Party). They became the first freely elected party in a Communist country. The use of organized labor to challenge government in a Communist state is particularly ironic, since in theory Communist states represent workers' interests.

GENDER AND RESISTANCE

In the nineteenth century, women's rights – then known as the "woman question" – were widely debated in European society. Male intellectuals such as the English philosopher John Stuart Mill, who supported improving the status of women, and the German

Figure 8.3 Economic Protest, etching by José Guadeloupe Posada (1852–1913). Irate housewives protest high food prices and threaten a foreign merchant.

philosopher Friedrich Nietzsche, who expressed deeply misogynistic views, debated the issue and influenced popular ideas about the role of women in society. In the 1830s American women in the northern United States joined the antislavery crusade and were active in the abolition movement. This experience in public life helped prepare women for organizing the women's rights movement.

Although European women took part in the revolutions that swept Europe in 1848, that year marked a turning point for women all over the world because of the women's rights meeting held at Seneca Falls, New York. Organized by Lucretia Mott (1793–1880) and Elizabeth Cady Stanton (1815–1902), this meeting of about 300 people was devoted exclusively to the problems of women and issued a document, "Declaration of Rights and Sentiments," that had a powerful impact on women's rights advocates in both the United States and Europe. Other meetings followed, and new leaders emerged. In 1851 a freed slave who called herself Sojourner Truth told a gathering in Akron, Ohio, that women were not the weaker sex, citing as evidence the conditions that black women endured under slavery.

Another important leader of the women's rights movement in the United States was Susan B. Anthony (1820–1906); Mott, Stanton, and Anthony worked for reform in higher education, employment, the status of wives, and suffrage. Following the Civil War, demands for full female suffrage began to increase; by the late nineteenth century, the issue of suffrage had become central to established politics because it was the key to bringing about political reform. The term "suffragette" popularly described any woman who demanded the right to vote. In early twentieth-century Britain, radical suffragettes such as Emmeline Pankhurst (1857–1928) chained themselves to buildings to make speeches advocating the right to vote or in other ways tried to gain the attention of people to support their cause. Some British radical women were imprisoned for their actions; Pankhurst ended up in Ethiopia where she lived in exile.

Around the world, women were active in movements to gain the right to vote. Women in the Habsburg empire organized to demand their right to engage in political activities and to vote. Socialist and communist parties in Europe, Australia, and the United States championed women's rights and supported female suffrage. For example, Adela Pankhurst Walsh (1885–1961), daughter of Emmeline Pankhurst, helped found the Communist Party of Australia and fought for women's suffrage there. Following the 1905 revolution in Russia, women became politically aware of their subjugation. Nadezhda Krupskaya (1869–1938), the wife of V. I. Lenin, wrote the first major Russian work on the woman question from a Marxist standpoint, *The Woman Worker* (1900). Alexandra Kollontai (1872–1952), born an aristocrat, was a radical advocate of women's rights and held positions in the Soviet government. New Zealand, colonized by the British, actually became the first country in the world to grant female suffrage (1893); South Africa granted African women the right to vote in the 1994 national election.

Race and class intersected with gender in the struggles for women's rights. For black women in the post-Civil War United States, discrimination on the basis of gender was complicated by racial discrimination. Black women leaders such as Ida B. Wells (1862–1931) worked for the female vote, but they also struggled for racial equality and justice. Middle-class women formed the backbone of the suffrage movement; working-class and poor women had neither the leisure nor often the education to participate in demonstrations or other activities that demanded time away from work and family.

After the First World War women gained the vote in the United States, the Soviet Union, and many European countries. From the early 1880s women in Japan had been active in the popular rights movement, and some enlightened intellectuals of the Meiji period, such as Fukuzawa Yukichi (1835–1901), advocated the improvement of the position of women. Japanese women were active in temperance organizations and in efforts to abolish prostitution. But legislation in 1889 and 1900 forbade political activity by women, and female socialists attacked such restraints. Other women were less concerned with emancipation and turned to activities associated with a more traditional female role. For example, the Patriotic Women's Association, founded in 1901, assisted wounded soldiers and bereaved families who suffered as a result of the growing militarism and imperialism of the Meiji state. In contrast, the Bluestocking Society, founded in 1911, was a middle-class intellectual movement advocating self-awareness of women; it lasted into the 1930s when all such organizations were either absorbed or suppressed by the state. Although universal male suffrage was achieved in Japan in 1925, like France and certain other European countries, Japan did not extend the vote to women until after the Second World War.

GLOBALIZATION AND THE STRUGGLE FOR EQUALITY

The struggle for equality highlights the tensions between the ideal model of democracy and the economic and political implications of global capitalism. For example, throughout much of the twentieth century, United States foreign policy seemingly ignored the political aspirations of peoples around the world in the quest for capitalist expansion, continued access to profits, and perceived national security interests. From Ghana and the Congo to Cuba, United States government policies tried to impose the values of capitalism abroad through covert and direct involvement, using military force and economic sanctions.

Third World economies

During the Cold War era, the developing nations of Africa, Latin America, and Asia gradually became associated with the label of "Third World" nations, suggesting their position on the periphery of industrialization and capital accumulation. Their economic

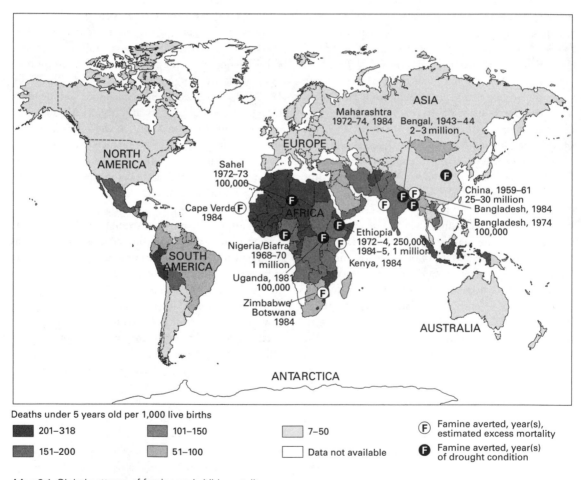

Map 8.1 Global patterns of famine and child mortality.

status was compared with that of First World superpowers (the United States and Soviet Union) and the Second World countries (industrialized Europe, Canada, Japan, Australia, New Zealand). Many of the so-called Third World nations, even oil-producing ones, were strangled by their indebtedness to Western banks through aid agreements that coupled high-interest loans with "development schemes." Contradictions also characterized domestic socio-economic conditions that both attracted immigrants and led to great disparities between the wealthy and the poor. While post-Cold War realities may have created a more nuanced understanding of the simplistic division between superpower and developing nations, the recent "Fourth World" designation currently applied to countries like Haiti and Bangladesh, also suggests the extreme impoverishment requiring a new category.

Globalization, like imperialism, has intensified inequalities. As globalization led to economic growth it also increased poverty. Global markets have strengthened the imperial forms of entitlement to unequal access to wealth accumulation. In India, for example, in the early days of independence (post-1947), nationalism reduced the impact of the preceding era of British imperialism and poverty declined. Then, after the 1980s, and especially after 1991, free-market-oriented economic policies can be likened to imperial days. Rapid growth increased inequality even faster in this democracy. Globalization has increased the inequality in social control of wealth in many parts of the world, not only in democratic states. Under the impact of globalization's forces, distance matters less (as mobility increases) and so the forces move capital, goods, and people with increasing rapidity to affect everyday life in almost every corner of the globe. Hierarchical ranks are defined by spatial location, gender, ethnicity, and class issues still entangled with state power and male authority.

Global feminisms

Global feminisms have also emerged as sites of resistance. By the 1970s the second wave of American feminism made use of the Marxist concept of class to represent gender. In 1969 a manifesto of a group known as the "New York Redstockings" claimed that women constituted a social class. At the same time

sexual identity was becoming a political issue, and gay men and women began to organize to achieve social acceptance and equal rights. In the same year that the New York Redstockings issued their manifesto, police raided a gay bar in New York's Greenwich Village; because patrons fought back, unlike in previous raids, this incident (Stonewall, after the bar's name) became the symbol of gay liberation. After Stonewall, activists called for gays and lesbians to publicly affirm their sexual identity and to reject the hidden lives they had led. The diversity of feminisms since the Nairobi Women's Conference (1985) suggest the opportunities for broader unity in common opposition to oppression and hierarchies.

Political resistance

Events of social or political resistance such as Stonewall or Seneca Falls, the Nicaraguan Revolution, Tiananmen Square, or the Ibo Women's War became defining moments in the lives of their respective communities. Whether remembered by participants, the survivors, or their descendants, subsequent generations seized upon such events as rallying points to continue to effect change. Whether successful or not, the acts of resistance produced communities whose identities were profoundly revisioned. Resistance to European and American hegemony took many forms, from Gandhi's nonviolent activism to the militancy of PLO *fedayeen* (commandos). Resistance also took different courses, shaped according to the targets of resistance. In some cases the direct controls of colonialism were resisted, as in the Indian nationalist movement. In others resistance was directed at national governments, as in Peru during the 1970s and 1980s where the Shining Path guerrillas carried out campaigns of terrorism to destabilize the Peruvian government.

The People's Republic of China was created in a revolutionary struggle that sought to overthrow the gross inequities of Confucian society and imperialism. Women were to be freed from the bonds of dependence on fathers and husbands and egalitarian principles were embodied into the first constitution of the PRC in 1950. The old Confucian elite had already lost its position earlier in the twentieth century, but a new elite was being produced by the Communist Party. Membership in the CCP was sought as a marker of social, economic, and political status, and over time the party cadres became members of an oppressive elite. Inequality grew as the Chinese economy modernized and industrialized in the 1960s, and, despite attempts by Mao and others to derail this development, by the 1970s – and especially after Mao's successors took power – Chinese society once again witnessed increasing inequality. This time it was not party cadres so much as prosperous entrepreneurs and urban residents who gained both wealth and power through access to education, jobs, and consumer goods. Rural people in remote regions continued to struggle on the margins of a global economy.

CONCLUSIONS

As imperialism succeeded in threading together disparate cultures into single political and economic systems and capitalism spread its tentacles worldwide, the experience of vastly different parts of the globe led to the recognition of a common identity. This identity, called by Franz Fanon the identity of "the wretched of the earth," was also the beginning of a common determination to end all forms of oppression and injustice. International solidarity and links across class, culture, and color lines increased dramatically after the turn of the twentieth century. Not only was the presence of any injustice viewed as a threat to all within the community, but the defeat of common enemies brought many causes into a single revolutionary vision.

Twentieth- and twenty-first century technologies have enabled individuals to be informed about and to participate in resistance and revolutionary struggles around the world. The earlier revolutions in America and Haiti would not have succeeded without the support of foreign allies with their own different goals. Through the solidarity of labor union activities, the Spanish Civil War had some followers in Latin America and the Caribbean. Cubans fought in Angolan and Mozambican struggles. Viewers around the world watched and listened to and protested against events from China to South Africa. Terrorist networks before and after September 11 relied on the worldwide web, cell phones, and satellite technology to further their aims and gain global attention.

As societies achieved greater technological and social complexity, they created grossly unequal systems of social, political, and economic order. The persistence of and even increase in inequality is seen in the estimated 27 million enslaved persons in the twenty-first century and in the growing economic disparities that separate the lives of the "haves" from the "have-nots" globally. According to the UN report *The Inequality Predicament: Report on the World Social Situation 2005*, the current trends of inequality are on the increase. The extent that order was imposed by imperialism rather than the result of an unfolding process, whether through material conditions or ideology, suggests to some degree the primacy of inequality in the maintenance and equilibrium of at least some modern societies. In its beginnings, the industrial age had held out a powerful promise of wealth, equality, and "progress." The global migration of labor and capital resulted in the cross-pollination of people, ideas, and technologies. Even as industrial capitalism connected the world in a global web of commerce and culture, it magnified persistent inequalities and differences. Modern slavery, imperialism, and industrial capitalism have depended largely on the global proliferation of difference and inequality. Globalization of inequality has accelerated the worsening of working conditions, class divisions, gender inequality, political and social instability, health, violence, and environmental degradation. Yet the rise and fall of societies and systems cannot alone explain the story of inequality. Instead it must be glimpsed both when hierarchies coalesce to funnel resources to the top and when they splinter through generations of resistance.

SELECTED REFERENCES

Curtin, Philip (1991) *The Tropical Atlantic in the Age of the Slave Trade*, with a foreword by Michael Adas, series editor, Washington, DC: American Historical Association. Classic work defining the creation of an Atlantic world through slavery.

Davis, Mike (2006) *Planet of Slums*, London: Verso. Examines the impact of the global explosion of disenfranchised slum-dwellers.

Frederickson, George M. (2002) *A Short History*

of Race, Princeton, N.J.: Princeton University Press.

Explores ideas of difference in the ancient and modern worlds, linking religious persecution and the rise of racism.

Hoogvelt, Ankie (1991) *Globalization and the Postcolonial World: The New Political Economy of Development*, Baltimore, Md.: Johns Hopkins University Press. Examines how global capitalism operates in networks, privileging some places over others.

Mann, Michael (1986–93) *The Sources of Social Power* (2 vols.), Cambridge: Cambridge University Press. Examines the evolution of political systems of domination from social networks of power.

Manning, Patrick (1996) *Slave Trades, 1500–1800: Globalization of Forced Labour*, Variorium: Aldershot. Volume 15 of *An Expanding World*, edited by A. J. Russell-Wood. Explores the global-ization of slavery and movement of forced labor after 1500.

Wiesner-Hanks, Merry (2001) *Gender in History: New Perspectives on the Past*, London: Blackwell. Examines the myriad ways in which gender intersects with family, economy, religion, social life, education, and politics.

ONLINE RESOURCES

Annenberg/CPB Bridging World History (2004) <http://www.learner.org/channel/courses/world history/>. Multimedia project with interactive website and videos on demand; see especially Units 14 Land and Labor Relationships, 19 Global Industrialization, 20 Imperial Designs, 23 People Shape the World, and 24 Globalization and Economics.

CHAPTER 9

Transmitting traditions

History, culture, and memory

The colossal stone monument known as the Sphinx stands guard to the Giza plateau's greatest pyramids of ancient Egypt. Towering more than ten times the height of humans, the Sphinx – a sculpture that is part man, part god, and part animal – was built about 2600 BCE. It serves as a powerful reminder of Egypt's past. Although we tend to think of such monumental treasures as unchanging cultural memories, such is not the case. By the time of the pharaoh Thutmose IV, living in 1401 BCE, the Sphinx was already ancient, already altered, and in need of major restoration. According to the inscriptions on a red granite slab erected in front of the statue, Thutmose cleared away the desert sand and restored the damaged lion body with large limestone blocks for protection against wind erosion.

After another thousand years, the Greeks and Romans visited and again restored the Sphinx. The Greek historian Herodotus (fifth century BCE) toured the valley and wrote the definitive tourist guide before the nineteenth century. Beginning with the Romans, visitors have also stolen smaller, more portable monuments, in attempts to appropriate their power as historical icons. The appropriation of history, it seems, is as enduring as the monuments. In the fifteenth century, Islamic leaders defaced the great sculpture, fearing that local Egyptians were still paying homage to its grandeur and durability. An Arab proverb claims that "man fears time, but time fears the pyramids." Modern plunder in the form of treasure seekers and scientists began in the time of the French emperor Napoleon, whose troops invaded the Nile in 1798 and uncovered the Sphinx again, followed by European explorers and archaeologists who began digging up hundreds of ancient treasures that eventually found their way into the museums and collections of the world.

Today, if the Great Sphinx could look backwards, it would gaze on a transformed landscape marred by fast-food restaurants, polluted air, and tourists. The view ahead remains the desert sands of the Sahara; like the sands of time they are constantly shifting. That the Sphinx and other Nile Valley monuments have survived the millennia was precisely the intent of the Egyptians, who built and painted them in bright colors in antiquity. However, their intent was also that they not be entered ever again. While later generations have treated the great structures as human monuments, for the ancient Egyptians these were monuments to something cosmic and eternal. Yet the deterioration of the stone surfaces of the Great Sphinx continues at an alarming rate. Perhaps it is fitting that the symbol of the Internet service America On-Line is a pyramid, since the hundreds of websites dedicated to ancient Egypt soon may be the only way to visit such monuments as the Great Sphinx.

Memory is neither as durable nor as monumental as a pyramid. Ideas about the past can be embedded in the tales historians tell or in the songs children sing. They can be reflected in objects or in the technologies that create the material world. Their specific cultural shape, the systems that transmit them across generations, and the meanings historians make of them are the focus of this chapter.

INTRODUCTION

Human memory is the stuff of history. Memory helps make sense of the past, selectively arranging its vastness into meaningful events. Memory can be individual or collective, and both are shaped by cultural experience. History is concerned not just with organizing the past along a linear timeline. The relationship between

Figure 9.1 Great Sphinx and pyramid at Giza, Egypt. Carved out of local limestone in the third millennium BCE, one of the world's oldest sculptures depicts the half-human/half-lion creature thought to be a pharoah.

history and memory is constructed through complex cultural and social processes. Cultural memory is the accumulation of all experiences, information, events, and remembrances of a society transmitted across generations. Memory is embedded in various cultural forms and media. In this sense, cultural memory is the "archive," not literally an archive of written documents but an assemblage of experiences, information, and totality of meaning attached to living in a particular cultural and social setting.

Cultural memory can be transmitted formally as instructions or informally through practice and habit. Changes in cultures can be responses to ideas or material conditions – either natural or human in origin – such as environmental and climatic shifts or war and conquest, and the memory of change is preserved in cultural memory systems. Since memory is a dynamic social process, memory systems do not preserve or reproduce knowledge without sometimes altering, shaping, or even inventing it, either consciously or unconsciously. And memory systems themselves can and do change. As agents of the changes they record

and preserve, memory systems exert powerful influence over the communities whose cultural experiences they store and transmit or selectively erase.

The practice of history is an exploration in the realms of cultural memory. How historians use memory depends on how we know what we know of the past, what the processes of remembering the past are, how those processes influence what is passed on, and how and by whom cultural memory is controlled. Writings, oral traditions, myths, sagas, epics, and traditions constitute the enormous domain of cultural memory, but so do artifacts from which historians can also reconstruct cultural memory and seek a more complete understanding of history. These archives of material culture include art, architecture, technology, institutions, and even performance – such as processions, music, and dance.

The modern discipline of history is but one of the memory systems by which community is defined and cultural knowledge is transmitted. Among the artifacts of cultural memory systems we consider are visual and performing arts, literature, institutions, architecture, and technology. Memory systems share with history the processes of shaping, defining, and perpetuating community cultural memory. Transmitters of community cultural knowledge, such as teachers and preachers, historians and dramatists, entrepreneurs and artists, help define the identity of the community whose cultural memory they shape. Historians, artists, scientists, religious leaders, and philosophers all shape the cultural memory systems of their communities, creating, propagating, and perpetuating communal culture over time and across spatial boundaries. Their role in transmitting and transforming cultural memory can either sustain and support or challenge institutions of power and the authority of rulers and elites.

Culture is shaped by all members of a community, but most humans individually have neither the power nor the ability to create cultural memory systems, which are often controlled by an institution or a group. Official memory, such as that produced by governments, churches, or other institutions, can impose a selective forgetting as well as a selective remembering. Popular cultural memory, however, manifested in a variety of forms such as performance arts and literature, often provides a means of expressing resistance to official cultural memory and thus can function as an agency of cultural change, following its own principles of selective remembering and forgetting.

This chapter offers evidence of a variety of cultural memory systems as they evolved around the globe, first as local, regional cultural systems and subsequently as global ones. We ask how the basic tools of cultural memory, the spoken and written word, and their institutions, perpetuate ideas and stories about the past. What are other kinds of memory systems? How do technology and visual and performance arts, which rely primarily on image and bodily practice, create cultural memory? Critical devices like the clock have also helped to organize and integrate human societies, while making the study of change over time possible. Examination of cultural memory systems in Asia, Africa, Europe, and the Americas leads to a consideration of resistance to politically sanctioned cultural memory. How does resistance affect changing historical consciousness? We examine more closely the process that transforms historical identity along the bridge between past and present.

ORAL TRADITIONS

The oldest system of cultural memory may be intimately linked to the evolution of the human capacity to communicate: first through bodily movements and eventually through the spoken word. Written systems of cultural transmission are less than 6,000 years old, but oral traditions, based on orally transmitted cultural knowledge, date from the time the human species became capable of speech and communication. Since that time, human communities have transmitted their shared cultures orally. Even in the age of the computer, oral tradition remains an important means of preserving and transmitting cultural memory. Many preliterate societies relied on oral traditions to record the past, but even the oral memories of literate societies present historians with alternative sources to the officially sanctioned past.

Oral tradition can be a formal and highly ritualized system of cultural transmission, but it can also reflect change. As human constructions, oral memory systems are subject to revision. Some aspects of oral narratives conform with and support current political and social realities of their communities, while others resist revision and remain historically valid, fixed features of orally transmitted memory. The revised and fixed aspects of oral histories are not as oppositional as they might at first appear. They reflect the tendency of oral evidence to provide both unchanging and historically dynamic cultural memory.

Many oral cultures relied on specialists, who, like the scribes, priests, or scholars in literate societies, either were themselves elites (by virtue of the cultural information they controlled) or were connected intimately to elites through relations of patronage. Across much of West Africa, the oral historian known popularly as the "*griot*" held a position of power and importance as the individual responsible for preserving and transmitting the records of the past in oral form. The historical role of the *griot* is described in the version of the Mande epic Sundiata (*c.* 1190–1255), attributed to the *griot* Mamadou Kounyaté. He sums up the importance of oral memory, explaining his role as the agent of cultural transmission:

> [W]e are vessels of speech, we are the repositories which harbour secrets many centuries old. The art

of eloquence has no secrets for us; without us the names of kings would vanish into oblivion, we are the memory of mankind; by the spoken word we bring to life the deeds and exploits of kings for younger generations.

(D. T. Niane, *Sundiata: An Epic of Old Mali*, Harlow, Essex: Longman, 1994, p. 1)

In Mande society in the Mali empire, the *griot* played a key role in political continuity. He was judge and counselor to kings as well as court historian, who, by knowing the past, was able to shape and control it. According to Mamadou Kounyaté, "history holds no mystery" and knowledge itself is a form of power. The influence of the *griot* was such as to make those who seek power envious. Their words not only brought to life the past but also profoundly affected the present course of events. Because they possessed and could shape knowledge of past events, *griots* could enhance the power of the king and his court and influence the cultural traditions they preserved.

In another West African society, that of the ancestors of the Yoruba in southwestern Nigeria, those who preserved cultural memory were known as *arokin*. They were court functionaries, official historians who performed as bards and drummers. The Yoruba people also reenacted founding myths of lineages, quarters, towns, and kingdoms in annual festivals and installation ceremonies associated with chiefs and kings. The *arokin* performed royal and religious rituals that helped preserve myths. Yoruba cultural memory categorized the past in several different ways. Their view of the past consisted of immutable views of their world that were publicly accepted and of myths and rituals that were constantly subject to review and revision by contesting political and social forces in their community. There were also "deep truths," the knowledge of spiritual realms, that might subvert shifting myths and rituals and thus were dangerous to the status quo because they undermined it and provided subversive resistance and opposition to those in authority, including those who controlled official Yoruba cultural memory.

MEMORY DEVICES

While memory can and does exist "virtually" today in online resources, nearly every cultural memory system helps make memory more permanent through a range of mnemonic "remembering" devices. For the Luba of Central Africa (called "Kamilambian" and "Kisalian" from about 600 CE), a rich vocabulary of images and words exists to describe ideas about historical memory and connectedness, about remembering and forgetting as interdependent sides of memory. Luba officials still stage oral recitations of local history. Traditionally, state historians were rigorously trained men called *bana balute* ("men of memory"). They recited genealogies and king lists and recounted the founding charter of kingship. They traveled with kings and, like the *griots*, spread propaganda about the prestige and power of their patrons' culture. They used mnemonics, visual devices or objects that aided in and ordered their remembering.

The Luba world is quite literally strewn with mnemonic devices, images, and objects that are used to remember and reconfigure the past. These include royal emblems, shrines and grave markers, staffs, thrones, bead necklaces, and the object known as a *lukasa* (memory board). The *lukasa* is a hand-held wooden board covered with colored pins and beads; sometimes painted or incised geometric markings are added to evoke particular events, places, or names from the past. Such objects visually represent the vocabulary of memory, to be "read" only by those skilled and trained to convey the complexity of meaning encoded therein. The *lukasa* is used in initiation ceremonies to teach initiates the stories of culture heroes, clan migrations, and sacred lore. It also provides a visual mapping of the complicated political and social ordering of society, the natural world, and the world of the spirits.

Like the traditional memory systems of the Luba, Mande, or Yoruba in Africa, that of the Incas in the central Andes of South America was oral. Incan oral traditions were organized in ways specific to their culture and transmitted with the help of mnemonic devices unique to it. Though their cultural memory system was fundamentally oral, Incan communities also used a knotted cord, called a *khipu* or *quipu*, the colors and lengths of which recorded important numbers such as census figures, chronological data, and everyday transactions. Like the Luba's *lukasa*, the *khipu* seems to have functioned as a mnemonic device, a shorthand tool to aid in the memorization of large bodies of information.

Figure 9.2 Luba memory board (*lukasa*), Zaïre. The *lukasa* is used to teach about collective historical events, like migration, culture heroes, and genealogies. Individual meaning is assigned to the particular spaces created by the deliberate placement of beads of different colors and shapes on the board.

The form of the device made it extremely portable in the vast mountainous region of the Incan empire. The recent discovery of a seventeenth-century Jesuit manuscript in Italy has raised the possibility not only of deciphering these string documents but also that the *khipu* was used to record information other than accounting, such as calendars, astronomical observations, accounts of battles, and dynastic successions, as well as literature. According to this European observer:

> Quechua [the Incan language] . . . is a language similar to music and has several keys: a language for everyone; a holy language, [which] was handed [down] only by knots; [and] another language that was handed [down] by means of woven textiles and by pictures on monuments and in jewels and small objects. I will tell you . . . about the quipu, which is a complicated device composed of colored knots. . . . There is a general quipu used by everyone for numbering and daily communication and another quipu for keeping all religious and caste secrets. . . . I visited . . . archives for those quipus that tell the true story of the Inka people and that are hidden from commoners. These quipus differ from those used for calculations as they have elaborate symbols . . . which hang down from the main string. . . . The scarceness of the words and the possibility of changing the same term using particles and suffixes to obtain different meanings allow them to realize a spelling book with neither paper, nor ink, nor pens. . . . This quipu is based by its nature on the scarceness of words, and its composition

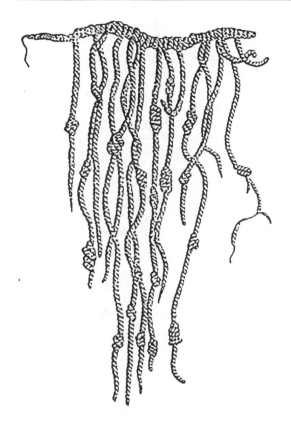

Figure 9.3 Memory devices like the *quipu* (or *khipu*) evolved in societies where oral memory systems were relied upon by all but the elite, such as in the Inca empire and its predecessor societies. It usually consisted of colored spun plied thread from llama or alpaca hair with numeric and other values encoded by knots in a base ten-positional system.

key and its reading lie in its syllabic division. . . . [It was] explained, "If you divide the word Pachacamac [the Inca deity of earth and time] into syllables Pa-cha-ca-mac, you have four syllables. If you . . . want to indicate the word 'time,' pacha in Quechua, it will be necessary to make two symbols [in the quipu] representing Pachacamac – one of them with a little knot to indicate the first syllable, the other with two knots to indicate the second syllable."

(Los Retratos de los Incas en la Cronica de Fray Martin de Murua. Oficina de Asuntos Culturales de la Corporacion Financiera de Desarrollo S. A. COFIDE, Lima, 1985)

If this manuscript is shown to be authentic, it should be possible to understand even Incan poetry, which was recorded using the *khipu*. However the scholarly debate about the authenticity of this manuscript is resolved, its discovery highlights the complexity of *khipu* in the Incan cultural memory system and reminds us that even the knotted strings used for accounting purposes can be a rich and enduring repository of cultural memory.

The general history of the Incan empire was secret and transmitted by specialists similar to the Yoruba specialists. They taught in schools reserved for members of the elite who were given room and board by the state. Like Mali *griots*, Luba memory men, and Yoruba specialists, the Incan *khipu* readers ensured state control of cultural memory. By preserving those aspects of a ruler's exploits that he wished to be remembered and thus censoring the past, they selectively reordered the past to serve present needs.

WRITING SYSTEMS

Among the most complex of memory systems was the invention of writing. Writing, wherever it emerged, has served a variety of different purposes in shaping and transmitting culture. Writing coexisted with other memory systems, which either supported or sometimes subverted written cultural memory. The interplay of written and nonwritten memory systems at times created significant political and social change. The development of cuneiform script among the peoples of Mesopotamia in West Asia during the early third millennium BCE and the later evolution of an alphabetic script transmitted by Phoenician traders around the eastern shores of the Mediterranean, were innovations related in part to the needs of commerce. Merchants needed a way of keeping inventories and financial records of transactions. Chinese and Mesoamerican pictorial writing systems were likely developed independently from the practice of record keeping. In the case of Mexican codices and some Egyptian tomb paintings, the pictographs are prompts or mnemonic devices for cultural memory. At what point did the attempt to display ideas visually result in written forms, with the ability to convey the information of a language?

The earliest writing systems appear to have been invented and adapted to meet multiple purposes, from royal display to religious and administrative functions. The development of writing was also associated with the exercise of power in early West Asian states, enabling scribes in service to rulers to record events, keep population records for taxation, and propagate and preserve law by around 3200 BCE. Written law codes, such as that of the Babylonian ruler Hammurabi, are examples of the lasting importance of written systems of cultural memory. The writing down of myths could sometimes support royal power, such as the myths surrounding the god Marduk in Babylonia. Writing thus contributed to the establishment of new states and rulers by establishing continuities with earlier cultural traditions.

In early North Africa, Egyptian hieroglyphics ("priestly pictographs") were a sacred script under the control of a priesthood who served the pharaohs after about 2900 BCE. Slightly earlier bone tags on pottery jars date from about 3200 BCE. Later scripts include those developed during the second millennium BCE in the kingdom of Kush and at Axum, where sacred and secular powers were recorded on stone engravings and inscriptions. A key element in the evolution of scripts was the invention of the alphabet, signs that related to each phoneme.

Some scripts were used on more perishable "documents." In the Americas, the Mayans created a script in the first millennium CE that was used in the keeping of historical and astronomical records. Ink and painted evidence has not survived, but the slightly earlier (mid-first millennium BCE) Mesoamerican glyphs experimented with developing markers of identity into representations of language in multiple forms. By the next millennium, the Mayan script was a mixture of ideographic and phonetic elements, using graphic symbols or pictures to represent both objects and sounds. It included a complete set of written characters, each representing a syllable, so theoretically everything could be written phonetically, as it sounded when spoken; however, the Mayan script was never used entirely to communicate phonetically since ideographs were considered to be religiously symbolic and thus to have great prestige. This probably reflects the desire of literate elites – priests and scribes – to maintain their monopoly of writing, knowledge of which gave them power. Scribes, who controlled astronomical, historical, and religious information, had their own patron deities, such as Itzamna, considered the creator and inventor of writing. Mayan hieroglyphics appeared on a variety of materials, including stone and bark paper, although relatively few manuscripts on paper have survived. When it was finally translated in the 1990s, the Mayan glyphs were understood to be comprised of both a phonetic system and a system of logograms, standing for whole words. The ancient Maya coordinated the strands of their

Figure 9.4 Cuneiform tablet, Iraq. The Sumerians developed writing on wet clay tablets, using pictograms and later syllabic signs. Those kept as records were then dried in the sun or baked and stored.

memory system through painting, narrative sculpture, architectural decoration, and pottery – all providing complementary information in written texts.

Sanskrit, the language of the Indo-Europeans who migrated into India in the mid-second millennium BCE, was transcribed in an alphabetic script and used to record religious texts of the Vedic tradition in early South Asia. The writing down of hymns to Indo-European gods, for example, helped to maintain the elite Indo-Europeans' cultural memory and consolidate their power as they moved into the Indian sub-continent. Much later, in the third century BCE, inscriptions carved to proclaim the Indian ruler Ashoka's belief in Buddhism and to assert his claim to secular power and to prescribe standards of behavior further illustrate the utility of writing to preserve and transmit a politically useful message. Later religious instruction in middle and northern India also took the form of narrative bas-relief panels as part of temple architecture and depicted the key stories, tales, and beliefs to the ordinary community member.

While writing systems may be found in virtually every region of the world, nowhere was the written word endowed with greater power than in China. In Shang China (c. 1600–1050 BCE) the development of the archaic script found on oracle bones was linked to divination practices. It was believed that the ancestors of the Shang kings, deities who could communicate with the supreme god, Di, would make their wishes known through the bones of animals used for sacrifice. To contact the spirits of these royal ancestors, a diviner would engrave a bone or turtle shell with written characters and then apply a heated bronze pin to them. Various lengths and patterns of cracks would appear on the shell or bone, and their relationship to the written characters would be interpreted by the diviner as oracles and kept as records. The characters on oracle bones are archaic forms of the modern written script and thus provide evidence of the foundation of Chinese writing.

The practice in China of using oracle bones for prophecy and guidance, known as scapulimancy, also illustrates the role of a priestly elite in the creation and preservation of cultural memory. As in Egypt and among the Mayas, a scribal priesthood controlled a memory system and imbued it with a sacred quality and ritual character. The close association of the Chinese scribal elite with those who exercised political

power provided the leaders of the early Chinese state with religious underpinnings. Even the earliest oracle bone inscriptions, which recorded events such as battles, harvests, and royal marriages and births, can be seen as historical records, and the keeping of written accounts of the past became a central concern of those who held power in imperial China.

More than 2,000 years later, the fully developed Chinese writing system spread to other parts of East Asia, primarily as a means of transmitting Chinese culture and Buddhism to Korea and Japan. Adapted by Koreans and Japanese to transcribe their own cultural memory, Chinese script was used by the emerging centralized states in Korea and Japan for the same purposes it served in China: the preservation of cultural memory to serve the interests of those in power. For example, the Kojiki, a record of myths and chronicles of the founding of Japan compiled under imperial sponsorship in 712 CE, was written using Chinese script in different ways, for both sound and meaning, an example of the process of adaptation. The writing down of myths that supported the claims of the imperial family to divine descent is a clear indication of the power of the written text as a cultural memory system.

TECHNOLOGY AND THE TRANSMISSION OF CULTURAL MEMORY

Technological innovations were integral to the development of memory devices, including those that contributed to creating writing and recording systems. Technology is also a category of cultural knowledge and, along with memory systems such as history, literature, and architecture, transmits essential cultural knowledge from generation to generation. Technology includes both tools and practices, the ways in which tools are used by people to manipulate their environment and to construct the physical world around them. Technology is itself a memory system, a cultural link that is as revealing of historical experience as art or literature. Technology has also aided and transformed cultural memory systems, especially in the roles they have played in the transmission of information across space and time.

Not only is cultural memory embedded in the history of technology, but the technology itself often aids in the preservation and transmission of memory. Technological innovations have made the storing and transmission of cultural memory increasingly external to the human body. Paper, which is essential to printing, was invented in China early in the Han dynasty (202 BCE–220 CE). The earliest extant printed texts on paper were made in eighth-century Korea and Japan by carving text onto wooden blocks, which were then smeared with ink and covered with paper, producing an impression of the text. The earliest surviving Chinese text made by woodblock printing is a Buddhist *sutra* from the mid-ninth century. Woodblock printing became the favored method of reproducing texts throughout East Asia, in contrast to copying by hand using brush and ink. This method allowed fewer errors and omissions or other changes to creep into texts because the carved woodblock, though subject to deterioration over time, was a relatively permanent and unchanging means of reproducing texts. In addition to propagating religion and spreading culture through literature, printing was used to spread new technologies for agriculture and silk production and in this way contributed substantially to the economic revolution of Song times.

In the eleventh century, movable type – in clay, wood, and metal – was invented in China 400 years before its appearance in Europe. Ultimately, because of the use of an ideographic script with thousands of characters as opposed to an alphabetic one with fewer than a hundred letters, movable type did not dominate printing in China because it was relatively more efficient to carve a woodblock page than to keep available the thousands of pieces of type necessary to set a page of text. Still, the development of a commercial printing industry in the Song period and the proliferation of printed books made learning and written culture more accessible to a wider population, aiding in the transmission of popular literature as well as the historical and philosophical texts used in studying for the civil service examinations.

The spread of papermaking technologies increased the impact of printing technologies in Europe, Asia, and Africa. Papermaking technologies made their way from China, where paper was invented in the first century CE, westward over the routes of commerce and conquest by the ninth century. In the twelfth century, papermaking spread from North Africa to Muslim Spain and Sicily, then beyond to the European continent. Much cheaper than the Egyptian papyrus or the vellum (calf- or kidskin) used in Europe, paper made possible the development and widespread distribution of books, stimulating literacy and the expansion of an educated elite, while more generally spreading knowledge in Africa, Europe, and West Asia.

In contrast to China, where woodblock printing remained important despite the invention of movable type, the introduction of movable type in Europe in the fifteenth century brought about changes in the way cultural memory was shaped, transcribed, and transmitted, changes comparable to those resulting from the invention of writing in the third millennium BCE or the introduction of the word processor and computer in the late twentieth century. Johannes Gutenberg (*c.* 1394–1468), a goldsmith from the German city of Mainz, was responsible for a series of inventions that eventually revolutionized the transmission of knowledge. Gutenberg's experiment with print technology resulted in the development of stamping molds for casting type; the printing press; and ink with an oil base that would produce finely printed, multiple copies of texts. Gutenberg's efforts were financed by loans from another goldsmith, Johann Faust, but when after five years no book had appeared from his printing press, Faust sued for his money and bankrupted Gutenberg. Faust then brought out the first printed book in 1456 with another type designer, Peter Schöffer; ironically, it became known as the "Gutenberg Bible."

The Gutenberg Bible was the first book printed in Europe using movable type, but Gutenberg's process was soon used to print books of many kinds. Greek and Roman classics were made available to a much wider audience, and printing became a commercial enterprise in which profit often mattered more than scholarship. Consumer demands, production costs, and marketing strategies all played a role in determining which books were published and who could afford them. Although initially most works printed in Europe were in Latin, the language of the Church and state, increasing numbers of works in European vernacular languages were printed. Printing in both Europe and China contributed to the expansion of vernacular and secular literatures. In so doing, printing made knowledge more widely and easily available to an increasingly literate audience.

The global expansion of these new technologies was accompanied by fears about how they might erode boundaries. It was thought by contemporaries that the printing press might displace individuals' jobs, including the Muslim scribes, who had colorfully illustrated manuscripts, and that it would allow propaganda to be widely disseminated and errors to be permanent and fixed. Some thought that this new technology might make people lazy since it did not require as much work to become literate. It was also thought that this new technology was too multimedia, that it allowed power of the image to subsume the power of language and of writing. These fears echo mightily in the early responses to the Internet and the worldwide web. In fact, both the printing press and the Internet allowed new knowledge to emerge globally. People from different locations were able to share knowledge through wider networks, enabling great leaps in knowledge.

INFORMATION TECHNOLOGY AND THE TRANSMISSION OF IDEAS

Key to understanding the increasingly frenzied pattern of technological change is the means by which ideas are transmitted. Most complex societies developed systems for recording the range of information, from economic transactions to the lineages and the feats of kings and queens and presidents. Sometimes information technology involved papyrus or textiles, sometimes stone glyphs or bronze inscriptions. The accumulation of knowledge resulted in the proliferation of specialists and eventually full-time scholars. New understanding of the Eurasian world among Renaissance humanists was initially inspired by the rediscovery of Greek thinkers such as Plato, whose works were translated from Greek and Arabic manuscripts into Latin. Until the introduction of the printing press in the mid-fifteenth century, manuscripts of texts were laboriously hand copied, often in single editions available only to learned men in scholarly settings.

Printing begins the continuum of innovations that contributed to the globalization of knowledge. As they explored new reaches of the globe, ship captains carried printed works about other parts of the world, maps, travelers' accounts, and descriptions of world cultures and histories on board their ships. Technological innovations in transportation were accompanied by even more rapid means of communication, as people began to gather news of events from every part of the world and with increasing synchronicity. As early as 1820 André-Marie Ampère (1775–1836), a French physicist, used electromagnetism to send a message over wire; by 1837 Samuel F. B. Morse (1791–1872) patented a practical system of electric telegraphy in the United States. In 1851 an undersea telegraph cable across the English Channel provided almost instantaneous communication between London and Paris, and in 1866 a trans-Atlantic cable successfully established telegraphic communication between Britain and North America. Ten years later, the Canadian Alexander Graham Bell successfully exhibited his telephone and, with improvements and modifications, it was adopted throughout America and subsequently in Europe.

Whereas photography, the moving picture, and television provided a whole new technology for storing and displaying pictorial information, the telegraph, the telephone, the phonograph, the tape recorder, and the radio have given us new technology for storing and transmitting auditory information, the computer's evolution has been able to integrate all these technologies into one system. The computer is unique, however, in that it has the capacity for manipulating and transforming information without human intervention.

Like the earlier invention of the printing press, contemporary social critics worried about the impact of the new technology. There is no doubt that computers have increased human productivity, whereas the impact of computers on the nature of work and leisure and on the quality of life is still debated. Computer technology originated to meet the needs of the most nationalistic of twentieth-century institutions, the United States military, yet the information superhighway, a worldwide network of computer networks, now delivers computer-transmitted information instantaneously to a much wider transnational community.

Figure 9.5 White men broadcasting from an *mbari* (ritual) house, Ibo, Nigeria. African artists borrowed images of the tools of the European empire, symbolically capturing their power for purposes of resistance.

THE COMPUTER REVOLUTION AND CULTURAL MEMORY

The Information Age refers to the late twentieth century, when cultural memory systems were revolutionized and proliferated by the ultimate external memory device, the computer. The notion that machines could replace the human body and its functions was a powerful catalyst to the development of the computer, probably one of the most important inventions of the twentieth century. The computer has revolutionized the speed of access to information. Many of the late-twentieth-century appliances and innovations, from telephone-answering machines to microwave ovens to air traffic control systems, would not have been conceivable without the development of the computer. No other invention has had such a revolutionary impact on global relations and daily lives. The first generation of computers relied on another innovation, the vacuum tube, the device that also enabled the invention of television. Early computers were enormous objects that filled entire rooms.

Major developments in computer technology created an information age; some of these developments can be credited to United States Navy rear admiral Grace Murray Hopper (1906–92), a mathematician recruited by the Navy to work on the Harvard University computer project. Dr Hopper, who realized that most people communicate better with prose than with mathematical symbols, created and standardized what came to be known as COBAL, a common business-oriented language for computers. The use of complex, mathematical data to translate and manipulate words and concepts also made possible the mass communications revolution that interconnects the globe, while revealing the information storage and retrieval potential of the new computer technology.

ARCHITECTURE AND CULTURAL MEMORY

We have seen how written and oral memory systems utilize both word and image to convey and remember the past. Equally important as a cultural memory system are the more material monuments of past cultures as well as the plastic and other representative arts such as painting. Buildings and monuments, sculpture and painting are tangible and visible means of maintaining cultural continuity across the centuries and also of engineering change. Like historians and poets, artists and artisans create works that reflect and help shape the culture of their times. And like the written (and orally transmitted) word, works in stone or paint – pottery and pictures, buildings and statues – are cultural records of religious and secular power.

Memorials and monuments are among the most powerful and politicized forms of memory. Part of the collective archive of cultural memory, non-verbal forms renew and rebuild potent patterns of meaning. Large buildings of permanent materials such as stone are among the oldest examples of artifacts that promote cultural memory. By constructing buildings that reflect the needs and ideals of their times, architects and artisans embed the memory of those times in their work. Architecture can be considered an archive of collective memory in and of itself, but also figured in the wide array of public ceremonies, parades, and other commemorations of community's past.

African monuments

No other record preserves the culture of ancient Egypt more clearly than the pyramid, a monumental stone form that represented the sun, a power nearly as important to the Egyptians as the Nile itself. Pyramids also intentionally commemorated the power of the pharaoh who ordered them built and, as one element of the royal burial complex, signified the survival of the ruler's power beyond his individual reign. The pyramid of Khufu at Giza is the largest single building ever known to have been constructed. It is recognized as an extraordinary achievement in workmanship, accuracy, and proportional beauty. The architects and artisans who built the temples and pyramids of ancient Egypt created monuments to their technical skill and artistic vision that are important repositories of cultural and historical information about Egyptian social and political practices and religious ideals. Monumental stone architecture also survives at the site of Great Zimbabwe, a southern African trading and ceremonial center from about the eleventh century CE, defined by a series of stone walls that housed the community's elite.

Elsewhere on the African continent, monumental architecture appeared not only in stone but also in mud or other perishable materials where stone was not available. The mud walls surrounding West African urban centers such as Jenne-Jeno (before *c.* 900 CE) or Benin (after *c.* 900 CE) required an impressive organization of labor and indicate the defensive needs and commercial purposes of those cities. Their maintenance was visible and ongoing, representative of the process of a centralized authority conscripting labor and thereby defining the limits of community. Modern works similarly function within memory systems. The Eiffel Tower in Paris, the world's highest structure until 1932, was conceived as a monument to the achievements of the age of iron and steel, when it was built in 1889.

Much of the visual art and architecture of the West African forest states was associated with divine kingship. Because the succession of kings relied in theory at least on genealogical claims, the knowledge and control of history were used to validate power and authority. Within the architectural structure known as the palace of the oba, or king, of Benin, shrines and altars were built to remember past kings and their exploits (*c.* 1400–1800). Linked by ritual and containing visual reminders such as ivory tusks carved with historical scenes of battles and cast bronze and brass memorial heads portraying specific kings and queen mothers, the shrines formed an important part of the extensive calendar of ritual life at the palace.

Another source of historical information in Benin was the collection of rectangular plaques cast in various copper alloys. The plaques were thought to have been attached to the pillars of the royal palace structure. Scenes on the plaques depicted events in the kingdom's history. They could be read like a history book of costume, technology, politics, and culture over time. The plaques were kept inside the palace, and their production was limited to members of the oba's guild of brass casters. Within an oral culture, they also served as mnemonic devices enabling the recovery of past knowledge for the purpose of recitation and ritual. Buildings and their decor such as the Benin plaques or Egyptian pyramids and other monumental stone architecture of the ancient world help preserve political and religious ideas as well as cultural memory.

Asian religious monuments

Architecture and arts around the world provide visual, aural and tactile expressions of religious ideas. In India, the homeland of Buddhism, religion inspired monumental art, which was also influenced by invading foreign peoples. Following the death of the devout Buddhist ruler Ashoka and the collapse of his empire in the third century BCE, waves of migrating peoples – Greeks, Scythians, Central Asian Kushans – brought new and foreign influences into the subcontinent. Early Buddhist art, reflected in the Bamiyan caves (fourth to fifth centuries CE) in Afghanistan, shows the influence of Greek and Roman sculpture transmitted by the Kushans from Central Asia. The Ajanta caves on the Deccan plateau in south-central India contain extensive remains of Mahayana Buddhist wall paintings, dating from the fifth through the seventh centuries, many of which illustrate the *jataka* tales of Buddha's previous incarnations.

Indian Buddhist temples, or *stupas*, which took their characteristic form between the third century BCE and the third century CE, were formal arrangements of gateways and stone railings that enclosed a burial shrine, or tumulus, of Buddhist relics, such as a bone or other physical remains of the historical Buddha. The dome of the *stupa* that covered the tumulus was a symbol of the dome of heaven, enclosing a world mountain. Worshipers walked around the circular terrace within the railings, which was a sacred space showing scenes from the life of Buddha as well as symbols of death and rebirth. Tactile sculptured frescoes adorn *stupas* in a continuous flow of images, somewhat like a narrative fresco painting. Many *stupas* are large, with domes raised on elaborate platforms, such as several ancient monuments in Sri Lanka.

The cave temples of Yun'gang and Longmen in north China are testimony to the powerful influence of Buddhism as it spread from India through Central and East Asia. Buddhist sculpture in China during the period when Buddhism spread (*c.* third to sixth centuries) reflected both Indian and Central Asian influences. Giant images of Buddha and numerous smaller carvings at Yun'gang and Longmen display the devotion of wealthy and powerful believers, such as the Empress Wu (r. 690–705) in China, who commissioned the Longmen complex as an act of devotion and perhaps a desire to legitimize her authority. Religious art was produced under the patronage of Buddhist temples and monasteries as well as rulers throughout East Asia. Wall paintings from the caves at Dunhuang in northwestern China dating to the sixth through eighth centuries illustrate Buddhist themes designed to appeal to a Chinese audience, but they are clearly influenced by Central Asian styles.

When Buddhism spread from China through Korea and Japan, influencing architecture and plastic arts as well as religious beliefs, images of Buddhist deities became objects of worship in the Buddhist temples and monasteries. Images that proliferated throughout Japan were symbolized by the erection of the statue of the Great Buddha at Nara in 752.

Under the Gupta (c. 320–540) rulers of India, who were Hindu patrons of the cult of Vishnu, Buddhism declined as an independent faith and was reabsorbed into Hinduism. The great age of Indian Buddhist art ended, and Hinduism became the primary source of inspiration for South Asian artists, though Buddhist images by no means disappeared. With the rise in the seventh century of Hindu devotional (*bhakti*) cults, centered either on Shiva, the Destroyer, or on Vishnu, the Preserver, and his incarnations Rama and Krishna, their images, both in round and in relief, joined figures of Buddhas and *bodhisattvas* as decorative art.

Hindu temple architecture and sculpture illustrate the unitary quality of Indian art, in which the erotic and the demonic are mutual expressions of cosmic unity. Sensuous sculptures showing such deities as Shiva and his wife Parvati locked in erotic embrace manifest the erotic aspect of divinity, while portrayals of Parvati as a fierce female brandishing weapons in preparation for battle illustrate its demonic side. By the ninth century, Hindu temples were covered with such relief carvings and sculptured patterns. There was a preference for human figures, though they usually represented gods or mythical beings, sometimes hybrid half human half animal, such as Ganesha, the son of Shiva, portrayed as a human body with the head of an elephant. Epic stories were also represented, and female figures, graceful nymphs and goddesses, were common.

The spread of Buddhism and Hinduism to Southeast Asia is exemplified by two impressive temple complexes, Borobudur in Java and Angkor Wat in Cambodia. Created in the eighth century, Borobudur is an artificial mountain that combines the concept of a Buddhist *stupa* with that of Mount Meru, the world mountain in early Indian cosmology. The entire complex represents a huge magic diagram of the cosmos. As pilgrims mounted the terraced sanctuary, they were believed to reenact symbolically the ascent of a soul from the world of desire to the world of spiritual perfection and ultimate union with the cosmic Buddha. Angkor, the sacred capital of the Khmer empire, was the site of numerous temples incorporating Hindu and Buddhist images during the height of Khmer power in the twelfth century.

European cathedrals

Religious themes similarly dominated European art in the medieval period (c. 1000–1300), when the Church was the dominant force in European society and the principal patron of the arts. Although religious themes dictated the subjects of painting and sculpture, such as figures of the Virgin Mary, Christ, and saints, religion inspired artistic genius most visibly in the architectural monument of the cathedral. As cities grew and flourished, their residents built handsome and impressive churches that were as much monuments to urban wealth and pride as they were dwellings of the Christian divinity.

One of the most celebrated of these monuments was the French cathedral of Saint Pierre in Beauvais, the vaulting of which exceeded 46 meters (150 feet), making it the highest of all Gothic churches. Having collapsed twice, this cathedral was never completed. It remains an impressive example of the civic pride and religious fervor that produced such art. Cathedrals represent the unity of sacred and secular functions in other ways as well. They served their communities as refuges for the homeless and destitute, thus embodying the ethical virtues expected of the wider cultural community, even Christians who did not live in areas immediately surrounding the structure. Most importantly their material artifacts and architecture served to transmit religious tradition. They depict the key stories and religious beliefs in the form of panels of decorative narrative on architectural components. Exposure to such visual information displayed through generations keeps the scriptural details and symbolic power of their beliefs alive in the minds of people visiting them.

West Asian and African domes and mosques

In West Asia, the counterpart of the Buddhist and Hindu temples in South and East Asia and the cathedral in Europe was the Islamic mosque, characteristically a domed structure. Although the dome was in use in West Asia before the Arab conquest, the Muslims subsequently raised this architectural form to monumental proportions; mosque domes are evidence of the unequaled skills of West Asian engineers and architects. Hundreds of domed structures, above all mosques, were constructed throughout West Asia and beyond when Islam spread. As domes were introduced to parts of West Africa by the spread of Islam, they were constructed of indigenous materials following local traditions, which dictated their construction out of mud, requiring a constant cycle of devotional upkeep and repair.

After the Ottoman Turks captured Constantinople in 1453 they devoted considerable resources to constructing an elaborate complex of cisterns, dams, reservoirs, locks, and aqueducts to supply water to their new capital, building on the Roman/Byzantine system. This system is still in use. One section of it is a beautiful aqueduct 500 feet long with eleven pointed arches. In addition to water systems, there were other public works projects whose construction required skilled engineers, such as bridges and domed buildings. Engineers and architects combined their skills to produce arches and domes for both aesthetic and other purposes, one of which was to cover a great space while avoiding the need for rows of pillars to support the roof.

By the early modern period, hundreds of domed structures, above all churches and mosques, had been constructed throughout Europe, West Asia, and North Africa. Localized styles of architecture emerged in West Asia among the Ottomans in Turkey, the Safavids in Iran, and the Mamluks in Egypt. The Ottoman style was symbolized by the immense domed mosques of Istanbul with their sleek pencil-like minarets; the Safavid Persian style by the dazzling, tile-covered mosques of Isfahan with their bulbous domes; and the Mamluk Arab style by the intricately carved and joined stone domes of the tombs of the sultans in Cairo.

The dome crowning the Suleymaniye Mosque in Istanbul epitomized the large-scale dome. It was designed for Suleyman the Magnificent by Sinan (d. 1588), the greatest Ottoman architect and a worthy rival of his close European contemporary Michelangelo. Completed in 1557 after seven years of labor, the Suleymaniye dome has a diameter of 80 feet and floats 160 feet above worshipers' heads. It rests on four massive piers and is extended at the front and back of the mosque by two half domes of equal diameter and 120 feet high. Even today the visitor is overwhelmed by the achievement.

Mughal culture in India was the product of Persian-Islamic and Hindu influences, and Mughal architecture reflected this cultural blend. The most famous monument of Mughal architecture is the Taj Mahal, built as a mausoleum for Shah Jahan's wife Mumtaz Mahal after her death in childbirth in 1631. In this way the monument reflects the individual's attempt to preserve personal memory. Designed by two Persian architects, it took more than 20,000 workers over twenty years to build. It has been called the greatest single work of Safavid art, but in its dependence on Indian materials and craftsmen it can be seen as an excellent example of Mughal cultural syncretism rather than as a Persian import. The Taj Mahal, however, was also viewed as a symbol of oppression by the Shah Jahan. Mumtaz Mahal died in the Deccan, a region of India that her husband waged costly wars to bring under control following the decimation of the local peasant population through one of India's worst recorded famines. Shah Jahan spent only 5,000 rupees of imperial funds each week to help relieve widespread misery and starvation in Deccan; not long after that, he lavished billions on a peacock throne and his wife's mausoleum, the Taj Mahal. The building reflects an attempt to elevate individual memory to the larger collective.

Monuments in the Americas

Architecture can thus be a source of cultural memory that reflects continuity and change. The tangible remains of North American communities suggest a spiritual basis for culture that was as pervasive as the Afro-Eurasian world religions. Many North Americans led nomadic lives requiring little in the way of permanent structures. Earthworks, such as the Great Serpent Mound (c. 500–1000 CE) in Ohio, appear to have been designed to function as sacred effigies and may have been built as reference points for settled peoples. There are others in the form of panthers, bears, birds, and humans, found at a variety of sites. Monumental mounds at Cahokia served political and religious purposes. Some were burial mounds, log tombs covered with earth piled up in various shapes.

The contents of these burial mounds provide evidence of the considerable artistic skill of Cahokia's inhabitants and reflect their religious practices and their conspicuous consumption of luxury goods (metals, shells, teeth). Public structures and residences were built on some of the mounds and reflect the ranked political and social structures of the community. Generally, the largest mounds are temple mounds. "Monk's Mound" at Cahokia contained 600,000 cubic meters (21 million cubic feet) of earth, all carried to the site in baskets. This was an engineering feat comparable to the building of the stone pyramids of Egypt.

It is possible that the monumental traditions of North America were imported by immigrants from the south or at least inspired by earlier Mesoamerican architecture. There is general agreement that the Olmec culture (c. 1200–400 BCE) provided a common foundation for the Mesoamerican cultures that came after it. The monumental Classic Mayan art (c. 300 BCE) reflects an environment in which stone was plentiful. Characteristic of Mayan remains are temple pyramids made of stuccoed limestone, multiroomed "palaces," causeways connecting groups of structures in cities, and cities themselves, including stone monuments often inscribed with Mayan hieroglyphics. At Tikal, the buildings of a central acropolis were built over earlier tombs of elites cut into bedrock. The acropolis was for ceremonial purposes and was surrounded by substantial suburbs. Stone was the primary medium of Mesoamerican art, and Tikal's monuments provide significant evidence of political complexity and cultural connections across the southern lowlands.

Deconstructing cultural memory

Later colonial powers destroyed many of the temples in the Americas and used their stones to build cathedrals, acts of cultural appropriation not lost on the colonizers or the colonized. The ability to control cultural memory meant having the power to "erase" as well as remember the past. Power, identity, and belonging could be reinforced by the establishment of recognized sites of authority.

After the demise of the Khmer empire, Angkor was gradually absorbed by the jungle, only to be rediscovered by Europeans in the course of their colonization of Southeast Asia. In the mid-nineteenth century a French expedition began to document the ruins at Angkor, and until 1972 when the Cambodian civil war forced them to leave, the École Française d'Extrême Orient worked steadily on restoration of the site. Despite the efforts of local workers to continue, little was done over the next twenty years as Cambodia was engulfed in war. Only in 1991 did the United Nations, through UNESCO, establish a presence at Angkor to provide international support for the recovery efforts to protect structures in danger of collapse due to the subsiding soils. Angkor thus was recognized as not only a monument of cultural identity for the Cambodian people but also a world heritage site. Such sites are embraced by legitimacy-seeking elites and their architecture is viewed as having witnessed a glorious past and able to reflect values that serve modern national identity. In the wake of devastating war and genocide, that manifestation of cultural memory became even more important to a country seeking to heal the wounds of fratricidal conflict.

Other sites of cultural and religious heritage were less fortunate. The Bamiyan caves in Afghanistan housed two huge Buddhist statues that had been carved into the hillside of the Hindu Kush between the second and sixth centuries CE. One of the statues was ten storeys high, and both were regarded as unique representations of the Buddha. When the Taliban came to power in Afghanistan in the late 1990s, they set out to create a pure Islamic state and this meant, in the most radical terms, the eradication of all images representing other religions. Despite international pressures to preserve the Bamiyan Buddhas, the Taliban destroyed them in 2001. The destruction of the Buddhas took place along with the town of Bamiyan and its inhabitants, Shi'ites of the Hazara ethnic group who were persecuted by the Sunni Taliban. In this case, both the cultural memory of

Buddhism and the existence of a people were erased by the actions of the Taliban.

INSTITUTIONS AND THE TRANSMISSION OF CULTURAL MEMORY

The various systems of cultural memory may be private products of individual creation or the results of public community design and effort. Whatever the forms of cultural memory or the means by which they are created, the storage, maintenance, and transmission of cultural memory are often associated with institutions such as churches, schools, guilds, brotherhoods, libraries, and universities. These institutions may be represented in physical structures or they may exist as patterns of social or political interactions. In the process of preserving and transmitting cultural knowledge, institutions are agents of cultural memory, adding a distinctly social dimension. Such institutions can consolidate the authority of social and cultural elites, but they can also act as agents of change by expressing resistance to prevailing cultural norms and ideals.

Religious institutions

Communities in which individuals dedicated themselves to spiritual goals, monasteries also served as institutions of cultural memory. They transmitted religious ideas through practice and sometimes became powerful agents in the political and social world outside the monastery. Though monks and nuns were removed from secular life, their main contribution lay in copying manuscripts and maintaining libraries, and the monastery thus served as a principal institution for the transmission of Eurasian cultural memory. Christian monasteries in Europe controlled the preservation and reproduction of cultural knowledge, much as Confucian institutions and ideas dominated this process in China, Buddhist and Hindu ones did in India, and Islamic ones did in West Asia and Africa.

Buddhist monasticism reached across Asia from India to China, Southeast Asia, and Japan. In China, independent Buddhist sects established networks of monasteries that housed hundreds of thousands of monks and nuns. By the Tang period (618–907),

Buddhist monasteries were wealthy landowners and Buddhist abbots and priests socialized with the court aristocracy and were highly educated members of the literati elite. Buddhist monasteries and temples also served as schools, providing primary education in Confucian texts as well as Buddhist ones. Buddhist monasteries, like their counterparts in Europe, often served as repositories of learning and also functioned as educational institutions that preserved and transmitted knowledge, including secular ideas such as Confucianism in East Asia. Buddhist monastic institutions in medieval Japan were centers of learning patronized by the military leaders of the time, much like monasteries in medieval Europe, although women might also seek refuge therein.

Like the community of monks and nuns in Buddhist and Christian monasteries throughout Asia and Europe, in the Islamic world Sufi brotherhoods, called *tariqas* (paths to union with God), sprang up in the twelfth and thirteenth centuries and established networks of lodges throughout West Asia. These lodges were typically organized around an outstanding mystic, whose tomb was usually incorporated into the main lodge. Branch lodges were subsequently founded wherever groups of his disciples and adherents might meet. Each lodge had its own rituals and costume, and some were restricted to particular professions or strata of society. The brotherhoods in the cities, especially those associated with the professions, often adopted their own code of ethics.

Tariqas played a major role in the spread of Islam and in the maintenance of cultural memory. One of the most famous brotherhoods was inspired by Jalal ad-Din ar-Rumi (1207–73), a Sufi mystic and poet whose tomb at Konya in Anatolia became a site of pilgrimage for his disciples and their followers. Jalal ad-Din had used music and dance to help induce a mystical state, and dancing became the outstanding feature of religious rituals associated with Sufi brotherhoods.

Tariqas appeared in West Africa with the spread of Islam that accompanied the expansion of the Mali empire (*c.* thirteenth and fourteenth centuries). Muslim brotherhoods proved compatible with indigenous West African cultural institutions and made conversion to Islam easier. Among linguistically related West African peoples, secret men's and women's societies centering on commerce and its regulation existed among the merchant classes. Such urban lodges, scattered throughout the Mali empire, increased cultural solidarity within the merchant community, defrayed the costs of individuals' trade and travel, and further enhanced the success of West African commercial and cultural connections within the Islamic world. Specialized information and historical tales were both controlled by family groups. After the arrival of Islam, local histories were appropriated, rewritten in Arabic, and transmitted through the new religion of converts.

European guilds

Counterparts to the Islamic lodges can be seen in the medieval European guild system. With the expansion of trade in Europe from about 1200 to 1500, associations for mutual aid and protection developed among town dwellers engaged in common pursuits. Known as "guilds," these societies were the means by which manufacturing, trade, labor, and even government in towns and cities were regulated and protected. Like the urban lodges of West Africa, occupational guilds provided a basis for the retention and transmission of specialist knowledge, offered community solidarity, and were among the agencies of political and cultural change in late medieval Europe. Guilds were among the most important institutions in medieval Europe.

There were almost as many guilds as there were different activities: there were guilds for bellringers, minstrels, candlemakers, masons, roadmenders, and weavers, to name but a few. Guild members participated in public rituals and ceremonies, such as the celebration of the Doge (ruler) of Venice in 1268, a parade in which each of the city's guilds marched in bands, sumptuously dressed, carrying banners and flags, and heralded by musicians. These colorful processions became an expression of the collective memory and identity of their community of participants and were likely witnessed by Marco Polo before he left on his voyages.

Universities, libraries and education

Many societies systematically developed means of acquiring and transmitting vital cultural knowledge through a variety of educational institutions, both religious and secular. In Islamic West Asia, educational institutions (*madrasas*) arose mainly to provide religious and legal instruction according to the Qur'an and its interpreters. Arabic was the language of instruction in the *madrasas*, which were established to train orthodox Sunni theologians. One or more of these colleges were built in most of the major cities of the empire, where they eventually became an element in the Muslim definition of a town or city as a place where there was a mosque, a *madrasa*, a public bath, and a bazaar. Generally, a *madrasa* was a square building with one to four arched halls (classrooms) that opened onto a central arcaded courtyard and that had residential rooms for students and teachers.

In northern India, the great Buddhist university at Nalanda was founded in the sixth century CE and had an enrollment of around 5,000 students, including

Figure 9.6 Sandstone sculpture of Indian woman writing with a stylus, north India, eleventh century CE. The tip of a stylus was pressed into the wet clay tablet making the desired sign. Manuscripts on palm leaves were also used throughout South and Southeast Asia. Scholars who were often supported by patrons included elite female scribes.

many foreign scholars and distinguished lecturers. Buddhist texts and the Vedas and Hindu philosophy were taught. Caste divisions were reflected in other educational institutions, as elite *brahman* boys (and occasionally girls) were educated in the Vedic tradition; members of the warrior caste were educated largely by household tutors, who taught them reading, writing, military arts, dancing, painting, and music.

In contrast to China, where elites endowed the written word with sacred power, there was far more regard for oral tradition in early India. Rote memorization of the Vedas was emphasized, although writing was eventually used as an aid to memorization. As in medieval Europe, libraries were established in monasteries and palaces. Manuscript copying on palm leaves was an industry involving professional scribes and was often considered a pious activity, also centered in monasteries and palaces.

Cathedral schools, along with the traditional monastic centers of learning, were the centers of education in Europe until the appearance of universities in the twelfth century. Students were considered clerks though they might never become priests. The earliest universities may be thought of as urbanized, expanded cathedral schools. The first appeared in Italy at Bologna in the early twelfth century, and the first north of the Alps was at Paris (1200). The University of Paris became the foremost center for theological and philosophical studies in Europe, an indication of its origins and the dominant role of the Church in the education of the time.

In China, the Confucian notion that schools were a responsibility of the state persisted from antiquity. By the second century BCE, there was an "Imperial University" in the capital that taught the Confucian classics. Educational institutions were closely linked to the operation of the examination system. Based on the use of systematic recommendations of those judged suitable for government service as early as the Han dynasty (206 BCE–220 CE), the examination system instituted in the Tang period (618–907) was designed to recruit and select men for office in the imperial government. Over time, it became the single most powerful mechanism for the reproduction of the cultural, social, and political elite in imperial China.

To acquire the vast learning necessary to pass the examinations, students would have to begin at an early age and work long hours for many years to master the entire corpus of the Confucian classics, the commentaries written on those classics, and historical works documenting the transmission of the scholarly tradition of Confucianism over time. Literary works, both poetry and essays, were included in this curriculum. Some early education took place in Buddhist monasteries, where Confucian texts were often transmitted along with Buddhist ones. The civil service examinations not only tested knowledge of the classics, their commentaries, and histories but also required candidates to propose policies to deal with problems of government administration, such as fiscal matters. In addition, candidates were asked to write poems of a certain form on specified themes in order to demonstrate their abilities as men of culture.

Prospective candidates from families deeply entrenched in this cultural tradition, or from those that aspired to status and power, were educated by private tutors in their homes if they were wealthy or through an extensive network of schools that radiated out from the capital to nearly every region of the empire by the twelfth century. These schools were not "public," in the sense of being open to everyone, but they were an important source of learning for the elite, whose sons filled these schools. Families sometimes endowed lands to provide income for a family school, and sometimes community leaders would promote joint efforts to establish a school to serve the sons of elite families. Private academies also began to proliferate by the twelfth century, and these academies were the seat of the new synthesis of classical learning called "Neo-Confucianism."

Magnificent libraries of paper books were also established throughout West Asia in the ninth and tenth centuries. Although all kinds of books were collected, among the most important were those on the Greek sciences. The libraries served as academies where scholars of all faiths and origins came to study, discuss, and debate the hard sciences as well as other subjects. Libraries had a major influence on the transmission of ancient learning throughout the Islamic world and from there to Christendom. Among the most famous Muslim libraries were one founded in Baghdad in 833 and another founded in Cairo in 1005.

Like its European, West Asian, and North African counterparts, the University of Sankore in Timbuktu,

Figure 9.7 The College of Henricus de Alemannia. Miniature/covering colours on parchment by Laurentius de Voltolina, 18 × 28 cm. Taken from "Liber ethicorum des Henricus de Alemannia," fourteenth century, this illustration depicts a typical European university of the time. Higher learning took place in a community under the tutelage of a recognized master, who guided subjects from mathematics and astronomy to music and rhetoric.

on the banks of the great Niger River, witnessed an intellectual awakening across the Islamic societies of fifteenth-century West Africa. The university actually consisted of a constellation of nearly two hundred small schools, mosques, and libraries, which together acquired and disseminated knowledge from the Arab world and various African oral traditions. Two famous *tarikhs*, or written histories, date from this period and were actually transcriptions in Arabic of local Sudanese traditions. For the most part, the university curriculum was controlled by the clerics, and it represented a privileged culture of elites that was reproduced through family ties. The curriculum included Muslim theology, jurisprudence, astronomy, geography, and history – subjects of interest to only a small minority of the urban elite.

Gender and institutions

Like other aspects of institutions, the transmission of cultural memory was not only shaped by social class and culture, it was also highly gendered. The Islamic tradition of compiling biographical dictionaries, somewhat like the lives of the Christian saints, forms the basis for understanding the history of the Islamic community as the cumulative contributions of individual men and women who created and transmitted Islamic culture. One such individual life is that of the female scholar Umm Hani (1376–1466), who appears in the twelve-volume dictionary by al-Sakhawi (d. 1497) as a "brilliant light."

According to al-Sakhawi, Umm Hani was born and died in Cairo. First taught by her grandfather, she studied with about twenty different masters of learning. Umm Hani eventually married twice, and her sons were educated in law. She became a teacher of other scholars, including al-Sakhawi himself, who wrote that she knew more than he was able to learn. As a young woman, Umm Hani memorized the Qur'an and could recite lengthy passages of *hadiths* (traditions). She was an accomplished poet and would make up verses instantly on the spot. When her second husband died, she inherited his fortune and his business – a textile workshop that she managed. Sakhawi also tells us that Umm Hani performed the *hajj* (pilgrimage) to Mecca thirteen times, often staying on for months in Medina and Mecca to teach.

The dictionary entry for Umm Hani is one out of a total of 11,691 entries, one of 1,075 women for whom citations were written. In the fourteenth and fifteenth centuries, women figured prominently among the biographical listings of Islamic scholars, probably encouraged by the assertive promotion of women's religious learning by the Syrian and Egyptian *ulama* (clerics). In later centuries, however, women practically disappeared from the dictionaries; by the end of the nineteenth century, al-Baytar (d. 1918) found room for only two women out of the 777 persons remembered in his biographies.

By controlling the transmission and dissemination of cultural knowledge, institutions of cultural memory, such as monasteries, churches, universities and brotherhoods, tended to reproduce the prevailing patterns of power relations and reinforce cultural hegemony, power or control exercised from above. Such institutions generated ideological authority that could sustain a social and political order as well as reinforce elite cultural ideals. At the same time, these institutions were sources of dissent and contributed to the revision of cultural memory through challenging or resisting inherited cultural knowledge. In the process of transmission and reproduction, transformation took place that fundamentally realigned power relationships or rejected the power of dominant elites by challenging the underpinnings of their authority.

RENAISSANCES: TRADITIONS AND THEIR TRANSFORMATIONS

Cultural memory systems can also be altered by reviving or promoting the past and replacing one set of ideas with an earlier one. Late medieval European culture and society (*c.* 1000–1200) had been dominated by the traditions of Christianity and the institution of the Catholic Church. After 1200, both were eroded by changes brought about in part by the expansion of commerce, the breakdown of feudal political structures, and, beginning in the fifteenth century, by the opening of the Atlantic frontier and influences from Asia, Africa, and the Americas.

The European Renaissance took place from the fourteenth through sixteenth centuries and meant to contemporaries, who coined the term, a rebirth of learned culture as they turned to Greece and Rome for a source of inspiration and cultural ideals distinct from those of medieval Christianity. These cultural ideals can be described by the term "secular humanism," emphasizing secular or worldly concerns over those of religious faith and humanistic concerns over those of God. Rejecting medieval preoccupations with Christian belief and the sense of community provided by the unity of medieval Christianity, Renaissance thinkers were attracted to the individualism they found in the works of Greek and Roman authors. The ideal of individualism was encouraged and supported by the social and economic realities of commercial capitalism and the process of urbanization that took place in the centuries between 1200 and 1500.

The European Renaissance signaled a "rebirth" of a European cultural memory system against the background of medieval Christianity. European thinkers were inspired by Greek and Roman writers, by values and ideals that were secular, not sacred, humanistic, not god-centered, and based on reason rather than on Christian faith. Similarly, a "rebirth" of Confucianism took place in China after the eighth century and culminated around 1200 in what is known in the West as Neo-Confucianism.

Like the rediscovery of classical Greek and Latin texts and the rejection of medieval Christianity that characterized the European Renaissance, the revival of Confucianism and the reworking of its fundamental ideas was linked to a rejection of Buddhist spiritual ideals as well as a response to the Buddhist challenge to Confucian social and political ideals. Neo-Confucian thinkers sought to provide Confucian answers to Buddhist metaphysical questions – about the nature of being and the universe – and to create Confucian institutions and practices that addressed the needs of society. In the realm of metaphysics, Neo-Confucians explained the purpose of existence in terms of Confucian sagehood: people should aspire to realize their true human nature, which was essentially good, and to utilize that in the service of the community.

In contrast, Buddhism called for people to reject their attachment to the world and to seek "enlightenment" in realization of their Buddha nature: the extinction (nirvana) of individual self in the oneness with all being. At the same time, Buddhist institutions provided not only refuge from society in monasteries and nunneries but also social welfare services, such as feeding the hungry and caring for orphans. The Buddhist clergy also provided important functions for people by performing funeral rites, long a central concern of Confucians, beginning with the elaborate prescriptions for proper funeral rites described in the ritual texts of antiquity. The Neo-Confucian thinker Zhu Xi (1130–1200) authored a new set of Confucian-based practices for family life and needs, such as funeral rites and marriage ceremonies that were intended to replace Buddhist practice and to eliminate dependence on Buddhist clergy and temples.

In Confucian thinking, identity had always been defined in terms of fundamental human relationships, such as that of father and son or husband and wife. The self was defined primarily in relation to others, especially to the family but also to the larger community. Neo-Confucianism laid new emphasis on the self as the source of order and harmony in the community, as thinkers such as Zhu Xi argued that self-cultivation of one's Heaven-endowed human nature was the key to social and political order. Neo-Confucian thinkers of the Song era (960–1279) and

after based this notion on ideas drawn from the Great Learning, a portion of one of the five Confucian classics, *The Record of Rites*. In this text, individual moral rectitude is linked to the regulation of the family, the order of the state, and harmony in the world.

KEEPING TIME

Religious institutions played a key role in the integration of human societies and promoting history itself by helping to introduce the role of timekeeping in our everyday lives. Essential to the practice of modern historians is being able to identify and measure change over time. Measuring time was essential to the rise of complex societies. The earliest systems for tracking the passing of time were various forms of sundials that relied on the observation of regular planetary movements. The Egyptians and the Chinese also used a time mechanism that involved the measured flow of water. Medieval European religious communities used sundials, water clocks, marked candles, and eventually, in the thirteenth century, mechanical clocks to synchronize the work and daily prayers of community members.

Other societies have made timekeepers in order to coordinate and make sense of the world, and modern societies continue to rely on shared external devices – from sundials and wristwatches to calendars and clocks. Chinese used astronomical water-wheel clocks both for making astrological predictions and calendrical timekeeping that some historians think was likely to have been even more accurate than the earliest European mechanical clocks. The earliest such water device, which dates to the tenth century and reproduced the movements of sun, moon, and selected stars, was described by Zhang Sixun in 979 CE. But the need for accuracy also changed over time in response to other technological innovations. A major stimulus to improving the accuracy and reliability of clocks was the importance of precise timekeeping for maritime navigation, which also relied on the observation of stars and planets. The breakthrough invention was the first highly accurate marine chronometer invented by John Harrison in the mid-eighteenth century and it allowed for longitudinal measurements. In the twenty-first century, the Global Positioning System (GPS) relies on extremely accurate atomic timekeeping to calculate positions in space, where an error of nanoseconds could translate into an error of distance of 1,000 or more kilometers.

It is not only historians, mariners, and astronauts who have depended on the clock. The use of standard time drives daily lives of much of the world today, but was unheeded by rural agriculturalists. It was in industrial cities that shared schedules became critical markers of urban life and allowed the control over individuals. Eventually time was made portable and worn and read on watches since the beginnings of the wristwatch in the early nineteenth century. In the mid-1880s, leather "watch wristlets" were considered desirable as a jewelry accessory for ladies. Within a few decades, the wristwatch was commonplace, though chiefly used by women. Not until the First World War was the practicality of the wristwatch irresistible to men.

As urban industrial life spread around the globe, timekeeping became a hallmark of the new scientific age. The common global adaptation of timekeeping systems represents one example of the impact of science on human memory systems. During the era in European history commonly labeled the "scientific revolution," culminating about 1700 CE, changing perceptions about ways of knowing began to assert the role of the scientist and scientific thinking over the received wisdom of cultural memory embedded in religious tradition. The world was considered knowable through the systematic investigation of evidence, experimental or observed, leading towards a new age in which empiricism played a key role. The emphasis on the material, rather than spiritual realms of cultural memory, gradually gave way to the concept of modernity as a secular world view.

CULTURAL MEMORY SYSTEMS AND NEW ENCOUNTERS

After about 1500, disparate cultural memory systems increasingly came into contact with each other through maritime travels and exploits. The spread of religions, empire, and trade served to bring together distinct systems of cultural memory. During the period of European exploration after 1500, Eurasian ideas and

technologies encountered the vastly different cultural contexts of Africa, the Americas, and Oceania. Encounters left both carrier and recipient as co-participants in an interactive process of cultural change. But it would be a mistake to think that cultural memory systems only served to preserve and promote "traditions." Maintaining a viable cultural system meant constantly filtering new ideas and reformulating them into a socially acceptable container. Cultures in the past were, as they are today, constantly changing. Cultural memory systems functioned to negotiate and regulate those changes.

The encounters that occurred with the expansion of Europe were marked by processes of selective borrowing in the collection of objects and ideas believed to be of value. The material world also provided sites for transformation as cultural memory systems encountered one another. The first tourist art appeared alongside the distribution of cultural objects to new shores. For example, local West African weavers unraveled imported silk textiles from Asia and rewove their silk threads into their own familiar patterns. Europeans sailing through Oceania mimicked the tattoos of Polynesians (tattoo comes from the Samoan *tatau*, meaning to strike twice), altering their complex symbology and cultural memories alike. Japanese silk-screen painters traveled to Mexico and painted indigenous festivals during the era of the silver trade. These are examples of cultural memory systems adapting to new locales and new media.

Cultural food ways formed part of the cultural memory systems that linked the external world, its foods and flavors, with the human body. What people ate expressed their identity, to themselves and to others, and what people ate changed over time. These changes shaped the cultures of consumption around the world, and sometimes even directed the movements of populations, the decline of some, and the dramatic increase of others.

COLONIZING MEMORY

Colonies were powerful crucibles for the transformation of the societies, which brought together colonizer and colonized. New studies of the colonial era emphasize the mutual impact of colonialism on both groups. The process of "decolonizing the mind" involved subtle and intentional changes in language, dress, and other systems of cultural memory. Just as colonizers extracted the colony's wealth in the form of natural resources, they similarly attempted to appropriate the past of the peoples they conquered. When the Nigerian writer Chinua Achebe wrote his first novel, *Things Fall Apart*, he described the historical experience of what it felt to be colonized from the perspective of Africans, whom colonialism had tried to silence.

The imposition of European languages furthered the colonial aims. In colonized parts of the worlds, such as Asia, Africa, and the Caribbean, European languages also represented an opportunity – through the use of a common language – for resistance by promoting solidarity and unity leading to independence. The languages of the colonizer also symbolized the continuing neocolonialism and cultural dependency experienced even after political independence was achieved. In Jamaica the writer Louis Bennett brought street talk and African-derived patois along with oral storytelling devices to literary heights, empowering a new generation of writers and rappers. Writing in the vernacular, the Jamaican poet Andrew Salkey (1929–96) used the African-derived spider folk hero Anancy to express outrage over a brutal dictatorship in Guyana. Anancy takes on the garb of freedom-fighter and works his magic in Salkey's short book *The One*, by avenging the murder of the Caribbean historian and political activist Walter Rodney (1942–80).

On the African continent Ngugi wa'Thiongo reverted to writing in his first language, Kikuyu, rather than the English language of the colonizer, because he believed the language itself colonized the mind. By contrast, the Nigerian Nobel Laureate Wole Soyinke used not only the English language but particularly Shakespearean English to ruminate on the twentieth-century Yoruba experience in *Death and the King's Horseman*, a book that few Nigerians can buy or even read today because the Nigerian government prohibits it. The Caribbean-African writer Frantz Fanon suggested that the literature of the former colonial world first passes through a cultural nationalist phase that romanticizes the precolonial past. The trend among African novelists was away from romanticism and toward realism and even surrealism (beyond or above realism) to describe their post-colonial worlds.

RESISTANCE IN MOTION: CULTURAL MEMORY, POLITICS, AND PERFORMANCE

Even in memory systems where tensions between experience and written knowledge were absent, resistance could threaten the elite's control over knowledge. Popular and elite cultures sometimes served different populations and represented conflicting versions of cultural memory, just as family histories and court histories might differ vastly in their interest in and interpretation of the past. For example, over the course of centuries the Yoruba of West Africa have conceived of rituals as both actual and virtual journeys. Transformation of cultural memory can take place whether rituals are performed as a procession or public parade, pilgrimage, masquerade, or possession trance in which practitioners dance and embody the identities of cultural heroes and powerful deities.

Ritual performance can as easily subvert the mundane order as it can reinforce it. What may be more difficult to capture in this written description of ritual and other experienced performance is its simultaneous links to tradition or cultural memory and to impermanency and change. The religion of the ancient Greeks was similarly focused on action: rituals, festivals, processions, athletic contests, oracles, sacrifices. The cult of Athena, goddess of wisdom, centered around splendid festivals rather than any fixed or written representation. Lived experience and nonverbal communication could create a powerful cultural memory system even where verbal systems were present.

Dance and ritual, in parts of the world where they are integral parts of cultural politics, have also played a significant role in storing and transmitting cultural memory and creating interstices of transformation and resistance. In ritual and in dance movements, bodies say what cannot be spoken. Cultural practice, including dance and kinesthetic practices like the Indian tradition of Hatha Yoga (a method of cleansing and purifying the body to attain spiritual ends) constituted bodies of teaching cosmological and spiritual vision and imparting identity to followers. Dance and body movements – from ritualized behavior to military marching – could preserve and communicate complex memory systems in support of or against the status quo.

Performance arts and resistance

For example, responses to colonial rule ranged from successful armed rebellions to forms of cultural resistance to active collaboration. African resistance to colonialism sometimes took the subtle and complex path of mimicry. Beginning about 1925 the Hauka movement of West Africa embodied colonial resistance in the rituals and dances of spirit possession in which European colonizers were mocked. Members of dance troupes traveled around the countryside of Niger proselytizing and spreading messages of derision and rebellion. The dancers dressed like European soldiers and imitated their colonial behaviors. By appropriating the European style and form of body movement, Hauka members hoped to empower themselves in opposition to the French administration of their territory.

In an era of globalization, the bodies of dancers also speak of their own complex history of identity formation through the motions of samba, a singularly unique dance form that mixes Amerindian, African, and European dances in Brazil. The samba's three-count, between-the-beat, intricate movement of swaying hips and feet resisting the contrary two/fourth beat became a metaphor that celebrates the fusion of separate traditions. In Brazil, African (Kongolese) and Amerindian (Cariri Indian) syncopation and rhythm work against the strong beat. A kind of layering of movements allows one rhythm to resist and alternately silence the others in the syncretic samba form. After the abolition of slavery in 1888, though some written historical documents pertaining to slavery were destroyed in attempts to eradicate a painful past, the stories have lived on in such forms as the samba.

In twentieth-century Brazil and other parts of the African-Caribbean world, the politics of resistance came to be performed as art and ritual just as they had under slavery. Dance and other performance arts were resistance in motion. The oppressed used religious expression to empower individuals, invert the social order, and sometimes even transform political identity and reassert cultural memory. Whether in the danced rituals and other ceremonies of the African-derived religion known as *candomblé*, the rituals and dance steps of carnival in Trinidad, the Brazilian martial arts form called *capoeira*, or in samba, which became the popular "national" dance of Brazil, elements of resistance and of cultural expression survived as intertwined cultural memories.

Dance steps and musical instruments had multiple meanings in a history of resistance. The Brazilian *berimbau*, a single-stringed bow with a resonating gourd attached, was played as an instrument, and according to one musician, "in the hour of pain, it stops being an instrument and becomes a hand weapon." *Candomblé*, a syncretic faith combining Catholic elements and Yoruba deities, originated in the violent cultural encounters of the Atlantic world. But it also emerged in the context of community and collective action. As creative expression dance was not only relevant to resistance, it remained at the core of historical identity. According to dance scholar Barbara Browning, "the insistence of Brazilians to keep dancing is not a means of forgetting but rather a perseverance, an unrelenting attempt to intellectualize, theorize, understand a history and a present of social injustice difficult to believe, let alone explain."

Cultural memory and the Cultural Revolution in China

One of the most violent clashes over cultural memory took place not as resistance against slavery or colonialism but against the past understood as the domain of elite culture. The Cultural Revolution in China began in 1965 with a critical review of a play about a Ming emperor's dismissal of a loyal official. The drama critic derided the play as a veiled attack on the emperor-like Mao Zedong's treatment of a Communist Party official. This seemingly artistic conflict was in reality a political strategy designed by Mao and his supporters to undermine his critics. The debate eventually erupted into increasingly virulent reactions from people throughout China who lashed out at what were perceived as "remnants of feudal culture." Red Guards, young people liberated from closed-down schools and universities, traveled across the country smashing icons of the old ways of life, including religion and traditional culture. Buddhist temples were destroyed, libraries were emptied and books burned – everything that was connected with the old society and culture came under attack, including people such as writers and teachers. Mao aimed to create a new culture in the name of workers, peasants, and soldiers, whose culture was glorified as a replacement for veneration of the educated intellectual, enshrined as it had been by the Confucian tradition. This Cultural Revolution was an echo of the May 4th Movement in 1919 that attacked Confucianism and traditional society, but in the name of Western ideals of "Mr Science and Mr Democracy" rather than the 1960s Cultural Revolution that was inspired by Chinese Marxist and Maoist rejection of the West.

TRANSNATIONAL TECHNOLOGIES AND GLOBAL CULTURAL MEMORY

It is not only institutions and states that have shaped cultural memory. Today, satellite technology and the distribution of television and film (and, most recently, print media) rights by multinational corporations have an impact on what gets seen and read and by whom. It was often said that film was the quintessential art form of the twentieth century. Modern technology, from televisions to computers, has made visual expression and communication paramount in people's lives. The invention of still photography in the nineteenth century was followed almost immediately by a consideration of the potential of stringing together photographic images to create a moving picture. By the late twentieth century, virtually every region of the world had begun to participate in the creation of visual culture through the images of photography, film and television. By the end of the twentieth century, global audiences had come together electronically as a single media community. The ascendancy of transnational images and their reproduction made possible the creation of global icons of cultural memory from national ones, such as the famous photograph of Cuban revolutionary leader Che Guevara that gained global currency in all of the Americas and in Eurasia.

Cinema has pondered the altered power relationships of the twentieth century's interwar years and the social and economic challenges of globalization. The ability of film to transcend and even manipulate time and space has made it a valuable tool for persuasion and propaganda, from the Nazi era films of Leni Riefenstahl to the Super Bowl advertisements. Although film has a rich background in various countries, some of the most distinctive, impressive, and powerful examples of this new art form have been produced in non-Western nation-states. Film has created the possibility for multidimensional expression of complex cultural and social questions. It has also provided a means of communication across cultures not limited to the translation of verbal expression, either written or oral/aural.

While the control over film production and distribution by multinational corporations since the 1950s has generally impeded independent filmmaking, some filmmakers have successfully used film and video to promote countercultural ideas, validating the early observation that film is "truth twenty-four times a second." For example, the Senegalese filmmaker Ousmane Sembene found ways to connect the traditional role of West African *griot*, an oral historian/ storyteller, with the medium of film. A pioneer of African film, Sembene sees the modern filmmaker as replacing the *griot* as "the historian, the raconteur, the living memory and the conscience of his people." His films (*Emitai* [1971] and *Ceddo* [1976], for example) were drawn from historical events. Sembene has also used the possibilities of the medium of film to portray the nonlinear nature of time and the magical/spiritual beliefs of his African culture. Unlike many filmmakers from developing countries, Sembene has successfully made films in African languages.

Japan's position since the late twentieth century as a major economic force is reflected in the richness of its cinema, although the greatest Japanese directors were making some of their finest films in the 1950s, not long after Japan's cataclysmic defeat in the Second World War. Ozu Yasujirô (1903–63) chronicled the inner life of the Japanese family, the core of Japanese society, in films such as *Tokyo Story* (1953). The technical aesthetics of Ozu's filmmaking are classically Japanese: spare, restrained, and subtle, with great emotional appeal, and they portray a social world that is slipping away in the face of modern, Western influences. The elderly couple in *Tokyo Story* represent the old life of the village and family, while their children are busy, urban professionals who have no time for their elderly, unsophisticated parents. Naruse Mikio, established as a director already in prewar Japan, sympathetically documented the continuities in women's lives amidst the dramatic changes of the postwar period in many of his films, such as *When a Woman Ascends the Stairs* (1960). The films of other Japanese directors, such as Kurosawa Akira (1910–98), blend both Japanese tradition and modernity along with global influences. Kurosawa, for example, adapted Shakespeare for the plots of several of his films.

In the recent worldwide success of the Japanese graphic novel (*manga*) and *anime* (animation), the Japanese have taken the fundamentals of American comic art and have reframed image and word into a new narrative cultural form. Japanese popular culture has as its core themes both globalism and nationalism, consumer culture, and traditional *kata* (patterned form). The expressive two-dimensional art plays on the mobile flat images of the digital screen and derives from a popular art tradition that dates back to earlier woodblock printing for mass audiences. Public discourse around new transnational identities is a key focus of these new media that serve cultural memory systems.

Filmmakers in the People's Republic of China began to experiment in the late 1970s and 1980s with previously forbidden topics, such as sexual relationships, the oppression of women, and the many flaws and failures of life in the new society. By far the most powerful and controversial film to be produced in this period was a six-part television documentary, "He shang" (River Elegy). The 1988 production uses the Yellow River as a metaphor for China. The central theme is that of cultural continuity and cultural renewal, familiar to the experiences of all non-Western "modernizing" societies. The question of cultural continuity in the face of profound change seems particularly acute in the case of China. Its history is portrayed in the rapid juxtaposition of various images with historical narration, and contrasts between images

Figure 9.8 Still from the film *Ran* by Kurosawa Akira. Kurosawa's films found global audiences because of their skilled and innovative cinematography as well as their powerful content, which often drew on both Japanese historical themes and on Shakespearean tragedies such as *Macbeth* ("Throne of Blood," 1957) or *King Lear* ("Ran," 1985).

provide dramatic statements about the complexities of culture change. The Yellow River historically was known as "China's Sorrow" because of its periodic flooding of the north China plain and the devastation it wrought. It has been a ubiquitous source of sustenance as well as tragedy for as long as human memory.

The filmmaker Zhang Yimou's *Raise the Red Lantern* (1991) portrayed in vivid and elegant cinematic style the ritualized oppressiveness of the traditional Chinese family system. The film was so powerful an evocation of cultural memory that government censors initially banned it as potentially critical of Communist Party authoritarianism. More recent films have used allegory, but some have drawn on their relationships to global cinema and the Chinese diaspora, from Hong Kong to Paris. In Wang Xiaoshuai's film *The Beijing Bicycle* (2001), the bicycle becomes a symbol of China, suggesting the rapidly changing and diverse perspectives of the protagonist from the rural countryside and the thief who steals his bicycle in the city. These filmmakers seem to be suggesting that China's culture, too, is both a source of strength and a heavy burden that modern Chinese have yet to reconcile with the demands of recent history and the model of the West as they construct a viable cultural memory system for the twenty-first century.

CONCLUSIONS

The traditional Japanese drama form *Noh* can serve as a useful metaphor for the theme of this chapter: the production and reproduction of culture and its transmission as cultural memory through distinctive memory systems. *Noh* plays are retellings of events that took place in the past, and there is usually a resolution, often religious, of some painful conflict that occurred. There is a chorus, somewhat like that in Greek tragedy, that chants background and commentary on the actors and the events. The *Noh* play *Atsumori* is based on an episode in the *Tale of the Heike*, in which the young warrior Atsumori is slain by his enemy Kumagai, although the latter wanted to spare Atsumori because of his youth and beauty. In the *Noh* play, Kumagai has become a priest and encounters the ghost of Atsumori, who forgives him in a demonstration of Buddhist compassion. In the case of *Noh*, the retelling of a past event functions as a means of dramatic catharsis, a way of not only explaining the event but also commemorating and controlling it by recreating it. The point is not the objective recounting of the story but the assignment of meaning to it. In a similar way, as human cultures reproduce themselves over generations they do so in part with intent. That is, people construct memories of the past embedded in cultural forms and practices through which they transmit that past in a purposeful way.

Some cultures stressed the keeping of formal historical records and transmitted the past in an explicit, conscious fashion through written texts, such as the Chinese, or through oral traditions, such as the Mande in West Africa. Other cultures paid greater attention to the transmission of religious ideas or cosmological conceptions, such as those influenced by Hinduism and Buddhism in India and Southeast Asia. But all cultures, whether explicitly or implicitly, found ways to impart a particular understanding of their past through formal and informal means, through institutions and organizations, community rituals and distinctive structures. In this way, they negotiated, produced, and reproduced their unique cultural memory in the very process of expressing and transmitting it. It is no accident that the words "memory" and "commemorate" are related. The institutionalization of memory through commemorative rituals of the past is an essential means of cultural reproduction and transmission.

In this chapter, we have emphasized the transmission of cultural memory through memory systems largely, though not exclusively, within cultures. World historians are not alone in their engagement with the processes of remembering the past. The transmission of ideas and practices across cultures as well as across time occurs using media as diverse as the history book you are reading or the continuing globalization of culture and cuisine you encounter down the street in the twenty-first century. Historians can explore the interaction of cultures through the development of global cultural idioms: information technology's digital web, visual arts and literature in translation crossing national boundaries, music created from the cross-fertilization of different forms, and film and video are defining art forms of the modern world. Their moving images document the speed of change, as well as the universal concerns that shape the human condition and explore the cultural memory of its profound differences and commonalities.

SELECTED REFERENCES

Apter, Andrew (1992) *Black Critics and Kings: The Hermeneutics of Power in Yoruba Society*, Chicago, Ill. and London: University of Chicago Press. Examines how Yoruba forms of ritual and knowledge shape history and resistance.

Assmann, Jan (2005) *Religion and Cultural Memory: Ten Studies*, Palo Alto, Calif.: Stanford University Press. Ten essays explore connections between religion, culture, and memory, arguing that cultural memory is both individual and social.

Connerton, Paul (1989) *How Societies Remember*, Cambridge: Cambridge University Press. This book treats memory as a cultural rather than an individual act, focusing on the means by which societies transmit the past.

Draaisma, Douwe (2000) *Metaphors of Memory: A History of Ideas About the Mind*, Cambridge: Cambridge University Press. Explores multiple frameworks for how human societies have conceptualized memory.

Fabian, Johannes (1996) *Remembering the Present: Painting and Popular History in Zaire*, Berkeley: University of California Press. Provides the example of one African artist's struggle to paint the past in a contemporary context of oppression and silencing:
raises critical questions about what historians do to represent the past and reproduce the power relationships of the present.

Halbwachs, Maurice (1992) *On Collective Memory*, edited, translated, and with an introduction by Lewis A. Coser, Chicago, Ill. and London: University of Chicago Press. Classic work proposing that all memory functions in a collective context.

Roberts, Mary Nooter and Allen F. Roberts (1996) *Luba Art and the Making of History*, New York: Museum for African Art. Brilliant consideration of art as cultural memory in Zaïre.

White, Jr., Lynn (1966) *Medieval Technology and Social Change*, New York: Oxford University Press. Classic view of technology as a memory system.

Zerubavel, Eviatar (2003) *Time Maps: Collective Memory and the Social Shape of the Past*, Chicago, Ill. and London: University of Chicago Press. Explores the social process of creating continuity and discontinuity.

ONLINE RESOURCES

Annenberg/CPB Bridging World History (2004) <http://www.learner.org/channel/courses/world history/>. Multimedia project with interactive website and videos on demand; see especially Units 1 Maps, Time, and World History, 2 History and Memory, 17 Ideas Shape the World, 21 Colonial Identities, 25 Global Popular Culture, and 26 World History and Identity.

CHAPTER 10

Crossing borders

Boundaries, encounters, and frontiers

Among the peoples who lived in provincial Spanish America (today's Mexico) in postconquest times were the Nahua, who, between 1550 and about 1800, produced numerous documents in their own language (Nahuatl) that were written in the European script. The Nahuatl sources show how the indigenous structures and patterns of Nahua culture survived the conquest on a larger scale and for a far longer period of time than if judged on the basis of Spaniards' reports alone. For example, although the Spanish "claimed" and "possessed" the land and determined its boundaries, land was granted to others, often reverting to the indigenous inhabitants. The excerpt from the document below describes a 1583 land grant in the town of San Miguel de Tocuillán, Mexico. Its recipient and the family spokeswoman is Ana:

> Ana spoke and said to her older brother Juan Miguel, "My dear older brother, let us be under your roof for a few days – only a few days. I don't have many children, only my little Juan, the only child. There are only three of us with your brother-in-law Juan."
>
> Then her older brother said, "Very well, my younger sister. Move what you have, let all your things be brought up." . . .
>
> Then Ana said, "Don't let us give you so much trouble; let us take a bit of the precious land of our precious father the saint San Miguel, and there we will build a little house." . . .
>
> Then Juan Francisco said, "Who is going to measure it out?"
>
> Then the lords said, "Who indeed? Other times, wasn't it good old Juan? He'll measure it out."
>
> Then they said to him, "Come, take the cattle prod in your hands and measure it out. Measure out six lengths on all four sides."

> And when he had measured it, then they said, "That's how much land we're giving you."
>
> Then Ana said, "Thank you very much; we appreciate your generosity."
>
> Then the rulers said, "Let it begin right away; don't let the stone concern you, but let it quickly be prepared to begin the foundation."
>
> Then Ana said, "Let's go back and you enjoy a bit more pulque [an alcoholic drink made of the agave plant]."
>
> Then the rulers said, "What more do we wish? We've already had (enough)."
>
> And Ana wept, and her husband wept, when they were given the land.
>
> Then Ana said, "Candles will be burnt, and I will go along providing incense for my precious father the saint San Miguel, because it is on his land that I am building my house." . . .
>
> When all five lords had spoken, everyone embraced.
>
> (James Lockhart, *Nahuas and Spaniards: Postconquest Central Mexican History and Philology*, Stanford and Los Angeles, Calif.: Stanford University Press/UCLA Latin American Center Publications, 1991, pp. 70–4)

Even in the context of their encounter with Spanish invaders who determined new territorial boundaries, Nahua people continued to practice their own customs surrounding boundary setting, including the ritual sharing of food and drink to signify agreement to the land contract. The boundaries drawn here designated the site of a house, but boundaries are also used to map out larger-scale territorial claims, such as those of states, nations, and empires. Spanish *conquistadores*, for example, mapped the Spanish empire in North

America, establishing boundaries at the farthest limits of imperial control. As they did so, the Spaniards relied on native geographical knowledge to find their way through what they called "New Spain."

INTRODUCTION

More than a defining of territory, the drawing of boundaries is also an assertion of identity, encircling, enclosing, and distinguishing self from the "Other." The concept of a boundary thus operates meta-phorically as well as materially: boundaries can refer to the physical body, to social and cultural categories, as well as to geographical space. Zones that lie between boundaries – which may be geographical, cultural, social, or political – are frontiers, spatially fluid arenas of cultural, social, and economic interaction. Like frontier, the term "borderland" is used to refer to areas along borders that are fluid and not yet clearly absorbed by territories on either side, even though both may lay claim to it. Frontiers or borderlands shift, change, and often disappear with the expansion or contraction of empires and the tightening of borders that accom-panies the consolidation of nation-states.

Both empires and states establish walls or other kinds of markers to designate not only territorial but also symbolic political and cultural boundaries. The Great Wall of China marked the division between steppe and sown land and was a powerful symbol of the northern frontier of the Chinese empire after its consolidation in the third century BCE. Hadrian's Wall, built in the early second century CE, distinguished the realm of Roman civilization from that of the "barbarians" north of it in present-day Scotland. In recent times, the Berlin Wall divided East from West during the Cold War, marking the line between communism and the "free world," as did the metaphorical boundaries of the Iron and Bamboo Curtains.

"Encounter," or "contact," describes the experiences of peoples – whether traders, pilgrims, missionaries, settlers, warriors, or tourists – who interact across boundaries or in frontiers and borderlands. Frontier and borderland inhabitants appropriate new cultures, create alliances, engage in conflict, and shift identities. Social mobility is a product of geographic mobility into and within frontiers and borderlands (see Chapter 1).

"Encounter" and "contact" are neutral terms that mask the often violent nature of encounters and the frequently unequal relationships between individuals and groups who experience encounters, although commercial and cultural encounters between relatively equal agents are likely to be peaceful and productive.

Whether on land or sea, boundaries, encounters, and frontiers are all related to the world historical processes of the movement of peoples, state formation, economic exchange, and the spread of religions (see Chapters 1, 4, 6, 7). At the edges of empires or the intersection of cultures, people who crossed boundaries produced hybrid cultures and historical transformations, often subverting the power and authority of states, empires, and nations. In this chapter we will focus on boundaries, encounters, and frontiers as ways of illuminating processes of world historical change from the peripheries rather than the centers. Individuals and groups who drew boundaries, engaged in encounters, and lived in frontier zones were the human agents of historical change.

MAPPING THE WORLD

The drawing of boundaries and exploration of territory in Spanish America described in the beginning of this chapter demanded maps that could represent both the physical landscape and the human claims made on it. From earliest times maps served many different purposes, depending on the needs of the people who made and used them. Early maps were made of various materials, even drawn on stone or made from sticks, such as the charts showing ocean currents and distances between Pacific atolls and islands used by Marshall Islanders.

The development of scientific cartography, however, was crucial to navigation across long distances for purposes of trade, exploration, and the spread of religion. Cartography was related to the sciences of the heavens, and the most famous astronomer-cartographer of the ancient Mediterranean world was Ptolemy (fl. 127–51 CE), the librarian of Alexandria, the center of the Egyptian and Greek community. Ptolemy devised maps of the world that provided a general picture of the relationships of the known oceans and landmasses. Ptolemy was the first to use parallels (of latitude) and meridians (of longitude) in his mapping, and his maps of the world were the best transmitted to medieval Europe from antiquity. Ptolemy was aware that the world was round, but errors, such as his underestimate of the circumference of the globe, hindered the practical use of his geography. However, Ptolemy's miscalculations did have one practical effect: they encouraged Columbus, who, based on information from Ptolemy, had greatly underestimated the distance westward to the Indies when he set off on his first voyage.

Maps have more than practical functions: they are also ways of representing the world, and so often reflect the cultural perspective of the mapmaker's world. Around the time of Ptolemy, the rise of religious cosmography (representations of the cosmos) in Europe retarded the development of scientific cartography. According to Christian cosmology, the world was represented as a disk symbolizing the relationship of man to heaven, and the grid system of coordinates mapping the world in parallels and meridians was abandoned. Just as this was occurring in Europe, a Chinese cartographer-astronomer and seismologist named Zhang Heng (78–139) made use of a grid system to map the world. Although religious cosmography in East Asia also played a role in the creation of maps, Zhang Heng's grid provided an independent, standardized framework for Chinese maps from his time forward to the present day.

Religious cosmography dominated Arab cartography until the world map of the North African scholar al-Idrisi (1099–1166). This sophisticated world map was made in the mid-twelfth century for the Norman ruler of Sicily, Roger II (r. 1132–54), who was known for his interest in foreign ideas and institutions. Al-Idrisi's map was drawn in the Ptolemaic tradition, based on a grid system that resembled Chinese grid maps, extant examples of which can be dated to the mid-twelfth century. It is not clear how the Ptolemaic tradition was transmitted or to what extent Chinese influence played a role in the revival of scientific cartography in Europe, but by around 1300 sea charts were in use in the Mediterranean, testimony to the reintroduction of scientific cartography based on the use of the mariner's compass, which became known in Europe just before 1200.

Refugees fleeing to Italy from Turkish attacks on Constantinople in the fourteenth and fifteenth centuries had carried with them precious manuscripts from the city. Among them were Greek texts of Ptolemy's *Geography*, a second-century work known to Arab cartographers since at least the ninth century CE. During the fifteenth century, Ptolemy's guide to making maps was translated into Latin, and later maps were added and updated. They had an enormous impact on the models and meanings attached to geographical discovery during the next century. The *Geography* included instructions for making map projections – maps that included meridians and parallels, longitudinal and latitudinal lines based on astronomical reckoning.

An important consequence of the invention of printing during the European Renaissance (see Chapter 9) was the creation and distribution of printed maps, including Ptolemy's world map (first printed in Ulm in 1486). The ability to reproduce identical copies permitted multiple copies to circulate and increased the quantity of cartographic information that could be added to or refined on drawn maps. Centers of Renaissance learning, such as Florence and other Italian cities, attracted scholars as well as master craftsmen who constructed maps and model globes during the years of European exploration, a time when the understanding of land and water relationships altered drastically.

The first maps to show the Atlantic world were the manuscript, portolan-style charts used by ship pilots. They were typically drawn on sheepskin. Used to guide ships, portolans were largely concerned with providing detailed, accurate information on shorelines and compass points for navigation, but they lacked the projection system of Ptolemaic maps, an orderly system of meridians and parallels. Juan de La Cosa's portolan-style map of 1500 shows the discoveries of Columbus's voyages and later explorations in South America, together with the voyages of the Englishman John Cabot (1497) along Newfoundland.

The first printed map showing the discoveries in the Americas appeared in Florence in 1506. Unlike de la Cosa's map, the map by Giovanni Contarini and his engraver, Francesco Rosselli, has a regular projection. This map and an engraved 1507 map by Johannes Ruysch, a Dutchman living in Germany, provided the means for the gradual recognition that a new world had been discovered (not the Indies or Cathay, as Columbus had wrongly imagined) and that another continent therefore needed to be added to the cartographic representation of the world. This recognition was dramatically illustrated on Martin Waldeseemüller's 1507 map; his printed map is also the first dated map on which the name "America" appears.

The many advances in knowledge resulting from the geographical exploration of the sixteenth century culminated in the great 1569 world map by Gerardus Mercator of Flanders. Mercator's projection bore lines of constant compass bearing that made it readable by navigators. Finally, a true world navigational chart had been achieved. The Mercator world map included European discoveries that permitted delineation of the Americas, the Strait of Magellan, and other discoveries. It placed Asia, the Americas, Europe, and Africa into a single global vision corresponding to the incorporation of much of the world into a new world system dominated by Europe.

SACRED ENCOUNTERS: CHRISTIAN, ISLAMIC, AND BUDDHIST PILGRIMS

Map-making was stimulated not only by the needs of merchants and explorers to navigate sea or land routes but also by the desire of pilgrims and missionaries to visit sacred sites or to seek new believers in distant places (see Chapter 4). Every culture in the world had

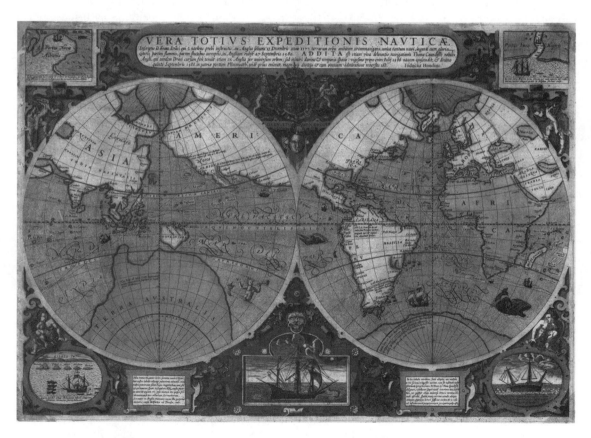

Figure 10.1 Jodocus Hondius, Map of the Earth (1595). Hondius was a Flemish artist, engraver, and cartographer who helped to publicize the earlier work of Gerardus Mercator. In his own map-making, Hondius made use of information gleaned from the voyages of the Englishman, Sir Francis Drake, who circumnavigated the globe in the late 1570s. Hondius's work helped establish Amsterdam as the leading center of cartography in seventeenth-century Europe.

its shrines, recognized and visited by its people as centers of power. Some were in sacred groves of trees, as in the case of Celtic Europe, or caves, as at Zimbabwe in Africa. Others were on mountain tops, on seashores, or in towns. And as some religions stretched far beyond their original cultural boundaries, spread by political or economic pressures and sometimes by persuasion, pilgrims became world travelers whose horizons expanded through encounters with other cultures.

By the fourth century, Christian pilgrims were visiting Palestine from Africa, Europe, and West Asia. At shrines in Bethlehem, Nazareth, and Jerusalem they sought God's intervention for healing, children, and wealth. Some sought God's forgiveness for past sinful acts, and later, after the eleventh century, many came from Europe to fulfill a vow. In part because of the large numbers of homeless wanderers and pilgrims on the road, it was customary Christian practice to open one's door to strangers and provide them with food and drink. Any poor or homeless person had the right and privilege to find shelter in churches. In the tenth century, Christians also traveled to shrines in Europe, most of which were either tombs of saints or churches holding the bones or other relics of saints. By this time towns had sprung up around the holy sites to provide services to the pilgrims. Guides knowing several languages, as well as restaurants and lodgings, were available in these towns. Downpatrick in Ireland, the site of a shrine to Saint Patrick, the patron saint of Ireland, was one such tenth-century resort town; similar towns could be found all over Europe. In eastern Europe, Christian pilgrims more often visited monasteries, seeking mediation with God by the holy men within.

Pilgrimage was more formally structured into Islam. By the tenets of the faith, all Muslims were expected to go on pilgrimage (*hajj*) to Mecca at least once in their lifetime. By the eighth century, that city was receiving thousands of pilgrims from all over West Asia during the month of pilgrimage each year. By the tenth century, still more arrived and from much farther afield: India, West and North Africa, and Spain. Mecca became the largest pilgrimage town site in the world. Muslim pilgrims also visited the tombs of prophets in Palestine and the tombs of saints elsewhere, but in smaller numbers.

The crusading expeditions by which western European Christians sought to recapture Palestine were in part an outgrowth of contacts between Muslims and Christian pilgrims visiting their "Holy Land." Through their experiences and contacts in the eastern Mediterranean, European crusaders were able to regain from the Arabs much knowledge that had been lost after the fall of Rome. In addition to making much Greek knowledge available to western Europe, Arab mathematics, science, and medicine were more advanced than either knowledge or practice in western Europe, and European trade and agriculture had much to learn from Arab business practices and horticulture. Common words such as algebra, alfalfa, and alcohol, and agricultural products such as oranges, nectarines, and eggplants, are examples of what Arab contact gave to western Europe.

Pilgrimage was also an important religious practice throughout Asia. For Hindus, in addition to visits to temple shrines to Shiva, Vishnu, and other gods and goddesses, bathing in the seven main rivers of India, especially in the Ganges, was considered a means of sacred purification. Pilgrimage tours to several temples in succession, each of them located in different parts of India, were popular as well. Hindu pilgrimage, however, except for a few instances in Southeast Asia, was primarily limited to India proper. Buddhists, on the other hand, took part in long-distance pilgrimages to sites associated with the life of the Buddha in India and later to places throughout Asia where Buddhism spread. By the first century CE, Buddhist pilgrims from Central and Southeast Asia, as well as from all over India, regularly visited places in northern India where the Buddha had lived and taught. By the seventh century, the Buddhist pilgrimage network had been expanded to include China, Japan, and much of Southeast Asia. Pilgrims traveled not only to India but also to temples holding relics of the Buddha in such places as Sri Lanka and Burma.

All these long-distance pilgrims returned to their societies different people than when they had left, and they brought knowledge of different cultures as well as material goods – art, literature, foods, clothing. Like returning modern tourists, they passed such knowledge on to their neighbors. Having completed their pilgrimage brought them a higher status and more leverage in business and social affairs in their own societies, and that position helped to disseminate the new knowledge they had acquired on pilgrimage. Routes followed by pilgrims were often also commercial arteries traversed by merchants, such as the Silk Roads across Central Asia or the gold roads in Africa. These caravan routes themselves, along with maritime pathways such as the Indian Ocean, became avenues of encounter, a kind of mobile borderland where religious, cultural, and economic exchanges took place.

SACRED ENCOUNTERS: JESUIT MISSIONARIES IN ASIA, AFRICA, AND THE AMERICAS

Like pilgrims, missionaries also traveled for a religious purpose, but their goal was different: to spread their faith through teaching and good works. One of the most widespread and influential missionary movements in world history was that of the Society of Jesus (Jesuits), approved by the Catholic Church in 1540 as a means to counter the impact of the Protestant Reformation (see Chapter 4). Because they received intensive religious and academic training, in addition to their activities in Europe Jesuits were major participants in the initial encounters between Europeans and peoples in Africa, the Americas, and Asia. They wrote and read accounts of other cultures, spreading information about these culture to Europeans as they sought to disseminate their faith to peoples across the globe.

Soon after the founding of their order, Jesuits made their way to Asia. Mid-sixteenth-century Goa had as many as eighty churches and convents. Following missionary work elsewhere in Asia, Francis Xavier (1506–52), one of the founding members of the Society of Jesus, landed on the southernmost Japanese island of Kyushu in 1549 and there began making converts to Christianity. Calling them "the best people that have yet been discovered," Xavier, like other Jesuits, was favorably impressed by the Japanese and their seemingly well-ordered society.

To the Japanese, Catholicism was the religion of the "southern barbarians," as the Portuguese and Spanish were known, and at first Christianity was assumed to be just another sect of Buddhism, like others that had

reached the shores of Japan from the mainland of Asia. Some of the *daimyo* (lords) of southern Japan believed that conversion to Christianity would bring wealth and power, and so they adopted at least the superficial aspects of the new faith. One of the most powerful *daimyo* in the late sixteenth century, Oda Nobunaga, enjoyed dressing up in Portuguese clothes and wearing a rosary. Jesuits and other missionaries initially gained a substantial number of converts; the sixteenth century is sometimes known as Japan's "Christian century."

Francis Xavier died in 1552 while waiting to gain permission to enter China. But others soon took his place. The most famous was Matteo Ricci (1551–1610), an Italian student of law, mathematics, and science, as well as cartography and mechanics. Ricci carefully prepared the way for Jesuits to be accepted by the Chinese by adopting the style of a Confucian scholar and impressing his Chinese hosts both with European knowledge and with his understanding of Chinese culture. Unlike the experience of the Jesuits in Japan, however, where their efforts at conversion were relatively successful, few Chinese converts were made. Chinese toleration of the Jesuits, and even imperial patronage of them, was largely due to interest in the European scientific and technological knowledge they transmitted. A German Jesuit, Adam Schall von Bell (1591–1666) was appointed court astronomer by the Manchu Qing dynasty; the Belgian Ferdinand Verbiest (1633–88) was similarly appointed court astronomer and became a favorite of the Emperor Kangxi (r. 1662–1722).

Jesuit accommodation to Chinese culture through the acceptance of such practices as Confucian ancestral rites, however, was denounced by competing religious orders in Europe. In the eighteenth century, the pope declared such rituals unacceptable for Chinese Christians to practice, and the influence of Catholic missionaries faded. In neither China nor Japan did Jesuits have more than a peripheral impact, and in both they were eventually expelled.

Probably the best-known African society the Jesuits tackled was the Kongo, a powerful Central African state. Its notoriety and status derived largely from the successful efforts of Portuguese missionaries; Kongolese royalty had converted to Catholicism and made it the state religion. The Kongolese king, Afonso

(r. 1506–45), not only remained a staunch Christian but in his lifetime saw his son Henrique ordained a bishop by Rome, which sent Jesuit missionaries at Afonso's request. Status as a Christian kingdom provided diplomatic and trading privileges to the Kongolese royalty, but the benefits soon gave way to political and economic dependency as Portuguese increasingly became involved in elite culture and local politics. In 1556, when local Portuguese tried to install their own choice as successor after the death of the king, the African commoners rebelled against the Kongolese aristocrats, killing the Europeans and gaining a reputation for xenophobia; henceforward, they resisted outsiders.

The religious conversion of the kings wrought great cultural transformations that seeped down from elite culture and eventually embraced much of Kongolese society. Through the efforts of the Jesuits, elites (including kings) and others became literate in European languages. The Jesuits produced a dictionary of written Kongolese and the correspondence between the kings of Portugal and the Kongo are valuable historical documents.

The transfer of European ideas was not a matter of superimposing them on a pristine canvas in the Kongo. The new beliefs were, rather, incorporated into the matrix of politics and traditional beliefs in ancestors and spirits. This syncretism is especially apparent in the local expression of Catholic rituals. Descriptions of the Jesuits' 1620 canonization feast of Saint Francis Xavier at Luanda in the Kongo suggest something of the interplay and even tensions between African and European beliefs. Luandan bards competed to write praise songs for the new saint. The Portuguese governor, a slave trader from one of the great Jewish finance houses, ordered naval salutes of musketry and night illuminations throughout the city.

The carnival procession associated with the Catholic feast in Luanda was a blend of Mbundu and Kongolese rituals and symbols together with inventive European pagan and Christian rituals. The procession satirically portrayed three African states ("Angola," "Ethiopia," and "Kongo") as three white giants dressed in formal wear accompanied by their "father," the European conqueror portrayed by a black dwarf captured in war. Such occasions permitted unprecedented criticism and role reversals, no doubt serving to relieve tensions and conflicts brought about by the social and religious transformations that were underway.

Other Jesuit activities extended to the Americas, where they helped ensure Europeans' interest in the newly established colonies. Their annual written reports encouraged settlement, and they actively participated in exploration. In 1549, the Jesuits launched what would become one of their largest missionary undertakings among the Guaraní Indians in South America. The missions became known as the Paraguayan Reductions (from the Latin *reducere*, meaning "to lead back" or "to bring into the fold"), and they encompassed thirty towns and more than 80,000 Indians. During the course of their missions, the Jesuits instructed the Guaranís in European language and skills. Embracing European technology and culture, Guaranís became magistrates, sculptors, classical musicians, calligraphers, and builders of baroque cathedrals.

Perhaps the best-known Jesuit explorer in North America was Father Jacques Marquette (1637–75), who was posted to the permanent central mission at Sault Sainte Marie in what is now the upper peninsula of Michigan, a territory inhabited by Huron Indians. Jesuit "missions" were scarcely more than outposts accommodated by Huron agricultural villages. Marquette accompanied voyages from Green Bay on Lake Michigan to the upper Mississippi and down the Arkansas River. Among the Illini in the Illinois country south of Lake Michigan, Marquette observed a high incidence of serial polygamy; others noted the accompanying abusive treatment of women in Illini communities in which the sex ratios were skewed by the reduction of the male population through warfare. In ways that could not have been anticipated by the Jesuit missionaries, Illini women found Catholicism to be a means of empowerment in their own communities.

The daughter of a prominent chief, a woman we know from her priest's records as Marie Rouensa, converted to Catholicism and initially at least rejected marriage to a French fur trader her parents chose for her. Eventually she effected a compromise, agreeing to marry the trader if her parents would convert to Catholicism. They converted, and she married – a monogamous official marriage sanctioned by the Catholic Church in contrast to the polygamous, informal marriages common in her own community where women greatly outnumbered men. She also successfully encouraged other Illini women to adopt the Catholic faith (Sleeper-Smith 2001: ch. 2). While notable, Marie's story is not unique. It provides a compelling example of the ways in which the Great Lakes frontier was a space, a "middle ground," where native peoples negotiated with French fur traders and Jesuit missionaries to secure their own positions. Her story suggests how women in particular were able to use new religious ideas to empower themselves in their own communities.

GENDER BOUNDARIES

Missionaries intentionally crossed cultural boundaries for the purpose of spreading their faith, although the outcomes of their efforts were always inflected by the cultures of their audiences. In both their own societies and those in which they established their missions, social boundaries also influenced the nature of their encounters. Gender was one of the most important social boundaries that circumscribed the thought and behavior of women and men, and profoundly shaped the communities they built (see Chapter 8).

The relationship between gender and religion is extraordinarily complex, ranging from the exclusion of women from spiritual pursuits to the sanctifying of women as having special access to divinity and spiritual power. In its persecution of heresy the Catholic Church in Europe condemned some women as witches, but religious communities often provided a means for women to escape social and cultural restraints on their lives and to acquire education. Education made it possible for women to express their ideas in often powerful literary forms as a means of resistance to restrictive norms within their own society, if not the Church itself. In Spain, Teresa of Avila (1515–82) led the Carmelite order and encouraged women to withdraw from the world to realize true devotion. Her writings and the example of her life inspired other women to become educated and to use their learning to promote the interests of women.

One such woman was Juana Inés de la Cruz (1651–95), a brilliant poet and independent thinker. Born in Mexico, she represents early stirrings of resentment there against control by Catholic Spain.

After a promising career at the court of the viceroy of New Spain, she spent the last thirty years of her life as the nun Sor Juana in a convent on the outskirts of Mexico City. She became a nun in part because that was the only way to be allowed to read, study, and write. The hundreds of poems she wrote are an important contribution to Spanish literature and represent an awakening of early feminist consciousness. "Stubborn men, who accuse women without reason" is the opening line of one of her most famous poems, written in the late seventeenth century while she was living in the convent.

Though Sor Juana's ideas were attacked by Catholic authorities in Mexico, women promoting heterodox beliefs in the New England colonies along the Atlantic seaboard of North America fared even less well. One of the more radical Protestant religious groups in England was the Quakers. The Quakers believed that every man and woman had access to God without the intervention of clergy or the sacraments of the Church. According to Quaker beliefs, both men and women could know the will of God through an internal state of grace, the "Light Within," which enabled them to attain spiritual perfection. Two women, Ann Austin and Mary Fisher, were sent as the first Quaker missionaries to the Puritan Massachusetts Bay Colony in 1620. Because of the radical nature of their beliefs, one of the early Quaker converts, Mary Dyer, was hanged in 1656, along with three men. The independence and assertiveness of women as part of Quaker beliefs threatened the Puritan social and religious order of New England communities.

The suppression of ideas and behavior perceived as a threat to gender hierarchy and community order took a violent turn in the infamous Salem witchcraft trials in 1692, which resulted in the executions of twenty people, most of them women. Accusations of witchcraft because of heretical beliefs or alleged sexual improprieties in New England were reflections of the witchcraft mania that swept England in the seventeenth century. In both cases, social and economic tensions within communities often exacerbated fears of the supernatural and led to accusations that certain individuals were agents of the Devil and threatened the welfare of the communities. By their outspoken expression of religious beliefs, these women crossed clearly defined gender boundaries.

Other transformations of power and identity appeared in the deep divisions and contradictions of the African-Atlantic world, which gave as many opportunities for change as it took away. One of the most successful transformations brought about by the crossing of gender boundaries emerged in the small central African kingdom of Ndongo during a series of disputes over royal succession in 1623. Authority was ultimately grabbed by Ana Nzinga (r. 1624–63), the deceased king's sister. She ruled over Ndongo and even expanded its territory to include Matamba, legitimizing her claim to rule by altering her gender. Queen Nzinga dressed like a man, married multiple "wives" (actually men dressed as women), and carried and used weapons in war and ceremony. Despite the fact that she found it necessary to undergo the transformation of her own gender, the success of her actions wrought lasting change since the majority of her successors were women, not men.

BOUNDARIES, ENCOUNTERS, AND FRONTIERS IN NORTH AMERICA

Both Sor Juana and her counterparts in New England lived in frontier zones of North America. The opening of the Atlantic frontier through the "voyages of discovery" enabled the colonization of North America by Europeans seeking both economic gain and religious freedom. Economic survival in an expanding global economy forced settlers to look back across the Atlantic. Expansion on land defined the colonies as the moving frontier of European culture, commerce, and Christianity, a zone of intensive interactions with indigenous peoples.

Most North American schoolchildren know one version of the story of the Indian Squanto, who brought food to the starving pilgrims of the Plymouth colony in their first dreadful winter and taught them how to cultivate maize. This version established the mythology

Figure 10.2 Anonymous, *Landing of Columbus* (1860). The encounter between Columbus and the peoples of the Caribbean was romanticized in this mid-nineteenth century hand-colored lithograph.

of the American Thanksgiving festival, celebrated annually to commemorate the sharing of food and the cooperative relationship between the pilgrims and the indigenous inhabitants of the land where these refugees from England settled. Similarly, the story of Pocahontas, who pleaded with her father, the chief Powhatan, to spare the life of John Smith and ultimately to ensure the survival of the Virginia colony of Jamestown, has become part of the mythology of the European settlement of the Americas. Rarely, however, is the end of the story for the two Native Americans remembered. Both Squanto and Pocahontas met unhappy fates: Squanto died in exile in his own land because of conflicts with his own people brought about by his relationship with Europeans, and Pocahontas died in England before she could return home.

Powhatan, Pocahontas's father, was the leader of a confederation of tribes that numbered nearly 9,000 in 1607; when the settlers arrived, the English were just another tribe to be dealt with. They came in large boats, carried powerful weapons, dressed oddly, and built in Jamestown – in his territory – a fort they named for their king. In 1614, Powhatan married his daughter Pocahontas to John Rolfe, an Englishman, who brought a new kind of tobacco plant from South America that could be grown in Virginia and sold for profit across the sea. By the time of Powhatan's death in 1617, tobacco plantations were sprouting up throughout his land.

In the same year her father died, Pocahontas, known by her Anglicized Christian name as Rebecca, sat next to her husband, John Rolfe, and King James and Queen Anne at a performance in London of Ben Jonson's play *The Vision of Delight*. This early interracial marriage in American history was the product of an effort to ally the English and Powhatan's people, as well as to bridge the enormous gaps in culture and politics. After Pocahontas's death her husband and their mixed-blood son returned to Virginia, where Rolfe died in an assault by Pocahontas's half-uncle, who had taken her father's place. Though both Pocahontas and John Rolfe met unhappy fates and their union did not become the pattern for relations between Europeans and Native Americans, it demonstrated the unrealized possibilities for accommodation and reconciliation through intermarriage of two vastly different peoples on the North American frontier.

In North America, the strategic corridor of the northeastern frontier was the site of intense struggle between Native Americans, the British, and French colonials. Dozens of fort and battle sites are the scattered remains of the frontier era. The era's commercial rivalry culminated in the French and Indian War (1756–63), which ended after the signing of the Treaty of Paris. The links between Europe and North America were tentative and potentially hostile. Several of the thirteen North American colonies along the Atlantic frontier – Massachusetts, Pennsylvania, and Maryland – were established by nonconformist religious refugees from England. Similarly, early French settlements in New York and Canada were almost always accompanied by priests. Some of the communities founded by Europeans fleeing persecution for their religious beliefs quickly turned their backs on the Atlantic world and pushed westward. Migrants and their descendants crossed the Appalachians in 1760, following a hundred years behind the first French, and they kept expanding.

Religious groups contributed to moving the frontier westward. To the extent that there was never an official religion on the Anglo-American frontier, organized religion was not a formal partner of government as it moved westward across the continent. Much later, groups such as the Mormons moved westward to escape hostility, eventually settling in what would become the state of Utah. Refugees from European religious intolerance, such as Hutterites, Mennonites, and others, also escaped to the empty spaces provided as the American and Canadian frontiers moved westward.

The European introduction of the horse, iron, and the gun to North America brought significant technological additions to frontier life, but they were no less important than the knowledge of geography, locally adapted technology, and foods that indigenous peoples brought to bear on the fur trade and other economic pursuits on the frontier. The impact of European diseases (especially smallpox and including alcoholism, encouraged by the lucrative trade in brandy, whiskey, and other intoxicants) was devastating to indigenous lives and lifestyles.

The final closing of the frontier came about through the removal of culturally assimilated peoples from their ancestral lands, followed by their enforced placement on reservations. By the early nineteenth century in

North America, the extermination of the Indians who refused to become subservient to white rule was predicted by French observer Alexis de Tocqueville, who traveled throughout America and recorded his observations in *Democracy in America* (1835).

BOUNDARIES AND FRONTIERS IN THE RUSSIAN EMPIRE

On the other side of the world from North America, Russia itself was a frontier, both to western Europeans moving eastward and to Asians moving westward.

Beginning with Charlemagne's ninth-century campaign, the Germanic peoples of Europe continued to push western Europe's frontiers east at the expense of the Slavic peoples who inhabited the area from the Danube basin to the Urals. In the late tenth century, the ruler of the principality of Kiev was converted to Eastern Orthodox (Greek as opposed to Latin) Christianity, an event that drew Slavic peoples into the cultural orbit of the Byzantine empire and separated them from the Latin West.

The earliest Russian advance eastward across the Urals occurred during the eleventh century, when Novgorod was the most powerful Russian principality.

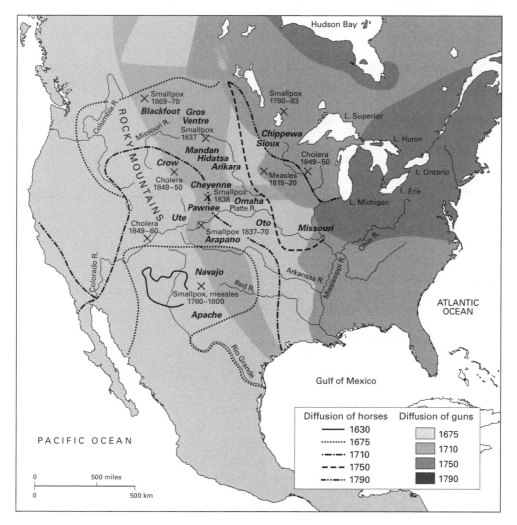

Map 10.1 The diffusion of horses, guns, and disease along the North American frontier.

Novgorod was made vigorous and prosperous by trade with western Europe and sought to exploit the great forests of northeastern Russia for timber, furs, wax, and honey for foreign export. In the thirteenth century, the Mongols under Chinggis Khan subdued and gained control over most of the people of Siberia and continued westward across the Urals, conquering Russia and moving on into the Danube basin. Russia remained the western frontier for subsequent Mongol khans until the sixteenth century. Ivan III (r. 1462–1505), who took the title of tsar (emperor), defeated the Tatars, the last of the Asian masters of Russia following the Mongol conquest. In the course of subduing the Tatars, Ivan III brought Novgorod under his control and Moscow became the center of power in Russia. In 1480, Moscow was declared the "Third Rome," claiming the lost legacy of the Byzantine empire as the center of Eastern Orthodox Christianity. Once the western frontier of Russia at the Urals was secured, Russians pushed their frontiers eastward toward the Urals and subsequently into Siberia.

Russians were lured eastward across Siberia to the Pacific for reasons similar to those that drew Europeans to cross the North American continent from the Atlantic to the Pacific coast. As in North America, one of the main attractions of Siberia was furs – sable, ermine, beaver – but in time exploitation of the land also became important. By the middle of the sixteenth century, Russian entrepreneurs such as the Stroganov family used northern land and sea routes to gain access to Siberia. Thousands of individual Russians, attracted by the potential wealth of the fur trade, crossed into Siberia to explore, build houses in the wilderness, and settle down. They were joined in time by refugees from serfdom (bondage to the land), military conscription, or religious persecution. Such communities settled in the almost inaccessible forests and vast steppes of Siberia, even on territory claimed by the Chinese.

The Russian frontier reached the North Pacific realm in 1648, when a Russian expedition sailed along the northern Arctic coast of Russia and rounded the northeast tip of Siberia, passing into the North Pacific through what came to be called the Bering Strait. Other Siberian expeditions reached the shores of the North Pacific, penetrating the Kamchatka peninsula in 1696. A Russian expedition in the early half of the eighteenth century undertook the task of mapping the North Pacific shores of Siberia. Vitus Bering, a Dane in the employ of Peter the Great, commanded an expedition that in 1728 charted the strait dividing Asia and North America that bears his name.

As Russians reached Pacific shores, Alaska was colonized by them in the first half of the eighteenth century, the only part of the Russian empire in the Americas. But the Russian North American frontier ran into British, Spanish, and American frontiers, and these fellow European powers proved more fatal to Russian interests in Alaska than the indigenes there had been. In contrast, eastward expansion on the Eurasian continent brought the Russian empire into contact with China. As the Russians expanded in the eighteenth century and began pressing the borders of the Chinese empire, they also came up against the

Map 10.2 Russian expansion into Siberia and the North Pacific.

Muslim states of Central Asia, the frontier of the Islamic world.

THE "ABODE OF ISLAM": BOUNDARIES, ENCOUNTERS, AND FRONTIERS IN THE ISLAMIC WORLD

The boundaries of the Islamic world were clearly delineated in Islamic thought: dar al-Islam was the "abode of Islam," the world of Muslim believers who followed Islamic law, and dar al-Harb was the world of infidels who lived outside the law of God. These were religious boundaries that transcended the politics of empires. A third notion developed to encompass the reality of Muslim rule over non-Muslim populations. Dar al-'ahd, "abode of the pact," referred to the agreement between Muslim rulers and their non-Muslim subjects, who were allowed to continue practicing their own religions and keep their property as long as they paid certain taxes.

In al-Andalus (Islamic Spain), Christians and Jews lived under Muslim rule for centuries. The non-Muslim population, called *dhimmi*, were subordinate to Muslims in terms of social and legal status, and subject to Islamic law. There were thus well-defined boundaries in Islamic Spain: the geographical one between Christian kingdoms and Muslim ones; the ideological one between the goals of *reconquista* and *jihad*; and the one between religious communities, Muslims, Christians, and Jews. But the latter boundaries were permeable, and religious identities, malleable. In ninth-century Cordoba, Ibn Antonian, a Christian who converted to Islam and held high office in the government, displayed an impressive command of Arabic and a rich knowledge of Arabic and Islamic culture. Although his career was tainted by political attacks that questioned the authenticity of his conversion, Ibn Antonian's rise in the official bureaucracy of Cordoba is evidence of the potential of conversion to allow substantial mobility across the boundaries between Islam and Christianity.

Elsewhere in the contemporary Islamic world, other examples of fluid identities abound. One of the most extreme cases was that of the Barmakid family, Buddhist priests originally from the Oxus region in Central Asia who converted to Islam and held office in

the Abbasid government in mid-eighth-century Baghdad. Although Islamic rule on the Iberian peninsula came to an end in 1492, with the fall of the last Islamic kingdom of Granada, Islamic empires rose elsewhere that also ruled over populations of ethnic, cultural, and religious diversity.

By the sixteenth century, the Islamic political world was divided into three distinct empires in a zone stretching from North Africa to the Indian sub-continent: the Sunni Ottomans in West Asia and North Africa, the Shi'ite Safavids in Iran and Afghanistan, and the Mughals in India. Each of these empires dominated culturally distinct regions, and each was a composite of languages, cultures, and ethnic groups. Within dar al-Islam, there were not only religious boundaries between Sunni, Shi'ite, and Sufi Islam but also cultural and political frontiers within each Islamic empire. The Mughals incorporated Hindu culture, language, and religion within their empire, and the Ottomans expanded the boundaries of Islam to confront both Christianity and European states.

In addition to representing dar al-Islam in the regions it controlled from North Africa to West Asia, the Ottoman empire straddled both the European and Asian worlds; and although the boundaries between dar al-Islam and dar al-Harb were distinct, they were not impenetrable. With the conquest of Constantinople in 1453, the Ottoman empire began to intrude on Europe's boundaries. The Ottomans took over the heritage of the Byzantine empire along with that of the Abbasid caliphate in Baghdad. This was most visible under the reign of Suleyman the Magnificent (r. 1522–66), the height of Ottoman power, when the Ottoman empire controlled perhaps a quarter of Europe in addition to the entire eastern Mediterranean coast. Ottoman expansion into Europe continued in the sixteenth and seventeenth centuries, but by the eighteenth century European states and the expanding Russian empire significantly reduced the territory controlled by the Ottoman empire.

The Sunni Ottomans were further weakened by frequent wars waged on their eastern frontier against the Shi'ite Safavids of Iran. In 1722, as a result of persecution of its Sunni subjects in the area of modern Afghanistan, revolts broke out in Safavid Iran. The leader of the Afghan revolts invaded Iran and forced the

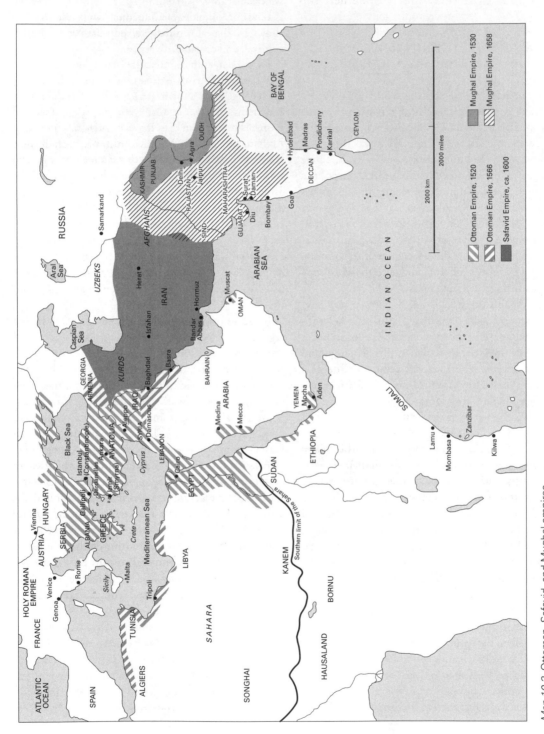

Map 10.3 Ottoman, Safavid, and Mughal empires.

Source: Ottoman and Safavid: Albert Hourani, *A History of the Arab Peoples* (New York: Warner Books, 1991), p. 473

Mughal Empire, 1530

Mughal Empire, 1658

Ottoman Empire, 1520

Ottoman Empire, 1566

Safavid Empire, ca. 1600

2000 miles

2000 km

last Safavid shah to abdicate. By the end of the eighteenth century, the Qajar dynasty took up the legacy of the Safavids and ruled for the next two centuries. Though the borders of Islamic empires, such as that of the Ottomans, defined the political boundaries of Islam, many Muslims dwelled outside these boundaries, from Africa to Asia.

BOUNDARIES AND FRONTIERS OF THE CHINESE EMPIRE

Muslims were also incorporated into the Chinese empire, a political and cultural framework that integrated vastly different peoples, languages, and cultures much as the Ottoman and Mughal empires did. From the perspective of the Chinese empire, the East Asian world shared a common culture with regional variations. Japan, Korea, and Vietnam were all part of this Chinese cultural world, influenced to varying degrees over centuries by Chinese ideas and institutions. The boundaries of Chinese culture, as perceived by Chinese, lay not with distinctions drawn between what was Chinese, Korean, Vietnamese, or Japanese but between Chinese "civilization" and the "barbarians" of the steppes. For centuries the Great Wall had defined the boundary between the pastoral peoples of the steppes and grasslands and the settled agrarian population of China. Alternating patterns of trade and warfare characterized the relations between these two ways of life; and the periodic invasions of nomadic warriors from the north culminated in the thirteenth-century Mongol conquest, when China became part of a Eurasian empire.

After the fall of the Mongols, native Chinese rule was restored in the fourteenth century under the Ming dynasty (1368–1644). The boundaries of Chinese civilization were redefined and two frontiers emerged: a maritime frontier and an inland frontier. The seven voyages undertaken by the Chinese Muslim admiral Zheng He between 1407 and 1433 bore witness both to the seafaring capabilities of the Chinese navy and to the Ming court's desire to command the maritime frontier. Zheng He's Muslim background made him well suited for the task, since many of the countries visited by the expeditions were Muslim. Hailing from the southwestern province of Yunnan ("south of the

clouds"), both Zheng He's father and brother were devout Muslims who had made the pilgrimage to Mecca.

The expeditions were huge in scale: 62 ships, more than 200 support vessels, and nearly 30,000 men made up the first contingent. The final voyage sailed more than 12,000 miles, and altogether the series of expeditions visited at least thirty countries around the rim of the Indian Ocean. Financed and supported by imperial patronage, Zheng He's voyages were designed to display the power of Ming China and to confirm its place as the center of the world, even though they discovered that the world beyond China was larger and more diverse than ever before imagined. Ma Huan (c. 1380–after 1451), who accompanied Zheng He on the voyages, wrote an account of them to record information about the lands and peoples encountered, thus enriching Chinese knowledge of the world.

Unlike their European counterparts later in the century, however, the purpose of the voyages was not to establish a presence in foreign lands, nor to seek either goods or markets, but to confirm the basic order of tributary relations by taking gifts from the Chinese emperor to rulers of other lands and accepting tribute in return. When the winds shifted at court under a new emperor, funding for the voyages was halted because of their great expense and because of distrust of maritime commerce. The government's interest turned instead to the country's inland frontiers and to the consolidation of Chinese civilization in its land-based realm.

A failed invasion of Vietnam in the early fifteenth century, and an expensive war in Korea against a Japanese invasion in the late sixteenth, limited the ability of the Ming state to exert its political control over countries regarded as part of its zone of cultural dominance. More dangerous, however, than the securing of its position in Vietnam and Korea was the threat from beyond the Great Wall. In the mid-sixteenth century, while a powerful coalition of Mongol tribes threatened the northern frontier, another threat emerged from the northeast: the Manchus. Like the Mongol conquest in the thirteenth century, the Manchu conquest in the seventeenth was a culmination of centuries of cultural, political, and economic interaction across frontiers. The Manchu Qing dynasty (1644–1910) brought about the integration of two different ways of life under the military domination of peoples from beyond the Great Wall.

The Manchus were an ethnic group whose homeland lay beyond the Great Wall in the region of modern Manchuria. When they conquered China in the seventeenth century, they carried out policies designed to maintain their ethnic distinction, such as forbidding intermarriage between Chinese and Manchus and prohibiting Manchu women from binding their feet in the manner of Chinese women. Over time, however, Manchus did intermarry with Chinese, and they gradually lost much of their language and culture. Manchu emperors learned Chinese, and in the eighteenth century the great Manchu emperors were skilled calligraphers, poets, painters, and patrons of the arts. Emperor Kangxi (r. 1662–1722), who was adept in the scholarly skills

admired by Chinese while maintaining his equestrian abilities, despaired over his sons' losing their skill at horsemanship and command of the Manchu language.

By the eighteenth century, the Manchu Chinese empire was the largest state in the world, covering nearly 13 million square kilometers (5 million square miles), stretching from the Himalayas to the East China Sea and from the Mongolian border with the Russian empire to Southeast Asia. It encompassed a vast range of territories and peoples and incorporated into its governing apparatus bilingualism, since government documents were written in both Manchu and Chinese, as well as sometimes Mongolian, and both Manchus and Chinese held high offices in the state bureaucracy. A vast array of languages was spoken within the realm of the Manchu Chinese empire, including (in addition to Manchu, Chinese, and Mongolian) Uighur, Miao,

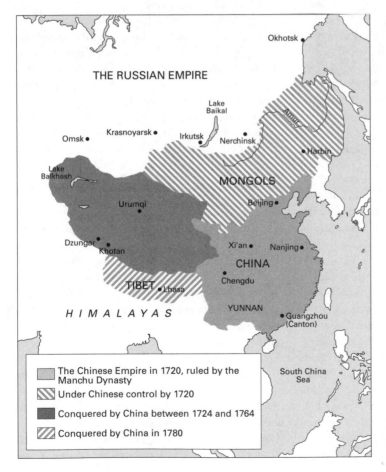

Map 10.4 Chinese expansion, 1720–80.

Source: Richard L. Greaves et al., Civilizations of the World (New York: Harper & Row, 1990), p. 451, with Martin Gilbert, Atlas of Russian History (London: Dorset Press, 1972), p. 44

Tibetan, Zhuang, Arabic, and Korean – and there were a great many religions as well. Besides Confucianism, Buddhism, and Daoism, Tibetan Buddhism or lamaism, Mongolian shamanism, Christianity, and Islam were all practiced by believers scattered throughout the empire. Although political boundaries were relatively fixed, within the empire cultural and religious boundaries were fluid and highly permeable.

A lengthy period of colonization of "new territories" (the modern province of Xinjiang) in the northwest took place in the eighteenth century. A frontier where Indo-Iranian, Islamic, Turkish, Mongol, Tibetan, and Chinese influences had mingled for centuries, Xinjiang initially was a land of exiles for both political and common criminals; only in the late nineteenth century did it become a province within the administrative structure of the Chinese empire. The exiled Chinese scholar Ji Yun, for example, made his journey to Xinjiang in 1769, remarking that he felt as though he had entered another world, one dominated by Uighur merchants in strange clothes and unusual foods and smells. Still, the capital, Urumchi, had a bookstore that sold Chinese classical texts, and Ji Yun found other things to admire and give pleasure, such as the huge chrysanthemums and marigolds he was able to grow in his garden there. Like other frontiers, Xinjiang was a place where people could make miraculous changes in their lives: an emancipated convict made a fortune in 1788 by opening a shop in the city of Ili selling delicacies native to the Yangzi delta region.

The southwestern provinces of Yunnan, Sichuan, and Guizhou had previously been brought under control by the Manchus but remained frontiers of complex ethnic and cultural mixes. The Miao people of Guizhou, for example, inhabited a region that was discovered to have rich mineral deposits and was consequently colonized and developed by the Chinese. The Dai people of Yunnan shared a common ethnic background with the Thais across the border in Southeast Asia, as did mountain-dwelling people, the Meng, who also lived both within China's borders and in Southeast Asia. The Manchu empire, despite its claims to control of its vast realm, was a multicultural empire that accommodated diverse peoples, cultures, and religions that shaped Manchu rule as much as the Manchus ruled them.

MARITIME BOUNDARIES, ENCOUNTERS, AND FRONTIERS

Seas and oceans formed natural boundaries of land masses, and they were also sites of encounters between people who navigated the waters, becoming frontiers in some cases when and where sea-going peoples routinely interacted with each other. Due to its relatively limited size, the Mediterranean was the first major body of water to be traversed on a regular basis by traders transporting goods along its shores as early as the seventh century BCE. Indian merchants were navigating the Indian Ocean to Southeast Asia by the fifth century BCE and were eventually joined, centuries later, by Arab and East African mariners. Not until the fifteenth century CE did technological innovations enable Iberian, English, and Dutch mariners to sail the broad Atlantic. People in Oceania sailed over sometimes long distances from island to island, and inhabitants in Asia and the Americas around the rim of the vast ocean we now know as the Pacific established coastal maritime connections as early as two millennia ago. The regular crossing of the Pacific awaited the whaling vessels and steamships of the nineteenth century.

Despite the navigational challenges encountered by early voyagers across the Mediterranean, Atlantic, Pacific, and Indian oceans, seas and oceans were highways linking land masses, not barriers between them. With the interconnection among these bodies of water established after the circumnavigation of the globe in the late fifteenth century, it was possible to conceive of the world's oceans as one vast body of water connecting lands and people everywhere. Like the peoples and cultures they encircle, seas and oceans have histories, too – names reflect the perception of bodies of water by inhabitants of islands or by those who live on the shores, as well as by those who navigate them.

Oceania was known to its inhabitants as "Our Sea of Islands," but to Europeans who sailed into the waters around Oceania the islands were part of the Pacific (from the Latin for "peaceful") Ocean. The Mediterranean (from the Latin for "middle" and "earth") was *mare nostrum*, "our sea," to the Romans, whose empire at its height completely surrounded this sea. Long after the fall of the Roman empire, a decisive sea battle on the Mediterranean helped to define boundaries on land as well. The Ottoman defeat at Lepanto in 1571 by a coalition of European powers established informal boundaries between largely Christian Europe to the north and west and Muslim North Africa and West Asia to the south and east. The Indian Ocean derives its name from the Arabic *al-bahr al-Hindi*, a direct translation (*Hind* from Sanskrit to Persian to Arabic, and then to Greek and Latin) reflecting the early presence of Arab mariners navigating this huge body of water long before Zheng He's expeditions of the early fifteenth century. The Atlantic Ocean takes its name from Greek mythology and the naming of the Atlas Mountains in Morocco. Before Columbus, the Atlantic referred only to the sea off West Africa, but as European discoveries expanded so did the extent of the Atlantic Ocean.

PIRACY, TRADE, AND THE POLITICS OF FRONTIERS

Naval battles such as that fought at Lepanto in 1571, or the defeat of the Spanish Armada in 1588 that defined the limits of the Spanish empire in Europe, were extensions of land-based political, and sometimes economic, struggles. All the major bodies of water – the Mediterranean, Atlantic, Indian, and Pacific oceans – were also sites of piracy, which sometimes supported and sometimes challenged the political and economic interests of states, empires, and nations. Piracy around the world reveals the permeability of boundaries as much as the defiance of authority.

Piracy can be seen as a form of trade in which individuals exact profits by acting as middlemen between merchants or by forcibly confiscating goods for sale or trade. Piracy everywhere signaled the existence of frontiers – zones of interaction – that emerged where political controls weakened. Vulnerable frontiers were often on the edges or seams of large polities. Piracy was a part of larger economic systems; it reflected instability, disorder, and chaos on the frontiers as much as it created them. At times piracy could also be sponsored by rulers or rebels who sought to use pirates as mercenaries to achieve political ends. Piracy was very much in the eye of the beholder, and whether it was piracy or trade depended entirely on the

perspective of the observer. Found in the Mediterranean, the Indian Ocean, the Atlantic and the Pacific, piracy was an extension of the experiences of boundaries, encounters, and frontiers on land.

Pirates and politics in the South China Sea

During the sixteenth century pirates plagued the southeastern coast of China. As Ming power weakened, central authority was less able to exercise control over local areas. The only officially sanctioned trade was the tribute system, which was under state control. Local officials and merchant entrepreneurs often participated in illicit private trade (behind the backs of state authorities) to enrich themselves and were thus reluctant to impose stringent sanctions against pirates. Initially, small bands of pirates – many of them common people who were excluded from the state trade and forced into piracy by economic circumstances – sporadically raided coastal settlements. Eventually, these groups organized into larger and more effective forces that could undertake private overseas trade in spite of the official sanctions that prohibited it. Their armed fleets plied the coastal waters, and one pirate leader was said to have commanded more than fifty large ships.

After the Manchu invasion and conquest of north China in the mid-seventeenth century, the remnants of the Ming court sought refuge in the south. Bolstered by other exiled supporters, the Ming emperor and his court attempted to stave off Manchu conquest of the south and to restore Ming rule. The deposed emperor was aided in this enterprise by Zheng Chenggong (1624–62), who eventually became one of the most flamboyant and popular figures in the Chinese folk tradition. Known by the Latinized name of Koxinga, given him by the Dutch, he was the son of a Chinese father, who had been baptized a Christian by the Portuguese at Macao, and a Japanese mother from the southern Japanese port of Hirado. In addition to his contacts with the Portuguese and the Japanese, Koxinga's father also dealt with the Spanish at Manila.

A supporter of the Ming against the Manchus, Koxinga controlled much of the southeastern coastline for over a decade in the mid-seventeenth century. The Manchu strategy to defeat Koxinga relied on policies adopted by the Ming in their attempts to eradicate coastal piracy: the restriction of foreign trade. In 1661, Koxinga was forced to retreat to Taiwan, where he expelled the Dutch. Originally named "Formosa" by the Portuguese, Taiwan had become part of the trading empire of the Dutch East India Company earlier in the seventeenth century (see Chapter 6). It was also the home of Chinese emigrants from Fujian along the southeast coast, but it had not been integrated into the Chinese empire during the Ming period.

In the eighteenth-century Cantonese "water world," a maritime zone that straddled the coast from the Pearl River delta at Canton to the Red River Delta in northern Vietnam, piracy became more than a temporary survival strategy for impoverished fishermen. As political events in Vietnam intersected with ongoing ecological changes (overpopulation, land shortage, increased trade), they produced an intensification of piracy and large-scale collective action in the form of

Figure 10.3 Zheng Yisao, Chinese woman pirate. At Zheng Yi's death in 1807, his wife, known only as Zheng Yisao (wife of Zheng), took over her husband's position. She moved rapidly to create personal ties that would bind her husband's followers to her – especially Zhang Bao, the adopted son of Zheng Yi. A former fisherman's son who had been captured by pirates at age 15, Zhang Bao was initiated into piracy by means of a homosexual union with Zheng Yi and rose rapidly through the pirate ranks. To assure Zhang Bao's loyalty to her after her husband's death, Zheng Yisao took him as her lover and eventually married him.

pirate confederations. The Sino-Vietnamese coastline was a "water world" inhabited by pirates who became mercenaries in the service of leaders of the Tay-son Rebellion, which captured power from the reigning Nguyen dynasty in Vietnam between the 1770s and 1790s.

When the Tay-son Rebellion was finally suppressed at the end of the eighteenth century, Chinese pirates who had served the Tay-son leaders returned to China and formed a confederation under the leadership of a man named Zheng Yi. By employing his male relatives as squadron leaders under his command and by marrying his female relatives to his supporters, Zheng Yi merged family loyalties and political power. By 1805, he commanded a confederation of between 50,000 and 70,000 pirates that controlled the coastal trade and fishing industry of the southeastern province of Guangdong, where the major foreign trading port of Canton was located.

Pirates and privateers in the Mediterranean, Indian Ocean, and Atlantic worlds

In other parts of the world, piracy similarly flourished on the boundaries and frontier zones between cultures. During the sixteenth and seventeenth centuries piracy reached its peak in the Mediterranean, where not all pirates opposed state controls. Privateers were pirates licensed by the state. Under the guise of privateering, two equally backed groups, the Barbary Corsairs and the Knights of the Order of Saint John, acted as warriors in an extension of the holy war between the Ottoman Turks and Catholic Spain. Actually, these two privateer forces carried out an exchange of goods between Muslims and Christians that would otherwise have been impossible. So integral were these pirates to the Mediterranean economy that the Ottoman sultan in Constantinople acquiesced to their trade by first appointing the Barbary leader to the post of governor-general of Algiers in 1518 and later making him high admiral of the Ottoman fleets in 1535.

Not unlike the close collaboration between pirates and governments in the Mediterranean, wide-scale backing by the elite who lived along the coastline supported piracy in the English Channel during the Elizabethan era (named after Elizabeth I, r. 1588–1603). Throughout the sixteenth century, British gentry along the southern coast turned quick profits by marketing the prizes of local marauders. These conditions accorded well with the monarchy's aspirations at the time: war with Spain was the prevailing international concern of the Tudor sovereign, but waging war was a problem because the monarchy was still dependent on voluntary forces. By sanctioning the pirates and transforming them into privateers – ships whose captains, during wartime, were given governmental authorizations to attack enemy ports and ships – Elizabeth gained an inexpensive navy at a time when the English monarchy was unable to support its own.

The ambiguity of pirate identities and the constantly changing nature of the environment in which piracy flourished were equally true of the Indian Ocean. In the early eighteenth century an independent mariner named Kanhoji Angre allied with the Maratha confederacy that had formed in resistance to the Mughal empire. He also allied with the Portuguese at Goa, who were interested in challenging the English and Dutch, allies of the Mughals. Kanhoji acted as an independent agent, however, despite his alliance with the Portuguese, one of whose ships he captured. He also captured an English ship carrying a British East India Company official, whose wife he held for ransom (Patricia Risso, "Cross-Cultural Perceptions of Piracy: Maritime Violence in the Western Indian Ocean and Persian Gulf Region during a Long Eighteenth Century," *Journal of World History*, 12, 2 (2001), pp. 293–319). Kanhoji and his counterparts in the Indian Ocean acted very much likes pirates elsewhere. They were by and large independent agents who were made use of by land-based political forces when it suited them. In turn, pirates shifted allies when it suited them and sought to enrich themselves and their supporters whenever and wherever possible.

European hegemony and fierce competition during the eighteenth century crossed the Atlantic into the Caribbean, where it was played out against a background of constant piracy and privateering. Not all piracy was profitable. One of the first pirates to traverse the Atlantic was Paulmier de Gonneville, who successfully seized goods from the Spanish but was not able to recover the costs of his expedition. Merchants and ships had to defend themselves from pirates and privateers.

Privateer status also meant that if they were caught by the enemy, pirates enjoyed the rights of soldiers. If captured, they would be made prisoners rather than hanged as criminals.

Criminals and buccaneers, or runaway bond servants escaping from their contracts of servitude, found safety from exploitation by their masters and profits by becoming pirates in the Caribbean. Buccaneers began as hunters of runaway cattle in Santo Domingo (where they took their name from the *boucan*, a wooden grill for smoking meat), and they soon began to combine hunting with piracy. Buccaneers traversed the Caribbean and Atlantic and reached as far as Madagascar in the Indian Ocean, where they established the Pirate Republic of Libertalia.

Like their counterparts from Asian and Mediterranean waters, pirates of the Caribbean often enjoyed political patronage. Indeed, it was often difficult to discern contraband from legitimate commerce, so unorthodox and unscrupulous were the dealings of merchants and pirates alike. The famous late seventeenth-century buccaneer Henry Morgan sailed under orders from the governor of Jamaica, a British colony. His last expedition was an attempt to seize and pillage Panama City, despite agreements between Spain and England to cease such lawlessness. More devastating to piracy than the British Navigation Acts, which limited trade to British ships, was the 1692 earthquake at Port Royal, Jamaica. The earthquake and subsequent tidal waves pushed this coastal center of piracy, known as the "wickedest city on earth," under the sea.

As in the Cantonese water world, women pirates were not all that unusual in the Caribbean frontiers. Two such women in the Caribbean were Mary Read and Anne Bonny, brought before the governor of Jamaica in 1720, convicted of piracy, and sentenced to hang. Women went to sea as passengers, servants, wives, prostitutes, laundresses, cooks, and, less frequently, as sailors. To avoid controversy and seize what was regarded as male liberty, the women pirates often cross-dressed, wearing men's jackets and pants and carrying pistol or machete or both. Read and Bonny also cursed and swore like any other sailors. Both came out of unconventional households, excelled in their chosen pursuits, and were recognized as leaders on their pirate ships. Such "warrior women" were celebrated around the Atlantic world in popular ballads, suggesting that their impact was both economic and cultural.

FRONTIERS OF RESISTANCE IN THE ATLANTIC WORLD

The Caribbean was not only a site of piracy but also the destination of slave ships originating in West and Central Africa. On the African side of the Atlantic world, large and small states originated in response to the dangers and requirements of the trade in slaves and manufactured goods, including guns. On the edges of these states in the new African frontier, chaos reigned and new cultural identities emerged.

From the slave trade's sixteenth-century beginnings, many of the slaves originated as war captives. Warfare

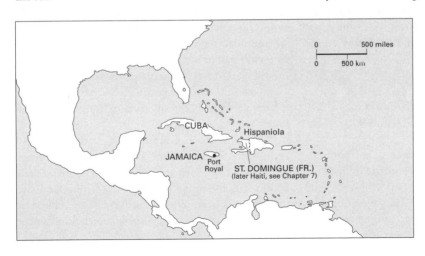

Map 10.5 European rivalry and piracy in the Caribbean, c. 1750.

Source: After Peter Ashdown, Caribbean History in Maps (Trinidad: Longman Caribbean, 1979), p. 20

was fed by fierce economic competition and political rivalry. The slave trade was so lucrative that not only did African states sometimes agree to participate, but freelance African kidnappers and mercenaries also attempted to acquire prisoners of war. Political enemies who were potential slaves and slaves who managed to escape fled the cities and towns near the African coast, taking refuge in less accessible mountains and hills of the interior.

These refugees from the slave trade existed on the frontiers of coastal communities. They organized themselves around powerful lords who preyed on the weak and vulnerable in opposition to the traditional authority of kings and nobility. Out of the amalgam of fringe populations speaking many different languages they came to construct a new and distinct cultural identity called "Jaga" or "Imbangala." Sent to the Americas, troops of "Black Jaguars" fought as mercenaries for European settlers, gaining a reputation for their fierceness in battle.

The transfer of African resistance across the Atlantic occurred when runaway slaves formed communities on the fringes of plantations. Successful communities of runaway slaves (called maroons) functioned much like the scattered communities on the edges of slaving frontiers in Africa. Sometimes they destabilized the authority of would-be oppressors; other times they accommodated and adapted to their new world of living apart. Moreover, runaway slaves often took African patterns of resistance as their organization model. The *quilombos* of Brazil were palisaded war camps modeled on the Jaga structures of Central Africa. These independent settlements followed African political and social examples, using their African identity to instill pride and possibility on the margins of European control.

CULTURAL BOUNDARIES AND FRONTIERS IN THE CARIBBEAN

After the initial European intrusion into the Caribbean decimated or sent into exile most of the indigenous populations, Africans and Europeans dominated the social interactions of the region. They were joined by other Amerindians and by Asians, as well as by the descendants of marriages between persons of various cultures. Creole populations, people born in the Caribbean of admixtures of Hindi, Yoruba, Dane, French, Kongolese (of Central Africa), Ewe and Fon (of coastal West Africa), British, Arawak, Carib, and other cultures, were created by these interactions.

The history of plantation life in the Caribbean reveals the changing boundaries of town and country, as well as the complex and shifting lines that distinguished race, ethnicity, and gender as the Atlantic world came into being. By the eighteenth century, land surveyors and cartographers were important instruments of those who ruled over estates, and they played key roles in the settlement of boundary disputes between claimants. The resulting culture they constructed was also known as "creole."

Some eighteenth- and nineteenth-century surveyors, such as Thomas Harrison (c. 1823–94) of Jamaica, were well versed in botany; they noted their keen observations about fencing materials or agricultural crops on the maps they produced, thus recording valuable historical information. After about 1700, surveyors used a standardized compass and chain, actually 100 metal links that were 66 feet in length and joined with brass rings and counters marking off every ten links. Harrison's cadastral (land survey) map of Jamaica, dating from 1891, required decades of measurements and individual plantation surveys. Such precise lines of demarcation contrast with the complexity of social and cultural interactions that characterized the plantation economy and its society.

Official maps were based on a European ideal notion of plantations and colonies as rigidly ordered and geometrically conceived landscapes. Plantation operations, however, reveal the ambiguity and limited usefulness of such an understanding. Plantations were international, multicultural zones with permeable boundaries. Most inhabitants and workers were non-Europeans, the majority of them African, whose different cultural backgrounds determined their use of space.

Slave provision grounds where Africans grew crops to supplement their diets and the maroon communities living independently in the mountains ran counter to the European maps. African land use patterns followed natural contours of the land and traditional African-derived organizational principles of settlement planning around a center courtyard, market area, or other communal space. Maroon thieves and marauders easily traversed the boundaries of field and farm; on occasion they even left the sanctuary of the territories they had won from the colonizers and appeared in towns, where they stole or traded for the goods they required for their survival. Sometimes maroons were employed by the estate elite as mercenaries and bounty hunters to capture runaway slaves in exchange for their own survival.

The contrast between the plantation Great House (the residence of the slave master) and the slaves' houses was great. Building materials for the great house were brought from abroad to re-create local versions of the houses of European aristocrats, while slaves' houses resembled West and Central African structures in their style and construction out of tropical materials. Persons of African descent who entered the Great House crossed a cultural boundary, as did the few who labored as house servants or became mistresses of the European masters.

The fluidity and permeability of boundaries were equally visible in the islands' informal economies. Internal marketing systems transcended state and plantation controls. Slave-crafted pottery and other goods, including foodstuffs from slave provision grounds, were exchanged among plantations and islands, producing a money economy to the extent that some observers complained about the fact that the smaller denominations of local currencies were almost entirely in the hands of slave marketers and higglers (bargainers). The interplantation access permitted communication across islands and even regions, and no doubt increased the effectiveness of slave resistance before the abolition of slavery in the 1830s.

BOUNDARIES, ENCOUNTERS, AND FRONTIERS OF THE PACIFIC

In contrast to the Caribbean, which was quickly brought under European political hegemony, the vast Pacific remained contested territory despite the European presence. First circumnavigated by Magellan in 1520 to 1521, the Pacific – from Chile to Guam – was far more difficult to explore and exploit.

The first permanent European presence in the South Pacific was Dutch. From their base at Batavia (modern Jakarta), the Dutch sailed southward and in 1597 advanced claims to what was known as "Terra Australis" (Australia). These claims were substantiated by a description of the landing and circumstantial details of the relationship of Australia to New Guinea, which lay to its north. Throughout the seventeenth century, a number of Dutch ships sailed southward from Java. Voyages in 1616 and 1622 made discoveries along the southwest coast of Australia and explored the Gulf of Carpentaria. These expeditions met Aboriginal resistance, but succeeded in providing the earliest descriptions of Australia, where the names given by the Dutch to prominent physical features have been retained, suggesting the outcome of European and Aboriginal conflicts thereafter.

Dutch claims to Australia were successfully challenged by the British, beginning in 1688 when the first English long-distance navigator, William Dampier (1652–1715), sighted Australia. That the continent ultimately became British is due less to Dampier than to Captain James Cook (1728–79), whose three voyages into the Pacific made him the most significant of all European explorers of the Pacific.

During his first (1769) Pacific voyage, Captain Cook coasted along the eastern shores of the Australian continent, and in April 1770 he hoisted the British Union Jack at Botany Bay, claiming what he named New South Wales for England. Following Cook's voyages, the next English to appear in Australia in 1788 were a fleet of settlers who started a British penal colony at Port Jackson on the shores of Botany Bay. Beginning with this settlement, Australia was to retain the character of a penal colony for the next half century, until transportation of convicts from Great Britain was virtually suspended in 1839.

Cook's second expedition, in 1772, went around the Cape of Good Hope at the southern tip of the African continent, across the Indian Ocean to New Zealand, and thence to Tierra del Fuego at the southern tip of South America, around Cape Horn into the Atlantic, and northward to England. This circumnavigation of the globe was a voyage of massive proportions, and the work that Cook did in mapping and sounding made clear the main outlines of the southern portion of the globe substantially as they are known today.

Cook's final expedition in 1778 took him to the North Pacific in search of the long-sought Northwest

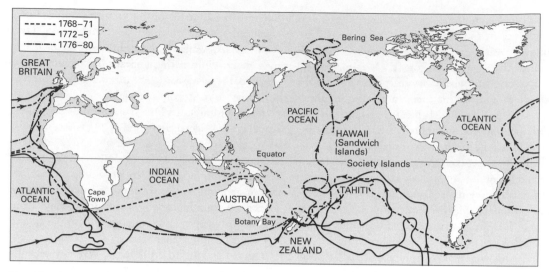

Map 10.6 Cook's voyages.

Source: National Library of Canada

Passage that would connect the Atlantic with the Pacific. On this voyage Cook reached the Hawaiian Islands, which he named the "Sandwich Islands" and claimed for Great Britain. From the first voyage to Hawaii he sailed up the northwest coast of North America, sighting land along the Oregon coast and sailing northward to the Bering Strait between North America and Russia, before returning to Hawaii where he met his death.

Not long after Cook's voyage into the North Pacific, the overland expedition of Alexander Mackenzie (1763–1820) reached the Pacific shores of present-day British Columbia in 1793. Mackenzie's expedition and Captain Cook's voyages established the North Pacific rim as a British frontier. Spanish claims to a North Pacific frontier in Alta California date from the sixteenth century, when Hernán Cortés sent an expedition there and Juan Cabrillo sailed along its coast. Spanish colonization of the region began with the founding of the mission of San Diego de Alcala (1769) by Father Junipero Serra. In the next half century, twenty other mission settlements stretched northwards along the California coast.

The Pacific powerfully attracted the French in the Saint Lawrence Valley and the English along the Atlantic seaboard from the time they arrived and settled in North America in the late sixteenth and early seventeenth centuries, respectively. Initially, they sailed westward in the hope of reaching Asia, and though this proved impossible it did not end the quest for the Northwest Passage, which continued into the nineteenth century. The quest for furs, for land, and in time for natural and human resources, including labor necessary to fuel the ever-developing and ever-expanding market economy, would result in continued European expansion across North America to the Pacific.

Russian expansion eastward across Siberia had also been in part generated by the search for furs, and Russian expansion into the North Pacific was motivated by the same quest. Sea otter furs found early favor in Russian court circles, and a state trading company was developed to exploit the trade. In the 1730s and 1740s, Russians from permanent settlements on Kamchatka were seeking furs in the Kuriles and Aleutians. Initially the Russian fur trade was a form of tribute, with indigenous people providing government agents payments of pelts as tokens of political subjugation. By the end of the eighteenth century private trade was allowed and merchants were increasingly important, especially in trading furs to China in return for Chinese tea, silks, and linens, which the Russians favored almost as much as the British did.

CULINARY AND DRUG ENCOUNTERS

Chinese tea was a commodity traded widely across Eurasia, from Russia to Britain. As the ritual of tea drinking was transported from its origins in China, it eventually became a new cultural custom in both Britain and Russia. From earliest times, the introduction of new foodstuffs was one important consequence of encounters across land and sea. The global exchange of foods and crops altered traditional patterns of consumption. Changes in diet that followed the adoption of new foods significantly transformed human physiology, identity, and cultures.

Foods and drugs used for religious experiences and medicinal cures constantly circulated between cultures. Whether an item was considered medicine, foodstuff, or recreational drug largely depended on its availability and use, as is illustrated by the changing available quantity, value, and use of opium, which was once a tonic for women, or by similar changes in the status of sugar, which was originally considered a spice. By the 1670s the Dutch were willing to trade New York to the British in exchange for the sugar-producing territories of Surinam.

Columbus returned to Europe with tobacco, originally a substance cultivated by indigenous peoples of the Americas for use in religious ceremonies. In Europe, its use as a cure for migraines and its initial condemnation by King James I in 1604 and by Pope Innocent X in 1650 were soon overcome by exceedingly popular recreational use. Though this indulgence was a male prerogative, European trade spread the knowledge of (and vocabulary for) tobacco from Lapland to Africa, where men and women smoked pipes and inhaled other substances for recreation and for the hallucinogenic and religious experiences that resulted. By the 1790s tobacco and opium were routinely smoked together in China, despite prohibitions of the Ming era. The Spanish began to use other substances, such as quinine, extracted from the bark of the South American cinchona tree, against malaria by 1638. The resulting protection and curative effects subsequently enabled Europeans to expand into more tropical parts of the world.

The era between 1500 and 1800 introduced new foods and beverages, including coffee from Africa and the Ottoman empire to North Africa and Europe. The first coffeehouse in Constantinople was established in 1554 and in Oxford, England, in 1650, where university students eagerly adopted the new drink. Both parts of the world relied on beans from Mocha, near Aden, at the southern tip of the Red Sea, for their supplies. In the eighteenth century, the Dutch began to grow coffee in Java, as did the English in the Caribbean. Chinese tea was known for some time before it was eagerly adopted in Japan and Russia; it first sold in England in the mid-seventeenth century. One pound of tea leaves could produce almost 300 cups of the drink; by the end of the eighteenth century, 1.8 million pounds of tea were consumed annually in England.

From the opposite direction, chocolate traveled from the Americas to Europe, and its trade was initially monopolized by Spain and Portugal. In Aztec society, cacao was a luxury item; the beans were used as currency and prepared in many different ways. In sixteenth-century Mexico cacao beans were dried, roasted, and then pounded to a paste with water; spices were added, and the mixture was shaken into a froth. The concoction was offered to early Spanish visitors at a banquet; they confronted the mixture with apprehension and fear. However, popular European opinion soon agreed with Bernardino de Sahagun, a Jesuit observer, who stated that "it gladdens one, refreshes one, consoles one, invigorates one."

The increasing populations of Europe, Africa, and Asia selectively embraced other crops from the Americas: the potato, the tomato, and maize. The potato reached England via Drake's voyage from Colombia, and it was immediately put into cultivation, though at first as an ornamental plant rather than as a food. As late as 1774, Prussian famine victims of Kolberg refused to touch a wagonload of potatoes sent by Frederick the Great. The potato, which originated in the Andes, enabled a huge population expansion to occur in Ireland after it was accepted there. The Irish reliance on a single variety of the potato as a staple, however, created a devastating dependence, as nineteenth-century famines made abundantly clear.

Population in China increased dramatically and cuisines were altered, thanks to the introduction of maize, sweet potatoes, and peanuts after 1500. In West Africa the introduction of the groundnut (peanut), chili pepper, cassava, tomato, and maize from the

Americas provided the basis for agricultural production on marginal lands and population expansion and supported diets during the transshipment of slaves. By the end of the eighteenth century these foods had become defining staples of local cuisine and were demanded by slaves on trans-Atlantic voyages, even while eschewed by their European masters.

South Asian diets were also significantly transformed after 1500. The establishment of Mughal rule in India brought new everyday foods and methods of food preparation. Kebabs made of bite-sized meats grilled on spits, pilafs (dishes of rice with shredded meat), fruits served with meats, nuts (sweetmeats), and the wrapping of foods with delicate sheets of hammered gold and silver (easily absorbed by the body), all created a sumptuous and distinctive cuisine. The introduction of peppers from the Americas forever altered the taste of curry blends of spice mixtures, which were in turn carried from the Indian subcontinent to the markets and cuisines of Africa, England, and other parts of Asia, and eventually back to the Caribbean.

BOUNDARIES OF THE NEW IMPERIALISM

Culinary and drug exchanges were just one aspect of global encounters beginning in the sixteenth century. As soon as Europeans began to explore and map newly discovered lands in Africa, Asia, and the Americas, they laid claim to them. By the nineteenth century, European colonial powers were busily redrawing the maps of continents. The Berlin Conference in 1885 created new boundaries for people under the control of European empires, which jostled with each other for their share of the riches of the African continent (see Chapter 7).

In late nineteenth-century China, Europeans adopted "spheres of influence," zones of commercial interests and political influence that inflicted humiliation on the weakened Qing dynasty and helped to bring about its eventual collapse. Although China was never directly colonized, unlike most of the rest of Asia (excepting Japan), it was carved up into "spheres of influence." Earlier, during the Opium Wars of the mid-nineteenth century, the forced opening of treaty ports employed the concept of "extraterritoriality,"

which meant that foreigners residing within Chinese treaty ports, such as Shanghai, were subject to their own laws rather than those of the Chinese (see Chapters 6, 7). This concept drew a boundary around foreigners living within the borders of the Chinese empire, effectively excluding them from its domain by creating enclaves. Foreign intrusion helped to precipitate rebellion and eventually the revolution that overthrew the Qing regime, ultimately leading to the founding of the modern nation-state in China.

NATIONAL BORDERS AND TRANSNATIONAL FRONTIERS

Reservations for the native populations – "First Nations" in Canada – of both the United States and Canada were also enclaves within the borders of these North American nation-states (see Chapter 7). They were territories that set apart one population, displaced from their homeland, to control and contain them, though not without resistance and conflict. Similar conflicts between indigenous peoples and the growing power of nation-states took place in South America. The eastern Andes and Chaco frontier, which today overlaps the borders of three different nation-states (Argentina, Bolivia, and Paraguay), in the nineteenth and early twentieth centuries was the site of ongoing resistance on the part of Indian peoples to the imposition of state power in the region. The conflicts eventually concluded with Indian defeat in a war fought between Bolivia and Paraguay in the 1930s (known as the Chaco War, 1932–5). Initially penetrated by Franciscan missions, this frontier zone was later the focus of nation-building through the forced acquisition of territory and labor. This frontier closed with the Chaco War, and most indigenous peoples were driven out to seek refuge elsewhere or be taken to prison camp.

Thailand's experience offers a different perspective on the relationship between imperialism, boundaries, and the nation. Like other states in Southeast Asia, Thailand's boundaries were elastic and permeable. The Thai state incorporated people of various ethnic identities, besides the Thai (also known as Dai or Tai). When the British and French colonized large parts of insular and mainland Southeast Asia, the Thai

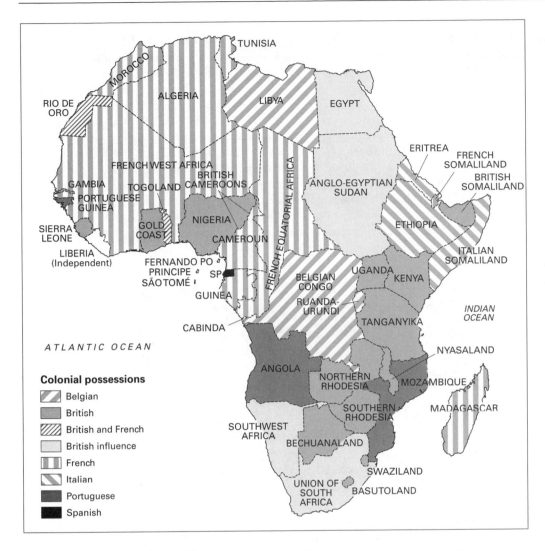

Map 10.7 Colonial boundaries in Africa.

kingdom quickly tightened its borders and began to construct the geographical body of the nation in order to resist the threat of colonization. Using maps and history to legitimize the new nation-state of Thailand that was coming into being, King Mongkut (r. 1851–68) and his son Chulalongkorn led Westernizing and modernizing reforms to maintain their independence in the face of British and French imperialism. Sharply demarcating territorial borders in a way that departed from traditional ideas of geographical space was an important part of this process. The modern map of Thailand clearly identifies the borders of the state, though the "geo-body" of the Thai nation, in the words of Thongchai Winichakul, is a historical and geographical fiction. Despite the official delineation of Thailand's national boundaries, its borders remain porous in many ways. The Golden Triangle, for example, is a geographic term that designates a frontier zone overlapping the national borders of Burma, Thailand, and Cambodia, the site of major drug trafficking beyond the control of any of these state authorities.

BOX 10.1 INDIANS AND ANGLO-INDIANS: *THE YOUNG LADY'S TOILET* (1842)

From "Sketches illustrating the manners and customs of Indians and Anglo-Indians," this nineteenth-century illustration was a visual means to familiarize British people with a foreign culture that was rapidly becoming part of the British empire. It shows a young Englishwoman in Victorian dress, attended at her toilet by Indian servants wearing native dress. Both the women's apparel (and that of what appears to be a very young male servant) and the physical surroundings suggest cultural differences in dress and décor that were traversed in the context of colonialism. In addition to the Indian servants, the room is Indian in its furnishings and evocative of the natural locale: the decorated screen, the parrot, the rush flooring, the canopy. In other ways, the scene could as well be in a young lady's bedroom in Victorian England: the elegant vanity and mirror and the portrait of a male officer hanging on the wall, possibly her fiancé or her father or another male relative. Even the Kashmiri shawl carelessly draped at the young lady's side could be found in nineteenth-century England as well as India.

Originally woven by Indian craftsmen from fine goats' hair produced in the far northern reaches of Kashmir, Kashmiri shawls were sold in markets across Asia, from Persia to China. Eventually their popularity spread to Europe and even across the Atlantic. Napoleon brought Kashmiri shawls for Empress Josephine, and they became fashionable among wealthy Parisians. The characteristic teardrop with a bent tip design is visible on the shawl here, a design that originated as a flower but became known after about 1850 as "paisley" for the Scottish town of Paisley where imitations of Kashmiri shawls were produced in the first half of the nineteenth century. Originally, merchants and agents of the British East India Company bought Kashmiri shawls as souvenirs and gifts, and as they gained in popularity among both the British population in India and as luxury items at home, British manufacturers sought ways to produce them more cheaply using industrial technology to replicate their fabric and design.

Kashmiri shawls, whether genuine or imitation, remained valuable luxury commodities in European as well as Indian society. In Europe and North America the cloth could be made into men's vests or dressing gowns, draped over pianos, as well as worn by women. At the time of this illustration, Kashmiri shawls were regarded as desirable items for a young woman's bridal trousseau. Just as the story of Kashmiri shawls weaves together the colonial appropriation of an Indian handicraft industry with the cross-cultural appreciation of fine cloth with beautiful designs, this illustration portrays both the richness of blended cultures and the dominance and submission of colonial interactions clearly depicted in the Indian servants attending the English young lady.

CONCLUSIONS

Twentieth-century global wars were precipitated in part by conflicts over national borders, and the end of these wars generated new states with new borders (see Chapter 11). In the aftermath of the First World War, efforts were made to create a supranational body, the League of Nations, and the Second World War saw the realization of those efforts in the United Nations. Still, nationalism and the borders of nation-states remained a primary focus of attention throughout the twentieth century. The decolonization of the post-Second World War era yielded many new states, and there was no decrease in the number of border conflicts. To the contrary, as the number of states multiplied so did the conflicts. State borders did not necessarily align with the geographical boundaries of ethnic groups, but there was a pervasive expectation that they should. This has led to the fracturing of many nations, such as Yugoslavia. The break-up of the Soviet Union in 1991 created fifteen new nations based largely – though not exclusively – on ethnic identities (see Chapter 7).

Borders are both symbols and reality, and they are also dual in meaning. Borders are bridges, along which migrants, refugees, workers, tourists, and traders move. As nation-states seek to protect their internal sovereignty and control, borders are also barriers to movement, defining by inclusion and exclusion those who are part of the nation and those who are not. The US–Mexican border is the historical consequence of the borderlands between New Spain and the United States disappearing as the US expanded its territorial grasp in the nineteenth century and established a border along the Rio Grande. In the twenty-first century, the US government expends substantial resources to try to keep Mexican immigrants from crossing that border, while US citizens cross in the other direction for tourism, shopping, and drug trafficking. Just as Ana (see p. 259) negotiated the shifting boundaries of her world in 1583, so do countless modern citizens of today's world negotiate, create, and cross borders.

Other forces beyond border-crossing groups and individuals blur the boundaries between nations and weaken the effectiveness of passports, visas, and other documents of citizenship used by states to exclude some and include others. Multinational corporations elude the grasp of national governments and create their own rhythms of continuity and change in response to the global marketplace and international investment. Technology has enabled transnational communication that has transformed political, economic, social, and cultural identities across the globe.

This process has had a double-edged consequence: as diasporic identities multiply, the nation-state seems reduced in importance; but at the same time, as consciousness of separate ethnic and religious identities increases, there is a counter-trend that produces new nationalisms. In this context, it is possible to imagine a borderless state made up of individuals who identify as a nation, but without "real" borders and able to communicate around the world instantly. Not unlike Benedict Anderson's "imagined community," these formations may herald a new kind of "internationalism" fostered by the technologies of the twenty-first century in which borderless virtual communities become the primary source of identities, and hybrid or creole cultures are the norm, not the exception.

SELECTED REFERENCES

Anderson, Malcolm (1996) *Frontiers: Territory and State Formation in the Modern World*, Cambridge: Polity Press. A global treatment of the concept of frontiers in the context of modern nation-states and international borders.

Axtell, James (1992) *Beyond 1492: Encounters in Colonial North America*, New York: Oxford University Press. Problematizing the concept of encounter in the context of colonial North America by focusing on the strategies that native peoples used to forge new identities in the face of European invasion.

Ballantyne, Tony and Antoinette Burton (2005) *Bodies in Contact: Rethinking Colonial Encounters in World History*, Durham, N.C. and London: Duke University Press. A collection of innovative articles that examine gender, sexuality, and the body in relation to colonialism and imperialism.

Barfield, Thomas J. (1989) *The Perilous Frontier: Nomadic Empires and China, 221 BC to AD 1757*, Cambridge, Mass. and Oxford: Blackwell. China's interaction with nomadic peoples and empires from its unification through the eighteenth century when China was ruled by the last of these empires.

Bentley, Jerry H. (1993) *Old World Encounters: Cross-Cultural Contacts and Exchanges in Pre-Modern Times*, New York: Oxford University Press. Cross-cultural encounters before 1500 examined through the spread of religion, empire, and trade in Afro-Eurasia.

Donnan, Hastings and Thomas M. Wilson (1999) *Borders: Frontiers of Identity, Nation, and State*, Oxford and New York: Berg. An interdisciplinary perspective grounded in anthropology that looks at borders in relation to transformations of identity in nations and states.

Klein, Bernard and Gesa Mackenthun, eds (2004) *Sea Changes: Historicizing the Ocean*, New York: Routledge. A collection of interdisciplinary articles offering new perspectives on the shaping of cultural identities through shifting conceptions of oceans.

Murray, Dian H. (1987) *Pirates of the South China Coast, 1790–1810*, Stanford, Calif.: Stanford University Press. A study of Sino-Vietnamese piracy in the "water world" of the eighteenth-century South China Sea.

Power, Daniel and Naomi Standen, eds (1999) *Frontiers in Question: Eurasian Borderlands, 700–1700*, New York: St Martin's Press. A collection of articles on the concept of the frontier in premodern Eurasia applied to a variety of case studies ranging from the Iberian peninsula to China.

Sleeper-Smith, Susan (2001) *Indian Women and French Men: Rethinking Cultural Encounter in the Western Great Lakes*, Amherst: University of Massachusetts Press. A study of the negotiation of gender and power by Native American women in the Great Lakes region of North America during the colonial era.

Thrower, Norman ([1972] 1996) *Maps and Civilization: Cartography in Culture and Society*, Chicago, Ill.: University of Chicago Press. The nature and uses of maps from prehistoric times to the present in relation to culture and society.

Weber, David J. (1992) *The Spanish Frontier in North America*, New Haven, Conn.: Yale University Press. A comprehensive study of conflict and accommodation between Spaniards and Native Americans on the North American frontier as these experiences shaped new societies.

Winichakul, Thongchai (1994) *Siam Mapped: A History of the Geo-Body of a Nation*, Honolulu: University of Hawaii Press. An argument that the modern nation of Thailand is a geographical construct created in response to the drawing of defined territorial boundaries in Southeast Asia by nineteenth-century imperial powers.

ONLINE RESOURCES

Annenberg/CPB Bridging World History (2004) <http://www.learner.org/channel/courses/world history/>. Multimedia project with interactive website and videos on demand; see especially Units 7 The Spread of Religions, 9 Connections Across Land, 10 Connections Across Water, 15 Early Global Commodities, 16 Food, Demographics, and Culture, 24 Globalization and Economics, 25 Global Popular Culture.

Electronic Cultural Atlas Initiative <http://ecai.org/>. Based at the University of California at Berkeley, this ongoing project uses both time and space to map human cultures and historical change.

CHAPTER 11

Imagining the future

The crossroads of world history

The Yoruba diviner Babalawo Kolawole Ositola sits before a carved wooden tray (*opon*) in the Porogun Quarter of the city of Ijebu-Ode, Nigeria. He begins the divination ritual in which he will explain the present and predict the future by invoking the past. First he traces the crossroads pattern, two lines that intersect at a right angle, in *irosun* powder on the surface of the tray. The crossroads symbolize the meeting place of all directions, all forces. Like any busy intersection, the crossroads from a place of danger and confusion that arises with the opportunity to change direction. The Yoruba experience of the universe is expressed by the carvings on the *opon* and the words of the diviner that speak of continuous change and transformation, amidst the social realities of interaction and interdependence. The divination will become a dialogue with the ancestors and spiritual forces. The divine messenger, the deity Esu/Elegba, will be called upon to assist with the deeper truths about nature and the dangers and ambiguities of human communication. Yoruba divination sculpture reflects an ideal world of balance: humans are in the balance with nature and the unseen forces of agency and energy; the past is in balance with the future. According to the Yoruba scholar Robert Farris Thompson, "If there is anything to learn from [Esu] the god of the crossroads, it is that all is not as it seems to be."

Not all social visions required the intervention of specialists in unseen realms. The Yoruba cultural metaphor of a crossroads reflects a far more universal human vision, which imagines the balancing of paired, opposing ideas – such as good and evil, war and peace. The certainty of religious fervor and the attachment to ideas of ethnic, cultural, or national identity have empowered individuals and societies to create goodwill and security as well as warfare and genocide. The same beliefs and ideas shape personal identity or community

solidarity in the modern world. When they intensify to extremes, these beliefs can provide individuals and groups with the strength not to create peaceful and integrative communities, but rather to use violence to kill, as Nobel laureate Amartya Sen argued in his book *Identity and Violence: The Illusion of Destiny* (2006). How has conflict shaped world history in the past and in the present? How have societies achieved balance

Figure 11.1 Babalawo Kolawole Ositola begins the divination ritual in Ijebu-Ode, Nigeria, 1982. Photo: Margaret Thompson Drewal.

among individual and community identities rooted in differing beliefs and ways of life, and pursued visions of a better world?

INTRODUCTION

Throughout history, conflict among societies has often been expressed in war, although the means for conducting warfare has changed from sticks and stones to nuclear weapons and chemical poisons. The fifth-century BCE Greek city-state Sparta was organized around the goal of war, cherishing martial values and training Spartan children to be soldiers. For the Aztec, humans lived against the backdrop of the daily cosmic battle of the sun across the sky. The culture of the

Figure 11.2 Greek vase of the black-figure period by the artist Exekias, showing Achilles and Ajax playing draughts but with weapons and military helmets alongside.

Yanomami people of the Amazon basin became known for the anthropological descriptions of their warfare – highly ritualized, constant conflict against their neighbors enabled men to obtain women for wives as well as other resources required for their material and spiritual survival.

Conflict both within and among societies, whether leading to war or not, has frequently been brought about by the pursuit of either religious or secular visions of the ideal society. Seeking utopia, societies have as often created its opposite, dystopia. One of the motivating forces in the twentieth-century creation of the field of world history was the possibility of understanding the global past as a reservoir of ideas about our shared future. What does world history tell us about the possibilities for humans to achieve what they have imagined? This concluding chapter examines the role of ideal visions of society against the backdrop of the realities of conflict in determining the success of ordinary and exceptional humans in creating the worlds they imagined. How did humans use these ideas to create balance or disorder in the variety of human experience? To what extent does the imagined world define our human future as much as it does our shared past?

IMAGINED WORLDS

Searching world history for imagined worlds, we find the envisioning of ideal societies almost as early as the first expressions of human thought in written and oral traditions and in art. Mythological depictions of the origins of the human and natural worlds were explanations drawn largely from experience of the world as well as imagination. Embedded in these myths were ideals of family and community life: how people should live together, share resources, and choose leaders among them. Religions inspired the imagination of worlds beyond the realm of human experience, and these worlds embodied the fullest realization of what it meant to be human as well as the most terrible ordeals human beings could suffer. Whether Buddhist, Christian, or Islamic, the envisioning of both heavens and hells encouraged people to believe and to practice their beliefs as individuals and as members of a community.

Religious visions also inspired millenarian movements that projected the hope of a new age – the coming of the Millennium that would usher in a new world – and exhorted followers to act to bring about the new age. Millenarian movements are found around the world and in many diverse religious settings, including Buddhist and Christian as well as numerous syncretic traditions (see Chapter 4). They arise from different historical conditions and often become violent in response to social, political, and economic oppression. There were Christian millenarian movements in medieval Europe and Buddhist ones in medieval China. The massive Taiping Rebellion in mid-nineteenth-century China – which resulted in the deaths of perhaps 20 million people – coalesced under the leadership of Hong Xiuquan (1811–54), who had a vision that he was the younger brother of Jesus Christ, sent by their father to bring the Chinese people back to their original belief in God and to create a "Heavenly Kingdom of Great Peace (Taiping)." Arawakan Indians in the northwest Amazon followed an indigenous shaman and millenarian leader, Venancio Kamiko, during the 1850s to resist colonial encroachment on their world. In the Kongo, a millenarian movement originated with the claims of a young Kongolese girl to be Saint Anthony in the first decade of the eighteenth century. Beatriz Kimpa Vita announced that she had come to teach the true religion: priests were imposters, God and his angels were black, and the kingdom of Heaven was near the Kongo country, where Christ had really lived and died. Suggesting such a radical alternative amidst the clash of cultures was a dangerous thing, and the founder of the movement was executed. However, the movement itself survived and became the first Zionist African Church; the name "Zion" referred to the biblical city that was a symbol of hope.

Along with religious visionaries, philosophers, artists, historians, and writers around the world have produced secular visions of perfect societies. In his *Republic*, the Greek philosopher Plato (427–347 BCE) described the ideal state as a commonwealth ruled by a philosopher-king. The material world of phenomena, Plato believed, is a shadow world dimly reflecting the real world of ideas. It is this world of ideas that philosopher-kings understand and what qualifies them to govern. Beyond the world of things and experiences, apprehended by the senses, there is another, more fundamental world of eternal forms and types. In everything we experience through the senses there is an essence of this unchanging reality, independent of the material "accidents" that surround it. The "accidents" of everyday life are transcended by eternal essences and forms, which are the goals of knowledge. The philosopher-king is by education, if not by desire, able to guide the state out of the chaos and illusions of the external world of sense phenomena to eternal patterns and order.

The Chinese philosopher Confucius in the sixth century BCE taught that the ideal society existed in the past, under the wise rule of the sage kings of antiquity. The notion of the Mandate of Heaven that developed as the sanction for rule in imperial China held that a ruler's responsibility was to maintain the order of Heaven in human society; if and when the ruler failed, then the Mandate was bestowed on a new ruler. The key to social harmony for Confucius and his followers was the proper performance of ritual, ceremonial practices elaborated in a text compiled between the late first century BCE and early first century CE. In this text, *The Record of Rites*, society under the sage kings of antiquity is depicted as an age of the "Great Harmony" in which everyone has his or her tasks and place, and all are cared for according to need. This ideal was resurrected by a late nineteenth-century Chinese reformer, Kang Youwei (1858–1927), who promoted the ideal society of the Great Harmony as central to Confucian thought. He argued that Confucius would have supported the modern reforms Kang advocated had he lived at the same time.

The term "utopia," used to describe an ideal society, was coined from the Greek by Sir Thomas More in writing about an imaginary island world, *Utopia* (1516), where private property did not exist and religious tolerance reigned. Like many utopias, this one was inspired by the writer's observations of his contemporary world, but also by reports from the "New World." Written nearly a century after More's *Utopia*, William Shakespeare's play *The Tempest* (1611) takes place on an island referred to as a "brave new world," in which there was "no use of service, of riches, or of poverty." To Europeans, this New World was a virgin space, a paradise filled with promise of human possibility; to indigenous peoples of the New World, the European presence brought death and destruction.

Paired with the concept of utopia is that of dystopia, the opposite imagined world of utter deprivation and misery. Long the domain of science fiction writers, one of the best-known dystopias is that of George Orwell's *1984* (1949), in which the main character is gradually deprived of his individual humanity to be absorbed by the "Big Brother" of the twentieth-century totalitarian state. Aldous Huxley's dystopian novel, *Brave New World* (1932), took its name from the phrase used in Shakespeare's *The Tempest*, and portrays a world where all human needs are satisfied and there is no war or poverty but also no religion, philosophy, family, or cultural difference to enrich human life. Drugged on *soma*, people in Huxley's *Brave New World* escape from anything unpleasant, including painful emotions and memories. As Huxley's novel makes clear through its depiction of a utopian world that is in fact a dystopia, visions of ideal societies – freedom from want, hunger, fear – did not always produce desirable results. The technological advances that made possible the worlds described by Orwell and Huxley were largely a product of the Industrial Revolution, which generated its own competing visions of utopia and dystopia.

CRITIQUES OF INDUSTRIALISM AND VISIONS OF COMMUNITY

As much as the explorations of the New World influenced utopian visions among Europeans in the sixteenth and seventeenth centuries, the impact of the Industrial Revolution also evoked a powerful and varied response among European thinkers. Some reacted to the technological promises of the Industrial Revolution with ideas about how to utilize what technology offered to create ideal communities; others saw the conditions produced for workers by the Industrial Revolution as something to be struggled against.

Robert Owen (1771–1858) was a practicing and successful textile mill entrepreneur who sought to mitigate the most disturbing effects of industrial capitalism: a decline in personal contact between employer and employee that characterized the factory mode of production and resulted in the alienation of laborer from employer. Owen's solution was not to return to precapitalist, preindustrial society, but to create a paternalistic industrial communalism based on the mutual interests of workers and employers. His scheme was implemented in communities such as New Lanark in Scotland and New Harmony in Indiana. The New Lanark factory community contained a mill and cooperative housing and stores. Free schooling was provided, for Owen believed that educated workers were better workers.

John Stuart Mill's (1806–73) father had been an enthusiastic disciple of Jeremy Bentham (1784–1832), the formulator of the philosophy of Utilitarianism, which argued that the goal of society should be the greatest good for the greatest number of people. Utilitarianism attacked unrestrained industrial capitalism, and Mill in turn continually questioned the economic structure and social patterns of nineteenth-century England. Mill proposed that more equal distribution of property and wealth could be accomplished by heavy taxes on land and by levies on inherited wealth. Progress, Mill insisted, lay in a better distribution of material goods and in social justice, including equal rights for women, which he championed.

One of the early French critics to begin a dialogue on achieving justice in capitalist industrial societies was Count Henri de Saint-Simon (1760–1825). He accepted that an economy based on industrial production would ensure a future of abundance that would put an end to human want. Though of an ancient noble family, Saint-Simon viewed the aristocracy as an idle class whose privileges were unjustified. For him, privilege should belong only to those who work to produce, those whom he called *industriels* – agriculturalists, manufacturers, and merchants. Society, he proclaimed, should be organized for the promotion and well-being of the most numerous and poorest class. In his last work, *The New Christianity* (1825), Saint-Simon undertook to reform society on the basis of Christian ethics.

Among those strongly attracted to Saint-Simon's ideas were professionals (including bankers and engineers), intellectuals, and some working-class women. By the 1830s about 200 French women identified themselves as Saint-Simonians, an early example of the appeal that alternative visions of industrial society had for women, who were often its most oppressed victims. In 1832 a group of Saint-

Simonian women published their own newspaper, *The Free Woman*, which printed only articles written by women and declared that "With the emancipation of women will come the emancipation of the worker." Although their movement collapsed, other feminist movements continued to offer criticism and alternatives to industrial capitalism in the later nineteenth century.

Charles Fourier (1772–1837), another French critic of industrial capitalism, differed from Saint-Simon by rejecting industrialism. Fourier proposed a visionary reorganization of society as an alternative to the industrial society that Saint-Simon sought to make just and rational. Particularly alarmed by large-scale centralized production, which he saw as a threat to small enterprise, Fourier proposed as a substitute his own conception of a community based on an agrarian handicraft economy. In his vision, labor would be necessary but also fulfilling and joyous, and life would be long and happy.

The utopian vision of society proposed by Saint-Simon and Fourier did not have the wide appeal to the working masses that other more practical strategies did. Pierre-Louis Proudhon (1809–65), a self-educated printer who wrote *What Is Property?* in 1840, was a working-class critic of capitalist society. For Proudhon, property was theft, profit stolen from the worker with the connivance of the state. Proudhon proposed a cooperative society of independent equals based on common ownership. Because he rejected private property he was called a socialist, and because he rejected the state in favor of cooperative organizations he was called an anarchist.

One of Proudhon's admirers was the Russian anarchist Mikhail Bakunin (1814–76), who believed that the state was the cause of the afflictions of the common man and woman. Bakunin, who espoused and engaged in violent action against the state, was an exile from Russia and familiar with the inside of many European jails. From his base in Switzerland, Bakunin continued to work for revolution against the social order in which he found himself. The true revolutionary, he wrote, "has severed every link with the social order and with the entire civilized world." Bakunin believed that industrial workers constituted a vanguard of revolutionary activity that would lead to the replacement of capitalist industrial society. Two other Russians, Prince Peter Kropotkin (1842–1921) and Count Leo Tolstoy (1828–1910), also contributed to criticism of capitalist industrial society. They, like many Russian intellectuals and similar to Fourier, saw small rural communes rooted in the traditional peasant village community, or *mir*, as the basis for an alternative society.

MARX AND THE CRITIQUE OF INDUSTRIAL CAPITALISM

The critique of industrial capitalist society that would have the greatest global impact appeared in the last half of the nineteenth century. Two Germans, Karl Marx (1818–83) and Friedrich Engels (1820–95), presented their case against capitalist industrial society in their *Communist Manifesto* (1848) and in Marx's *Capital* (published between 1867 and 1883). These two works became the basic texts of "scientific socialism" or communism. Indebted to earlier German and French thinkers and based on his study of history, Marx combined a critique of industrial capitalism with a theory of historical change (see Chapter 7). His ideas offered both a basis for understanding the problems and conflicts of his own time and the vision of an ideal society that could be achieved by human action as part of an inevitable historical process.

According to Marx, material conditions – technology, natural resources, and, above all, modes of production (slavery, serfdom, the factory system) – determined all other aspects of human society and culture (political institutions, social organization, thought). Human consciousness, he believed, is formed from these material conditions; for example, the thought of an industrial worker will differ from that of a farmer because each is part of a different mode of production. Marx also introduced the concept of "class," divisions of society arising from economic and social differences. Conflict between classes – "class struggle" – was driven by changes in the modes of production and became the "engine" of historical change. The characteristic conflict of capitalist industrial society was between those who worked in factories (wage earners, whom Marx labeled "the proletariat") and the capitalists who owned the factories.

Marx analyzed nineteenth-century contests between workers and industrial capitalists on the basis of a labor theory of value. The true value of an object, he argued, is determined by the labor that goes into it. The difference between the cost of production (wages and material) and the market price is the surplus value, of which those who own the means of production (capitalists) rob those who produce (the proletariat). Keeping surplus value for themselves permits capitalists to get richer while the proletariat grows poorer as a result of rising costs and stagnant wages. The widening gap between capitalists and the proletariat increased class consciousness in both and culminated in increasing conflict between them. The outcome of this conflict would be the victory of the proletariat, leading to the creation of a classless society in which conflict would disappear, since producers themselves would own the means of production.

As the unsavory aspects of industrial capitalism – poverty amidst plenty, repetitive labour, urban blight, economic cycles, the slow progress of change by political processes – became common in the second half of the nineteenth century, Marx's vision gained widespread appeal in Europe and ultimately found wide acceptance outside Europe. But before Marx's ideas would have an impact on world history, global war claimed the attention of Europeans and the rest of the world, creating a grim landscape of dystopian horror across the globe.

GLOBAL WAR AND PEACE IN THE TWENTIETH CENTURY

In the twentieth century, conflicts among European nation-states, reflected in imperialist rivalries in the non-European world, twice led to global war. European nationalisms forged in the aftermath of the Napoleonic wars in the nineteenth century fed the fires that led to global conflagration in the First World War. The new national boundaries drawn after the war split groups that were bound by language and culture, heightening tensions caused by a global economic depression to the point that the Second World War broke out. Together, the two global conflicts demarcate a shift from a world dominated by Europe, a condition dating from the sixteenth century, to one dominated by the United States and increasingly by new nations born from the dismantling of European imperialism worldwide. The impact of these struggles ranged from the diplomatic and political arenas of nation-states to the intimate, daily lives of individuals.

The First World War

By the beginning of the twentieth century the major European powers were grouped into two hostile military alliances created by diplomatic strategies stemming from late nineteenth-century power politics and imperialism. The Triple Alliance was made up of Germany, Austria-Hungary, and Italy; the Triple Entente (or Entente Cordiale) included Great Britain, France, and Russia. Tensions among these nations extended beyond Europe. From the end of the nineteenth century to the outbreak of the First World War, economic rivalry in Africa – the Sudan, East Africa, Morocco – fueled tensions that on several occasions nearly led to war between France, Great Britain, and Germany. Economic and political rivalries, military expansion, the maintenance of large standing armies, and naval competition provided the volatile background for war in 1914.

The Great War, as it was known to Europeans, began in 1914 as a local European war waged between Austria-Hungary and Serbia, which championed the cause of Slavic nationalism. The event that precipitated hostilities in 1914 was the assassination of Archduke Franz Ferdinand, heir to the Austrian and Hungarian thrones, by a 19-year-old Serb nationalist at the Bosnian capital of Sarajevo. This central European conflict quickly extended into a general European war because of the two opposing systems of alliances into which Europe was divided. Germany honored its pledge to come to the aid of Austria, and Russia rallied to the aid of Serbia, which also involved Russia's French and British allies. Britain's participation in turn involved its Asian ally, Japan.

The war eventually spread beyond Europe and involved thirty-two nations, including European colonies in Africa and Asia. Twenty-eight nations, known as the Allies, including Great Britain, France, Russia, Italy (which joined the Allies in 1915), and the United States (which did not enter the war until April 1917), opposed the coalition known as the Central

Powers, consisting of Germany, Austria-Hungary, the Ottoman empire, and Bulgaria. Though precipitated by a political assassination, it was the intense nationalism rampant in nineteenth-century Europe, together with economic competition stemming from the growth of industrial capitalism and its extension through imperialism, that lay at the heart of the conflict that engulfed Europe and other parts of the world in the early twentieth century.

The war lasted four years, and after initial rapid advances the struggle became virtually fixed along a series of fronts: a western front in France; an eastern front along the frontiers of Russia, Germany, and Austria, and a southern front along the Austrian–Italian frontier. The Germans constructed a labyrinth of trenches, which were complicated ditches designed to provide cover for troops. The French and their British allies in turn ordered trenches as defense against the possible German advances. The digging of trenches, some of them 4 feet deep, meant that soldiers were held fixed in their defensive positions, awaiting face-to-face combat and death. In the meantime they lived through cramped, miserable, unhealthy, and dangerous days and nights of constant gunfire and bombardment, relieved only by the even more dangerous efforts to break through the lines and advance.

The horror of trench warfare was dramatically evoked by the German author Erich Maria Remarque (1898–1970) in *All Quiet on the Western Front*, a powerful indictment of war published in 1929. Remarque was drafted into the German army at the age of 18 and wounded on the western front, where he observed the horrors he later described in his novel: "The sun goes down, night comes, the shells whine, life is at an end. Still the little piece of convulsed earth in which we lie is held. We have yielded no more than a hundred yards of it as a prize to the enemy. But on every yard there lies a dead man." Remarque's book was a plea for peace, but for those engaged in the war the prospects for peace held little hope as they lived through endless days of misery and bloodletting in the muddy trenches and scorched landscapes of Europe. When Germany and its allies were finally defeated in 1918, over 10 million lives had been lost, and the lives of 20 million more were permanently scarred. Many millions more died in the worldwide influenza epi-

demic of 1918 than in the entire span of the First World War, and both this epidemic and the civil war that engulfed Russia, beginning with the Bolshevik Revolution of 1917, were related to the devastation wrought by global war.

Peacemaking and the League of Nations

Two contradictory conceptions of peacemaking dominated the negotiations at the Paris Peace Conference that ended the First World War. One was the traditional idea that "to the victor belongs the spoils," the assumption that a defeated state would have to sacrifice territory and wealth to the victor. Contrary to this in spirit and content was the peace envisaged by the US president Woodrow Wilson, a "peace without victors or vanquished." In presenting his war aims in April 1917 before the United States entered the war, Wilson proclaimed that the war was being fought "to make the world safe for democracy," and that it would be a war to end all wars if the self-determination of all major nationalities in Europe were the basis for peace. Wilson embodied these ideas in his Fourteen Points, which concluded with a proposal for a League of Nations – "a general association of nations . . . formed under specific covenants for the purpose of affording mutual guarantees of political independence and territorial integrity to great and small states alike" – a world organization that would guarantee peace.

Despite Wilson's idealism, the terms exacted by the victors in the 1919 Versailles treaty with Germany were harsh: Germany was forced to dismantle its armed forces, to surrender most of its merchant fleet, and to agree to extensive reparations – compensation for economic damages inflicted on the Allies by Germany during the war. Among other reactions, the Versailles treaty provoked an outpouring of nationalistic opposition in China (the May 4th Movement) because of the decision to grant former German concessions dating from the nineteenth-century "spheres of influence" to Japan, as an ally of Great Britain, rather than return this territory to direct Chinese control. What few, if any, at Versailles foresaw was that Japan was positioned to reap much larger political, economic, and military rewards from China and the rest of Asia. The seeds of the Second World War were already sown by the impact of the settlement on Germany as well as by the repercussions outside Europe. The League of Nations proved incapable of balancing national interests in an international arena, especially without the participation of the United States, which, despite Wilson's efforts, never joined the organization.

The interwar years

The two decades between the Paris peace treaties that ended the First World War and the outbreak of the Second World War (1919–39) were years of growing tension and uncertainty that undermined domestic order nearly everywhere and contributed greatly to the collapse of international cooperation and peace that the League of Nations had attempted to ensure. Political tensions created by the failures of peace-making after the First World War were coupled with severe economic crisis stemming from the Great Depression that gripped the world in 1929 (see Chapter 6).

By destroying so much of the traditional framework of European society, the First World War had greatly strengthened revolutionary politics on both the left and the right. In Germany, Italy, and Russia, mass revolutions led to the rise of both fascism and communism. These political ideologies were radically opposed to each other in terms of the ideals they proclaimed, but both gave totalitarian power to the state to order society and the lives of individuals (see Chapter 7). The rise of these conflicting models of the state in an international context set the stage for global conflagration at mid-century in the Second World War. Despite its origins as a European conflict, the Second World War truly engulfed nearly the entire globe because of connections among Europe, Asia, Africa, and the Americas created by imperialism.

In the same year as the signing of the Versailles treaty, Adolph Hitler (1889–1945) joined with other unemployed veterans who were disillusioned by German defeat and embittered by the German government's acceptance of the Versailles treaty to form a National Socialist German Workers (Nazi) Party. Shortly thereafter, he became its leader. The specter of socialism also reared its head in disillusioned Italy. Italy had joined the Allies in 1915, but experienced great hardship, loss, and humiliation in the war and emerged with only a small portion of what

the Allies had promised as the price of its participation. Postwar bitterness, inflation, and unemployment increased general discontent and, inspired by events in Russia, encouraged the spread of radical ideas. Out of this morass of confusion and disillusionment, Benito Mussolini (1881–1945) offered himself as a national savior who would protect Italians from both Bolshevism and the bankruptcy of nineteenth-century precepts of liberty and democracy. The term "fascism" (state dictatorship over society) was coined by Mussolini in 1919 and referred to the ancient Roman symbol of power, the *fasces*, a bundle of sticks bound to an axe.

Japan's rise as a modern nation-state and its role as a powerful player in both Asian and global politics by the early part of the twentieth century is a potent reminder of the influence of European imperialism as a model. Both Japan's industrial economy and its military had grown quickly in the late nineteenth century, and the defeat of China in 1895 and Russia in 1905 signalled Japan's success at achieving the military and industrial goals of the Meiji Restoration (1868). Japan adapted rapidly to the developing global system of nation-states and emerged as an Asian imperialist power by end of the First World War. Japan, which had modeled itself on European nation-states such as Prussia in the nineteenth century, like its European allies Germany (formerly Prussia) and Italy in the Second World War, rejected parliamentary government and came under the dominance of the military in a Japanese form of fascism. Having profited economically during the First World War, and politically by its peace, Japan was also severely affected by the international financial collapse in 1929. During the 1930s, economic crisis intensified the political appeal of fascism. Japan took military actions on the Asian continent to assert its position there and to protect its industrial economy, first colonizing Manchuria in 1931 and then launching a full-scale invasion of China in 1937.

A World's Fair and the Second World War

Although the conditions leading to the second global war of the twentieth century were already in place, the planners of the New York World's Fair that opened in 1939 attempted to create a futuristic vision of the union of science, technology, and industry in the World of Tomorrow. Like the city of Oz in the film *The Wizard of Oz* that opened the same year, the fair's planners dazzled visitors with its constructed vision of an imagined world. The fairgrounds were dominated by a slender pyramidal tower called the Trylon, soaring more than 600 feet into the air, and a giant globe, 180 feet in diameter, called the Perisphere. These white stucco monuments were the hub of a wheel from which spokes radiated outward in the form of multi-colored zones devoted to communication, food, government, and other concerns of "civilization." As the US president Franklin D. Roosevelt's opening address put it:

> [T]he eyes of the United States are fixed on the future. Our wagon is hitched to a star. But it is a star of good will, a star of progress for mankind, a star of greater happiness and less hardship, a star of international good will, and above all, a star of peace. May the months to come carry us forward in the rays of that hope.
>
> (Quoted in Larry Zim, Mel Lerner, and Herbert Rolfes, *The World of Tomorrow: The 1939 New York World's Fair*, New York: Harper & Row, 1988, p. 9)

But the rays of that hope were already dimming, even as Roosevelt spoke. The United States was just emerging from a decade of economic depression, and war had already broken out in Europe.

While the New York World's Fair was being planned, ideals of racial supremacy drove political and social change in Nazi Germany. Pseudoscientific historical notions of German descent from white "Aryan" and racially pure stock were derived from widespread nineteenth-century racist assumptions about the superiority of some people and the inferiority of others, based on inherited qualities. The ultimate expression of this vision of supremacy was contained in the Nazi propaganda films by Leni Riefenstahl, *Triumph of the Will* (1936), the depiction of the Nuremberg Nazi Party rally of 1934, and *Olympia* (1938), a documentary on the Olympic Games of 1936 in which the Nazi leaders were extolled as a superhuman pantheon.

In January 1939, before the New York World's Fair officially opened, the Spanish republican government fell to the fascists under General Francisco Franco, supported by both Italy and Germany, and the Spanish pavilion was closed. In March, Hitler's Germany absorbed Czechoslovakia, and Czech immigrants took over the Czech pavilion. Poland was invaded by Germany in September, and the Polish pavilion closed. In the spring of 1940, Denmark, Norway, Belgium, the Netherlands, and France fell to German forces, and their participation in the fair ended. On one level, the 1939 New York World's Fair bore little resemblance to the real world, and yet on another level revealed sharply the dissonances of that world on the eve of the second global war of the twentieth century.

Despite the Nazi–Soviet Non-Aggression Pact of 1939, Hitler believed that the Soviet Union constituted a threat to German security and ambitions. Anxious to gain control of food supplies and raw materials, especially oil, in the Soviet Union, the Germans launched their invasion in June 1941. When the United States joined Britain and Russia against the Axis powers in late 1941, following the Japanese attack on Pearl Harbor in the Hawaiian Islands, the second phase of the Second World War commenced what was known to the Russians as the "Great Patriotic War." Within four months the Germans reached the vicinity of Moscow, when a combination of the extreme Russian winter and a Soviet counteroffensive checked them. In 1943 the Russians halted a German offensive into the Ukraine in a bitter siege at Stalingrad. In June 1944 the Allies launched their invasion of France, while the Soviets pushed westward, and within a year Germany was defeated. The Pacific War, as the Japanese knew it, raged on, largely carried out by the United States on behalf of the Allies. On 6 and 9 August 1945, the United States dropped two atomic bombs on the Japanese cities of Hiroshima and Nagasaki, forcing the surrender of Japan on August 15, 1945 and ending the final phase of the Second World War.

THE IMPACT OF WAR ON SOCIETY

War tends to encourage the growth of state power for the mobilization of resources and the mobilization of citizenry. Control of the economy, government regulation and planning, and even requisitioning and

Figure 11.3 Trylon, Perisphere and Helicline, photo by Sam Gottscho (Library of Congress). These futuristic forms symbolized the dreams of the World of Tomorrow. The Helicline was a spiral ramp on which visitors descended from the Perisphere after viewing "Democracity," a multimedia diorama designed to show the possibilities for future peace and prosperity through cooperation.

Figure 11.4 Indian troops in East Africa. Indigenous troops from Africa and Asia served in European colonial armies, often stationed outside the colonial boundaries of origin.

rationing were necessary in the pursuit of wartime goals. The demands of technological innovation and the expense of new technology showed that the concentration of power in the hands of political leaders was an effective and essential way to increase production and contribute to national power through military successes.

Leaders in both world wars depended heavily on conscripted soldiers. The mass production of weapons required the mass production of soldiers. By the Second World War fighting units were highly diversified in terms of function, and the new dependence on technology required many units dedicated to servicing and supplying that technology. The traditional division between soldier and civilian disappeared, as mechanics were as necessary as other soldiers to the war effort. The importance of scientists and engineers grew as the realization dawned that new weapons could tip the balance quickly in favor of one belligerent over another. During the Second World War, European refugee scientists fleeing Hitler's Germany persuaded the British and American governments to mount an effort for research and development that produced the first atomic bomb. Science and other aspects of culture were harnessed to serve the nationalist goals of societies.

Figure 11.5 Old German woman standing between advancing US Seventh Army troops (1945). Both the victors and the defeated were faced with the daunting task of rebuilding Europe in the wake of the devastation of the Second World War.

In contrast to nineteenth-century conflicts such as the Crimean and the Franco-Prussian wars, which were relatively limited in scope and scale, the global wars of the twentieth century were of long duration and exacted very heavy tolls in human lives and resources. The First World War was unique up to that time in the numbers participating in and affected by it. Previous wars, such as the French Revolution and Napoleonic Wars, had required the active participation of large portions of the population, but never before 1914 had war so extensively called into play all the human and material resources of the participating nations. In the Second World War conscription and the displacement of people fleeing war or persecution made huge demographic changes across the European landscape. Between September 1939 and early 1943, at least 30 million Europeans were deported or had fled from their homes. By recent estimates close to 60 million men, women, and children lost their lives in the Second World War, and many millions more suffered the indelible pain of loss and hardship. Twenty-seven million people are estimated to have succumbed to war and its effects in the Soviet Union alone.

Material costs were also too vast to be readily comprehended. Combatant nations in the First World War spent at the rate of $10 million an hour, and the grand total of war expenditure (including property damage) has been estimated at $186 billion. The Second World War cost the United States $341 billion and Japan $562 billion; the Soviet Union lost approximately 30 percent of its national wealth. These staggering figures take on true meaning only in terms of what might have been accomplished by the expenditure of so much energy, effort, and money for peaceful purposes such as feeding, housing, and clothing people.

The alliance between industry and the state in war was exemplified in Germany by the history of the Krupp family firm. After the unification of Germany in 1871, the Krupp firm became the chief arms supplier for the German state, often keeping ahead of the military in the development of new weapons, such as its cannon "Big Bertha." Following the First World War, the Krupp family firm turned from weapons to nonmilitary production, from railroad equipment to stainless steel dentures. During the interwar years, however, the Krupps also secretly manufactured weapons banned by the Versailles Peace Treaty and developed new ones.

Not only did they participate in Hitler's rearmament of Germany in the 1930s, but during the Second World War 70,000 forced laborers and concentration camp inmates toiled in Krupp factories on behalf of Hitler's armies. The relationships between military industrialism, armament, and security were ones with which the world, teetering between war and peace in the twentieth century, would continue to wrestle.

People felt the impact of war in many ways. Rationing of sugar, gasoline, tires, automobiles, coffee and other goods, shortages, and inflation were endured by millions. Welfare measures and expanding roles for labor unions in the organization of the labor force were utilized in the interests of the war effort. The war permitted the intrusion of states into the daily lives of individuals and families, sometimes promoting motherhood while taking away husbands and sons. The provision of guaranteed health care likewise was a product of the need to ensure workers' health so that they could achieve maximum productivity. In the postwar era technology that had been created to meet military demands was applied to the production of consumer goods

WAR AND RESISTANCE

The Second World War subjected most of Europe and much of East Asia to foreign military occupation. The responses of occupied peoples varied from one place to another and among peoples – sometimes even among members of the same family – in the same community. In the colonized Dutch East Indies, the Japanese invaders were initially welcomed as liberators from Western colonial rule. In Norway most citizens resisted both the Nazis and the handful of Norwegian collaborators set up by the Nazis as a puppet government. Sometimes the path of resistance offered impossible moral dilemmas. For example, those who spied for the enemy or hid Jewish children and other refugees were often required to act in ways that endangered their own lives and the lives of their families, neighbours, and colleagues.

Not all resistance occurred as individual acts of moral conscience. Following the fall of France in 1940, two forms of French opposition to the Germans emerged. French patriots led by General Charles de Gaulle

(1890–1970) organized resistance to the Germans from abroad. Within France and outside France in French North African territories, a secret, underground resistance movement operated with much success to hide Jews and downed British and US airmen, and to help some of them escape from the German authorities. Many men and women gave their lives in the Resistance. There were also resistance movements in communities in Denmark and the Netherlands. In Yugoslavia resistance took the form of guerrilla warfare against German and Italian occupation forces conducted by two groups: loyalists to the monarchy and "partisans" supported by the Soviet Union and led by Josef Broz (1892–1980), known as Tito.

Resistance movements within both Germany and Italy opposed the Nazis and Mussolini's Fascists. For example, the White Rose was the name of a small group of German students, professors, and intellectuals who opposed the war and distributed pamphlets urging the German people to resist the Nazis and the war effort. Two students and a professor at the University of Munich were executed in 1943 for their activities with the White Rose society. Jewish resistance was extremely difficult in the heavily guarded camps, though there were isolated but remarkable instances of protest. In the Warsaw ghetto, where thousands of Polish Jews were confined to a quarter of the city and subjected to overcrowding and starvation, an armed rebellion broke out in 1943. The resisters received no outside backup, and most were ultimately killed by the Nazis.

Documentation of large-scale resistance to the Nazi government in German society is harder to find. One example of mass resistance by German women did occur in 1943, when about 600 unarmed women marched on a building near Gestapo headquarters in Berlin and demanded the release of prisoners who had been rounded up as a result of the laws restricting marriage between Jews and non-Jews. The women protesters succeeded in securing the release of those accused; their actions saved the lives of many Germans.

WOMEN IN WAR AND PEACE

The conditions of global war ironically also provided opportunities for women around the world to challenge gender roles. As early as the French Revolution, the services of women had been requisitioned during wartime, but at no preceding time had the role of women in war been so organized, planned, and complete as in the First World War. Women took over customarily male jobs so that men could go to the battle fronts. Factories employed women, and their work in the munitions industry was a major contribution to the war effort. Women also assumed a variety of service and administrative jobs in transportation, worked in offices, and entered teaching and government to lead more public lives. In Russia a "battalion of death" made up exclusively of women (80 percent of whom were killed) was sent to the front in 1917. Women also served in combat as nurses and ambulance drivers for military hospitals. As a result of the war, a generation of young women remained unmarried or were widowed, childless, or single parents. The contributions of women to the war efforts led some postwar societies to reconsider their roles. In Great Britain, where a massive women's suffrage movement in the decade before 1914 had failed to get women the right to vote, women over the age of 30 were given the right to vote in 1919. In the United States, President Woodrow Wilson (in office 1913–21) recommended that women be enfranchised as a war measure.

Many women, as well as men, did not support the war. Between 1890 and 1920 a women's rights movement had spearheaded a wave of political activism. Women began to support progressive causes that were critical of the plight of urban and rural families and fought for social reform, economic justice, and international peace. Organized opposition to war by women was not new in the twentieth century. *Lysistrata*, a fifth-century BCE play by the Greek dramatist Aristophanes, tells the story of women uniting to stop war by making a pact to withhold sex from their husbands until the war ends. From their origins in the seventeenth century, people of the Quaker religion were committed to peace. Secular peace groups were established in New York and London in the aftermath of the Napoleonic Wars. But it was the end of the nineteenth century that saw the formation of a viable international peace movement. Its political ideology was broad based, including progressive reformists, anarchists, and socialists, and its members were mostly women, many of whom worked through the American Union Against Militarism

(AUAM), a lobbying group that attempted to keep America out of the war. The link between growing pressure for women's rights and the peace movement was symbolized in the organization of a Women's Peace Party in January 1915 in Washington, DC, led by suffragists and social reformers such as Jane Addams.

Delegates from the Women's Peace Party joined European women at an international conference in The Hague in April 1915. Though vilified by the mainstream press and called "hysterical women" by Theodore Roosevelt, the Women's Peace Party persisted. The traumas of the First World War gained support for the peace movement, and in 1919 the International League for Peace and Freedom was founded to promote the goals of the 1915 International Women's Congress. At the end of the war, one of the leading suffragists, Carrie Chapman Catt, established the National Conference on the Cause and Cure of War.

During the Second World War women aircraft workers such as Rose Will Monroe (1920–97), known as "Rosie the Riveter," became celebrated symbols of United States patriotic womanhood. There were actually many "Rosie the Riveters," women for whom gender boundaries were temporarily lifted, allowing them full access to jobs and skills normally available exclusively to men. The Rosie the Riveter who appeared in wartime films and posters promoting war bonds worked in an aircraft parts factory in Ypsilanti, Michigan. The Ford Motor Company's bomber plant recruited women for delicate technical work. A pamphlet claimed: "The ladies have shown that they can operate drill presses as well as egg beaters." Some firms made deliberate efforts to recruit the wives and

Figure 11.6 Women carrying peace banner (1915). Women march down Fifth Avenue in New York City in an international protest against the war, symbolizing the link between growing pressure for women's rights and the peace movement.

daughters of servicemen whom they had employed before the war so as not to encourage the women to consider their jobs permanent. But war also created new kinds of hardship and oppression for women as well.

Women served in combat roles. In 1939 the Soviet Union drafted women for the first time, mostly to take support jobs. After the German attack in 1941, many Soviet women took part in combat. Of the million women serving in the Red Army and the Soviet navy, about 800,000 of them saw combat. Over 100,000 won military honors and eighty-six earned the coveted rank "Hero of the Soviet Union." Female pilots in the Soviet Union flew numerous combat missions. One fighter regiment had only female pilots, navigators, mechanics, and handlers of munitions; it was so successful in its bombing raids over Germany that the Germans called its pilots "night witches."

At the same time that new roles for women and new opportunities were created by the demands of wartime, traditional roles were promoted by the policies of some leaders. Hitler, who viewed the role of women as confined to the domestic sphere, encouraged motherhood as the fulfillment of a woman's destiny and her duty to the Nazi state and society. On Mother's Day in 1939, 3 million women were given the "Cross of Honor of the German Mother" for having four or more children, because of the need for more soldiers and despite labor shortages. On the opposite side in the war, but with similar goals to raise the birth rate, in 1936 the Soviet Union drafted a new law prohibiting abortion, supported by fines and prison sentences. In 1944 the Soviet government launched the "mother-heroine" campaigns that awarded cash bonuses to women who bore more than two children, with the amount increasing as each additional child was born.

Women also served in the war in roles associated with traditional modes of oppression outside the family. Young Japanese girls from impoverished families had been sold to brothels in the prewar period to help support their families or pay off debts. As the Japanese empire expanded in the early twentieth century, Japanese brothels were established all over Asia, including Siberia, Korea, China, Manchuria, Hong Kong, Singapore, and Southeast Asia. Often tricked into servitude and sexual slavery by promises of lucrative jobs in foreign places, the Japanese women

were called *karayuki* ("going to China," i.e., abroad). Cut off from home and family and lured into prostitution, they lived their lives without any comfort or hope.

The Second World War created a new and more miserable extension of prostitution for women in Japanese colonies such as Taiwan and Korea who were forcibly sent to provide sexual services for Japanese troops stationed all over Asia. In 1941 Japanese authorities conscripted Korean women as "comfort women" for Japanese troops in Manchuria. With the beginning of the Pacific war, between 50,000 and 70,000 Korean girls and women were sent as unpaid prostitutes or sexual slaves to Japanese troops throughout Asia. During the course of the war, other women in areas occupied by Japan, such as Taiwan and the Philippines, were also forced into state prostitution by the Japanese army.

TECHNOLOGY AND THE HUMAN COSTS OF GLOBAL WARFARE

Improvements in mass-produced weapons and new experimental weapons intensified the conduct of both world wars, sometimes with unpredictable results. Each side introduced new weapons to try to gain an advantage, but many of them had not been perfected. The Allies introduced tanks in 1916 as a means for spearheading advances into German-held territory. These new armoured, motorized vehicles provided mobile fire power, but they also broke down frequently and could be easily trapped in trenches. The Germans developed flamethrowers to attack the mobile tanks. The military prototype of the Wright brothers' 1903 airplane proved to be of problematic military use until pilots could figure out how to shoot without hitting the propellor blades. Accordingly, despite the fame of "ace" fighter pilots such as the German, Baron von Richthofen, air warfare was basically ancillary to land fighting. Airplanes provided reconnaissance behind enemy lines and served as a substitute for artillery, attacking and bombing the enemy far beyond the front lines, where civilians as well as soldiers were killed and maimed.

The most terrifying new weapon was poison gas, first used by the Germans in April 1915. The use of poison gas was unpredictable: it could drift back and kill or disable those who launched it as well as those for whom it was intended. Even the invention of gas masks provided little protection from the searing, blistering chemicals. The British poet Wilfred Owen (1893–1918), who was killed just before the end of the war, described from personal experience the horror of poison gas:

> . . . the blood
> Come gargling from the froth-corrupted lungs.
> Obscene as cancer, bitter as the cud
> of vile, incurable sores on innocent tongues.
> (Alfred J. Andrea and James H. Overfield,
> *The Human Record: Sources of Global History*,
> Vol. II: *Since 1500*, Boston, Mass.:
> Houghton Mifflin, 1994, p. 370)

Other weapons were more controllable but equally deadly. Rifles fired quickly and accurately. The Gatling gun, first used in the American Civil War, could fire several rounds of ammunition a minute, but the machine gun, invented in 1884 by Hiram Stevens Maxim (1840–1916), had proved superior during the British conquest of Africa. Bullets were fed into this new weapon by a belt that contained thousands of rounds of ammunition. Maxim manufactured and sold his machine gun to the leading nations of the world, and it became the major weapon of the First World War. The Germans developed efficient, long-range cannon that could effectively bombard the enemy from a great distance behind the front lines. The most famous cannon of the First World War, known as "Big Bertha," was produced by the Krupp munitions works, the chief German arms supplier. It was able to hurl 1-ton shells a distance of more than 15 kilometers (9 miles).

Improvements in maritime technology affected the war at sea. By the end of the nineteenth century, German efforts to build a navy competitive with that of Great Britain resulted in a race to construct new fleets of heavily armoured and heavily armed battleships. In 1914 Britain and its allies were still ahead in the naval race. When Britain declared a blockade of enemy territory, it had the naval means to make the blockade effective. This tactic forced the Germans to retaliate, which they did by using submarines, thus

beginning a new chapter in the history of naval warfare. The development of the submarine from a short-range vessel for coastal protection to an ocean-going vessel enabled Germany to retaliate against the British blockade with terrible effectiveness. It also extended the war across the world's oceans.

Atrocities were carried out by soldiers around the world. One of the most dramatic instances was the "Rape of Nanjing" in December 1937, when Japanese troops engaged in random and merciless slaughter of an estimated 200,000 civilians in Nanjing and the surrounding area over a period of six weeks. The secret documents of Unit 731, a Japanese military unit in Manchuria whose doctors and scientists performed institutionalized murder in the form of lethal medical experimentation, only came to light publicly long after the end of the war. Experiments on captured prisoners of war included spreading bubonic plague virus among the local Chinese population or the vivisection of captured US airmen at Kyushu Imperial University in 1945. These mirror the Nazi medical experiments on the inmates of concentration camps.

All sides committed atrocities. Toward the end of the war in Europe, the British put the German city of Dresden to the torch in a massive incendiary raid that killed 135,000 people, many of whom had fled westward from the Soviet advance. The firebombing of Tokyo on March 9–10, 1945 razed 16 square miles of the capital city and killed between 80,000 and 100,000 civilians, who were "scorched and boiled and baked to death" in the words of US general Curtis LeMay, the architect of the bombing raid. The detonation of a terrifying new weapon just a few months later brought an end to the Second World War, and nuclear warfare had become a global reality.

Secretly developed by an international team of scientists working for the US government in various laboratories and tested in the deserts of New Mexico, the atomic bomb was a weapon of incredible terror and destruction. The question of whether the bomb should have been used twice, or even developed, raises an issue that has never been resolved. The military justification for the dropping of the bomb was that it would put a quick end to a seemingly interminable war and accordingly save lives, particularly Allied lives. Nevertheless, much of the world continues to ask whether other means, such as stringent blockading, would have

Figure 11.7 Atomic bomb (1946). Mushroom cloud rising from Bikini atoll after the 1946 atomic bomb test.

accomplished the same ends. Was it necessary to drop the bomb on a city? Above all, why was it necessary to drop a second bomb so quickly? What of the environmental results of atomic explosions? Peace replaced war at the cost of enormous uncertainty and questioning.

POSTWAR ORDER/DISORDER

The Second World War recapitulated the experience of the First World War in attention given to the shaping of the postwar world even while warfare was still raging. President Wilson had pinned his hopes on a League of Nations that would guarantee a peace without victors or vanquished and "make the world safe for democracy," a vision that faltered in the face of nationalistic ambitions on the part of all, including the United States. The Allied vision of the postwar world, reflecting the powerful influence of President Franklin Roosevelt, was perhaps less idealistic and more pragmatic.

Like Wilson, Roosevelt believed that an international organization would help establish and maintain a rule of law among nations, and advance US interests; once again the United States took a leading role in creating such an organization. Roosevelt's proposals, which were less skeptically received than Wilson's, resulted in the San Francisco Conference (April–June 1945) that created a United Nations organization even before the war in Europe was completed, though not before Roosevelt's death in 1945. The new international organization came into existence before, and apart from, subsequent peace treaties. More than a half century after its creation, the United Nations continues to wrestle with the maintenance of international order in a global climate of rapid change and instability.

The rivalry between the two superpowers, the United States and the Soviet Union, resulted in the era known as the "Cold War," a period between the end of the Second World War and 1990 in which arms and security continued to play a defining role. The Cold War was a global political chess game of moves and countermoves in which tensions between the two superpowers varied in intensity. The division of Germany into Allied and Soviet zones of occupation after the war created the front line of the Cold War in Europe, which persisted in the division of the city of Berlin and the two Germanies, East and West, until the fall of the Berlin Wall in 1989. The division between the United States and the Soviet Union deepened as a result of the Marshall Plan, by which the United States provided about $22.5 billion to aid the recovery of western Europe between 1948 and 1952. The Soviets perceived the 1949 military alliance of western governments (NATO) as a threat to their security. They responded with the economic integration of central European satellite states and the Warsaw Pact, a counter-military alliance. From West Asia to Ethiopia to South Africa, the superpowers extended their perspectives through conflicts and strategies involving "national security interests." The Cold War found expression in technological ventures, including the space race to the moon, and in the continued development in military arms and nuclear capability. The Cold War became global in scale; no part of the world could be uninvolved.

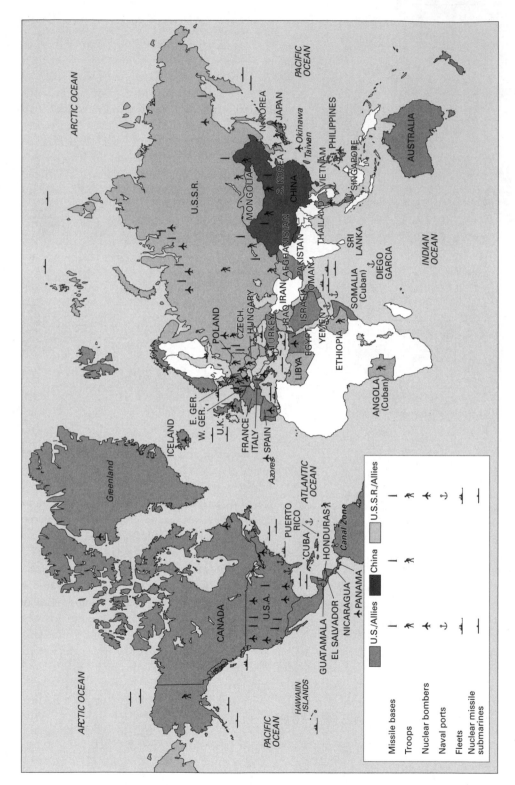

Map 11.1 Strategic Cold War sites.

The Korean War erupted in 1950 as tensions between the United States and the Soviet Union heightened on the Korean peninsula following the postwar drawing of a line at the 38th parallel demarcating the Democratic People's Republic of Korea in the north from the Republic of Korea in the south. The People's Republic of China, an ally of the Soviet Union, felt threatened by the landing of United Nations troops led by the American general Douglas MacArthur, who advocated crossing the northern border of the Yalu River into Chinese territory and eradicating the specter of communism in Asia. The conflict ended in a ceasefire in 1953, and symbolized the growing strategic concerns of the United States in Asia, reflected in the shift of Occupation policy toward Japan, and the division of Korea paralleled the division of postwar Germany and later of Vietnam between the two superpowers and their client states.

Fearing the spread of communism in Asia, especially in the wake of the Korean War and the build-up of the Cold War, the United States supported the French until the French defeat at Dien Bien Phu in 1954. An international meeting in Geneva following the French defeat partitioned Vietnam at the 17th parallel, with North Vietnam under the Communists and the government of South Vietnam under Ngo Dinh Diem, a former collaborator with the Japanese who was backed by the US. During the next two decades, US involvement in Vietnam steadily escalated, from sending military advisors and material support to committing thousands of troops.

Domestic opposition in Vietnam to the Diem government crystallized in the opposition of Buddhist monks to the Catholic-led government, some of whom burned themselves alive to demonstrate their resistance. But the guerrilla activities of the Vietcong, who infiltrated the south in increasing numbers, were by far the most serious threat to the South Vietnamese government. In 1963 Diem was overthrown in a military coup that the US government knew to be imminent but did not stop. Succeeding Vietnamese military governments were dependent on US aid to prop them up.

The Vietnam War delivered the United States its first modern military defeat, at high cost to both Vietnamese and Americans. More bombs were dropped on Vietnam than were used by the Allies during the Second World War, and the use of defoliants to clear jungle vegetation that provided enemy ground cover left widespread destruction and pollution of the countryside. The Vietnam War's reliance on guerrilla combat and the use of the helicopter in difficult terrain marked a major turning point in modern warfare. Guerrilla warfare also made it a "people's war" because there was no clear division between the civilian and the military populations. Vietnam proved the strength of guerrilla war on home territory against even such a powerful force as the United States, with its tremendous financial, material, and human resources. The Vietnam War also fragmented American society as conflicts erupted between the generation that remembered the Second World War with its clear enemies and the generation of the 1960s whose Peace Movement protested a seemingly hopeless, morally wrong, and pointless war.

The collapse of the Soviet Union and the fragmentation of Eurasia in the closing decade of the twentieth century ended the Cold War. The costs of this "war" were higher than those of any other global conflict. Human, capital, and technological resources were drawn into the worldwide competition of the superpowers for political influence and strategic advantage. World military spending from 1960 to 1990 was $21 trillion. Despite major arms reductions (especially after the Strategic Arms Reduction Talks in 1991), the international perspectives on the role of weapons in creating security have not altered. Nuclear dangers persist. Japan's economic achievement and the united postwar European economic community, as examples of successful transformations in which global interdependence is balanced with limited military spending, are exceptions to the pattern of conflict and development. The persistence of world poverty among 1 billion of the planet's peoples and the oppression of many more reminds us that "global politics in the human interest" reaches beyond the dualistic and perhaps overly simplistic perspectives of war and peace.

SCIENCE AND UNCERTAINTY: TWENTIETH-CENTURY PHYSICS

Belief in the ideals of science and reason – that the natural world is subject to laws that can be investigated and known – stemmed from intellectual transformations commonly termed the "scientific revolution" and the Enlightenment that took place in Europe between the sixteenth and eighteenth centuries. These changes drove transformations in world history through the Industrial Revolution, when progress was seen in terms of advances in technology that improved the material conditions of life for many inhabitants of the planet. Advances in science and technology have been responsible for many transformations in twentieth-century life, ranging from the new view of the universe introduced by physicists early in the century to the uncertain benefits of atomic fusion at the end of the century. These "advances" can no longer be seen in terms of the simple progress of the nineteenth century; rather, scientific and technological change has been increasingly understood as adding an ambiguous complexity to twentieth-century lives, and the changed ways people comprehend their world are reflected in developments in psychology and philosophy. Many of the technological advances were born of war and many contributed to making modern warfare horrific in terms of planetary consequences.

In some ways physics has been the most significant science of the past 300 years. The modern ways of knowing the world and the very precise language used to describe that world were developed by physicists. The scientists Isaac Newton (1642–1727) and Robert Laplace (1749–1827) established the criteria of rational objectivity for natural science in which the scientist was a pure spectator. The classic expression of this was Laplace's image of the ideal scientist as the omniscient calculator, who, knowing the initial positions and velocities of all the atoms in the universe at the moment of its creation, would be able to predict and give running commentary on the entire subsequent history of the universe. Thus the nineteenth-century world was not only knowable but existed as a result of its past, which was the cause of its future. The physicist's cause-and-effect view of the universe was soon applied by many other disciplines besides physics, including history.

The problem with the cause-and-effect view, however neat and believable it may have been, was that it depended on an artificial construct: the separability of observer and observed, the belief in the scientist as an objective spectator. Take that away and, like a house of cards, all else would (and did) follow in a tumble of uncertainty and chaos. Among the scientists who created a post-Newtonian view of the universe, the most important was Albert Einstein (1879–1955). Einstein questioned the concepts of the stability of matter, time, and motion that had been received wisdom since Newton. In 1905 Einstein proposed his theory of relativity, which made time, space, and motion relative to each other as well as to the observer, rather than the absolutes they had been believed to be.

Objectivity was no longer possible. According to Einstein, "this universe of ideas is just as little independent of the nature of our experiences as clothes are of the form of the human body." That is, theories about the world are like garments in that they fit the world to a greater or lesser degree, but none fits perfectly and none fits every occasion. And all are manufactured by humans. Einstein also said that we cannot even compare our theories with the real world. We can only compare our theoretical predictions with observations of the world, and these observations are subjective and therefore inherently uncertain.

Uncertainty was also suggested by the work of Joseph Thompson (1856–1940), Hendrick Lorentz (1853–1928), and Ernest Rutherford (1871–1937), who, by unlocking the secrets of the atom, cast doubt on accepted beliefs about the nature of matter. Thompson and Lorentz independently discovered that the atoms of which all matter is composed are in turn composed of small particles, which Lorentz named electrons; Thompson and Rutherford imagined each atom as a miniature solar system consisting of a nucleus (the sun), electrons (the planets), and (mostly) space. They further suggested that the particulars of the atomic solar system might themselves not be matter at all, but energy: the positive and negative charges of electricity. Their work made possible the practical impact of twentieth-century physics by bringing to light the details of the microscopic, subatomic universe. Devices such as transistors, silicon chips, integrated circuits, superconductors, and nuclear power all depended on knowledge of the electron.

Another major contribution to the twentieth century's scientific revolution was the work of the physicist Werner Heisenberg (1901–76), who is credited with conceiving the Uncertainty Principle, a principle that sought to explain the unlikelihood that science can know a predictable and orderly world independent of the observer. Heisenberg argued that what scientists observe is not nature itself but rather nature exposed to our method of human understanding. The new quantum mechanics has shown that motion cannot be described by location and velocity since there is a trade-off between the precision of measuring each.

Since the 1940s more subatomic particles have been identified, including quarks. The set of scientific studies of the subatomic world since about 1925 is called "quantum theory," but while its impact has been great it is hardly a finished story. Contrary to the Newtonian world-view, quantum theory implies randomness – the constant movement and unknowable arrangement of atoms – and a lack of predictability. During much of the nineteenth century the mechanical universe of Newton had exuded confidence in an independent reality that existed essentially unchanged whether or not we observed it. In the twentieth century quantum theory has transformed this certain world into chaos.

Reality understood is reality changed, since the capture and perception of information is fundamentally flawed by the scientist whose presence intrudes on and changes the scene. In the world of physicist Niels Bohr there are no atoms, only observations made by scientists. According to Bohr, the atom is a creation of the human mind; science is imposed and fabricated order – human-made, not natural. These scientific ideas questioned the very nature of matter and furthered a creeping sense of uncertainty, a sense that the more we learn the less solid and reliable the natural world seems. Beginning in the 1970s the development of string theory promised to resolve some of the gaps in particle theory, especially related to the problem of gravity in quantum field theory. String theory posits that strings, rather than point-like subatomic particles, are the fundamental components of matter and can better explain the structure or "fabric" of the universe. The universe has many more dimensions than science can currently explain, and these appear more frenetic and violent the more closely their movements are examined. As astronomers and astrophysicists continue to explore the origins of the universe and the way it works, new discoveries undermine previous assumptions about the infinite space that surrounds the planet

and lend greater force to the sense of prevailing uncertainty of scientific frontiers.

THE IRRATIONALITY AND UNCERTAINTY OF KNOWING: PSYCHOLOGY AND PHILOSOPHY

In the late nineteenth century and the early twentieth, people working in the new field of psychology undertook the systematic study of human behavior, including relationships between mind and body. One of the first such psychologists was Wilhelm Wundt (1832–1920), who tested animal and human reactions in laboratory conditions. The Russian Ivan Pavlov (1849–1936), like Wundt, carried out controlled experiments on animals under the assumption that the results would be applicable to humans. One of his experiments with a dog resulted in "Pavlov's response," the concept that many human responses are not rational but purely mechanically products of stimuli of which we are often unaware.

The most provocative leap in understanding human nature in the twentieth century was created by the work of Sigmund Freud (1856–1939), the father of the method of investigation and treatment called psychoanalysis. Freud concluded that much of human behavior is irrational, rooted in the unconscious, and instinctive. Conflict, he believed, not reason, is the basic condition of life. Freud believed that conflicts exist mostly on an unconscious level and begin in childhood. They cause frustation, which festers in the subconscious and results in neuroses and psychoses (mental disorders of varying degrees). Neuroses may be dealt with by making the neurotic person conscious of the facts and circumstances of the original frustration. Such consciousness was the objective of psychoanalysis. Freud's ideas have gone through three-quarters of a century of evolution, modification, and rejection. Despite the criticism that Freudian ideas are time-, place-, and especially gender-bound, psychoanalysis persists as one response to the confusions and fears of individuals living with modern uncertainty.

Philosophical responses to the changes of the twentieth century have been many and varied. European reactions have often been couched in extreme pessimism, an insistence that European civilization has collapsed and is doomed. The German metahistorian Oswald Spengler (1880–1936) put forth this argument in *The Decline of the West* (1918). For Spengler, the First World War was the beginning of the end for European (German) civilization. The works of the Spaniard José Ortega y Gasset (1883–1955) express a similar sense of decay and crisis. His *Revolt of the Masses* (1930) is a lament for the dehumanization and decline of rational society, which he believed was the result of the rise of popular material culture and the tendency of the masses to use destructive force to achieve their goals.

Another reaction to twentieth-century uncertainty was Existentialism. Rooted in the disenchantment and anxiety produced by two massive twentieth-century wars, Existentialism became especially prominent in France after the Second World War. According to this philosophy, there were no absolutes or permanencies or universal truths, only personal inspiration and individual commitment. Existentialists argued that there is no ultimate meaning, rational or irrational, to existence. Individuals are simply born and exist. They are free and are responsible for the decisions they make and the actions they take. There are no final, ultimate rights or wrongs, so individuals must establish their own rules and standards and be responsible for living up to them. These personal rules are their blueprint for living, after which they die.

MODERNISM, ART, AND UTOPIAS

Systematic efforts to understand and interpret the twentieth century, the relationship of people to each other and to the universe they inhabit, have found various forms of cultural expression. Modernism has come to symbolize the complex ideas and global culture that came into being in the urban centers of the early twentieth century. The built environment – from buildings to chairs to advertising's graphic design – was imagined and then created by the aesthetics and the ideology of Modernist design. Modernism was not only conceived as a distinctive design style but also as a collection of ideas, which included the rejection of ornamentation in favor of abstraction. Modernists had a utopian desire to create a better world and they believed in technology as the key means to achieve social improvement. In Modernist thinking, the machine became a symbol of the ability of art and technological design to transform society.

At the core of Modernism lay the idea that the world had to be fundamentally redesigned. The carnage of the First World War led to widespread utopian fervour, a belief that the human condition could be healed by new approaches to art and design. Focusing on the most basic elements of daily life – housing and furniture, domestic goods and clothes – artists, designers, and architects reinvented these forms for a new century. Art was to become part of everyday life, and technology was to be extended to its limits and beyond. Avant-garde architects and artists threw themselves into the collective effort of engineering social change.

After the Revolution of 1917, Russian designers and artists working from a socialist perspective believed that utopia could be achieved by using the machine and industrial production as ways of creating greater equality. The Dutch group De Stijl believed in the spiritual as well as in the social dimensions of their work. The Bauhaus school in Germany sought what they called the "New Unity" of art and technology. Much of Modernism was formulated in opposition to the perceived evils of the present – above all, the repressive authoritarian and totalitarian states and glaring social inequalities of the modern world. At other times, the utopian solutions of the early and mid-century modern view were rational and practical. A new environment – clean, healthy, light and full of fresh air – would be sufficient to transform daily life.

A major aesthetic movement of the twentieth century, Surrealism, grew out of a rejection of all aspects of Western culture, a rejection also associated with a cultural movement known as "Dadaism" (from the French for hobbyhorse, suggesting nonsense). Both of these movements emphasized the role of the unconscious in creative activity and were represented in literary and artistic works in which dream imagery and the unconscious play a large role. The work of the Spanish artist Salvador Dali (1904–89) exemplifies surrealism in painting. His most famous painting is called *The Persistence of Memory* (1931), depicting limp, fluid watches strewn about a dreamlike landscape. Though based on the sixteenth-century artist Hieronymous Bosch's famous painting *The Garden of Earthly Delights*, Dali's work is a product of the twentieth century and suggests the breakdown of the certainties of the mechanical Newtonian universe (the limp watches sliding over the landscape) as well as the human perception of time itself. Surrealist writers, painters, and filmmakers extended the Western notions of reality beyond what was known and visible to the human eye or the eye of the camera.

MORALITY, HUMAN RIGHTS, GENOCIDE, AND JUSTICE

The two world wars focused attention on the extremes of human behavior and values and on the different interpretations of "human rights" that cultures and governments constructed to promote domestic or international interests. After the Second World War organizations dedicated to international peace and order began to discuss universal human rights – basic human needs, decencies, participatory rights, and liberties. Could peoples from vastly different cultural and political perspectives agree on a basic covenant of human rights?

In the wake of the Nazi extermination of Jews, homosexuals, gypsies, and others, a campaign ensued for the universal acceptance of international laws defining and forbidding genocide. This was achieved in 1948, with the promulgation of the *Convention on the Prevention and Punishment of the Crime of Genocide*. Sadly, this did not prevent further genocides, defined as a variety of crimes against humanity committed against a targeted national, ethnic, racial, or religious group. The former Yugoslavian state of Bosnia (site of ethnic cleansing, rape, and massacre during wartime); Cambodia (where the Khmer Rouge slaughtered over a million of their countrymen between 1975 and 1979); Rwanda (where as many as a million Tutsis were massacred from April to July 1994), and Darfur (a conflict beginning in 2003 that has killed or threatened the survival of more than 5 million Africans) are several of the most recent sites of modern genocides since 1948. Historians are also uncovering historical examples of concentration camps and massacres, such as occurred in the British colony of Kenya or the Belgian Congo.

Global wars in the twentieth century resulted in the deaths of more than 100 million people. While most of those were casualties of war, both military and civilian, some were the result of deliberate policies of genocide. From the slaughter of 2 million Armenians by the Turks in 1915 to the 15 million Jews, gypsies, Slavs, and homosexuals murdered by the Nazis during the Second World War, genocide was practiced by governments and by people who bore responsibility for carrying out these acts of institutionalized murder. Though genocide was not unique to the twentieth century, technology made it more efficient, as the gas chambers of German concentration camps bore witness. At Auschwitz as many as 12,000 victims a day were gassed to death.

The Nuremberg and Tokyo War Crimes trials at the end of the Second World War attempted to assign guilt and to punish those who had transgressed the bounds of civilized human behavior in the conduct of war, as defined by the international community in such forums as the League of Nations. The Geneva Convention, for example, established rules for the humane treatment of prisoners of war, though these were nonetheless violated by belligerents in the Second World War.

The dropping of two atomic bombs on Hiroshima and Nagasaki ostensibly to bring about a rapid capitulation by Japan brought moral questions sharply into focus. Yet numbers of those killed in the atomic holocaust or the Nazi Holocaust quickly become numbing statistics, just as photographic records by their very clarity and objectivity make us all too familiar and comfortable with the grim realities of war and human inhumanity. The German-born American political philosopher Hannah Arendt (1906–75) wrote of the "banality of evil," the idea that evil is commonplace and that trying to define it as something atypical of human behavior is fruitless. Nevertheless, in the aftermath of the Second World War, though neither genocide nor war ended in 1945, people continued to question the morality of war, to oppose it, and to struggle to prevent it.

In contrast to the Yoruba's acceptance of the potent ambiguity of the world illustrated in the work of the diviner, nineteenth-century Europeans believed in the possibility of understanding the world through scientific observation that would lead to discovery of the orderly, rational laws that made it work. Europe's domination of the world through imperialism reinforced confidence in European civilization. As the end of the nineteenth century approached, however, contemporaries considered the meaning of the past and made predictions about the future, not unlike the Yoruba diviner. For example, the term *fin de siècle* ("end of century") came to represent an attitude of despair, discomfort, and uneasiness that went far beyond the literal meaning of the term in French. The term suggested the possibility of tectonic shifts in cultural meaning and identity that could arise from a new era and an uncertain future; it also came to be associated with the perception of decaying moral codes.

At the end of the nineteenth century, the philosopher Friedrich Nietzsche (1844–1900) was one of many Europeans who made predictions about the age ahead. Writing in 1888, he warned that lives in the new century would be characterized by the onset of catastrophic wars beyond imagination; by the death of god; and by feelings of self-loathing, skepticism, lust, greed, and cynicism. Certainly some twentieth-century survivors would see the fulfillment of Nietzsche's prophecy in the world wars; the threat of a nuclear holocaust; the dark night of fascism; and the contradictions, inequalities, and injustices exhibited in the twentieth-century world. Whether or not cultures view the human condition as inherently filled with contradiction and ambiguity, as in the world of the Yoruba diviner, there is no doubt that the history of the past century leaves humankind at just such a crossroads as the one overseen by the Yoruba deity Esu.

CONCLUSIONS

Ideas by themselves are intellectual abstractions. However, when ideas inspire people to action, they become powerful agents of change in the material world. We often identify individuals with the discovery or creation of particular ideas – such as Isaac Newton and gravity – but those ideas only have an impact through the cumulative and collective actions of others. All ideas are products of particular times and places, of specific historical and cultural contexts. At the same time, ideas are not limited by these historical and cultural boundaries. Instead, ideas are frequently transmitted widely over time and space, where they take on new meanings in new settings.

The people who transmit ideas are those who use them as tools for analysis or for action. Frequently, these are people who move between cultural boundaries themselves, including scholars, rebels, travelers, sailors, pilgrims, and journalists. Those who promote new ideas may not accept them in their entirety, but rather tend selectively to adapt or reject certain aspects that fit their own political, social, or cultural circumstances. In this way, ideas of all kinds are refracted through the lenses of specific cultures. However, these altered and adapted ideas can still be powerful agents of change, whether they advocate the creation of a new world or urge a revival of past ideals.

The past five centuries of globalization have created economic and social links that provided avenues for the rapid exchange of ideas across the globe. Globalization has also revealed the differences, ambiguities, and contradictions of the modern, ever more integrated world. World regions were found to be so diverse that ideas were rarely transplanted unchanged into new cultural contexts. Even so, when opportunities presented themselves, individuals with access to new ideas strove to put them into action in a wide variety of places.

In the nineteenth and twentieth centuries, the transformations of industrialism, nationalism, imperialism, and global war have undermined the stability and security of individuals and their communities. The collapse of certainties embedded in traditional cosmologies has produced anxiety about who "we" are and where we are going. The intrusion of constantly changing technology in our daily lives has created a sense of persistent unfamiliarity and alienation at the same time that the technology of communication has brought people closer together.

In the late twentieth century utopian visions continued to inspire social change. In the mid-1950s, for example, Mao Zedong promoted the creation of "people's communes" in the People's Republic of China. These were to be models of a new kind of social organization, breaking down the old patterns of family and village to create communal living, eating, and working spaces. The people's communes were meant to embody a Marxian communal ideal, but the intensified economic and social changes implemented under Mao's leadership during the "Great Leap Forward" – also a utopian scheme to adapt industrial development

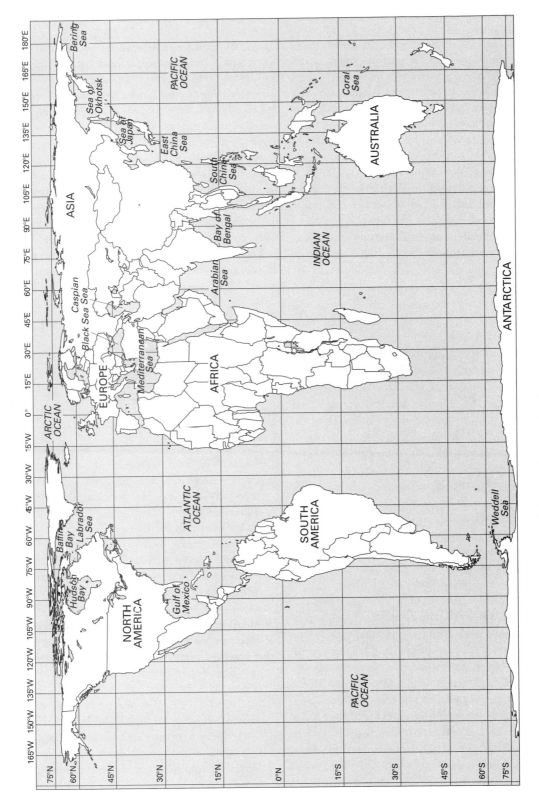

Map 11.2 Peters Projection, accurately conveying the relative size of the continents.

to agrarian production – resulted in the deaths of between 20 and 30 million people from famine. In the 1960s United States, there was a movement among young people to live in communes, where they shared life, work, and family and returned to a kind of agrarian ideal of self-sufficient farming. But these communal visions were overshadowed by the utopian ideals of a world designed by technological innovations that speeded up change on a global scale.

Such late-twentieth-century technology as infrared mapping, an ancillary product of satellites that record images of the earth from space, has altered perceptions of peoples and places. International boundaries have never been more accurately drawn than by space-age cartographers, yet these boundaries have also been made irrelevant in some ways by satellites, which invade the cultural and social space of even the most isolated corners of the globe on a daily basis. Telecommunications and computer technologies make possible intimate and immediate links between Los Angeles and Lahore, or London and Lagos.

Both the material bases of human cultures (including technology, environment, and demographics) and the resulting changes in the way people understand the world provide the sources of individual as well as community, national, or even global identity. Accelerated change has affected issues such as ethnicity, race, class, and gender in the lives of individuals and communities.

Never before has the human race faced the possibility of extinction as a consequence of the meeting of the forces of technology and population. The combination of increasing population and advances in industrial technology has altered the physical landscape of larger and larger portions of the globe, and caused a growing imbalance in the relationship between nature and human life, while drastically reducing the resource base that supports life on the planet. At the same time that technology has provided the means to raise the standard of living of a portion of the world's population while damaging the environment through deforestation and the pollution of water and air, progress in transportation and communication technology has brought the peoples of the globe closer and closer together, enhancing awareness of humanity's common fate and interests.

As the world has become technologically interconnected, the emerging global culture has been constantly and rapidly transformed; increasingly unstable, fragmented, and ambiguous cultural and social identities have been but one consequence. Another is a rich sense of possibility that the dynamic interaction of cultures has created. Culture, the patterns of behavior developed by societies in their efforts to understand, use, and survive in their environments, is a basic form of power no less important than the political or economic power that it underscores and helps shape. Culture is also simply a people's "way of life," concerned with how people understand themselves, their communities, and their world, as well as how writers, artists, and musicians represent that world. The singer John Lennon urged his listeners to "imagine" a world without war. So far this has not been possible. But like generations before, today's population is situated at the meeting place of past and future, where universal concerns shape the human condition at the twenty-first century crossroads.

SELECTED REFERENCES

Adas, Michael (1987) *The Prophets of Rebellion: Millenarian Protest Movements Against the European Colonial Order*, Cambridge: Cambridge University Press. Explores millenarian visions, their use, and impact in the colonial world.

Bartov, Omer (2000) *Mirrors of Destruction: War, Genocide, and Modern Identity*, New York: Oxford University Press. Four provocative essays relating total war in the twentieth century to utopian dreams, genocide, and ethnic and national identities.

Dower, John W. (1986) *War Without Mercy: Race and Power in the Pacific War*, New York: Pantheon. A powerful study of race, propaganda, and culture in wartime, focusing on Japan and the United States.

Fussell, Paul (1977) *The Great War and Modern Memory*, New York: Oxford University Press. A vivid recreation of the First World War through the eyes of major literary figures who fought in it and whose literary works were shaped by their wartime experiences.

Goldman, Wendy Z. (1993) *Women, the State, and Revolution: Soviet Family Policy and Social Life, 1917–1936*, Cambridge: Cambridge University Press. Women and family life in Soviet society between the wars.

Havens, Thomas R. H. (1978) *Valley of Darkness: The Japanese People in World War II*, New York: W.W. Norton. A close study of the war at home for the Japanese.

Hochschild, Adam (1999) *King Leopold's Ghost: A Story of Greed, Terror, and Heroism in Colonial Africa*, New York: Houghton Mifflin. Haunting account of the Belgian Congo, an extreme dystopian relic of the colonial venture.

Keegan, John (1996) *The Battle for History: Re-Fighting World War II*, New York: Vintage. A thoughtful review of the historical literature and perspectives on the Second World War by a leading military historian.

McNeill, William (1982) *The Pursuit of Power: Technology, Armed Force, and Society since A.D. 1000*, Chicago, Ill.: University of Chicago Press. A survey of the relationship between technology and war from medieval through modern times.

Segal, Howard P. (2006) *Technology and Utopia*, Washington, DC: Society for the History of Technology and the American Historical Association. A useful historical overview of the relationship between technological changes and ideas of utopia.

ONLINE RESOURCES

Annenberg/CPB Bridging World History (2004) <http://www.learner.org/channel/courses/world history/>. Multimedia project with interactive website and videos on demand; see especially Units 22 Global War and Peace, 26 World History and Identity.

Index

Related titles from Routledge

Themes in World History series

Editor: Peter N. Stearns, *Carnegie Mellon University*

Pre-Modern Travel in World History

Stephen Gosch

Featuring some of the greatest travellers in human history, this survey uses succinct accounts of the most epic journeys in the pre-modern world as lenses through which to examine the development of early travel, trade and cultural interchange.

ISBN13: 9780415229401 (hbk)
ISBN13: 9780415229418 (pbk)

Alcohol in World History

Gina Hames

From the origins of drinking to the use and abuse of alcohol in the present day, *Alcohol in World History* combines archaeological evidence with historical case studies to produce a fascinating exploration of drink and its cultural meanings in contemporary society.

ISBN13: 9780415311519 (hbk)
ISBN13: 9780415311526 (pbk)

Education in World History

Mark S. Johnson

This comprehensive overview of the history of education, from ancient times to the present day, is a thematic survey of the history of education throughout the world.

From Confucius to the Greeks and the Egyptians, Mark S. Johnson takes an integrated look at ancient education, and the development of various education traditions separately. Examining the implications of empire for the history of education, he goes on to look at the rise of vocationalism, the decline (in some places) of religious education and the effects of globalization on education.

Suitable for introductory courses and students new to the subject, this book is a must for anyone studying the world history of education.

ISBN13: 9780415318136 (hbk)
ISBN13: 9780415318143 (pbk)

Agriculture in World History

Mark Tauger

The survival of the human race since earliest times has depended on its exploitation of the land through agriculture. Mark Tauger looks at farming in early civilizations – from ancient Mesopotamia and Egypt and beyond, in early China and India, and asks how it is that although farmers have played a critical role in the fate of the species, they have never enjoyed high social status.

Following medieval farming through to imperialism, agricultural revolution, then to decolonisation, the Depression and the Cold War, this wide-ranging survey brings the story of farming right up to the present day. It examines contentious current issues such as contrasting aspects of overproduction and famine, the role of the World Bank and the IMF, environmental issues and GMO.

ISBN13: 9780415773867 (hbk)
ISBN13: 9780415773874 (pbk)

Available at all good bookshops
For ordering and further information please visit www.routledge.com

A History of the World
From the 20th to the 21st centuries

Second edition

J. A. S. Grenville

Thoroughly updated with recent events such as 9/11 and the Second Gulf War, and including recent historical research, this second edition of a popular book is a comprehensive account of key events and personalities of this period worldwide.

ISBN13: 9780415289542 (hbk)
ISBN13: 9780415289559 (pbk)

Available at all good bookshops
For ordering and further information please visit www.routledge.com

---

International History of the
Twentieth Century and Beyond

Second edition

Antony Best, Jussi M. Hanhimaki, Joseph A. Maiolo, Kirsten E. Schulze

A completely revised and updated authoritative account of the history of international relations in the twentieth and early twenty-first centuries, covering events in Europe, Asia, the Middle East, Africa and the Americas. A new chapter explores the history of European integration and the decline of Britain and France as world powers and the rise of supra-governmental organizations worldwide. A new and final chapter explores the war on terror in a globalized world.

ISBN13: 9780415438957 (hbk)
ISBN13: 9780415438964 (pbk)

Available at all good bookshops
For ordering and further information please visit www.routledge.com